Rob Evans is a journalist on the *Guardian* ne worked for the *Sunday Telegraph, Financial 1* programmes. In 1999, he won an award from the Campaign for Freedom of Information for challenging official secrecy. His articles prompted the current Labour government to launch two independent inquiries into the safety of germ warfare experiments which had been conducted over large parts of Britain. He has been researching and writing this book for the past five years.

GASSED

ROB EVANS

HOUSE OF STRATUS

Copyright © 2000 Rob Evans

All rights reserved. No part of this publication may be reproduced, stored in a retrieval system, or transmitted, in any form, or by any means (electronic, mechanical, photocopying, recording, or otherwise), without the prior permission of the publisher. Any person who does any unauthorised act in relation to this publication may be liable to criminal prosecution and civil claims for damages.

The right of Rob Evans to be identified as the author of this work has been asserted in accordance with sections 77 and 78 of the Copyright, Designs and Patents Act 1988.

This edition published in 2001 by House of Stratus, an imprint of Stratus Holdings plc, 24c Old Burlington Street, London, W1X 1RL, UK.

www.houseofstratus.com

Typeset, printed and bound by House of Stratus.

A catalogue record for this book is available from the British Library.

ISBN 0-7551-0353-X

This book is sold subject to the condition that it shall not be lent, resold, hired out, or otherwise circulated without the publisher's express prior consent in any form of binding, or cover, other than the original as herein published and without a similar condition being imposed on any subsequent purchaser, or bona fide possessor.

Cover design: Karen Stewart.
Front cover images: Reproduced courtesy of the Maddison family (Portrait); *Daily Mail* (Newspaper); Hulton Getty; Fred Morley/Fox Photos (Gas mask); Wesley/Keystone (Chemical exercise); Keystone (Sign).
Back cover image: Public Record Office.

To my father and my late mother.

ACKNOWLEDGEMENTS

Chemical and biological warfare has often been sensationalised. I have sought to write this book as dispassionately and fairly as possible. It is up to the readers to make their own judgements on the rights and wrongs of these experiments.

I would like to thank all those who have helped me to research and write this book over the past five years. Originally, I had hoped to talk to both the volunteers and the scientists to get all sides of the story. But this ran into difficulties. The human subjects in the tests were willing to be interviewed, but the scientists who were behind the trials were less inclined to talk.

I am grateful to all the volunteers who gave up their time to speak to me and to send me documents relating to their experiments. In total, I interviewed more than 100 human 'guinea pigs'; many of them were speaking publicly for the first time. They had been to Porton at different times stretching from the early 1930s to the late 1970s. It could be said that, since these trials happened a long time ago, their memories may not be reliable. Indeed, their recall of their tests inevitably varied. Despite the years, however, it is apparent that for many, being gassed at Porton is one of the more striking experiences of their life. Not surprisingly, it is something which sticks in the memory quite vividly.

Given Porton's reputation, it is understandable why the scientists are less keen to speak than the volunteers, so I am especially grateful to those who were prepared to talk to me. Their views and perspective were invaluable in giving a more rounded picture of the experiments. Some of them did not want to be identified publicly; their anonymity has been made clear where necessary. Unfortunately the current management of Porton refused to grant me a formal interview. It appears that this decision was taken because I had written what they perceived to be 'negative' articles about Porton in the *Guardian* and *Sunday Telegraph* newspapers. I believe that this was a misguided decision, since Porton needs to go out and explain its side of the story, however arduous this is, if it is to have any chance of changing the public perception of its experimental work. Retreating into a kind of laager

ACKNOWLEDGEMENTS

is the easy option, but ultimately futile. The Porton management also refused to provide any photographs for reproduction within this book. Porton began to open up markedly under the directorships of Rex Watson (1974-83) and Graham Pearson (1984-95), but currently seems to be more closed again. During Graham Pearson's time, I was invited three times as part of various groups to visit the establishment and discuss its work. I am grateful for those opportunities, which I accepted. Rupert Cazalet and Sue Ellison, Porton's press officers, have answered my questions as best as they could.

The backbone of the book comes from declassified government documents in the Public Record Office (PRO) at Kew, south-west London. Many myths surround Porton and chemical warfare for a variety of reasons, not least inaccurate accounts in books and the media from secondary sources of information. One Porton veteran has commented that the subject is frequently bedevilled by a 'mixture of half-truths, nonsense and sheer speculation'. As far as possible therefore, I have sought to locate primary sources to establish what actually happened – the original documents produced by Porton and Whitehall departments. For instance, descriptions of experiments are based on the technical reports which were written by Porton scientists at the time to record their work. Such documents, while essential, do not always give a full picture of what went on, and so I have aimed to weave in the first-hand testimonies of the volunteers and scientists.

In recent years, more documents have been opened up at the PRO, mainly due to an initiative by the last Conservative Government to flush out unnecessary secrecy in all departments. This Open Government Initiative (OGI), started in 1992, has meant that in particular, more documents about Britain's chemical warfare policy have been made available at the PRO. At times, it almost seemed that so many previously closed files were emerging from Whitehall's archives that it was difficult to keep up with this flood of new information. The MoD's archivists in Whitehall have been helpful, not only in releasing these new documents under the OGI, but also in responding to my requests to open up specific files.

The written record of Porton's work down the decades is uneven in the PRO. There are two classmarks at the PRO covering the establishment (WO 188/189), but there are substantial gaps. For instance, there are hardly any files about Porton's chemical warfare trials between 1941 and 1945, although there are quite a few for the period between 1939 and 1941. There is relatively little within these classmarks on the internal discussions about the ethics and proper conduct of the human experiments; the available papers on this subject have emanated from elsewhere in the PRO. Something approaching a full inventory of unclassified reports within the Porton

Technical Papers series only recently appeared in Porton's classmarks, although ironically many of these papers had been available in other classmarks – chiefly WO 195 – for some years. As ever, it always pays to search the files of related departments, however laborious it may be, to uncover interesting material. It appears that the MoD's archivists in Whitehall have had much trouble persuading Porton to release its records. Of course there are no state papers on Porton's work since 1970 because of the thirty-year rule banning the release of such papers; it remains to be seen whether Labour's proposed Freedom of Information Act will significantly open up this area. I am also grateful to the staff of the PRO, whose service in a number of respects (for example, retrieving and photocopying documents) has greatly improved over the past decade.

Special thanks also to Andy Thomas for his trailblazing research in the PRO. His early work in identifying files about chemical warfare was published in *Effects of Chemical Warfare: a selective review and bibliography of British state papers* (Taylor & Francis, 1985). He was commissioned by the Stockholm International Peace Research Institute (SIPRI), partly in the hope that it would stimulate further research in the PRO. It certainly did that in my case. The vastness of the PRO flummoxes many researchers when they first go to this archive, but Andy's book proved a valuable guide for my initial research, saving much time and helping to locate relevant files which may have been missed.

In particular my thanks go to Julian Perry Robinson, of the Science Policy Research Unit (now Science and Technology Policy Research) at Sussex University. An acknowledged authority on the subject of chemical and biological warfare, he generously spent time reading chapters in their draft form and making invaluable comments to correct potential errors and misinterpretations. The first two volumes of the six-part study of CBW produced by SIPRI are largely his work. Even though they were written nearly thirty years ago, they remain indispensable guides to be consulted for reliable information. Some of the more obscure references in this book come not from my own research, but from his files, an archive which must be one of the most comprehensive on the subject of chemical and biological warfare. The Harvard Sussex Program on CBW Armament and Arms Limitation paid for the photocopying of nearly all the official papers which I obtained from the PRO – a useful source of funds, since each page costs forty pence to be copied.

A number of MPs have been helpful. Ken Livingstone, Labour MP for Brent East and now London's mayor, and his efficient secretary Maureen Charleson, tabled more than 150 Parliamentary Questions and sent a series of inquiring letters to Porton and defence ministers, which yielded much important new information. (I am grateful to Graham Pearson, the then Porton director, who sought to answer these Parliamentary Questions as fully as possible, and not simply reply with the bare minimum). Thanks also to Matthew Taylor, Liberal Democrat MP for St Austell and Truro, and his researcher Abbe Frigerio, Harry Cohen, Labour MP for Leyton and Wanstead, and David Atkinson, Conservative MP for Bournemouth East, who diligently promoted the volunteers' campaign, including his constituent Michael Paynter.

The meticulous work of Gradon Carter in recording the history of Porton from an official point of view has been useful. I have drawn on both his book, *Porton Down – 75 years of chemical and biological defence*, (HMSO, 1992), and the articles which he has written (often with Graham Pearson) on various aspects of Porton's past. The book omitted aspects of the establishment's historical activities because they were still classified secret at the time. An updated, expanded version of his history was published just as this book was being completed. As described in chapter one, there are two earlier histories of Porton. I have referred to Gradon Carter as Porton's official historian since he has worked at the establishment for many years since 1948 and is currently part-time consultant on historical matters. For many years, there were two distinct establishments, covering chemical and biological warfare, at Porton. Moreover, the names of these establishments have changed over the decades. To make it easier for the reader, I have simply used the term Porton to refer to them. In any case, this book mainly covers the chemical side of Porton.

The now-defunct Observer Films made an hour-long ITV documentary on the Porton volunteers which was transmitted in October 1994. The team behind the film were Callum Macrae (reporter), Kim Shillinglaw (associate producer), Matthew Davies (researcher), Ray Fitzwalter (executive producer), Kimi Zabihyan (producer) and Bill Lyons (director). I was also employed to carry out some of the research. This film broke important new ground, particularly in locating human 'guinea pigs'. Observer Films kindly passed on all their research to me after the programme was broadcast. In places, I have used untransmitted material from interviews with Porton staff which were carried out in preparation for the programme. I also conducted some research for a section on Porton's LSD experiments in the *Dispatches* programme 'Purple Haze' which was transmitted on Channel Four in April 1996. The producer was Sarah Manwaring-White, the reporter Callum Macrae, and the researcher Mark Handscomb.

Acknowledgements

Other programme-makers who have been helpful are Sally Davies and Greg Myers of BBC Wales, whose radio programme on the Porton volunteers was broadcast in November 1999, and Jonathan Elliott of BBC Close Up North, whose film about the death of Ronald Maddison was transmitted regionally in October 1999 and repeated nationally in April 2000.

Others who have been given me help and encouragement in various ways include Adam Coulter, Kamala Hayman, Alistair Hay, Alan Care, Mike Kenner, Richard Guthrie, Elizabeth Shepherd, Joshua Latimer, John Ashton, Andrew Gilligan and Henrietta Wilson.

I am also grateful to my literary agent Andrew Lownie for securing a publishing deal for this book. As a first-time author, I was making rather heavy weather of getting this book published before he agreed to represent me. Thanks also to David Lane, group chief executive of Stratus Holdings, who agreed to publish the book. I have also appreciated all the hard work of House of Stratus employees – Jenny Rayner, Justine Bell, Karen Stewart, Emma Bottomley and Sasha Morton.

I would be interested to hear any comments about this book and will be willing to help individuals seeking further information. I can be contacted through the *Guardian* newspaper in London, or via email – robevans55@hotmail.com. I am also setting up a website which will feature the latest developments, new documents and a discussion forum. Its address is www.portonexperiments.org.

I believe that this book was only made possible by the ending of the Cold War. It meant that many PRO documents could be opened up, volunteers started to come forward, and scientists felt freer to talk. However there are still some layers of secrecy surrounding Porton's past work. I hope that these can be lifted some day.

CONTENTS

Chapter		Page
	List of Illustrations	xv
	Introduction	1
1	Pioneers of Pain	21
2	The Pursuit of Bodies	47
3	Burning Issues	79
4	Cleaning up after the Nazis	111
5	Death of an Airman	139
6	Breaking the Code	165
7	Conscience Explored	197
8	Britain's Psychedelic Soldiers	231
9	Tears of Volunteers	261
10	A Solitary Battle	289
11	In Whose Interest?	315
12	Into the Twenty-first Century	337
	Afterword	349
	Appendix 1	365
	Appendix 2	368
	Appendix 3	371
	Appendix 4	373
	Notes	377
	Index	471

LIST OF ILLUSTRATIONS

Guards outside the Porton Down Germ Warfare Establishment
(Hulton Getty) — 8

Protestors outside the Porton Down Germ Warfare Establishment
(Hulton Getty) — 8

Porton in the First World War
(Public Record Office – MUN 5/386/1650/4 no. 94) — 20

Artillery detachment loading gun
(Public Record Office – MUN 5/386/1650/4 no. 151) — 20

Livens Projector emplacement
(Trustees of the Imperial War Museum, London – Q14944) — 28

Salvo from Livens Projector firing trial
(Public Record Office – MUN 5/386/1650/4 no. 165) — 28

Automatic Straight Line Machine, 1920s
(Public Record Office – WO 188/318) — 75

Two blisters on arm (Public Record Office – WO 188/472) — 75

Indian soldier (Public Record Office – WO 33/1776 no. 2037) — 101

Chemical weapon for use against the Japanese
(Public Record Office – AVIA 15/896) — 101

Exposure of men to GB vapour – confidential report
(Public Record Office – WO 195/11264) — 112

Extract from 'Report on Exposure of Unprotected Men and Rabbits to Low Concentrations of Nerve Gas Vapour', 1949
(Public Record Office – WO 195/10813) — 129

Ronald Maddison (private collection) — 138

Ronald Maddison's death certificate
(Death Certificate – Office for National Statistics – © Crown copyright. Reproduced with the permission of the Controller of Her Majesty's Stationery Office. Also with the permission of Maddison's family) — 151

Gordon Bell, 1959 (North News and Pictures) — 174

Gordon Bell, 1999 (North News and Pictures) — 174

LIST OF ILLUSTRATIONS

Soldier on bike, 1964 (Hulton Getty)	200
Protective clothing, 1964 (Hulton Getty)	200
Experiments carried out at Porton Down in the 1960s (Hulton Getty)	244
A technician at work (Hulton Getty)	244
Testing a respiratory mask at Porton Down (Hulton Getty)	292
Porton's laboratories in the early 1960s (Hulton Getty)	292
Official Porton map (Public Record Office WO 195/14973)	354

INTRODUCTION

On a sunny summer's day, Porton Down, the British government's chemical and biological warfare establishment, was about to be hit by a political bombshell from a very unexpected source. On 19 August 1999, Detective Superintendent Gerry Luckett of the local Wiltshire police force stepped in front of the television cameras to make a short, simple announcement. The tall, soft-spoken veteran of the rural force revealed that police officers had decided to carry out an inquiry into the death of a young human 'guinea pig', Ronald Maddison, in a nerve gas experiment in 1953. Detectives were also going to investigate allegations that unsuspecting servicemen had been duped into taking part in chemical warfare experiments. Operation Antler, the codename for the investigation, had been born.

It was the first time that the long programme of human experiments at Porton Down had ever been subjected to a criminal investigation by a police force.

Wiltshire Constabulary are investigating whether crimes have been committed against the human 'guinea pigs'. In the case of Ronald Maddison (see chapter five), the police are considering whether Porton Down should be charged with the offence of corporate manslaughter. It is notoriously difficult to mount a successful prosecution on this offence, which was not even on the statute book until relatively recently. The officers are also considering whether Porton should be prosecuted for administering noxious substances and perpetrating a form of assault – under the Offences Against the Person Act – on many servicemen. These men claim that they were tricked into agreeing to be subjects in poison gas tests when they believed that they were participating in research to find a cure for the common cold (see chapter six).

The surprising turn of events had been triggered by a dogged sixty-one-year-old Gordon Bell who had been a human 'guinea pig' at Porton in the Cold War. He was one of the many who believed that they had volunteered for common cold research, but ended up in chemical warfare tests. He says

INTRODUCTION

that it was not until 1996 that he discovered that Porton had never carried out common cold research. Sensing a cover-up, he angrily sought the truth behind the experiments, enlisting the help of his MP and writing numerous letters to the government. By 1999, he had hit a dead end. He then tried a different tactic. He decided to lodge a complaint with the police, alleging that he had been the victim of a criminal deception. He also told police about the case of Ronald Maddison, whom he claimed had in effect been murdered in a 'reckless and irresponsible' experiment. On the face of it, this appeared to be another brick wall; a last, desperate resort which held little prospect of success. But police took it seriously. Detectives came to see Bell and talked to him for several hours. After further preliminary inquiries and official discussions behind the scenes for some weeks, Wiltshire police force decided to launch a full-scale investigation into the 'hush-hush' government laboratory on their patch. It was undoubtedly a major breakthrough for Bell and other human 'guinea pigs'.

Wiltshire police's announcement of the investigation led to widespread media coverage. Some of the press had a field day. In a pithy editorial, the *Mirror* weighed into 'Porton's dark past'. The tabloid opined: 'What went on at Porton Down chemical warfare centre has always been a mystery... At least one [serviceman] is said to have died – and if one did, you can be sure there were others. If the charges against Porton Down are proved, the establishment will be shamed. It will be a sobering lesson that over-eager warfare scientists need to be controlled.' Other papers were more moderate in their opinions. In *The Times*, science-writer Nigel Hawkes cautioned that the police inquiry was an attempt to impose the attitudes of the 1990s on events of the 1950s. 'The 1950s are now bathed in a glow of nostalgia: an Ovaltine decade of steady jobs, stable families and innocent enjoyment. Crime was low, roads were empty, to be middle-class was very heaven. But it is easily forgotten that it was also a decade of suspicion and paranoia, when a world tired of war was forced to face up to the threat of Soviet Communism.' He agreed that the Porton experiments had broken the Nuremberg Code of ethics, but argued that 'a police inquiry is not the right way to investigate what appears to have been a tragic error of judgement'. He warned that detectives faced great obstacles in their investigation, not least tracking down witnesses and even finding the surviving Porton staff to charge with an offence, if it came to that.

Wiltshire police officers have said little about the details of their investigation, except to stress that their inquiry would be 'full and impartial' – and 'lengthy and protracted'. The small force has been prepared to commit money and staff to carry out a comprehensive investigation, one of the highest profile in its area. As each police force in England is independent, Wiltshire Constabulary had the power to launch its own inquiry without needing permission from Whitehall. Detective Superintendent Gerry Luckett – with his deputy, Detective Inspector Sid Kimber – assembled a team of fourteen officers. With palpable determination, they started to interview hundreds of the human 'guinea pigs' from around Britain. In a laborious process, each was questioned about their experiences in Porton's experiments many decades ago, and an official statement taken. Widows of former Porton human 'guinea pigs' were also interviewed in an attempt to establish whether their husbands' deaths or illnesses were in any way connected to the chemical warfare tests. Officers were despatched to hunt through official archives, especially those at Porton itself. After a year, the team had talked to more than 300 people and the inquiry was stepped up with an extra five investigators recruited from the military services.

All this activity was welcomed by many of the human 'guinea pigs'. The Wiltshire police inquiry is expected to last well into 2001. No one knows how the inquiry will end – and whether it will give Porton a clean bill of health, or lead to a damning condemnation of its treatment of young, naive servicemen.

The military establishment of Porton Down sprawls over thousands of acres of picturesque English countryside, on the edge of Salisbury Plain. The land occupied by Porton is one of Britain's most abundant areas of natural life. It is the largest continuous tract of undisturbed chalk grassland left in the country and is a richly filled habitat with a huge variety of plants, particularly orchids, and some rarities. It is also a paradise for beautiful butterflies, and probably the one place in Britain where the highest number of species can be spotted in a single location. Half Porton's 7,000 acres have been designated a Site of Special Scientific Interest, and are protected to some degree as a result.

The Porton acres are unspoilt and undisturbed because farming stopped on this ground eighty years ago. Instead, the land was taken over by the military for a completely different activity – poison gases and, later, bugs. And this is why many view Porton Down to be a place, not of colourful butterflies and rare plants, but something much more malign, perhaps almost evil.

Set up in 1916, Porton Down is the oldest poison gas research establishment in the world. The thousands of acres have acted as a magnificent buffer zone to hide the work of Porton's scientists from prying eyes for eight decades. Deep in this pretty countryside, behind barbed wire,

Introduction

'keep-out' signs and guards, scientists have toiled to produce a panoply of lethal poison gases and germs. They have also striven to devise more and more secure defences against such insidious and frightful weapons. Yet their work could not be done so successfully without one vital ingredient – human 'guinea pigs'.

Porton started to use humans in tests within months of being established and these tests have continued with few interruptions over the past eighty years. These experiments have been carried out so relentlessly that Porton now holds a peculiar record. It is the chemical warfare establishment which has conducted the world's longest-running programme of human experiments. Moreover, Porton has recently built a new gas chamber (at a cost of £3.5 million) which has a projected lifespan of at least twenty years.

It is no longer possible to compile an exact total of the number of individuals who have been subjected to Porton's chemical warfare tests over the past eight decades, but a figure of around 30,000 would be a good estimate. As well as running the longest programme of human tests, Porton is also likely to hold the record for subjecting the largest number of people to chemical warfare tests. If Porton's total is not the highest in the world, it is certainly among the largest.

In this particular field, Britain is one of the world leaders, if not, *the* world leader. Far from being an unusual occurrence in this country, poison gas tests on human subjects have actually been a very British activity. They could be said to be as British as Buckingham Palace.

The story of Porton's experiments is the story of chemical warfare itself, from the blinded victims of the First World War to the threat of Saddam Hussein's arsenal. Throughout the decades, Porton has frequently been at, or near, the forefront of the latest developments in chemical warfare, be it a new lethal poison gas or an improved gas mask. The hard work of Porton scientists over the years resulted in large stockpiles of poison gases which were, for many years, judged to be essential by politicians. With their considerable skills, the scientists also toiled to ensure that since 1916, Britain has been equipped with some of the best possible defences against the horrors of chemical weapons. That is certainly true today when the menace of these weapons is reckoned to be all too real.

But this appears to have been achieved at a cost. The long line of experiments has left a sad legacy today. Many human 'guinea pigs' now angrily complain that their health was damaged by Porton's tests. There are no reliable figures for the total number of these complainants but many bitterly believe that they have been shabbily mistreated by the government – twice over. Firstly, they maintain that they are now suffering illnesses which were caused by the experiments. Secondly, as if to worsen the wound, they are angry that the government has rebuffed their sometimes forlorn pleas for compensation and official recognition of the cause of their ill health. Isolated and scattered around the country, they feel neglected and badly let down, cast aside as if they were worthless.

Many regret that they ever volunteered to take part in the tests, especially since other countries – Britain's allies – have been more sympathetic to their human 'guinea pigs' and have compensated them more generously. As already mentioned, one young man died in the experiments. Others believe that they were 'green behind the ears' and were simply exploited by Porton – conned into taking part in the tests through the 'common cold' ruse or allowed to walk into something about which they knew nothing. In the view of some, many of the human 'guinea pigs' were unwitting innocents who had trusted their superiors to make sure they would not be harmed by the experiments. In this more knowing, modern age, it now may seem quaint that the volunteers were prepared to place such faith in their commanding officers and 'white-coated boffins'. The scientists themselves believed that the pain and discomfort the human 'guinea pigs' endured was worth it for the discoveries that would benefit the armed forces and the country as a whole. It should not be forgotten that a fair number of the volunteers themselves have no complaints about their time at Porton, also believing that the tests were just one part of their service to the nation. They make no allegations of being abused and believe that their well-being has not been affected in any way since. These volunteers are 'in the majority', according to Porton.

Human experiments have been part of the fabric and tradition of Porton. Within the internal, covert culture of the installation, testing on humans has long been considered normal and commonplace. Few other countries may have been experimenting on their people, but that did not seem to deter Porton scientists. It appears that in this atmosphere, human experiments were for many years conducted without any alternatives being seriously considered. At times, it was almost as if human testing was far from being the last resort of scientists seeking answers to the latest conundrum. Rex Watson, Porton's director between 1974 and 1983, commented, 'One of the problems of Porton was that there was a history of mustard gas experimentation which had become part of the way of life, which was accepted. I don't think it was done thoughtlessly. I think it was done with the agreement of the relevant committees, people who ought to have known what they were talking about. They were satisfied that the processes were as safe as they could be.'[1] A scientist who worked at Porton during much of the

INTRODUCTION

Cold War commented that the human trials were just 'one of those things' and 'part of the ongoing work'. He added, 'We happened to believe that before you start issuing products, you should prove their capacity first, both their safety and effectiveness.'[2]

This idea had its roots in the early days of testing, during the First World War, when Porton staff were prepared to expose themselves to painful poison gases, and it just continued and thrived from there for years on end. It has however faded in recent times. Looking back down the ages, the sheer volume of experiments is quite breathtaking – almost like a surging supertanker which was difficult to stop, and so just ploughed on and on.

Some of the experiments which were carried out before the 1960s are quite staggering, and the human 'guinea pigs' undoubtedly suffered greatly in such trials. However Porton staff adamantly argue that the tests should be judged by the circumstances and standards of the time, not by today's. They believe that too many people jump to judgements without considering the tests of yesteryear in the full context of what was then going on, and what was believed to be acceptable, at that time. Dennis Swanston, who worked as a toxicologist at Porton between 1966 and 1992, said, 'There are things which would probably not be done now, but I would not criticise Porton at all for doing what they did in the past. Provided it was commensurate with the culture of the times, you cannot attach blame.'[3] He added that it is 'terribly easy' for people to look at tests through the mores and values of the modern age and ask 'how could they possibly have done that?'

The culture of the installation is undoubtedly one of the major reasons why Porton's programme of human experiments has been so extensive. Another key reason is the tight secrecy. The trials, and much of the rest of Porton's work, have been swathed in so much official secrecy that few outsiders really knew what was going on within the establishment. In such circumstances, Porton scientists could get on with their experiments without much threat of having to explain themselves to the public or members of parliament. It is clear that they would have been forced to curtail the concealed programme of experiments if had they been subjected to the spotlight of publicity and prolonged questioning by politicians. Indeed the first time Parliament appears to have debated these human experiments with any vigour was in 1994, and even that took place in the relative obscurity of the House of Lords.[4]

The British government is renowned for being among the most obsessively secretive in the developed world. Ministers and civil servants have long had the deep-seated habit of keeping information hidden from public scrutiny – often to protect their own interests, not the electorate's.

They sometimes forget that they should be serving the electorate. Secrecy courses incorrigibly through the blood of the British bureaucrat. It has been so profoundly embedded in the system that huge amounts of even quite mundane information have been routinely locked away from the public. Most civil servants seem to have an automatic reflex to say 'no' to the release of information, and then reach for a suitable reason to justify the non-disclosure. In recent years, ministers — both Tory and Labour — have been claiming that the government as a whole is being opened up, with the 'cobwebs of secrecy' being swept away. But past records of Porton's human experiments are still handled with care by the government censors. The Ministry of Defence's own manual for releasing official papers admits that the gas tests are a 'particularly sensitive' area.[5] The experiments are not something that the authorities are keen to have picked over.

This secrecy has fed the public's suspicions and mistrust of Porton. All manner of myths and rumours have swirled around the institution. Government officials have admitted that an unhealthy reputation has grown up around Porton. It inspires limp jokes about scientists with two heads, or animals with too many legs. One mandarin told Downing Street that Porton had the image of 'a sinister and nefarious establishment'.[6] Another official noted that the installation was 'already sufficiently unpopular' with the public.[7] In this common mythology, 'perfidious' Porton scientists are virtually seen as heartless Nazi-style scientists who sadistically carried out deeply repugnant experiments.

The secrecy surrounding Porton is not however unique. Chemical warfare is such a furtive business that the poison gas activities of most nations are laden with layers and layers of concealment. Often basic facts are not even made public. Whole programmes of human experiments may have been conducted in some countries without a whisper of it ever reaching the outside world. Sometimes, sporadic reports do seep out into the public domain, but it is this worldwide secrecy that makes it almost impossible to draw up a reliable comparison of the level of human chemical warfare testing programmes in the various countries.

For many years, Britain has co-operated closely with three other nations in the field of chemical warfare — the United States of America, Canada and Australia. Britain has had the longest and biggest testing programme of this circle of allies. The Americans began chemical warfare work in 1917 and still maintain poison gas facilities today. 'Only a few subjects' were used in gas experiments between the First and Second World Wars according to one authoritative account.[8] An estimated 5,000 human 'guinea pigs' were subjected to chemical warfare tests in the Second World War. After 1945,

Porton with its 'sinister' reputation has attracted many demonstrations.

another 7,000 or so took part in such tests during the Cold War until 1975. The American programme was then abruptly halted after the experiments came under the glare of scrutiny and publicity in the media. Details of the human tests were publicised at a time when the wider American public were learning about Watergate and the excesses of the CIA and other state agencies. In this atmosphere, many American citizens were growing more distrustful of clandestine government activities. The government felt that these human tests could not be justified and so they were stopped (and, so far, not re-started). In total, the American experiments which ran from the 1930s to 1975 used up to 15,000 human subjects. The American programme of tests has been well-aired in the media through Congressional inquiries, the disclosure of documents via the Freedom of Information Act, and the testimony of the human 'guinea pigs' themselves. However the American government admits that precise figures for the number of individuals used in the tests no longer exist.[9] This is a common feature of poison gas tests in countries around the world.

In Canada, chemical warfare research did not begin until the late 1930s. The Canadian Government has estimated that more than 2,000 volunteers have taken part in its chemical warfare tests in total,[10] with significantly more than half of these during the Second World War. Some human tests did continue after the war; military scientists in particular were testing on themselves. Up to 1968, there was a 'small' number of nerve gas tests, involving probably fewer than 100 people. Since then, a limited number of human subjects has been tested with drugs designed to protect against nerve gas but they were not exposed to the gas itself. In Australia, chemical warfare tests were confined to the Second World War only, involving between 750 and 2,000 human 'guinea pigs'. As we shall see, Britain funded much of the poison gas research in Canada and Australia during the Second World War, thereby allowing Porton staff to direct human experiments in those countries themselves.

Information on the extent of human tests conducted by other developed nations with a history of poison gas work is skimpy. It is known that Germany used human subjects for chemical warfare experiments in both World Wars. Human experimentation may have been curtailed for many years between these wars, since the scope for German poison gas work as a whole was restricted for a number of reasons – the terms of the peace settlement at the end of the First World War prohibited Germany from manufacturing chemical weapons; the country was short of cash in the 1920s; and many of the military commanders were not keen on poison gas. After the fall of Hitler and the Third Reich, Germany's substantial chemical arsenal was destroyed and its poison gas research outlawed. It is unlikely that Germany has carried out a substantial number of human tests, if any, since 1945. Like Germany, Italy was also barred from researching and developing poison gas from the end of the Second World War. The Italians had started work on chemical warfare in the First World War. Afterwards, they devoted significant effort towards gas, firing considerable stocks of chemical weapons in Ethiopia in the mid-1930s. It is not publicly known if human subjects were used in Italian experiments before 1945.

Two countries each with a long history of weighty involvement in chemical warfare are France and the former Soviet Union. Both of them have been intensely secretive about their activities in this field. The French began work in this field during the First World War and have continued ever since, with a gap in the Second World War after the country was overrun by the Nazis. They produced chemical weapons during the First World War and continued developing them after the Second World War. Poison gas had strong advocates within the French military. It would be surprising if the French had not tested human subjects at some point during their chemical warfare work. Beyond that, little is known. The Soviet Union dedicated sizeable resources to chemical warfare during the seventy years of Communist rule, producing many thousands of tonnes of poison gases. It ran a large-scale research programme throughout these decades. Soviet propagandists sought to make hay in the 1980s when a Porton volunteer spoke out about human experiments which he had undergone. Their self-righteous criticisms were very much part of the claim and counter-claim culture of the Cold War. However, details of Soviet gas tests on humans are now seeping out.[11] It has been reported that troops were exposed to chemical weapons in a series of tests carried out in 1935. Scientists released clouds of some sort of poison gas, and then sent a tank crew into the cloud, ordering them not to don their gas masks until the irritation became unbearable. The crew coughed and experienced 'strong irritation' to the chest, eyes, nose and respiratory tract from only fifteen minutes in the stinging clouds. One man who has persistently spoken out is Vladimir Petrenko. He says that in 1982, as a twenty-two-year-old lieutenant, he and others were exposed to supposedly harmless dosages of a substance, which appears to have been a nerve gas. He adds that he was not told what was going to be tested on him and that since then, he has suffered ailments, such as skin and thyroid problems, chronic respiratory and stomach disease. He has sued for compensation. The similarities between his story and that of some of the Porton volunteers is noticeable.

INTRODUCTION

It can be seen that part of the reason behind Porton's long, uninterrupted programme of chemical warfare tests is that Britain has experienced continuity and stability; unlike these other countries, it has not been overrun by another nation, undergone a revolution, or been defeated in a major world war.

Information about gas testing in the developing, or Third World, is similarly scanty. Reports of such experiments in these countries are very sporadic. It has been alleged that on the orders of the callous regime of Iraqi dictator Saddam Hussein, biological weapons were tested on Iranian prisoners of war in the 1980s. If this is the case, there seems little reason why Iraq would not have undertaken their own programme of chemical warfare testing on humans.[12] It was reported in early 1997 that the Israeli military had been testing nerve gas antidotes and other drugs on soldiers since the 1970s.[13] The reviled apartheid regime in South Africa ran an active and covert chemical and biological warfare programme during the 1980s and early 1990s. An in-depth investigation by the Truth and Reconciliation Commission (TRC) found that the South Africans had developed a range of chemicals and germs for assassinating opponents of the apartheid system and manufactured large quantities of street drugs (apparently to control crowds). In its report published in 1998, the TRC painted a picture of a programme which was effectively out of control and run by a 'self-serving and self-enriching' clique. Interestingly, the TRC apparently did not uncover any hard evidence that human experiments were carried out during this cynical programme. One of the key officials claimed that chemical and biological warfare tests on humans were 'definitely not for us'.[14]

Allegations of the military use of poison gas by a raft of countries have been bandied around throughout past decades. Proving these claims is usually impossible. In recent years, the idea that chemical weapons are the 'poor man's atomic bomb' has taken hold around the world. The mere existence of gas tests in most countries is simply not known, but it seems a fair assumption that human subjects would have been used in experiments at some time by most developing countries seeking to develop and manufacture chemical weapons. However it is doubtful whether any country from the developing world has been conducting human experiments on a scale to rival that of Porton, especially since none of these countries appears to have been involved in poison gas for such a sustained period of time.

Even the number of nations which are, or have recently been, building up a chemical and/or biological arsenal has been shrouded in uncertainty. Imprecise figures of anything up to twenty nations have often been cited by analysts, intelligence agencies and other sundry experts in the past, usually

INTRODUCTION

naming Libya, Israel, Syria, Iran and China. The extent of Iraq's chemical and biological weapons was confirmed following the 1991 Gulf War. However, the total number of nations with poison gas fluctuates over time. The United States of America and Russia – two of the largest holders of gas munitions – are currently in the process of getting rid of these weapons following the signing of the 1993 global treaty banning this form of weaponry. It is hoped that this treaty will deter other nations pursuing chemical stockpiles.

Porton's gas testing programme may be the largest and longest in the world, but the British experiments are not the most horrific. The most grotesque chemical warfare tests on humans (which are known to the world at the moment) were done by the Nazis and the Japanese during the Second World War. Military personnel and scientists from both countries went as far as deliberately killing large numbers of humans during their macabre tests. The terrible human experiments in Nazi concentration camps included a series of chemical warfare tests. Many victims of these tests died after they had been intentionally poisoned with chemical weapons.

The notorious Unit 731 of the Japanese army secretly conducted gruesome biological and chemical tests on prisoners during its thirteen-year existence. This unit mainly used humans for biological warfare experiments. It is however apparent that humans were also exposed to poison gases in appalling tests, many of them experiencing agonising deaths. Victims were tied to a pole – some naked, and some with masks – and shoved into a chamber where they died in a lethal dose of gas. A young mother and baby perished in this way; she tried to protect her child from the fumes by covering it with her body. She failed and died lying on top of her offspring. Other victims were tethered to posts without protection as they were enveloped in huge gas clouds. According to one eyewitness, nearly 100 people were killed in an experiment with a new gas bomb; their cadavers were later dissected by scientists.[15] (The Japanese and Nazi experiments are discussed further in chapters four and six.)

An illicit air often hangs over chemical warfare. Governments of all hues frequently do not want to own up fully to what they have been doing in this field. The 'dirty war' image of poison gas grew from the muddy battlefields of the First World War. Many members of the public saw poison gas as a weapon of unique horror, which caused excruciating deaths among the young soldiers. Gas was feared to be a sort of all-powerful force which killed every living thing it touched – it could creep up silently and catch victims without the slightest warning, damaging their bodies before they could do anything about it. Many believed that gas was immoral and beyond the pale.

Introduction

Just as chemical warfare is perceived to be morally ambiguous by many people, the same can also be said of human experimentation. Together, poison gas and human tests make a controversial brew. In general, ordinary people are repulsed by the thought of scientists carrying out experiments on other humans. It sends shivers down spines. Many instinctively dislike it – and are even more wary when the experiments are being done by government scientists. We are living in an era when many have become more suspicious and sceptical about governments. People will readily believe that shadowy government operatives are perpetrating all kinds of dubious misdeeds and are then telling lies to cover up this wrongdoing. It creates a climate in which conspiracies are rife – and The Truth is being hidden by malign government forces. The popular television programme, *The X-Files*, has had a huge following because it skilfully taps into these beliefs. The plots chime with the views of a sizeable section of the population. It is not surprising that dodgy experiments on unwitting humans are a regular theme of the programme.

It is also apparent that as a whole, the public's trust in scientists – as well as governments – has been receding. In days of yore, 'boffins' were portrayed in films and books as absent-minded, slightly mad inventors who threatened no one in their pursuit of batty and innocent discoveries. But since – say – the Second World War, scientists have been depicted in the popular media as more menacing figures who invent dangerous machines such as death rays or deadly lasers – contraptions that can inflict death and destruction on a vast scale. They are also seen as being naive fools who are easily manipulated by evil men. Their image has shifted from one of fun to one of folly. This lack of confidence has surely been brought on by the development of nuclear weapons, and their power to blow up the world. This can be seen today in people's current fears over the controversies of genetic engineering and 'mad cow disease', to name but two. It would seem that all these views – on chemical warfare, human experimentation and scientists – have compounded to influence the British public opinion of Porton's tests.

Chemical warfare and biological warfare – or CBW – are invariably lumped together. They are however two different things. This book deals only with chemical warfare experiments. This is because Porton has not tested real biological weapons on human 'guinea pigs'. However Porton scientists did organise biological warfare trials – with simulants – over many populated areas of Britain between the early 1950s and the late 1970s. (These trials, and some aspects of biological warfare testing, are described in the afterword.)

INTRODUCTION

Chemical warfare can be defined as the use of chemicals against the enemy to inflict toxic damage of varying degrees on man, animals or plants. It also, of course, embraces the development of defences against such chemicals. Biological warfare – also called germ warfare – is the use of organisms, or 'bugs', against the enemy to cause diseases or death in man, animals or plants and the design of protection against such a threat. Chemical warfare tests can be defined broadly as being any experiment which is aimed at developing either chemical weapons or defences against such weapons. This therefore includes trials in which humans are exposed to poison gases (with or without protective equipment) or are used to test a wide variety of defences, such as protective clothing or anti-gas tablets. Nowadays, Porton is still using human volunteers in tests to develop defences, which fall within this definition of chemical warfare. It is by this definition that Porton is responsible for conducting the longest-running programme of chemical warfare experiments on human 'guinea pigs' in the world.

Within the realm of chemical warfare, there is a range of different types of chemical weapons whose toxic effect varies from short-term incapacitation of the mind or body to serious injury and death. There are also several categories of chemical weapons. At one end of the scale are irritants which simply harass the enemy. These include tear gases (also known as *lachrymators*) because they produce a flood of tears in the victim. Another class of irritants are known as the *sternutators*, because they induce excessive sneezing. These include arsenicals such as adamsite (DM), DA and DC. The military purpose of these harassing chemicals is to rapidly disable the enemy for a short period of time and therefore put them out of action for the duration of that time. Similarly, the *psycho-chemicals* were developed to incapacitate the enemy for temporary periods, primarily by affecting their minds. Chemicals such as BZ and the mind-altering LSD were explored in this respect.

Moving along the scale are chemicals which maim or kill. *Choking gases*, or lung irritants, attack the lungs, causing them to fill with liquid. Typical among this group are phosgene and chlorine. Another group are the *blood gases* which are absorbed through the lungs and then impede the movement of oxygen around the body. These include hydrogen cyanide and hydrogen sulphide. *Blister gases*, or vesicants, are chemicals which principally attack and burn the skin of the enemy. Examples of these are mustard gas and lewisite. The most deadly of these chemicals are the *nerve gases*, such as sarin, soman, tabun and VX. These disrupt the functioning of the nervous system and are so potent that minute amounts can result in a very rapid death. (Anti-plant chemicals, such as defoliants, have not been tested on human 'guinea pigs', and so they are not examined in this book). Scientists and staff within the world of chemical warfare often refer to chemical weapons as 'chemical agents'. I have tried to avoid using this jargon, unless it is in a document which is being quoted. Instead, I have used the terms 'chemical warfare' and 'poison gas' more or less interchangeably. Poison gas is the more common name for this type of warfare among the public. It is, however, a loose term, since chemical weapons can be gases or vapours, aerosols (mist/smoke) or liquid droplets.

One dispute which frequently bedevils chemical warfare research is the division between *offensive* and *defensive* work. Under an offensive policy, a country will actively seek to develop and manufacture chemical weapons in bulk for use on the battlefield. Such a country would manufacture the known poison gases. Some may even have the technical ability and the financial resources to try and seek out new compounds which could be used as poison gases. Defensive preparations are fundamental to an offensive policy. A country with gas stocks would also seek to develop defensive equipment and measures to protect its own troops against chemical weapons. This would enable its own armed forces to operate efficiently on a battlefield which had been contaminated with poison gases. It would also shield its own armed forces from chemical attacks if its enemy retaliated with poison gas. Many countries, however, announce that they are not developing or manufacturing a chemical arsenal and have instead a purely defensive policy – one in which they are solely seeking to devise protective measures against chemical attack.

Since the First World War, the public's distaste for poison gas has on the whole forced and obliged countries to shy away from admitting that they are manufacturing poison gases in an offensive policy. These countries – including Britain – have therefore concealed offensive activities in a heavy blanket of secrecy to avoid the inevitable public criticism. These governments have often denied point-blank that they are producing chemical stockpiles, only to have the truth revealed at a later date. This secrecy and duplicity has, over time, created so much doubt over chemical warfare work that many members of the public no longer believe official statements. Chemical warfare research usually takes place behind closed doors in a clandestine establishment as many governments believe that even a purely defensive research programme must be carried out in secret in order to conceal it from potential enemies. If it was all in the open, according to this argument, an enemy could spot the weaknesses in defensive preparations and invent ways of exploiting these deficiencies. However, despite this, many members of the public remain sceptical and suspicious of any official statement claiming that the work is only defensive, if they cannot see for themselves what is really going on.

There is another factor that muddies the picture. Military scientists need to study offensive techniques to a certain extent in order to develop defensive preparations against them. Some governments feel that it is necessary to carry out research into finding new chemicals which may be developed into weapons by a potential enemy at some point in the future. This would enable that country to produce defences against these novel poison gases. But this work at the same time can be misinterpreted by a suspicious public as being evidence that that country was itself seeking to develop these new chemicals as a weapon. The dividing line between offensive and defensive work can be fluid. A secretive chemical warfare installation could use the same knowledge for either purpose. For example, research to establish how much mustard gas affects the human body and causes casualties can be used to aid the development of defensive equipment; equally it can be used to predict how effective a mustard gas attack on a particular area of the body can be.

For many years, Porton has been dogged by murmurs and whispers that offensive work was being done behind its long fences, when officials were insisting that all its research was for defensive purposes. Rex Watson, Porton's director from 1974 to 1983, said these suggestions originated from 'misguided people' and created a 'certain amount of tension'. 'One of the things I found difficult to cope with was the fact we were always referred to as a top-secret establishment, when most of our work was not secret because it was to do with protecting people. There's nothing much secret about a gas mask or protective suit.' (His obituary recorded that he 'once had the discomfiting experience of having his effigy burnt in the street' by angry animal rights protesters.)[16]

It is now confirmed that Britain pursued an offensive gas policy from the First World War until the 1960s. In a key decision, the British Government decided in 1956 to halt the development of nerve gas, the premier chemical weapon then and now. This decision, and the real reasons behind it, was not properly spelt out for some years. As it turned out, the 1956 decision was not a clear-cut move to renounce poison gas stocks completely. After much secret Whitehall deliberation, the government decided in 1963 to rearm with a 'limited' chemical arsenal. Although offensive preparations were carried out, this decision was never fully implemented and chemical weapons were not actually manufactured in great quantities. These plans drifted in abeyance and by 1968 they had been clearly abandoned. During the 1960s, public interest in Porton and chemical warfare flourished, but it is now clear that the government was less than truthful over the real nature of its gas policy at that time. The existence of the 1963 decision was not revealed until the mid-1990s. Since 1968, Porton's work has been solely directed towards defensive research. Over the years, this policy was reviewed periodically, but not changed. It appears that the Conservative administration of Margaret Thatcher came closest to reversing this policy in the mid-1980s. With all Porton's accumulated knowledge of chemical warfare, Britain would have been in a relatively good position to restart gas production, although it would have been expensive.

Porton's human tests have been an essential and central part of both its defensive and offensive work. Experiments for defensive purposes have included testing the effectiveness of new masks and equipment in clouds of poison gases; exposing human subjects to these gases to try out possible treatments and antidotes; and wearing protective clothing in hot or cold temperatures or while undertaking heavy exercise to gauge if the clothing will hinder fighting efficiency. Human experiments are needed to check that a new invention in chemical defence will actually work in the confusion and chaos of the battlefield. These tests for defensive purposes have been carried out throughout Porton's history since 1916.

Developing chemical weapons, however, is a complex business. Military scientists searching for substances to turn into flawless poison gases do not simply select the most toxic compound. The potency of the chemical is only one of an array of factors which are taken into account. One former Porton scientist has outlined other considerations which are equally as important as the toxicity of a given substance – whether the chemical can be readily manufactured in large amounts; whether the compound can be easily stored and will not deteriorate over a long time; whether the compound can be dispersed effectively without being destroyed in the munition system; whether there is robust protection for your own troops against the chemical; and indeed whether the chemical can 'do the job' better than the existing poison gases.[17] A secret British document listed eight attributes for the 'ideal' chemical weapon, such as 'able to kill or incapacitate immediately and without warning – by its poisoning, blistering or irritating effects...effective in small concentrations – preferably more than one route of entry into the body...persist long enough to be effective in most climates...difficult to detect and counteract...[and]...considerable powers of penetration'.[18]

Satisfying all these criteria can be a difficult job. Many of the chemicals that have been examined at Porton Down and other poison gas establishments around the world were cast aside, leaving only a small number to be developed into weapons. The initial stage of any evaluation of

INTRODUCTION

a promising chemical is to test it on animals. However Porton scientists have, as a rule, felt that animal experiments are inadequate and that ultimately the chemical has to be tried out on people. Like many scientists, one of Porton's histories notes that the 'final' evaluation of the effectiveness of a chemical weapon depended on 'many and varied' tests on humans.[19] As one senior British official commented, 'As a general principle, in the chemical warfare field of investigation there is no doubt that, in the absence of tests on man, estimates of the hazard from potential chemical warfare agents will be unreliable and a dubious backing for weighty decisions concerning UK defences.'[20] He added that experiments with various species of animals to determine the toxicity of chemicals often produce differing results and so 'crucial' tests on humans had to be done to discover just how poisonous a compound was to mankind.

A large number of Porton's human tests have been done to establish exactly how a chemical attacks the human body, especially since humans are, after all, the intended targets of the weapons.[21] The scientists needed to know how susceptible the body would be to the chemical entering via the skin, the eyes, and through the mouth and nose. In a 1942 guide to human testing, for instance, Porton officials wrote that when a new gas is tested, volunteers 'are employed to discover the effect on the skin, the detectability by smell and the irritant properties, if any, on the eyes and respiratory tract; finally observations are carried out in the field.' It counselled that 'from the chemical warfare point of view, the effect of gas on the human organism depends greatly on the tactical objectives in the [battlefield] and method of dispersal. The problems which face the physiologist are thus far more complicated than those which face the chemist; accurate predictions are difficult to make, and cannot be made at all if the target is not clearly stated.'[22] As a general, and rough, rule scientists can learn more about a poison gas if human 'guinea pigs' are exposed to high dosages, thereby almost replicating the actual conditions of a military conflict. The dosages were, on the whole, higher in Porton's earlier tests than they have been in its more recent ones.

Porton's human trials have been invaluable for estimating the dosages of gases which would kill or injure an enemy. In this way, this experimental work has yielded much-needed data to facilitate the development of chemical weapons up to the late 1960s. Only a proportion of the human subjects have been exposed to chemicals of some kind; the exact ratio of the total number is unknown.

Porton's human trials are a hidden part of Britain's history. Some may say that the experiments in Porton's gas chambers are one of Britain's dirtiest secrets. Even though the testing programme has been so large, the public still knows relatively little about the experiments. Indeed, an internal history of the establishment notes that the role of Porton's human 'guinea pigs' was 'little known to the outside world'.[23] This book is the first in-depth investigation of these long-running human trials and seeks to shine a light into the dark recesses of Porton's work over the past eighty years.

The following chapters look at why the tests were conducted by Porton scientists, how the human 'guinea pigs' ended up in the gas chambers and what they experienced during the trials, and how the scientists felt about subjecting fellow human beings to poison gases. This book will examine the allegations of abuse hanging over the experiments – whether the volunteers were genuine, if they knew enough to give properly their consent to be human 'guinea pigs', if they were tricked into taking part in the gas tests instead of research into the common cold, if they were unnecessarily exposed to danger, and if their health has been ruined by the trials. It will scrutinise the ethics of the trials against the changing circumstances of the times, in both war and peace.

Porton's human experiments are an extraordinary story. Put yourself in the shoes of the human 'guinea pigs' and the scientists as you read the descriptions of the gassings.

Porton towards the end of the First World War.

Artillery detachment loading a gun in the First World War.

CHAPTER ONE
Pioneers of Pain

Modern chemical warfare burst into reality in the late afternoon of 22 April 1915 when clouds of chlorine gas rolled towards the Allied lines near Ypres in the First World War. German commanders had released around 150 tons of the chemical from 6,000 cylinders across a four-mile front. The Germans had waited eleven days for the right moment, when the wind changed and started to blow towards enemy lines. As soon as the liquid was freed from the cylinders, it turned into a dense yellowish-green cloud and billowed over the Allied trenches.

The attack heralded a grisly new chapter in the history of warfare. It had a devastating, spectacular impact. This form of warfare was so new that the victims in the front line trenches simply did not know what had hit them. There was virtually no battle – the Allied lines quickly disintegrated. Their commanders were similarly bamboozled by what was the first large-scale military assault with a chemical weapon.[1] In a despatch, Sir John French, the British Commander-in-chief in France, despaired of this new weapon, saying that it was 'practically indescribable'. He wrote, 'The effect of the gas was so overwhelming that the whole of the positions occupied by the French Divisions was rendered incapable by any resistance. It was impossible at first to realise what had actually happened. Fumes and smoke obscured everything. Hundreds of men were thrown into a stupor, and after an hour, the whole position had to be abandoned together with 50 guns.'[2]

No one knows how many died or were wounded in the attack. The British have estimated that as many as 5,000 were killed, and another 15,000 injured.[3] The unfortunate men were the first to suffer the effects of chlorine in warfare. The gas lays waste to the lining of the air passages, producing large amounts of liquid which block the lungs and windpipe – the victims drown in their own fluid. Some soldiers frantically attempted to bury their mouths and nostrils in earth to avoid inhaling the deadly gas. Others ran away, but could only make their poisoning worse as they breathed more heavily. Several men burst their lungs trying to suck in more air and survive their horrifying fate. One official account vividly describes how the victims suffered 'a burning sensation in the head, red-hot needles in the lungs, the throat seized as by a strangler. Many fell and died on the spot'. Others – 'gasping, stumbling, with faces contorted, hands wildly gesticulating, and uttering hoarse cries of pain...fled madly through the villages and farms', spreading panic as they went.[4]

The Germans had executed a perfect surprise attack, punching a hole four miles wide in the Allied lines. Ironically, they were too astounded by the sheer scale of their success to take advantage of their assault. If they had been more prepared, they could have rammed through the Allied front line for many miles and gained a decisive victory in the war.[5] Stung by the attack, Sir John French cabled London the very next day, demanding that the British retaliate against the Germans with their own chemical weapons.[6] Lord Kitchener, the War Minister, stepped onto the moral high ground when he replied on 24 April saying that, 'before we submit to the level of the degraded Germans' the request would have to be put before the Cabinet because the use of poison gas in war was outlawed by international agreement. He added, 'These methods show to what depths of infamy our enemies will go in order to supplement their want of courage in facing our troops.'

But, within weeks, the British Cabinet had agreed to the request. The politicians decreed that the British could only use chemicals which were no more harmful than those used against them by the enemy, although 'preparations and experiments might proceed for the employment of more deadly things'.[7] The British Army selected Major Charles Howard Foulkes to be in charge of 'gas reprisals' against the Germans. Foulkes was an eye-catching figure who had lived a life of adventure in the British Empire.[8] He had already served twenty-three years in the Army in various colonies, during which time he had narrowly avoided being shot several times, explored hostile country by horseback and canoe, and worked as a secret agent. He had also found the time to shoot big game, compete in the 1908 Olympic Games, and play football.

He believed that the Germans had cast aside 'civilised warfare', and that it was his duty to give them a 'dose of their own medicine.'[9] Foulkes was well aware of his predicament – he later reflected that 'our entire ignorance of the whole subject was particularly evident to me'.[10] As one military official wrote in 1919, at the time of the first gas attack, 'there was no organisation in this country for dealing with such an emergency. Little was known as to the possibilities of substances which might be employed in warfare, and there was only a trifling amount of manufacturing plant available for their production.'[11] From a standing start, and with little personal scientific knowledge, his task was to search out chemicals suitable for warfare, produce one or more of them in bulk as weapons, transport them to the battlefront, work out the most effective way of employing them, and train soldiers to use them. All this had to be done quickly at a time when chemical warfare was in its infancy.

Foulkes and his staff, comprising military officers and scientists recruited from universities, set to work. He was to receive much support from Lord Kitchener, whose instructions were simply 'do your damnedest.'[12] In late May, Foulkes reported to his superiors that experiments were being conducted on a number of gases.[13] One avenue focused on gases which could be propelled in some kind of missile or 'projectile', but 'no suitable filling was in sight'. Another idea was to adopt the Germans' form of gas attack – chlorine released from static cylinders. But there was just one factory in England which could produce chlorine in liquid form. This factory – the Castner Kellner chemical works at Runcorn – could only fill fifty cylinders a day; the military wanted at least 1,500 cylinders to mount their retaliation. Foulkes knew that releasing gas from cylinders was unsatisfactory, but he had little alternative for the time being.

Trials with the new chlorine cylinders took place on 4 June at the Runcorn factory. Employees of the factory were lined up at measured distances downwind from the cylinders.[14] Some of them were given the respirators that were used at the factory for protection (this consisted of several layers of soft cotton held over the mouth and nose), whilst others wore some kind of 'protective helmets'. The chlorine was then freed from cylinders of different sizes. Foulkes reported that the factory workers 'who were accustomed to inhaling small quantities of gas, were instructed to make a signal the moment the gas cloud reached them, but not to put on the respirators until compelled to.' Foulkes did not record either the quantity of gas released nor the reactions of the factory workers but he did however comment that he was very pleased with the results.[15]

During the trial, he had been impressed by the flow of the gas cloud along a thirty-foot high bank between the factory and the Manchester Ship Canal. The cloud had crept up the bank 200 yards from the cylinders, passed along the top of the bank for another 200 yards, and then rolled down the other side of the bank to the canal towpath. Foulkes noted that the moment he walked onto the towpath, the chlorine was so strong that he immediately donned a respirator. But the cloud, perhaps unsurprisingly, provoked the anger of people who were sailing past on barges – they shouted abuse at Foulkes and his colleagues. Foulkes found that his report of the trials 'created lively interest and satisfaction' at his headquarters; he was given a free hand in organising Britain's first gas attack. This finally took place, with chlorine from cylinders, at the Battle of Loos on 25 September 1915 – five months after the German gas strike at Ypres.

In the following weeks, more chemical attacks were launched by the British, but before long, many of their own soldiers came to loathe the gas cylinders.[16] The cylinders were too unreliable because they depended completely on the direction of the wind to carry the cloud towards the enemy. Unfortunately, the wind often changed and the gas was blown back over British lines. In the three weeks after the British first released gas at the Battle of Loos, 2,000 of their soldiers were struck down as casualties of their own cylinders.[17] The British claimed however that it was 'consoling to know that the Germans suffered similar and some rather worse accidents in their own early discharges'.[18]

Gas warfare had arrived and was not likely to disappear. The British expected gas to play a large role in the rest of the war, and so they decided to devote greater resources to it. An experimental establishment was needed. In September 1915, military officials began to scour the country for a suitable site, looking mainly in Dorset, Suffolk, Hampshire and Wiltshire.[19] One early favourite was an area in Cannock Chase in Staffordshire; so much so that some trials were conducted there in December that year. But residents were far from keen on the trials because some chemicals floated off and caused 'great discomfort' in the surrounding neighbourhood.[20] One of the chemicals used in these trials was hydrogen sulphide, known for its smell of rotten eggs. Foulkes recalled that this chemical, although 'well-known to most schoolboys who have employed it surreptitiously in many an escapade in class, was found to be surprisingly toxic.' One of those present at a particular trial was Captain William Howard Livens, who was to become known for inventing a projector, in collaboration with his father, which fired 'drums' of chemicals at the enemy. It was hailed by Porton as the 'outstanding gas weapon of the war'.[21] Foulkes regarded Livens as an energetic 'go-getter' who was 'always full of ideas'.[22] Livens 'entered the path of the cloud as the [hydrogen sulphide] emerged in high concentration from a cylinder. He was testing the protection afforded by a service gas helmet, but the latter was penetrated almost at once and Livens fell unconscious, though he recovered quickly when dragged out of the cloud.'[23]

Livens and many of the early pioneers of British chemical warfare believed that they should test gases under scrutiny on themselves. They were prepared to take the risks, since they were devout believers in gas. Foulkes, for example, went to great lengths to proclaim the advantages of poison gas to audiences, organising open days and demonstrations for the unconverted.

He stressed, 'I tested, personally, every gas which we took into use – repeatedly in the case of those for which the penetration of the German mask was claimed.'[24]

In early 1916, the site for the experimental establishment was chosen – around 3,000 acres of grazing land near the small country villages of Porton and Idmiston near Salisbury in Wiltshire.[25] The establishment was to become known as Porton Down. Its first member of staff, Sergeant Major Dobbs of the Royal Engineers, reported for duty on 7 March 1916, although it is not clear if there was anyone actually there to report to.[26]

The establishment was founded by constructing two Army huts, one for an office and the other a store. A few roads were prepared, along with some trenches for gas experiments. That month, the first load of gas arrived at Porton – 100 cylinders of hydrogen sulphide. Slowly more staff arrived, and a rudimentary laboratory was erected where 'a few desultory experiments' took place but it was not until 26 May 1916 that the establishment held its first major chemical warfare trial on the site.[27] This trial had been delayed as the staff were waiting for suitable weather. In front of a crowd of scientific and military visitors, 120 cylinders of hydrogen sulphide, spread out over 100 yards, were opened over a series of trenches. Rats were placed in cages and in the open. Meanwhile six men, borrowed from a mine rescue team, took samples of the passing cloud as it moved over them. They were protected by self-contained oxygen breathing apparatus and were required to open bottles which had been dug into the ground. Porton hailed this first trial as a success: 'the weather obeyed the meteorological forecast, the sampling arrangements worked, there was no analytical contretemps and lethal concentrations were produced at a distance of at least 300 yards.'[28]

Porton's first chief was appointed in June, a respected chemist called Arthur Crossley. A Fellow of the Royal Society, he had been helping the chemical warfare effort already and, with the rank of Lieutenant Colonel, had served in France.[29] Porton regards him as the 'outstanding figure' at the establishment during the war – 'from the moment Crossley arrived work was done all day and most of the night'.

Porton was now beginning to grow. Originally, it was only intended to be a site where gas cylinders could be released in open-air trials, away from the general public. But the British realised that this role was too narrow as there was a growing demand for research. Crossley recorded that it soon became evident that the gas cylinders tests would form only a small portion of Porton's work, since it was also necessary to investigate the 'very large problems of the use of gas in artillery shell and trench mortar bombs.'[30] Slowly other departments were set up, with their own buildings and facilities on the site. In the two years until the end of the war, Porton expanded substantially from its initial two huts to become a fairly large establishment.[31] By November 1918, its staff topped 1,500 – around 50 officers, 1,000 other ranks and 500 civilian workers. (In comparison, the modern-day Porton has only around 580 staff in total).[32] Its size had doubled since another 3,000 acres of land had been compulsorily purchased.

One of the first departments to be set up was the Physiology Laboratory in January 1917. One of Porton's most vital tasks was to establish how the various gases affected the human body and how toxic these chemicals were. The new laboratory was necessary because 'the effects on human volunteers who submitted themselves to gas in experiments demanded proper medical assessment.' Experiments on humans – which until then had been conducted in an apparently ad hoc manner – were now going to be carried out in a more systematic way.[33] Information had to be built up through gas chamber experiments, field trials and 'scanty reports from war operations in France'. As Porton now acknowledges, 'much use' was made of humans who were exposed to chemicals during the war – such human 'guinea pigs' were 'unmasked, but with his respirator at the ready, to act as the ultimate sensor and recorder of the effects on man.'[34] Porton's commandant, Crossley, acknowledged that the human experiments were 'some of the most important work' at Porton in the war – 'exposure which apart from its highly dangerous nature, has frequently meant much pain and violent discomfort.'[35]

In Porton's parlance, the human 'guinea pigs' were quaintly called 'observers' – because they literally observed and recorded the effects of the gases on themselves. (This term, which sanitises the sound of the poison gas experiments, lingered on at Porton for many decades.) In the two and a half years from its founding until the end of the war, Porton carried out a considerable number of trials and tests, both in the open air and in gas chambers, on an intense and almost feverish basis. The total is unknown but at least 800 reports were written recording the results of these experiments, the equivalent of virtually one a day. These reports (which were only made public in 1970) show that groups of humans, typically five or ten at a time, were exposed to gas in a substantial number of these trials and experiments.[36] As a rough estimate, it would appear that the number of times humans were exposed to chemicals would easily be in the thousands.

Porton examined the toxicity of around 200 substances during the war.[37] How many of these were tested on humans in that time, and on how many humans, remains unclear. It is difficult from the surviving public records to calculate reliable figures for the number of exposures for each particular substance. (This is not surprising since firstly, writing reports is not always a priority at a time of war, and secondly, many records from that time may have been destroyed, lost, or locked up forever.) One survey – compiled in 1918 – showed that Britain's chemical warfare department had obtained data about the effects on humans of ninety-six compounds.[38]

The final tally may be higher than that though. Another report shows that between 1917 and 1919, the chemical warfare department discarded 208 chemicals as being unsuitable for chemical weapons after they had been investigated.[39] (Some of that work would have been done outside Porton.) Although plainly many of the chemicals have been tried out on humans, the report does not state exactly how many were. The chemicals on the list were ditched for a number of reasons, such as 'killing power of a low order', 'very unpleasant irritant properties, but not incapacitating', 'evil-smelling substance of little value as an irritant or lethal agent', or most commonly, 'inferior' to chemical weapons which had been pressed into action by the British.

Many of Porton's human experiments in the Great War were done at a time when its scientists were groping around in the dark, desperately trying to understand this new subject. They had to build up their knowledge from scratch, since there were 'no known techniques for field trials or methods of taking samples of gas clouds, and no knowledge of safety distances or the influence of weather on gas diffusion'.[40]

On the offensive side, the British came to realise that releasing gas from cylinders was a very cumbersome and inefficient form of chemical warfare. Porton's official historian, Gradon Carter, comments that research on cylinders 'preoccupied the British for an untoward period' since they were 'slow' to catch up with the Germans.[41] The obvious innovation was to propel the gas in a container onto the target, and so each side began to investigate artillery shells, mortar bombs and grenades. Porton began to devote more and more of its time and energy in test-firing shells and the Livens Projector. The Livens was 'fired in batteries so that "crash shoots" of several thousand projectiles or Livens "drums" could produce an instantaneous and massive concentration of gas in the enemy lines.' In many of these artillery trials, observers were placed at staggered distances – some protected, others not – to document the effects of the gases on themselves. Crossley wrote that these firing trials presented a 'grave risk to the gunners involved and to the observers taking part in them, but it is gratifying to note that among the 2,000-odd trials fired no single accident occurred.'[42]

On the defensive side, much work was done outside of Porton in the Anti-Gas Department in central London. Based firstly at the Royal Army Medical

Many human subjects were exposed to gases fired from the Livens Projector.

College in Millbank and then at University College in Gower Street, this department worked on designing British gas masks and other protective equipment. However, as the war progressed, the amount of defensive work at Porton began to grow; the main task being to evaluate German, British and French gas masks under 'realistic conditions'.[43] This meant that the observers had to wear the masks and expose themselves to a range of toxic gases both within chambers and outside to determine, in a nutshell, whether or not the masks were effective. Clearly, finding out whether German respirators were vulnerable to particular gases would yield invaluable information, albeit at the price of the agony suffered by the British human 'guinea pigs'. In the last year of the war, this unpleasant work became more important – and onerous – since the Germans had developed a new mask – the 11.C.11. Experiments were undertaken not merely to determine if poisonous gases penetrated this mask, but to discover exactly how much penetration occurred. Crossley comments that it was 'particularly during the conduct of these experiments that the observers – officers, NCOs and men – suffered so much pain and discomfort, readily and cheerfully'.[44]

As we have already seen, the senior figures of Britain's early chemical warfare activities firmly believed that they should personally be exposed to gas if it helped the war effort. This created the atmosphere in which, it appears, the lower ranks at Porton were also obliged to subject themselves to poison gas in experiments. Whether the subordinates believed the same credo as their superiors, or whether they simply had no choice, is not known, since the voices of the underlings were not recorded.

The burden of the human experiments appears to have fallen on one particular unit within the Porton staff – the Royal Engineers Experimental Company. This unit was responsible for providing 'trained observers...to make observations on the travel of the lethal gas at various distances from the point of burst of the shell' and 'for the return of a detailed report on the observations.'[45] The size of this unit grew from fifty one in late 1916 to over 250 in 1918. Crossley claimed that Porton 'always' asked for volunteers for the experiments, 'since such work could not in any sense of the word be regarded as a duty'.[46] He added that 'in all cases' every member of the Experimental Company volunteered.

But what about the ethics of these experiments? To make any sense of what went on, these must be judged in the light of the ethical standards of that time and not of today. A universal code of ethics governing human experiments did not really emerge until after the Second World War when the Nuremberg Code was drawn up in the wake of the Nazi war crimes trials. However, even if there had been an overriding code of ethics in Britain at the time, it is probable that Porton's superiors would have seen the experiments as being absolutely necessary at a time of war and national emergency, and therefore above any such regulations. They would almost certainly have considered the information which was derived from the experiments as being essential to winning the war, particularly the chemical conflict, on the battlefront. This is shown in the way senior figures at Porton, foolishly or otherwise, chose to subject themselves to poison gas willingly, knowing the dangers and risks. This may not, however, have applied to some of the lower ranks of the Porton staff who had less scientific knowledge and were under orders. Even Crossley hints that there may have been some subjects who had not volunteered. He wrote that in Porton's first six months, 'the greatest difficulty was experienced in getting sufficient men to carry out the experimental work.' The 'necessary' solution, he noted, was 'time and again' to divert 'the cooks, orderlies, clerks, etc.' from their usual jobs to participate in the experimental work.[47]

Crossley singled out all the human 'guinea pigs' for praise in his final report at the end of the war. 'In a special word of admiration and commendation', he applauded all of them – from the highest to the lowest ranks – for exposing 'themselves to danger and intense pain always with cheerful loyalty.'[48] He said that, aside from the troops fighting on the front line, it was doubtful whether any other men in the entire British forces had endured 'so much discomfort entailing actual pain and so many hardships'. One history of the establishment comments: 'Risks were taken and sufferings were endured in a manner which was only possible by men of high morale under the urge of war.'[49] In the reports of the experiments, many of the same names keep on cropping up as human 'guinea pigs'. It is truly remarkable that large numbers of staff – caught up in the mood of the time – were prepared to subject themselves, time and again, to the painful gases.

Porton believes that during the war, the team spirit within the establishment as a whole was so strong that it drove the staff on to achievements 'which otherwise could not have been obtained'. (The officers at Porton sought to keep alive their wartime camaraderie through regular reunions and newsletters until the late 1930s.)[50] Crossley said, 'The main cause which has made possible the work accomplished was the patriotism, keenness and devotion to duty of all ranks.'[51] He summed up the efforts of all the staff in one word – 'Splendid!'

The staff in the Physiology Laboratory have been portrayed as being typically plucky British. At first, the department was merely one hut, which was to act as both an office and a laboratory. The original hut was burnt down, but 'work was carried on temporarily in a tent without stopping the research in hand'.[52] In the early days, one of the staff, Captain 'Bunny' Peters (later to become Sir Rudolph Peters and to be involved with Porton for many decades), slept on the floor of the Physiology Laboratory and bathed in a round tin tub on the floor of the post-mortem room.[53] 'Bunny' was described by colleagues as a 'very congenial' member of the department, who, apart from his 'valuable work as a medical officer', was 'a first class messing officer (the mess bills, however, were rather high!)'.[54]

One of the junior staff, Austin Anderson (later knighted), remembered that life in the department was 'pretty strenuous' – spending 'a lot of time dodging in and out of gas with our gas masks on or at the ready. However there was no real risk of suffering serious damage unless you did something silly and allowed familiarity to breed contempt of the poisons we handled.' He added that when it came to measuring the potencies of chemicals, 'we had to rely on our own skins, lungs and eyes.' He recalled that he was given 'all kinds of odd jobs' because he was 'by far the youngest and probably the best cross country runner' in the department. One of his tasks was to go to a field about a mile away. Arsenical smoke clouds were then released and he 'had to watch their progress across country, get into them, and judge their potency by sniffing.' He commented, 'As the clouds were apt to change direction unexpectedly, considerable fleetness of foot was needed to get into position to receive the cloud.'

As with many institutions, the memoirs of Porton staff are peppered with light-hearted anecdotes and tales. Many years later, Anderson reminisced about one particular incident which the British, with our 'crude sense of humour, thought was funny, though I do not think the French victims did'. He recalled that the British and the French were having a dispute over respirators and a particular arsenical smoke. This smoke produced a 'distinctly painful choking' for an hour which could only be alleviated by chloroform. The British believed that this smoke gave them a military edge because it penetrated respirators unless they were fitted with special filters to keep the smoke out. They therefore modified their respirators with the filters. However the French were convinced that their respirators gave complete protection against the smoke and did not need to be modified in any way. The British disagreed, drawing on their own experiments with the French respirators. To resolve the dispute, the French sent over an officer who would walk around in a cloud of the arsenical smoke wearing one of their respirators. He was to be accompanied by some of the British who were protected by their own respirators. Anderson recalled, 'The poor man got a very painful lesson in his superior's fallibility. He used up so many chloroform ampoules to alleviate his suffering that he passed out after telling his British companions that his life had been endangered by their diabolical negligence. However I do not think that he bore us any ill will after he had recovered.'

In charge of the Physiology Department was a very unlikely figure, Professor (later Sir) Joseph Barcroft. He was a distinguished physiologist, and also a Quaker. Because of the Quakers' opposition to war, the military hesitated for a while before appointing Barcroft to the post. Throughout the war, he 'consistently and successfully resisted being put into uniform.'[55] One of his staff later wrote that without doubt, Barcroft was 'the unquestioned leader of all the work in that department...we had some little difficulties as he was the only civilian in an entirely service establishment; but somehow we managed to build up a kind of aura around him as the mysterious "Professor Barcroft", and he was accepted as a superior being.'[56]

Barcroft has become renowned for one particular incident in the war. It was a tale which Austin Anderson described as 'but one illustration of his habit of proving the accuracy of his theories by trying them out on himself.' He adds that it was the one occasion on which Barcroft 'our much admired leader did subject his life to a wisely calculated but definite risk.' Once again, it was done to settle a dispute with their French allies.[57] Both nations were experimenting with hydrogen cyanide (HCN) as a killer gas. The French were testing it on dogs, while the British were trying it on goats. A large proportion of dogs were being killed in the tests, but equal numbers of goats were left unscathed. On the basis of their experiments, the French were intending to use hydrogen cyanide as a battlefield weapon, but Barcroft suspected that it would be next to useless.

The argument revolved around the point of whether a human being would be as vulnerable to the gas as a goat or as a dog. Anderson recalled, 'One night, Barcroft without telling anyone of his intentions waited until the rest of us...had gone back to the mess. He then got hold of a corporal to help him and to act as a witness. He then raised a fairly high concentration of hydrogen cyanide in the chamber, and accompanied by a dog on a lead walked through the air lock into the gas without a gas mask. He waited the few minutes necessary for the HCN to knock out the dog and came out of the chamber very much on his feet. When he got back to the mess, he reported what he had done, but went to bed early because he "still felt a bit muzzy".'

Barcroft reported that the only real effect on himself 'was a momentary giddiness when I turned my head quickly. This lasted about a year, and then vanished. For some time it was difficult to concentrate on anything for any length of time.' As for the dog, it had collapsed after fifty-five seconds in the chamber and 'commenced the characteristic distressing respiration which heralds death from cyanide poisoning' and at around ninety seconds, it stopped breathing and was carried out of the chamber. In many versions of this tale, the dog did indeed die. However, this was not so, as Barcroft himself reported later in a scientific journal: 'Although the corpse was set aside for burial [at] about 6.30p.m., the dog did in point of fact recover and was found walking about next morning.' A colleague reported that the dog was 'bouncing around the lab complaining that its belly was empty and needed filling'. Barcroft felt that he had proved his argument and that the French were over-estimating the potency of hydrogen cyanide.[58]

The 'Barcroft's Dog' incident did wonders for the scientist's reputation. King George V was even told about the tale during a visit to Porton in 1918. Barcroft — who fretted about the correct way to greet the King since he was a civilian, not an officer — records that he had just finished explaining his department's work to the King when 'to my dismay events took an unlooked for and alarming turn.' Crossley began to retell the experiment with the dog to the monarch. Barcroft tried to beat 'a hasty retreat' but a general 'caught me by the arm and gently, but firmly led me back, commenting, "Oh no, Barcroft, you can't escape like that." The King exclaimed, "Good God, what a wonderful plucky thing to do."'[59]

Prime Minister Lloyd George sent a personal letter to Barcroft expressing 'the most intense admiration' for his 'outstanding courage, gallantry and devotion' in exposing himself to gases in two particular experiments.[60] Commenting on the 'Barcroft's Dog' incident, the Premier wrote of his 'high appreciation of your brave action which obtained information of quite exceptional value.'

Lloyd George also commended Barcroft for another experiment with an unspecified gas. In this instance, Barcroft was 'called upon to ascertain the immediate and subsequent effect upon troops of a new gas...you voluntarily exposed yourself to a strong concentration of the gas for a period of half-an-hour — subjecting yourself to the certainty of severe pains and to serious danger of permanent ill effects.' In one of Porton's official histories, a senior member of staff has scrawled, alongside an account of the incident, 'Barcroft was a great showman.'[61]

Aside from the human experiments, Porton conducted an enormous number of tests on animals from early 1917 onwards. It is said that the Porton scientists 'had considerable difficulty in working with a good many soldiers because the latter objected so strongly to experiments on animals, and did not conceal their contempt for people who performed them'.[62] The tests on animals helped to establish the toxicity of chemicals before they were tested on humans. Porton founded a farm within its grounds to breed the necessary number of animals. At the end of the war, the farm had 2,990 animals, including goats, cats, dogs, rats, mice, rabbits and monkeys, although there were 'considerably' more when the experimental work was going at full tilt.[63]

As the war ground on, both sides investigated not only new weapons for propelling gas at each other's lines, but also new toxic chemicals which could be loaded into such weapons. One of the most important breakthroughs was phosgene, a colourless gas which smells like mouldy hay.[64] Although it was first employed by the Germans, it was to become the main battle gas of the Allies. Initially phosgene was mixed with chlorine and released from cylinders, but later it was fired at the enemy in projectiles. The Allies first uncovered the war potential of this gas in the summer of 1915. A French captain had alerted Foulkes to a derelict factory near Calais which had manufactured the chemical in peacetime for use in the dyeing industry. They visited the factory and witnessed some experiments on animals which indicated that the gas was much more toxic than chlorine. Foulkes said, 'Some of it was also liberated in a closed chamber, and when I entered it, wearing the British gas helmet, I found that the latter gave no protection against the gas whatever. Here was a valuable find!'[65]

Phosgene is between six and ten times more lethal than chlorine,[66] but Foulkes extolled it as being 'still more valuable as it possesses other dangerous properties.'[67] The delayed effect of phosgene is extraordinary. A person can inhale a lethal dose and feel nothing other than a mild irritation of the eyes and throat which passes quickly. For a day or so, he or she can feel perfectly normal and even mildly euphoric, but this is fatally deceptive. During that time, the lungs are filling up with liquid at a steady rate which increases during physical activity. All of a sudden, the victim collapses since the oxygen is now being blocked from the lungs. A painful cough develops, the skin and lips turn blue, and breathing becomes hurried, shallow, and spasmodic. The victim dies a terrible lingering death, their lungs spewing out a frothy white or yellowish liquid.

Phosgene caused sheer desolation when it was first used by the Germans in December 1915 – six days before Christmas. A total of 1,069 British soldiers were gassed that day with 116 fatalities.[68] Troops in the First Leicestershire Regiment heard a 'loud hissing sound' at around 5.20a.m. on 19 December; within ten seconds, they had detected the 'strong smell of gas'. An army doctor recorded that in his section, around three men died from the gas, with another dozen 'suffering slightly'. At noon, he visited the trenches and found that all the gassed men were 'merry and bright and no one had any complaint to make' and by late afternoon, the medic, Captain W J Adie, reported that he was 'very pleased' to see that so few of the troops had been killed or injured in the attack. But as darkness grew, the phosgene was beginning to take its lethal grip. Around thirty to forty 'slightly ill' men left their trenches to report sick. As they crossed the 100 yards of very rough muddy ground, they began to succumb to the mysterious gas; this exertion wore them out as it made the effect of the phosgene worse. Captain Adie wrote, 'The road was strewn with exhausted men, and we did not get them all in until 7a.m. the next morning.' The men who stayed in the trenches were 'still more striking. One man, feeling fairly well, was filling sand bags, when he collapsed and died suddenly. Two more men died in the same way that evening.' Confusion reigned as more and more men perished abruptly.[69]

The British had already been striving to manufacture bulk quantities of phosgene, but sufficient supplies were not produced until the Battle of the Somme six months later. Foulkes believed that 'ignorance of this peculiarity' of phosgene was responsible for most of the casualties among the British when they first used it. His men 'knew to what extent they could breathe small quantities of chlorine without harmful results. With phosgene, however, death sometimes occurred after only a whiff or two of it had been inhaled, an insufficient dose even to cause coughing...' He added that there were constant cases of men who declared positively that they had not breathed in phosgene, but who – one, or even two, days later – dropped dead. One man, Sergeant Harrower, 'got a slight smell' of phosgene while disconnecting a pipe: 'He paid no attention to it, did not even report it and carried on with his work.' That night he slept well, but collapsed the next morning during breakfast and was dead within twenty-four hours.[70] One German prisoner captured in a raid after a gas attack ridiculed the effect of the gas and 'expressed supreme confidence in his mask'. He died from gas poisoning a day later. Such incidents were caused by 'even a small intake of gas, varying in amount with the idiosyncrasies of individuals,' according to Foulkes.

He recalled that the British were unaware of this 'remarkable' delayed action when it was initially discovered. In the early days of phosgene, he had been 'frequently' exposed to the chemical, while being totally oblivious of its delayed effect.[71]

Porton carried out many experiments with phosgene during the war. Observers were used in Porton's trials to develop suitable phosgene-filled weapons. In one trial, on a Friday evening in September 1917, the scientists were trying to establish how phosgene would spread after it had been exploded from Livens drums.[72] Rats and goats were tethered at various distances from the drums to see which ones died. Captain 'Bunny' Peters strode through the cloud wearing a British gas mask which gave 'perfect' protection. Later, he walked to a position 200 yards from the drums and removed his mask, but had to put it straight back on because his eyes had begun to stream severely. Two observers had been placed 1,500 yards from the drums. Six minutes after the explosion, they noticed the phosgene 'in sufficient quantity to make their eyes smart and to cause them to put on respirators.' Other observers – 100 yards and further from the drums – were equipped with oxygen breathing apparatus and had the task of opening bottles to catch samples of the drifting cloud. Some of these observers reported that the cloud was not 'distinctly visible' so 'they had to be guided as to when to take the samples by the effects produced on their eyes and skin.'

Observers were also exposed to phosgene in trials to test out the reliability of captured German gas masks. In one set of experiments, two teams of ten observers went into the gas chamber in relays for three-hour stints so that a number of gas masks could be exposed to a mixture of phosgene and chlorine for twelve hours. This mixture – half and half of each chemical – was known by the British as 'white star' and was used in vast quantities during the war. In the experiment, the men were instructed to wear the masks until they could notice either the phosgene or chlorine penetrating through the respirator. 'In a very few instances' the observers had to be sent back into the chambers after their superiors had found that only a small amount of phosgene had penetrated their respirators.[73] 'In most cases, however, the observers remained in until very distinct amounts of phosgene were penetrating, and they were evidently most anxious to carry out the tests fairly and not to withdraw too soon,' noted the report of the experiments.

In the first round of tests, the observers managed to expose four of the ten respirators for the full twelve hours. The rest had to be withdrawn before the target time because 'small quantities' of phosgene were seeping in. Two days later, the experiment was repeated, mainly with the same respirators. The observers rotated between two gas chambers every thirty minutes. In one chamber, the concentration of the chlorine/phosgene was the same as before, but in the other, it was ten times stronger. This time, the observers were 'decidedly' more confident, and 'as a rule did not withdraw until considerably larger quantities of phosgene were being breathed. No harmful after-effects were caused.' On this occasion, seven of the ten masks were worn for eleven hours or more in the gas before the observers left the chambers. 'Considerable quantities' of phosgene penetrated four of the masks – 'one observer withdrew coughing violently'. However, the report noted, 'Owing to the delayed poisonous effects of phosgene, it was not considered advisable to make the observers continue to breathe small quantities of this gas for a long period, since it would be impossible to know at what point they ought to retire before injurious quantities were taken in.'

A few months later, another batch of observers was subjected to 'high concentrations' of phosgene to try out the latest type of German respirator, the 11.C.11.[74] The observers were selected from officers, NCOs and men who had 'special knowledge and experience of this kind of chamber experiment.' They were sent into the chambers to see how much phosgene would enter the respirators in a set time. Once again, the Porton scientists stressed that they had to take precautions because phosgene is 'highly toxic': all penetration was 'treated as dangerous and the observers were ordered to retire even though they might have found it possible to remain somewhat longer.' At the time – summer 1918 – Porton had devised a simple system for grading the degree of penetration of the gas masks, ranging from 'complete protection' to 'distinct penetration noticed but no discomfort' and then to 'marked penetration so severe as to cause observer to leave the chamber.' According to Foulkes, a concentration of one part phosgene in 50,000 parts air (1/50,000) would kill an unprotected person in ten minutes.[75] From these experiments, Porton was able to learn the lesson that while phosgene could not penetrate the newest German respirator at concentrations of 1/1000 and weaker, the gas at a concentration of 1/500 could do so 'to the extent of fifty percent to one hundred percent'. The danger of the experiment was plain. The observers – protected by their gas masks – were being exposed to much stronger concentrations, between 1/5,000 and 1/500 for up to 30 minutes. Many of them had to flee the chamber after as little as 30 seconds once the phosgene had breached their respirators.

Observers were also used to test German respirators with another class of chemical weapon – arsenical smokes. The Germans had been the first to use one of these compounds, called DA, on the battlefield in 1917. DA produces an intolerable irritation of the nose and throat, provoking protracted sneezing, intense and quite unbearable headaches, runny nose, pain in the chest, breathlessness, nausea, vomiting and retching. 'The victim has unsteady gait, a feeling of vertigo, weakness in the legs, and trembling all over the body,' according to one account.[76] DA, along with two other major arsenical smokes, DC and DM (adamsite), are known as sternutators (because they cause sneezing).[77] Through human experiments, the British established that no model of German respirator could protect the wearer from either DA or DM. In one such test, ten observers, 'selected on account of their experience of such work', entered the gas chambers in successive tests with seven different concentrations of the two gases.[78] Their instructions were to remain in the chamber for up to an hour until 'penetration of their protection was so marked as to render it impossible' to stay. They then had to quit the chamber and report to the officer in charge. This officer would then 'record their observations and satisfy himself as to their accuracy' and note down the time they left the chamber. A variety of German gas masks were worn by the observers during these tests, but the results were always the same: 1/1,000,000 of DA was enough to run through the enemy's respirators rapidly and completely. 'The effect produced upon experienced observers was quite startling, for although they retired from the chambers in a very few minutes, they were suffering acutely.'

A short while later, Porton conducted another set of experiments with these two arsenical smokes to discover for how long the gases would retain their power to penetrate the German respirators.[79] Observers donned the masks and went into gas chambers for more than five hours. When the toxicity of the gas appeared to be fading or disappearing altogether, observers who were not protected in any way entered the chamber to check. Porton reported that, approximately, the potency of DA seemed to wear off after an hour, while DM was still effective after four hours.

The vulnerability of the German gas masks to the arsenical smokes was an important discovery for the British. On the battlefront, Foulkes considered that it was 'his business' as expert adviser to Britain's Commander-in-Chief in France, to use it to its best advantage. He proposed that the arsenical smokes should be released on a 'vast scale' before an infantry advance.[80] Although the Germans were in fact the first to introduce arsenical smokes, they did not, however, have an efficient weapon with which to disperse it among enemy lines. But the British had developed one, the so-called 'M device'.[81] By using thousands of these devices at once in a surprise attack, Foulkes believed that the 'most effective chemical weapon ever devised' would be used to maximum benefit, 'in contrast with the waste of opportunity which was the result of the first use of gas by the Germans' in April 1915. Complete success was 'absolutely certain' if the secret of the M device was kept. As it turned out, the war ended before the M devices were used in France. But Foulkes believed that if it had been used and exploited properly and to the full, it would have made a bigger impact on the course of the war 'than any other measure that was put to a practical trial on the battlefield or that was even considered.'

Several experimental versions of the M device were tried out in trials at Porton. One of the first trials took place from noon on Saturday, 16 February

1918.[82] Observers – who were either unprotected, or wearing British or German gas masks – were placed at intervals of 100, 200, 400 and 800 yards from the devices. At separate times, four of the experimental devices were set off, generating clouds of DA, and 'the effects experienced by the observers were recorded.' Porton was encouraged by the trial, since the performances of the devices were 'promising' despite a very high, blustering wind on the day. 'The effects produced on unprotected observers even at distances of 600 yards are extremely distressing, and it would not appear necessary to use unprotected observers at any distance less than 800 yards in future experiments,' noted the scientists.

Throughout 1918, Porton strove to perfect the M device, with experiments to refine its efficiency and to establish, for example, at which distances it would be effective for specific lengths of time. The reports of these experiments are littered with descriptions of the pain suffered by the observers; sometimes this is recorded as being 'extreme distress' or 'intense discomfort' and other times it is more specific – burning in the throat, coughing, pains in the chest. One of the worst hit was an unnamed man who was stationed fifty yards away from the M device in a trial in May of that year. The DM arsenical smoke punctured through his gas mask within three minutes. 'Observer forced to retire at 10 minutes with intense discomfort. For 15 minutes afterwards a feeling of illness, a desire to vomit, violent coughing and extreme mental depression. The distress then began to subside. 14 hours afterwards a "tightness" in the chest and general feeling of lassitude were noticed.'[83] Clouds of arsenical smoke generated by the M devices could travel fair distances, and according to one Porton experiment, still rapidly penetrate German respirators for distances up to 2,000 yards.[84] This sometimes resulted in clouds billowing over people, including civilians, who were not part of the experiments. In one trial, an 'experienced observer' was posted to a road 2,700 yards from a cluster of fifty M devices (one of the previous jobs described by Austin Anderson). The observer detected the cloud of DA after fifteen minutes and felt 'very marked' symptoms of poisoning. Nearby workmen too 'were obviously affected and withdrew after a few minutes' exposure.'[85] In a previous trial, a cloud of adamsite (DM) 'apparently touched' buildings within Porton 'some 1,000-1,200 yards away and men were driven from their huts with sneezing and general slight throat effects.'[86]

Mustard gas was the most important chemical weapon discovered during the First World War. This fearsome compound was soon to become known as the 'King of the Battle Gases'. It was first used by the Germans in July 1917 and its power soon became evident. In the first three weeks of using this new gas, the Germans inflicted as many gas casualties on the Allies as in the entire previous year from chemical weapons.[87] The Germans had covertly manufactured an enormous amount of mustard gas so that they could deliver a resounding surprise attack on the unsuspecting enemy when it was first unleashed. Within ten days, they had fired off more than a million shells containing 2,500 tons of mustard gas.[88]

As with the first use of phosgene, the impact of the new chemical was devastating. Those exposed to mustard gas do not initially experience any pain. But – like phosgene – this only makes the gas more dangerous, as the victim is unaware that the damage has begun. The main effects are on the skin and eyes. Within six hours, the eyes become inflamed with an intense burning pain. Slowly, they begin to water and feel gritty, becoming more and more sore and bloodshot, with the eyelids reddening and swelling up like balloons. Blisters on the skin begin to appear, along with stiffness, throbbing pain and swelling, with the burns being most severe in the most moist parts of the body, such as the groin, neck and armpits. After a day, there may be a fresh crop of blisters and the skin may then become very itchy, preventing sleep. Victims may also be temporarily blinded. The blisters can take up to four to six weeks to subside during which time they are prone to bursting and becoming infected.

The British called the new gas 'HS' (Hun stuff).[89] The first German attack with mustard gas occurred at Ypres in the late evening of 12 July. Initially, the British troops felt little; one expert was later to write, 'There is no doubt that the immediate effects...were quite trifling.' This lulled them into complacency – many did not think that it was worth putting on their gas masks and they unsuspectingly carried on as normal, with many even going to sleep. This was to be the cause of many of the 2,000 casualties that night. Within five hours, they woke up with 'intolerable' pain in the eyes; some were treated with morphine and cocaine to ease their terrible distress as the medics struggled to cope with the huge number of victims. Those who died did so agonisingly over several days.[90]

It took the British fourteen months – until September 1918 – to manufacture enough supplies to retaliate with mustard gas. Ironically, a British chemist had suggested mustard gas as a weapon of war back in 1916, but it had been rejected at that time by the military. As the story goes, the chemist had put the idea to a general. ' "Does it kill?", asked the general. "No," he was told, "but it will disable enormous numbers of the enemy temporarily." "That is no good to us," said the man of blood; "we want something that will kill." '[91]

Porton realised that mustard gas was a 'highly dangerous weapon against troops' because of its 'extraordinary' capacity to blister, its ability to cause 'serious eye casualties' with low doses, and capacity to lie around on the ground for a long time.[92] The first task was to protect British troops. The respirator could block vapour and safeguard the eyes and lungs, but the mustard gas liquid threw up an additional problem – all the skin from head to toe had to be completely protected as well. It only took the minutest amount to cause, after a few hours, reddening and blisters which proved very difficult to heal. Porton ran large numbers of experiments in an attempt to discover the best method of removing mustard gas from contaminated clothing and boots, dugouts and craters, and to establish how long the gas would remain on various types of soils, surfaces and rubble.

Mustard gas has a particular characteristic: those who have been burned by it once often subsequently become much more sensitive to it, and are therefore prone to be more quickly and badly blistered when they later come into contact with even very small amounts. This phenomenon was confirmed in experiments which compared the effects of the gas on two types of human 'guinea pigs': those who had never been exposed to mustard gas and those who had. In one test, for example, some of the latter group had previously had a 'single rather severe blister' and others had had 'repeated experimental burns over 12 months or more.'[93] After this test, Porton recommended that trials with mustard gas 'must be made on persons who have not been previously used for similar experiments.' Foulkes commented: 'The only satisfactory course was to use "virgin skin". There was, of course, no scarcity of this commodity in the country, even late in the war, but provision had to be made for a constant supply of newcomers among the experimental staff.'[94]

Mustard gas was given its name because it smelt like mustard. Oddly, though, people have described the smell of the brownish liquid in many ways. One of the 'vagaries of the human sensation of smell', commented Foulkes, was that 'although everybody agreed that mustard gas had a distinct and unpleasant odour, it was variously described by patients in hospital and others as resembling mustard, rubber, vulcanite, dead horses, diseased vegetables, petrol, garlic and lamp oil!'[95]

However one of the perils of the liquid was that troops were failing to detect its odour in the heat of the battle and had been struck down as casualties as a result. At Porton, groups of between ten and twelve observers – 'officers and men with considerable experience of the smell of mustard gas' – were exposed in a series of experiments to see whether other smells would disguise the gas.[96] They were each sent for two minutes into the chambers which were polluted with mustard gas and alternatively, fumes from a black powder, and phosgene. Porton noted that the observers were working under 'favourable conditions' for recognising the mustard gas, since they knew all about it and could guess that it would probably be in the chamber, an artificial atmosphere in itself. But it became evident that 'the smell of mustard gas in atmospheres of low concentration may be readily masked by other odours such as explosion gases, lethal gases, etc.' Another set of tests in the chamber revealed that observers could no longer smell the gas after as little as two minutes; in other words, its distinctive smell would fade away.[97] However they were able to smell it again after having worn a gas mask for a few minutes.

Other experiments focused on determining how much mustard gas was needed to induce harmful effects on a person's eyes.[98] Three observers were exposed to concentrations of mustard gas for up to seven minutes. All three developed conjunctivitis within twelve hours with damage ranging from 'severe' to 'slight', along with chest and throat symptoms – one even suffered 'almost complete loss of voice five days later.' In further tests, observers, with their mouths protected, wore goggles with one of the eyepieces removed so that it was naked to the gas. By late 1918, Porton had come to believe that if mustard gas could be smelt, it would also be strong enough to be dangerous to the eyes.[99]

Before the end of the war, both sides were unable to devise satisfactory defences to protect the skin of soldiers against mustard gas. One proposed solution was clothing of impermeable oilcloth, but it proved to be too cumbersome and uncomfortable.[100] But relatively few soldiers actually died after their skin had been contaminated with mustard gas. It was responsible for at least 120,000 British casualties – by far, the highest of any chemical weapon – but only around two or three percent of them actually died. The power of mustard gas was to keep soldiers away from the front line for weeks and even months, since the burns and eye problems generally took a long time to heal, and also would sometimes reappear. Many soldiers became tormented with unending depression and eye pains. Since mustard gas tended to lie around for a long time, it contaminated the trenches, causing casualties long after the shells had been fired, and this prolonged hazard did much to undermine morale.

If inhaled, mustard gas can corrode the breathing passages and – like phosgene – liquid can fill up the lungs and kill a person, or foster infectious diseases. However, neither side in the war was able to develop the weapons needed to generate a sufficiently dense cloud of mustard gas to kill in this way. The MoD estimates that phosgene killed eighty-five percent of all those on both sides who died from chemical weapons, a much higher percentage than mustard gas.[101]

Porton was not the only British establishment during the Great War where staff were being exposed to chemical warfare gases in experimental work. The Anti-Gas Department – in Millbank and later at University College, London – had been set up back in 1915 to provide protection to troops. As well as overseeing the production of fifty-five million respirators, the department ran 'daily tests' in which its staff were subjected to many poison gases to examine the effectiveness of masks. According to a privately-printed history of the department, there were a 'considerable number of chamber tests on the unprotected observer'. Another history acknowledges that this work was always 'done ungrudgingly and without complaint despite its trying nature', but it also caused 'much personal discomfort and some disturbance of health to officers and other ranks who carried it out'.[102]

Forty staff were constantly in jeopardy at another chemical warfare establishment, the Central Laboratory of the British Expeditionary Force. Based in France, its hazardous task was to open up German gas shells to analyse their contents and discover what chemicals they contained. They also had the job of 'systematic and regular' testing of British and enemy gas masks and equipment. The Central Laboratory organised one of the first experiments in which British people were deliberately exposed to chemical warfare gases.[103] The laboratory's official history claims that the experiments 'were the first conducted by any of the Allies in which an actual gas cloud was used.' They were started on 30 April 1915, eight days after the first German gas attack at Ypres. The British were desperate to find a defence against the gas. They hoped that a 'cotton-waste respirator' might do the trick. Chlorine was released over a trench 'to imitate the conditions of an actual gas attack'. It was found that the respirator was 'satisfactory at first, but that after a short time it broke down.'[104]

Ernest Rudge, one of the Central Laboratory scientists, later recalled their risky work. For example, unexploded mustard gas shells would be brought to the laboratory where a hole was manually drilled into the shell and its hazardous liquid drained. Late in the war, the huge stock of bottles filled with drained mustard gas smashed to the floor after an entire rack of wooden shelving collapsed. 'For weeks, we lived and worked with the persistent odour, with the inevitable result. One by one we began to feel the effect upon our lungs,' wrote Rudge. He was sent back to England where he suffered weeks of delirium before recovering.[105]

Some of the pioneers in British chemical warfare experimental establishments lost their lives because of their work. Lieutenant Colonel William Watson, head of the Central Laboratory, died in 1919 after being repeatedly exposed to chemical weapons.[106] Colonel Edward Harrison, head of the Anti-Gas Department, perished a week before the end of the war at the age of forty-nine and was dubbed a 'poison gas martyr'. Soon after, another officer of the Anti-Gas Department – Captain Alexander Gemmell – also died and was hailed 'the second victim of these researches'. A number of staff in the Anti-Gas Department suffered permanent ill health from their involvement in the testing of such large numbers of gas masks. One military official commented that the country had reason to be grateful 'for their zealous labours.'[107] It is not known how many of Porton's staff experienced lasting bad health. After the war, the Allies discovered that the Germans had employed a unit of forty 'specialist observers' who acted as their human 'guinea pigs' in the gas chambers. They submitted themselves to 'not more than one test a day'. One of them had died after 'prolonged exposure to phosgene'.[108]

One of the abiding memories of the First World War is the dreadful deaths and injuries caused by chemical weapons. The image of the shuffling line of soldiers blinded by mustard gas stuck in the public psyche of many for years to come. The terror of gas was captured most vividly by Wilfred Owen's famous poem, 'Dulce Et Decorum Est'; it portrays the panic of 'fumbling' and 'fitting the clumsy helmets just in time' and the horror of 'drowning', as 'under a green sea'. But for all the desolation and misery wreaked by gas, the question still remains as to whether chemical weapons were a great success in the war. To this, there is no clear answer. British official historians of the Great War concluded that gas achieved only 'local success, nothing decisive; it made war uncomfortable, to no purpose'.[109] Gas greatly weakened morale, while armies wasted a lot of time and energy moving perilous chemical weapons up to their front line and striving to protect their own troops. While gas did not win any battles, it did have a military impact on battles which would almost certainly have turned out differently had chemical weapons not been used.[110] However, gas was responsible for far fewer deaths and casualties than the public perceive.[111]

In one sense, chemical warfare in the 1914-18 conflict was a scientific struggle to gain the upper hand. The ingenuity and determination of scientists on both sides was taxed and tested, but although much energy was expended, neither side managed to come out on top. The development of new offensive weapons was met by new defensive measures, forcing the other side to unearth even more potent weapons which once again had to be neutralised by another set of defences. Official Porton historian Gradon Carter concluded: 'The story of gas in the Great War on all sides is one of experiment and imitation conducted on a background of uncertainty and hurriedly assembled arrangements for both development, production and use. This was compounded by unfamiliarity and a lack of confidence, both to exploit gas warfare to the fullest and to seize the initiatives revealed after successful attacks. Further some methods of use were patently crude.'[112] The Germans, for example, were unable to turn the war their way despite for a year being the only country to possess the most potent chemical weapon of the entire conflict – mustard gas. One British military commander wrote immediately after the war: 'When the Germans introduced the use of poison gas into civilised warfare, they stumbled on to one of the most destructive of weapons. But, fortunately for us, they did not know how to use it to the full.'[113]

Porton summed up that its effort during the Great War was 'one of extremely hard work and some frustration'. The establishment was sorely disappointed that the results of much of their work did not reach the commanders and fighters on the front line soon enough to be useful; and vice-versa, the experiences of those on the battlefront were not channelled back regularly and promptly to the Wiltshire installation.[114] In his final report in 1919, Crossley reveals how Porton felt a profound sense of isolation from the rest of Britain's chemical warfare effort, since the establishment was never in direct touch with either the armies in the field or the scientists of other Allies. He added that Porton 'never had any pretence of a liaison with the Artillery in France, though nearly one half of the total work carried out affected artillery problems'.[115] It appears that to a large extent, the pain and sacrifices endured by the human observers went to waste because the fruits of their experiments were not used efficiently and effectively.

Foulkes paid tribute to the 'most valuable and careful scientific work' at Porton, much of which was 'unpleasant' and some 'dangerous'.[116] He appreciated the actions of the human 'guinea pigs', commenting that 'volunteers were always to be found who exposed themselves fearlessly in the chamber tests'. But the man in charge of British chemical warfare on the battlefield discovered that Porton's theoretical results were not always the same as the practical experience gained in the fighting. He believed that there was no substitute for learning from the battlefield. 'Actually we had in the theatre of war itself a vast experimental ground, which, in its way, was of far greater value than Porton.'

He and his staff could observe at first hand the casualties produced by a range of gases, evaluate the tactics employed, interrogate German prisoners and so on. 'Human beings provided the material for these experiments on both sides of No Man's Land, and the various weaknesses of human nature – ignorance, fatigue, carelessness etc – were vital factors.' None of these realistic conditions, he added, could be reproduced at Porton.

Armistice in November 1918 brought both general rejoicing and a 'sense of anti-climax' to Porton.[117] Sir Austin Anderson tells how some of the staff celebrated by freeing some of the monkeys. A long way away from Porton, some farm labourers were 'peacefully eating their lunch under some trees when they were frightened out of their lives by some hideous chattering and grinning faces in the branches above their heads.' The men fled in terror, leaving the monkeys to gobble down their food.

When Barcroft heard on the morning of 11 November that peace had broken out, 'it took a good while to dawn upon me…I had a lot to do and by lunchtime it still meant nothing more than a probable change in the next day's programme.'[118] In a letter to his wife, he wrote that the day itself was 'wonderful' – troops in camps around Porton were 'all firing cannon and blowing bugles and putting up lights and raising bonfires.' But by the next day, everyone seemed 'rather flat and at a loose end. No one of course knew quite what is going to take place – so my chief news is that I bit a piece off one tooth.'

The end of the war left the future of Porton hanging in the balance.

CHAPTER TWO

The Pursuit of Bodies

Gas had been used heavily by both sides in the First World War, but at the end of the conflict, it was far from an accepted form of warfare in the court of popular opinion. The enduring diabolical image of chemical weapons dates from the Great War. Many people saw poison gas as 'dirty war'. War is a nasty business, but many believed that poison gas was something different – inhumane, sinister and unfair.

Across the globe, many countries doubted whether gas was legitimate. Much time was spent at international conferences discussing whether chemical weapons should be banned forever. In this atmosphere, it looked as though Porton would be permanently shut down. Moreover, there was considerable doubt among military commanders that chemical weapons were in fact useful on the battlefield.

This uncertainty compelled many staff to leave Porton 'in a massive exodus' at the end of the war.[1] Much of the work virtually ceased; one military chief warned that 'our gas organisation is at a standstill, or rather is threatened with extinction'.[2] This 'limbo' was to be resolved by a committee set up in May 1919 to make recommendations on the future of chemical warfare in Britain. The Holland committee saved Porton.[3] It was staunchly supportive – the committee had 'no shadow of doubt' that 'gas is a legitimate weapon in war'. It was a 'foregone conclusion' that it would be used again in battle, 'for history shows that in no case has a weapon which has proved itself to be successful in war ever been abandoned by nations fighting for existence'. The committee recommended that work on all aspects of chemical warfare must be carried out 'in the most wholehearted and energetic manner, in order that the safety of the Empire shall not be left to chance'.

Porton came out very well from the Holland committee. A 'well-equipped' research station at Porton was the 'only guarantee of the safety of the fighting forces of the Empire' against the threat of gas. All chemical warfare activities were from then on to be centralised at Porton. Crucially, the establishment was to be responsible for both producing chemical weapons and developing defences against such weapons. This ended the division between the offensive and defensive aspects of chemical warfare which had been evident in the war. The committee believed 'it was impossible to divorce the study of defence against gas from the study of the use of gas as an offensive weapon, as the efficiency of the defence depends entirely on an accurate knowledge as to what progress is being or is likely to be made in the offensive use of this weapon'. The distinction between the two was an argument which was to reverberate for many years to come.

The committee wanted scientists of the highest calibre to work at Porton. Unless 'the best brains of the country' were recruited, the British Empire could find itself exposed – just like the first gas attack by the Germans in April 1915. 'Considering the possible advances which are likely to be made in chemical warfare in the near future, such a state of affairs might easily lead to national disaster,' added the committee. To get the best brains, the government had to offer 'substantial inducements' such as handsome salaries and pension, job security, and the freedom to publish unclassified research. Moreover, 'very liberal' leave had to be offered 'in view of the fact that work with gases, in spite of all the precautions, involves a large degree of risk'. The committee pointed out that 'the health of the officers at Porton and similar establishments suffered considerably during the war owing to continuous exposure to gas'.

The report was endorsed by the Cabinet in 1920. It was to lay the foundations for the expansion of Porton over the next two decades. The lengthy process of recruiting staff and rebuilding the establishment – including a new 'special' gas chamber – was begun.[4] In particular, lots of new recruits were needed for the physiological department – which was responsible for testing humans – since many of its wartime staff had left. The new staff came into a department that was 'in a state bordering on the chaotic'.[5] One report noted, 'As the equipment was extremely meagre, a good deal of time had to be spent in procuring the apparatus and materials wanted, and in installing and standardising the various instruments'. Despite these 'considerable difficulties', they managed to bring the department up to scratch by late 1921. However, within two years, Porton came to realise that the number of its existing staff was 'inadequate to cope with the large amount of work in hand', especially to research new potential poison gases.[6]

The end of the war had temporarily stopped experiments on people.[7] The rate of human experiments dropped off during the first couple of years after the war, since the new staff had to be trained.[8] Any question of permanently banning human experiments was dismissed by Porton.

As the number of tests began to rise from the early 1920s, Porton ran into a problem that has dogged the establishment in varying degrees ever since – a shortage of suitable human bodies to experiment on. The tests were then being carried out solely on the Porton staff themselves and in April 1922, officials noted that 'repeated tests on individuals of the staff' were ruining their health.[9] By the next year, the position had become 'even more acute in view of the extension of [Porton's] work in many directions'.[10] One long-serving Porton scientist commented that at that time, 'the staff were testing on themselves and they were getting quite ill. The point was that they were exposing themselves to, say, chlorine again and again and were unwell.'[11]

An investigation was launched to see how the staff – a mixture of military personnel and civilian scientists – could be 'relieved' of this 'duty'. Porton's commandant, Colonel Rawlins, argued that 'these sources were inadequate' and demanded volunteers from outside the establishment for such experiments. However his requests for 'external assistance' from the Army and Navy 'had not met with any response'. The commandant also resisted a suggestion that only the civilian scientists should be subjected to the experiments, maintaining that 'only small numbers were available and hence the work would be held up'.

The sensitive issue was referred up the chain of command to the Army Council, the most senior body in the service. In late 1923, Porton told the council that in 'special tests', humans were being deliberately exposed to toxic compounds, firstly to check respirators and secondly to obtain data on new chemicals.[12] However since the 'supply' of men had now ceased, and since this work was so dangerous, Porton wanted to offer the incentives of extra pay and a compensation scheme if anyone were to be injured.[13] But in a surprising setback for Porton, the Army Council banned all human tests at the establishment.[14] The ban was, however, soon revoked after heavy lobbying by chemical warfare officials, who insisted that the 'risk of injury, or of serious impairment to health was negligible'. Mr S C Peck, the president of the Chemical Warfare Committee, commented that 'the imposition of a ban on all deliberate exposures of personnel to gas will practically stop the work at Porton'.[15]

Over the next year, the difficulty of getting staff to volunteer for the tests became a 'serious' hindrance to Porton's work. This was only eased when the establishment won permission to offer 'danger money' for each test. The lure of cash yielded a 'considerable improvement' in the number of volunteers from the staff. Officials noted that, although the danger money was small, the human 'guinea pigs' believed that the authorities appreciated their willingness to undertake extra work outside of their normal duties.[16]

And yet despite this, the supply of volunteers was still 'not equal to the demand'. Porton had compiled a 'very large' list of chemicals that needed to be tested on humans, but their lack of volunteers now forced them to consider whether to 'limit the number of compounds submitted for examination, or to carry out the preliminary examination of new compounds elsewhere'.[17] In 1925, the shortage of bodies become 'more acute' when Porton wanted to carry out a series of experiments on ways of treating skin burns by mustard gas. The War Office agreed that volunteers could be called from troops based in the local area, and in return, Porton had to promise that 'the greatest care would be taken to prevent serious burns'. The volunteers would also be given an extra day's leave for each test they undertook.

Officials now found that the 'response was most gratifying, and the number of volunteers was far in excess of the demand' causing The War Office to comment that this 'arrangement has proved most helpful and will be continued for all similar experiments'.[18] This was the start of a system which has existed from the mid-1920s to the modern day. For the past seven decades, almost all the human subjects in Porton's experiments have been drawn from the armed forces who have gone to the establishment for short periods of time (between one week and a month, but usually two weeks). It was a key change in the type of human 'guinea pig' used in Porton's experiments. In the First World War, many of the subjects were Porton staff who knew about chemical warfare and willingly subjected themselves to gas (although it remains unclear as to whether the junior staff felt the same way). Since the mid-1920s, the majority of the human experiments have used young military personnel from outside the establishment.

Under this long-running system, Porton's pleas for volunteers have been distributed to military units across the country. In turn, the commanding officers of these units have broadcast the pleas among their ranks. Since 1964, Porton has advertised for volunteers through Defence Council Instructions (DCI), 'a form of internal notices which are issued to all military units'.[19] An example of these DCIs for 1998 draws the attention of unit commanders to the 'requirement for servicemen and servicewomen to volunteer to take part in studies and tests of chemical and biological warfare equipment' at Porton.[20] It adds that Porton 'is well aware of the many pressures on Commanding Officers and the difficulties of releasing personnel for duties outside the role of their command.' It is however stressed that volunteers 'play an essential part in the development of chemical and biological defence equipment'. Unit commanders are asked 'to give this requirement maximum publicity by repeating it in daily/unit routine orders'. The DCI notice outlines the number of volunteers for particular dates, the gender required, the duration of the stay, and any 'special requirements'. One recent 'special requirement' was the simple instruction – 'no beards'![21]

One wry scientist involved in Porton's human experiments for many years recalled in jest, 'We always had the feeling that some military commanders had persuaded certain people to go to Porton in the pious hope that there would be a fatal accident.' Why? 'Because they were a bloody nuisance. They wanted to get rid of them.'[22]

Since 1925, Porton has frequently struggled to attract enough volunteers from the military services to take part in the tests. These troubles have been catalogued in an internal history.[23] In 1927, volunteers were being recruited from units in the immediate area, but Porton complained that the flow of men was 'insufficient', pointing out that 'much of the work' on the most important chemical weapon – mustard gas – was dependent on an ample supply of volunteers for the experiments. To ease this 'considerable difficulty', a 'special appeal' was addressed to the three services.[24] There was, however, no response from the RAF, while the Navy could not spare any men. The War Office therefore agreed to extend the areas from which the men could be drawn. This did indeed temporarily solve the problem since the Western and Scottish commands of the Army supplied six volunteers a fortnight for nearly a year. By 1932, men from the three services all over the country were volunteering for Porton experiments – 'when the Army ran dry, the Air Force or Navy were tapped in turn'.

In 1937, the 'number of observers required rose to 16 per week, but this was immediately followed by complaints with regard to irregular supply'. In the following year, the system was reformed so that each of the three military services had to send eight volunteers a week throughout the year. It was hoped that the weekly target would be met in this way. 'Almost immediately, however, the Air Force and then the Navy ceased to supply volunteers and the full responsibility fell again on the Army.' Recruitment of the human 'guinea pigs' proved to be no less difficult during the Second World War. 'The flow of volunteers fell off in 1944; application was made to the Air Ministry, but no men could be spared.' In this instance, it was the Americans who came to the rescue, sending sixty men until British troops 'became available' again later in the year.

Porton lamented that every year in the late 1940s 'saw the perennial crisis with regard to the supply' of volunteers, but 'nothing new was introduced' to boost the flow. In the early 1960s, the numbers of volunteers 'continued to diminish and it became obvious that the Services could not maintain the supply of observers at the rate of 20 men each week'. It was suggested that this decline 'was closely linked with the run-down of National Service which had provided some 30 percent of the total number of volunteers'. The flow of volunteers for certain tests in 1963 was 'still inadequate'[25] and continued to be poor for the remainder of the decade.

And this pattern has continued today. In recent times, Porton has run into trouble trying to get the total number of volunteers it has aimed for each year.[26] Professor Malcolm Lader of the Institute of Psychiatry in London, the current chairman of the Independent Ethics Committee which oversees Porton's experiments, said there were a variety of reasons why recruitment of volunteers was a problem. 'The volunteers get paid, but it is a piffling amount. There is a concern of "what are they going to do to me?" There is a feeling maybe that medics in the armed forces don't actually know entirely what they are doing. The Gulf War business with the vaccinations, and so on, did rather shake confidence, although maybe it was perfectly reasonable. It is disruptive – they have to come for two weeks. We know that the army is understaffed anyway. You can imagine commanding officers not being too pleased when half his squaddies disappear to go to some study down at Porton Down.'[27] He believes that because of these recruitment difficulties, Porton's experiments 'go a little more slowly than expected [but] they do get completed'. His committee would not authorise experiments if members thought that there would not be enough volunteers to complete the test. 'There is no point having a study that collapses half way through. You just expose half the numbers that you need to, to the dangers, without getting a clear answer.' Graham Pearson, Porton's director between 1984 and 1995, explained that there are so many different proposed experiments and far too few volunteers that 'the numbers [of volunteers] go quite rapidly'.[28]

From time to time, Porton has considered different ways of attracting more volunteers. One notable suggestion in the mid-1960s was a short promotional film, 'showing volunteers at work and at play', which was screened in military units. Unsurprisingly, the film put the best gloss on the human experiments, portraying Porton as a kind of holiday camp. It opened with an invitation that 'invites you to take part in the tests which are held at this establishment'.[29] It assured potential volunteers that staff explain the tests to them 'in detail' beforehand, emphasising that they are 'perfectly free' to withdraw from the experiments at any time. The commentary informed them that 'every care is taken to ensure the safety and well-being of volunteers' both in and out of the tests – 'the billets, while not being luxurious, are made as comfortable as possible'. It described an array of alluring amenities – their own clubhouse, billiards, table tennis, darts, television, bar, football, and badminton – and added that the 'food is plentiful and varied'. Against a background of lively music, the film stated that there were frequent buses into nearby Salisbury for those who liked 'urban, as opposed to rural, nightlife'. The volunteers would also be excused from doing menial military chores, or fatigues, during their stay.

Volunteers recall that they were treated well whilst at Porton, as if they were being cosseted after the harshness of the usual military accommodation. Airman Alan McBray went to Porton in 1959: 'I thought it was absolutely wonderful for a start. You were used to living in barracks with 30 other guys. Here I was given a lovely room on my own, in secluded countryside, absolutely delightful. We were fed like kings.'[30] He was 'hugging himself with delight' and – with only two months left of his National Service – would have liked to have spent the rest of his term at Porton. While this may have been the positive side of his time at Porton, he is, however, now annoyed that Porton resorted to 'deliberate subterfuge' by not telling him that he was to be tested with nerve gas. If he had known beforehand, he would have refused to take part in such an experiment. He adds that he says it is 'conceivable' that the nerve gas tested on him may have contributed to his recent ill health.

Porton's 1960s promotional film states that the 'main business' of the volunteers was to undergo experiments which 'of course vary and depend on the current work of the establishment'. It gave examples of some of the tests – volunteers in protective gear walking on a treadmill to see how they cope with the anti-chemical warfare suits during heavy exercise; material from protective suits being placed on their skin to find out if it irritates humans; volunteers crawling across ground contaminated with chemicals – said to be harmless – to establish how much of the compounds are picked up on the protective suits. Only once does it show volunteers being exposed to chemicals – a soldier's eyes were shown as smarting as he shot his rifle in a cloud of tear gas. This was to test the reactions and accuracy of their shooting in such conditions.

The film emphasises Porton's defensive research, without any mention of its work in developing gas weapons. In a short history of the establishment, the film stated that Porton's efforts between the First and Second World Wars provided every British civilian with a gas mask in 1939. This 'helped to deter the enemy from using gas. The onus of testing the prototypes of those respirators was borne by the volunteer observers. It can be said that these men were at least partially responsible for the enemy not using chemical agents against us.' It added that the only way that scientists could ultimately ensure that the masks were practical was by testing them on man himself. Using a cartoon of an elephant, it explained: 'A respirator designed to protect a human being cannot be tried on an elephant. It must be fitted to a man to get the necessary answers.'

The volunteers in the film were smiling and looking happy. At the end of the film, to complete this reassuring picture, a Porton staff member was shown asking a group of young volunteers if they had any complaints about their stay. The volunteers answer 'no'. The staff member then urged the volunteers to 'tell their pals' about Porton: 'We'd like as many volunteers as we can get to help us with our work. We hope to see you here again in the not too distant future.' The commentary added that volunteers returning to their unit were 'not only better off financially', but also had the 'sure knowledge' that they have made a 'definite personal contribution to the defence of their country and the advancement of science'. It describes how the experiments were used to produce defensive equipment against poison gas. The film was very much how Porton wanted the potential volunteers, and the public, to see the work of the establishment.

Initiatives such as this promotional film may have sporadically paid dividends in the short term, with spurts of volunteers arriving at Porton, but they were almost always followed by another dip in numbers. In Porton's eyes, the 'basic difficulty in securing volunteers' was ignorance, firstly of the experiments themselves and secondly, the importance of the tests to the nation's defences.[31] Fundamentally, officers and men in the units had to be convinced through constant publicity that volunteering was vital to 'their own fighting efficiency' and recognised as a 'direct contribution to the defence of the country'. In almost stirringly patriotic tones, senior Porton scientists argued in 1968 that volunteering should be given the 'esteem that such a contribution deserves'. Instead, they grumbled, some potential volunteers were actually being dissuaded from coming to Porton by their commanding officers. One scientist who worked at Porton during the 1970s and 1980s said that it was a continual battle to get the right message across to potential volunteers. 'We seemed to [be] failing to publicise ourselves adequately. There was some misunderstanding as to the purpose of coming to Porton, which was traditional of course.' He added that the stumbling blocks were not only the reluctance of commanding officers to release their men, but also the 'incredible stories and folklore' surrounding Porton that deterred volunteers. The problem was especially acute since the overall size of the armed forces – the pool of volunteers – was also gradually declining.[32]

Over the decades, at least 20,000 service personnel have journeyed to Porton to participate in experiments, although even these numbers were frequently not enough to satisfy the scientists' demands. To many members of the general public, it is utterly unbelievable that service men and women have willingly volunteered for poison gas tests. A common reaction was expressed, for instance, by Tony Banks, Labour MP (and later a government minister), when a former Porton volunteer first drew his attention to the tests: 'It beggars belief that anyone would genuinely volunteer to be used for experiments involving chemical warfare.' He thought that the only possible explanation was that service personnel had been 'cajoled' into volunteering for 'potentially dangerous experiments' because they were facing a disciplinary charge and hoped to get it dropped in return for becoming a human 'guinea pig'.[33] Another sceptical politician was veteran Labour MP Tam Dalyell who questioned: 'When is a volunteer, not a volunteer? When he is a serviceman, and the company sergeant major wants participants for experiments at Porton Down.' He added, 'Probably the experiments do, as ministers claim, make a vital contribution to Porton's work in ensuring the protection of our forces against the threat of chemical attack. But don't let's pretend that sometimes it isn't "Volunteers! You, you and you, there."'[34]

The very thought of poison gas immediately fills many people with horror, conjuring up images of unspeakable pain and suffering. So why would anyone in their right mind voluntarily agree to subject themselves to experiments with such ghastly weapons?

In fact, it is clear from the testimonies of volunteers that many actually had little idea of what they were volunteering for. Most were young, mainly in their early twenties,[35] with some even under eighteen years old.[36] Many confess that they had been naive and had simply believed that the tests would be benign and harmless. They had not the considered the implications of the tests as much as they would had they been older. Once they had arrived at Porton, they would ideally have been informed of what was going to happen in the tests, but, as discussed in chapter six, many maintain that they were still kept in the dark.

Porton rarely described the tests fully when appealing for volunteers, as a sample of the circulars sent around military units since 1945 shows.[37] These appeals did not spell out in any great detail what the volunteers would undergo in the tests. One from 1953 merely states that the volunteers will take part in 'physiological experiments'.[38] It appears that the wording remained much the same until late 1963 when the appeals sent to Army units became more expansive – but only briefly. Army chiefs had warned that 'it was becomingly increasingly difficult to obtain volunteers' and suggested that 'better results might be obtained if potential volunteers could be given some idea of the type of tests which they would be required to undergo'. As a result, the amplified appeals therefore stated that the experiments 'were designed in order to develop means of protection against chemical warfare agents. It is not possible to list all the many varieties of tests in which volunteers are invited to participate, but they include work with respirators, protective clothing, decontaminants, and studies of the effects of small, safe concentrations of various drugs whilst carrying out different activities'.[39]

But by 1964, the description had shrunk back – an Army circular from that year merely stated that Porton 'relies on a regular supply of volunteers to take part in physiological and medical studies' in connection with its work to 'develop means of protection against chemical warfare'.[40] An appeal for Army units' notice boards from 1967 stated that 'servicemen have been volunteering to go to Porton since 1925 to take part in tests of equipment that the scientists are developing to protect our country against the possibility of an enemy attacking us with chemical agents. The service that the volunteer gives is still as important today as it has ever been'. However it added the proviso, 'Details of the tests cannot be published in advance.'[41] The recent appeals are noticeably quite spare and just mentioned that volunteers would take part in 'studies and tests of chemical and biological warfare equipment'.

Porton's promotional film to recruit volunteers in the 1960s also baldly admits that 'it is not possible to publish details of the tests in advance'. There may have been several reasons for this – Porton would have wanted to keep tests secret during the clandestine atmosphere of the Cold War, and possibly the schedule of experiments for the months ahead had even not yet been formulated. However there was another, more cynical reason at work. Porton officials were clearly aware that an explicit description of the tests would simply scare off servicemen. This was plainly expressed by a senior Porton official in August 1961.[42] Discussing the wording of the appeals circulated to military units, the official commented, 'Experience has shown that detailed description tends to deter the serviceman and so now very little is said. Also, any wording might be reproduced in the press and has therefore to be very carefully phrased. The fewer details the better, but we must not be accused of "insulting the public's intelligence".'

Porton often misled volunteers in their warnings about the level of pain that they might experience.[43] According to the 1953 appeal, 'the physical discomfort resulting from the tests is usually very slight'.[44] This phrasing seems to have stayed the same until Porton officials noted in 1962 that even this mild form of warning 'was unfortunate as it probably deterred some potential volunteers'. The appeal was therefore changed so that 'any reference to physical discomfort and danger' was omitted.[45] However, some measure of honesty did creep in again during 1967 when the appeals cautioned that 'indeed, some of the tests are arduous'.[46] This term hints at heavy exercise, but certainly not the sort of pain experienced when exposed to toxic gases. It is not known whether this wording has stayed the same since then, although the appeals in the 1990s did not warn volunteers of any impending discomfort at all. Many, but not all, volunteers endured pain in Porton experiments. It is apparent that many human 'guinea pigs' who did suffer physical distress and discomfort were deceived, since they had been led to believe that the pain would only be 'slight'.

Since the 1920s, the volunteers have been offered inducements in the form of extra pay and leave. In many cases, the extra money has been a substantial addition to the often low wages of the volunteers. As an indication of the amount, volunteers in recent times could earn between £125 and £500 on top of their usual income for undergoing the tests, usually for two or three weeks.[47] However officials have seen the amounts of money as being merely nominal. According to the MoD, the level of pay was 'deliberately set not so high that anyone with doubts would be induced to participate purely for the sake of the money'.[48] One Porton scientist who organised human experiments said the extra pay amounted to 'piddling' sums – and intentionally so. 'Nobody wanted to be accused of luring some innocent soul to take part in experiments with deadly chemical agents for £5 or something like that.'[49]

The amount of leave and pay offered has fluctuated over the years, but has usually correlated to the number of experiments that the volunteers underwent. In 1941, 'as a greater inducement', Porton decided to pay the volunteers 'on the spot, rather than let him wait for his reward until his return to his unit'. Since many service personnel took their leave immediately and so wanted the cash in their hands straightaway, this proved to be an alluring prospect.[50]

The human 'guinea pigs' often cite the enticement of extra money and leave as one of the reasons why they volunteered for the experiments. It seems, however, that this was not the main reason. As one Porton report noted in 1965, the 'financial rewards, while essential, are not sufficient in themselves' to lure recruits.[51] It is apparent that throughout the decades, there has been another, more startling reason that motivated many of the volunteers – they simply hankered for a break from their normal monotonous routine in the military. The human 'guinea pigs', usually from the lower ranks, wanted to get away from the boring, humdrum grind of service duties, be it square-bashing or whatever. They were sufficiently fed up to volunteer for anything that would be different for a couple of weeks. When the Porton notices came along, they put up their hands, frequently without knowing virtually anything about the tests. This is surely a reflection of how tedious and dull military life could be for many service personnel. From interviews with the volunteers, it seems that for many, this desire for a change proved a stronger incentive than the money.

Take for example, Ron Ross, who took part in a nerve gas experiment in July 1952.[32] He went to Porton because he was 'cheesed off and fed up' in his last year of National Service in the RAF. He thought to himself, 'I'm going to have a go just to get away for a wee while. It was something different'. He admits that 'to be quite honest', he had no idea what he was volunteering for, since he was a naive nineteen-year-old. It just happened to be Porton that was calling for volunteers at the time. 'If it had been something else, it would have been that.' He recalls that it was not the extra money that made him volunteer, even though the payments for the experiments equalled his then weekly income. He claims that he was 'one of the fortunate' volunteers who did not in fact suffer much pain in the gas chamber and has not had recurring health problems.

Infantryman Henry Fudge, then in his twenties, went to Porton in 1943 from his unit because he wanted a short interlude from the 'very boring' and 'endless' route marches.[33] 'I was fed up walking around Kent with a heavy pack on my back. One lane looks like another in the country. It was a break from the daily grind of infantry training,' he says. 'All we knew was that we would be testing new respirators. Of course, when you volunteer for these things, you don't know what is going to happen to you.' On every third day for three weeks, he was sent into a chamber filled with different gases for varying lengths of time; the longest was two-and-a-half hours. He was never told what the gases were. He wore his army uniform and a respirator, but no other protective clothing. He did not experience any ill effects whilst in the chamber. He was also used in an experiment in which a chemical, probably mustard gas, was dropped on the arms or back of the neck. This produced 'enormous blisters', with yellow pus which itched so much that he could not sleep at night. Ironically, he found the whole experience at Porton dull.

Porton's own research shows that the opportunity to escape from a boring routine has been the main reason why service personnel have chosen to become volunteers at Porton. Three studies into the psychology of the human 'guinea pigs' were carried out by Porton scientists in the late 1950s and 1960s. In the first of these, 117 volunteers – who were at Porton between November 1959 and February 1960 – were asked to fill out a questionnaire which was designed to assess their personality.[34] These volunteers were shown to have an average age of twenty-two. Porton scientists were keen to discover whether the volunteers represented a 'normal cross-section of the population', as this may be affecting the outcome of their chemical warfare experiments. They noted that 'where the primary effects of tests are discomfort and pain', the psychological make-up of the 'experimental subjects' may sway the length of time they were prepared to remain exposed to chemicals.

Porton speculated that there were two types of people who might be expected to volunteer for chemical warfare tests. 'On the one hand, the hysteric and neurotic eager for the glory of "secret tests" and on the other hand the conscientious individual anxious to serve his country. Experience with units such as the Parachute Regiment has suggested the first type of volunteer is much more common than the second.' However, the volunteers' responses revealed that the majority came to Porton simply because they 'were very bored with their normal work'; the payments were 'unlikely' to be an incentive for volunteering. According to Porton scientists, the results 'suggest that the typical volunteer may be more neurotic and introverted than the average serviceman'. They added: 'This will inevitably influence the result of any trial that is at all unpleasant or requires the co-operation of the subject.'

A much bigger study – involving 503 volunteers – was started soon afterwards.[55] As well as undergoing the usual chemical tests, these volunteers completed two sets of questionnaires which gauged their personality and intelligence.[56] As further evidence of the inexperience of the human 'guinea pigs', the volunteers in this batch also had an average age of twenty-two. The research showed that, once again, the main reason for volunteering was 'boredom with Service life'. Most volunteers went to Porton either 'for a change' or 'out of interest or curiosity'. Relatively few came for 'the money', 'a rest' or to be 'near home'.

According to this study, Porton volunteers included a greater proportion of more intelligent men than the British population and the services in general, but were also 'significantly more neurotic' than the other categories. It also suggested that volunteers were more extroverted than the general population, but were in effect no different from the rest of the services (in contrast with the previous study). However, the validity of such personality and intelligence tests must be viewed with some scepticism, and Porton scientists concluded that, as a whole, the volunteers were 'abnormal with regard to intelligence and personality when compared with the general civilian and Service populations'. They even suggested that perhaps the results of experiments performed on them should be extrapolated to other people only 'with caution'.

A few years later, Porton conducted a further investigation into the typical personality of volunteers.[57] The most striking was an attempt to see how much the men were motivated by money. Thirty-seven volunteers were exposed to a potent riot control gas – known as CR gas – in a gas chamber. The men had been told that the longer they stayed in the chamber (playing dominoes), the more money they would receive as a reward. The maximum time was four minutes. As it turned out, the results 'gave only very slight support' to the idea that the motivation of volunteers might be improved by small money prizes.

The motives of the volunteers were also briefly touched upon during two nerve gas experiments in the early 1950s. These two experiments were looking at the psychological effects of nerve gas on men (they are described in chapter four). After the first experiment, Porton scientists commented that 'the men's reasons for volunteering were not exhaustively probed, but appeared sensible. Most had come for a change and out of a mild curiosity, with the prospect of a small payment as a secondary inducement.' They added: 'The awkwardness of the few references to higher motives – of helping others etc., – was taken as a good sign. One or two noble martyrs had been diverted to other work.'[58] The report of the second experiment found that 'far and away the main reasons for volunteering were the desire for a change from camp and various kinds of curiosity. These were mentioned five times as often as all other reasons, which included the money, doing good, revisiting that part of the country'. Candidly, the report admits that 'few had more than the vaguest idea of the sort of things they would be asked to do'.[59]

One scientist who worked at Porton for many years joked that staff were cynical about military personnel who claimed they had volunteered mainly 'for the good of the country'.[60] 'We were always a bit nervous about accepting them! They were very few, but always some who were there for the "common good", not the money, nor to get away from their units.'

Some volunteers have in fact been to Porton for experiments on repeated occasions, which, to the general public, seems particularly strange. In the short recruiting film produced by Porton in the 1960s, a medical officer is shown asking a group of volunteers if any had taken part in the Porton experiments before. One replied that he had, prompting the officer to tell the others, 'Good...it can't be all that bad – he's come back for a second try.'

Porton's research shows that in a fifteen-month period in 1960-61, twelve percent of the volunteers had been to Porton on more than one occasion. Of these fifty-seven individuals, seven had been three times, while one man was on his fourth trip.[61] (According to Porton, people can volunteer as many times as they like to take part in the experiments.)[62]

This phenomenon may strengthen Porton's argument that the volunteers were treated properly and fairly, since the men would presumably not go back had they had a rough experience the first time around. However, it is apparent that some volunteers regret going a second time, since they now believe that their health was damaged on the return trip. One of these is Mick Roche, who was exposed to nerve gas in 1963 on his second visit to Porton, whereas the first time around, the experiments on him had been fairly benign. As a result, he later became a staunch campaigner, founding the Porton Down Volunteers Association and suing the Ministry of Defence for damages (see chapter 10).

Another volunteer who went twice is Henry McKay who served in the RAF for thirty years.[63] He first went to Porton in 1954 because 'you were young, stupid, you thought that you were doing some good'. He had 'four blobs' of liquid put on his arms which produced mildly irritating blisters as well as undergoing 'pretty exhausting' exercises, such as pedalling a bike for as long as possible whilst wearing a gas mask. Five years later, he volunteered again because he thought that it had been fairly reasonable the first time. He says, 'Somebody had to do it. It had to be done.' He was paid for his tests on both occasions, and although the money was 'worthwhile', it was not the main reason he went. On the second visit, he was exposed to nerve gas but did not feel any effects from it. However, he has recently been trying to claim a war pension since he now suffers stomach problems which he believes are a result of coming 'into contact with unknown chemicals' whilst at Porton.

Up until 1972, the volunteers for Porton's experiments were men, since there was a bar on women being used. Other than simple old-fashioned chauvinism by the mainly male Porton establishment and the military in general, the reasons for this bar are not particularly clear.[64] At one point in the Second World War, three women were rejected as human 'guinea pigs' on the grounds that 'medically it is unsafe to use females as observers, since their reactions are not the same as with men'.[65] But pressure to remove this bar increased when Porton was short of volunteers. One instance was in 1963 when the scientists needed a pool of suitable candidates to undergo experiments with mind-altering drugs. At a meeting with advisers, Dr Bill Ladell, then in charge of Porton's human tests, suggested that female volunteers would increase the total number of 'guinea pigs'. However, one scientist retorted that 'in many women, the psychological state alters' prior to their menstrual period, and a brigadier chimed in saying that 'if it became widely known that women were subjected to tests at Porton, there might be the most unfavourable repercussions'.[66] In 1965, Eric Haddon, then Porton's director, commented that 'the use of test subjects was very difficult in a small community such as Porton, and the military authorities had advised against their [women's] use'.[67]

As described earlier, Porton produced a short film in the mid-1960s to distribute around military units to recruit volunteers. In one passage, the film commentary said, 'Unfortunately volunteers from the women's services cannot be accepted for administrative, amongst other, reasons.' It then showed a naked woman in the shower, being interrupted by a towel-clad man entering the room.

Sue Berrecloth, a corporal then stationed at the famous Sandhurst training school, volunteered for Porton's tests around 1977, and was one of around half a dozen in a completely female intake for two weeks.[68] (She was given the task of trying out some sort of tablets over three days.) It appears that the intake was restricted to one gender so that it would be easier to accommodate them within Porton's sleeping quarters. Sue Berrecloth said she can understand why women were barred from Porton's tests for so long, since the military has traditionally viewed women as a 'totally different breed' who were suited only for support roles. Recently, however, women within the armed forces are being allowed to do more duties and jobs which had previously been confined to men, so she believes that with regard to Porton's experiments, women should now be treated no differently from the men.

Whatever the success or failure of gas in the First World War, chemical warfare was in reality here to stay. Chemical weapons had been used on a massive scale in the war, and most expected that, despite the public's hatred, they would again be used in the future. Like the other military inventions of the war – the tank, the submarine and the fighter plane – gas was another weapon which countries had to take seriously.

After the war, there was a series of international negotiations in an attempt to banish chemical weapons from the world. This resulted in the 1925 Geneva Protocol. Under this agreement, countries were banned from employing chemical weapons first in any future war. Although a landmark treaty, this agreement had a number of crucial flaws. Chiefly, the protocol barred countries from using chemical weapons first, but it did not stop them from retaliating with gas if they had already been attacked with such weapons. In effect, this meant that countries could carry on researching and developing weapons (so-called offensive work) which they could argue were only for retaliation. Moreover, countries were also entitled to produce gas masks and other defences, and clearly, knowledge of existing and future weapons was needed if such defensive research was going to be effective.

'By about 1930, the international arguments had died down and most countries were quietly carrying out as much research and development as they believed was necessary for their safety and which they could afford in cost,' comments one of Porton's histories.[69] In this respect, Britain was no different from many other nations. At Porton, work for both offensive and defensive purposes continued. One of its official histories states that 'any actual development of weapons had to be done "under the rose",' away from the public gaze. 'As a gesture', the names of departments were changed, so that the Offensive Munitions Department became the Technical Chemical Department. 'In 1930, the term "chemical warfare" was expunged from official language and titles, and "chemical defence" was substituted. Thereafter all offensive work was done under the heading "study of chemical weapons against which defence is required".'[70]

Offensive work on actual weapons was in practice limited and restricted, according to Porton. Weapons trials 'could not be done openly', and there was little impetus to finish the designs of such weapons since there were no manufacturing contracts or target dates to be met. There were limited funds at a time when there were widespread financial restrictions across the whole of the military. 'Funds for chemical warfare and defence research peaked in 1929, but dropped in 1933 before rising only gradually throughout the remainder of the 1930s,' states one official account.[71]

The military services were also unsure of the gas weapons that they might have cause to need in the case of an outbreak of another war, so they were hesitant to outline their required arsenal. They wanted Porton to improve many World War One weapons, including gas shells, mortar bombs, the Livens' Projector and toxic smoke generators, but Porton also studied the development of 'many new items, such as apparatus for mustard gas spray from aircraft, bombs of many types, airburst mustard gas shell, gas grenades, weapons for attacking tanks'. The establishment congratulated itself on making 'a good deal of progress' on all this offensive work in the years between the two World Wars, although actual production of gas weapons did not in fact restart in earnest until the late 1930s.[72]

As for the defensive work, Porton had much to do in the inter-war years. One of the first tasks was to assess the condition of nearly a million respirators which had been manufactured in the Great War. It appears that there was only one, very painful, way to do this. Men had to breathe the arsenical smoke adamsite (DM) through the canisters, literally to see if the gas masks were working. One percent of the masks were sent to Porton for testing, and by working sixteen hours a day, Porton managed to finish in double quick time, but at a cost. One of its official histories discloses that 'apart from the long working hours, these particular tests were a severe physical strain on the staff and several of them suffered from the effects for long afterwards'.[73]

Much of the adamsite did in fact penetrate the masks which had become 'largely useless through deterioration'. But this proved to be a 'blessing' for Porton. Extra money was then allocated to fund urgent research into the design of new masks. This 'opened the door more quickly for the entry of new ideas' for the masks, and Porton was able to develop a better mask, of which around twenty-five million were manufactured before and during the Second World War for the British military and civilian population.

The armed forces also wanted other kinds of defensive equipment – 'devices for detecting any gas which an enemy might use, for protecting the rest of the body as far as was necessary, and for means of decontaminating any type of material or ground surface which was contaminated with mustard gas'.[74] As a result, Porton became engrossed in a large-scale research programme to invent reliable equipment.

This research, both offensive and defensive, however needed a fair number of human 'guinea pigs'. Quite how many is difficult to establish. Porton admits that it is 'impossible to find out' how many people were used – either in total or annually – in its experiments before 1945.[75] The records of the committees which oversaw such experiments are not available to the public.[76] It appears that as a rough estimate, the totals would certainly have been hundreds each year for this period between the wars. Evidence for the annual totals is fragmentary. One Porton report suggests that the establishment demanded more and more volunteers as the Second World War approached. In the twelve months prior to August 1934, the military services supplied, or promised, at least 504 volunteers to Porton. In 1937, Porton required sixteen human 'guinea pigs' a week, implying a total of 832 over the whole year.[77]

As an indication of the scale of testing, it appears that around 4,000 human subjects were exposed to tear gases between 1925 and 1936.[78] In a five-year stretch in the 1930s, around 1,500 people were tested in one kind of experiment alone – to discover how sensitive they were to mustard gas.[79] As World War One tests at Porton had shown, people who have been burned by mustard become much more sensitive to it, and are subsequently liable to be badly and quickly blistered by even minuscule amounts of the gas. (Surgeon Commander Archibald Fairley, who was in charge of Porton's human experiments at this time, had himself become 'highly' sensitive to the gas and 'had to place the length of a corridor between himself and any room in which testing involving mustard was going on').[80] As with many Porton experiments, a proportion of the humans in these tests were staff at the establishment.

One human 'guinea pig' from this time was Joseph Crowther, who went to Porton twice in the 1930s.[81] The first time was in 1932 as a seventeen-year-old RAF apprentice. He decided to go after he saw an appeal for volunteers on the notice board of his station. The tests were described in 'very mild terms... There was no mention of any danger or anything like that. It was all very suave. I went like a mug.' In return, he received a month's leave which was 'very welcome' since he only got a month's holiday anyway. He remembers that a patch contaminated with mustard gas was placed on his wrist, producing a blister. This scab was punctured and then bandaged to heal. A few days later, lewisite, another blister gas, was also placed on his wrist. (Lewisite was tested on human subjects by Porton for many years.)[82] Once again, a blister appeared. He recalls that both tests were 'not very painful', although — all these years later — he still has the two small scars that they caused. In 1935, he was sent to Porton as a punishment for failing to get permission to get married. However this time, he was not subjected to any experiments, but had to monitor the temperature of an ammunition dump instead.

Another seventeen-year-old serviceman who took part in Porton's tests in the 1930s was machine-gunner John Fortescue.[83] During the two weeks he was there in 1938, he said he was tested with gases more or less every day. He commented that the Porton scientists got their money's worth from him as a human 'guinea pig': 'I thought that they were going mad, or that I was going mad — one of the two.' His father Arthur, who had been gassed on the battlefield in the First World War, told him that he had been an idiot for volunteering for Porton's poison gas experiments. However, Fortescue had seen a notice in his unit's canteen and decided to go to Porton to relieve the boredom of training — 'something better to do than marching up and down like a fool'. He was told that he would be exposed to different gases, some of which were 'very dangerous'. He remembered going into a gas chamber with glass walls with other volunteers, where he had to take off his mask and describe the effect of the chemical on him whilst scientists stood outside with notebooks to record what they said. He reported that the gas hurt his teeth, eyes, nose, and ears while blood seeped from his gums. Later, he suffered two-inch, pus-filled blisters after having been told to put his arms over four holes from which some sort of gas was released. The following day, while still nursing the blisters, he was sent onto nearby Salisbury Plain to be tested with more gas. In one trial, he and others — standing five feet apart — were sprayed with mustard gas from a plane, while wearing a tin helmet and a cape for protection. This resulted in more blisters, this time to his legs. For all this, he was rewarded with a week's leave and extra money. Before his death in 2000, he was very angry that, after a long battle in the 1990s, the government had refused him a war pension for his ailments.

Daniel Fraser worked at Porton for two and a half years from 1936. It was his first posting as a young army plumber. He is bitter that, during this time, he was forced to undergo gas experiments against his will:[84] 'They told you that you could refuse, but then up came the Sergeant-Major [saying], "You're in the British Army. Do as you are told."' According to Fraser, the subjects of the experiments came from the traditional military way – the commanding officer lined everybody up and picked out the 'volunteers' with a simple order: 'You, you and you'. He adds that Porton needed people for the experiments and this was simply the best way of getting them, but, to Fraser, this form of 'volunteering' amounts to abuse. 'You are a human being, not a guinea pig. That's the main thing that angers me.' He appreciates Porton had to do the tests, 'but they could have done it a better way.' Like others, he was paid for each test. 'When I was down there, it meant extra cash. Your pay was not very good in those days. It was handy.'

He was subjected to a series of experiments – 'as soon as you were fit enough, they tested you again.' In one test, he had three drops of mustard gas put on each arm which caused 'very painful, big' blisters. For the next three months, he had to wear clothing impregnated with a chemical to stop poison gas penetrating through to the skin and the state of the blisters was monitored during that period. However, it was so uncomfortable that he could not sleep at night on the rough army blanket. It was 'torture', he says. 'The ones who could stick it, stuck it, the others just dropped.' But the longer they stayed in the experiment, the more money they received. In another test, he had to wear a very coarse undercoat while standing guard all night. 'It was very horrible stuff. I think it was goat's hair. You were glad to get it off in the morning.' He believes that the material – treated with an unknown chemical – was being tested to see if it irritated too much to be worn as protective clothing. He says that the scientists never told them what the unknown chemical was.

On one occasion, he and others were sent into a hut to try out a gas mask. Mustard gas was sprayed around the hut, but it started to seep underneath the edges of the mask. 'We had to make a rush for the door. There were sixteen of us in there, all trying to get out of the single door. It was very painful.' He believes that the scientists did not expect the mustard gas to penetrate the mask – 'They thought that the mask was tight and gas-proof.'

As a result, he had blisters around his face for a week, from which some of the marks are still visible today.

In other tests, he had to go onto the vast Porton ranges and stand in the centre of large white cards. Planes would then fly over and spray red dye (which did not contain poison gas) to ascertain what size of droplet would fall on marching troops.[85] Residents from neighbouring areas complained when the spray fell, as it inevitably did, outside Porton – 'somebody's underclothing and stuff which had been hung out to dry was full of red spots', and a pink-spotted baby was once discovered after some married quarters were inadvertently sprayed. Fraser also worked on the trials of weapons – including the Livens Projector – which fired various gases such as phosgene around the Porton ranges. There proved to be 'quite a lot of mishaps' with the Livens Projector.

Many of the buildings were erected whilst Fraser was at Porton. He spent six months building solid lead tables for experiments on animals. (At least 206 chemicals were tested on animals during the inter-war years, although the number of animals used is unknown).[86] He recalls that the atmosphere at the secretive installation was perpetually 'very tense' because nobody was allowed to talk to each other about their work.

Now in his eighties, Fraser believes that the Porton experiments caused some of his ill health in the past years, including skin cancer. But he is sceptical that the government would ever admit this. 'They don't want to know. If you blame it on such and such, they turn around and say that's not possible. I still maintain that we are due some recompense.'[87] Campaigning for such compensation is however 'a waste of time'.

In the years after the First World War, Porton tested a steady stream of new compounds on humans. Chemical warfare officials had argued that such tests with novel substances were 'essential' when military superiors had attempted to ban human experiments in 1923. It was one of the key reasons given for the continuation of the experiments.[88] Porton's commandant, Colonel Rawlins, claimed that it must surely be 'obvious' that the military potential of a new compound could not be 'definitely determined' until it had 'been tried out on the human'.[89] Experiments on animals would show whether the new compound was toxic, but without experiments on people, 'its noxious effect on human beings would be largely unknown, and properties of considerable military value might in this way be overlooked'. He argued that this could prove to be 'serious', since important new poison gases might be missed, and it would impossible to guarantee completely secure protection against a chemical which suddenly appeared on the battlefield out of the blue.

The testing of new compounds did take up 'considerable amounts of time'.[90] Such compounds came from a variety of sources, for example, British colonial authorities in Nigeria sent in 'botanical specimens' of allegedly poisonous beans, which turned out to be innocuous when tested on volunteers.[91] Some of these new compounds proved to be painful for the human 'guinea pigs', while others seemed to be fairly harmless.[92]

A number of human tests at this time repeated experiments which had been done during the First World War. Officials recognised that some of the data collected from human experiments in the war was inaccurate and unreliable, whereas in the new experiments, the dosages of chemicals to which humans were being exposed could be checked more precisely. It is unclear how much of the data from the war was considered dubious. The wartime experiments had been carried out at a time of extreme urgency and Porton had had to rush to solve the problems thrown up by the conflict. Some of the work was inevitably haphazard, especially since poison gas was such a new form of warfare. However the discovery of unreliable data raises the question as to whether the distress and agony experienced by the human 'guinea pigs' in the war was all in vain. As previously noted, Porton's wartime commandant, Crossley, had already lamented that the results of their experiments were rarely channelled to the battlefield commanders on the front line who could then capitalise on this work.

Porton staff spent much time re-examining the existing mainstream poison gases. This was done for a variety of reasons: to find out more about their poisonous effects; to try and see how they could be better exploited in battle; or to investigate their related compounds to discover if any proved to be more toxic. The arsenicals in particular consumed much of Porton's time. The principal arsenicals during the war had been adamsite (DM), DA and DC. As described in chapter one, they were extensively tested on humans during the war, and were found to be capable of inflicting unbearable pain along the victim's nose and throat, provoking, among other traumas, intense headaches, prolonged sneezing, nausea, vomiting, unsteadiness, and trembling all over the body.

Arsenical smokes had first been pressed into action by the Germans in 1917, although they had been unable to produce an efficient weapon for dispersing the chemical along enemy lines. The British had countered by developing the M device, but the war had ended before this new weapon could be employed. Instead, the devices were used by the British in Russia in 1919 during the civil war against the Bolsheviks. The British had intervened along with the French and Americans to try to smother the new revolutionary regime in its infancy. More than 2,700 devices were hurled out of planes into forests around Archangel to attack Red Army forces. One despatch claimed that the 'recent successes' in that area 'have been due almost entirely to Gas'. The weapons spread 'great panic' among the enemy. Winston Churchill, then Secretary of State at the War Office and a keen advocate of poison gas for much of his life, said that 'of course' he 'very much' wanted to hit the Bolsheviks with gas.[93]

A plethora of tests with the arsenicals was carried out by Porton, many involving humans. In one, successive clouds of DC were released over a detachment of six gunners, and all but one suffered 'severe' symptoms as a result. It was found that the detachment's rate of firing was reduced because of the gas. All agreed that it would have taken 'considerable mental and physical effort' to continue firing.[94] In another, thirty-four human 'guinea pigs' – with no respirators – went into gas chambers filled with DM to test firstly how long they took to detect the compound, and then how long they could bear to stay in the chamber.[95] This was taken to be the 'limit of tolerability' (defined by Porton as 'when a strong desire to flee from the irritation became manifest'). They experienced 'some distress...from coughing and pain and a sense of tightness in the chest'. Two of them showed 'marked' agony, turning slightly blue.

Porton were determined to explore substances related to the existing arsenical weapons in the hope of uncovering a new, more effective poison gas (as did many chemical warfare scientists around the world at this time). Wave after wave of these arsenicals were tested on human 'guinea pigs' in the gas chambers. These men entered the chambers and breathed in the clouds of different arsenicals so that their reactions could be compared to DC, DA and adamsite (DM). For instance, one substance – 'of very great interest' – drove out many volunteers, gripped by pain along their nose, throat and chest, before the allotted time of ten minutes was up.[96] But despite this extensive programme of testing, none of the scores of arsenicals proved to be a more attractive alternative to those that had already been discovered during the Great War.

Many of Porton's human experiments in this inter-war period concentrated on mustard gas. It had emerged from the First World War as the premier chemical weapon – the so-called 'King of the Battle Gases'. Another legacy from the war were the illnesses suffered by victims who had been attacked with mustard gas during the conflict. Poison gas had been so horrifying for the ordinary soldier that many people believed that it would inflict lingering ill health on victims for many years after the war.[97] The official treatment of these gas victims after the war is important to Porton's human 'guinea pigs' who have been struggling for some time to win recognition and compensation for their own ill health. Gathering dust in the Public Record Office are declassified documents which show how much Porton knew about, and had accepted at that time, the long-term dangers of mustard gas exposure.

In 1920, around 19,000 British veterans who had been gassed during the war were still so ill that they were drawing a disability pension from the government. However this number steadily slid in the following years – down to 9,250 in 1922 and to just 683 in 1926.[98] The government came under heavy pressure from both war veterans and MPs to award pensions to more gas victims. This is evident from meetings in 1930 between government ministers and veterans' groups. At one meeting, ministers admitted that the issue was 'most difficult' and that there had been 'strong complaints...from a number of MPs'. But the politicians insisted that 'before the State, in 1930, could accept liability in respect of gassing in 1917 or 1918, there must be very definite proof that the man did suffer from gassing and also that the remaining effects of it were still present'. One veterans' representative 'felt that hardship was involved in cases of gassing where it was very difficult to get a favourable decision'.[99]

Porton staff were unhappy in the late 1920s about the 'almost daily' articles in the press regarding 'the dire results of chemical warfare'. Surgeon Commander Archibald Fairley, in charge of human experiments at the establishment, fumed about one article which stated that 'every day human beings are dying in agony from the effects of gas infection received in the war'. He commented tartly, 'Possibly the author of such an article might be invited to produce the evidence on which his views are founded.'[100]

Porton officials were sceptical that large numbers of gas victims were experiencing lasting illnesses after the war. Nevertheless, they were 'keenly interested' in the long-term effects of the wartime gassing.[101] Secretly, Porton staff devoted much time to researching this question. It was the Ministry of Pensions, however, and not Porton, that was responsible for deciding whether war veterans were experiencing ill health from their gassing and should therefore be awarded a disability pension. Porton officials were given permission to attend Ministry of Pensions medical boards at which such claimants put their case.[102] Porton found that these boards believed that the majority of gas victims receiving disability pensions were suffering badly from chest illnesses, caused mainly by mustard gas. Surgeon Commander Fairley reported in June 1927 that 'the most interesting and most definite cases are undoubtedly the pulmonary cases resulting from mustard poisoning'.[103] 'Some of these have chests like men of over 60, chests definitely and permanently damaged. The evidence suggesting that mustard [gas] is the cause appears to be conclusive. These pensioners, young and fit before the War, have a definite history of having spent some weeks or months in hospital with conjunctivitis, laryngitis, bronchitis and in some cases skin burns in addition. The bronchitis has been maintained ever since, and...these cases do not tend to improve with time,' he wrote.[104]

Porton pursued its investigations by obtaining from the Ministry of Pensions the files of seventy-two invalids who were receiving a pension as a result of gassing. However, Porton later dismissed the quality of the records as being too unscientific to draw any concrete conclusions. Surgeon Commander Fairley wrote caustically that the pensions were being awarded for reasons of 'political expediency' rather than on 'unimpeachable' scientific grounds. Nonetheless, he stated once again that there was one 'common type of injury' which Porton 'definitely' did believe was caused by chemical weapons in the war – 'chronic bronchitis and emphysema resulting from severe mustard gassing'.[105]

A further inquiry by a consultant, Colonel J C Kennedy, looked at thirty-three mustard gas victims from the war. Of the thirteen victims that he could trace through the files of the Ministry of Pensions, three had recovered fully, but the rest were still ill from the gassing, mainly from bronchitis and 'disordered action of the heart'. Military officials commented that 'although the number of cases studied is not large, the investigation confirms the figures generally accepted as representing the after-effects of mustard gas poisoning.'[106]

Further evidence came from a board of chemical officers in America who, in a 'specific and exhaustive analysis', studied the entire medical histories of 'a fair cross-section' of gas victims over a ten-year period.[107] In 1928, this board found that a decade after the war ended, there were gas victims who were 'definitely' suffering lasting illnesses 'due to either one or a combination of gases'. It also found that these illnesses were usually pulmonary (most frequently 'a bronchitis of varying severity'), and much more likely to be caused by mustard gas or phosgene than chlorine gas. British chemical warfare officials noted that these conclusions were 'in agreement with observations made in this country'.

Two other significant pieces of work came from American officers who had been involved in chemical warfare during the First World War. One by Lieutenant Colonel E B Vedder was dismissive, suggesting that most of the illnesses claimed by veterans were actually psychosomatic.[108] The other, by

Colonel Harry L Gilchrist, took a very different view. In an extensive study, he examined gas victims and charted the progress of their health for some years. By 1933, he concluded that exposure to mustard gas on the battlefield had left these victims with two kinds of long-term illnesses – respiratory illnesses (principally chronic bronchitis and emphysema, bronchial asthma) and eye illnesses (mainly chronic conjunctivitis, corneal opacities and keratitis). He found that twenty-seven out of the eighty-nine men in his study were still suffering ill health ten years after they had been gassed in the war.[109]

As the arguments continued, British chemical warfare officials once more made their view plain in 1934: 'There is no doubt...that a peculiarly chronic and progressive form of bronchitis results from severe gassing with mustard gas... In our experience, this chronic bronchitis, with the further resulting disabilities which it itself produces, is the general and almost the only definite residual condition from the inhalation of gas.'[110]

Government officials were on the whole unconvinced that war veterans could recover from mustard gassing, lead healthy lives, but then after some years, succumb to illnesses which could be directly attributed to the original chemical attack. They did however accept that this pattern could occur with one particular disease – delayed keratitis of the eye. This illness was largely unknown until cases began to emerge in the early 1930s. One, for instance, was Mr E M Cross, an 'inmate of the Kingston Poor Law institute'.[111] Cross was in a trench in 1918 when he was exposed to mustard gas. 'After many hours, his eyes closed up, became severely painful and he was unconscious for some hours,' according to one account. He was in hospital for nine months – his eyes were 'completely closed' for the first four months. His sight slowly improved and after two years, he 'was able to read and to resume his work as a plumber'. But he began to experience 'slight attacks of irritation of the eyes and swelling and redness of the lids'. These became more and more frequent and by 1939, he was completely blind. The Ministry of Pensions – recognising that mustard gas victims could be free of symptoms for a decade or so and then start to lose their sight progressively – awarded a significant number of disability pensions to delayed keratitis cases.[112] It is likely that Porton was aware of the development of this ailment by 1934 at the very latest.[113] Nowadays, Porton concedes that this delayed effect can indeed occur 'following exposure to very high concentrations' of mustard gas.[114]

In summary, the declassified documents help to establish that by the late 1920s, Porton admitted that at the very least, mustard gas could cause chronic lung diseases, particularly bronchitis. They also show that in the

1930s, the Ministry of Pensions, responsible for awarding disability payments to gas victims, recognised that delayed keratitis resulted from mustard gas. These illnesses were produced by limited exposure (once or perhaps twice) to mustard gas – similar to the human 'guinea pigs' in the Porton experiments. However, Porton insists nowadays that its mustard gas experiments could not possibly have damaged any of the human 'guinea pigs'.

It is clear that before the Second World War, Porton was aware of the arguments about the delayed effects of mustard gas and even accepted some of them. In the light of all this, Porton scientists still decided to continue exposing humans to the gas in many experiments until 1978.[115] It was only then that Porton finally banned human experiments with mustard gas (see chapter 11).

During the inter-war years, Porton conducted a myriad of human tests with mustard gas, with some experiments picking up on research done during the First World War. For example, 'a large amount of experimental work' during the war had focused on finding out if soldiers could detect mustard gas by smell, and would therefore be able to put on their protection in time. Experiments with 'trained observers' had shown that humans could smell the gas relatively quickly, but after they had been exposed for a while, they could no longer detect it – 'a state of affairs which obviously tends to lead to disastrous results'. Porton acknowledged that this research was 'difficult and somewhat dangerous', but more work needed to be done.[116] Developing protective clothing was also an important target for Porton, and occupied much of the scientists' time.[117] Volunteers were used to discover how much mustard gas vapour penetrated through various kinds of clothing, and whether some types of clothing would be capable of absorbing the poison gas to shield the skin.[118] In one such test, a 'well-marked blister' developed after 'large drops of liquid mustard gas' were smeared over the outside of a greatcoat. Porton scientists commented that 'the striking point about this experiment was the severity of the injury', showing that even the heaviest battlefield clothing then available 'gives a very limited degree of protection from large drops of liquid mustard gas'. Depressingly, it was concluded that soldiers – even with the heaviest coats – would become casualties 'unless his outer garments and probably the whole of his clothing were removed within the matter of minutes'.[119]

Another experiment looked at whether the prolonged wearing of contaminated clothes could wreak damage, even after the victim had left the poisoned atmosphere.[120] Two men were exposed to mustard gas vapour and took off all their clothes. Two other men – 'never previously exposed to mustard gas' – then put on these clothes for ten hours. The first two men were fine, but the latter two 'showed a sharp reaction' about a week later. The scrotums of both men became very irritated, turned red, and within days had become 'scabby'. Both were off sick for a week. This highlighted a delicate problem for servicemen. As Porton noted, 'It has been shown once more that the scrotal area is very vulnerable to mustard gas vapour. This confirms the war experience. How can it therefore be protected without the "incubus" of complete protective equipment? If a satisfactory method can be found for affording a degree of protection to those parts, it is not unlikely that a considerable saving in casualties would result.' Porton resolved to investigate if 'short trunk drawers might be valuable' in this respect.

Human experiments with mustard gas are inevitably hazardous and, as Porton itself admits, 'occasionally...a rather larger burn...occurred than anticipated'. It is difficult to know how often volunteers were injured more than the scientists actually intended. Porton claimed in 1927 that such instances 'have been few and far between, and the greatest care is taken to avoid their occurrence'.[121] One such occasion involved Privates Allmark and Evans of the Cheshire Regiment who were badly burned in February 1928 during tests to determine if bricks contaminated with the gas could inflict casualties.[122] The bricks had been wrapped up in oilskin, leaving a small circle uncovered. The two privates had been required to place their forearms above this circle for forty-five and sixty minutes respectively. 'The results were unexpectedly severe,' commented Porton staff. The vapour of the gas produced large blisters – six by four inches – on their arms and Private Allmark was in pain for weeks as Porton scientists tried to treat the wound, while the blister of Private Evans filled with pus and also took weeks to disappear.

Porton investigated many substances to see if they could find one that would prevent, or treat, mustard gas burns effectively.[123] The mustard liquid was deliberately placed onto the skin of the human 'guinea pigs' to induce burns so that the various substances could then be tried out. In one series of experiments, for example, twenty-three possible remedies were tested on forty-seven men in 1929.[124] Drops of the mustard gas were spread over the arms, and then left for three minutes before the potential remedy was applied for five minutes. Bleach, mixed with Vaseline, emerged as the most promising treatment and was, of course, subsequently tested on many volunteers.[125] In one such experiment, mustard gas was smeared onto both arms of the men; the right arm was then treated with the bleach ointment, and the left arm with an inert substance which would do nothing to prevent burns.[126] Blisters of varying size erupted on the left arms of almost all the

Rudimentary machine for filling chemical weapons in the late 1920s.

Two blisters on the arm of a volunteer named Hayton after he had been exposed to mustard gas.

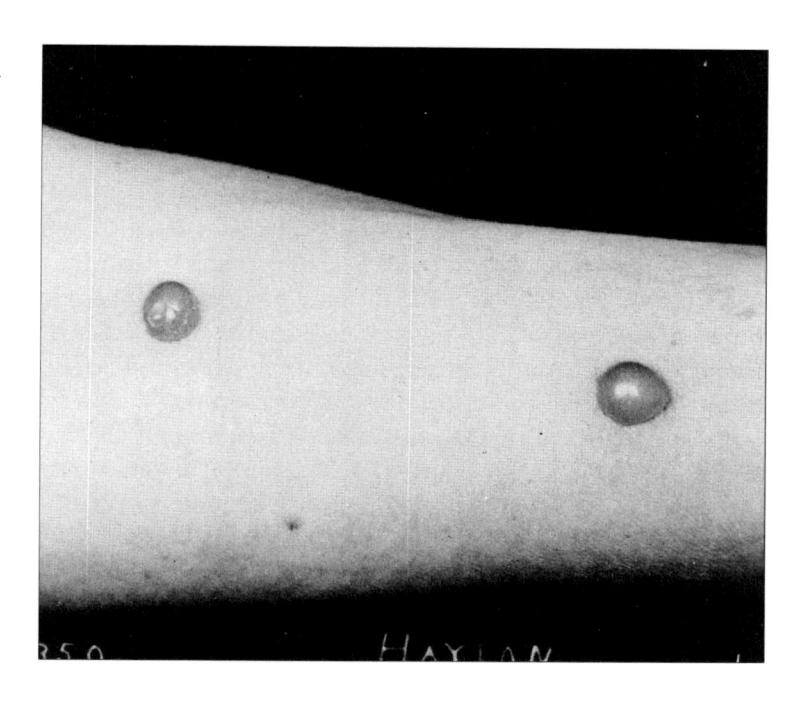

men. Over many decades, Porton and other military scientists have researched a large number of substances to discover one which would be a good treatment for mustard gas burns. Despite all these experiments, no specific therapy has ever been uncovered – burns are best treated using bland lotions and other such creams.

The countless mustard gas experiments continued throughout the period between the two World Wars – sailors were exposed to see how much gas seeped through the edge of naval gas masks; volunteers marched across contaminated ground to find out if the gas would penetrate boots; men were used to establish the potency of mustard gas produced through different manufacturing processes; and so on.[127]

Britain began to build up its chemical armoury in the late 1930s as tensions in Europe escalated. The political issue of rearmament was fiercely argued. British military officials had been especially alarmed by the widespread use of chemical weapons by Italy when it invaded Abyssinia (now Ethiopia) during 1935-6. The Italians had unleashed the weapons even though they had signed the 1925 Geneva Protocol banning gas. This was the first major breach of the treaty. An estimated 15,000 Abyssinian troops were killed or wounded by gas as a result – almost a third of all their casualties. Abyssinian Emperor Haile Selassie described how groups of up to eighteen Italian planes 'followed one another so that the liquid issuing from them formed a continuous fog…soldiers, women, children, cattle, rivers, lakes and pastures were drenched continually with this deadly rain'. Many peasants suffered horrific injuries as mustard gas was scattered over the ground and bushes. Many of them – in their usual clothes and therefore unprotected – did not know that they were being poisoned as the gas lingered on. A reporter from the *Times* newspaper saw helpless peasants with 'large areas of skin removed from the legs and thighs' and 'extremely painful burning of the genital organs'.[128] It is noticeable that since the First World War, chemical weapons have characteristically been used against unprotected troops, most frequently by technologically-sophisticated nations with a well-armed military against ill-equipped, Third World peasants or guerrillas.

By the thirties, Britain's gas stockpile had become depleted so, in 1936, the military approved plans to manufacture a new arsenal of chemical weapons. By the following year, it was decided to set up a mustard gas factory at Randle, near Runcorn in Cheshire, and in 1938, the first batch of mustard gas was produced.[129] Inevitably, as war with Hitler loomed, the steady rearmament permeated into the atmosphere at Porton. Extra staff were recruited and the pressure on the human 'guinea pigs' also intensified.

In 1937, as we have seen, Porton staff demanded more subjects for their experiments – the target now rose to sixteen men a week. At the same time, Porton began to carry out 'more "realistic" trials'.[130]

Gradon Carter, Porton's official historian, believes that, as the Second World War approached, Britain's anti-gas defence was better than that of any other country. 'We had emerged from the Great War of 1914-18 with a respirator, techniques for gas-proofing dugouts and buildings, and little else. At the end of the 1930s superior quality and scales of anti-gas equipment were available to the forces to cater for all known hazards.'[131] He highlights a long list of such equipment, including eye-shields, capes, impregnated battledress, protective dubbin for boots, detector papers and paints, gas identification sets for military units, respirators and anti-gas covers for horses, mules and dogs. He adds that the basis for Britain's superiority in chemical defence 'lay in the research and field trials done at Porton'. As with the First World War, Porton's human experiments between the two wars once again proved to be a vital contribution in developing this proclaimed superiority.

At the outbreak of the Second World War, many feared that poison gas would wreak widespread damage – just as had happened in the First World War.

CHAPTER THREE

Burning Issues

In the early days of the Second World War, many in the British armed forces and the general population expected gas warfare to erupt at any moment. They believed that since chemical warfare had figured so largely in the First World War, there was little reason why it would not also break out in this war. War leader Winston Churchill warned, 'We must expect gas warfare on a tremendous scale'.[1] The atmosphere was understandably jittery, and reports and rumours of chemical attack were rife. Just two weeks into the war, British diplomats in France sent a stark telegram back to London: 'Germans using gas Western Front today'.[2] Thankfully, it turned out to be untrue. Most of the false alarms were caused by nervous tension. One of the most widespread, and in retrospect, ludicrous alarms was that the Germans were releasing over Britain a kind of cobweb that blistered the skin. This scare was soon quelled by Porton scientists who confirmed that it was in fact a harmless natural phenomenon.[3]

Many people of course knew victims who had been gassed in the mud and trenches of the Great War, where the chemical horrors had largely been confined to the battlefield. The advent of the bomber threw up a fresh, yet awful, prospect – that civilians would be bombarded with deadly poison gas in their own homes, gardens and streets. Such fears had been widely aired in the run-up to the outbreak of war. Since the mid-1930s, the British government had been trying to reassure the public that they were by no means defenceless and could actually protect themselves against such a chemical attack. The first official booklet on air raid precautions dealt solely with anti-gas defence, and by 1939, every civilian had been equipped with a gas mask (designed by Porton) – and there were even helmets which could shelter babies. More than ninety-seven million gas masks were produced during the war, and Britain was unique in distributing these respirators to every citizen free of charge.[4]

While Porton believed that Britain's anti-gas defences were among the best in the world, the picture was very different on the offensive side – the country possessed few actual chemical weapons. A small number of RAF bombs had been loaded with mustard gas, while Army weapons were non-existent except for some empty World War One shells. 'Had the Germans initiated gas warfare in 1939, our immediate ability to retaliate would have been negligible,' a Porton history noted.[5]

Churchill was prepared to spray chemical weapons on any German invading forces the moment they hit British beaches. However, when he discovered in 1940 that the country's poison gas armoury was so meagre that all stocks would quickly be used up within a matter of days, he was absolutely livid. Back in 1938, the Cabinet had agreed proposals to produce 300 tons of mustard gas a week, with a reserve of 2,000 tons.[6] Soon after the outbreak of the war, these proposals had been approved once again. Churchill therefore demanded to know why these political orders had been flouted, placing the country in 'very great danger'. He was determined to discover who had been 'responsible for disobeying War Cabinet orders without even reporting what was going on'. He ordered that the production of gas be speeded up, and to ensure that the order was implemented this time, he insisted that the updates of gas production be brought to him personally each week. He scrutinised them, often scribbling observations on the reports, such as 'Press on. We must have a great store. They will certainly use it against us when they feel the pinch'.[7] As a consequence of this, Britain's gas stockpiles steadily grew to the size demanded by Churchill.

Both the Allies and the Nazis were in theory committed to not using poison gas in the war, but it was an uneasy truce. Neither side could trust the other to honour this commitment. Churchill resolved that Britain would not be the first country to use chemical weapons, but if Hitler resorted to such weapons, then Britain had to be in a position to retaliate immediately. Throughout the war, Porton played a vital role in evaluating and authenticating allegations of gas attacks. This work was crucial since a mistake could trigger gas warfare. Both sides feared that it would only take one gas strike on one front to provoke an instant reply which would rapidly escalate to an all-out chemical conflict across all the theatres of war. To prepare for this, Britain's chemical arsenal was steadily built up as the war progressed, contingency plans in the use of chemical weapons drawn up, and stocks of poison gas secretly moved closer to front lines.

Unsurprisingly, Porton was intensely busy. The establishment 'expanded considerably' in the early months of the war, with a great influx of scientists from universities and industry. Within three years, the number of staff had trebled, but the volume of work had grown nearly ten times. A strategic change was also made at the top. Government officials had come to realise that Porton needed a new leader 'to overcome the semi-stagnation into which the station has tended to fall in peace, because of the official cloud – largely due to the Geneva convention – under which work on chemical defence has had to be conducted'. Unfortunately there was 'much inertia' to be overcome before Porton could be moulded into the efficient organisation that was essential for wartimes. A 'young and virile' commandant was appointed – Colonel Watkinson – who soon made a 'splendid success of the job'. He was judged to be 'breaking down the old inter-section jealousies and getting them to work together as a team in a way which none of his predecessors ever did'.[8]

At the start of the war, Porton 'expected that the work of the past 20 years would very soon be put to the test'. Since the defensive preparations for war were 'fairly complete', the major effort at Porton was 'very quickly' swung over to offensive work, particularly 'the great need to accelerate the design and production of gas weapons'. Staff were reallocated and more land was bought as space for Porton to test out the weapons.[9]

Porton's physiology department – responsible for human testing – was 'of great importance' since it provided 'the final assessment of the offensive and defensive value of most chemical warfare agents and materials'. In 1940, the list of the valuable tasks of the physiology department included testing new compounds to see if they might be effective chemical weapons; finding ways of treating gas burns with a variety of ointments; determining how quickly gases penetrated various fabrics, oilskins, and rubber gloves; conducting 'routine' tests of tear gases; and checking the efficiency of new methods of decontaminating clothes. Much of this work built on the research that had gone on before at the establishment.

Porton needed contingents of twenty volunteers each week to carry out this work (an increase from the number required just before the war).[10] This amounted to around 1,000 a year if sufficient subjects could be recruited. It is not known whether this target was met each week (or indeed if this target was altered during the war). One monitoring report, for instance, from mid-1940 recorded that one of the 'difficulties holding up progress [was that a] steady flow of volunteers…[was]…not being maintained'.[11] It is conspicuous that few of the documents which record the planning and results of the 'many and varied' human experiments that went on during the Second World War have been released by Porton into the public domain.[12] As previously noted, Porton maintains that it is no longer possible to ascertain how many people took part in its human experiments before 1945.

It is apparent, as shown in chapter two, that Porton had its usual troubles in getting enough volunteers to be human 'guinea pigs' during the war. As ever, Porton's pool of volunteers was drawn from military units around the country, and the establishment, to some extent, had to be reliant on the goodwill of unit commanders to promote the idea of volunteering and a favourable image of its work. This caused some notable bust-ups.[13] In 1943, acrimonious arguments flew back and forth between Porton and various units when some servicemen were found to be unfit to resume their normal duties after they had been burnt by mustard gas in Porton experiments. Two years later, the number of volunteers from the RAF slumped considerably after 'some false impressions had unfortunately been disseminated' by a group of men who had just been to Porton. This had to be corrected by 'energetic action' from Porton and unit commanders.

Throughout the war, officials argued over the rewards that should be dangled in front of servicemen to induce them to volunteer for the tests.[14] 'In an effort to give additional incentives to volunteers' in April 1941, Porton's Commandant suggested that extra money should be given to each person 'suffering from severe mustard burns incurred during a trial which was considered to have a special risk'. But Whitehall replied that this suggestion could not be authorised 'in case of legal complications'. This objection was overcome and the extra money for the payments was found from another budget. Other officials soon objected that the scale of payment was 'over-generous'. However it was pointed out that the payment, for example to one volunteer who had been blinded for more than three days by mustard gas could 'scarcely be considered excessive'. The incentive of extra leave, which had traditionally been on offer to volunteers, was stopped in 1941 when the War Office argued that this time away from military duties could not be justified in the emergency. To this, Porton lodged a strong protest.

Whatever the attractions on offer at any one time to entice volunteers, they proved irrelevant to some servicemen. These men claim they never in fact chose to take part in the gas tests and so cannot be classed as volunteers. It seems that members of chemical warfare units, especially those stationed in Porton's vicinity, were often ordered to take part in gas tests at the establishment, without any choice. These units – called chemical warfare companies – were trained to fire chemical munitions and to implement defences against gas. It appears that the units, although independent of Porton and actually part of the Royal Engineers, were required to supply human subjects for Porton's experiments on a regular basis, as is shown in their various records and war diaries.[15]

Wilfred Hall was a young sapper in a chemical warfare company based near Porton over three months in 1940. During that time, he was regularly sent to Porton to undergo 'quite a lot of different tests'.[16] How many tests, however, he cannot recall. He reels off a list of chemicals to which he was exposed – mustard gas, lewisite, tear gases and so on. 'You name it, we did it.' He says that he was twice hospitalised for around a week because he was coughing so badly from the tests. 'I was coughing for about 36 hours.' He does not know, and was not told, which chemical caused this illness.

He firmly maintains that he did not choose to participate in the tests. 'I was not a volunteer. We was in the army. It was a matter of you're going and that's it. It was a matter of you have got to go. You had to do what they told you.'

After three months of tests, he and many others refused on the parade ground to go back into the gas chambers. 'We told the people [his superiors] that we were not going in no more. We had a bloody enough of it. Absolutely everyone refused. We all stood fast and said "That's it, we are not doing it any more."' Faced with such solidarity, their superiors had no option but to back down and move them to other duties. 'There was a lot of bad feeling, naturally. After that, they had to put the conscientious objectors through it.' He says that unlike the volunteers, he did not receive either extra pay or leave for undergoing the tests. He has since suffered from chronic bronchitis, but is unsure if this was caused by Porton experiments. 'You don't know whether it is or whether it isn't. They [the authorities] won't tell you.'

Terence Barnes, then a young sapper in a chemical warfare company, was also stationed near Porton when he and his section were detailed to take part in experiments around 1941. He remembers that at the time, he just saw it as being 'part of his soldierly duties',[17] and did not question it. 'If one was given orders in the army, you carried them out. That's it.' Now he regards it as 'a damn cheek and a bit of an imposition' to be used as a human 'guinea pig' in this way. 'There was no question of choice,' he adds. During his time at Porton he had to go into the gas chamber and then take off his mask. He was left with a 'hefty' cough for a day or so. He remembers little about the experiments in the chamber or even what the gas was. In another test, he and the twenty or thirty in the section had to walk over unknown poison gas on a piece of ground within Porton. He was given no protection and suffered no effects. Afterwards, 'a few bigwigs' including a brigadier asked them various questions, specifically whether they could detect gas by smell.

Another sapper, Godfrey Henman, had a similar experience when he was based near Porton. One day in the early part of the war, a thirty-strong section in his chemical warfare company was collected together and sent to Porton to take part in an experiment.[18] Like Barnes, this section was also told to walk slowly through a field within Porton. He assumed that the field had been contaminated with poison gas in some way. 'It was all a bit vague. We were not told in detail what it was all about.' They all took some kind of intelligence tests before and afterwards. He assumed that this was to measure if the gas had had any effect on them. He cannot remember anyone experiencing pain. Henman was twenty-one at the time. 'We did not really know what we were going to, or going through. We were told nothing.' He felt that they had no choice but to accept it. 'Being young and sort of innocent in those days, we didn't feel unduly frightened about it, but it was just one of those things that happened.'

Other human 'guinea pigs' believe that they were deceived when they were used in the gas tests. One was Harry Hogg, then a corporal in armaments in his late twenties. In late 1942, an appeal on the notice board of his station, RAF Honington in Suffolk, caught his eye – service personnel were needed to join another base to maintain a stockpile of chemical weapons.[19] Before he could take up this new job, he was posted to Porton for what he thought was training to carry out maintenance of such gas weapons. But when he got to Porton, he found himself being sent into a gas chamber. It was an experience that has been seared on his memory. He and the other human 'guinea pigs' were 'herded' into a small chamber: 'There was no ventilation. There were no windows. There was just a small light in the ceiling. And a thick door of course, with a peep hole in the door.'

He recalls that Porton staff told them that a canister on the floor would be opened and that 'no man would be let out until everyone was on their hands and knees'. 'They released the gas and closed the door. I can hear the bang of that door to this day.' Porton staff then watched them through the peephole in the door. 'Sure enough every man was on his hands and knees. We were scrambling about with our heads at the door, trying to get air.' The 'fumes spewing out' of the canister were 'pungent and acrid'. The men felt was if their lungs or head were 'bursting'. 'It seemed like an eternity. They opened the door and we all piled out. Hands and knees, groaning and moaning and crying and oh goodness...one man in particular, who was a little bit older than I was, was just like an animal. He was trying to eat grass. He was out of his mind. It was horrendous what we went through. Horrendous.'

He adds, 'I did not know what concoction it was and was not told.' He recalls that he could detect 'a sort of smile' on the face of one officer and remembers thinking that 'this so and so got pleasure and delight at our distress and helplessness, writhing and groaning with the awful pain'. He was subjected to other similar experiments in 'this hellish chamber' during his ten or twelve days at Porton. 'We could not refuse – not in wartime. We was in uniform.'

He insists that he did not 'volunteer for this "guinea pig" stuff', since he actually elected to look after a gas stockpile. 'But then they took advantage. Whenever they got you there, they experimented on you.' He did not talk in public about the tests for fifty years because he was scared of breaking the Official Secrets Act and being sent to jail. 'Porton Down – you just had to keep everything to yourself. It is like Fort Knox.' He believes that Porton has 'got something to answer for...How they can live with that on their conscience, I just don't know.' Hogg has suffered several illnesses including breathing problems and depression over the past decades. He believes that he is the only Porton human 'guinea pig' to have won a war pension for his later ill health (see chapter 10).

Another human 'guinea pig', Thomas Case, was more sanguine about being unexpectedly thrust into the tests. In 1943, as a private in the Royal Norfolk Regiment, he was sent on a course to learn how to make water safe and drinkable in military situations.[20] He said that the course was held at Porton – and that he too was suddenly roped into the gas experiments. 'I didn't think I did volunteer. When I got there, various things started to happen.' He had mustard gas and lewisite dropped on his arms four times, producing painful blisters of 'quite a size' of which the scars remained visible until his death in 2000. He was also sent into the gas chamber to try out a new kind of respirator. 'We just thought that it was part of the course. I just joined in. Everybody else seemed to do it.' He felt as if he could not object to the tests, since he was serving in the military in a war. 'I just took it all in my stride.'

By 1942, most of the human subjects were being drawn from the Pioneer Corps and, according to a Porton report, 'included Germans and other foreigners; one week German scientists were included'.[21] Porton, however, complained at the time that the physical condition of the human 'guinea pigs' was 'too low.' The Pioneer Corps were essentially a labouring force within Britain which carried out unpleasant tasks such as digging ditches, cleaning lavatories, unloading lorries, and humping coal. 'The Pioneer Corps enjoyed a sad reputation as the dumping ground of the British Army; all human dross, it was once unkindly said, was there. It was the natural home of illiterates and former criminals,' according to one account.[22] From this description, it is questionable whether any member of the Pioneer Corps had the choice when they were sent to Porton, and how many of them went is unknown.

Around 25,000 Germans, Italians and other foreigners had been interned in the early part of the war, since the government viewed them as possible spies and a threat to British national security. Most of them were released around 1941, and those who wanted to help the British war effort had only one option open to them – to join the Pioneer Corps. It appears that it was via this route that some of them came to be subjects in Porton's experiments. It is unlikely that the 'Germans and other foreigners' referred to by Porton were actually prisoners of war.

It must be said that although it appears that some of Porton's human 'guinea pigs' were plunged into the experiments against their will, it is however clear that many others did actually volunteer for the tests throughout the war.

Many of these volunteers had vastly different experiences. Sydney Pepper, of the Bedfordshire and Hertfordshire Regiment, seems to have had a mild time when he went to Porton in January 1940.[23] Aged twenty, he had volunteered because he wanted the six days' leave on offer. 'You were told never to volunteer, but I did,' he jokes. He recalls that the appeal for volunteers on the notice board specifically mentioned mustard gas and lewisite, and he wanted to get an idea of what to expect from these gases, in case they were used in the war. 'Nobody knew at the beginning of the war what was going to happen. People were frightened of those things in those days. I would then know that is what it is and it could be treated,' he explains. Over two days, he had dabs of both gases on each arm; his blisters were then tended with an experimental treatment. 'It hurt a bit. It was like a burn. It was not too bad.' For the rest of the week, Porton staff inspected the blisters twice a day to see how they were healing. The remaining time was his own. He spent it either reading, practising semaphore, or in the canteen. He remembers it as 'a pleasant break', but dull. In his case, the marks from the blisters faded over time and all but disappeared.

Kenneth Henson believed that he was volunteering for one day of tests at Porton in April 1941, but ended up for two weeks in the establishment's hospital.[24] He was a thirty-four-year-old sapper in a Royal Engineer chemical warfare company at the time. His superiors quipped that he would get a military funeral with full honours as his reward for volunteering. He was given an army blouse – apparently sprayed 'with a mixture of mustard gas and some other toxic substance' – which he had to wear. He walked around Porton's grounds for some hours, talking and watching a cricket match, so that the chemical had a chance to sink through to the skin. Later that afternoon, he was put into a ward in the hospital on his own. He says that the Porton staff told him nothing about the experiment or what was happening to him. 'I got it into my mind that they wanted to find out how long it would take for me to die. I was lying there. I was not allowed visitors. I had plenty of time to think. In those days, so many people were getting killed that it [did] not seem so terrible as it does nowadays.' As it turned out, the contaminated blouse gave him a rash, but little else. 'Half-a-dozen high-powered doctors came to look at me over the two weeks to see how I felt.' Afterwards, he was allotted extra leave and money for volunteering.

Richard Daykin, then a twenty-six-year-old driver in the Army Service Corps, found the experiments more painful than he had expected when he had volunteered in 1941.[25] He had decided to go with some mates because they were bored at the time. They had been evacuated from France and were waiting to be sent abroad again to fight in another military campaign. At his base, it was 'all parades and maintenance'. He was not offered any extra leave or money for going to Porton for a week. In hindsight, he wishes 'that he had damn well not gone there', since 'you felt like a bloody fool'. He has had illnesses for many years, such as chronic bronchitis, bad colds and creeping deafness, but he is unsure if these are directly connected to the Porton tests. He has never bothered to claim a war pension, because, as he says phlegmatically, 'it would take some proving after all these years'. He believes that some Porton volunteers have suffered badly and should be compensated. 'Our government has hushed it up. They won't tell you nothing.'

In his first experiment, he and others ran through a cloud of choking gas of some sort without a respirator. They then had to put on their gas masks and go around an assault course. He felt 'breathless' from the gas and 'just collapsed' at the second obstacle, as did the others. 'I could not run any further. It was painful.' The scientists then took his temperature and checked his heart rate.

After a day's rest, he was put onto his second test. He was dressed in a real German uniform and helmet. He and others were led onto the fields within Porton and spaced out under a tower with a target board on it. 'We were stood at ease with our rifles, looking down at the ground', he says. In front of them were white sheets, about a yard square. A mustard gas shell was fired at the target board, exploding and spraying the chemical at them. He suffered a small blister on his hand (the resulting scar is still slightly visible). They were then required to wear the contaminated uniform for twenty-four hours, sleeping in it in a marquee. It seems that this experiment was aimed at seeing how the liquid penetrated the German clothing and affected the men. In the early hours, they were woken by the moans of a man who was in agony. This man was 'in a hell of a state'. His clothes were stripped off, revealing severe blisters under his armpits and genitalia causing him to be taken straight to hospital. Daykin says that he never saw this man again, although he had been from his unit.

In his last experiment, a group of men, numbered one to six, were put in a glass-fronted gas chamber where they were observed by Porton staff as they walked around. Gas was dispersed into the air, and the men had to point to the parts of their bodies where the gas was hurting them. 'It started on your ears, your nose, your eyes. You felt as if your teeth were coming out of your gums.' They were shut in for ninety seconds. 'You were in such a state that you wanted release. You would have honestly shot yourself. It only lasted for a few minutes and then it went away.' Daykin felt that the guards posted outside the chamber were there to stop the men harming themselves in any way. The chemical involved, according to him, was 'a suicide gas', known as 'Arthur'. This was in fact the code name of a potential lethal chemical weapon – arsine.

'Arthur' had been at the centre of a scare during the war. A single specimen of a new German gas mask had been captured in France in the early part of the war. It was found that this new mask afforded greater protection against arsine, at a time when British masks gave inadequate protection. It was also learnt that the Germans had cornered all the available arsenic on the world market before the war. These combined discoveries heightened British fears that the Germans were planning to use arsine as a chemical weapon. Emergency measures were therefore devised to defend British troops fighting in France against this threat. These consisted of a special detector paper which turned yellow in the presence of arsine, and a new (but rather 'awkward') canister which was latched onto the regular gas masks. Both were hurriedly manufactured in great quantities and rushed over to France. During the war, Porton carried out a fair amount of research into arsine, but when the fighting had finished, the British learned that the Germans never actually had any intention of using arsine whatsoever. The Nazis had bought up the arsenic for other military purposes, and it was merely fortuitous that their masks gave them better protection against arsine. In fact, the Germans had intensified their previously low-level research into arsine after they captured some of the British detector paper, causing them, in turn, to believe that Churchill might employ arsine.[26]

This chain of events is an example of how research priorities in chemical warfare fluctuate in response to the perceived actions and intentions of the enemy. Throughout the war, both sides sought to find out what the other side was up to. Reliable intelligence on either new gases or defensive equipment was crucial. A novel poison gas could inflict great damage on the other side if they were not prepared for it, and so time and resources had to be devoted to inventing new methods of protection. This process of reacting to the enemy's innovations, whether real or not, often dictated the pattern and direction of Porton's human experiments.

Porton's permission to experiment on humans was briefly examined by military and political authorities in 1940 in a curious affair. Since 1925, Whitehall officials had laid down certain regulations governing the use of human subjects who were recruited from outside Porton from the armed forces. According to one account, experiments with such volunteers were 'subject to conditions and safeguards approved from time to time by the Army Council'.[27] However, it is unclear how onerous these regulations actually were. With the passing of the years and a paucity of surviving and released documents, details of such restrictions are now quite obscure. As Porton accepts, it is difficult to establish the rationale behind these regulations, the exact years in which they were supposed to have been enforced, whether they were actually obeyed by Porton, or if they curtailed Porton's experiments to any degree.[28]

In 1937, the then head of the chemical warfare department in London set out his understanding of the regulations. Whitehall had authorised the use of outside volunteers for experiments to test and develop measures to decontaminate victims of gas in a war. He does not say when this authority was given. In 'recent years', this permission had been extended to include tests to establish whether other protective measures (such as clothing impregnated to shield against gas) worked. He adds that 'the one thing which the War Office have repeatedly refused to authorise is the employment of outside observers for *breathing tests* against arsenicals or other gases'.

At first glance, this categorical statement appears to imply that many Porton tests in which volunteers breathed in chemicals – such as arsenicals, tear gases and sundry new compounds – before 1937 were, in fact, unauthorised. However, it seems that under Porton's definition, a *breathing test* refers specifically to one kind of experiment – when the effectiveness of respirators was gauged by placing humans in 'very high concentrations of gas in a chamber where breakdown of the respirator is anticipated'. This definition is contained in a revised set of regulations produced in 1930. These same regulations clearly state that Porton's tests cover 'exposure of the unprotected body, eyes, *lungs*, or skin to the action of any toxic substance for experimental purposes' (author's emphasis added).

In March 1940, Porton chiefs requested permission from wartime commanders in Whitehall to carry out 'occasional' experiments on outside volunteers with sternutators. These were the arsenicals, such as adamsite (DM), which produce very irritating effects including protracted sneezing, unbearable headaches, vomiting, unsteadiness, trembling and pain in the chest, nose and throat. Porton argued that its work on sternutators had become increasingly more important and that such experiments must surely be justified in wartime. However, it is mystifying that Porton should now apply for this permission since it had already been carrying out human experiments with these arsenicals before the war (see chapter two). It raises the question as to whether Whitehall officials had ever been fully aware of what was happening in the secretive installation. (Interestingly, arsenicals were tested heavily on human subjects during the First World War, but the issue of restrictions and permission does not appear to have arisen then, mainly, it would seem, because the subjects were at that time Porton staff.)

The pressure and urgency of wartime inevitably pushed back the boundaries of what was previously considered to be acceptable in the field of human experiments. This is very evident in many of the particularly brutal tests which were conducted abroad – in Australia, India and Canada – with Britain's allies under the supervision and control of Porton scientists.

The Allies in the Far East feared that Japan could well use chemical weapons against them. A plethora of reports had indicated that the Japanese had already employed a variety of chemical weapons – including mustard gas and arsenicals – in their war against China since 1937. These reports continued to come in during the Second World War. In 1942, Freddie Gorrill, a British major who had been working at Porton, was despatched to Australia to help set up a research unit.[29] Gorrill, who was to be in command of the experimental unit until the end of the war, was depicted as a real powerhouse of a leader, who cajoled and drove the unit on. 'He was a compact man with a round head, round glasses and an infectious grin. He still had something of a Devon accent in his speech, which was fluent and persuasive,' according to one description.[30]

Chemical warfare in the Far East, if it did break out, was to be fought in an entirely different environment from Europe. The war in the Far East was mainly in tropical forest where the atmosphere was warm and highly humid. Porton lacked reliable data on how effective poison gas would be in such clammy, dense forests. One of Gorrill's key tasks was therefore to discover how mustard gas harmed the human body in a tropical climate. The first experiments were done in northern Australia (at Townsville, Queensland) so that they were as close to tropical conditions as possible.

The initial experiments with humans suggested that mustard gas was roughly four times more potent on hot and sweaty skin in the tropics than in the cooler climates of Europe.[31] For instance, the human subjects had started to vomit severely far earlier and at lower dosages than in the temperate climates where vomiting in such tests was 'comparatively rare'. In his seven-page 'most secret' report back to Britain, Gorrill painted a grim picture.[32] He disclosed that 'many of our protective measures are of very limited value in the tropics', and advised that because liquid mustard gas and lewisite penetrated the skin much more rapidly in the tropics, Porton's anti-gas ointments would have to be applied to the skin within one minute, or else they would be useless in preventing burns and blisters.[33] 'How often this would be practicable under battle conditions would be debatable,' he pondered morosely. Anti-gas powders seemed to be even worse than the ointments.

These early findings were a sharp warning of how gas warfare in the tropics differed greatly from temperate zones. Gorrill advised that Porton's great body of knowledge accumulated in temperate climates would have to checked and completely revised before the Allies could understand gas warfare in the tropics. Until that time, the Allies would be all at sea if chemical warfare was started with the Japanese.

The Allies were sufficiently alarmed to authorise the expansion of their research unit in Australia. Returning to Britain, Gorrill recruited half a dozen staff from Porton in the summer of 1943. One of these was a British doctor, David Sinclair, who became the unit's deputy in charge of the human experiments. With the arrival of more Australians, the unit was essentially a combined British and Australian effort, although there were also a few Americans present. The unit was relocated to the banks of a river in Innisfail, further north in Queensland, where the landscape more closely resembled the tropical forests of islands in the south-west Pacific.

The human 'guinea pigs' were obtained in a similar way to the test subjects at Porton, and an appeal letter was circulated around the Australian armed forces. Australian biochemist, Jack Legge, concedes that the initial letter was 'a little obscure, simply mentioning "experiments in the tropics"'. Sinclair indeed now concedes that it was 'possibly a mistake' that the letter was 'less than detailed', suggesting that 'part of the problem of this whole operation was the intense security which was imposed by everyone concerned. Nobody was willing to say that this unit was dealing with mustard burns in the tropics and that they would be exposed to mustard gas.' One volunteer, Maurice Maunder, recalled, 'The whole situation was a very hush-hush affair. I knew nothing about it. I am afraid that I didn't even think of my health. I didn't even think that we would suffer as much as we did.'

The volunteers' reasons for agreeing also echo those of the human 'guinea pigs' at Porton. As Sinclair says, 'Many of these men had seen war service overseas and would volunteer for anything in order to escape for a time from the boredom of their existence.' Legge, the Australian biochemist, also remembers that many were 'only too happy' to volunteer, since they were tired of all the 'drilling, cleaning, webbing and polishing their boots'. Jack Baird, another volunteer, recalls that he had just come back from abroad. 'We were getting a bit sick of the route marches.' When he heard about 'volunteers for a gas school', he went with his friend, since both thought that they could learn something about tear gas. 'We did not know much about what mustard gas was like until we copped it.'

As the batches of fifty or so volunteers arrived, Sinclair, in charge of human experiments, says that he 'used to give them the introductory harangue, telling them something of what the unit was trying to do and what they could expect.' He adds that they were told that they would be exposed to mustard gas in some way, but admits, 'I didn't make it quite as full as I perhaps should have done.' He says that the volunteers were given the opportunity to withdraw from the tests beforehand, but none in fact did. Baird attributes this reluctance to leave to the essential Australian character: 'Being Australians we don't want to let our mates down.' British doctor Sinclair adds that 'in typical Australian fashion', the volunteers 'weren't going to let their mates down and once they'd started, they would carry on.' It is noticeable (as shown later in chapter six) that few of the human subjects at Porton withdrew from the experiments after they had arrived at the establishment, and it may be that they felt they had no choice in the disciplined and rigid atmosphere of the military.

A stainless steel gas chamber had been built at Innisfail; Sinclair hailed it 'our fine new gas chamber, the status symbol of the unit'. This chamber allowed the scientists to expose the volunteers to mustard gas at varying dosages, temperatures and humidities in precise experiments. Sometimes the men wore protective clothing; sometimes they did not. Some had to undertake heavy exercise in the chamber, such as carrying bags of sand from one corner to the other. One rather surprising feature of these experiments was that the volunteers themselves ran a sweepstake – the person who got the worst burns from the gas was the winner and pocketed all the money. Strangely, volunteers often asked to go through the chamber again – to have a 'proper crack of the whip' – if they had fainted the first time around because the humidity or temperature was particularly high. At other times, some men scarcely suffered any ill effects, since, as Sinclair says, 'we had to proceed cautiously as the last thing we wanted was to produce severe burns'. Although these men had got off lightly, they then complained that 'it wasn't fair that they had not been burned as badly as their mates' in the chamber and wanted another go!

This was not the only unusual part of the experiments. The female members of the unit were detailed to gee up the men while they were in the gas chamber. Volunteer Maurice Maunder recalls, 'The girls kept us going by singing songs of Australiana. In fact I can still hear the songs coming through the PA.' Fay Brazill, an Australian laboratory assistant, explained that, 'When we had gas chamber duty – everybody took their turn at it – we would sing to them, tell them funny stories, or even just poke faces at them through the windows – anything to keep them amused because even though they did some physical labour in there, there were times when they were resting and it must have been very boring for them.'

A main objective of the experiments was to see how long soldiers could continue fighting after they had been poisoned with mustard gas. This was done by first exposing the men to the gas in a chamber and then – in a daily routine for three weeks – sending them on a six-mile route march with full equipment and two runs over an assault course. According to Sinclair, 'the point of this was to give them a standardised task to do each day so that it could be determined whether they were fit to do it or not.'

His fellow scientist Legge admits, 'We designed a most vicious assault course, which was designed to rub off blisters and abrade injured skin... There was a particular refinement on the assault course to exacerbate the pain they were feeling from their burns. We built a sort of cage out of tangled liana vines which was extremely hard for everyone to go through without rubbing their arms and shoulders. The bravery of the Japanese soldiers was well understood. Many might stay in a foxhole, injured almost unto death, and still have a grenade ready to throw at our people who came past. It was therefore explained that only by going to the limit of their own endurance with the burns could they even manage to equal the courage of the enemy they had to fight.' Legge (described as 'a slight, mild-mannered man') claims that after 'open discussion', the volunteers 'willingly' accepted the assault course.[34]

The men could pull out of the daily routine at any point over the three weeks and recover in a hospital bed, but they kept on going day after day. Lab. assistant Fay Brazill recalls, 'Unfortunately, perhaps fortunately, we had Australian volunteers who are extremely pig-headed and they would carry on for ages, long after you thought it would be possible for human beings to do so.' Sinclair believes that the men were prepared to suffer the pain for two reasons. One was to demonstrate to each other how tough they were. 'They used to take bandages off their burns in order to negotiate assault course obstacles.' The second reason was to perform well in front of the female sergeant who supervised the assault course and 'encouraged them with words and gestures to do their best'.

However, many of the men suffered shocking burns and blisters. Military film footage shows the men hauling themselves over the assault course in a crab-like motion and trying to hold onto ropes with blistered hands. Mustard gas vapour harms the moistest parts of the body most severely. The exertion of the assault course in the tropical heat made the volunteers exceedingly sweaty which of course exacerbated the burns. As volunteer Maurice Maunder says, 'The worst areas affected were obviously where the dampness was – in-between the crutch, under the armpits and around the backs of the legs where the sweat accumulated.' Official film of the experiments shows the men afflicted with raw, skinless genitals. Jack Baird, one of the human 'guinea pigs', recalls, 'I reckon I was burnt over 90-95 percent of my body. It was all around my privates and I could hardly walk in the finish, it was that bad.' He felt 'great relief' when he finally gave up. Collapsing before he could get to the hospital bed, he was treated for three weeks before he could walk properly. 'The sister used to come around each day and peel off big sheets of skin and it was red raw underneath. You couldn't bear the sheets on you. We were like pieces of raw steak.'

Sinclair concedes that 'perhaps I would have been happy to see little less dramatic results', adding, 'We didn't know how far we could go, and some of the dosages we gave at the upper end of the range did, in fact, produce burns which were worse than we had thought they would be.' He remembers that people in the nearby town 'widely believed that we were a kind of punishment unit and that this was why we made them run over the assault course with such savagery'. Australian biochemist Jack Legge says that when they came to collate the results of the tests in a report, 'We found that we had been able to push the experiments rather close to conditions we felt might have had lethal consequences.'

Sinclair regrets the horrible burns, but believes that 'it was necessary. Unless we had done this, you wouldn't know at what stage acceptable burns change into unacceptable burns.' His report on a large tranche of these experiments – 258 men – commented that under tropical conditions, the scrotum was the 'most commonly and most severely affected area of the body' in clouds of mustard gas.[35] 'The healing time of raw areas on the penis tends to be longer than that of raw areas elsewhere,' he wrote, deducing that 'the condition of the scrotum is by far the most important single factor' in determining whether a man was a casualty. In general, the burns emerged after several days, and were at their height on the tenth day after the gassing in the chamber and healed on about the nineteenth day.

The scientists believe that the results of the tests were valuable since they devised for the first time an objective system for assessing whether mustard gas victims were casualties or not.[36] This was to create a 'revolution' at Porton and other chemical warfare installations. Previously, a medical officer would examine a gas victim and decide himself whether he should be consigned to hospital. The process relied solely on the opinion of one person but, as Sinclair explains, opinions in different stations varied widely. 'It wouldn't be an exaggeration to say that in one station, a man would be assessed as being a casualty and sent to hospital; in another station, the same man would have been said not to be a casualty at all.'

The objective assessment was done with some precision. The volunteers' ability to finish the assault course and marches was rated on each of the twenty-one days after they had been exposed. If they could not finish on any of the days, they were classed as 'partially disabled' for that day; if their burns and injuries had become so painful that they were incapable of defending themselves by the relatively simple task of firing a rifle, they were categorised as 'totally disabled'. Sinclair invented a scoring system using sketches on the front and back view of the human body on cards. Details of a volunteer's exposure – such as dosage or temperature – were entered on the card. Every twenty-four hours, the scientists would examine the men and shade in the areas which had been burnt.

The scientists produced other research data which they believed to be very useful.[37] Some troops took part in trials wearing anti-gas clothing which had been impregnated with the standard British protective chemical. The concept of impregnating clothing with a compound capable of neutralising mustard gas before the poison soaked through to the skin had been much researched by Porton scientists before the war, particularly since 1935.[38] This impregnated clothing was widely issued to troops during the war; all the troops which invaded occupied Europe in June 1944 were equipped with it. Unfortunately, it was discovered that the standard British impregnated chemical was worse than useless because it degraded in tropical heat into a toxic substance. Unwittingly, a batch of men who had been sent on a four-day march were badly poisoned and fell sick as a result.[39] A more structured experiment later confirmed this unexpected danger and American suits which used a different compound were adopted instead.

Volunteers also took part in trials to find out how long they could wear anti-gas protection in the sweltering heat and humidity of the tropics. In temperatures of ninety-five degrees and togged out in 'thick, impregnated, long-legged underwear, closely woven impregnated suits, respirators, woollen hoods, and rubber boots', they set to work hacking their way through scrub with machetes. The scientists noted down how long they lasted before keeling over. It was not long. Even at night without any exercise, the men could only wear the clothing and masks for between two and three hours. Sinclair comments: 'This demonstrated that attack by gas could have been very effective against the Japanese in the south Pacific, since even at night and at rest the defenders of the islands could not have worn their respirators long enough to resist concentrations which could easily have been maintained for several days.'

While some of the Australian trials were aimed at developing defensive measures, others were designed explicitly to illuminate the offensive possibilities of using poison gas on the Japanese. In 1943, thousands of American troops perished while trying to capture a series of fortified Japanese islands. The massive losses prompted the Allies to consider other ways of driving the tenacious Japanese out of these heavily defended islands. Poison gas was one such way. A large trial was held in February 1944 on Brook Island off Queensland to compare mustard gas and the conventional high explosive bombardment.

Sinclair calls the Brook Island trial 'dramatic' and the 'highlight of the whole set-up' in the Australian gas experiments. Brook was a small coral island, covered by rain forest.[40] Mock Japanese fortifications – including foxholes and tunnels – were built on the island, and animals were tethered among these fortifications. Aircraft flew over the island and dropped four tons of mustard gas bombs in a pre-arranged pattern. This initiated some intense activity. Scientists and soldiers in protective gear landed on the island and began to examine the bombed animals and take readings from the sampling apparatus to see how long the contamination remained. 'The mustard had been dyed to allow us to see it, and there were heavy splashes of it all over the place. Some of the bombs had burst on the canopy [of the rain forest], but others had got through to the ground,' says Sinclair.

Parties of volunteers 'clad in various kinds of British, American, Japanese, and experimental' protective clothing went onto the island soon afterwards. According to one account, 'jungle-trained troops with the minimum of protection carried out manoeuvres for several hours over the contaminated territory'.[41] One group of volunteers wore masks, but no other protection. With liquid mustard sticking to leaves and branches, their forearms and arms were burnt as they had to force their way through the dense jungle. According to Sinclair, 'Some of the resulting burns were really the most severe that we ever had', and four men's burns took between three and six weeks to heal completely.[42] One volunteer, Ron Nosworthy, reckons that 'about 80 to 90 percent' of those volunteers who went onto the island were burnt from the gas.[43]

Tom Mitchell, then twenty, was sent back onto the island a day after the gas attack as the scientists wanted two soldiers to spend twelve hours in the contaminated zones. They had absolutely no protection. They were told not to rub any bushes or foliage. 'There was a terrible stench of the gas everywhere...we went up to where the bombs had dropped and I put my net up and I sat on my blanket all night in the gas. The goats were bleeding and they were sick. A lot of them were in trouble.' After a night, he came off the island, feeling ill. He had a few burns, but believes that he must have breathed in a lot of mustard gas. 'They didn't tell me much and I didn't know how much damage had been done.' Soon afterwards, he was frightened when he suddenly lost his voice for a few days. He later suffered ill health and won some compensation (see chapter 11).

British leader Gorrill was furious when two American medics refused to go onto the island themselves, telling them that they were lucky not to be shot for refusing to obey orders. Sinclair believes that the Brook Island trial was successful in showing that 'it would be perfectly possible to winkle the Japanese out of their burrows and in fact render them totally incapacitated'. Moreover it demonstrated that it was safe for Allied troops to land and capture the island after 'a certain lapse of time' to allow the mustard gas contamination to subside. More of the Japanese occupying forces would have been killed by mustard gas than by the same amount of high explosive. Further trials were later carried out with low-level spraying of beaches and tropical forest fringes with mustard gas; again, men were sent into contaminated areas and suffered bad burns.[44]

With the backing of the British and the Americans, the chemical warfare establishment at Innisfail was expanded greatly and relocated in 1944 to Proserpine, also in Queensland. Gorrill was appointed to be the head of the new establishment, with a staff of around 650. It is estimated that by the end of the war, up to 2,000 human 'guinea pigs' had been involved in the gas tests in Australia.[45]

The Australian tests were 'of considerable value' in deciding whether to use poison gas against the Japanese, according to one top secret Allied appraisal.[46] This report – in late 1943 – argued that 'recent work in the tropics' proved that chemical weapons were much more powerful than was previously believed. 'A ruthless application of chemical weapons under tropical conditions will produce destruction and desolation upon a scale scarcely surpassed in the history of war,' it noted. The report's author, Major General Lethbridge, was convinced that the Japanese would be unable to survive such an onslaught, with a mixture of gases which not only 'cause mutilation and death' but also 'terror and panic in the minds of the victims'. The American military were prepared to carry out such an attack, but it was then vetoed by American President, Franklin D Roosevelt. However, in the later stages of the war, poison gases were to be transcended by nuclear weapons.

British-run gas trials with human 'guinea pigs' also took place in India. The British had been carrying out some chemical warfare experimental work in their dominion since 1920.[47] They then set up a poison gas research establishment in 1930 at Rawalpindi in north-west India (now Pakistan).[48] Staffed by British scientists, it acted as a branch of Porton to investigate a wide range of both offensive and defensive chemical warfare problems in a hot climate.[49] Back in 1919, the British government had authorised the use of chemical weapons to quell rebellions in their colonies. Winston Churchill, then Secretary of State at the War Office, in particular had been 'strongly in favour of using poisoned gas against uncivilised tribes', declaring that he could not 'understand this squeamishness' of officials who objected.[50] Major Salt, the Army's chemical warfare adviser in India, crowed that 'after a tremendous lot of bother and argument', the government had decided to use gas against Afghan rebels on the North-West frontier.[51] 'There was the usual talk about "clean hands" and "low-down tricks against the poor ignorant tribesmen", but in the end, we won our points,' added Salt. Although it is alleged that gas bombs were used against the neighbouring Afghan tribes, hard documentary proof appears to be lacking.

One set of experiments appears very bizarre today – tests to determine whether mustard gas burnt Indian skin more easily than European skin. Major Salt had raised the issue in 1920 'in connection with the possible use of mustard gas against frontier tribes'. He had noticed that his 'native' staff – 'my laboratory bearer and sweepers' – 'have all sustained burns whilst cleaning out my apparatus, and their burns take longer to heal than mine under the same treatment, in spite of my being now extremely sensitive' to mustard gas.[52] Officials in Britain commented, 'It is probable, however, that there is great variation in susceptibility among the different tribes. It is interesting...that tests made in America during [the First World War] have shown that Negroes are much more resistant than white men; the latter, however, vary considerably in their susceptibility.' It was agreed that Major Salt should therefore carry out experiments to 'obtain some information regarding the susceptibility of the various native races in India'.[53]

These experiments, however, had to wait until the Rawalpindi establishment had been set up.[54] In a 'mass test', 590 British and Indian troops were exposed to liquid mustard gas in 'severe' hot weather in 1934. The test was repeated in the country's colder weather two years later. At first, the British researchers believed that 'marked' differences could be detected between European and Indian skin. In hot weather, eighty-two percent of the British troops were classed as being 'sensitive' or susceptible to the gas, compared with fifty-nine percent of Indian troops. However doubts were raised that the 'test employed may not be a true measure...and too much importance must not be placed on the results.' By 1937, 'efforts...[were]...now being made to devise a more satisfactory test to overcome the objection to the former method', recorded one report.

The 'characteristic facial differences between Europeans and Indians' were also investigated so that gas masks could be fitted properly. All castes of Indians – with 'the exception of the Burma classes' – were fitted with respirators and scrutinised. It was found that 'on average the Indian's forehead is rather shorter, thus limiting the area in which fitting takes place and also the frontal prominence is not so pronounced in the case of Indians as that of Europeans'.[55]

Both Indian and British troops were used in a raft of experiments, both before and during the war. It seems unlikely that Indians were able to exercise complete free will when they took part in these experiments organised by their British masters, but this question remains clouded. The number of people who participated in these experiments in India cannot even be estimated, since only a few of the relevant papers have been declassified. One British scientist who was out there during the war admits that it is still 'a delicate political subject'. Although the entire extent of the Indian tests remains hidden, a flavour of the work is given in short summaries in regular progress reports which were submitted back to Porton.[56] For instance, humans were burnt with mustard gas so that many possible ointments to treat such burns could be tried out in the Indian climate, the penetration of mustard gas through Indian military clothing was measured, and troops tramped across ground contaminated with mustard gas to see how much seeped through their boots in the weather of the sub-continent.

Two full reports of these Indian human experiments have been released to the British Public Record Office. In one test in the summer of 1942, seventy British and Indian soldiers were sent into a chamber to see the effect of mustard gas on their eyes in hot weather.[57] They went into the gas clouds, wearing 'ordinary tropical service uniform of drill shorts, and open-necked, khaki, cellular cotton shirts'. At a given signal, they removed their gas masks. The groups were exposed to rising dosages of the gas. 'A number of actual casualties' were produced at the highest dosage, requiring up to a week's treatment in hospital. The soldiers exposed to the strongest dosages suffered 'well-marked and generalised' conjunctivitis for between ten and fifteen days. Many had sore eyes or felt pain in strong light. They had obviously breathed in the gas, and some felt huskiness or were unable to speak properly for around five days. The scientists suggested that mustard gas was slightly more potent on the eyes in hot weather than in cooler temperatures, and planned to repeat these experiments on eyes with 'very high and very low concentrations' of mustard gas in the following year.[58]

'A large number' of mustard gas burns were produced in British and Indian military subjects between April 1942 and July 1943, according to one official report.[59] The burns ranged from mild and very small to severe and extensive (for example, across the entire back), requiring them to be hospitalised. 'Severely burned patients are often very miserable and depressed and in considerable discomfort, which must be experienced to be properly realised,' commented the report.

'Intense and crippling pain' was also inflicted on five Indian men during the summer of 1943, especially to their genitalia. 'After a month, two were diagnosed as having developed neuroses, "a slightly morbid genital consciousness",' according to one account. The report of this experiment is apparently still too secret for the British to release to the public.[60] These five had been selected for long exposures to mustard gas without any protection in the second phase of an experiment. In the first phase, 'dozens' of men had paraded around in the midday heat on mustard gas-soaked ground with varying degrees of protection.

Porton's global reach stretched not only to India and Australia but also to Canada.[61] Early in the war, Porton staff wanted a huge space to carry out full-scale testing of chemical weapons. With Churchill's blessing, they began to search for a suitable site somewhere in the British Empire.[62] The Canadians, who had fortuitously requested expert advice from Porton at the same time, agreed to co-operate, and so in 1941, a jointly-funded establishment was set up on 1,000 square miles of semi-arid grassland at Suffield, Alberta.[63] The head of Suffield until the end of the war was Emlyn Llewelyn (E Ll) Davies, a British scientist who had previously worked at Porton for many years rising to become superintendent of experiments. Other Porton staff joined Suffield during the war. One of the main advantages of the site was that it experienced extremes of cold and hot weather, and so the scientists could test, for example, the effects of gas on humans and equipment in freezing temperatures. In conjunction with their work in India and Australia, Porton was thereby able to conduct trials in a range of temperatures during the war.

One of the unknown Indian soldiers exposed to mustard gas in 1942; his eyes recovered after a month.

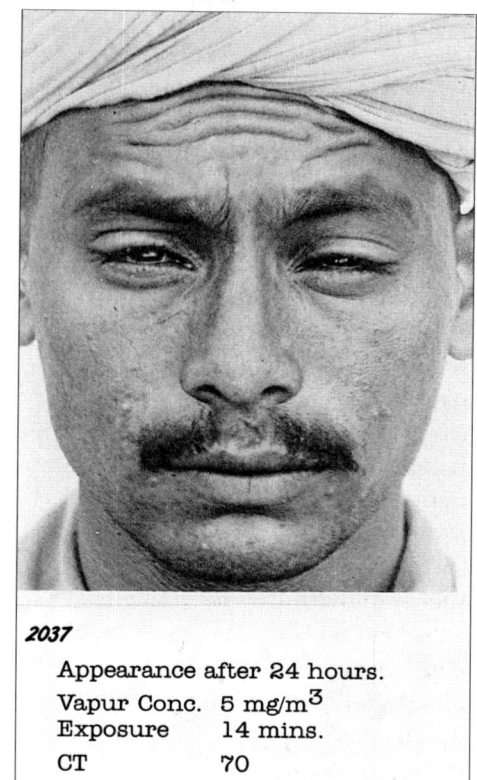

2037

Appearance after 24 hours.
Vapur Conc.   5 mg/m^3
Exposure   14 mins.
CT   70

One of the chemical weapons developed by Porton for possible use against the Japanese.

Porton officials were able to direct Suffield to carry out the specific experiments they wanted investigating since they were paying half the establishment's bills.[64] 'Suffield was run essentially as a British establishment with Davies receiving direction as much from London as Ottawa, often dealing directly with his colleagues at Porton or...the British Ministry of Supply. As a result, the British were free to do whatever human trials in Canada they liked short of causing death,' one author has observed.[65] The British were particularly keen to investigate how mustard gas could be sprayed from aircraft, but the 7,000 acres at Porton had simply been too small and constricting. One trial in 1939 had to be cut short because the gas had drifted beyond the Porton perimeter, provoking complaints from neighbouring residents.[66] One of the major innovations in poison gas since the First World War was the capability to deliver gas bombs from aircraft. Some work had been done to develop this aspect of aerial warfare during the Great War, but nothing important was produced or perfected before peace arrived. It was also claimed that the air forces of all sides refused to allow their planes to take part in the gas war.[67] The British use of the M device in Russia in 1919 is believed to have been the first time that chemical weapons were dropped from aircraft in combat. Porton dedicated much effort towards developing aerial gas warfare in the years after the First World War in trials, often involving human 'guinea pigs'.[68] However, by the Second World War, gas bombs from aircraft were seen by many countries as the dominant chemical weapon.

In Canada, human subjects were sprayed with mustard gas from aircraft in a series of experiments on the wide-open prairie land. In early 1942, for example, the spraying of humans from a great height was given the 'highest priority' at Suffield, following insistent requests from Porton.[69] The problem at the time was that spraying mustard gas from low-flying planes was dangerous because of the risk of anti-aircraft fire. The chemical would therefore have to be released from a higher altitude, but this too was problematic – the mustard had to be thickened with additives so that it did not evaporate on the way down; it was difficult to ensure that these chemical bombs would accurately hit their targets; and it was not even certain whether these high-altitude sprays would actually produce casualties.

On 2 May 1942, Privates L V Devitte and R H Caldicutt were among a group of men who stood on the prairie wearing a helmet and ordinary battledress. Since it was freezing, they also wore winter underwear. As they heard a plane droning in the distance, they were ordered to put on their gas masks. They were then sprayed by the plane. After a while, the men sprinkled a kind of decontamination powder over each other and then marched three miles back to their camp where they changed their clothes. As a result of the gas, both became casualties for two weeks – Caldicutt suffered 'sharp' burns on his entire back, right side and flank as well as one 'between buttocks developing into opposing ['kissing'] blisters in fold'. Devitte had 'mild burn on shoulders', 'sharp burn on lower back', two blisters on left buttock and 'large intense burn' on back of right knee.

After another trial that summer, 'eight people were hospital cases, six of whom were really bad'. The trial was deemed to have been 'successful from the offensive point of view'.[70] Three months later, at least nine men were turned into casualties in the sixth trial of spraying mustard gas on troops from a high-flying airplane.[71] Around 160 men were sprayed in a series of eight 'very valuable' trials around this time.[72] The following spring, twenty-nine men received eye injuries in an experiment entitled 'The casualty-producing power of mustard spray on troops'. They were kept in darkened rooms in hospital for between five and twenty-one days whilst their eyes were inflamed with the eyelids tightly stuck together. According to one account, doctors noted that they were 'usually silent, depressed and introspective at the height of the eye effects'.[73] At least one aerial trial was also conducted with lewisite.[74]

These glimpses of the trials come from the few reports that have slipped past the censors. As with other human experiments from the war, only a handful of Suffield tests have been declassified and placed in the public domain.[75] More than 1,000 Canadian soldiers were exposed to mustard gas in trials at Suffield during the war, according to an official estimate. The Canadian government says that the main objectives of these trials were to develop new treatments for mustard burns and to determine exactly when a soldier had become a gas casualty and should be taken to hospital. They were keen to avoid repeating the mistakes made in the First World War when 'many men suffering from minor mustard gas burns were evacuated to rear areas unnecessarily, clogging hospitals and throwing a tremendous strain on the supply of reinforcements'. Originally, chemical warfare volunteers had to be completely covered in protective clothing, except for a small patch on the arm to allow the mustard burns, but in 1942, the Suffield staff were allowed to rewrite and relax these constraining regulations.[76]

Like Porton, the Suffield scientists ran into trouble recruiting enough human 'guinea pigs' to take part in the experiments.[77] Davies, the British chief, complained that the shortage of men made it difficult to complete the full programme of tests. The men were being recruited by quotas from military districts in the country and were paid for each test they endured. Volunteers responded to notices posted onto unit bulletin boards which informed the potential recruits of the purpose and nature of the tests in a 'general way', but also reassured them that the experiments 'were carried out under scientific control, so that no personal injury is likely to result'. This was blatantly untrue, especially since the scientists had been authorised to pay extra money to volunteers who suffered severe burns or injuries. In 1944, the situation became critical since Davies wanted to double the number of volunteers and the military districts were struggling to supply even half their quotas. It transpired that some 'previous volunteers' were advising their colleagues not to step forward for the gas tests. After pressure from Suffield, the Army headquarters sent out a letter to the districts, imploring them to meet their quotas and give Suffield a favourable gloss: 'The observers are not to be given the impression that they are 'guinea pigs' to some weird scheme. They are not called upon to make sacrifices. Their job is merely to render co-operative understanding to those who conduct the trials.' It is reported that some soldiers bitterly renamed the establishment 'Sufferville'.

The Americans also carried out thousands of human experiments during the war, at various locations in the US and in the tropical conditions of San Jose Island, Panama.[78] Many of these were similar to the Allied chemical warfare tests. One kind of experiment was the so-called 'man-break' tests. Men would be togged out in masks and experimental protective clothing and sent into gas chambers filled with mustard gas for between one and four hours. They were required to go back into the chamber repeatedly every day or every other day until their skin started to blister. Some of the human subjects say that they were threatened with court martial if they refused to go back into the chamber. They became intensely fearful because other men had collapsed in the chamber and were removed, never to be seen again. They assumed that these men had died.[79] They felt trapped in the chamber because the door could not be opened from the inside. Many of the human subjects say that they were misled about the tests and that they did not know they were going to be taking part in poison gas experiments until it was too late to back out. Many were very young at the time, sometimes just seventeen, and had had little education. (As described in chapter 11, the treatment of the American human 'guinea pigs' in the war was later severely criticised by an inquiry.)

Collaboration in chemical warfare grew very strong between the United States of America, Britain, Canada and Australia in the war. Porton believes that this co-operation 'probably surpassed that in other defence fields' during wartime.[80] Information was freely swapped between the countries with staff going over and working in the chemical warfare installations of the other nations. The British and Americans sought to develop chemical weapons which could be easily interchanged and used by either country. American stockpiles of gas, for example, were stored in Britain. Work was co-ordinated between the nations. In 1944, an international body was set up to share information in case gas warfare should break out in the war against the Japanese. A clearing house distributed the results of research – including reports detailing human experiments – among the countries. None of the individual nations was able to carry out research in all the various climates and terrains in which poison gas could have been used in the war, so these co-operative arrangements meant that all the results of experiments could be pooled. Potentially, some human experiments could have been avoided if they duplicated tests which had already been carried out but it is however unclear whether this was actually the case.

Between them, the Allies conducted thousands of chemical warfare experiments on humans across the globe during the war. Many of them now appear gruesome and brutal, inflicting great agony on the subjects of the experiments. However, the ethics of these experiments must be judged by the circumstances of the time. A war was on and the Allies faced grave threats from the Nazis and the Japanese. Wartime is clearly different from peacetime. Whatever was needed to be done to protect themselves had to be done. Many saw ethics as a mere nicety at such times. Harold Stranks, a chemist who worked at Porton during the war, said: 'To a large extent, [ethics] did not occur to you. One finds it very difficult in the present climate to explain what it was like to live through a war.' In these dire circumstances of life or death, it was as if nothing was beyond the pale, especially if a superior officer was ordering you to do something. 'You did not think twice if it was thought necessary'.[81]

It could also be argued that the hardship experienced by the human 'guinea pigs' was no worse than what many of their compatriots were suffering elsewhere in the war while serving their country. War is, after all, a nasty business. Sinclair, the British doctor in charge of the human experiments in Australia, defends the experiments for two reasons. He claims firstly that the volunteers did not withdraw from the tests beforehand when they knew that they might get badly burnt, and had therefore given their consent. Secondly, he says that this information had to be obtained somehow. 'Animals were no use to us, it had to be humans that we used.' He argues: 'The way I look at it is that the experiments were indeed ethical, given the circumstances. I wouldn't do these experiments in peacetime, but in the conditions in which they were done they were essential.' Graham Pearson, Porton's director between 1984 and 1995, says that 'there would have been a huge public outcry had there not been any research to improve the protection of the armed forces against chemical weapons' at the time.[82] 'History had already shown that this kind of warfare was more likely to be used against unprotected and poorly protected personnel,' he adds.

These arguments can be deployed to justify the need to carry out such experiments, but did these tests go too far in harming the subjects and, for example, causing unnecessarily bad burns? Some of the human 'guinea pigs' were forced to undergo the tests, while others volunteered not really knowing what they were letting themselves in for. It is apparent that the scientists took advantage of the willingness of the volunteers in the Australian tests. Sinclair, for one, concedes that those experiments were essential, but unfortunately caused too much pain for the subjects.

In hindsight, it could be argued that the scientists should have held back when they had a fair estimation of what the results would be, without continuing to gather more and more finely-detailed data. Porton, for instance, had 'a great deal of evidence' by 1939 to show that mustard gas was more potent in the tropics than cooler climates, so it is arguable as to whether further tests were really necessary.[83] The experiments during the war meant that Porton and their Allied counterparts could more accurately quantify how potent the gas actually was in the hotter weather. This data was derived from many, many human experiments. Perhaps too many humans were exposed to the gas after the required conclusions could reasonably have been drawn.

The point of poison gases is that they damage and harm people in different ways. The best way of finding out how these gases damage people is to expose humans to them under experimental conditions, and then study their effects on the human body. The more extreme the damage, the more the scientists discover, on the whole. Many of the experiments pushed the limits so much that before this war, they would not have been permitted or carried out in peacetime. The scientists argue that priceless data did emerge from these experiments, both to prepare against the threat of gas attack and to learn about poison gases in general. It is clear that the Allied experiments 'greatly extended' the body of knowledge about the military value of mustard gas from that existing at the end of the First World War.[84] But the price for gaining this knowledge was paid by the human subjects who often endured much pain, and in some cases, suffered illnesses in later years.

It appears that there were few external constraints on the scientists over how far they could go in the experiments. The chemical warfare installations were wrapped in such tight secrecy that no outsiders knew what was going on. The political and military authorities do not seem to have had the time, nor the inclination, to monitor the installations. The Canadians, for example, issued passes with special pink slips to politicians who came to inspect Suffield. According to one scientist, this indicated that the staff had to be careful in what they told the politician, and 'especially don't let him know anything' about the human experiments.[85] It is unlikely that explicit descriptions of the injuries suffered in the human tests were passed to the Allied commanders; only the main conclusions of the tests which were apparently sufficient for them.

The excessive and horrific experiments perpetrated by the Nazi scientists in the concentration camps during the war led to the Nuremberg Code, the first significant move to establish a universal set of ethics to control human experiments (see chapter six). Details of these terrible tests were aired after the war, particularly during the war crimes trials. Fortunately for the Allied victors, they were not forced to reveal their chemical warfare experiments in public in such court cases. The full scope of their experiments only began to emerge and attract public attention much later.[86] The reticence of the Allied countries to remove the secrecy surrounding their gas tests shows how embarrassing and controversial such experiments are perceived to be nowadays.

Many fair-minded people would believe that whatever the rights and wrongs of the experiments themselves, anyone who subsequently suffered long-term illnesses from the tests should be compensated adequately for their troubles. As shown later, winning compensation has been an uphill battle for many of the human 'guinea pigs'. By the start of the war, Porton knew that mustard gas could cause chronic lung diseases, especially bronchitis, while war pensions were being awarded for gas victims of the First World War for at least one illness which damages the eyes (see previous chapter). But it is clear from the wartime experiments – run by Porton staff both in Britain and overseas – that the eyes and lungs of human subjects were at times exposed to mustard gas, sometimes by accident.[87] Depending on the dosages used, Porton staff were running the risk of inflicting long-term illnesses on the subjects of their tests, which at the very best appears highly irresponsible.

The Second World War turned out to be the unfought chemical war – gas was carefully considered at many stages of the fighting by the Allies and Germans, but was never actually used during this conflict.[88] In the Far East, Japan almost certainly used gas against China. Aside from accidents such as the Bari harbour disaster (see chapter 11) and among those who produced and stored gas weapons, the only other people who were exposed to gas in the war were human 'guinea pigs', and that was by their own side.

The protagonists had produced half a million tons of chemical weapons by the end of the war – around five times the total used in the First World War. There appears to be no single reason why gas was not unleashed in the Second World War, although several explanations have been put forward. At certain times, there would have been no military advantages to resorting to gas. Armies sweeping through countries such as in the German Blitzkrieg of 1940 or the Allied invasion of 1944 would only have been slowed down had they employed gas. Once fired, they would have had to be constantly putting on their protective clothing and cleaning their equipment and vehicles. Sometimes, war leaders were unable to use gas because they were militarily incapable of doing so; for instance, the British did not have enough chemical weapons in 1940 to halt the Nazi Blitzkrieg in France; Hitler was restrained in the closing stages of the war because the Germans had lost their supremacy in the air. Nations were deterred from using gas by the threat of massive retaliation by the opposition. On the whole, it appears that military chiefs on both sides were unconvinced by the advantages of chemical weapons. The high level of defensive preparations – the product of the work of Porton and other such installations – had reduced the attraction of gas.

It is also suggested that the personal beliefs of the war leaders played a part. It has been frequently said that Hitler was opposed to chemical weapons because he had been gassed during the First World War. American President Roosevelt was also believed to be morally against gas. On the other hand, Churchill was always a fervent supporter. In one infamous memo, he implored his military commanders to address seriously the possibility of drenching German cities with gas so that the inhabitants would need almost continual medical help in retaliation for the V-rocket attacks on British cities. 'I do not see why we should always have all the disadvantages of being the gentleman while [the Germans] have all the advantages of being the cad. There are times when this may be so but not now'. Churchill wanted this idea to be 'studied in cold blood by sensible people and not by that particular set of psalm-singing uniformed defeatists that one runs across'.[89] But he could never gain any backing from the upper echelons of the British military. It is noteworthy that many remained opposed to poison gas during a conflict which saw other horrors such as the massive bombing of civilians and cities and the first use of nuclear weapons.

Porton believes that 'without doubt', its greatest concern during the war was 'to intensify the development of new chemical weapons and munitions'.[90] Around 1,500 trials with weapons (often involving human subjects) took place on the ranges around Porton, much like they had done during the First World War. 'Many new and ingenious' weapons were designed and tested by Porton.[91] They were given nicknames. The 'Flying Cow' was a 'gliding bomb which rained gobbets of thickened mustard gas' onto the ground during its flight. Another version of this – with unthickened mustard gas – was known as the 'Flying Lavatory'. The 'Squirt' was a 'portable high pressure generator which threw two gallons of liquid hydrogen cyanide in a jet to a range of about 25 yards'. The 'Warfin' generator emitted a cloud of mustard gas droplets. One Porton history records that 'perhaps the most ingenious of all the offensive devices' was an anti-tank projectile which first punched a hole through armour and then squirted enough hydrogen cyanide into the tank to kill all the crew; 'no acceptable nickname was ever found for this unsporting weapon'.

Such weapons were devised because military chiefs specifically needed to attack targets such as pillboxes, bunkers or tanks. David Sinclair, who was in charge of the Australian human experiments, recalls some of trials at Porton in which tanks were attacked with chemical grenades or armour-piercing projectiles. He sat inside the tanks with crews of volunteers. 'I was the lucky one who had a respirator on, and I had to observe the reactions of the unfortunates who had not. Few crews were able to get far before they had to stop the tank and come out, where they vomited on the grass.'[92] One Porton report remarked that some bombs were 'virtually biscuit tins filled with mustard gas', but were still effective in projecting 'considerable quantities' of poison into the tank.[93]

Three major poison gases were manufactured in bulk by the British in the war – mustard gas, phosgene and a tear gas called BBC.[94] In another 'important' aspect of the offensive preparations, British scientists examined 'a very wide range' of compounds during the war to try and discover new chemical weapons (or, as one official put it, in the hope of pulling 'a quick one on the Hun').[95] This exploratory work was done either at Porton or in universities, and most notably in Cambridge.[96] A large number of these compounds, probably in the hundreds, were tested on human subjects to assess their potential as poison gases.[97] Many were capable of causing pain and injury, but the vast majority were discarded as being inferior to the existing poison gases for a variety of reasons. A few of the most promising compounds had been manufactured on a small scale in experimental production plants.[98]

By the end of the Second World War, the chemical arsenals of the Allies comprised much the same range of poison gases as at the end of the First World War. Since 1918, they had managed to devise more sophisticated ways of delivering those gases at the enemy. However they had failed to uncover any new outstanding chemicals which were superior to the known range of poison gases. The main thrust of the work of Porton and their counterparts had concentrated on mustard gas, but they had missed the most important new poison gas to be uncovered in this era. This discovery – nerve gas – has to a large extent dominated chemical warfare ever since.

CHAPTER FOUR

Cleaning up after the Nazis

As the Allies swept through Germany to defeat Hitler, they began to uncover the secrets of the Third Reich. One of the most startling discoveries was that the Nazis had developed and produced thousands of tonnes of a new chemical weapon which was far more toxic than the known poison gases. The Allies would have been incredibly vulnerable against this latest weapon – the so-called nerve gas. Within two weeks of uncovering the deadly gas, stunned Porton scientists had tested it out on volunteers, even though they had very little idea of its effects on the human body. Astounded by the new weapon, they frantically set about investigating the disturbing discovery. For the next four decades and more, Porton ran an extensive programme of testing nerve gases on humans in often painful and unpleasant experiments. It is probably the biggest such programme of human experiments with nerve gases in the world.

The origin of nerve gases dates back to a German scientist, Dr Gerhard Schrader, in 1936. For two years, he had been studying a group of chemicals known as organophosphorus compounds with the aim of finding new insecticides. He had been steadily synthesising a series of these compounds when he came across one with enormous power. In December 1936, he tested a minute amount of the new chemical on some lice – all the insects were killed. In early 1937, he realised that the putative insecticide had 'extremely unpleasant' effects on humans and was an 'unusual new compound'.[1] 'The first symptom noticed was an inexplicable action causing the power of sight to be much weakened in artificial light. In the darkness of early January, it was hardly possible to read by electric light, or after working hours to reach my home by car.' A tiny quantity spilt on the laboratory bench caused the pupils of Schrader's eyes to shrink to pinpoints, and he found it difficult to breathe. Normal vision returned after three days, but he and his assistant needed three weeks at home to recover their health after they had worked with the compound for a little while. They had become the first to suffer the effects of the first nerve gas – the compound was later to be called tabun (GA).

T.P. 218   SECRET   WO 195/11264   P.T.P. 218

CONFIDENTIAL   Copy No. 23

MINISTRY OF SUPPLY

DIRECTORATE OF CHEMICAL DEFENCE RESEARCH AND DEVELOPMENT

CHEMICAL DEFENCE EXPERIMENTAL ESTABLISHMENT

EXPOSURE OF MEN TO GB VAPOUR

PART 1

GENERAL SYMPTOMATOLOGY

By

SURG. CDR W.H.E. McKEE R.N.   &   B. WOOLCOTT

PART 2

EFFECTS ON THE EYES

By

R. FOSTER - MOORE

PORTON TECHNICAL PAPER No. 218

C.D.E.E.
Porton.
Wilts.

CONFIDENTIAL

SECRET

Porton's report of one of the larger-scale nerve gas experiments, 1951.

Nerve gases disrupt a key element of the nervous system. A human's muscles contract when a chemical substance – known as acetylcholine – is released from the nerve endings. Muscles do not exist in a permanent form of contraction because the acetylcholine is destroyed in a split second by an enzyme (acetylcholinesterase) thereby allowing the muscle to relax once again. Nerve gases inactivate this important enzyme, and since it is prevented from working, the muscle goes into a state of spasm from which it cannot be relaxed. Victims die because the most important muscles in the body – those of the heart and the rib cage, which control the emptying and filling of the lungs – are paralysed. They suffocate swiftly in a horrifying death.

The new nerve gases were a big advance in chemical warfare because they were more lethal and killed more quickly than the existing poison gases. Even very tiny quantities of the deadly liquid are enough to kill a person, with a minute drop the size of a pinhead being sufficient to inflict death. The consequences of this were that more people could be killed on the battlefield with smaller amounts than with previous poison gases. Nerve gas kills very rapidly, within one to ten minutes. This compares to phosgene, the most toxic of the previously known chemical weapons, which took between four and twenty-four hours to kill.[2]

Since 1935, Hitler's regime had ordered the German chemical industry to report any toxic substance which could be exploited by the military. Schrader passed on the news about tabun to the German military, which quickly grasped the significance of the find. By 1940, the Germans had started to build a huge nerve gas factory in a forest at Dyhernfurth in what is now Poland. The heavily camouflaged factory was capable of producing 1,000 tons of nerve gas a month. Schrader had also uncovered another organophosphorus compound which was even more toxic than tabun. This was sarin (GB) – a name culled from the four key individuals who were involved in its production. By 1944, the Germans had discovered a third nerve agent – soman (GD) – which was even more lethal than sarin. It was too late in the war for the Nazis to develop soman as a weapon, but, by early 1945, the Germans had already produced a considerable quantity of nerve gases at the Dyhernfurth factory, approximately 10,000-12,000 tons of tabun and some tons of sarin, and also developed the munitions to fire the lethal liquid.[3]

Of all the chemical warfare work carried out by both sides during the war, the nerve gases were by far and away the most outstanding development. But Hitler did not use this new 'super weapon'. As outlined in chapter three, there are a range of complex reasons why gas warfare did not break out in the Second World War. Ironically, one of the main explanations was that the Nazis mistakenly suspected that the Allies too had developed nerve gases. They reckoned that, since organophosphorus compounds had been discussed in scientific journals before the war, the British and American chemical warfare experts could not possibly have failed to take notice.

Porton scientists were certainly caught out by the Nazi discovery of nerve gas. But to what extent were they and their Allied counterparts at fault? Firstly, the British and Americans themselves had in fact come close to unearthing the nerve gas secret during the Second World War. They had been studying some of the organophosphorus compounds to see if they could be used in warfare. (Both countries had tested these compounds on men in some painful experiments.)[4]

They went as far as building an experimental plant for manufacturing one of the compounds, PF-3. However by 1944, 'after careful assessments', they had discarded PF-3 because they believed its effects would only harass victims and would not kill them any more effectively than the existing chemical weapons.[5] Crucially, they had not managed to make the breakthrough and uncover the more toxic members of the organophosphorus group — the nerve gases. One of Porton's official histories claims that before 1945, the establishment had had a 'high opinion' of the military potential of the organophosphorus group.[6]

Secondly, the Allies received reports from their spies during the war that the Nazis had some sort of new powerful gas. According to an American official account, there were 'vague, but persistent rumours...from time to time through intelligence channels', but 'no reliable information' until the Germans were being overrun.[7] Porton's own history records that 'no intelligence report from the year 1937 when Germany started working on [nerve gas] had given any tangible clue to its existence'.[8] Perhaps due to luck more than cunning, the Nazis had managed to keep their nerve gas discovery a secret for eight years, especially since the scale of research and production was so large.

However with the benefit of hindsight, it is evident that there was compelling intelligence which should have convinced the Allied gas experts that the Nazis did in fact have a super weapon which could beat their defences. The most detailed report came in 1943 from a German prisoner who had worked at one of the Nazis' chemical warfare laboratories.[9] He described a chemical which 'cannot be classed with any of the other war gases as it is a nerve poison'. The smallest concentrations could cause the eyes to shrink in only a few minutes 'to a pinhead and [cause] asthma-like difficulties in breathing. In any heavier concentration, death occurs in about a quarter of an hour'. He even disclosed that the chemical was an organophosphorus compound. He added: 'Tests with this gas are extremely dangerous as there is no perceptible threshold of irritation as is the case with other gases.' He revealed ominously that manufacture of the gas had begun a year ago 'so that by this time, a large quantity must be ready'. The evidence of this chemist should have immediately set the alarm bells ringing, since no other poison gas could kill so quickly. British and American tests on humans with organophosphorus compounds, such as PF-3, in the middle of the war had produced similar symptoms. With hindsight, it is perhaps easier to see that this intelligence, and other signs, should have impelled Porton to persist in its investigations of the organophosphorus compounds.[10] One Porton official has admitted that it was 'the one time that we were really caught with our trousers down'.[11]

The first hard evidence of the nerve gases was discovered by the Allies on 6 April 1945 when advancing British soldiers captured a dump of chemical weapons. The weapons consisted of the known poisons such as mustard gas and phosgene. But there were also artillery shells – coloured with green and yellow rings – whose contents were a mystery and so a sample was sent to Porton for examination. At first, Porton greeted the unknown chemical with disdain, dismissing it as having a 'nuisance value only; undue alarm is to be deprecated. Existing methods of protection appear to be fully adequate'.[12] The establishment was 'already familiar' with this type of compound since it was related to PF-3 which had been 'thoroughly investigated'. From various tests and animal experiments, Porton commented in an assessment on 12 April that there was 'as yet no reason' to believe that the unknown substance 'would offer any advantages in the field' over the already discarded PF-3. Within days, the evaluation began to change – one note dated 16 April commented that 'it is perhaps going too far to say that it is of nuisance value only, since inevitably if it were used a number of troops would be killed in spectacular fashion'.[13] In the dying days of the war, the fear remained that Hitler could 'recklessly' fire off chemical weapons in desperation during the 'final stages of the disintegration' of the Third Reich.[14]

The unknown chemical was tabun. Porton first tested the potent chemical on human subjects on 18 April.[15] Former Porton staff have commented that the scientists' initial 'lack of awareness' was evident in one of the establishment's early reports on the human experiments with tabun: 'Before the substance was identified, 1 mm and 2 mm drops were placed on the skin of the arms of human observers to ascertain whether or not it was a vesicant [blister gas]. The results were negative.'[16] The scientists were testing to see if the lethal liquid burned and blistered the skin, like the then premier chemical weapon, mustard gas. It didn't – the new gas attacked the body in a completely different way. According to an extract from the still-secret report, 'a 1 mm drop was also placed in the eye of a rabbit to show whether the substance caused eye damage. The rabbit went into convulsions and died in a few minutes'.[17]

Like Schrader, Porton scientists also experienced dimmed vision and pains in their heads before they had fully realised the potency of the deadly chemical. In a single weekend – while suffering from its effects – they managed to unlock many of the secret properties of tabun.[18]

Porton is reluctant to release the reports of this early work, although many salient details have already been made public elsewhere.[19] In the first study, forty-nine unprotected human subjects were exposed in batches to dosages of tabun ranging from 0.7 to 21 mg min m^{-3}.[20] (As an indication of the toxicity of these exposures, current estimates of tabun's lethal dosage range between 150 and 400 mg min m^{-3}.)[21]

Five volunteers who received the highest dosage were 'severely harassed' and developed the classic symptoms of nerve gas poisoning – tightness in the chest, coughing, the pupils of their eyes reducing to pinpoints, watery eyes, 'tingling' of the eyelids, runny nose, headaches, difficulty in seeing. A second batch of ten human 'guinea pigs' was exposed to 14 mg min m^{-3}. 'Shortly after exposure, all subjects had markedly contracted pupils. Sunlight seemed less bright and on entering a shaded room the light appeared to be very dim. Severe headache followed in all cases, accompanied by pain in the eyes, especially during attempts to focus.' These symptoms persisted for the next two days. Four of the subjects vomited the day after they had been poisoned. Some of this batch had been exposed twice in four hours to the gas. Another three men were not treated with the nerve gas antidote, atropine, and suffered symptoms, such as headache and congested nose, for 'several days'.

In a related experiment, one man had 'very severe harassment' after he was exposed to 30 mg min m^{-3}, with one eye and his mouth protected. He was unable to sleep for two nights because of an extreme pain 'above and behind the exposed eye'. His vision was to take seventeen days to recover properly.

Porton was transformed by the arrival of nerve gas. The German gases were so powerful that work on the other poison gases was downgraded drastically. Porton had been engrossed with mustard gas until then, but the so-called 'King of Battlefield Gases' had been knocked off its throne. Soon the majority of Porton scientists were focusing their attention on the deadly new gases from the Third Reich.

For Porton, the new weapon was a great shock to the system, triggering a 'vast programme of work' on the new gases. Porton's official historian, Gradon Carter, comments that it is difficult to appreciate the enormous impact of the nerve gases. He points out that few of the earlier chemical weapons 'were quite so insidious'. 'The well-trained British serviceman was familiar with the characteristic smells' of gases such as mustard, lewisite, chlorine, phosgene. 'A few whiffs of most of these at low concentration before the gas mask was donned would do little harm.'[22] But there was no such warning with the nerve gases which were 'highly potent, odourless, colourless' and capable of killing very rapidly through the skin, eyes and mouth.

In a comment which may seem ironic to Porton's human 'guinea pigs', Carter adds that, 'Demonstration of the actual effects of nerve agents on man and personal experience of the effectiveness of protective measures could not be built in to service training, as they were with the older agents. Unprotected men could not be put through gas chambers or allowed to see that if nerve agents were decontaminated swiftly from their skin, no effects were exerted. Unlike most of the older agents, the margin between mild effects at low doses and death at higher doses was small – nerve agents could not be used in troop training.'

The new discovery did, however, ensure the survival of Porton. As the war ended, doubts about the establishment's future had risen because gas had not been used during the conflict, begging the question that perhaps it was not an essential military weapon. The dropping of nuclear bombs on Japan had confirmed the power of the nuclear bomb as a weapon of mass destruction, placing another query over the usefulness of chemical weapons. But Carter states that the nerve gases were 'undoubtedly a major factor' in ensuring that poison gas would still play some part, of whatever size, in Britain's military plans. 'In the years immediately following [the Second World war], there was little of the uncertainty about the future that had been evident at Porton after the Great War.'[23]

Porton's first task was to investigate the new German nerve gases and find out exactly how they worked. The British and their allies took what they could from the vanquished Nazis, appropriating the captured facilities for their own ends. Soon after the Third Reich capitulated, a team of Porton scientists was sent over to the chemical warfare research establishment at Raubkammer in north-west Germany. This was the German equivalent of Porton. For four months over the summer of 1945, the scientists fired off salvoes of chemical weapons in a panoply of trials, investigating tabun and other gases in the German arsenal. One of the twenty-six trials, for example, was to gauge the effectiveness of tabun when dispersed in German and British shells and bombs. 'Many distinguished visitors' from America, Canada, and Australia dropped in to inspect Raubkammer and watch the trials, while each week, visiting parties were flown over from Porton. It appears that during these trials, there were no human experiments, and animals were used instead.[24]

The British confiscated 10,500 tons of tabun-loaded weapons from the Germans – virtually the whole GA stockpile. The Chiefs of Staff wanted this huge stock of tabun bombs, but were aware of potential controversy: 'If the information leaks out that we are removing stock of poison gas from Germany and storing them in England, we shall inevitably meet with hostile comment and protests from other Powers.'[25] Without any publicity, the British managed to transport the 71,000 bombs back to the mainland and store them in a disused airfield at Llandwrog in Wales. This large store was procured 'primarily' to provide the raw material for experimental research, but also as weapons to be used in a war if necessary by the British.[26] It is possible that some of the confiscated tabun was later used to test British human 'guinea pigs' at Porton, although this cannot be confirmed. (As part of the drive to disarm Germany, Britain and its allies dumped the rest of its chemical weapons – amounting to thousands of tons – into the sea as they did not want them.)[27]

The British also seized German chemical warfare equipment, including parts from the sarin manufacturing factory, and took them back home.[28]

Another key source of information was of course the German scientists themselves. As the Nazis succumbed to defeat, intelligence officers from the Allied nations had raced to track down the scientists to capture and interrogate them. These intelligence officers crawled all over the German chemical warfare facilities, hoovering up every possible detail they could. This intensive process was repeated over every part of the Nazi war machine. It was a priceless opportunity to capture the scientific secrets of one of the world's industrial leviathans and foremost technical innovators. At its peak, this effort consumed the energy of 10,000 intelligence officers from the US, Britain, France, Belgium, Holland and Luxembourg.

Investigators from Porton and their American colleagues compiled compendious reports, packed full of the minutiae not just of the new nerve gases, but also of every aspect of the Nazis' poison gas activities. For instance, the results of at least 165 Luftwaffe trials with weapons, including tabun, were scooped up and taken home.[29] Such knowledge was not only invaluable, but also fascinating to the British chemical warfare scientists. It was a chance to compare and measure their work with that of other experts in the field.

The Allied investigators also gathered information about the Nazis' dreadful experiments on the inmates of concentration camps. Soon after the camps had been discovered, the Allies had decided that the 'exact data' of these experiments 'would be most valuable'.[30] Many of the unfortunate subjects had died in the numerous tests, a proportion of which involved chemical weapons.[31] At one concentration camp, mustard gas was tested on 220 people, of which fifty died, and, at another, eight victims had their arms contaminated with mustard gas. Three days later, their blisters were deliberately infected so that a potential remedy could be applied. Forty people were also exposed to phosgene at another concentration camp, killing four and inducing 'severe' pain in others when their lungs filled up with liquid. At another, 150 inmates were forced to drink water poisoned with lewisite and mustard gas. (As discussed in chapter six, these chemical warfare experiments were part of a wide range of horrific tests).

As for human experiments in chemical warfare facilities outside of the concentration camps, the Allies were rather bemused. One senior investigator commented that in tests with blister gases, 'the Germans seem to have been afraid of using human observers directly'.[32] An extensive report on the German chemical warfare effort was compiled in 1945 by a team of seventeen Allied investigators, almost all of whom were British.[33] They ferreted out details of the German gas tests with humans and then compared them with their own experiments during the war. They concluded that the Germans appeared to have had 'a curiously unrealistic approach'. The Germans had made 'no real attempt' to find out how much mustard gas vapour was needed to produce casualties through human skin. They had, moreover, never exposed humans directly to mustard gas spray from aircraft to see how effective it would be on the battlefield. 'The method that they did use we have found to be open to grave errors,' commented the mainly British team.[34]

The Allied investigators appear to have been unimpressed by the German experiments in which unprotected 'volunteer officers and workmen on the staff' stood downwind of irritant gases and tried to stay in the cloud for two or three minutes. The volunteers would then describe their experiences to a scientist, but the investigators noted that no objective tests were used to assess the effects of the gas: 'We know how misleading subjective observations can be in this case.' In other tests, chemical weapons were fired against tanks and 'afterwards men, waiting behind moveable shelters, ran out and put their heads into the back of the tank...the symptoms suffered were noted'. The Allied investigators suggested that 'again' the tests were flawed since the subjects had not been inside for the duration of the experiment.

It suggests that while the Nazis were prepared to inflict unspeakable horrors on the prisoners of concentration camps, they held back in chemical warfare experiments on their own troops. This may not, however, be the full picture, since many documents were destroyed or concealed in the last days of the Third Reich, and many captured German scientists denied all knowledge of experiments.

Britain's spy chiefs placed a high priority on gathering information about the nerve gases from Germany in late 1947.[35] At that time, Porton official, Major D C Evans, was sent over to Germany on a mission which had two secret objectives. His first was to assist in the prosecution of Nazi scientists at the Nuremberg war crimes trials, whilst his second was ethically more delicate – he was to obtain 'details of chemical warfare experiments on human beings and of mass exterminations by hydrogen cyanide (HCN)' and bring them back for the British military.[36] The British officials spent 'considerable' time in an attempt to collect reliable data to calculate exactly how the Nazis had managed to kill millions of Jews and political prisoners in concentration camps with HCN, also known as Zyklon B.[37] Evans reported, 'It would appear, however, that no controlled experiments were carried out on a scientific basis. The chief object was to kill the victims as quickly as possible so as to make room for the next batch.' However, the question remains as to why the Porton scientists wanted this data. The reason seems to be that this information would add to their store of knowledge on hydrogen cyanide which, up to 1945, had been developed as chemical weapons by at least five countries. As a chemical weapon, hydrogen cyanide – although it killed rapidly – was not successful for several reasons, mainly because it was difficult to build up a lethal concentration on the battlefield. Porton itself had tested hydrogen cyanide on humans, although the most well-known experiment was the 'Barcroft's Dog' incident (see chapter one). In any case, hydrogen cyanide was soon to be eclipsed by the nerve gases and dropped as a poison gas.

The British had apparently been finding it difficult to acquire the detailed results of German chemical warfare experiments on human beings.[38] But on this occasion, Major Evans announced triumphantly that he had been able to get records of human experiments with mustard gas, phosgene, and lewisite. There was however one problem. He said that 'no record could be found of any experiments with the nerve gases. It is thought highly probable, however, that such experiments would have been carried out, and the results (if available) might provide invaluable data as to lethal concentrations for man'. Porton scientists were dismayed by this, and one member of an advisory committee remarked that 'it was somewhat disappointing that no experiments employing nerve gases had been traced'.[39] It is clear that at some point, Porton did manage to obtain German data on these experiments and on the toxicity of nerve gas to humans.[40] However, two former Porton scientists stated recently that, 'German workers investigated the effect of nerve agents on man during World War Two, under concentration camp conditions, but comparatively little information has been gleaned from these studies.'[41]

Major Evans also reported that he was dumbfounded when he came across the treatment of one Nazi scientist. Luftwaffe doctor Karl Wimmer, among others, conducted poison gas experiments on human beings at a military institute which was part of Strasbourg University. 'The inmates of the adjacent Natzweiler concentration camp provided the necessary human beings,' noted the major. The British had long suspected that the university 'was closely connected with such crimes' but had found no proof. It was therefore 'with particular satisfaction' that the major uncovered documents confirming that Wimmer had 'definitely' performed the experiments. But he was 'astonished' to learn from the Americans that Wimmer 'was at present living in a small Bavarian village'. The major demanded that Wimmer be arrested immediately for two reasons – firstly, so that he could be put on trial for war crimes and secondly, so that he could be interrogated about the human experiments as he was 'probably one of the few surviving individuals who might be able to provide' information about the nerve gas tests. The major reported that the Americans 'readily agreed' to arrest Wimmer. But Wimmer was never in fact prosecuted. According to one account, he was guaranteed his freedom in return for handing over to the Americans the detailed reports on the human experiments.[42]

The case of Wimmer is just one example of how the Allies allowed many Nazi scientists to escape justice after the war. Hundreds of German and Austrian scientists, engineers and technicians were recruited by the Americans in a conspiracy known as Operation Paperclip. Britain, France and the Soviet Union also competed to recruit these Germans. The new recruits were selected by the Americans after they had been interrogated, and the chosen ones had a simple paperclip slipped onto their personal file. In defiance of an order from President Truman, American officials allowed them to settle in the US. As a result, these ardent Nazis became respectable American citizens working on a range of scientific projects, including assisting in the design and development of the technology which landed the first man on the moon in the Apollo voyage in 1969. They had traded their scientific knowledge for their liberty. (The Americans did a parallel trade with Japanese scientists who had carried out awful biological warfare experiments on humans in the war. The results of their research were exchanged for a guarantee that they would not be prosecuted for war crimes. The cause of justice was thus outweighed by the Allies' desire for this knowledge, which could advance their own biological warfare programmes.)[43]

Eight German scientists worked at Edgewood Arsenal, Porton's counterpart in America, between 1947 and 1966 developing chemical weapons, including nerve gas, and assisting experiments on humans.[44] It is not known how many, if any, German scientists were recruited to work at Porton Down. The British certainly drew up lengthy lists of the German scientists they wanted, some of whom were described as being chemical warfare experts. The British and Americans haggled over who should have them, but it remains uncertain who actually won.[45]

There has been a long and continuing controversy over obtaining and using experimental data which has been derived from unethical human tests. On the one hand, some argue that such data should be banned since it is deeply immoral to use research which has so grossly violated human beings. They maintain that using the data dishonours those who died in the concentration camps and offends those who managed to survive. It would also legitimise the use of such data and may even encourage more unethical research in the future. But others advocate the free use of such research since it could actually expand scientific understanding and assist humanity, especially as the Nazi experiments are perceived to have generated data which had not been produced anywhere else. They believe it would be wrong to ignore information which could help save lives, and, in this sense, a practical benefit could be retrieved from the nightmare of the death camps. Some, however, have argued that this debate is irrelevant since many of the Nazi experiments were so badly conducted, without any attention to proper scientific methods, that their results are worthless and should be disregarded anyway. This has been shown in the case of tests in which prisoners at the Dachau concentration camp were deliberately immersed in tanks of ice water to find ways of treating victims of hypothermia.[46]

Any qualms over searching for such data, and employing Nazi scientists, were however overshadowed and cast aside, since another conflict – the Cold War – was looming out of the ashes of the Second World War. Expediency bested morality, as it frequently does. Back in April 1945, soldiers of the conquering allies – America and Russia – had met at the River

Elbe as they overran the Third Reich and, amid joyous scenes, had greeted each other like great friends. But the mood of the relationship between the two countries had later soured and the coalition was splitting apart. Instead of a lasting peace, East and West were sliding into precarious confrontation. By March 1946, Britain's wartime leader, Winston Churchill, famously declared that 'from Stettin in the Baltic to Trieste in the Adriatic an iron curtain has descended' across the continent of Europe; the Russians were imposing communism on their neighbouring countries. This heralded the start of the Cold War.

As the relations turned more and more frosty, both sides scrambled to deny their opponents information which had been culled from the vanquished Nazis. To the dismay of the British and Americans, it turned out that the Russians too had been filching the secrets of Germany's nerve gas. Dr Gerhard Schrader – who had discovered both tabun and sarin – was found by the British to be 'more useful than all the other German chemical warfare personnel'.[47] He had quickly disclosed the secrets of the two nerve gases to American investigators in a long account of everything he knew.[48] He claimed that in the closing stages of the war, the German bomber planes had been sent in to destroy their own huge nerve gas factory at Dyhernfurth. Encouragingly for the West, he considered that 'the job was completed'. But he was wrong – the Russians had in fact dismantled the installation and transported its equipment piece-by-piece back home. Even the factory's technicians were taken back to Russia.[49]

By October 1945, British intelligence chiefs were predicting that the Russians were in a position to begin producing tabun and sarin 'very shortly'. The increased potency of these two chemicals could encourage the Russians to see poison gas 'as a more useful and efficient weapon than she has done hitherto', cautioned one top-secret appraisal.[50] Furthermore, one Porton official pointed out that the German chemists in the hands of the West had 'talked freely' on the subject of the nerve gases 'and it is probable that any other chemist in Russian hands would talk as freely'.[51]

And so, in this atmosphere of growing mistrust of the Russians, Porton scientists were thrust into the front line of the chemical Cold War. In a 'desperate preoccupation', they frantically worked to understand the new nerve gases.[52] Porton scientists, in collaboration with their American colleagues, had to analyse all the data gathered from the Nazis and quickly check that the results were correct. One Porton veteran said staff were 'genuinely and absolutely terrified' about the Russian chemical threat. 'There was good evidence that the Russians had chemical-filled weapons and were extensively training with these weapons. Plausible scenarios were written about what was going to happen when and if [a] Third World War broke out. The idea was the Russians were going to saturate areas of East Germany with very high concentrations of chemical weapons, which meant that troops could not be transferred from one part of the front to the other. They would then concentrate on the small part of the front, and carry through to the Channel coast as a battering ram, before the Americans could act. Porton staff had to find out all they possibly could about the nerve gases.'[53]

Porton's early investigations, both in its laboratories and at Raubkammer, had 'amply confirmed' the 'very considerable' potential of the gases.[54] However, after the first, and rather precarious, experiments on humans in 1945, Porton did not in fact test the nerve gases on people again until 1948.[55] It appears that once Porton scientists had realised the enormous power of the nerve gases, they had waited to find out more about them before testing them again on humans. An update in early 1947 reported that the 'present knowledge of the nerve gases' did not permit 'extensive' experiments on humans. Instead the 'supply of volunteer subjects' (a total of 286 volunteers came to Porton between 1946 and 1948) were used for 'further minor work' with mustard gas.[56]

Volunteers faced a kind of roulette wheel when they went to Porton. Depending on the timing of their visit, they could either be subjected to some very painful experiments, or else might merely undergo some relatively innocuous tests. This was particularly true of that period between 1945 and 1948 in which the nerve gas experiments were in abeyance. Steve Mills, who served in the Royal Navy for fifteen years, believes that, compared to other volunteers, his tests were relatively harmless, 'not like some of these other poor devils'. He went for three weeks in late 1946, but was only required to take part in two tests. In one, a small amount of mustard gas was put on the back of his hand. 'The next day we had one dab on each forearm,' and from then on, they treated it and it was photographed at various intervals to see how it progressed. 'The mustard gas did not hurt, but stung a bit.' He had a blister for a couple of weeks which has left a permanent, but not very noticeable, scar the size of a one-pence coin.[57]

Mills says he spent the rest of the time 'lazing around and visiting local hostelries' with other volunteers. They were free of any other duties apart from one appointment with the doctor each day. 'You virtually looked after yourself and came and went, as long as you were there to see the doctor. Other than that, you were on your own. It was a holiday, really.' Like many others, he had volunteered to get a 'few extra bob' and to 'get away from the humdrum life' of his barracks. He does not believe that his health problems have been caused by the Porton tests, but adds that those volunteers whose health is ailing from the experiments should be given their 'due recognition... These people acted in good faith, and as they thought for the benefit of the country and its defence, the country and Government now needs to honour that faith and see that justice is done'.[58]

The post-war government under Labour Prime Minister Clement Attlee determined to be 'in a position to wage chemical warfare from the start of hostilities' in the case of any future war.[59] Since nerve gases were likely to be the main chemical weapons, Porton's sister station at Sutton Oak had begun to research ways of manufacturing them in bulk.[60] This research was helped by the fact that the Allies had managed to acquire the fruits of German efforts to produce tabun and sarin in large quantities.[61] Much early work concentrated on checking the German work before moving onto investigating other methods of generating nerve gas in great amounts. Manufacturing nerve gas in bulk, if it was to be done, was a huge undertaking; it would be expensive and technically complicated. The British were in favour of building an experimental nerve gas factory before committing themselves to a full-scale plant. However it was considered too dangerous to use Sutton Oak because it was in a built-up area and too close to neighbouring houses. The new gases were so much more toxic than the chemical weapons which had been previously produced there, and any explosion or spillage would have been disastrous, both for the civilian victims and the military. An extensive search was therefore launched for an isolated site which had a large supply of water, electricity and local skilled labour as well as a nearby sea or river into which waste could be discharged.[62] By 1949, officials had settled on a disused RAF base at Nancekuke in Portreath, north Cornwall.[63]

Since the bulk production of nerve gases was a firm goal, Porton conducted a series of experiments to learn whether the various ingredients of the gases would be hazardous to the factory workers who would actually manufacture them. There are several ways of manufacturing nerve gases. Each method involves particular chemicals – known as intermediates or precursors – which are mixed together to form the required type of nerve gas. Porton needed to know if the intermediates were in any way as dangerous as the finished products. Five of these intermediates were tested on fifty-eight men. The liquids were dropped onto the web area of the fingers and forearm of the men, repeatedly for between three and eight days. The men were instructed that 'if possible the hands were not to be washed until inspected the following day'. The chemicals produced varying degrees of 'mild' erythema – reddening of the skin – and occasionally 'superficial burns'. Some of the men complained that the chemicals stung when they were dropped onto their skin, although this sensation quickly passed. Porton therefore concluded that the intermediates were not a 'serious hazard'.[64]

Britain's chemical warfare effort was concentrated totally on the nerve gases by 1948.[65] One of the most important tasks was the 'systematic' investigation into the effects of the nerve gases on the human body and the 'detailed assessment' of the toxicities of sarin, tabun and soman. Such research was 'necessary to furnish data for the exploitation' of these gases as offensive weapons. It was also 'essential' for defensive purposes, because there was then no satisfactory treatment against the deadly chemicals. 'This is obviously so grave a gap in our defences as to call for the most intensive research to solve the problems involved', warned one top-level official.[66]

After three years of extensively testing the nerve gases on animals, Porton scientists believed that they now knew enough about the chemicals to restart the experiments on humans,[67] and in the year 1948-49, 129 servicemen were tested with nerve gases.[68] David Smith, then an eighteen-year-old private, went to Porton in 1948 with a mate who had volunteered him without his knowledge.[69] He did not know for certain what he would be doing: 'They never sat us down and explained anything.' He says now that if they had, he would probably have refused to take part in any test, especially since he had seen nerve gas kill a caged rabbit in seconds. Back then, however, he had never heard of nerve gases, and was only told afterwards that he had been exposed to tabun by a technician during a casual conversation. One afternoon, he spent around fifteen to twenty minutes in a chamber without a mask, but wearing an army uniform which he believes had been treated to absorb gases. The tabun was spread by fans through the chamber: 'You could not smell any gas. You could not see any gas – it was cloudless. You thought that there was nothing there whatsoever.' He became breathless and his eyes started to 'nip a bit'.

Smith felt as though he had a heavy cold until that night when he and the other volunteers went for a run in the countryside. When they returned, they started to feel sick. 'The pupils of my eyes contracted to pinheads. My chest was congested as if somebody had kicked me in the back. I was not focusing right. If you went to step over a step, you actually banged into it.' He remembers that it felt much like having flu, i.e. hazy and dozy. 'That night, we were all sitting looking at each other, miserable and in a right state. We could not see each other.' Ironically, the impact of exercise on the human effects of nerve gas was not studied by Porton until a decade or so later.

Another volunteer who was exposed to tabun was nineteen-year-old National Serviceman Gerry Ashton. He was warned that he would experience 'a bit of discomfort' from the experiment, but he would be completely cured of its effects by the end of the week.[70] 'The amount that they would be giving us was very small and would not affect us. The idea was to give us enough of it to make us ill to a certain extent, and then to give a rabbit the equivalent dose so as to make it ill to the same extent, and then to give the rabbit more to kill it. From those three parameters, they could work out how much would kill a human being.' Ashton was told he was being given nerve gas, but knew nothing of its effects. He was sent into the gas chamber, with scientists watching through glass walls. After five minutes, 'they brought me outside and told me to go back to my billet, which was not very far away, about 100 yards that's all.' But, even though it was broad daylight, he had to grope his way back: 'My eyes seemed to grow dark and everything went sort of dark on me. Although I could see, it was just shadows. As it happens, there was someone passing at the time, and he helped me to get back to my billet.' He was blinded by the time he got back there, and for the next two or three days, he could only fumble around. 'When I'd begun to be able to see a bit better, I went into the bathroom and looked in the mirror at my eyes. The pupils of my eyes, instead of being round had actually turned kidney-shaped, which I thought was most unusual.' He was treated with atropine and by the end of the week, he was fine.[71]

However a few years later, he started to suffer the first of a series of illnesses, some of which he believes were caused by the Porton experiments. Over the years, he has suffered from impotence, high blood pressure, an enlarged heart, severe abdominal muscular spasm and blackouts, and believes that these health problems ruined his first marriage. He had originally volunteered for Porton to impress his commanding officer's daughter whom he was courting at the time. The notices calling for volunteers had gone onto the noticeboard of his station. 'Nobody at all volunteered. This went on for a week or two. The commanding officer was saying to me how disappointed he was that nobody had volunteered for this thing.' And so he volunteered to impress her and her father. 'In those days, I was young and foolish. It is right what they say about the Army – "never volunteer for anything".' Ashton states categorically that he would not undergo the tests today because of the 'short shrift' that he has been given by the MoD – he has not received any compensation from the government.

Porton produced two landmark reports from its human experiments in 1949 and 1950. Former Porton scientists have hailed them as 'classical papers' containing 'excellent accounts' of nerve gas poisoning with a 'wealth of information'.[72] In the 1949 trial, Porton sent around fifty-six men – with an average age of twenty – into the gas chambers and exposed them to 'low concentrations' of sarin. The human 'guinea pigs' were given no protection as well as no treatment 'in any instance, in order that the course and duration of effects might be fully observed'.[73] The results of the tests on humans were compared with those on rabbits, which had apparently been put in the chamber at the same time as the men. This test established just how little sarin vapour was needed to trigger a reaction in the humans. The scientists were watching to observe when the men started to suffer miosis – a classic symptom of nerve gas poisoning where the pupils of the eyes are reduced, in its most marked form, to mere pinpoints, and sometimes for several days. In the trial, miosis began to appear after twenty or thirty-five minutes, and even though the concentrations were relatively low, many of the men had the condition for two days, with some experiencing it for five days. A few of the men also complained of headache, runny noses, and lethargy.[74]

Fourteen men were also subjected to repeated doses of sarin. Some of them were sent into the chamber on three or four successive days and exposed to 3.3 mg min m^{-3} of sarin. On the second and third days, they were put back into the chamber when they were still suffering miosis. In the evenings, six or eight hours later, the men complained of headaches, blurred vision, and a pain in their eyes if they looked at strong light. Others were exposed on eight successive days to a dosage of 1.65 mg min m^{-3} on each occasion – less than the amount which Porton believed would produce a reaction in humans. (It is not known if Porton regularly exposed volunteers to more than one dose of nerve gas. The report of another test in 1949 shows that five volunteers were exposed three times.)[75]

A fresh amount of sarin was often administered to these men before there was enough time for the symptoms caused by the previous tests to subside. 'Repeated exposures produced, after the third or fourth occasion, an aggravation of effects, viz, a more marked and persistent miosis, more severe headache – frontal, or described as constant aching behind the eyes – and blurred vision,' observed the Porton scientists. While repeated exposure helped to build a clearer picture of the effects of nerve gas, it was unlikely that soldiers on a real battlefield would ever actually be exposed so many times. To give an idea of the strength of these dosages, it is currently estimated that upwards of 35 mg min m^{-3} of sarin produces casualties, while between 70 and 100 mg min m^{-3} will kill.[76]

One man who was gassed twice by Porton was Gerry Beech, an RAF fitter for eight years, who took part in the experiments during the summer of

SECRET

TABLE 2

SUCCESSIVE EXPOSURES AND RESULTS

Subjects & No.	Time of Exposure	Nominal Dosage (Ct.) mg.min/m³	1st Day 1st exposure	2nd Day 2nd exposure	3rd Day 3rd exposure	4th Day 4th exposure	5th Day 5th exposure	6th Day 6th exposure	7th Day 7th exposure	8th Day 8th exposure
1) 2) Group I 3) 4) 5)	20 min.	1.65	No symptoms.	No symptoms.	No symptoms during or immediately after exposure. 4/5 complained of pain at back of eyes same evening, i.e. after 6 – 8 hours. No Miosis present. No other complaints.	Miosis present in all subjects at end of exposure. All complained of headache same evening, i.e. after 6 – 8 hours. 24 hours later miosis still present. No other complaints.	Following a 3 day interval, all subjects normal. No signs or symptoms during or after exposure.	No signs or symptoms following exposure.	No signs or symptoms during exposure. After 1 hr. interval all showed partial miosis. Condition similar after 24 hours. No other complaints.	Miosis present in all subjects at end of exposure period. No other complaints. Partial miosis present after 24 hours.
6) 7) Group II 8) 9)	40 min.	3.3	1st exposure Onset of miosis 30 – 35 min. No other signs or symptoms.	2nd exposure All subjects miotic before exposure. Ditto after exposure. Complained of headache (frontal & aching behind eyes) 6-8 hrs. later. Photophobia +. (Painful to light cigarette). 24 hrs. later:- As above. Pin point miosis present. General condition & appearance approaching definite harassment.					
10) 11) Group III 12) 13) 14)	40 min.	3.3			1st exposure After exposure no miosis present. No subjective symptoms.	2nd exposure Onset of miosis in 30-40 mins. All complained of headache 6-8 hrs. later, ache 6-8 hrs. later, & 3/4 of running nose. 24 hrs:- No complaints. Miosis present.	3rd exposure All subjects miotic before exposure. All complained of headache during & after exposure. Pin point miosis exhibited. 6-8 hrs. later:- All complained of headache & aching of eyes. 24 hrs:- Pin point miosis in all subjects. Photophobia present and conjunctivae suffused.	4th exposure All complained of headache & pain in eyes during exposure. Pin point miosis present. 4-5 hrs:- Headache & blurring of vision. 24 hrs:- Complete miosis in all subjects. Symptoms as above with suffusion of conjunctivae and photophobia present. Complete recovery in 48 hours.

NOTE: Group I. All rabbits showed miosis at end of each test. Eyes normal in 18 – 24 hours.
Group II. Onset of miosis in all rabbits in each test in 18 – 20 mins. approx. All miotic at end of test.
Group III. As in Group II. Eyes normal in 18 – 24 hours.

SECRET

Porton scientists record the effects of repeated doses of nerve gas on the human guinea pigs.

1950.[77] He was told that Porton needed volunteers because a new unnamed gas – discovered by the Germans – posed a threat to Britain who had yet to find a defence against it. Then in his early twenties, Beech had not heard of nerve gas at the time, nor was he told that it was nerve gas before he was put into the gas chamber. 'When we went in, we took in a load of rabbits which had been shaved on the back. They said to us when we went in, you have got to fear nothing because it is the mildest, mildest of mildest dose.' Porton staff – behind the glass walls – told the volunteers to stand facing them, and one of them came in with a gas mask. 'We stood there without gas masks, and then while we were looking at them through the window, they injected this liquid into a fan, like an atomiser…it sprayed about.'

He remained in the chamber for four or five minutes breathing in the gas, but did not suffer any obvious effects then or later that day. The rabbits had been wheeled away on a porter's truck, and Beech presumed that they were dead. One or two days later, they were sent back into the chamber and gassed again so that the scientists could measure the pupils of their eyes afterwards. 'This time, our eyes are gone to little pinpoints. It was like you were blind all day, but you could see at night. It was like you had a black spot in front of your eyes all the while.' It stayed like that for four days, even after he had returned home. A month or so later – back at his base – he started to feel ill from breathlessness, but he was unable to tell his military doctor about the experiments because he had been ordered by Porton to keep them secret. For decades after, he suffered mysterious breathlessness, but never told any of his doctors until the mid-1990s. As he got older, the breathlessness and dizziness got worse. He said, 'Whenever I do anything, it makes me feel sick. I have got to sit down.' His application for a war pension was refused. He died of cancer in May 2000.

Following on from the 1949 trials, Porton pursued this work by exposing further groups of men to 'considerably higher dosages' of sarin in a large experiment.[78] Porton noted that due to 'improvements in chamber technique', and since the young volunteers were 'in all instances "fresh subjects" without previous exposure', the nerve gas could on this occasion be measured 'with accuracy'. It appears that a total of 133 men took part in this experiment in 1950. Teams of four to five men – without masks or any other protection – were dispatched into the gas chamber for one exposure only. Porton catalogued – in great detail – the mounting severity of the symptoms, as the dosages of sarin were increased (from 6.5 mg min m^{-3} to 14 mg min m^{-3}) for successive waves of volunteers.

In the gas chamber, the volunteers felt constriction in the throat and a tightness in the chest within a minute. Some experienced 'twitching of the eyelids' and a 'sensation of "heaviness" or pressure in the eyes'. A runny nose was 'usually noticeable within a few minutes'. The men began to get a headache within five minutes, and after they left the chamber, other symptoms set in within thirty minutes with the 'peak of discomfort' being between six and twelve hours. The men were plagued by a constant severe headache for two to three days, 'causing dejection and insomnia' and even nausea and vomiting. Other symptoms included runny nose for twenty-four hours, miosis for days, and eye pain. The human 'guinea pigs' took up to five days to recover.

One volunteer – exposed to 14 mg min m^{-3} – suffered so badly that he had to be 'detained in bed under strict supervision'. He had complained that he could not see properly within a few minutes of being exposed, and had vomited several times within the hour. He was 'feeling really very ill' and suffering from a 'general weakness, lethargy and mental dullness'. 'He found great difficulty in trying to remember in detail recent events and in trying to concentrate on anything.' He was flushed and sweating and had an intolerable headache. He slowly improved over three days, although the miosis stayed for nearly a week. From this, Porton commented that the dosage of 14 mg min m^{-3} 'may be near the maximum to which men, even when breathing quietly, may safely be exposed without protection'.

Some men were exposed to higher dosages of sarin, up to 37.5 mg min m^{-3}, but only with their mouth and nose protected. (One Porton report suggests that the dosages actually went up as high as 45 mg min m^{-3}).[79] Porton wanted to 'determine if the effects of sarin vapour on the eyes alone would cause the test subjects to be casualties when exposed to high dosages'.[80] Over fourteen trials, the scientists found that the eyes of the men did not get progressively worse as the dosages increased, since there was a 'levelling off in the severity of symptoms'. Soldiers – although troubled by 'considerable' distress in their eyes – would be able to fight on, they concluded.[81]

Throughout this large experiment, Porton had paid particular attention to the impact of the gas on the volunteers' eyes, trying out possible remedies. For days, the men endured 'aching eyeballs' which was often intense and worsened by 'focusing on near objects, close reading or precision work'. Porton remarked: 'This symptom is well demonstrated by the often abortive attempt to light a cigarette, when the intense stabbing pain in the eyes on sighting the flame causes the subject hastily to avert the gaze or shield the eyes.' The pain was not relieved in the dark nor by rest – in fact the agony was 'aggravated by closing the eyes in attempted sleep'. Miosis – if left untreated – could last for five days, with the redness continuing for three to five days. The vision remained blurred and dimmed for up to three days – they described it as a 'darkness or haze, with a lack of definition'. Volunteers themselves described how it was like wearing a pair of blinkers: 'can't see out of the corners of my eyes'; 'like a misty shutter to the outer side'; 'seem as if boxed in, as if he had a pair of horse goggles on'.

The effect of the nerve gas on their eyes was often the most striking of many volunteers' experiences. Lewis Birt was blinded for two days after he was tested with nerve gas in 1951. He says that before he went into the chamber, his eyes were very carefully photographed in a mask similar to the one worn by actor Anthony Hopkins in the film *Silence of the Lambs*.[82] When he came out, he felt nauseous and had headaches for days – 'Light became an enormous problem'. The scientists were testing out certain eye drops as possible antidotes. He says that the effects 'very gradually wore away' after two weeks, and although he had been told nothing about nerve gas, he had confidence in the competence of Porton scientists. 'I do feel in many respects that at that particular point in time, they probably took advantage of the naivety of young people. You are not able to make the full assessment.' One reason he had volunteered was out of a sense of duty for his country. 'In the afterglow of the Second World War, patriotic feelings were enormous at that time.'

Tony Mallard, then a nineteen-year-old National Serviceman, remembers that the pupils in each of his eyes turned to different sizes – one large, the other to a pinpoint – after he had been subjected to nerve gas.[83] The scientists had told him that the experiment in 1951 was to test various antidotes for the eyes – 'to get people who had been gassed in action back into action as soon as possible'. They informed him that he was to be exposed to nerve gas, but this meant little to him. After a couple of minutes in the chamber, he rapidly began to suffer a splitting headache and lost his sight for a day or so. A day after the experiment, Porton scientists began to treat his eyes, while he was confined to his room for the rest of the week. At the weekend, his eyes 'began to play up' and he felt off-balance at times, since he could not focus properly with the different-sized pupils. It appears that antidotes had been dropped into one eye, but not the other.

Porton had requested more volunteers in 1950 because it wanted to step up its programme of testing nerve gases on human 'guinea pigs'.[84] The scientists wanted more than the ten to twenty a week that were then being supplied. The number of volunteers who were exposed to nerve gases increased noticeably afterwards – from 159 in 1949-50, to 234 in 1950-51, to 384 in 1951-52, to its highest-ever level of 531 in 1952-53.

By any estimation, these were remarkably large numbers of men who were being exposed to nerve gas in each of these years, and hundreds more volunteers – as appendix one shows – were also being used in other experiments during this time. The men were being exposed to a clutch of nerve gases – sarin (GB), tabun (GA), soman (GD), and the less well-known GE and GF.[85] Although some of these experiments have been made public, many are still classified secret. However it appears that a sizeable number of tests were not written up in formal reports by Porton, suggesting either a certain lack of scientific rigour or an overload of experiments.[86] One scientist who joined Porton later found that it was difficult to see clearly from written records what the staff had been doing during the 1950s. 'A lot of work was inadequately explained. We did not feel that we could interpret the results,' he added.[87]

Sarin was the nerve gas which was being tested most frequently on humans at Porton since Britain had chosen this as the most suitable nerve gas for its proposed chemical arsenal.[88] A variety of weapons for the gas were being designed and developed at the time, while construction of the nerve gas factory at Nancekuke had begun in 1951.[89] This work was helped by the deepening collaboration with the United States of America and Canada since 1947. Fostered in the Second World War, this co-operation in chemical warfare evolved and flourished into a long and fruitful partnership during the Cold War – one of the most intimate partnerships between the three countries in any of the military fields in those decades.

It nestled comfortably into the so-called 'Special Relationship' between Britain and America. Senior Porton staff have described the co-operation as being so close that the chemical warfare efforts of the two countries were virtually integrated,[90] and long-serving American official Saul Hormats commented that Porton and their American counterparts were like 'all the same family'.[91] Personal bonds between them were forged during frequent meetings and secondments. The three countries held regular conferences – known initially as Tripartite meetings – in which raw ideas were tossed around for discussion, tasks were divided up and allotted to specified countries, and results of research shared almost immediately they had been collated.[92] In particular, reports of human experiments were automatically exchanged across the Atlantic by both sides. The Americans too had started an extensive programme of testing volunteers with nerve gases by the early 1950s.

The obvious main advantage of this collaboration was to save money and effort.[93] An early example of this was when two chemicals – sarin and GE – vied to be the main nerve gas which would be manufactured in bulk. More costly research into the benefits of both gases was needed before a final decision could be made. Dividing up the two gases, the Americans and British investigated one each, thus conserving their resources.[94]

With a large pool of volunteers at its disposal, Porton was now able to investigate a variety of different questions which had been thrown up by the nerve gases. One in particular was to see how much sarin – when inhaled – was actually retained and absorbed into the human body. This was of 'some importance' in calculating how much sarin would kill a person and consequently how much should be loaded into weapons to make them efficient and effective.[95] From 'a port in the wall of a gas chamber', the eight volunteers each wore a mask in which they could inhale the gas through their nose and exhale it through their mouth. From this they concluded that 'practically all inhaled sarin vapour is absorbed'.

Another problem which interested Porton was how nerve gas would affect the mental performance and intellectual ability of humans. This was done by exposing unprotected volunteers to sarin and measuring how well they then completed a set of intelligence and aptitude tests. During the first study in 1952, twenty RAF men – with an average age of twenty – took part in the three-day experiment. On the first afternoon, they did the tests and were given marks for their performance. For example, one test was to circle particular patterns of crosses on a page in a given time; another was to cut out a light when it came on. On the second morning, the men were exposed to 10 mg min m^{-3} of sarin in the gas chamber. They then had to repeat the same tests in the afternoon and the following morning.[96]

Porton scientists recorded that the men suffered the 'typical symptoms' of 'mild to moderate' nerve gas poisoning – breathlessness, runny nose, headaches and eye pains. One volunteer vomited four times. But, in this experiment, Porton was more interested in the psychological effects on the men. The scientists found that in the first hour or two, the men went through a 'slow collapse into apparent dejection. From this state, however, the subject could easily be roused to normal animation by such events as the routine taking of a blood sample'. By the afternoon – five hours later – many of the volunteers felt marginally better and so made an effort on the tests, even though they were feeling lethargic. Only two of the twenty volunteers were able to get a good night's sleep after they had been exposed, whilst the rest went to bed early because they did not feel well, then struggled for two hours to get to sleep, woke four or five times because their eyes were hurting, and eventually got only two hours of sound sleep before waking at 7a.m.

The next morning, the men reported unusual dreams, or nightmares, of two kinds – the first was 'the anxiety dream [which] was really just an extension of the restless quality of the night ('tossing and turning') of which most spoke'. The second was prompted by the eye pains. One man dreamt of 'three big broad needles pointing at his head, which was very sore. Woke in a sweat and was told he had shouted out'; another 'threw a knife at a vulture which was about to molest a smaller bird. He missed, the vulture picked up the knife in its beak and came at him'. He then woke up 'very sweaty, with a horrible pain just above the eyelids'; a third man had 'an extreme and prolonged series of confusedly fearful nightmares' which he could not describe; a fourth 'was going home on leave; called for his girl, and was told she'd fallen off her bike and was in hospital'; a sergeant reported that he had had 'several unpleasant fragmentary dreams, especially one of a soldier getting killed' and was confused when he woke. On the morning of the third day, the men – taking the tests again – were still suffering pain in their eyes and from a bad night's sleep. Almost all said that they could not be bothered to carry out the later tests, as they were experiencing 'poor concentration and tiredness'. It appears that they were not given any treatment for the poisoning until after the three-day experiment ended.[97]

Peter Harper, an RAF driver for six years, took part in this experiment at the age of twenty-two and was blinded for three days. 'I was one of the unfortunate ones who was given nerve gas. We were assured that we would suffer no ill effects,' he says.[98] He underwent the tests on the first day. He remembers a few of them – one was to select specified coloured objects from a mass of symbols on a piece of paper, another was like a fairground game in which you have to use a steering wheel to keep a car on the road on a screen. The next day he was exposed to sarin in the chamber, and did manage to do the tests in the afternoon. 'I was not too bad to start with. I was a bit jumbled, but I did get through. By teatime of that day, I had lost my eyesight altogether. I could not see nothing at all – I had to be led to the cookhouse.' He had a good night's sleep, but he could not even attempt the tests on the following day because he was still blinded. 'When they [Porton staff] saw that you couldn't see, they said that's nothing to worry about. They don't push you on this point. It [the gas] affects different people in different ways. We all went in together, but some people's eyes were not affected. They could see alright. Some could not see very good at all. I think there were three of us who couldn't see nothing at all.'

A day later, he was treated for the first time when drops were put into his eyes. Since it was a Friday, he was hoping that his eyes would clear up so he could go home. 'My pupils sort of went the other way. They opened too wide, so it was out of focus that way, so I had to stay over the weekend for them to settle down.' His eyes finally recovered to normal after the weekend.[99] Harper had initially volunteered for the experiments 'because they sounded interesting', but the first thing he saw when he arrived at Porton was a batch of dead monkeys being brought out of a laboratory which he admitted he found 'a bit upsetting'.

From this experiment, Porton inferred that after exposure the men's visual co-ordination was worse, but their reasoning and intellectual capability had not deteriorated. The scientists quickly followed up this experiment with another in 1953. This three-day test was more or less the same, but this time, the twelve volunteers – with an average age of nineteen – were exposed to a stronger dose of sarin, 14 mg min m^{-3}, without any protection whatsoever.[100] Porton found that the severity of the physical symptoms suffered by the volunteers in the two studies was 'almost identical', despite the difference in doses. On the mental side, similarly, the men appeared 'behaviourally much less disturbed than the increased concentration (of sarin) would lead one to expect'. Indeed the volunteers seemed, if anything, less affected than those in the initial experiment.

The volunteers' sleep was once again disturbed, but to a lesser extent. Compared with the first study, fewer men suffered a restless night or had trouble getting to sleep. Two said they did not sleep at all – the next day, one of them saw 'transparent blotches' drifting slowly across his sight, a dozen at a time. One man dreamt that he was surrounded by stetson-wearing cowboys shooting a machine-gun at him. Another went to sleep at his usual time, but when he had got comfortable and warm after ten minutes, he 'started to shiver and shake. His heart seemed to beat very slowly, then quickened as the shivering began to die away'. He then slept normally.[101]

The scientist in charge of the two experiments was baffled by this unpredicted outcome, suggesting that perhaps the men in the second test were brighter than the first. He stated baldly, 'Some differences in the human material were tentatively thought to be responsible for some of the unexpected results, notably the mildness of the clinical picture, but such differences could only be a partial explanation.'

Porton also found 'some unexpected dramatic' results when six men were exposed to concentrations of soman (which is more toxic than sarin and tabun).[102] A thirty-year-old human 'guinea pig' suffered 'rapid onset of miosis to pinpoints', 'severe headache' and vomited within thirty minutes of leaving the gas chamber. He had a sleepless night because of the intense headache and eye pains. The next morning, he could not shave since a fierce pain shot up the back of his head every time he moved it. Later that morning, he developed 'a strange weakness in the legs' and collapsed since he simply could not stand. He recovered during the rest of the day. Over the next forty-eight hours, he was in a quietened state, interrupted by periods of foreboding and depression. Four days after he had been exposed to the gas, he suddenly felt his chest constricted, along with 'pain, disorientation, and a choking sensation'. All six experienced much more severe effects than the Porton scientists believed would be caused by this dosage of soman.[103] One senior scientist commented that it was 'a salutary reminder that soman vapour can be dangerous'.

Experimenting on humans with such potent gases is inherently perilous, and the risk of a calamity in such tests can never be eliminated. The larger the number of experiments, the larger the chance that such a calamity may actually happen. In one experiment in late 1952, Porton exposed 105 men to sarin vapour which had been pumped into a gas chamber.[104] The men sat outside the chamber and breathed in the gas through a kind of siphon. A quarter of them inhaled more than 14 mg min m^{-3} of sarin – the amount which Porton had earlier said could be the maximum to which volunteers could be safely exposed.[105] During the early 1950s, more and more people were being exposed to nerve gas, while the strengths of the doses were steadily going up. Soon Porton was to witness a grave tragedy which has haunted the establishment ever since.

Ronald Maddison. *Image taken from a video still.*

CHAPTER FIVE
Death of an Airman

The sad story of Ronald Maddison must rank as Porton's darkest hour of all its human experiments. At the age of just twenty, Maddison died after a dose of nerve gas had been intentionally dropped onto his skin in a sealed gas chamber. Chillingly, as subject number 745, he was part of a huge experiment to find out exactly how much nerve gas would kill a human. His death in May 1953 nearly ended Porton's experiments altogether.

His death, one of Britain's squalid secrets of the Cold War, has now come back to rattle and embarrass Porton. In a remarkable step, local Wiltshire police launched an official investigation into Maddison's death in August 1999, more than forty-six years after the event. Not only is it unusual for the police to start an inquiry into a fatality so long after it occurred, but moreover, it is a case in which one arm of the state is investigating a government establishment.

Maddison was born and grew up in Consett in County Durham. His younger sister Lillias described him as a 'popular person and a great personality... Everybody liked him. He was a real nice chap. Everybody will tell you the same thing. He was quiet, but at the same time, he was full of fun'.[1] She remembers him fondly, them playing tennis together, riding bikes and generally messing around in their childhood. He passed the eleven-plus exam and went to a grammar school. Lillias recalls, 'He did well. He was bright, there's no doubt about that. He was pretty talented.' He liked music – playing both the drums and piano – and had tried to get a band together with his friends. He had seven other brothers and sisters. His father John worked many nights cleaning and maintaining trains. Like millions of Britons, the County Durham family was full of bright, optimistic hope – looking forward to peace after the long war against Hitler, and to a decent future from Clement Attlee's newly elected Labour government.

Fascinated by aeroplanes, Ronnie joined the RAF at the age of eighteen and, by 1953, was stationed as a mechanic at Ballykelly in Northern Ireland with the rank of Leading Aircraftsman. He responded to a notice sent around RAF units calling for 140 volunteers to go to Porton between 25 April and

5 June. Porton 'required' airmen volunteers at a rate of twenty a week 'to undergo physiological experiments' at the establishment. To encourage them to volunteer, the airmen were specifically to be told that 'the physical discomfort resulting from the tests is usually very slight' and that the 'tests are carefully planned to avoid the slightest chance of danger and are under expert medical supervision'.[2] In hindsight, these words are cruelly ironic – and little more than false reassurance for Maddison. As shown in chapter two, Porton often misled volunteers by playing down the level of pain which they would experience. The human 'guinea pigs' were routinely informed that there was no danger in the experiments.

It is unclear, however, why Maddison chose to go to Porton. His cousin Ella Forster believes that he volunteered for the tests because he was homesick and wanted to visit his family. 'He was promised he would get extra leave if he volunteered.'[3] The notice sent to RAF units specified two inducements which were to be dangled in front of potential volunteers – each person would get extra pay, and would also be excused all military duties and would be free every evening while at Porton.[4] However, John Milliken, one of his Ballykelly colleagues, thinks that he responded to a request for volunteers for research into the common cold. 'Other research was hinted at, but not detailed.'[5] As Milliken says, 'The prevailing attitude of serving men to these volunteer requests was one of a "jolly", meaning that for a little discomfort one could have a small break from work with some travel.' He adds that Maddison – 'a friendly, likeable person' – was keen to go.

His close friend Jack Wilson says that Ronnie had told him that he was going to Porton for some 'mild' experiments to find a cure for the common cold or flu.[6] Ronnie himself had been told by other servicemen who had already been to Porton that 'it was a holiday camp he was going to'. Jack, however, warned him that he should never volunteer for anything while he was serving in the military. 'He told me what he was going to do and I played hell with him...I had met a lot of people who had been in the forces prior to Ronnie joining and they had all told me the same thing – "you never volunteer".' He believes that Ronnie would never 'in a million years' have volunteered had he known that he would be exposed to a dangerous chemical like nerve gas.

It was a choice which was to cost him his life. Two days after arriving at Porton, he was dead. He was one of 396 volunteers who were subjected to a massive experiment with one aim: 'to determine the dosage of GB (sarin), GD (soman) and GF (another nerve gas), which when applied to the clothed or bare skin of men would cause incapacitation or death'.[7] Teams of men were sent into the gas chamber with respirators, over many months from early 1952.[8] Varying amounts of liquid nerve gas were dropped through pipettes onto their arms which were wrapped in one or two layers of clothing.[9] The scientists aimed to compare how much the varying amounts penetrated through these layers. However, for another tranche of men, the liquid was applied directly to their bare skin on the inner part of their forearm.

To gauge the potency of the nerve gas, the scientists were relying on a particular technique. They were measuring how much different quantities of nerve gas reduced the amount of cholinesterase enzymes in the human body. Nerve gases work by destroying these cholinesterase enzymes which are a vital part of the mechanism by which the brain controls the muscles. In effect, the Porton scientists were seeking to establish a ratio between the level of cholinesterase reduction – known in scientific terminology as cholinesterase depression – and 'sub-lethal' quantities of nerve gas, and then extrapolate these figures to arrive at the lethal dose for humans. As we shall see, the validity of measuring these cholinesterase levels is now open to doubt. It is however clear that a fall of fifty percent and more in cholinesterase levels indicates that the victim has been poisoned, seventy to eighty percent and more implies that a person is seriously poisoned and is in danger, and so on upwards. The victim dies if the cholinesterase plunges by one hundred percent.

Some of the quantities of nerve gas administered to the men in this huge experiment are astoundingly high. In 1949 and 1950, Porton had twice estimated, mainly from its tests on animals, that 'any contamination greater than 200 milligrams [of sarin] on the bare skin would present a serious hazard, and possibly prove fatal, to man'.[10] And yet shortly afterwards, Porton started a large-scale experiment in which around a quarter of the subjects, ninety-nine men, were contaminated with this amount of sarin – and more – on their bare skin. According to the report of the experiment, 300 milligrams was dropped on the naked skin of forty-five volunteers, 250 milligrams on twenty-four volunteers, and 200 milligrams on thirty volunteers. In addition, quantities ranging from 200 and 300 milligrams were dropped through one layer of clothing on sixty-five volunteers, in another phase of the experiment.

Porton's full report on Maddison's death is still secret, but the main details have slipped out or have been released.[11] Maddison was one of a batch of six men who went into the gas chamber on 6 May 1953. He sat next to Mike Cox, then a twenty-two-year-old mechanic 'very reluctantly' doing his National Service.[12] Cox had gone to Porton not even knowing that it was a chemical warfare establishment. By the morning of the experiment, he had learnt that they were going to be exposed to nerve gas. However, he was not worried: 'In those days, although faith in the authorities was beginning to wear a bit thin, there was still a feeling that they knew what they were doing, that they would not willingly subject us to anything that was in the least bit nasty, or likely to have horrendous consequences.'

The human 'guinea pigs', wearing gas masks and a woollen hat, were asked to roll up their left sleeve. Two strips of military clothing were loosely taped to the arm. Porton scientists then dropped liquid sarin through these two layers of flannel and serge battledress onto the arms of the men. They had been told to sit at a table in the chamber for thirty minutes with their arms extended before they could leave.

Maddison was the fourth in line to receive his dose at 10.17a.m. Twenty-three minutes later, he 'complained of feeling "queer" and was seen to be sweating'. Cox remembers that they were playing noughts and crosses to while away the time when Maddison 'went quiet and then sort of flopped over'. Porton technicians immediately helped him out of the gas chamber into the open air. It was the last time that Cox saw Maddison – Porton staff did not tell him or any of the others that someone in their experiment had died.

At first, Maddison was able to walk on his own and seemed to be fine. But suddenly his condition deteriorated. At 10.47a.m., an ambulance arrived and whisked him off to Porton's hospital. He was injected with a nerve gas antidote, atropine. Within minutes, however, the muscles in his face began to twitch and his breathing 'became laboured'. At 11a.m., 'his colour turned ashen grey'. Then, his skin turned bluish and 'the pulse at the wrist could not be felt'. More Porton scientists rushed to the hospital as 'every effort was made' to resuscitate Maddison. He was placed on the floor – his limbs massaged, hot water bottles pressed onto his body, his legs raised. As the horror unfolded, the scientists struggled to revive the twenty-year-old, but, despite all their knowledge and experience, they were helpless. They continued trying until 1.30p.m., but it was all in vain. He had actually died at about 11a.m. because of 'sudden heart failure'.[13]

No one had anticipated that the convulsions Maddison suffered would be so great that it would become 'extremely difficult' to inject him with the life-saving antidote or to perform the 'vigorous' artificial respiration which was needed. The staff had pumped his chest so hard to restart his breathing that it caused 'severe bruising and vein congestion, so that over a pint of blood was found in the abdomen.' Lots of mucus was also found to have 'badly obstructed' his throat and mouth.[14] His cholinesterase level had plummeted by a huge amount – ninety-six percent.[15]

Porton's report of the experiment reveals that a second man had also come close to dying after he stopped breathing. A few weeks before Maddison's death, this man – subject number 702 – had been poisoned with 300 milligrams of sarin through one layer of clothing. He felt ill after leaving the chamber, and 'sat on a chair, salivated profusely and had spasms of the hands and arms'. Atropine was administered, but he 'rapidly became unconscious'. His whole body went into spasms, his skin started to go blue since his blood was being deprived of oxygen, and his breathing was 'strident'. He was admitted to Porton's hospital where his breathing stopped, but he thankfully recovered. 'Consciousness gradually returned' and he spoke for the first time four and a half hours after he began to feel ill. He continued vomiting intermittently throughout the night and the next morning.[16] His cholinesterase had been depressed by ninety-six percent. He too was considered to be such a serious case that Porton wrote a full report on him, but again it is being kept secret.[17] It appears that following this near tragedy, Porton scientists cut the dosage of nerve gas from 300 milligrams to the amount of 200 milligrams which was used in Maddison's fateful test soon afterwards.

Five other human 'guinea pigs' in this huge experiment also suffered particularly badly and required treatment in Porton's hospital, their cholinesterase level falling by at least eighty-five percent. Below are extracts of Porton's descriptions of what happened to them. (Other than their subject numbers, no names are given in the report.)[18]

Subject number 603 received 250 milligrams of sarin on his bare skin. After twenty minutes, he was sweating profusely, feeling ill, with a headache, and cold and clammy skin. He more or less collapsed and had to be helped from the gas chamber and injected with atropine. On the way to hospital, he vomited. During the night, he again threw up several times. He recovered after nearly two days. His blood cholinesterase had gone down by eighty-eight percent.

Subject number 562 was given a dose of 300 milligrams of sarin through one layer of clothing. When he walked out of the chamber, his knees went weak and he complained of dizziness, nausea and a cold sweat. He was given atropine, but vomited. He was taken to the hospital – during the night, he could not sleep and complained of a feeling of 'being pressed down'. He had recovered by the following morning. His blood cholinesterase had fallen by ninety-four percent.

Subject number 567 was exposed to 250 milligrams of sarin through one layer of clothing. After his spell in the chamber, he ran to the barracks and vomited. He was admitted to the hospital eight hours after he had been exposed. He said he was 'feeling queer and behaved hysterically, laughing, crying and saying stupid things'. His muscles were twitching, although this 'could be controlled at will.' He suffered these again during the following day, although they improved after he had been administered with atropine. He 'felt normal' thirty hours after the gas chamber. His blood cholinesterase had been reduced by ninety percent.

Subject number 708 was poisoned with 300 milligrams of sarin through one layer of clothing. He vomited ninety minutes later and twice later in the day when he 'still felt weak and complained of nausea'. That night he could not sleep. The next day, he was normal, but that night, he slept 'only intermittently, complaining of "noises in the ears" and feeling "stiff all over".' His cholinesterase level had decreased by ninety-three percent.

Subject number 714 also needed to be hospitalised a day after he was received 300 milligrams of sarin on one layer of clothing. He had been suddenly taken ill and threw up. He vomited from time to time over the next six hours. His cholinesterase had dropped by eighty-five percent.

But while those men suffered bad reactions, others got off lightly. Many of the men only felt sweating, blanching, itching, or a cold feeling on the skin where the liquid had been dropped. In February 1953, Mike Gray, a Royal Navy electrician, had 250 milligrams of sarin dropped on his arm which was protected with either one or two layers of clothing.[19] 'I don't recall feeling any adverse effects at all. In the gas chamber, you came out choking and breathless, but you went into the air and you got some wind on you and it clears fairly quickly.'[20] According to Porton, he had only experienced a cold feeling on his skin.[21] Gray added, 'I didn't know if it was nerve gas or what it was. We were never told.' At the time, he had 'vaguely' heard of nerve gas. 'We did not have much information on these nasties which were around.' He actually volunteered twice for Porton – the first time in September 1952. On both occasions, he had nerve gas dropped on his skin, but had little reaction.[22] He had chosen to go to Porton because he wanted the extra leave on offer to court his future wife. But he has been unable to have children and has often wondered if this had been caused by the Porton tests.

Mike Cox, who sat next to Maddison, also felt little except for a coldness in his arm about an hour after the test. Remarkably, his view of the experiment has been preserved in an account which he wrote two days afterwards.[23] This contemporaneous document shows how benign his experience was. He wrote, 'I felt no fear of the actual test because I really don't know what the stuff can do. A case of ignorance breeding contempt.' He says now that he knew that nerve gases killed, but not how they killed. He added at the time, 'The whole period went very smoothly, and I enjoyed it very much. The cooking was very good, and the Sgt cook gave us every opportunity to complain. Nobody needed to. The quarters are rough, but in summer this is no great handicap. I would very much like to come again if it is possible.'

An internal history of Porton's human experiments programme referred to Maddison's death as an 'unfortunate accident'.[24] Within a week of his death, a Court of Inquiry had been convened. Held over three days in secret, all except one of the nine members of the inquiry were officials in the Ministry of Supply, the department responsible for Porton. The committee heard evidence from eleven Porton staff and studied various documents.[25] By the end of May, it decided that 'in the light of knowledge available', the test had been 'reasonable' and properly conducted. The court was 'impressed by the smoothness' of the Porton scientists in dealing with the emergency, since all known treatments 'were promptly and efficiently applied by medical personnel of great experience'. It concluded that the death was caused by 'personal idiosyncrasy' – Maddison either had an 'unusual sensitivity' to the effects of nerve gas or the physiological behaviour of his skin 'allowed an unusually rapid absorption' of the lethal liquid. It added that no test for 'detecting any such idiosyncrasy' had been discovered.

Conveniently, this report did not blame Porton staff for the tragedy. But is this really a fair verdict? The current investigation by Wiltshire police is looking afresh at the death of Maddison and, if necessary, may bring charges against Porton and even staff who were working at the establishment at the time. Some aspects of Maddison's death still remain secret, and so any conclusions about Porton's culpability must be tentative. With hindsight, it appears that there are two factors which are probably central to whether Porton scientists were criminally responsible for his death. Each was like a warning light, which, if recognised by alert Porton staff, could have avoided his death.

The first is the amount of sarin which was administered to Maddison. Nowadays it is estimated that the lethal dose of sarin on the skin of an averagely built man is estimated to be around 1,800 milligrams.[26] At the end of the massive experiment, Porton scientists had observed that 'for obvious reasons', the lethal dose 'cannot be determined directly on man' and had estimated that the LD50 of sarin (the amount which would kill half of those exposed) lay between 1,500 and 1,700 milligrams through bare skin. But the key question remains — what did the scientists estimate to be roughly the lethal dose, before and during the course of their huge experiment? Back in the early 1950s, Porton scientists were unsure what was the lethal dose. As we have already seen, Porton had twice estimated, in 1949 and 1950, that anything above 200 milligrams on the bare skin could kill a man. But within three years, Porton scientists felt sufficiently confident to apply significantly more than this amount, rising to 300 milligrams, to the naked skin of around 100 men. This is potentially damning evidence. The report of the experiment does not explain why Porton believed that it was safe to go beyond 200 milligrams. What happened in those three years is at the moment somewhat of a black hole and is moreover crucial to the Wiltshire police investigation. Detectives will surely need to discover whether Porton scientists ever came across other information which reassured them that dosages up to 300 milligrams would not harm the human 'guinea pigs'. If this cannot be explained satisfactorily, then Porton is vulnerable to the charge of acting recklessly in this experiment and causing Maddison's death. That is a truly shocking prospect.

The second important factor is the measurement of cholinesterase levels in the human 'guinea pigs'. As already shown, the Porton scientists were seeking to establish a correlation between the level of cholinesterase reduction and non-lethal quantities of nerve gas, and then extrapolate these figures to calculate the lethal dose for humans. Porton scientists believed that measuring the level of cholinesterase was the 'only quantitive and objective' way of assessing the extent of nerve gas poisoning during this large-scale experiment. But this may have been an error, since nowadays it is accepted that cholinesterase levels are only a crude way of estimating the extent of nerve gas poisoning.[27] A key question therefore is: did the Porton scientists place too much reliance at the time on an unproven technique which is now used only as a rough guide to the effects of nerve gas? Again, their state of knowledge at the time is the crucial question. Some of Porton's papers from this era show that there was already some doubt that cholinesterase depression was a reliable method of assessing the extent of nerve gas poisoning.[28]

Porton and other scientists have spent much time and effort investigating the relationship between cholinesterase levels and nerve gas symptoms.[29] It is evident that the more severe the nerve gas poisoning, the larger the drop in cholinesterase. But it is also apparent that victims can suffer identical symptoms of poisoning, but experience widely different cholinesterase levels, and vice versa. One senior Porton scientist, for example, commented that 'one man may be nauseated at 70 percent depression and vomit at 80 percent, while another may feel perfectly fit and well, and even enjoy a good meal when he has 75-80 percent depression'.[30]

It appears that the scientists started by exposing the groups of the 396 human 'guinea pigs' in this test to lower amounts of sarin to ascertain what effects the chemical had on the cholinesterase levels. It appears that, working on the assumption that such levels could be directly correlated to the degree of poisoning, they believed that the quantities of nerve gas could be increased safely. But the data in the report of the experiment shows up what, in retrospect, should have been a warning for the scientists. From the appendices of the report, there is a noticeable trend in which a small proportion of human 'guinea pigs' suffered large drops in their cholinesterase, compared to their colleagues, even though they received exactly the same dosage of nerve gas. For example, of eighteen men who were contaminated with 250 milligrams of sarin on their bare skin, sixteen men had cholinesterase drops of fifty-three percent and below. However the other two men suffered huge reductions of more than eighty-five percent. By any statistical measurement, this was a very large variation in reactions, and should surely have indicated that there were in effect two populations among the human 'guinea pigs': those who were not greatly affected; and the smaller number who were acutely sensitive and for whom the dosages could have been potentially dangerous. As it turned out, Maddison was put in jeopardy and died. This could explain why Maddison died from 200 milligrams, an amount which is very much lower than the recognised lethal dose (nearly a tenth of this dose).

It seems that this experiment was the first time that Porton scientists appreciated fully that sarin can affect victims in vastly different ways. Porton concluded in its report that the 'most striking aspect of the results is the great variation in response of different individuals to the same degree of contamination'. In other words, some subjects suffered greatly, while others did not, even though they were poisoned with the same amount of nerve gas and wore the same layers of clothing. In very dry tones, the scientists wrote that this variation was 'dramatically emphasised when one of the 18 subjects receiving 200 milligrams of sarin (GB) through two layers of clothing developed major signs of GB poisoning and subsequently died'. The other seventeen men, such as Mike Cox, showed no signs or symptoms of poisoning.

Nerve gas experiments on humans are undoubtedly hazardous. Porton scientists were working in a complex, little-understood area of science. Obviously, actually exposing humans to nerve gas was the best way of finding the answers, but if scientists believe that such tests are absolutely necessary, they face a heavy onus of ensuring that the subjects are properly protected. As declassified papers make clear, Porton was well aware that estimating the toxicity of liquid nerve gas on the skin was a complicated matter. Important considerations including the rate at which the nerve gas evaporates from the skin, the speed at which skin in different parts of the human body absorbs the deadly liquid, and the difficulty of translating the results of animal tests to humans have to be taken into account.

Equally unknown was the effect of clothing on increasing or decreasing the hazard of sarin. In their report, the scientists speculated that flannel, one of the two types of clothing used in the experiment, may have trapped the sarin and caused more of it to penetrate into the skin, rather than acting as an effective barrier against the nerve gas.[31] Maddison was one of those men who wore flannel in the experiment. Previous Porton reports had warned that covering the skin – and therefore restricting the evaporation of the nerve gas – 'dangerously increases the hazard [of the] gas'.[32]

At around the same time, Porton was also investigating how quickly sarin penetrates through the skin in an experiment on humans and rabbits.[33] The sarin was laced with radioactive material – phosphorus-32 – so that the scientists, with the aid of a Geiger counter, could trace the progress of the nerve gas. This particular experiment therefore had a double hazard – not only from the sarin, but also the radioactive material. This compound emits beta radiation which, once inside the body, can damage soft tissue. Substances such as phosphorus-32 were being used quite extensively in medical experiments in many countries at this time to keep track of chemicals in the human body. In the 1950s, many scientists believed that there was a threshold dose of radiation under which it was possible that cancer or genetic defects would not develop. But now it is accepted that there is no dose of radiation so small that it cannot produce those diseases; the size of the dose simply determines the person's chances of getting such diseases. Although nerve gas mixed with phosphorus-32 had been tested on animals before, this experiment appears to be the first time that this hazardous mixture was tried on humans at Porton.[34]

Drops of 2 milligrams of sarin – tagged with the phosphorus-32 – were placed on the naked forearms of twenty men. This procedure was repeated with another fourteen men whose arms had been soaked in a solvent, acetone, to remove any fat from the surface of the skin. Comparing these two groups, Porton suggested that the amount of skin fat may affect the degree of penetration of the nerve gas. From this experiment, the scientists observed that the sarin penetrated at a regular rate, although there was some variation among the subjects. This underlined again how individuals were affected differently by nerve gas.

The day Ronnie died is vividly etched in the memory of his sister Lillias. She and another sister had been out celebrating their birthdays. The other sister had her birthday on that very day, while Lillias' was three days earlier. With money from her father, Lillias had gone to Newcastle with this sister and bought a new dress. When they came back in the evening, they were told the awful news that their brother had died earlier that day. Another sister fainted. The family was in shock. 'For days afterwards, everybody walked around as if they were treading on eggshells. Everything was quiet. It was a dreadful time,' she says. Lillias went and told Ronnie's girlfriend.

Rigid secrecy enveloped the death of the young airman at the time. Whitehall officials were keen to hide both the extent of British work on nerve gases and the human experiments with these potent chemicals. Ten days after his death – on 16 May – an inquest was held, but behind closed doors.[35] Inquests are normally open to the press and public, but coroners can decide 'in the interests of national security' to hold them in secret.

The only people permitted to attend were officials and Maddison's father, John. But he was sworn to secrecy by the authorities – he could not even tell his wife, Jane, the rest of his family, or Ronnie's friends. And until his death in 1956, John Maddison would never talk about the inquest, or what he had been told by the authorities. About three weeks before he died, Lillias asked him what had happened to Ronnie. 'My dad said to me, "Just don't ask".' Jack Wilson tried many times to persuade him to reveal how his close friend had died. 'On every occasion I got the same answer: "I have been sworn to secrecy, I cannot tell his own mother how he died and unfortunately I can't tell you". Now to me this was one hell of a shock. This was my best friend, and I thought we lived in a free country and I wasn't content with that.'

Ella Forster, Ronnie's cousin, points out that in those days, more people accepted the word of the authorities without questioning it. She says that the family were 'devastated' by the news of Ronnie's death. As for his parents, she adds, 'I don't think there are words to express how they felt. They were expecting him coming home and he didn't. They never came to terms with that ever, until the day they died. A real tragedy it was to them. It knocked the life out of them. They were never the same after that.' She believes that it was worse for Ronnie's father because he could not talk openly about his son's death at a time when he needed to speak about it to grieve properly and deal with his emotions. 'It's the only way you get it out of your system, but he couldn't.' She believes that the authorities were unfair to the family in hushing it all up.

The result of the inquest on 16 May was immediately reported to the government, but the public were kept completely in the dark. A newspaper article on 24 May highlighted the extent of the intense secrecy: 'Nobody outside official circles knows why he died. Nobody outside official circles knows what the inquest verdict was. Even his name, age and home town have been hushed up.'[36] The newspaper reported that the Wiltshire coroner, Harold Dale, was not the one who had decided to hold the inquest in secret: 'It was the result of official instructions. I have been told that no details concerning the inquest must be made public.' Whitehall spokesmen were disclosing only one fact: 'We can only confirm that there was a fatal accident. Beyond that we have no information.'[37]

Slowly the wall of secrecy began to crumble, if only because Maddison's death certificate could not be kept confidential. A reporter from the now-defunct *Sunday Dispatch* was able to look at the register of deaths and, on 31 May, disclose information from it, such as Maddison's name and his birthplace. Under the headline '"Guinea-pig" serviceman died from suffocation in hush-hush experiment', the newspaper revealed that the Wiltshire coroner had decided on a verdict of death by misadventure. The cause of death, however, made no mention of nerve gas – it merely recorded that the airman had died of 'asphyxia from blocking of the bronchi'.[38] When a local MP raised the question of his death in Parliament, the government stuck to the bare minimum, saying that Maddison had died from 'the effects of asphyxia' after taking part in a trial with an unnamed 'war gas'.[39]

Maddison was buried in a big funeral in Consett. His cousin Ella recalled the day, saying, 'It was packed. People were very emotional. People all over were finding it hard to deal with – the war was over and then this boy had to die like that. Everybody was going to try and be happy again. And then this sadness hit a little family in Edith Street.' He was buried with military honours, with representatives from the RAF.[40] A local newspaper reported that there were many tributes for the airman whose 'untimely death' had came 'as a great shock to relatives and friends in the Consett area, where he

Ronald Maddison's death certificate
(Death Certificate – Office for National Statistics – © Crown copyright. Reproduced with the permission of the Controller of Her Majesty's Stationery Office. Also with the permission of Maddison's family.)

was well known and highly respected'. Porton paid for the funeral, a suit for his father, and flowers.

Milliken and Maddison's former colleagues at Ballykelly gradually learnt of his death. Milliken himself commented that, 'It is sad that one life was snuffed out like a candle at such an early age.'

According to volunteers who went to Porton after the catastrophe, Maddison was blamed for his own death in a series of clearly false stories that were circulated. Robert Grandison, then a twenty-two-year-old national serviceman, remembered that on the first morning of his stay in December 1953, a senior officer, in an introductory talk, told them that the dead man had not followed the instructions which he had been given. 'He had been told not to go out drinking after the experiments – and he had gone out. He was found dead in his bed the next morning. Whether that's true or not, I don't know.'[41] Another volunteer, Bill Rodgers, who went to Porton in 1957 and 1959, heard that the RAF man had died after taking his mask off too early in the gas chamber.[42] 'We were told during the course of our experiments that "we have only lost one guy here in so many years, and he did not do as he was told".' He adds that the message from the Porton staff was, 'If you do exactly what you were told, you are going to be all right.'

Although some volunteers speak of other deaths among the human 'guinea pigs', Porton maintains strongly that Maddison has been the only one throughout the entire programme of human experiments who has died while at the establishment.[43]

As well as the Wiltshire police investigation, Porton is also under new pressure from the Maddison family. With the help of lawyer Alan Care (now with the London firm Russell Jones and Walker), the family won legal aid in October 1999 and is demanding an apology, compensation, and the truth about his death after all the years of silence from the authorities. Care believes that Porton were 'dicing with death' in the experiment on Maddison. 'They were taking risks that were at the very edge of what was known about the effects of sarin. I believe that particular attitude was reckless.' Chemical warfare expert, Alistair Hay, commented, 'They were playing with fire. They were exposing people to concentrations which in the event only killed one man, but were not far off, perhaps, killing a number of others.'

The grandson of Ronnie's sister, Lillias, has followed Ronnie into the RAF himself. But he went with strong words of warning from his relatives – never volunteer for anything in the military, especially Porton.

The death of Maddison cast a dark shadow over Porton for many years. It was not a subject which Porton liked to be aired. A veteran scientist recalled that, 'it was highly embarrassing, and rather frightening.'[44] He added that although not a taboo subject, staff who were there at the time did not really discuss it with their colleagues. 'Maybe they were told not to talk about it,' he added. Gradon Carter, Porton's official historian, comments that this death and other mishaps 'always exacerbated public unease and Ministerial anxieties'.[45] In the immediate aftermath, it seriously threatened to end or curtail Porton's human experiments' programme. The number of volunteers coming through Porton's laboratories had rapidly risen since 1950 when the establishment had requested more to be supplied, and in the three years leading up to Maddison's death, Porton had used an incredibly large number of volunteers in the experiments. The annual total of volunteers in the three years from 1950 rose from 637 through 789 to 836. As we have already seen, the proportion of these men who were exposed to nerve gas was substantial and also rose over this period – 234, 384 to 531.

It surely cannot be a coincidence that the number of men tested with nerve gas was at its all-time peak when Maddison was killed. It was almost as if it had been building up to a crescendo, and his death brought immediate silence. The tragedy triggered instant repercussions – all experiments with nerve gases were suspended while the government launched an investigation.[46] (Human experiments with other chemicals were, however, not banned, and a total of 704 men were used in non-nerve gas tests during the year 1953-54). The Court of Inquiry – which had judged Maddison's death to be due to a 'personal idiosyncrasy' – recommended that Porton's work was so important that the human experiments should be continued. It ruled that there should be no ban of any kind on nerve gas tests and the decision to resume such tests should be left up to the head of Porton. It suggested that small quantities – up to 10 milligrams of sarin – could be 'applied without foreseeable danger' to the skin of volunteers. Such doses were 'necessary' since Porton needed to clarify how chemical substances were absorbed through the skin.[47]

But these recommendations did not settle the question, since the Ministry of Supply, nominally in charge of Porton, wanted expert advice on the matter. In July 1953, the ministry decided to set up a special committee of eminent scientists to investigate whether humans should in future be exposed to nerve gas. The committee was headed by Dr (later Lord) Edgar Adrian, then the President of the Royal Society and winner of the 1932 Nobel Prize for Medicine for his work on nerve cells. He asked two other distinguished scientists to sit on the ad hoc committee – Sir Rudolph Peters and Professor (later Sir) Roy Cameron. Porton has claimed that this inquiry was carried out by 'independent scientists'.[48] This is not true. All three had done work for Porton.[49] The trio were also involved for many years with the network of official committees – made up of outside scientists, military officials and Porton staff – which advised Porton. These influential committees sat behind closed doors and had access to most, if not all, of Porton's secrets.[50] There was even a family connection – Dr Edgar Adrian's son appears to have been working on the nerve gas experiment which used Ronald Maddison as a human 'guinea pig'.[51]

This ad hoc committee reviewed the evidence and interviewed senior Porton staff in charge of the experiments.[52] In its report produced a month later, the Adrian committee recommended that the nerve gas experiments should be allowed to continue, but with specific restrictions.[53] The trio stressed that human experiments were important to chemical warfare research. They acknowledged that although a great deal could be learnt from animal tests, it was still necessary to experiment on humans to gauge the toxicities of chemical weapons. 'Many thousands of tests with various chemical warfare agents have been made at Porton on human subjects. They have been made until recently without serious results and have supplied essential information which could not have been gained in any other way. Such a record inspires confidence in the general standard of work at Porton and in the precautions adopted in human tests and we are also confident that the standards are no lower now than they have been in the past.' They stipulated that in all experiments, only sarin was to be used.

The Adrian committee was 'satisfied' that experiments in which men breathed in low concentrations of nerve gas were 'without serious risk', provided that the usual stringent precautions were employed. They argued, 'If all such experiments were banned, it would be impossible to study the effects of [possible treatments], to estimate the likelihood of minor casualties, the effects of repeated exposures etc. Animal experiments can give little quantitive information on such matters and although human experiments have already supplied much of the evidence, there are still some which should be made and could be made with safety.' The committee therefore recommended that for tests in which volunteers breathed in nerve gas, they should not be exposed to dosages of more than 15 mg min m^{-3} of sarin.

But the committee imposed a much stricter restriction on experiments aimed at determining the lethal dose of nerve gas. They recommended that in such tests, no more than 5 milligrams of sarin should be dropped on the skin of the human 'guinea pigs'. This was a minute amount, and a substantial reduction, compared to the quantities of 200 milligrams and more administered to Maddison and many others in the fateful experiment. This vast reduction was due to the three scientists' concern that when the liquid was dropped onto the skin, the amount of nerve gas which was actually absorbed into the body varied greatly from one person to another. They decided that until the cause of these variations was better understood, it would be unsafe to drop high doses to the skin. 'The application of [nerve gas] in liquid form to the skin is clearly too dangerous a procedure if the dose is within the toxic range for the majority of the subjects.' But the committee added that it was 'clearly important' that Porton should continue to study how nerve gas passed through the human skin under various conditions such as from contaminated clothing or straight onto bare skin. 'We are therefore in agreement with the authorities at Porton that direct tests on human subjects are desirable and that they can be made without risk by using very small doses of radio-active sarin.'

Officials were aware that Maddison's death made it difficult to carry out more experiments with liquid sarin on the skin of the human 'guinea pigs'. One high-ranking mandarin commented that the death was 'dramatic and certainly important', but was an 'exceptional' result out of a 'large number'. 'Unfortunately the risks of further accidents are clearly so high that we must proceed slowly and carefully and it will be sometime before it will be known whether, for instance, droplets of sarin are much more effective when dropped on to clothing than when applied to the bare skin.'[54] Another official noted, 'We know at present very little about its possibilities as a liquid, because the liquid is so dangerous that it is almost impossible to determine with any degree of exactness its effects on man.' As it turned out, it seems that after 1953, few, if any, volunteers from the armed services had nerve gas dripped onto their skin in the kind of experiment experienced by Maddison. Porton had permission to do so, but appears never to have risked that particular experiment again.

In another recommendation, the Adrian committee removed some of the responsibility for the human tests away from Porton officials. They decided that the biology committee – one of the official external committees consisting of academics and military officials which advised Porton – should be the 'authoritative advisers on any question' to do with human tests. This committee was to be the only body which decided whether the restrictions could be altered. As we will see, Porton staff were pushing to have the restraints relaxed within four years.

The Adrian committee's report is in some ways not surprising, given its members' close ties with Porton. Arguably all three scientists on the committee were imbued with Porton's mindset and were biased towards allowing the experiments to continue, albeit with restrictions. A truly independent committee, which had not had any previous contact with Porton, may have been shocked by the experiments when confronted with the details for the first time – and so ordered their immediate banning. It is an old and familiar trick of many an institution under threat to appoint a 'safe pair of hands' to carry out such inquiries for them. These 'safe pairs of hands' will know the institution's work and will often share many of their fundamental beliefs. Porton could get away with appointing such an insular committee because the human experiments were not subject to proper political accountability at the time. Throughout its eighty-year history, the programme of experiments has only recently been exposed to the sustained glare of outside scrutiny from politicians and the general public.[55]

The recommendations of the Adrian committee were accepted by government ministers. Significantly, this meant that these rules from then on carried the force of ministerial authority. It appears that this was the first time that government ministers had in effect imposed restrictions on the human experiments. By and large, decisions about the trials had previously been taken by Porton's director or, more usually, the official in charge of experiments, free from the interference of ministers. Judging from declassified papers, ministers had rarely even been notified of the details of Porton's human experiments in the past.

The MoD routinely insists that it has used 'very low and medically safe' amounts of nerve gas in its human experiments. In a memo in November 1959, a military official wrote that, out of the 2,771 volunteers who had been exposed to nerve gas in Porton's experiments since 1945, only 'four lost consciousness which might or might not have been' caused by the gas (excluding Maddison).[56] According to the military, in one case, a man in the late 1950s 'fainted momentarily while sitting on a stool still under observation 30 minutes after coming out of the gas chamber; he recovered consciousness before any first aid measures could be applied.' A leading Porton adviser commented that this man probably had a 'simple vaso vagal attack' (involving the blood circulation and the nerve supplying the heart, lungs and gut), although it was 'impossible' to say whether the attack had been triggered by the exposure to sarin (GB).[57]

Whether or not only four volunteers lost consciousness is difficult to verify. Two volunteers however who did pass out were Frank Stacey and John Nelson. Stacey, an RAF electrician for five years, volunteered in the summer of 1956 at the age of twenty-five because he was a 'bit bored' on his base.[58] He did not know what Porton was, but he certainly did not expect to have to do anything hazardous. He knew very little about nerve gas. On the last day of his stay, he was one of about sixteen men who were split into groups of four and directed into a glass cubicle – like a square goldfish bowl – in a gas chamber. They wore denim suits and a hood, but not gas masks or any other protection. The Porton scientists, on the other side of the glass, had donned gas masks. Stacey remembers thinking, 'If it's not harmful, why are they wearing gas masks?' The scientists told the volunteers that they would neither see nor smell the gas but would feel a smarting in their eyes and a tightness of the chest. They added that if the volunteers started to suffer anything more severe, they should indicate and the scientists would come in and take them out.

To monitor their concentration, the volunteers were to sit at tables playing cards after the vial containing the gas was broken in the chamber. Stacey recalled that after a few minutes, 'I started to feel a burning sensation, runny nose, and a tightness in my chest. I put my hand up and got up to start to walk to the door. I can't remember anything else. I passed out. The next thing I knew I could feel water being poured over my head and somebody saying, "He's coming around, thank God".' He believed he was out for around five minutes and had been carried to a room next to the chamber. The scientists said they were glad he had volunteered for the experiment because 'he was one of their prized specimens' – the pupils of his eyes had shrunk so small that they had not seen anything like it before. He could see virtually nothing. His eyes recovered after a few days. (In later life, however, he developed high blood pressure and bad eyesight, which he suspected were 'enhanced' by the nerve gas experiments.)

John Nelson also volunteered for Porton in the mid-1950s to get away from the dull routine of his National Service. 'Life was pretty boring at the time so I thought "What the hell?".'[59] He recalls, 'There was between eight and ten of us. We went into the gas chamber and I noticed lots of pipes at ceiling height. I remember hearing fans as if air was either being pumped in or taken out. We were told via a loudspeaker to remove our gas masks, which we did. And the last thing I remember was what felt like a clamp being sprung around my temples and around my chest. I don't remember anything after that. The next thing I knew I was in a hospital bed.

'I couldn't see very well at that time, and if somebody moved past me, it was like a grey shadow. Everything was different shades of grey, so I was completely disorientated. I felt nauseous. I was perspiring a lot. I felt very uncomfortable. Everything was very, very vague after that for the next three to four days.' He believes that the tests may have caused the chest and breathing problems he has suffered since.

Following the Adrian committee, the Ministry of Supply lifted the ban on nerve gas experiments in September 1953, four months after Maddison's death.[60] However, in true bureaucratic style, the tests could not be resumed until each of the military services had given their approval. The Admiralty gave their consent in November, the War Office in December and, after a few clarifications, the Air Ministry in January 1954. The resumption of tests was not announced to Parliament, nor, apparently, did any vigilant MP remember to follow up the matter and ask any questions.[61]

Porton's programme of human tests had survived the calamity of Maddison's death. The establishment was – so to speak – back in business. The number of volunteers exposed to nerve gas grew again over the next few years, and although only eight were tested in the year 1954-55, the total rose to 303 in the following year and fluctuated around the 200 mark for the rest of the decade.[62]

Despite its tight secrecy, Maddison's death had received a fair amount of publicity in the press. One volunteer who remembers reading about it was army regular William Guest. In early 1953, he had been injected three times with unknown chemicals which had forced his tongue to swell up, making it difficult to breathe, and on reading the news of the death, he thought, 'My God! It didn't come as no surprise to me because [the experiments] were so severe.'[63] However, many of those who later agreed to go to Porton may never have heard about it. Whether it would have altered their decision to volunteer is another matter. Robert Grandison, a national serviceman who went to Porton seven months after the tragedy, remembers that around fifty volunteers from his camp at Catterick in Yorkshire pulled out after finding out about the death, leaving just him and two others. Why did he still go? 'We were young and daft. You just went on with it,' he says, adding that they were not bothered.

With the ban lifted, Porton pursued a number of different objectives in its nerve gas experiments in the mid-1950s. One was to determine how well servicemen would be able to conduct military operations after they had been attacked with nerve gas. Opinion within Porton and the military was divided on this question. From their previous experiments, the scientists knew the signs and symptoms caused by low concentrations of sarin in the air. One side of the debate believed that such symptoms would 'so "harass" the soldier that his efficiency would be significantly impaired', whereas others felt that 'well-trained, well-motivated troops would suffer little more than minor embarrassment and would be capable of performing their duties with their usual efficiency.'

To settle the argument, a mock exercise – code-named Hangover – was organised on the large ranges around Porton in July 1954.[64] A total of 139 infantrymen from the 1st Battalion of the Wiltshire Regiment took part in the exercise and were exposed with no protection to dosages of sarin of between 11 and 13 mg min m^{-3}. In the first phase of the operation, more than 100 of them were required to march for around an hour and then attack a defended position in daylight. In the exercise's scenario, they were fired upon with artillery shells containing nerve gas during the battle. Since Porton did not want to actually unleash the nerve gas in the open air, the men were temporarily withdrawn from the mock battlefield and taken to a gas chamber in another part of Porton where they were exposed to the sarin. They were then returned to the battlefield to continue the fight and assessed on how they performed.

Military assessors commented that only a few troops attacked in a way which was below the usual standards. They noted that although there was 'little trouble in handling weapons and equipment', the troops' main problem was that they could not see as well as usual. The sight of the officers in charge also suffered, slowing down the delivery of their orders. The observers wrote that 'all ranks were very cheerful and only one case of undue irritability was observed. Mental reactions were possibly a little slow, particularly immediately after exposure to (sarin), and there was a certain amount of apathy, lack of confidence and loss of initiative.'

In the next phase of the exercise, thirty-two soldiers had to drive across open countryside at dusk and then set up weapons such as mortars and anti-tank guns. The watching military observers commented that on the whole, the poisoned troops performed well. For example, they drove quite competently, even though they could not see properly, 'One driver was observed to be completely incapable of judging distance and had to drive entirely on the tail light of the truck in front.' The observers wrote that, once again, morale was good with 'nearly everyone being cheerful, apart from a few complaints of tiredness and headaches'.

In the third and final phase, thirty infantrymen went on night patrols following set routes with a compass for an hour or so – a couple of hours after being exposed to sarin in the chamber. There were mixed and inconclusive results. Of the four patrols, one was completed satisfactorily. The others were affected because the patrol leaders were inexperienced in working a compass, some of which did not light up adequately. 'Morale on the whole was good, but again patrol commanders tended to be irritable and easily ruffled.' The report of the exercise shows that of the 139 men, all suffered miosis in their eyes, half had a runny nose, and fewer than half experienced headaches and a tightness in the chest. Porton thanked them for 'so cheerfully accepting the physical discomforts entailed in the exercise'.

Porton's scientists believed the lesson of the exercise was learning that the biggest hindrance to the fighting soldier gassed with this concentration of sarin would be the effect to his eyes. Another problem was that he would be more tired than normal, and as for the officers, 'commanders became rather irritable and unduly flustered'. The scientists believed that the infantry company had performed well in the military manoeuvres during the daytime, but not so well at night. They thought that the physical effects of the sarin poisoning would not impede the 'determined infantryman' in daylight. They were, however, not so sure about the psychological effects on the men. They speculated that during the day, 'a unit of intact morale' could cope, but at night, the men would have been vulnerable because they would be prone to panic or plunging morale, especially since their sight would have been hampered.

In April of the following year, Porton organised a second, similar exercise code-named Hangover Two.[65] This time, 169 unprotected servicemen – again from the 1st Battalion, Wiltshire Regiment – were gassed with sarin in 'minor' dosages ranging between 9 and 14 mg min m^{-3}. Porton wanted to assess how the men, after poisoning, would react to being treated with atropine and wearing a respirator.

Once again, on the ranges around the establishment, the men had to enact a mock assault and go on night patrols. As with previous experiments, the men were afflicted with the usual symptoms of nerve gas poisoning. One of the main ways of alleviating such poisoning is the antidote, atropine, itself a poisonous chemical first isolated in 1831 from the deadly nightshade plant. However, atropine is by no means trouble-free. Since it is first and foremost a powerful poison itself, ungassed soldiers who are injected with atropine run the risk of being incapacitated by it. On trial in the Hangover Two exercise was a device being developed by Porton – the semi-automatic injector. The troops pressed the injector against their leg, which in turn compressed a spring which punched a hidden needle through the skin and injected 2 milligrams of atropine sulphate.

One group of men who were treated with only atropine and did not wear respirators found that although it did relieve the symptoms of running noses and tightness of chest, this was 'outweighed' by the increased number of headaches, nausea, dry mouth and difficulties in seeing. Porton concluded that, had this been a real battle, the men would have probably been killed – they could not see the enemy and they had also become 'hopelessly lost' on patrol, since their leaders were rendered helpless in using their compasses. Porton concluded that 'eyesight and mental alertness are so impaired that operations such as patrolling may be hazardous by day and would be definitely dangerous at night.'

A second group in the experiment was allowed respirators but was not treated with atropine. Surprisingly, they discovered the respirators prolonged the inhaled effects of nerve gas, such as the tightness of the chest and runny nose, as well as restricting the sight of the men. The respirators also caused mental discomfort during intense physical effort – at least fifteen men were seen surreptitiously lifting the facepiece of the respirator at one stage in the assault. Porton concluded: 'Further sustained effort, such as against an enemy counter-attack, would not appear to be possible.' The third group, who were both injected with atropine and wearing respirators, experienced the combined effect of both and so suffered the worst.

The exercise emphasised how difficult it would be to treat and protect troops who have been attacked with relatively low levels of nerve gas. At the time, servicemen were being trained to don their respirators and inject themselves with atropine whenever nerve gas was believed to be present. And yet both the respirators and atropine had added to the distress and pain of the gassed men in the exercise. Porton concluded that there was no alternative since, if soldiers were attacked with nerve gas, it would be impossible to detect on the battlefield whether it was in fact a lethal amount or a smaller quantity. Commanders simply had to accept that troops protecting themselves against nerve gas would fight less efficiently.

One volunteer who was – and still is – happy to take part in these trials was Michael Beck, then a private in the 1st Battalion of the Wiltshire Regiment.[66] Aged about twenty, he volunteered to help the country: 'We are talking about a very different time. What we have got to remember is that, back then, we were fully expecting a war with Communist Russia. Porton knew that the Russians had found nerve gas. What Porton wanted was to get an antidote against it. It may sound stupid these days.' Like many others, he also found the extra money and leave useful. He went along with his twin brother, who was in the same regiment, and once at Porton, he says that he was fully warned that he was to be exposed to nerve gas. In the trial, he and the others went over the assault course and fired some rounds with his rifle. He was then tested with nerve gas with no protection in a chamber. 'When we came out, we had our eyes smarting as if you had something in your eyes.' A little while later, they again went over the assault course and fired their rifles. 'For three or four days, one had like little pig eyes. We all smoked then. To strike a match to light a cigarette was painful – the actual light of the flame coming into your eyes would make your eyes smart. You shut your eyes to protect them.' However, he thinks little of this discomfort.

'It was all part and parcel of a day's soldiering. You suffered more pain than that when you were on a route march, and things like that.' Beck is now 'incensed' by some of the volunteers' complaints and their coverage in the media – 'as if we were a heap of bloody idiots being marched into Porton Down like the Nazis marched them into Belsen. This is what annoys me. People talk as if we did not know what was happening. There was no pressure put on anybody to go up there.' He strongly believes that the tests have done him no harm in the long run.

A large nerve gas experiment in the mid-1950s was run by Dr Van Sim, an American scientist who, for two decades, carried out human tests in the US chemical warfare programme.[67] Dr Sim spent a year or so on attachment to Porton. He used 211 human 'guinea pigs' in a set of experiments to determine how long it took for the pupils in the eyes to contract after they had been exposed to sarin.[68] These 'guinea pigs' were sent into the gas chamber wearing respirators and protective clothing. At a given signal, they were told to remove their respirators for either one or two minutes. One batch of 136 men were not allowed any protection for their eyes, while another thirty-three had their eyes bandaged. A further forty-two went into the chamber thirty minutes after being injected with atropine. The dosages of nerve gas ranged up to 15 mg min m^{-3}. Only the effect of the poisoning on the eyes is recorded in Dr Sim's short report of the experiments – no other clinical symptoms are described. As with previous experiments in which eyes have been exposed to sarin, the volunteers commented that they felt 'they had blinkers on' or that 'it feels like you are looking down a gun barrel.' Dr Sim himself added, 'Bright lights or exposure to bright sunshine definitely increased the eye pain. Focusing on nearby subjects, such as looking at the finger close to the nose, caused an increase in pain.' In one rather obvious conclusion, he commented that the eyes contracted more slowly and less severely at the lower dosages of 5 mg min m^{-3} than at the higher dosages of 10 or 15 mg min m^{-3}.

Porton again attempted to assess the psychological effects of nerve gas poisoning as a continuation of two previous studies carried out in 1952 and 1953 (see previous chapter). Eight men – aged between eighteen and twenty – were put into the gas chamber, without respirators or eye-shields, and were exposed to just under 15 mg min m^{-3} of sarin.[69] Before and after this, they underwent a variety of intelligence and aptitude tests and were measured for 'changes of mood, alertness, and social participation'. As before, the results showed that the subjects' intellectual capacity was not seriously spoilt. Their ability to process information was slightly reduced. However there was a 'marked' plunge in their moods. Outwardly, the men, although lethargic, were 'moderately cheerful', but Porton believed this was only 'superficial'. From a list of 102 traits, the volunteers had to choose which ones best described their personalities. Porton found that the men were distinctly unhappy and depressed after being exposed to nerve gas, emotions which were combined with a 'feeling of reduced mental alertness and a tendency to social withdrawal'.

Perhaps it is surprising that a few years after Maddison's death, Porton was back testing large numbers of human 'guinea pigs' to nerve gas relatively quickly. They were able to do so because Porton was protected by the utmost secrecy and was not open to democratic scrutiny. The nerve gas experiments could be run at such a high level precisely because the work of Porton scientists was concealed. Behind all the secrecy, they were left to regulate themselves without much interference from the public. In one respect, Maddison may be seen as a victim of a failure in this system of self-policing.

In the fraught climate of the Cold War, the scientists were driven on by fear of the Soviet Union and the threat of its nerve gas arsenal. In these circumstances, it is difficult to see how the scientists could have been restrained. Hundreds of men were being exposed to deadly nerve gases. It certainly appears an uphill task for Porton to prove to the public that the safety of each and every one of these individuals was properly respected and cared for. In the Maddison experiment, one human 'guinea pig' died, another one almost died, and at least five others suffered badly. It is indeed fortunate that more did not die in this era.

Maddison's death has always been a raw subject for Porton and Whitehall officials, as it is difficult for any government to admit a mistake. It is an emotive charge to claim that Porton was out of control in this era, using human subjects as the scientists pleased, in a Wild West atmosphere. Many believe that Maddison was killed in an irresponsible experiment. The outcome of the current Wiltshire police investigation is likely to shed more light on how he died. It may even settle the outstanding question of who, if anyone, is responsible for his death.

CHAPTER SIX
Breaking the Code

The ethical standards of Porton's human experiments have now come under scrutiny in the Wiltshire police investigation. As well as the inquiry into the death of Ronald Maddison, the Wiltshire force is also currently considering whether to prosecute Porton over allegations that human 'guinea pigs' were tricked into taking part in the experiments when they thought that they were volunteering for common cold research. If proved, this is a very serious and highly damaging condemnation of Porton's ethics.

The atrocities committed by Nazi scientists during their experiments on people triggered the first substantial attempt to formulate a universal code of ethics for human testing. A ten-point code was drawn up in an optimistic atmosphere in which nations strove to build a lasting peace and to ensure that the horrors of the Second World War could never be repeated. This code – set out in 1947 in the judgement of one of the numerous war crimes trials – has become known as the Nuremberg Code and has been the cornerstone and origin of modern debate on the ethics of human experimentation. (The full code is reproduced in appendix three.)

Seven Nazi scientists were sentenced to death after a lengthy war crimes case called the 'Doctors' Trial'. The court heard sickening accounts of how the scientists had deliberately and methodically killed and tortured large numbers of human 'guinea pigs' during experiments in concentration camps. For example, many victims died after they had been forced to stay in a tank of ice-cold water for up to three hours. Others were intentionally infected with diseases to investigate the causes of such illnesses and possible treatments. Thousands were made barren and impotent by scientists in experiments involving surgery, X-ray and various drugs. The scientists were seeking to develop the most efficient method of sterilising millions, requiring the least amount of time and effort.[1] (For further discussion of Nazi chemical warfare experiments on people, see chapter four.)

German science had long been respected and honoured around the world; many of the famous names in science were German, while the industrial might of the country had been built on its scientific and technical prowess.

With this in mind, these horrendous experiments exemplify how German science had been subverted by the ideology of the Third Reich.

Sadly, these awful experiments were mirrored by a secretive germ warfare unit run by the Japanese military. Set up in 1935, scientists in Unit 731 conducted experiments for years on thousands of humans, mainly captured prisoners of war. The unit was dedicated towards developing a biological weapon which could bring victory for Japan.[2] Human 'guinea pigs' were intentionally infected with harmful organisms, often being injected with deadly diseases, or tethered to posts so that germ-filled bombs could be exploded next to them. Many victims were killed and dissected so that the effects of the viruses and bacteria on their bodies and internal organs could be tracked. These experiments by German and Japanese scientists are the most notorious and barbaric known to the world.

As already stated, it is only fair to judge the ethics of Porton's experiments by the circumstances and yardsticks of the ethical standards which were in place at the time. Accordingly, the human experiments after 1947 must therefore be measured against the Nuremberg Code and the developments in ethics which have flowed from it.

The first and most important principle of the Nuremberg Code concerns voluntary and informed consent. This means that the subject of an experiment must have freely agreed to participate in the test, without having been forced or duped. Specifically it lays down that the subject must be able to 'exercise free power of choice' without 'any element' of fraud or deceit. To this end, the scientists in charge of the experiment are obliged to give the subject a full explanation of the test before the experiment so that he or she fully understands what will happen and can therefore make an 'enlightened decision' whether or not to participate. The subjects should be told the nature, duration, and purpose of the experiment, how it is to be conducted, 'all inconveniences and hazards' which can reasonably be expected, and any possible effects on their health. This principle, according to the code, is 'absolutely essential' to any ethical human experiment. Compared to previous codes and regulations, this principle of the Nuremberg Code broke new ground in being so adamant in its intention to protect human subjects.

Porton officially maintains that all its human experiments have been 'morally acceptable' and complied with the Nuremberg Code, particularly its first principle of informed and voluntary consent. The establishment has claimed that volunteers 'have always, as a matter of course, been informed of the name, nature and possible short-term outcome' of the chemicals before they participated.[3] (The only admitted exception to this was in the experiments with hallucinogenic drugs in the 1960s, described in chapter eight). This claim is fiercely disputed by many Porton volunteers who were tested after the Nuremberg Code was introduced in 1947. When interviewed, many volunteers have repeatedly said they had little idea of what was tested on them, and did not even know the names of the chemicals to which they had been exposed.[4] Many maintain that they were told little of what they were to expect in the experiment. It is difficult to see how the human 'guinea pigs' could have possibly made an informed decision to participate if they did not know the name of the chemical or what was going to happen to them. Some of the volunteers confess that they barely even knew what Porton was. For many volunteers, they only found out the details of their experiments (such as the names of the chemicals, the doses and the point of the test) many years or decades later when they wrote to Porton requesting such information.

It is, however, also evident that a proportion of volunteers were in fact told beforehand what was going to happen to them. As a rough rule of thumb, the human 'guinea pigs' seem only to have been aware of the chemical to which they were to be exposed if it happened to be a well-known chemical weapon. So, for example, many volunteers can name mustard gas as being the chemical involved since it has been around and in the public consciousness since the First World War. Moreover, Porton scientists seem not to have been so secretive where mustard gas was involved.

It is clear that, despite its claims, Porton did not strictly enforce the most vital principle of the Nuremberg Code – informed consent – in many instances. One major reason for this lies with its tight secrecy. The human rights of the volunteers clashed directly with the traditional 'need-to-know' rules of military security. During the Cold War, all military activities were clothed in intense layers of secrecy to protect the defences and capabilities of the nation. Especially sensitive were the programmes for developing weapons of mass destruction – chemical, biological and nuclear weapons. Porton saw it as unthinkable to disclose details of a newly-discovered chemical (which could after all turn out to be a crucial weapon) to volunteers who had generally been drawn from the lower ranks of the services. This issue of stringent security was quickly raised by a War Office official in 1959 when – during the highly delicate V-agent debate described below – it was suggested that it should be made 'mandatory for volunteers to read a description of the tests, supplemented by oral explanation'.[5] Porton officials were worried that the volunteers – intentionally or otherwise – could have blabbed about the chemicals to others, and their secrets would have slowly leaked out.[6] In this atmosphere, the human rights of the volunteers, those on whom the chemicals were being tested, were sacrificed for the sake of national security.

Porton's work has always been carried out behind closed doors, and during much of its testing programme, the ethical standards of the experiments have been governed from within. The human experiments were subjected to limited scrutiny from outside the establishment. Peer review – in which work is laid open to the critical judgement of other scientists – is an important method of controlling standards in the scientific world. However, the only outside scientists who were permitted to examine the human tests sat on the official advisory committees.[7] The job of these committees – which were a mixture of external experts, Porton staff and military officials – was to review and give advice to the establishment, particularly when problems arose. But, as argued in chapter five, the outside scientists on these committees were sympathetic to Porton's work and so were unlikely to challenge fundamentally its ways. Indeed they would never have been appointed to the committees and given access to Porton's secrets if they had been hostile to, or even sceptical of, the establishment. The death of Ronald Maddison in 1953 was a key episode in this respect. Outside scientists from these committees sat on the ad hoc committee which reviewed the future of human tests after his death. However, these scientists uniformly had a close relationship with Porton, and they recommended that the programme of experiments should continue, albeit with some restrictions. A truly independent committee is likely to have been stunned by the nerve gas experiments and closed them down completely.

Members of Parliament and the public have more or less been barred from scrutinising the human experiments in detail during the last eight decades. Without such scrutiny from outside, Porton was for many years under little pressure to justify its programme of human experiments, and could therefore operate in the dark without any awkward questions from members of the general public which – if they had known more – may have demanded tighter ethical controls or indeed an end to the experiments altogether. It is interesting that when details about the American chemical warfare experiments on humans became widely known in 1975, the public outcry was so loud that the Pentagon stopped the tests and has never restarted them. The British testing programme was threatened in a similar way by the death of Maddison; the full details of the circumstances of his death had the potential to shock MPs and ordinary citizens, thereby forcing a permanent end to the testing. But very little information was released about the death or the tests at that time, and the inevitable outcry was avoided.

Another factor in the lax enforcement of the Nuremberg principle of informed consent results from the very nature of military life. Junior members of the Armed Forces are trained to follow orders. This is the essence of military discipline which commanders believe is crucial to an effective fighting force. In this sort of climate, many volunteers did not expect to be informed about the tests or treated with respect. They simply did as they were instructed. However they did have an inherent measure of trust in their commanding officers that they would not be placed in jeopardy in the experiments or suffer lasting ill health.

As already seen, many volunteers were very young servicemen – in their teens or early twenties – who were, as some of them admit, naive. These raw recruits certainly did not believe that they could query the experiments or demand more information before they were exposed. Eddie Roberts from Lancashire, who was in the Army for seven years, was a typical teenage volunteer for Porton in the mid-1960s.[8] He says, 'There was a lot of tests that we were not told what they were,' particularly concerning tablets. On arrival, he and the other volunteers were given an introductory briefing by Porton staff. They were 'told not to worry about anything because nothing untoward will be used on you' and that they would not come to any harm. 'When you are eighteen and you have somebody standing there in front of you with a white coat, you tend to believe them. You never questioned anything. You never questioned authority. You took what was told to you at face value. When you are a young squaddie, you are the lowest of the low. You just do as you are told.' He now believes that he was tested with nerve gas in the chamber, but he was not informed what the chemical was. 'When we got outside, five or ten minutes afterwards, quite a few of the guys keeled over. There were guys vomiting and all sorts.' He felt 'very queasy' for a couple of hours. A year later, back on army duty, he had an unpleasant experience when his legs seized up suddenly. He was immobilised for weeks: 'I could not move at all. My legs would not work. It frightens you'. Since then, he has suffered various illnesses which he believes were caused by the Porton experiments. There are occasions when – for no reason – he starts to tremble from head to toe. 'I can't stop. It's embarrassing at times'. He is bitter that he was treated in an 'unethical and disgusting' way by Porton. He angrily regrets ever going to the establishment, adding that he would now be a lot more sceptical about the reassurances he was given before the experiments.

Did Porton take advantage of young people's gullibility in their search for sufficient volunteers for their experiments? Looking back, it is apparent that Porton had an extra responsibility to inform naive volunteers of the perils and pain of the experiments. Once again, it appears that the needs of the military triumphed over the rights of the individual.

One former Porton scientist who helped run the Cold War human trials acknowledged that in hindsight, the volunteers should have been told more before they went into the experiments. 'Obviously, scientifically, it is very difficult to tell somebody what will happen, a) because it does not always happen, and b) if you tell them they are going to see little green men, they are going to see little green men.'[9]

One curious mystery of Porton's experiments after the Second World War is the significant number of volunteers who believed that they had volunteered to take part in tests to find a cure for the common cold – and then unexpectedly found themselves at the painful end of a chemical warfare test. It is a persistent story told by volunteers who were at Porton at completely different times and have never spoken to each other.

As we saw in chapter five, Ronald Maddison died in a nerve gas experiment in 1953 when, according to a colleague, he believed that he was going to participate in a common cold test. Some volunteers feel that, purely and simply, they were duped into going to Porton in this way. One of them is Douglas Shave, who was a nineteen-year-old National Serviceman at RAF Bicester in Oxfordshire in 1950. He says he saw a notice at his base calling for volunteers for common cold research at Porton Down. 'I can remember that notice as clearly as if it was today. There's no question about that. I think that it was all very unfair. In those days, we were all very naive and green. We were all mummy's boys. Nineteen-year-olds are completely different now. They have all grown up somehow.' Instead of common cold research, he was put into a gas chamber for five successive days at Porton for between fifteen and forty-five minutes without a gas mask or any protection, and to this day, he has no idea which gas was pumped into the chamber. 'It made me cough and splutter quite a bit. My eyes were watering badly.' He later suffered severe skin problems – such as boils on the face and eczema on his back – which he attributes to the Porton experiments. He has been left angry and bitter by the experience, believing that he and others were 'absolutely conned' into going to Porton through 'complete subterfuge'.[10]

Ray Hutchins, then eighteen, recalls that he was a 'frightened little lad' when he was blinded for days after a nerve gas test.[11] The army gunner had volunteered around 1951 believing that he was taking part in research for the common cold. He cannot now remember whether this was written down on the appeal notices or whether he was told this by commanding officers. As a 'broke, homesick lad', he jumped at the chance to earn some extra money and leave. 'When I got there, I was assured that it was not painful, there were no after-effects, it was a simple thing.' Coming from a military family, he trusted the scientists as he did not have a clue what was going to happen. But he realised that it was 'sod all' to do with the common cold when he was blinded, albeit temporarily. He had been sent into the glass-sided gas chamber, protected except for his eyes. 'Two or three hours afterwards, the pain came. Oh god, it was excruciating. I remember it well. It was dreadful.' He is in no doubt that 'the buggers took advantage of us'. 'They owe us,' he laments. He has demanded both an apology and compensation, but has won neither so far. He says that he has been 'tormented' for years by a constant pain just behind the eyes, which he believes 'absolutely' has been caused by the Porton test. Despite his feelings now, Hutchins initially kept quiet for a long time about the experiment. 'Everybody was terrified of the MoD, you know, "big brother". We had a different generation. We cared about the Official Secrets Act, we came through the Cold War.'

RAF regular Lawrence McAndrew volunteered in the early 1950s after he spotted an appeal for subjects for common cold research on the noticeboard of his base. Instead he was exposed to nerve gas.[12] He had been warned beforehand that his vision would be harmed. The pupils of his eyes went to pinpoints for five or six days, and he was issued with dark glasses. 'With the glasses on, you could see for miles. Without them, you could hardly see in front of you.' He says that nowadays, his eyes go all red, puffed up and sore from time to time. On the common cold research, he says, 'They told us a lie.' He adds that if he had had been told that he was actually going to be tested with nerve gas, 'you would have to be a nutter to do it'. He regrets volunteering, especially since the enticement – weekend leave – was not worth it.

One National Serviceman who did not end up at Porton was David Clutterbuck, who was in the Royal Signals in 1953. He remembers that the notices sent around military units appealing for volunteers did not state that the research was for chemical warfare. 'It was definitely only for common cold research. There was nothing else at all.' He adds that he was pressurised by his superiors to volunteer, and after he refused to go, he was called 'a wimp' by the officers. 'To volunteer in National Service meant you were virtually forced to do it. You had no option. It was like being on a different planet in those days. You had no chance.'[13]

A crucial target of the Wiltshire police investigation must therefore be to find out exactly what was on the notices calling for Porton volunteers which were circulated all those years ago around military units. Alan Walton, a former RAF mechanic, is certain that the notice, which went up on the

NAAFI board of his base in 1954, appealed for volunteers to take part in common cold research at Porton Down. 'I can remember it as if it was yesterday, written down. I would put my life on it.'[14] Like others, it was not until the late 1990s that he finally realised that he had actually taken part in chemical warfare experiments. During his time at Porton, he says that he was told nothing, and never questioned what was going on. 'I just trusted them because they were officers and I was there to do the common cold tests. That was it.' Then a 'naive' twenty-year-old, he had originally volunteered because he liked the idea of a bit of extra leave and pay, and he thought that he was helping the country. Of course, he also believed that he was going to be involved in common cold research. He did not know what Porton was, nor would he have fully understood what nerve gas was if he had been told that he was going to be exposed to it. He says that he only took part in one day of tests – and then spent the rest of the week in Porton's hospital. He was put into a gas chamber with five others without a mask for a matter of minutes. He says he will never forget what happened when he came out. 'I thought I was dying. I could not breathe. I had severe pain in my eyes, in my head.' Staff were 'shouting at him', asking what he was feeling. Nowadays, he suffers from multiple sclerosis and epilepsy, which he is convinced have been caused by the Porton tests. He has had difficulty winning a war pension, and Porton staff claim that they have no records of him being sent into a gas chamber or being exposed to any kind of poison gases. Today, Walton is livid at the way he perceives he had been 'tricked' and treated 'really badly'. 'I know they are lying and withholding things.'

RAF National Serviceman Michael Paynter says that he was 'silly enough' to volunteer for Porton twice, but is firmly convinced that he too was lured there on a bogus pretext on both occasions.[15] He angrily maintains that he went to Porton in 1954 and 1955, knowing little about the tests, except that they were somehow related to common cold research. 'I was a naive eighteen-year-old lad. I got into my head at the time that this was all to do with inhaling things that caused the colds and things like that, so I was not suspicious of the gas mask. It was forty years later that I discovered the actual extent of this.' He says firmly that on both occasions he saw an official memo on the noticeboard of his base calling for volunteers for common cold research which was to be conducted at Porton Down. The memo looked the same both times, even though he had moved to another base on the second occasion. He had assumed that they were going to be 'quite innocent tests' which would do him no harm, but now says that he has suffered decades of illnesses because of this 'deception…a lifetime of hell. I am so angry you would not believe my anger. As far as I am concerned, these people have got to be made accountable for things that have happened. They could not care less about me, once I had left there. We go for these tests, once our usefulness has run out, they don't want to know about us. It is an absolutely incredible situation.' He insisted, 'I would certainly not have volunteered if I had known the true nature of these tests.' According to Porton, Paynter took part in various trials – wearing protective clothing and backpacks in different temperatures while running on a treadmill, and testing whether his skin would react badly to rubber compounds which were to be used in gas masks.[16] They claim that he was not tested with any poison gases, but he and hundreds of others were exposed to an artificial fog as Porton scientists were investigating the terrible smogs which were afflicting London.[17] Paynter does not accept this version of events.

Another RAF National Serviceman, Gordon Bell, from Sunderland, went to Porton three times in 1959 and 1960. Aged twenty-one, he first went after seeing a notice asking for volunteers for common cold research at an unspecified military establishment. 'That's undoubtedly true. That's why I volunteered. It was for a bit of extra money, a bit of leave and it was doing a bit of good. I would never have set foot in Porton if it was for chemical warfare. No way.' He is livid that he and others were conned into going to Porton. 'I am mad as hell. It is a betrayal and the lowest trick in the book. I am furious that they violated the Nuremberg Code willy-nilly. They could not have cared less about it because they thought that they would never get caught. It was rampant.'

He maintains that he was never told any information about the chemicals to which he was exposed. In one experiment, he had to stand in front of a stream of gas – 'They told us to stand there as long as we could' – but could not endure the acrid gas for even a minute. 'My face was stinging, my eyes were running, my throat was red raw, my lungs were burning.' Afterwards, he was put on a static bicycle and told to pedal for as long as he could. A chemical in another experiment made him 'weak at the knees and nauseated', and in a further test, he was told to lie down on a bed where an unknown substance was injected into his arm. 'I never could find out what I was injected with.' The chemical had little obvious effect on him, although nurses continued to monitor him for the rest of the day. A few years later, however, he started to get skin problems, such as red blotches on the arms, legs and chest, which have flared up from time to time ever since. He also thinks that these were caused by the Porton experiments.[18] He was deeply shocked and angered when he finally found out thirty-five or so years later that he had not taken part in common cold research at Porton all that time

Gordon Bell at the beginning of his national service in 1959, the same year he went to Porton for the first time.

Gordon Bell, 1999. His complaints triggered the Wiltshire police investigation.

ago. It was his complaint to detectives in 1999 which sparked the investigation by the Wiltshire police force into Porton's human tests.

Royston Clarke, another volunteer who thought he was going to take part in common cold tests, experienced 'frightening' hallucinations during experiments in 1958 (described in chapter eight).[19] He says that when he arrived at Porton, a member of staff explained that the experiments were 'just injections for colds and things like that.' Later he queried this, just prior to being injected with the chemical that produced the hallucinations. He says the scientists replied, 'Well it is really, but we're testing other things as well.'

It appears that this confusion continued throughout the 1960s and at least into the early 1970s. Typical, it seems, are the recollections of three men from the Staffordshire Regiment, one of the myriad sources from which Porton sought to recruit volunteers. Jim Buxton, a private with the regiment from 1960 to 1969, recalls that Porton was 'always' sending circulars around his regiment appealing for volunteers.[20] He believes that common cold research was 'definitely written down' on the appeals which went up on his regiment's noticeboard. He adds that when he and his colleagues asked what they would actually do at Porton, they were told by older soldiers and others that 'they get so many of you with the common cold, so many without the common cold, and then they put you in a battle situation to find out how long it is before the ones with the common cold go down'. Despite the offer of extra pay, he was never tempted to volunteer because 'I just don't want stuff pumped into my body'. Mike Underhill, a lance corporal in the late 1960s, remembers these Porton appeals 'regularly' going up on the noticeboard.[21] He recalls that 'most' of the experiments were concerned with the flu and the common cold – 'to give you flu and see what the effects were'. He believes that the soldiers then had to undergo 'extreme exercise'. He says that this was the impression he gained from those who had actually gone to Porton.

Another man, who worked on the administration side of the Staffordshire Regiment in the late 1960s and early 1970s, received and processed the Porton circulars as part of his duties.[22] He remembers that the circulars did not spell out the details of the proposed experiments; instead the appeals stated that the volunteers would take part in various chemical warfare and medical tests – 'quite of a lot' of which were for the common cold. Even an airman serving between 1971 and 1976 recalls that the official circulars of his RAF base contained several requests a year for volunteers to assist in common cold research at Porton Down.[23]

Porton has stated categorically that it has never carried out any research to find a cure for the common cold.[24] The establishment also vehemently denies that military personnel were duped into participating in poison gas experiments when they believed that they were volunteering for common cold research. One Porton scientist who worked on the human experiments during this era maintains firmly that there was no conspiracy to con the volunteers. 'I don't think there was ever any deliberate dishonesty.'[25] No documentary evidence has so far surfaced to confirm that such a conspiracy existed.

So why did so many volunteers go to Porton under the illusion that they were taking part in such experiments? There may be a genuine reason behind the long-running muddle, since there was a research unit near Porton which did study the common cold. This civilian unit – based at Harnham Down, Salisbury between 1946 and 1990 – was managed by the Medical Research Council. It used to appeal regularly for volunteers from the British population.[26] Porton, however, has stated that it has never collaborated with the Common Cold Unit and that volunteers for the two establishments were never exchanged.[27]

Another explanation may be that the confusion was deliberately sown by Porton. As described in chapter two, Porton has been issuing appeals for volunteers through military units since 1925, but has frequently struggled to recruit sufficient numbers of human 'guinea pigs'. The appeals which were posted onto the noticeboards of these units were, however, never very fulsome in describing the experiments. As one senior Porton official frankly wrote in 1961 of the wording of these appeals, 'Experience has shown that detailed description tends to deter the serviceman and so now very little is said... The fewer details the better, but we must not be accused of "insulting the public's intelligence".'[28]

This economy with the truth appears to have created a vacuum in which misconceptions flourished. Without clear written descriptions, commanders of military units – under pressure to find volunteers – may have told waverers that the research was for the common cold in order to encourage them to volunteer.[29] It may have been used to play on the good nature of volunteers who wanted to help banish a persistent and irritating illness suffered by the general population. However, whatever their role, Porton appears to have done little to correct some of the volunteers' misconceptions once they had arrived at the establishment.[30] Ultimately, the responsibility for properly obtaining the informed consent of volunteers lies with Porton. At best, the confusion over the common cold was a lapse by Porton, at worst it was a deliberate and callous deception by scheming officials. The Nuremberg Code expressly forbids the use of 'fraud or deceit' in securing the consent of subjects. Whatever the suspicions, it is hard to establish the absolute truth because so many years have passed.

Porton has admitted that it never issued any directives to its staff to implement the provisions of the Nuremberg Code on human experiments which significantly weakens Porton's claim that it has always complied with the Code.[31] The public papers on Porton's experiments contain almost no discussion or reference to the Nuremberg Code. However, some commentators have suggested that the actual influence of the code throughout the scientific world in the first two decades after the Second World War has been exaggerated.[32] They have argued that the Code rarely figured in the minds of scientists and medical researchers in civilian, let alone military establishments. It appears that many in the scientific world regarded the code as only an ideal, and not something which should be rigorously applied in practice; it was associated more with war crimes and atrocities, but not run-of-the-mill research. One study described hundreds of experiments – published in open literature – conducted by civilian researchers around the world in the first twenty years after the Second World War which were to varying degrees unethical, unkind and dangerous. Not only did these tests carry a high level of risk, but the informed consent of the human 'guinea pigs' was also rarely obtained.

Little is known about the ethical standards of other chemical warfare establishments around the world which were conducting human experiments after the Second World War. Some light has been shed on the attempt to police tests carried out by Britain's ally, the United States of America. In 1953, the US Defence Secretary set out the Pentagon's policy on human experiments in a memorandum, adopting completely the Nuremberg Code's principle on informed consent. However an investigation many years later by the US Army's Inspector-General found that volunteers were not 'fully informed, as required, prior to their participation'.[33] It found that, although written consent forms had been drawn up in the 1950s, they were used merely to inform the volunteer of the general aims of the experimental programme, but did not provide him with detailed information about his specific test.[34]

Although Porton can be criticised on the first – and the most important – principle of the Nuremberg Code, there are nine other points in the code on which Porton appears to have a better record. Porton has conformed well with some of the points. For example, point three lays down that human experiments should be based on, and follow, animal tests. From the reports of experiments, this has been standard practice for many years. Equally, as required by point eight, the experiments have been conducted by qualified scientists.

It is more ambiguous whether or not Porton has obeyed some of the other points. Point nine states that human subjects may withdraw at any stage of the experiment if they feel mentally or physically unable to continue. Porton claims that this safeguard has always been in force, even before the Nuremberg Code, and that volunteers did not need to give a reason if they wanted to quit.[35] Whether this was appreciated by the volunteers in practice is however another matter.[36] One Porton doctor commented in 1959 that he could not recall any volunteers refusing to do the tests completely after arriving at the establishment; however some men turned down individual experiments 'largely because they might feel a little off-colour after a previous test or because they were not prepared to have another blood test taken'.[37]

It is apparent that scientists in many laboratories around the globe were quite unaware of the Nuremberg Code until the 1960s. Since then, ethical standards in medical research in many countries have gradually developed over the decades so that the public and scientists now generally believe that it is unacceptable to conduct experiments without gaining the informed consent of the subjects, or to risk their health unnecessarily. In line with such trends, ethical practices at Porton started to be improved steadily from the early 1960s. It is hard to judge if Porton has been ahead or behind the best practices of the rest of the scientific world during that time. Porton staff argue that its standards were always as stringent as they could be according to the ideas and customs of the time.

For Porton, a significant milestone was the establishment of the Committee on the Safety of Human Experiments (COSHE) in 1963.[38] This was the first committee in the post-war era whose primary purpose was to monitor the safety of the Porton volunteers.[39] The COSHE committee consisted almost entirely of the Porton medical staff, indeed all the scientists and doctors who were involved in the human experiments in any way. Crucially, no experiment could commence without the committee's express permission, and the committee similarly had the right to veto any experiment if it was not satisfied that the proposed test was safe or that the proper precautions were being taken.[40] However, Porton is unable to state how many times this veto was in fact used to halt experiments, nor can they specify exact occasions on which the right was exercised. The establishment itself has said the committee was 'more importantly' concerned with modifying proposed experiments and maintaining the register of work carried out.[41]

One long-serving Porton scientist who attended COSHE meetings has given a flavour of the committee's deliberations. He recalled that COSHE acted in a democratic way – approval for experiments had to be unanimous. Any member of the committee could theoretically therefore block a proposed trial if he had any reservations whatsoever. 'Whenever a proposal was brought before the committee, it was discussed. Of course, during the discussion, there was a lot of to and fro of ideas, possible reasons for change, so in a sense, it would never have got to a situation where 99 percent of people agreed to something, and one did not. It would not have got that far – it would have been squashed, or redesigned, or re-thought-out, or put aside.' He could remember only one or two occasions when there were serious, unresolved deadlocks on the committee.[42] He did, however, insist that the safety of the volunteers was the first consideration of the members of the committee. 'The standard of the ethics and safety of the human experiments at Porton was as good as anywhere else. We never imposed any dangers on the volunteers.' He pointed out that, as well as seeking to look after the health of the human 'guinea pigs', staff were very aware that, given Porton's image, any mistakes or accidents would result in a political row. 'We had to consider the safety first. Having decided on safety, we then had to decide whether it was worth the time and effort and finance of actually proceeding with a particular line of investigation. There was a multiplicity of issues involved, but the principal one was the safety of the volunteers.' Another Porton official said that the requirement to gain the agreement of all committee members meant that it acted as a 'fail-safe' so that proposed experiments could not be 'steam-rollered through'.

In its first two years, COSHE met virtually every month to thrash out Porton's future work and to lay down some general rules for the safety of experiments. These ranged from limiting the doses of some chemicals to regulating temperatures of clothing trials.[43] COSHE existed for eighteen years. Although some documents have been released, most of the minutes and papers of the committee are still secret, making it hard to assess its record on policing the ethics of Porton's experiments.[44]

Porton introduced a major change in July 1991 (which is still in force today) when it finally allowed outsiders to judge whether proposed human experiments should be allowed to go ahead. COSHE was wound up and replaced by a new eleven-member ethics committee, of which nine are drawn from outside the Ministry of Defence. They include 'representatives of the medical and legal profession, senior academics and lay people'.[45] The chairman of the committee has, so far, always been an outsider. Its first chairman was Hugh Dudley, a retired professor of surgery at London University, who helped establish the committee.[46] The idea of an ethical committee with a significant degree of independence from Porton had been growing over a period of years, in response to evolving ethical standards in the scientific world as a whole. Graham Pearson, Porton's director at the time, said he readily and strongly supported the establishment of such a committee, which was 'very much the thing to have'.[47] He commented that the previous set-up had worked well, but it became necessary to move with the times and institute the best practices of ethical oversight.

As with COSHE, no human experiment can go ahead unless it has been scrutinised and approved by this committee. The Independent Ethics Committee only permits an experiment to proceed if there is a clear military need, and everything has been done to minimise 'any possible risks, however slight'.[48] Porton has stated that the committee has never rejected outright a proposed experiment, although some proposals have been modified following comments from the committee.[49] In reality, the relationship between the committee and Porton scientists is not confrontational – Porton staff take informal soundings from the committee before submitting a proposal so that they have a good idea whether or not it will succeed. In this way, Porton scientists are very unlikely to put forward a proposal which they perceive would be turned down. However, the specific deliberations of the committee remain confidential.[50]

Professor Malcolm Lader, the current chairman of the committee, believes that, like Caesar's wife, Porton has to be seen to be 'whiter than white, purer than everybody', especially since the establishment is 'so high-profile'.[51] This is a view which is often voiced by the staff themselves. Lader said that when he became chairman in 1996, he tightened up the committee's rules to ensure that everything was being done by the book. He stated that if Porton was not adhering to the proper ethical standards, he would resign his post. Professor Lader is confident that his committee is as independent as any other ethics committee in a British research institute. He maintains that a 'fundamental principle' of the committee is that defence considerations do not override ethical concerns. 'I think that Porton understands this – if they undermine the credibility of this ethics committee, then the whole thing goes to pieces. It is not in their interest to devalue us.' He also stressed that Porton staff do not put any pressure on the committee to approve proposals, adding 'We have never had any problems in that way.'

The make-up of the membership of the Independent Ethics Committee is one positive way of improving the public's confidence in Porton's human experiments. Many people are repulsed or at best suspicious of the experiments, and in this climate, Porton was doing little to soothe the hostility by filling its ethics watchdog committee with its own staff. The ethics committee was in fact set up in response to the publication of an updated set of guidelines in 1990 by the Royal College of Physicians, the body which oversees the standards and quality of medical practice in hospitals in England, Wales, and Northern Ireland.[52] In these guidelines, the Royal College comments that the public will only have confidence in the committee if its membership is broad, not exclusively medical and contains strong lay members. Porton believes that its ethics committee fulfils the Royal College's criteria, since 'its membership includes lay members, members of both sexes from the local community, a nurse and a GP'.[53]

However, it is not likely that anyone who is fundamentally opposed to the idea of chemical warfare experiments on humans is sitting on Porton's ethics committee. Indeed the Royal College's guidelines comment, 'Those who are totally opposed to research investigations or experiments on humans should be left to attack the system from the outside and should not be invited on to the committee. On the other hand, individuals who are acquiescent and may be thought likely to give automatic approval are also not suitable members.' The other advantage of the new committee, according to Graham Pearson, was that for Porton's managers, it separated the ethical considerations of an experiment from their need to achieve results to reach the establishment's objectives.

Other innovations appear to have tightened up ethical controls at Porton, most notably on the crucial question of obtaining the voluntary informed consent of the human 'guinea pigs'. To this end, Porton introduced written consent forms in the late 1980s.[54] Previously, the experiments were, in theory, explained verbally to the volunteers, but, according to many of them, this did not happen at all. Graham Pearson said the new forms 'were all part of moving into the modern age' so that Porton adopted the best practices of ethical review. 'I was always conscious that with both the animal and human experiments, we needed to be going the extra mile and be seen to having done so,' he added. As director between 1984 and 1995, he said that his general approach across the establishment was to make sure that everything was done 'above board, not swept under the carpet...I am a great believer in doing it that way. It never caused problems.'

These written consent forms are given to the volunteers to sign. Each form is different, since they describe individual experiments. Two recent consent forms – released by Porton – demonstrate that they contain an in-depth explanation of the proposed experiment, outlining the point of the test, what the volunteers will have to do, how long it will last, any ill effects they may expect and so on.[55] (Volunteers are permitted to take away copies of these signed consent forms after their experiments, although Porton staff say they are not aware of any volunteers asking to do so. This itself is another indication of the changing ethical standards at Porton, since it would have been inconceivable in the Cold War era that volunteers would have been permitted to walk away with printed details of their experiments since such pieces of paper could have inadvertently fallen into anyone's hands.) The forms inform the volunteers that they can withdraw from the test without giving a reason at any stage – 'it will not be held against you in any way'. These written forms are surely integral to implementing the principle of informed consent fully and correctly. Their detailed explanations are in stark contrast with the vaguer practices of the Cold War era. Porton should therefore now be more honest and admit (in, for example, their official statements to Parliament) that their observance of the informed consent principle was not as it should have been during the Cold War, given the peculiar circumstances of those times, and explain that significant steps to rectify this have been taken since then. An inkling of this more honest approach was shown by the then Porton spokesman, Rupert Cazalet, in late 1997 when he was questioned over the common cold claims: 'We are certain that once the [volunteers] got to Porton, they were given sufficient knowledge for informed consent.' But he added that the concept of informed consent in the 1950s and 1960s was less strict and detailed than it was in the modern era.[56]

One secret long-running debate tested how far the British were prepared to go in exposing human 'guinea pigs' to the most lethal poison gases so far discovered. It was in a sense the high-water mark of Porton's experiments with potent chemicals on volunteers, and an episode which illuminates official attitudes towards the ethical and safety dilemmas of these experiments. Interestingly, the Nuremberg Code was never raised once in the surviving official papers of the saga.

In the early 1950s, Porton learnt of a new class of nerve gases which was much more potent than even the G-agent group.[57] These new nerve gases – the most toxic uncovered to this day – were nicknamed V-agents because 'of their venomous nature'.[58] Both the British and the Americans were quick to see the potential of the novel compounds,[59] and Porton stated that the V-agents were a 'considerable advance on previous chemical warfare agents'.[60]

The new gases were at least 200 times more toxic than the older G-agent nerve gases through the skin, according to Porton. The V-gases were so lethal that 'experiments may never be carried out in this country on men', counselled Dr Ted Perren, Porton's then director.[61] Initially, both Britain and America estimated the toxicity of the V-agents by testing them on animals, acknowledging that it was simply too hazardous at that time to try them out on humans. Porton was then still constrained in its nerve gas experiments on humans by the limits set down after the death of Ronald Maddison in 1953. In April 1957, however, Porton applied for permission to relax these limits, since scientists wanted to inject sarin (GB) straight into the veins of humans. Under the rules, only sarin of all the nerve gases could be administered in experiments, and then only in certain specified ways. Volunteers could only be used if they either breathed in the nerve gas or had the liquid dropped directly on their skin. Porton argued that these two methods had produced 'acceptable estimates' of sarin's toxicity to humans, but were still too inaccurate. The scientists desired a 'more exact assessment' through intravenous tests.[62] One reason for this need for greater accuracy was a 'difference of opinion' between Britain and the US. Porton and their American counterparts at Edgewood Arsenal had by then carried out hundreds of experiments on humans, but still disagreed as to the true lethal dose of sarin to men.[63]

However, it transpired that there was another motivation behind Porton's request – the establishment wanted 'eventually' to test V-agents on volunteers.[64] This ultimate aim of testing the V-agents was not included in the early Porton request written in the summer of 1957, although it did appear subsequently.[65] Dr Bill Ladell, then in charge of human experiments, believed that injection into the veins was the only sure way of obtaining 'a really accurate estimate' of the toxicity of nerve gases. He suggested that they could in effect build up to intravenous tests with V-agents by firstly injecting sarin, of which much more was known, and then eventually the V-agents. A later Porton memo went further, stating that determining the true lethal dose of sarin was 'of academic interest only'; the real purpose of injecting sarin was as a pilot test to give Porton 'useful experience' for the later injections with the newer V-agents.[66]

Porton's request could only be approved by authorities outside the establishment. Under the rules laid down after the death of Maddison, the authorising body in the first instance was one of its external advisory committees, the Biology Committee. After some discussion and some differences of opinion, this committee gave its permission in 1957. However the go-ahead was delayed, since it had been decided that Lord Adrian's committee – which had laid down the initial rules after Maddison's death – should be reconstituted to consider the request.[67]

But, while this process for obtaining official permission was chugging along in the Whitehall machine, Porton remained keen to carry out human experiments with V-gases. They found a way through the impasse – by testing it on members of their own staff. Two Porton scientists noted that, although permission for volunteers had not yet been obtained, 'there is no bar, however, to the medically-qualified members of the [establishment's] Medical Division staff offering themselves for such an experiment'. Ten months after the experiment, Dr Ladell put the report of the test before the Biology Committee. He admitted that some members of the committee might have been surprised by the existence of such an experiment, given that a request to carry out human tests with V-agents had still not been approved. He explained that Porton staff believed that 'they were at liberty to use their own skins, while awaiting approval to use volunteers'.[68]

The experiment on two members of staff on 2 January 1958 appears to be the first human test with V-agents in the West, and probably in the world.[69] The test was aimed at finding how quickly one of the V-gases, VX, would penetrate through the skin. Just before Christmas 1957, Porton had received 'a very active sample of VX' which had been tagged with a radioactive isotope. Porton at this time believed that the VX could be tested on man 'with complete safety' using a dose which was around one half of the then assumed lethal dose. Two members of staff stepped forward. A fifty microgram droplet of the radioactive VX was placed on their forearms in a marked circle and left undisturbed for thirty minutes. The skin in the circle was then cut back to the muscle. The brief report does not record what they experienced, although a later memo said there had been 'no detectable effects'.[70] One of the human 'guinea pigs' in this experiment appears to be Dr Ladell, himself then in charge of Porton's human experiments. (According to one assessment, Ladell was 'a civilised man, but with a hair-trigger temper'. He had a tendency to go off half-cocked, but had the grace to admit if he was wrong.)[71]

Porton scientists urgently wanted official permission to test volunteers with V-agents because they and their American colleagues needed to solve a critical conundrum. The problem was set out in a secret memo by Dr Ladell in May 1959. He reported that the scientists may have had to completely rethink the military power of V-agents. Recent experiments had 'suggested that human skin may be penetrated by V-agents so slowly that, to ensure a lethal build-up of V-agent within the body, a very much more massive contamination than had hitherto been considered necessary may be required'.[72] Clearly the V-agents – even though they were very much more toxic than the G-agents – would be less effective if they sank through the skin so slowly. It could, for example, alter calculations of how much V-agent would have to be loaded into each shell to kill a person quickly. This was an important consideration for the US which was then in the process of starting to manufacture VX on a massive scale to build up its arsenal. (Over the next decade, the US was to manufacture up to 5,000 tons of VX.) On the defensive side, however, if the V-agents were found to be absorbed slowly, there would be more leeway to administer treatments.

The recent experiments had been carried out with excised human skin, but, as Dr Ladell wrote, their results had been queried 'chiefly because excised skin is dying if not dead tissue.' He added, 'The only way in which an acceptable measure of penetrability can be obtained is by actual experiments with V-agent on intact human beings.' He contended that the tests with the two Porton staff and others in the US and Canada 'show decisively that 50 micrograms of pure V may be placed on the skin of an intact human being and left there without any untoward effect'. He therefore wanted permission to place a maximum of 20 micrograms of radioactive V-gas on the skin of volunteers. He was 'sure' that this amount was very safe.[73]

The Americans were anxious that the British should start testing V-gases on volunteers to help solve this crucial problem. Both agreed that 'every effort should be made' by both countries 'to execute, with the highest priority' a programme of such tests.[74] But, for all its lobbying, Porton was stuck without the all-important green light from higher authorities. Although Lord Adrian's committee gave their go-ahead in 1959, the issue had now been referred up the chain of command – to government ministers themselves – because it was such a sensitive subject.[75] Such a move was exceptional, since – as we have seen – traditionally, ministers had rarely been consulted on proposed experiments at Porton. It may even have been the first time that ministers had even seen the specifics of any trial before it occurred.

These proposals had to be sent to the top because the V-agents were seen as being so much more lethal than the G-agents and so there was a larger chance of something going wrong. Moreover, it was felt that injecting sarin would be more hazardous than Porton's permitted tests with the gas. Ministers were therefore being asked to give their approval to two related proposals – one to drop V-agents onto the skin of volunteers, and the other to inject sarin and later V-agents straight into the bloodstream of volunteers. It was envisaged that if these proposals were approved, the number of volunteers tested would be in the 'low hundreds'.[76] Senior officials conceded how touchy the issue was. The Permanent Secretary of the War Office said the experiments were 'an extremely emotive' subject for the public, whilst another mandarin called it 'a particularly hot potato politically'.[77]

In the late summer of 1959, the upper reaches of Whitehall began to discuss the twin proposals. The mandarins' deliberations, of which not a word leaked out, lasted for around three years, and many of them remained deeply sceptical of Porton's proposals for much of this time. One Air Ministry official was unconvinced of the essential need to check more accurately the toxicity of nerve gases, viewing the intravenous tests as being merely 'science for the sake of science and therefore ethically unjustifiable'.[78]

The awful death of Ronald Maddison hung constantly over the discussions between Whitehall and Porton. Another death would undoubtedly have provoked a severe political backlash. This was apparent from one high-level meeting of officials: 'All present were conscious of the danger that another fatality like that of 1953 might mean the closure, or restriction, of activities at Porton using human volunteers and thus jeopardise other valuable experiments there.'[79]

One issue which preoccupied the mandarins was to what degree the proposed tests risked another death. On the whole, the officials, advised by their medical experts, appeared to believe that dropping V-agents on the skin was safer than the intravenous tests and were more prepared to approve those particular tests.[80] An Air Ministry official warned that 'there is considerable risk of death if human subjects are used for nerve gas tests of either G or V agents by intravenous injections'. The risk from the skin tests was on the other hand 'slight', according to the same official.[81] It was argued that, if anything went wrong, there was less time to put it right since the deadly gas would have shot directly into the bloodstream. It was a point conceded by Eric Haddon, a long-serving chemical warfare official, who wrote that 'injection of a poison – however close the medical supervision and however accurate the checking and re-checking of dosages – is an irrevocable step'.[82] Indeed, a Porton scientist has noted that sarin 'is only equalled or surpassed by cyanide among poisons for its speed of action when given intravenously'.[83] One Whitehall official highlighted a different point, commenting that 'injecting the stuff as distinct from putting it on the skin sounds much more alarming to the laymen', adding that ministers – who ultimately had to give their approval for the tests – were 'only laymen'.[84]

Porton scientists asserted that intravenous tests were actually safer than inhalation and skin experiments because they had more control over the amount that was absorbed by the human 'guinea pig'. It was argued that, for example, when liquid nerve gas was placed on the skin, not all of it would penetrate uniformly through the skin; some would evaporate, depending on temperature of the skin and the surrounding air, the volatility of the gas, and the shape and size of the drop. Different individuals would absorb varying amounts of the liquid, depending on the toughness of their skin. Similarly, volunteers would breathe in different amounts of nerve gas when they were in the chamber.

Dr Ladell – exasperated by 'our long battle' to obtain official approval for the intravenous tests – complained that his staff were 'in the peculiar position of having to fight for permission to do something which is considerably less dangerous than things for which we have already been given permission'.[85] He specifically cited a series of experiments in which nerve gas was being breathed in by volunteers, arguing that Porton had easily been able to win permission for those inhalation tests, even though they used 'the equivalent of more than double the dose' of the proposed intravenous tests. 'It seems to me that there is a grave danger that if the Minister is shrewd enough to ask the right questions, he will appreciate this and he might consider it his duty to clamp down not only on the intravenous but also on the inhalation work.'

Sir Owen Wansborough-Jones, the then chief scientist at the Ministry of Supply (the department in charge of Porton) who had worked at the establishment during the Second World War, identified two sources of risk in the proposed tests. The first was human error: it was possible to make a mistake with a syringe containing nerve gas as with any other liquid. But to this, he was assured that Porton had 'elaborate precautions to cross-check the dosages before they were administered'. The second risk was the 'outside possibility of a human idiosyncrasy', which, after all, was Porton's explanation for the death of Ronald Maddison.[86] (He had been given a dose of nerve gas which killed him, but others who had been given the same amount suffered no ill effects – see chapter five.) This was an inevitable hazard since there is no sure test for spotting if a person has a particular susceptibility to nerve gas.[87]

The death of Maddison emphasises how there is always a risk of a fatality when humans are exposed to deadly gases, especially when those in charge of the experiments cannot be absolutely certain of the lethal dose. One Porton memo commented that its staff could only define the 'small doses' which were 'safe' to test on humans, once the true lethal dose had been established. To some degree, the proposed tests were therefore a stab in the dark, since Porton admitted at the time that it could only guess the lethal dose of the V-gases to humans. The quoted figures were 'based entirely' on the calculations of the fatal doses to various species of animals in experiments. Porton staff commented, however, that these could be 'misleading' because there was, in fact, a very wide variation between the amounts which killed different species.[88] As we shall see, the predicted fatal dose of V-agents was revised on occasions by Porton and the Americans. But in a classic chicken-and-egg scenario, the scientists had to carry out the tests so that they could find out more data about the V-agents and so forecast more accurately the amount which would kill humans.

A senior Porton adviser, Professor Jack Gaddum (the pharmacologist and pioneer of probit analysis), believed that it was 'never possible to abolish' risk completely. He said that with all Porton's safeguards, the risk of these tests 'would be no greater than the risks we all accept every day. Some people are allergic to aspirin and have been killed by small doses, but no one suggests that aspirin should, therefore, be forbidden.'[89] Gaddum pointed out that not doing the proposed tests would also pose a risk – this time to the defences of the nation. 'If these gases were used in war, this country would not have the best possible information about them,' he wrote. Whatever the degree of the peril, Porton and their Whitehall supporters believed that the risks – which in their minds were minimal – were in any case justified on military grounds. In their view, the needs of 'national security' were greater than the slight risks of the experiments. Intelligence gathered by British spies indicated that in 1959, the Russians were 'likely' to have developed V-agents or something similar and that 'production of V-agents could by now be in progress'. One mandarin commented, 'This seems to imply that the threat is real enough.'[90] They therefore believed that the tests were necessary in order to discover more about the V-agents and to develop protection against them. Furthermore, there was also the possibility that Britain might start producing V-agent weapons themselves in the near future.

Another of the hotly debated issues was how to present the risk of the two sets of proposed tests to potential subjects. It was a 'difficulty' summed up by one sceptical official: 'If we tell them that the experiments could be lethal, there would inevitably be a sharp fall-off in numbers and probably a degree of embarrassing publicity. On the other hand, if no more warning of the danger is given than at present, we may be quite rightly accused of deliberate misrepresentation in the future.'[91] Pressed on whether the previous human 'guinea pigs' had been genuine volunteers, a Porton doctor replied that they were, 'although many of them had no idea of the nature of the physiological tests for which they were volunteering'.[92] This remark, made at a meeting in 1959, seems to be a fair reflection of Porton's sustained breach of the most important Nuremberg principle at that time – informed consent.

The Navy – which did not 'like the sound of these new tests' – would only sanction them on one 'indispensable' condition. Since the 'element of risk in the new tests may be decidedly greater' than in previous ones, there had to be 'tangible evidence' that the subject 'has firstly clearly understood what he is in for, and has said that he is prepared to face it'. The Navy proposed that each volunteer should be handed a printed description of the test with an explanation of the 'danger and discomfort' and after reading it, they should sign a declaration that they had understood the test and were willing to undergo it. 'This would have to be done on each and every occasion of applying one of these experiments, on the basis of "no signature, no test".'[93]

Such a signed declaration would have been a new practice at Porton, since, as noted earlier, written consent forms were not introduced until the late 1980s. In so far as the volunteers were ever informed of anything about the tests, they had always been told verbally. The idea of a written form divided officials. A War Office official argued that a signed certificate would neither help the volunteer, nor protect the government. 'Either the certificate would become pure routine, which the men would sign without reading, or it would make them suspect that they were about to be subjected to something very dangerous, the responsibility for which we are trying to pass to them.'[94] Another official claimed that there was 'some danger' in such 'blood chits', since the certificate would replace 'patient and careful explanation to a man who may find the subject difficult to follow, even when put in allegedly non-medical terms'. He added that the men were 'more used to absorbing ideas by listening than from the written or printed word'.[95] Volunteers, who claim they were never told anything, no doubt would have appreciated this allegedly 'patient and careful explanation'!

Exactly who would be the subjects of the tests also provoked much discussion. John Profumo, the War Minister later disgraced in the famous scandal, was in mid-1961 'quite happy' to allow the experiments to go ahead on an assurance from Porton that the 'risk of untoward effects was very small'.[96] He warned that if anything went wrong, it was likely that all human experiments would be stopped from then on. However he imposed two conditions before he would give his final permission. One was that, 'for political reasons', he could not restrict the human 'guinea pigs' to military personnel only. He requested that civilians also be asked to volunteer. This raised an immediate problem of which civilians, and whether those civilians would keep quiet about their involvement. This was tricky. One official said 'it was very difficult to find suitable civilians to use in the tests [since] clearly the general public could not be called upon'. It was therefore necessary 'to find a suitable organisation to tap'. Mandarins briefly considered using prisoners, with one official writing, 'I understand that in America, they call for volunteers from the prison population for this sort of thing. Is this a possibility here?'. But this proved not to be an option. 'There would be no difficulty about getting a plentiful supply of prisoners but there would be no possibility of keeping it secret. Prisoners are great gossips, and the full glare of publicity is on every unusual incident in prison,' noted an official. Civil defence workers were deemed to be the most suitable source of volunteers, but they too presented problems. These individuals 'can be assumed to have a favourable background to this sort of thing and on the whole can be trusted to be reasonably discreet. But it was emphasised that there could be no guarantee that there would not be a leak.'[97]

Porton's own medical staff were willing to volunteer to be the 'guinea pigs' in the tests. But whether they were officially allowed to was another, more confusing matter. An Air Ministry memo written in 1959 stated categorically that after Maddison's death in 1953, Duncan Sandys (the government minister who was then formally responsible for the establishment) had expressly forbidden Porton staff from exposing themselves to nerve gases. 'This embargo is still in operation', added the memo.[98] This ban appears to have been ignored, or lost in the bureaucratic jungle. Declassified papers show that Porton staff openly discussed self-testing with Whitehall officials and their outside advisers. For example, a Porton adviser wrote in 1960 that in the four or so years that Dr Ladell had been in charge of human experiments at Porton, around 600 volunteers had been tested with nerve gas and that it was Dr Ladell himself who had suffered the highest degree of cholinesterase depression of all in that time.[99] A year later Dr Ladell noted that he and his medical staff were 'offering themselves for experiments and being used,' adding that 'there is not a medically qualified member of my staff who has not been the subject of several experiments involving a depression of their cholinesterase within the last year.'[100] Such self-testing had been going on at Porton ever since the establishment was set up in the First World War. For years, staff had been jumping in and out of gas clouds, or rolling up their sleeves to drop chemicals on their arms; the most notable such example was, of course, the celebrated incident of 'Barcroft's Dog'.

Porton staff were officially banned from testing all chemicals on themselves around 1961, according to one insider.[101] From then on, only the director of Porton himself could authorise such experiments, provided the scientists made a good case in writing. It appears that permission has been given from time to time, although unofficial self-testing still continued, particularly with tear gases. At one point, in 1968, Porton staff complained that the ban was 'restricting', although the director agreed to consider requests 'sympathetically' provided that 'such tests were essential' and the 'only means of obtaining the information required'.[102] Nowadays, staff are not allowed to test any chemicals on themselves under this 'long-standing' policy.[103] Porton says that staff were banned because such experiments 'would not be consistent with the proper ethical control, oversight and experimental design required for work of this nature. The scientific value of such studies would be very limited.'[104] Eric Haddon, Porton's director between 1961 and 1968, added that it was 'wasteful' to test on 'highly-qualified staff' since it would surely affect their other work.[105] Tom Inch, a chemist at Porton between 1965 and 1986, considers that this ban was justified. 'Your judgement can fail you sometimes, if you really believe in something. You can make wrong choices. If you want to prove your theory, you will prove your theory, whether it is right or wrong, and not look at the science and that could expose yourself to unnecessary risks.'[106]

Another controversial issue concerned the Americans, with whom there was a 'very free exchange of information' in the field of chemical warfare.[107] Some mandarins questioned whether it was necessary to run British tests with the V-agents, since their close allies in chemical warfare were already conducting similar experiments. Porton's riposte is embarrassing for the Americans. Dr Ladell did not want to 'leave it to the Americans' because their human experimenters had a 'rather slapdash and dangerous ad hoc approach'. He was particularly critical of one experiment with nerve gas in which the Americans had only discovered in the middle of the test that the batch of the proposed antidote was defective. This was 'almost unforgivable', railed Ladell. He added that Porton scientists would have been left open to 'severe censure' if they conducted human experiments in a similar way to the Americans.[108] A year earlier, Ladell had similarly criticised American experiments with VX as being 'not satisfactory' and 'liable to be dangerous'.[109] Whether Ladell passed on his views to his opposite numbers across the Atlantic is not known, but would seem unlikely. He was fully aware of the sensitivities, arguing that Porton's failure to conduct the proposed tests 'will seriously hamper' the exchange of information with the Americans and 'may even upset' the goodwill between the allies.[110] Other mandarins argued that 'systematic' V-agent tests on humans had to be done by Porton because the Americans were not prepared to carry out 'more careful scientifically controlled testing of nerve gases'.[111]

Of all the V-agents, the Americans tested a total of 740 humans with VX, with another thirty-two being exposed to an 'experimental VX-like compound'. One summary of this work shows a variety of tests – subjects were injected, had the liquid dropped on their skin, drank water contaminated with the nerve gas, smelt concentrations of the vapour and tried out antidotes.[112]

Like Porton, the first human experiment with V-agents in America was carried out on a member of staff in its chemical warfare department in 1959. He was Dr Van Sim, who had run the human experiments at Edgewood Arsenal since 1956. According to one account, Dr Sim had 'arranged for himself to be given slow intravenous injections of VX' spread over five-and-a-half hours.[113] He 'had said he was incapacitated, but some observers reported that he had been merely too frightened to move'. Dr Sim later described this experience to a US Congressional committee: 'There was some difficulty with breathing. First, I had the sensation of my nose running, and I was having difficulty with vision...sweating, tremors, nausea and vomiting.' Questioned by Senator Edward Kennedy, he denied that the experiment had almost killed him. Dr Sim explained that he had tested VX first because he would never administer a chemical unless he had experienced it and knew the hazards of the compound himself. 'This is a personal thing as far as I am concerned... That has been my credo since I have been in charge of the [human experiments] programme. People do not agree with me entirely on this. They say it is not entirely objective, but I have to live with myself and I have to conduct this programme.'[114]

After years of secret Whitehall deliberation on this 'vexed question', Porton ultimately won little joy. The government did not approve the proposal to test volunteers by injecting sarin and later V-agents into their bloodstream. The head of the chemical warfare department in London commented in early 1962 that 'the fact of several years' negotiation failing to gain permission for the tests is a clear indication of the profound difficulties in the way of such tests'.[115] He recommended that in view of these obvious difficulties, the proposal should be shelved. Instead, he and others, including Porton director Eric Haddon, 'doubted whether it was politically expedient to pursue the proposal at the moment'.

They now conceded that Britain's defences would, after all, not be compromised if these tests were postponed. Porton's advisers agreed that while 'the scientific necessity [for the intravenous tests] remained paramount for a proper understanding' of nerve gases, there was no longer a 'vital national risk in not conducting such experiments'. A rough measurement of the lethal and casualty doses of the V-agents could be made, based on the substantial body of previous experiments with nerve gases, both at Porton and America.[116] The shelved proposal, it appears, was never seriously raised again. Porton insists that its scientists have never injected any volunteers with nerve gas of any kind.[117]

Whitehall mandarins were, however, 'readily' prepared to approve a small number of tests in which VX was to be dropped onto the skin of volunteers. This set of experiments were seen as 'relatively trivial [as] only a few such tests will be necessary' and the dose to be used was 'extremely small'.[118]

While the issue of permission had been bogged down in Whitehall, Porton staff had been left stymied without any volunteers on which to test V-agents. They had therefore resorted to exposing themselves to the extremely potent gas.

Some seemingly hair-raising experiments were undertaken. A Porton scientist had carried out a series of tests on pigs and found that only a small amount of VX had penetrated very slowly through two layers of clothing and into the animals. Dr Ladell thought it 'desirable' to repeat the experiment on men in an attempt to validate them. Three of Porton's medical officers 'exercised their professional privilege to experiment on themselves' and volunteered for the tests in late 1960.[119] The dose used was 200 milligrams; strikingly this was the amount which at that time Porton believed would kill a person if their battledress had been contaminated with VX for twenty-four hours.

The three officers were prepared to take a large risk – and potentially put their lives on the line – to see if this figure was accurate. In the first experiment, the dose was dropped onto two layers of battledress, serge and flannel, which was wrapped around their arm. The contaminated clothing was worn for eight hours, but the 'guinea pigs' felt no symptoms of nerve gas poisoning, nor did their cholinesterase levels fall. So the same experiment was repeated, this time with two medical officers, who kept the clothing on for twenty-four hours. This time, their blood cholinesterase dropped by large amounts, but they did not suffer any malaise. Dr Ladell claimed that the outcome 'fully justified' the 'ad hoc' experiments, since it showed that the 200 milligrams figure was wrong. At the time, military chiefs had been using this figure in operational assessments – to calculate, for example, how many people would be killed in a real battle with VX. The experiments had shown that very little of the VX had actually permeated the clothing and reached the skin. However the tests are remarkable because the *current* estimate for the lethal dose of VX – when it is a liquid on bare skin – is 10 milligrams.[120] If only five percent of the poison had penetrated through the clothing, the medical officers would have been in serious trouble.

Over the following year, eight Porton medical officers once again volunteered and were exposed to VX a total of fifty-four times in a set of trials.[121] Porton admitted that these trials had started off on an ad hoc basis and that an attempt was only later made to make them 'more scientific'.[122]

Porton reasoned that the same eight could be repeatedly exposed because cholinesterase levels recovered 'relatively rapidly' after VX poisoning, compared to other nerve gases.[123] The establishment noted that using the same eight people had the 'additional advantage that serial observations could be made on the same subjects at different dosages, thus reducing, to some extent, a major source of variation'. The staff were placed in a wind tunnel, facing into a stream of VX vapour and exposing their heads and necks. In nineteen trials, the subjects did not have any protection over their mouths. In the other trials, the subjects received some protection since they were able to breathe clean air through a tube while their noses were clipped to stop any inhalation. As an indication of the dangers involved, staff were allowed to leave the tunnel immediately they suspected that either the tube was slipping out of their mouths or that there was some kind of leakage, and on two occasions, the subjects did flee the tunnel. Some of the subjects were believed to be breathing very hard 'because of the anxiety at being the first to inhale this highly toxic vapour experimentally'.

In one category of the trials, the VX dosages were increased to a maximum of 6.3 mg min m^{-3} for the unprotected subjects.[124] To get an idea of how perilous these trials were, the current estimations of the lethal dosage of VX range from just 10 mg min m^{-3} to 50 mg min m^{-3}.[125] As a result of these trials, Porton gauged at that time that the dosage which would kill an unmasked man lay somewhere between 48 and 82 mg min m^{-3}.[126]

The 'guinea pigs' experienced symptoms of nerve gas poisoning – miosis with some fluttering or twitching of the eyelids, runny nose, lethargy – to varying degrees. One individual, apparently Dr Ladell, suffered the most in both types of the tests. (Soon afterwards, Dr Ladell was congratulated for his 'skill and courage in doing the work to provide direct evidence of the toxicity of V-agent to man'.)[127] In one trial, this unprotected individual was exposed to 5.5 mg min m^{-3}; his blood cholinesterase fell by seventy percent – far more than the others in this trial – and he suffered a 'transient malaise (sweating and some nausea)'. However this individual had 'severe' symptoms when he was exposed to the highest dosage of VX vapour in the second type of trial, those in which the men were protected with the tube of clean air and nose clips. After being exposed to a dosage of 25.6 mg min m^{-3}, 'he felt perfectly well at first; then about six hours after exposure, malaise came on suddenly, with waves of severe nausea, culminating in vomiting about eight hours after exposure. He also had some cold sweating...the subject retired to bed. He had a nightmare when he first went to sleep, but awoke from it, went to sleep again and woke next morning feeling reasonably fit and with a good appetite.'

These experiments had underlined that soldiers on a battlefield could not be considered safe from VX vapour if they were only wearing a respirator – all the skin from top to toe had to be covered. Porton scientists believed that, from the trials with protected men, it was clear that the VX vapour had been absorbed through their skin, even though only a small amount of skin – the head and necks – had been exposed. The gas penetrated 'relatively rapidly', concluded the scientists.[128]

Staff also underwent experiments in late 1962 which showed that VX penetrates the skin of various parts of the body at different speeds.[129] A Geiger counter was used to track how much radioactive VX went through the skin and how much evaporated. The effects on the staff are not recorded in the report. The results showed that over six hours, less than one percent of the poison penetrated through the palm, while eight percent went through the back and fifteen percent through the forearm. Before this test, Dr Ladell said he had previously been 'unduly cautious by doing very few experiments with radioactive material.'[130]

Porton's director, Eric Haddon, praised the medical staff who had volunteered for the VX experiments as being 'valiant people' whom he trusted 'to look after themselves',[131] and Porton advisers, although having 'misgivings' about these experiments, 'saluted the bravery' of the staff.[132] By spring 1963, Porton believed that no more VX experiments were 'really necessary' since they had enough data on the lethal poison. One Porton adviser questioned whether the experiments should be continued on the medical staff 'as the repeated exposure of the same volunteers was not good'. Dr Ladell himself did not believe that 'there would be a strong case for continuing the experiments from a chemical warfare point of view, as [Porton] had some good results now, plus those from the United States, but continued work would be of scientific interest'.[133] It appears that a 'few' more VX experiments were carried out on staff later in 1963, which brought to an end Porton's V-agent tests on human beings.[134]

Porton still maintains that all its V-agent experiments were done on its own medical staff, and not on volunteers from the armed forces.[135] Although they had in fact won permission to drop VX onto the skin of volunteers from the forces, it appears that they were not needed because the experiments were all conducted on medical staff.

The long Whitehall debate over the proposals to test servicemen with V-agents and inject them with sarin was dominated by political considerations. Porton and officials lobbied hard to justify the proposed experiments on military, safety and scientific grounds, but in the end, the government was simply not willing to lay itself open to political criticism if details of these experiments leaked out. There would inevitably have been a political storm if another serviceman had died in the experiments. The proposed tests were scuppered, not by ethical objections, but by the fear of political repercussions.[136] The threat of scrutiny from outside Porton had curbed the scientists' experiments. Since they had to conduct the tests on themselves, the number of VX experiments was undoubtedly smaller than it otherwise would have been.

The V-agents – discovered and developed by the British and the Americans many years ago – are still very much with us. These chemicals, the most potent of all nerve gases, were found to be in the arsenal of the Iraqi dictator Saddam Hussein during the 1991 Gulf War. During the recent crises in the Gulf, the Americans and the British led the world in lambasting Saddam for producing chemical and biological weapons. Ironically, both nations had been among the first countries to uncover and develop these same weapons. This is a familiar pattern. Third World governments which are seeking to produce these munitions rarely discover their own types of poisons and germs. In reality, they take them, as it were, off-the-shelf, choosing harmful chemicals and micro-organisms which have already been identified by military scientists in technologically advanced nations. There is a certain amount of hypocrisy about the politicians of the developed world, condemning Third World governments for producing the so-called 'poor man's atom bomb'. These governments are, after all, only copying what the developed countries once did.

CHAPTER SEVEN
Conscience Explored

In the popular imagination, there is a tendency to see Porton scientists almost as little more than wicked Josef Mengele-types who enjoyed inflicting pain on vulnerable, young servicemen in gas chambers. But that is far too simplistic a view. The reality is, of course, more complex. The reasons why military personnel volunteered for the trials have been examined in chapter two, and so in this chapter, what the scientists themselves felt about carrying out chemical warfare experiments on fellow human beings is examined. Many people outside the establishment are horrified at the thought of these experiments; they wonder how scientists could possibly have experimented on humans in this way, what drove them to do it, and whether they ever experienced heart-wrenching pangs of conscience, or if they slept easily at night. Previous chapters have looked at the motivations of the scientists during the First and Second World Wars, so this will concentrate on the years after 1945, when Britain was locked into the Cold War but not all-out war.

For scientists, Porton is a curious place to work in some respects. For a start, its infamy goes before it; many potential recruits are deterred simply by its sinister reputation. Many also do not want to be involved in chemical and biological warfare research, even if it was for defensive purposes alone. They feel that they may be tarred with the odium of poison gas, especially since the majority of the general public do not make the distinction between developing chemical weapons and producing protective equipment against such weapons. Even if one felt that they were doing honourable, useful work, they would still be faced with the continual caustic comments and jibes from many outsiders at, say, run-of-the-mill social occasions, even having to go through a tiresome justification of one's job time and time again. Indeed, one former member of staff recalls that it was a 'conversation-stopper' at do's outside Porton: 'Either they were thinking "people with two heads" because it was all very secret, or they did not agree with it, or they did not know what to say, because they assumed that you could not say a thing. Either way, they were baffled.' That inevitably bred some frustration.

Before the 1950s, Porton had a lower profile and fewer people knew about it, but after that time, its notoriety began to spread throughout the land. As a result, many staff worked there in full knowledge of its reputation, but prepared to put up with the opprobrium. That is in a sense a distinctive characteristic of many who have been employed at Porton.

In general, many scientists throughout research institutions are motivated by the desire to earn the esteem and recognition of their peers. They want to write papers detailing their work in respected scientific journals, so that they can win the critical acclaim of other scientists in their field. This is an important consideration for most scientists. But for scientists in military research establishments, there is an obstacle – they have to sign the Official Secrets Act. They therefore cannot publish anything which may give away sensitive military secrets and imperil the defences of the country. They may be doing great work, but it may well not be recognised outside the installation among the wider scientific world. Instead, their worth is admired among a close circle of colleagues and counterparts in allied countries, but not much beyond that.

Porton management have recognised that this can be frustrating and have therefore sought to allow staff to publish as much as possible. It is interesting that in the 1920s, Porton staff were able to carry out their own private research in their spare time, and permission to publish the results of this work had to be sought but would not be 'unreasonably withheld'.[1] More recently, Porton's declared policy was to 'encourage staff to publish their research and to contribute to the scientific community through presentations at national and international meetings'. The rule of thumb was not to disclose any information which would expose vulnerabilities in British protective equipment, indicate Britain's evaluations of other countries' capabilities, or aid another country in its development of chemical and biological weapons.

It appears that the Official Secrets Act was less of an impediment after the 1960s when Porton was dedicated purely to defensive work. Dennis Swanston, a toxicologist between 1966 and 1992, believed that the restrictions on publication were steadily lifted during this time.[2] He said, 'Within the confines of the Official Secrets Act, there was quite a lot of room in a way. What you have got to realise is that when you work in industry, you are just as constrained, if not more, by industrial intellectual property, industrial espionage and sensitivity with competitors'. On a related question, he felt that he was given the liberty to roam widely in his research. He came to see Porton as 'more like a university', with a 'lot of scientific freedom', where he was confronted with taxing scientific questions and had the time to pursue the answers in a stimulating environment among 'very bright minds', whom he personally admired. 'Given a problem, in the early days, you had quite a lot of leeway to do individual research.' In his previous job in industry, however, he had been required to work 'in response mode', directed merely to complete specific tasks, such as a standard set of tests, and was unable to publish research because other firms would learn commercial secrets. One senior Porton scientist from this time pointed out that a number of his colleagues built up 'considerable' scientific reputations whilst at the establishment and subsequently moved on to prestigious jobs in industry and elsewhere.

Military research establishments have traditionally been compartmentalised under 'need-to-know' rules – staff in one section are not permitted to discuss their work with fellow workers from another section. This is a mechanism for restricting access to secrets, preventing too many people from having a complete overview of what is going on in an establishment. But it also stops staff from indulging in one of the normal, routine activities of the workplace – chatting and gossiping about your job to all sorts of colleagues in different divisions of the institution. Sometimes, scientists do not know what another is doing even in the next-door laboratory. Moreover, scientists in these establishments are not supposed to talk to anyone – their wives, husbands, friends, casual acquaintances – about how they earn a living. Sharing the ups and downs of your job with others is something we all need to do, but this cannot always be done by scientists in these establishments. This can breed a sense of isolation, a feeling of working in the dark.

Tom Inch, a chemist who worked at Porton between 1965 and 1986 and is currently Secretary General of the Royal Society of Chemistry, does not believe that this problem applied to Porton during this time. 'Defence against chemical and biological agents is multi-disciplinary. You need to bring in all the skills right across the place.'[3] He says Porton sought to encourage staff from different parts of the establishment to talk to each other, exchange ideas and work as a team. 'The fact is that we had chemists, physicists, biologists and medics all working together to provide protection, evaluate toxicity and so on.' He adds that it was very exciting to work across the usual boundaries alongside scientists from other fields.

Another problem facing some Porton staff was (and still is) that they could be trapped by the kind of work they were doing. They became very knowledgeable about a particular field of science, but one which was limited. Knowing all about arcane chemical weapons did not necessarily help someone get a job elsewhere in another research establishment. One

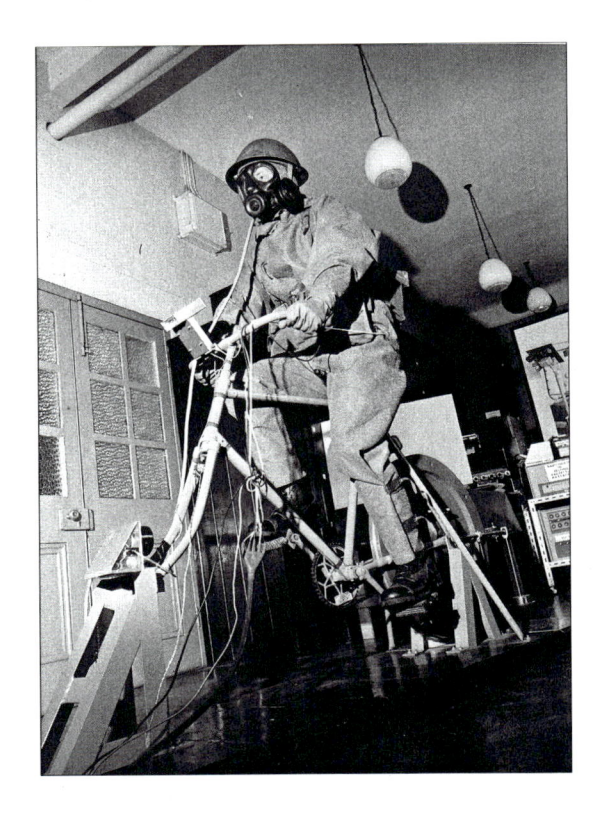

A soldier tests a gas mask and suit by peddling furiously on a fixed bike in 1964.

A soldier in protective clothing at Porton Down.

retired scientist who worked at Porton for many Cold War years jested, 'The more I think about Porton, the more I think that the place is bizarre. If you worked there for five years, you were unemployable anywhere else. You were useless, you could not do anything else. You were a world expert in some very, very esoteric field. The only place that they would employ you was Moscow or Kiev, and that was against the law.'[4]

Dennis Swanston acknowledged, 'There were people who became experts and ploughed a very narrow furrow.' When he joined in 1966, he says he found 'very much an old, closed culture,' in which long-serving staff were focusing their attention on a few of the traditional chemical weapons, such as the nerve gases. 'Good pioneering work was done. It was done in great depth. You can look at it in two ways – do you want a jack-of-all-trades or an expert in a narrow field?' He recalls that Porton was a 'funny old place' when he first joined – 'polished benches, a leisurely way of going on, all very nice, like going back in time a bit in the Sixties'. But he believes that the 'comfortable' culture of Porton soon began to alter and open up, partly in response to the outside world and to the influx of new scientists. It is apparent that the establishment was also beginning to take on new work. Furthermore, the innovation of allowing a series of open days in the late 1960s, in which anyone could come and look round Porton, was, according to Swanston, 'a bit of a watershed' which sent out 'irrevocable ripples'. He added, 'The 1960s were very much a revolutionary period and people were questioning. Also, it was very much an anti-war period...Porton's image was going down and down and down and so they had to do something and [so] had the open days.'

The British Government has always been very successful in hammering home the Official Secrets Act to its officials across the state. Porton – soaked in secrecy – is no exception. It is not derogatory to call this a form of indoctrination by a closed government. One Porton veteran admitted that some of his colleagues were frankly 'paranoid'.[5] In hindsight, some of this secrecy may be seen as a little ridiculous. Richard Cookson, a chemistry professor at Southampton University who was a member of a Porton advisory committee in the 1960s, said, 'There was enormous mumbo-jumbo about security, even though, I think, nearly all the members [of the committee] felt that it was well over-the-top by what was justified of what was going on.'[6] He recalled one occasion when an official messenger waited all morning at his university's offices so that he could personally hand him an envelope when he returned. Inside the envelope covered in secrecy markings was merely a circular telling him that a meeting of the advisory committee had been cancelled! Secrecy however can hold its own glamour for some people. The frisson of knowing secrets which the general public does not know has a particular allure for them.

The peculiar circumstances of Porton deterred many from joining, and it would be surprising if this had not affected the quality of scientists who did work there. One eminent scientist was invited to work at Porton, but refused, saying that he regarded the establishment as a 'blot on the landscape'. However it is difficult to judge the quality of the work which has been done by Porton scientists over the years to achieve their specified objectives, and to know if the results would have changed had the pool of scientists been different. Staff, however, insist that the work was high-class, with some brilliant minds working on the research.

In general, scientists seek to check the calibre of their work by exposing their results to the criticism of their fellow scientists. This process of review is an important way of guaranteeing the excellence of their research. It could be argued that another impact of the Official Secrets Act was to restrict the number of scientists who were actually able to give this kind of invaluable feedback on Porton's research, thereby affecting the quality of the establishment's work. The only other laboratories that could check Porton's research are those chemical warfare establishments in allied countries, such as Edgewood Arsenal in America and Suffield in Canada. By its nature, however, this was a smaller number of scientists. Graham Pearson, Porton's director for eleven years from 1984, said this kind of peer review from experts among their allies was 'an immense benefit... It meant that if we in the UK did a study of some "hot" subject, bounced it off our American and Canadian counterparts and they could not fault it, then it gave us tremendous confidence that we had the right appreciation and assessment.'[7]

Another source of critical assessment of Porton's work has been the advisory committees which have overseen what goes on at the establishment. For decades, these were full of top scientists from universities and external institutions who advised Porton scientists on particular issues and quandaries. Professor Richard Keynes, a former Cambridge University physiologist who sat on one of these committees for a few years in the 1960s, commented that one of Porton's troubles was to attract very distinguished scientists to work at Porton because of the mainly classified nature of the research.[8] He recalled that he was not 'gigantically' impressed by the staff there, but added, 'They did their stuff all right. They were perfectly competent.' He believes that Porton scientists were hindered by the secrecy – they were directed to solve particular, narrow problems, but since they were unable to discuss possible solutions with outsiders, potential avenues were inevitably closed off. 'It was difficult to make progress, because usually the progress comes from looking outside,' he added.

There has been something of a bunker mentality among Porton scientists, fostered by both the secrecy and the notoriety. They are often prickly and distrusting, drained by what they perceive to be an incessantly hostile media and, to a lesser extent, the general public. They feel almost demonised. The resulting bitterness seeps through the words of Gradon Carter, a long-serving Porton scientist (and its official historian) when he records the 'suspicion and opprobrium' in parliament and the public: 'This was however of little concern to most at Porton. The tradition of heaping abuse on Porton and Portonians was after all well-established; the press was an ever-ready means.'[9] They believe that the media misrepresent and twist what Porton has been doing in order to create alarm and trouble. However, and perhaps like many drawn together through any kind of adversity, former staff do say that it was an enjoyable place in which to work. They speak of a solid camaraderie. Recruitment material promotes Porton as having 'quite a tradition as a family employer', and indeed a core have stayed at Porton for most of their working lives, up to thirty or forty years. Undoubtedly, some did this out of intense loyalty for the institution. One scientist who worked there for many years in the Cold War put forward a series of reasons – 'There was a lot going for it. There was a lot of job satisfaction. I know that this sounds trite but you were in a nice part of the country. Certainly in those days, up to the 1970s, 1980s, there was absolute security in the scientific civil service, no privatisation, no threat really of sacking...the pay compared reasonably with outside. Because of the Official Secrets Act and everything else, it became a closed community...you get a lot of stability. There was very little motivation to move.' Another Porton scientist also pointed out that in days gone by, it was 'not remarkable' for civil servants to stay at a place for many years. He reiterated that Porton's highly specialised work made it difficult to move onto another posting.[10]

As a generalisation (and as far as one can generalise), 'Porton man' as a type (and most were men) has been conservative-minded and patriotic in varying degrees. They considered that they were working for the best interests of Britain, doing what had to be done. As one recent Porton official said, they were ordinary people with a wife (or a husband), a cat, a dog, going home every night to their semis, believing that they were protecting the defence of the realm.[11]

Porton's human experiments have been conducted by the medical division, one of several sections within the establishment.[12] A relatively small number of scientists and technicians within the installation were closely involved in organising the trials; others who worked in different parts of the establishment did not know much about the experiments. Indeed, it is noticeable that staff from other divisions quickly point out that they were not connected with the experiments, and therefore were not responsible for them and have no knowledge of them.

Many former scientists who are still alive and did organise tests on human 'guinea pigs' are reluctant to discuss the experiments in public. Some cite the Official Secrets Act as the reason why they cannot talk. This could be seen as a convenient cover. Harold Whitcher, who conducted nerve gas experiments in the late 1950s, politely and efficiently parried enquiries by saying that he would need clearance from the Ministry of Defence before he could say anything, adding, 'I feel that this is a very difficult area. I would much rather not talk as it was thirty, forty years ago. That's just too much to recall the details.'[13] Others squirm or put up a host of reasons. Frank Beswick, who was in charge of the human experiments for many years from the late 1960s until the late 1980s, said that his memory was not reliable enough to remember the details of the tests and that he was too busy. He added, 'Quite honestly, the subject is always one which is met with sheer unsympathy, if that's a good word. People are not prepared to listen. I am not prepared to talk.' He insisted the ethics of the human experiments were 'fine, and that's as far as I am prepared to go.'[14]

The beliefs and thoughts of one scientist who worked for a long time at Porton during the Cold War are illuminating. This scientist helped to run many of the human experiments, exposing volunteers to a series of poison gases and other chemicals. Like some others, he spoke about the tests on the condition of anonymity. He admitted that the ethics of testing military personnel with poison gases were 'very thorny' and 'in retrospect, dicey'. He says that back in the 1950s, many Porton staff felt that ethically, they had to be prepared to test the chemicals on themselves before they could subject other human beings – the volunteers from the armed forces – to such compounds. Like many others, he was exposed to a range of chemicals as he felt a 'moral obligation' to do so. This was a common view among Porton scientists, who had frequently tested poison gases on themselves since the establishment was set up in 1916. By the 1960s, such tests were banned unless the director's formal permission was obtained; it appears however this practice continued unofficially (see previous chapter).

He says that most of his colleagues thought about the ethics of the experiments to some extent so that they were in a position to justify the tests; otherwise, they would not have done them. He adds that a minority believed that they were like a 'special agent of God' and had no doubts whatsoever about what they were doing. Asked how he felt about subjecting his fellow human beings to painful chemicals in experiments which he had set up, he confessed, 'It is the not the sort of thing one can give a straight answer to.' It was an issue which he had often contemplated, both during his time at Porton and in his subsequent retirement.

He acknowledged that although the quantities of nerve gases used in many of the human experiments were very low, the volunteers still experienced 'very uncomfortable' effects. This made him, in turn, feel uncomfortable. 'When one sits down and thinks about the ethics of the whole thing in cold blood, one is very slightly worried about this. We did not believe there were any health risks. We were assured that these things were completely safe. Things had been medically investigated in some detail and we were assured that there was absolutely no danger, either immediately or long-term, not from the sort of concentrations we were using.' He took it upon himself to investigate the safety of the chemicals, and not just blindly accept the word of his superiors.

He insists that every possible safety precaution was taken at the time: 'On the whole, Porton tried to err on the safe side. We believed that were being as prudent as we possibly could. The trouble was that if we knew exactly the answers, we would not be doing the tests anyway. It is a Catch-22 situation.'

The controversial nature of both the establishment and the human experiments put Porton staff on their guard. As he said, 'You never see anything in the press, apart from "secret", "nerve agent establishment", or allegations about secret experiments on the deaf and dumb, or something like that. It is always made sensational. We were some of the most careful people on human experimentation, simply because a doctor in a hospital carrying out an experiment on somebody could always convince himself that he was doing it for the good of humanity. Porton was theoretically doing it for the good of humanity – if there was a war and if somebody dropped nerve gas, you had to have a way of treating it. But it was never quite the same, so people did lean over backwards to try and do it as ethically as they could.' He stresses that Porton scientists were not paid 'vast sums of money to salve our consciences', just the usual quite low civil service pay.

Many have sought to justify the tests in the Cold War on the grounds that the West was under threat and needed to defend itself against the perceived peril of the Soviet Union. 'There was certainly a feeling in the 1950s that there was a danger in the Cold War,' he says. Although he worked in a military establishment, he was a civilian scientist and has been less willing to believe that human trials could be justified solely for the sake of defence.

This, he believes, was in contrast with the military doctors who served at Porton.

As he gets older 'and feels the advancing Grim Reaper', he sometimes wonders whether his Porton tests are 'on a continuum with the German experiments in the concentration camps, or is there a break?' He ponders if there is a clear dividing line between his and their experiments. He can never reach a satisfactory conclusion, but he does on balance think that there is a difference between the two sets of tests. He would like to believe that he would have refused to carry out the excesses of the Nazi experiments had he been requested to by his bosses.

He does not regret carrying out human experiments for many years at Porton. 'Looking back, I don't think there is anything I did which actually caused anybody any harm. We genuinely believed there was no possibility of any harm. Everything had been checked beforehand.' However, he does not have a clear view of his exact feelings about his involvement in the chemical warfare tests. He sums it up thus: 'I am not suffering from guilt. I am not suffering from self-satisfaction. I am vaguely unhappy with it, slightly uneasy. It is not black and white.' He adds that while he is not complacent about the ethics of the tests, he is not so wracked with guilt that he would commit suicide. It seems that old age has loosened his tongue about these matters as, he quips, 'Old Nick gets interested'. In his low moments, he does now wonder 'what the hell' he did for so many years at Porton.

Other Porton scientists are known to have voiced concerns. Dr David Gall, who worked in the medical division of Porton in the 1970s, is said to have believed that the nerve gas tests on humans were 'on the borderline of safety'.[15] Similarly, an unnamed, retired Porton scientist admitted in the late 1980s that within the establishment, there had been 'shifts of opinion' about the safety of nerve gas tests. He was quoted as saying, 'It was believed that this was a 100 percent safe procedure. We still believe that, but we are less certain about it and today you have to be 100 percent sure or things can blow up in your face.'[16] Declassified documents contain little evidence of Porton scientists strongly objecting to the conduct and ethics of experiments, or the treatment of the human 'guinea pigs', over the years. Maybe there was little dissent, or maybe the relevant papers have simply not been released by Porton.

For many Porton scientists, the ethics of the tests boiled down to a simple consideration. The experiments were safe and therefore they were ethical. Indeed, one scientist who organised some human trials in the Cold War said the safety of the human 'guinea pigs' was paramount and Porton's prime concern: 'I certainly would not have worked there if I thought there was any potential danger to individuals. I would not ask the volunteers to do anything I would not do.'[17] It seems that this belief that the experiments were safe provided the main internal justification within the establishment for doing the tests. The scientists were working at an institution where, for a long time, experimenting on humans was the norm. If these experiments were not being done, then it would have been a big step to have suggested that tests on human subjects should be done. But since human testing was already part of the mindset of the institution, many simply adjusted to it, and so became involved in organising the tests. These experiments did, after all, frequently provide very useful data for the scientists seeking answers to tricky problems. They therefore signed up and became assimilated into the prevailing mores of the institution. Given the right conditions, it is evident that individuals will adapt and fit into their environment; in this case, so much so that some scientists were able to conduct even the most startling of the experiments which were carried out under Porton's auspices. The scientists were transformed by their circumstances.

Over the decades, there may well have been some scientists who were nasty individuals who positively enjoyed seeing others in pain; we just do not know. But it is likely that they were few and far between. As noted before, the scientists were mainly individuals who believed that what they were doing was a good thing – that the tests were necessary for the defence of the country and that they posed little risk to the human subjects. They considered that they were doing no wrong. In some years, the tests were so numerous that they became quite commonplace – even banal.

Away from the scientists at the coalface of the human experiments are Porton's directors, who have overall responsibility for the activities of the establishment. The buck, as it were, stopped with them, although ministers were ultimately answerable for the work of Porton at a higher level. Take, as an example, the views of Dr Rex Watson who was director between 1974 and 1983 when the size of the testing programme was still significant. He believed that the trials were justified because of the military menace of the Soviet Union during the Cold War.[18] He explained, 'It seemed to me not unreasonable for the armed forces themselves to contribute to the work that was being done for their protection and in that sense, a soldier or sailor or airman coming to Porton as a volunteer was offering his services to help himself and his fellow servicemen to be defended against the threat of chemical warfare. We were working on the basis that there was a threat, and at that stage there was.' As others in officialdom have argued, it is after all, members of the armed forces who were most likely ultimately to benefit from the product of Porton's research. Dr Watson himself considered that the dosages used in the human trials were safe: 'The experiments were being done at levels well below those where one expects any real problems.'

Watson was comfortable with the ethics of the tests. When he took over at Porton, he looked at how the experiments were being conducted and found that the 'drill for ensuring that the volunteers understood what they were volunteering for' was sound. He also felt that, as director, he could rely on the sound opinions of the advisory committees of outside scientists – 'high-fliers' with no axe to grind – who gave advice to Porton. 'I depended on my own judgement of what was good science, and the views of a pretty high-ranking lot of people coming in from outside who looked at the experiments and discussed them with the doctors and scientists involved and gave them the okay. If they were not happy, they said no.' He added, 'I had to be satisfied that every little detail had been covered. I had to accept the judgement of my peers in areas in which I am not necessarily directly competent. You cannot be a scientist who covers every possible subject. You have to rely on the advice of people who you have learnt to trust.' He however still had the responsibility of giving final approval to the tests.

He also believed that the tests were being done for the right reason – to develop Britain's defences against poison gas, and not produce an arsenal of chemical weapons. 'I don't think that I would have been happy, as a director, if we had been working on an active [chemical] capability, partly because I am not sure it is a very effective way of waging war. I felt that as a nation, our emphasis on defence to discourage its use was a reasonable one.'

During his time, many of the human 'guinea pigs' were being tested with tear gases, antidotes and some to nerve gas. Dr Watson was himself exposed to tear gas, although not nerve gas. Unlike Porton staff who organised human trials, he did not do this out of any sense of moral obligation, or feeling that scientists should test themselves with each and every chemical they were going to try out on others. It was for a very different reason. For many of the years he was in charge of the establishment, Porton was developing tear gases to control and dissipate riots in Ulster (see chapter nine). Watson therefore exposed himself to tear gas because, 'I wanted to know what it felt like because we were using the stuff in Northern Ireland. I was watching on television this going on, and people were telling me that it was effective. I thought that it was a good idea; if I was ever going to be asked by a reporter if I had ever exposed myself, I would be able to say yes.' (An exceptionally tall man, at 6ft 7in, Watson has been described as 'an imposing figure with a competitive edge, who was treated with due respect by his subordinates'.[19])

He believed that there was no option but to test human subjects, even if other nations did not carry out such experiments, to make sure that Porton's research was on the right track. 'What was the alternative? How did [other countries] know that their respirators were effective? By and large, the result of the work we did at Porton was to produce the safest sort of discouragement to mobs and civil violence that was available across the world. That was what we were trying to do, but we did not get a lot of thanks for it.'

As part of his duty to oversee the work of the establishment, he quite often watched gas chamber experiments in which human subjects were exposed to chemicals. He considered that one of the director's jobs was to wander around the installation, and observe what was going on. 'A director who sits in his office all the time is not much [of] a director. Basically, I was always a frustrated bench-worker, stuck behind a desk. If there was an excuse to go and look at something, I used to go and look at it.'

Dr Watson was relieved that he was not director of Porton in the 1940s and 1950s when he would have been responsible for the human experiments that were carried out then. He found the human tests in Australia during the Second World War arresting and 'rather dramatic', saying, 'I am glad that I was not the chap that said yes to them. One of the problems that we face is translating ourselves into the circumstances of that time. I was a schoolboy during the war, so I did not experience the way in which the armies had to operate, but some of the things they did to the soldiers – to see how long they lasted after being exposed to mustard gas – were a bit over-the-top. But then it is a difficult to understand why those decisions were made.'

He appeared to voice a note of cautious criticism about the experiments carried out in the 1950s, when equally there was felt to be a threat from the Soviet Union. He said, 'I would not have been in favour, nor was I, of the shot-gun approach to science.' Instead, he wanted to find a way of using resources, such as human volunteers and time, more economically. He said that by the time he became director, 'I was glad that we were able to refine the quality of our testing so that fewer experiments had to be done'. He noted that he had not been 'in the dock for what went on' at Porton while he was director.

The scale of Porton's nerve gas tests on human subjects is truly substantial. More than 3,100 human 'guinea pigs' were exposed to these potent gases in secret tests spanning four decades of the Cold War, from 1945 to 1989.[20] This total is three times the number of exposures conducted by the US military, which tested nerve gas on around 1,100 soldiers up to 1975.[21] Aside from Britain and America, Canada is the only other country which has admitted testing nerve gas on human subjects, saying that a 'small number' of trials were carried out before 1968.[22] It is likely that other countries, such as the former Soviet Union, Iraq, and France, which have had considerable chemical warfare programmes over the years, have also tested human subjects with nerve gas, but details are sketchy and unconfirmed. It seems probable that Porton has tested more human subjects with nerve gas, for the longest period of time, than any other nation in the world, but the secrecy which cloaks such a sensitive and controversial topic does make such a comparison difficult to prove. If Porton is not top of the league, it surely must come close to being so. This would be in keeping with the chemical warfare establishment which, after all, has run the most prolonged testing programme on human 'guinea pigs' in the globe.

Porton scientists have acknowledged that the human experiments were 'an integral part' of the British and American programmes to investigate the effects of the nerve gases and to develop them as weapons.[23] The majority of Porton's nerve gas tests occurred in the early part of the Cold War, when Porton scientists were rapidly striving to crack the secrets of how the new weapons harmed the human body, and Britain was actively preparing to manufacture massive quantities of the gas to counter the Russians' chemical arsenal. In the fifteen years after the Second World War, around 2,600 human 'guinea pigs' were exposed to nerve gas.[24] From the 1960s, the rate of these tests slowed down. In the twenty-three years between 1966 and 1989, 545 volunteers were tested with the gas.[25]

The later tests were indelibly influenced by the death of Maddison and the need to avoid any further fatalities, which almost certainly would have spelt the end of Porton's human experiments. The scientists had to work within the official rules laid down by the Adrian committee of experts after Maddison's death. These regulations had been drawn up specifically to prevent another death and to ensure the safety of the volunteers. Moreover, they had been backed by government ministers and bore their political authority.

It is now clear that Porton staff breached these safety rules at least once without the required approval of higher authorities. This breach occurred between 1962 and 1964 when Porton exposed human 'guinea pigs' to an unauthorised type of nerve gas, which had been barred under the restrictions set down by the Adrian committee. Under these rules, only sarin, also known as GB, could be tested on the military volunteers. Over two years, fifty-six volunteers were exposed to GF, a less well-known nerve gas within the G-nerve gas group.[26] One of these happened to be Mick Roche, who later went on to head the campaign of volunteers alleging that their health had been damaged by Porton tests (see chapter 10). In July 1963, he was exposed to GF after being assured that 'the amount used would be minute and would not harm a mouse'.[27] He recalls, 'The immediate reaction was a tightening of the chest muscles and lungs. For some volunteers, this lasted a period of several seconds, for others, several minutes. These quickly wore off, and for the next twenty-four hours, blood samples were taken at hourly intervals.' Porton has claimed that this breach occurred by accident. According to one explanation, scientists had misconstrued the rule which stipulated that the volunteers could only to be exposed to sarin (GB). The trials with GF were 'stopped when this misinterpretation had been pointed out'.[28]

To some, the use of one nerve gas and not another may seem like a minor infringement in the great scheme of things. However these were rules designed to protect the volunteers and were supported by the political authority of government ministers. Breaking these rules deliberately therefore amounted to defying the democratic will of the government. The toxicity of the GF compound to humans was, and is, less understood than sarin and the other main nerve gases. (A year before these human experiments, Porton had suggested that GF was as much as twenty-five times more toxic than sarin in at least one respect).[29] In that sense, it was more of a leap in the dark than testing the mainstream nerve gases. Indeed Porton itself suggests – slightly opaquely – that in the human experiments with GF, there were 'some intrinsic faults in technique which mitigated general safety'. A senior Porton official was asked to 'investigate the possibility of devising safer and more accurate ways of testing men with GF', if such experiments were to be done in future. As it turned out, it appears that in keeping with the safety rules, only sarin – and no other nerve gas – was tested on the volunteers after Maddison's death.

From time to time since the late 1950s, Porton staff have sought permission to loosen these safety rules so that they could carry out particular experiments, which they had to justify as being not dangerous. As described in the previous chapter, Porton waged a long battle to win approval for the twin proposals to drop V-agents onto the skin of volunteers and inject both sarin and V-agents into the bloodstream of human subjects, but eventually lost this battle in Whitehall in the early 1960s. It was not an issue which Porton felt could be raised again.[30] However, Porton did win other struggles to relax the constraints of the safety conditions which had been introduced after the Adrian committee.

One particular debate revolved around the effect of exercise on a person who had been exposed to nerve gas. After Maddison's death, it was stipulated that volunteers could not be required to undergo 'arduous exercise' after they had been tested with nerve gas. For the next few years, this embargo was observed, except 'for a few trials in which men have been marched up to 15 miles' after they had been poisoned with nerve gas. It was argued that the term 'arduous' had not been defined precisely enough. By 1958, Bill Ladell, the Porton scientist then in charge of human experiments, sought permission to ease this restriction.[31] He argued that it was important to find out how nerve gas affected volunteers who were undergoing vigorous exercise, and to see if they suffered any greater or lesser symptoms than men who had been resting having been exposed. Usually, the volunteers sat relatively still in the gas chamber when they were tested with nerve gas. Yet it was felt that these results could have been proved futile when applied to military situations, where troops on a battlefield may have to move quickly whilst being attacked with poison gas. Porton had already noticed that a few volunteers – exposed to a high dose of sarin – had vomited after they had exerted themselves, and so wanted to investigate the effects further.

As an indication of his awareness of safety concerns, Ladell suggested some safeguards for proposed trials in which men would undergo some sort of exercise before, during and after they had been exposed to sarin. This proposal was approved by the relevant authorising body, the Biology Committee.[32] It appears that Ladell stopped these experiments after a few initial trials which had started with light exercising. One of the safeguards was that the tests would be halted if the men experienced cholinesterase depressions of sevety-five percent or more. 'In the very first test on 10 men, the 75 percent limit was reached by one man, so I never authorised any more strenuous exercise,' he noted.[33] However this was not the end of this line of experiments, and further tests of this type were subsequently approved. It is known that in 1963, forty men were exposed to sarin and told to pump an exercise bike as quickly as possible for five minutes.[34] Later, in 1973, fourteen volunteers carried heavy objects – weighing a third of their body weight – up and down a step rapidly for five minutes before and after they had been poisoned with a dose of sarin.[35] On the whole, it did not seem that exercise exacerbated the effects of the nerve gas.

Another debate centred on tests with human volunteers in hot temperatures. Under the safety rules introduced after the 1953 death, tests had to be 'confined to normal (non-tropical) temperatures'. By 1958, Porton was pushing for these regulations to be adapted so that volunteers could be exposed in artificially-heated gas chambers. Scientists wanted to see if 'simple alterations in body temperature' would make people more or less susceptible to nerve gas.[36] A few years later, a batch of fifteen volunteers spent nine days getting used to both hot and cold temperatures in rooms at Porton. On the eighth day, half of them entered a gas chamber and breathed in sarin, while the rest inhaled only normal air under identical conditions.[37] The point of this experiment was to see if the body's ability to acclimatise to great variations in temperature was interrupted by being exposed to nerve gas. It was concluded that the 'stress' of exposure to the gas did not interfere with this process.

It is apparent that the safety rules laid down after Maddison's death restricted Porton's nerve gas experiments after 1953 to quite an extent. Apart from one breach in the early 1960s, these restraints appear to have been obeyed by Porton scientists. They knew that it was advisable to keep within these rules, and also to be seen to be doing so. Bill Ladell, who was responsible for Porton's human experiments for around a decade, stressed at one point, 'I should make it quite clear that we scrupulously observe all the conditions and limitations laid down by the Adrian Committee and by the Biology Committee...and they are fully satisfied as to the safety of what we do.'[38] These rules were important since they had the political backing of government ministers. The somewhat laborious procedure of having to obtain permission to alter the safety rules meant that a certain degree of control was exerted over the scientists. This contrasts with the years leading up to Maddison's death, when controls appear to have been laxer. There seem to have been few brakes on Porton scientists in the early phase of the Cold War, a period when they knew less about the power of the nerve gases, were under greater pressure to unlock the secrets of the terrifying gases, and were exposing more volunteers to the deadly chemicals at ever-increasing doses.

After the mid-1950s, Porton may still have been exposing human 'guinea pigs' to nerve gas, but at least there was some semblance of a system to check and regulate the experiments. Porton seems to have devoted more care and attention to deliberating about the nerve gas experiments post-Maddison, in a way which did not apparently happen before 1953. In the 1960s, for example, there was lengthy debate among Porton scientists about raising the dose of sarin nerve gas that they were allowed to administer to human volunteers. It is difficult to believe that such a debate would have even occurred prior to 1953. On this occasion, the proposal was dropped 'in favour of further exhaustive trials at lower doses' after they concluded that 'there was insufficient evidence to justify on safety grounds an extension of the limit'.[39] One staff member believed that 'any substantial rise in the present limit might get near the danger levels' in some human volunteers. The limit set down after Maddison's death was 15 mg min m^{-3}, and it appears that this dosage has never been exceeded in the human experiments since then. It seems that even before Maddison's death, Porton scientists had not often gone above this dosage in the human trials. To put this in context, it is currently estimated that between 35 and 75 mg min m^{-3} of sarin will injure a human being, while between 70 and 100 mg min m^{-3} will kill them. One scientist, who worked at Porton for a long time in the Cold War and was involved in the human experiments, insisted that after Maddison's death, 'the sort of quantities used in experiments with nerve agents were very small and in no way life-threatening'.[40]

From the late 1950s, the tempo of the nerve gas experiments appears to have been significantly more unhurried and leisurely than before the tragedy of 1953. As before, Porton scientists had a sizeable pool of volunteers to use as they pursued a variety of experiments. In one particular trial in 1958 scientists were attempting to discover whether a person's hearing was impaired by nerve gas.[41] It was concluded that it was not, after a group of forty-six 'normal, healthy' men exposed to sarin had their hearing tested, alongside volunteers who had not been exposed. However, if it had been found to have an effect on hearing, troops could have had difficulty in, say, hearing instructions or orders in the heat of the battle following a gas attack.

Porton studied the effects of nerve gas on specific parts of the human body in a set of tests around 1959. One involving twenty-three human 'guinea pigs' looked at whether sarin hindered the circulation of blood through the veins of their legs.[42] The scientists had suggested that this perhaps could have led to a new way of treating gas victims, but there was found to be little difference in circulation. Scientists had noted in this experiment that measuring the circulation of blood 'in untrained volunteers presents certain problems. Standard techniques, such as the recording of pressure within isolated segment of vein, require more co-operation than can be expected of many subjects.' Another related experiment concentrated on the impact of sarin on the hearts of twenty-five volunteers.[43] It found that there was a small increase in their heart rates. Ten men inhaled sarin to allow scientists to see if particular muscles between the ribs were responsible for one of the classic nerve gas symptoms, a feeling of 'tightness in the chest'. It was concluded that these muscles played no part in producing this symptom.[44]

One huge trial in the late 1950s used 253 unprotected men to investigate how they reacted to prolonged exposure to sarin. Without masks or protective eye shields, they were put in the gas chamber for periods ranging between twenty-five minutes and two-and-a-half hours so that Porton scientists could log their symptoms at the various dosages.[45] The men were told to keep their eyes open in the chamber where 'they sat and read, or played cards or talked'. Curiously, the scientists spotted something totally unpredicted – the human 'guinea pigs' suddenly became overjoyed in the gas chamber. 'From sitting quietly, the subjects would become elated. Over a very short period of time, they stopped their quiet pastime and started laughing, joking and indulging in general horseplay. So much so that considerable efforts of persuasion were sometimes required to keep them physically still. This mood would subside almost as rapidly as it had begun.' The scientists, however, remained uncertain as to whether or not this had been caused by the sarin – 'it is possible to explain the change of mood as being caused by the confinement of the men in the chamber, or by transitional hysteria in one or more of the men having an effect on the rest.' Porton found that at dosages of 15 mg min m^{-3}, it was impossible to predict the symptoms which would be experienced by the men. 'He is just as liable to show any or all of the classical symptoms of sarin poisoning as to show none whatever.'

Many of the human trials in the years around 1960 used an apparatus which had been developed by Porton, known as 'single-breath administration'.[46] Previously, the volunteers had been put into a gas chamber filled with a set amount of nerve gas and then just breathed in the contaminated air. Under the new technique, volunteers 'were seated comfortably...their confidence was gained by a few minutes of general conversation and instruction in the use [of the apparatus]'. They then had to put their mouth tightly around a tube, take a deep breath and hold it in their lungs to a count of three. They were sucking in a set amount of sarin which had been vapourised in a side flask attached to the tube. Porton scientists believed that this technique was a safer and more reliable method because the amount of sarin actually inhaled by the volunteer could be more carefully measured.

In the last two decades of the nerve gas tests, Porton seemed to have concentrated mainly on exploring how the potent chemicals spoil people's vision. One former scientist suggested that these most recent trials were 'very minor and limited', examining the effect of the gas on a specific part of the body, not the body as a whole.[47] Previous human experiments stretching back to 1945 had shown that one of the classic symptoms of nerve gas poisoning is miosis, in which the pupils of the eyes can be reduced to mere pinpoints, and it is often said that miosis is one of the first symptoms to appear when a victim is hit by a nerve gas cloud.[48] Bill Ladell, nearing the end of his tenure in charge of Porton's human experiments, set out the difficulty in 1967. He said the 'problem of miosis had exercised Porton for 20 years...[and]...there has been a tendency to regard this rather as a nuisance than as a real military effect'.[49]

The scientists still did not know exactly how nerve gas harmed the eye. As Ladell wrote, 'From the military point of view, the question is simply: to what extent does exposure of the eyes to low concentrations of nerve [gas] affect military efficiency and under what circumstances.' Porton needed to know, for example, how little nerve gas would trigger miosis. Their detecting equipment would need to be capable of picking up such minute amounts that military personnel would be warned to don their gas masks immediately. Furthermore, military personnel, such as pilots – in jobs where excellent vision was essential – would be prevented from working well if their sight was impeded by miosis.

That year, Porton exposed forty-nine men to different doses of sarin ranging from 2 to 15 mg min m^{-3} and assessed their ability to carry out various tasks, comparable to certain military skills. Officials had drawn up a list of military occupations 'considered to be vulnerable in that they would be poorly performed by men suffering from miosis'. The results of the tests confirmed that doses of as low as 2 mg min m^{-3} would induce miosis.[50] A few years later, twenty-seven volunteers were exposed to doses of sarin ranging from just under 2 up to 15 mg min m^{-3}.[51] Porton recommended that the crew of an airplane could still function well during daylight after they had been poisoned with 15 mg min m^{-3} of sarin, but at night, they should not fly if they had received a dose higher than 2 mg min m^{-3}.

In a subsequent experiment in 1971, Porton sought to compare the sensitivity of human and rabbit eyes to nerve gas.[52] The gas was 'administered in air flowing through tightly fitting goggles' to both the humans and the rabbits. This time, just over 3 mg min m^{-3} was estimated to be the lowest amount that would provoke miosis in humans. The scientists also found that a tiny amount of VX caused miosis in the animals; this quantity was so worryingly small that it was felt it might prove impossible to be perceived by the detecting equipment. They added however that this episode illustrated why rabbits were 'felt to be very effective detectors' of poison gases, rather like canaries in the coalmines of old.

One volunteer whose eyes suffered in a nerve gas trial was Alan Knowles, a stoker who served in the Navy for twenty-two years. In 1971, he went to Porton for a number of reasons – he would get a bit of extra pay, could get home easily for leave, and was not doing very much since his ship was being refitted.[53] He thought it would be a nice break. He was, however, subjected to tests virtually every day for two weeks, being exposed to sarin, riot control gases and mustard gas. He was told that he could refuse to do any of the tests. On the penultimate day, he was gassed with sarin (GB). 'They told us it was nerve gas, but that it was such a small amount that it would not hurt us. They spoke to you as though it was nothing, as though you would have no side-effects at all on you.' At that stage, he had no idea what the effects of nerve gas were. 'They didn't explain anything to you at all about what it did to you.' He went into the chamber with only a gas mask for protection, and, after a short time walking around, he and the other volunteers were told to take off their gas masks. He believes that they stayed in there for around five minutes. He began to suffer miosis. 'Your eyes started to go dark. When we came out, we could not see properly. They gave us some dark glasses to wear and said your eyes will probably be like that for three weeks before they get back to normal. You couldn't read a paper for a few days – it would give you a headache.' The next day, he left Porton to go home on leave and the establishment had no further contact with him.[54] His eyes gradually recovered over the next couple of weeks, but he suspects that the experiments may have caused him long-term damage. He had to start wearing glasses within a year and developed high pressure in 1978, which he has to control with a daily dose of tablets.

Porton's tests on the eyes continued. In a test around 1973, six volunteers were exposed to 15 mg min m^{-3} of sarin, 'well below the dose which would induce signs of systemic poisoning'.[55] The aim was to see if a specific mydriatic (substances which enlarge the pupils of eyes) could be used as an antidote to counteract the contraction of the pupil through miosis. After the experiment, two men complained of 'peripheral dimness', one suffered 'discomfort on looking at close objects', another believed that he had blurred vision when looking at far-away things (scientific tests, however, showed that actually his sight had improved). It was concluded that generally, mydriatics would not be useful as an antidote, unless the victim's eyes were very bad or he had to work in very poor light. In a test two years later, Porton exposed five 'unprotected' volunteers to a similar dose of sarin to clarify further how the nerve gas attacked the eyes.[56]

Only snippets of Porton's nerve gas experiments in the last three decades are known. Most of the experiments are hidden from the public because they fall within the official thirty-year ban on releasing government papers. A few papers have, however, been published in the scientific press. In a rather ironic incident, Porton recently refused to release two internal reports describing 1970s nerve gas tests on humans to the Labour MP Ken Livingstone, even though it had listed the reports as being unclassified just a few months earlier. Porton apparently decided to reclassify the reports as secret as soon as Livingstone asked for copies of them. The MP jested that there must be a special secrecy classification known as 'not to be released to Ken Livingstone'. (Paradoxically, the essential details of these reports had already, in fact, been published by former Porton scientists.[57]) Senior MoD sources insisted that these reports were not kept secret merely to avoid political embarrassment.[58] Instead Porton argued that the reports could have helped countries around the world which wanted to produce poison gases.[59]

The number of volunteers exposed to nerve gas has been steadily dropping since the early 1970s, and this seems to be in relation to the overall number of total volunteers which was also falling over this time. There was, however, a sudden leap in nerve gas tests for a few years around 1980. According to Porton, the rise at that time was due to 'the need to carry out studies into aircrew protection' and so a number of trials 'were carried out to determine the lowest acceptable level for exposure to nerve agents'.[60]

At the time of writing, the last time that Porton volunteers were tested with nerve gas was in 1989. For just over six and a half hours, twenty-three volunteers were again exposed to 'low levels' of sarin to see what effect the gas would have on their eyes. Compared to early Cold War trials, the amount of sarin used was small – 2 mg min m^{-3}. 'The response of the volunteers exposed was variable,' according to Porton staff, who concluded that this level of sarin contamination would not have prevented RAF aircrew from carrying out their combat duties.[61] Graham Pearson, Porton's director between 1984 and 1995, said that at this time, the scientists were trying to establish what was the lowest amount, or threshold, of sarin which would begin to produce a physiological effect in the human body. They were looking to see the first tightening of the pupils in the eyes of the volunteers, using a 'tiny' dosage of sarin. This information could be used, for instance, to assess the distance at which nerve gas would begin to affect military personnel downwind from an actual attack. Pearson added that with such a low dosage, 'the chances of it actually causing any harm to any of the volunteers was absolutely remote'. He believed that the volunteers would not experience any discomfort, except for a little change in the eyes. There seems to have been a temporary halt in these nerve gas tests after this experiment, but the exact circumstances are unclear. As recently as 1995, the Ministry of Defence proposed to subject volunteers to a 'prolonged exposure' of a 'low dose' of sarin for ten hours, but the idea was eventually shelved in favour of an alternative technique.[62]

So far, the government has not imposed an absolute ban on experiments in which human subjects are exposed to poison gases. Officially, Porton argues that there could be extreme circumstances when such experiments would have to be carried out to safeguard the country. Such tests have never been 'categorically ruled out', but would only be done if there was a 'compelling' reason. According to Porton, 'the use of human volunteers is kept constantly under review and people are only ever used when it is both necessary and safe to do so'; in recent years, there has been no need to expose them in this way.[63] It does seem unlikely that experiments with nerve gas (or other poison gases) will be conducted by Porton in the foreseeable future, but it is remarkable that the MoD did plan to expose volunteers to nerve gas in 1995, at a time when few other Western countries would even contemplate such a thing. Politically, such tests in the future would be hard to justify, especially since government ministers are so aware of public opinion, and now keep a tighter rein on these experiments, in contrast to the Cold War and before. Back then, Porton scientists routinely conducted human trials and seldom notified the politicians beforehand. Now ministers have to be consulted on *any* proposal to test human volunteers with poison gases.

Also, Porton staff would have to get the approval of the establishment's Independent Ethics Committee, which consists mainly of outsiders (see previous chapter). The committee's current chairman is Professor Malcolm Lader of the Institute of Psychiatry in London, who said, 'At the moment, we don't allow nerve gas to be tested because there is no safe low dose, basically.' He added, 'I think we would be very, very reluctant to change our minds on that'.[64] A few years ago, the committee was asked for its opinion on the use of nerve gas in tests – 'We felt that it is not a safe procedure at whatever dose, mainly because it is very difficult to know what the long-term effects might be. There was a lack of reassurance about the safety of these procedures'. He said it was difficult to be absolutely sure that, as with many other chemicals, nerve gas will not cause illnesses in the long run, commenting, 'You don't get certainty in science'. Furthermore, he also said that the Independent Ethics Committee believes that Porton should always choose alternatives to testing human subjects with nerve gas and other such chemicals – 'modelling it, or using safer chemicals that give the same answers'. There was, for example, another way to find out if humans see properly after they have been exposed to nerve gas. 'The question is – are you going to give nerve gas to soldiers and see if they can focus. You don't need to do that. You can work out how impaired their fighting capacity is by giving them a much safer compound which has the same effect. That's the sort of strategy we have adopted,' he added. Moreover, the end of the Cold War removed a key reason, and justification, for human trials with poison gases. It may be coincidence, but it is noticeable that the last nerve gas trial was conducted in the last year of the Cold War.

While Porton's nerve gas trials could in theory resume at any moment, Britain's closest allies in the field of chemical warfare have drawn a definite halt to their human tests with the deadly chemicals. The United States of America stopped testing humans with nerve gases and other chemicals in 1975 after the intense outcry from the public. Canada similarly ended its tests with such compounds in 1968, while Australia is not believed to have conducted any human tests after the mustard gas experiments in the Second World War. Despite this, data arising from Britain's recent tests on human volunteers has been shared with these allies under the collaborative agreements which have existed for many years between these countries.[65]

Britain's official policy on the production of chemical weapons has inevitably shaped the course and volume of Porton's human experiments. The task of Porton scientists was to support and help achieve the aims of the policy and so the experiments were tailored to meet those ends. From the First World War to the mid-1950s, Britain had been committed to manufacturing chemical weapons, but that has changed since then.

A major landmark was in 1956 when the then Conservative government resolved to stop the development of nerve gas weapons, effectively abandoning Britain's offensive posture.[66] This U-turn was not announced at the time – indeed, news of the new policy dribbled out and was not stated unequivocally in public until some years later, and the papers relating to the decision were not declassified until September 1995. It is yet another sign of Britain's secretive government that these papers – which explain such a significant milestone in the country's chemical warfare policies – were kept concealed for so long. The crucial decision was made in Downing Street on 10 July 1956 at a top-level meeting of the Cabinet's defence committee, attended by, among others, the then Prime Minister Sir Anthony Eden and Chancellor of the Exchequer, Harold Macmillan.[67]

In front of the meeting was a three-page memorandum by Sir Walter Monckton, then Defence Minister. In this, he advocated that Britain should no longer develop nerve gases. He wrote that on the one hand, it would mean that 'the United Kingdom would not be able from its own resources to retaliate in kind if chemical weapons of this kind were used by an enemy or to contribute to the deterrent threat against their use'. He pointed out that as a signatory of the 1925 Geneva Protocol, Britain's policy had always been to be prepared to retaliate if attacked with chemical weapons, but never to use such weapons in the first place. On the other hand, he reasoned, 'we are however faced with the necessity of restricting our defence expenditure to what is absolutely essential', adding that 'our American allies are devoting a considerable effort to the development of nerve gas weapons and this will provide a powerful deterrent' against the Russians. He therefore concluded that Britain's nuclear weapons – together with the 'massive nuclear armoury and chemical warfare potential' of the Americans – justified the decision to abandon 'our own capacity to wage offensive chemical warfare...in our own present economic circumstances'. According to the minutes, the committee heard that in general, Britain relied on nuclear weapons as its deterrent against weapons of mass destruction, and that it was 'difficult to reconcile' this with the 'substantial resources' which were being spent on developing nerve gases. Monckton spelt out once again that 'in the present circumstances, it seemed best to devote these resources to other purposes and to rely on the capacity maintained by the United States as a deterrent' against chemical attack by the Russians.

The decision to shelter behind the American chemical deterrent was made possible by the close co-operation and exchange of information between the two countries in chemical warfare. It was not the first time that the British had sought American help. In 1953, Britain had, without success, tried to buy huge amounts of nerve gas from the Americans as a stopgap until Nancekuke was up and running.[68]

Britain's reliance on the Americans' nerve gas armoury was the blunt reality of the shift in world power. Since the end of 1945, Britain's position as a superpower had been ebbing away, along with its empire. Two new superpowers – the United States of America and the Soviet Union – had taken over. Britain had aligned itself with the US in the famed 'Special Relationship', but, in reality, this was a relationship of unequals. With its superior economic and military power, the US was in control, and Britain was struggling simply to stay in the game and remain a key player in world politics. It was this desire for status which drove the British on to acquire nuclear weapons – at a huge cost to the nation's finances. But because of its declining economic might, Britain could no longer afford to produce another set of weapons of mass destruction – poison gas. The British defence policy since 1945 has to a large extent been driven by the unavoidable need to make cuts in the budget. As top-secret papers now declassified in the Public Record Office show, defence chiefs grappled for years with the painful task of selecting which part of their beloved military should be cut or closed down.

In a bizarre coda to the decision in 1956, the British had agreed that it was 'desirable' to inform the Americans of their intention to halt the development of nerve gas and in effect rely on the US for the production of chemical weapons. The Prime Minister was to communicate personally with the then US President, Dwight Eisenhower. An official letter was drafted, but Downing Street decided to delay sending it because of the intensifying Suez Crisis. But the missive was never actually sent as the furore over Suez in the autumn of 1956 plunged Anglo-American relations to its lowest point since 1945.[69] (The humiliating Suez Crisis was yet more confirmation that Britain was no longer a superpower.) The lack of a formal notification of this decision caused a few awkward moments for Britain at a senior level, but in reality, the American scientists at the lower levels quickly learnt from their Porton counterparts.

According to the surviving written record, the 1956 decision to discard nerve gas arose out of the overwhelming need to cut Britain's military expenditure. Whitehall's Defence Research Policy Committee had been charged with finding ways of keeping the total budget of defence research and development contained within a certain ceiling. The committee's report makes it clear that specific commitments would have to be cut if the ceiling was to be kept to.[70] The report compared Britain with the US and the Soviet Union. 'We know that the United States have deployed vast scientific and technological resources in defence R&D... Some considerable bodies of opinion in Parliament and public apparently expect us to match the results of both the United States and [the] USSR in every field.' The committee brusquely stated that 'it is obvious that this cannot be done with the resources likely to be available to us for defence R&D... In some fields, we have fallen behind either the United States or the USSR, or both, in the development of modern operational equipment and weapons. The wider we spread our effort in an attempt to keep up on a broad front, the more likely are we to fall further behind.'[71]

The 1956 decision did not spell the end of Porton. The establishment's life-saver was an agreement from the Cabinet's Defence Committee to continue 'research work in the chemical warfare field' as well as developing defensive measures against chemical attack. Defence Minister Sir Walter Monckton acknowledged that the possession of nerve gas by an enemy 'would still pose a serious defensive problem' especially since 'we have not yet reached the stage of knowing all about defence against these gases'. He added that this necessary defensive work 'would keep knowledge of chemical warfare in general alive in this country even though we cut back very heavily on the expensive field, that of production'.

In later years, the 1956 decision was often presented by the government of the day as being a virtuous move towards disarmament. An example of this is shown in an exchange in the House of Commons in March 1990 about proposals to reduce chemical weapons stockpiles in the world when a junior defence minister asserted that 'Britain had set the example about 30 years ago by renouncing chemical weapons'.[72] Since the papers detailing the decision were kept under wraps even longer than the usual thirty-year period, defence ministers were able to make this claim. The reality, however, is admitted in a recent MoD document which stated that official papers 'often reveal that the motivation for [the 1956 decision] was economic rather than the unilateral enthusiasm for arms control that has been emphasised in recent years'.[73]

Nancekuke was cut back, but not closed. According to the MoD, Nancekuke never got as far as actually filling real weapons with nerve gas. By the time of the 1956 decision, Nancekuke staff had managed to build an experimental plant which could produce a limited amount of sarin — about one ton a week. The purpose of the experimental plant was to gather data to design and build a larger factory which would, in turn, be able to churn out around fifty tons a week. The MoD says the only nerve gas produced at Nancekuke was twenty tons of sarin, and this was produced irregularly between 1954 and 1956.[74]

The design and planning of the larger nerve gas factory had been finished by 1956. But following the Cabinet's decision, the government stopped this work, folded up the blueprints and put them away. The smaller, experimental plant was decontaminated, although not dismantled until some twenty years later. Nancekuke's staff was cut back drastically, and, as for the twenty tons of sarin, these were used in other work to research into the stability and corrosion of nerve gas when it is stored, and all but 110 gallons had been destroyed by 1968. The remainder was transferred to Porton on an irregular basis where it was to be used for research. It was transported by road which provoked protests from West Country residents who were worried about the safety of the convoys. This campaign led to an official inquiry which — like the earlier Adrian committee into Maddison's death — was once again carried out internally by the MoD, with help from outside scientists, who were supposedly 'independent', but had in fact been associated with Porton. The 71,000 tabun bombs — which had been confiscated from the Nazis at the end of the war and stored at a Welsh airfield — were dumped in the Atlantic in 1955 and 1956.[75] The British had initially kept these bombs because they were the only nerve gas weapons they possessed. The military had wanted to adapt these bombs so that they could be fitted onto British aircraft, but this plan had been abandoned in 1954 because the weapons were unsafe and leaking occasionally.[76] Recently environmentalists have been worried that the deadly gas in the dumped bombs is seeping into the sea.

By 1956, the British had amassed a sizeable working knowledge of the arcane and sophisticated world of nerve gas production. Only a few nations – Germany, the US and possibly the Soviet Union – had embarked on such production at that time. This knowledge had been accumulated through the work of Nancekuke, Porton's experiments, and the data filched from the Nazis. Another important source of information had been a series of nerve gas trials in one of Britain's colonies, Nigeria. Between 1951 and 1955, Porton had sent over a number of expeditions to Obanakoro in the Sobo Plain area.[77] The twenty-seven-square mile testing site was isolated with a mixture of open grassland and jungle.[78] These expeditions fired nerve gas in artillery shells, mini-cluster bombs and mortar bombs, with the main aim being to assess the performance of sarin in a hot climate. Porton insists that there has been no lasting contamination on the site, since sarin is not a persistent chemical and disappears quickly. They also maintain that no human volunteers were exposed to poison gases at Sobo.[79]

But the British had not entirely closed the door on the possibility of manufacturing nerve gases in the future. The policy soon began to be reconsidered within government circles, and high-level reviews were initiated. During this secret Whitehall debate, some argued, for instance, that the true potential of the V-class of nerve gases and the incapacitating weapons had not been fully appreciated.[80] This reassessment – which had lasted for more than two years – eventually culminated in a critical change of policy at a meeting of the Cabinet's Defence Committee on 3 May 1963. Under the chairmanship of the then Conservative Prime Minister Harold Macmillan, the committee was told that the Russians were well equipped to use poison gas 'as normal weapons of war', but Britain had 'no stocks'.[81] According to a top-secret memo, Porton carried out 'small scale though highly effective research...to keep abreast of techniques' and to ensure the flow of information on chemical warfare matters from the Americans. In this fearful Cold War atmosphere, the committee members approved proposals to increase the research and development of lethal and incapacitating chemical weapons. They authorised the 'limited' production of lethal weapons so that they could have a 'small capability' to retaliate against any enemy which had used gas against Britain. This change of policy was tinged with tentativeness, as the politicians could not agree at that time that the weapons, once produced, should actually be deployed on the ground among military units in this country and elsewhere. That particular authorisation was held back for the time being. (Incidentally one of the committee members was the then War Minister, John Profumo, who made some of his last decisions before resigning a few weeks later in the famous scandal).

Ministers were acutely aware of the political sensitivity of this decision. 'If we manufactured them it would be desirable to keep the fact from becoming known,' noted the committee. The new policy – one of the most secret decisions within Whitehall at the time – was not announced and did not emerge in public until three decades later.

Officials therefore began to draw up plans to acquire munitions filled with nerve gas. It was proposed to load sarin into 22,000 artillery shells and spray VX from 320 tanks fitted onto aircraft.[82] But these proposals began to run aground, eventually disappearing into nothingness. Civil servants realised that, with the demise of the Macmillan government, the new administration under Labour Prime Minister Harold Wilson would have to approve the 1963 decision. But this never happened for a variety of reasons, according to official explanations.[83] There were 'economic pressures and political reluctance to rearm with these weapons'. Even research on defensive measures at both Porton and Nancekuke was being reduced in a programme of massive cuts in military spending. In the late sixties, there was intense public concern about chemical and biological warfare, triggered mainly by the American use of chemical weapons in Vietnam. Members of the public began to question the work going on at Porton, and especially whether Britain too was producing poison gas. It has also been suggested that ministers were too preoccupied with other, more pressing issues, such as the crisis in Rhodesia and the 1966 general election, to even discuss it at the Cabinet.

It appears that the drive to implement the 1963 decision petered out. The decision did not result in the production of any chemical weapons on a large scale, nor indeed the facilities to do so. In January 1968, the Chiefs of Staff, who had been supporting chemical rearmament, decided that, given the political and economic climate, they would not press their case at that stage and instead wait at least two years.[84] But it appears that it soon became widely recognised that the issue had been 'deferred indefinitely'. The Ministry of Defence agonised over whether to confirm publicly in 1968 that Britain had no stockpiles of chemical weapons. In a risible episode, a Foreign Office minister had stated this fact in a letter to a member of the public, who then asked the minister whether he could show the letter to others. Defence officials opposed this because 'they were not denying the truth of the statement, but they are not inviting attention to it and do not want it repeated more than absolutely necessary'. Foreign Office mandarins called it 'the worst sort of obscurantism...of the kind that makes everyone concerned look very foolish'.[85] It was on a par with the secrecy that has surrounded British chemical warfare ever since the First World War.

Since 1968, Britain has not made any renewed effort to manufacture chemical weapons in bulk, although the policy has been periodically reviewed.[86]

Aside from other arguments about the benefits of such weapons, Whitehall was very conscious that it would be hard to sell chemical rearmament to the general public. Given the thirty-year ban on releasing official papers, details of these Whitehall discussions are still secret, but from time to time, glimpses of these internal deliberations have surfaced.

In the 1970s, British politicians do not appear to have placed much, if any, priority on developing chemical weapons. This was clear during the wholesale review of the MoD's budget under the then defence minister Roy Mason in 1974-5. As a result of this review, the Labour government announced in 1976 that Nancekuke was to close as part of a hefty round of cuts.[87] The continuing existence of the Nancekuke factory could be seen as an indication that Britain was not prepared to renounce a chemical capability completely, in effect leaving the door ajar to return if the political will changed.[88] But this possibility was a cost which could no longer be justified in the harsh financial circumstances. Dr Rex Watson, Porton's director between 1974 and 1983, commented that, 'The pressure to close Nancekuke was an economic one,' adding, 'It employed over a hundred people. It was a pretty unpleasant thing to go down and tell them that they had lost their jobs.' Some of its work and senior staff were transferred to Porton. Its closure, however, was found to have a silver lining – literally. The equipment in the installation contained a lot of silver, and 'around about that time, there was a chap trying to corner the market and we sold the silver at the top of the market.' The sale netted a large sum, helping to boost government coffers, and the experimental nerve gas factory which had been mothballed in 1956 was finally dismantled in 1979.[89]

Porton itself had even come under threat of closure during the 'exceptionally ferocious' Mason defence review.[90] Senior Porton staff were sufficiently worried of this danger that they quickly organised a delegation to go over to seek help from their allies in the United States. Dr Watson explained, 'The Americans kicked up a fuss. They made it very clear to the then British government that they would be very unhappy. At the time, there were people in government, CND-ers, who were very anti-Porton.' Rather like Neville Chamberlain's famous Munich letter of 1938, the delegation came back with a letter in which the Americans stressed Porton's important work in the field of chemical defence. This American intervention was used to convince the government to reprieve Porton – 'It helped to do the trick. We survived. We went from strength to strength after that,' Watson added. The Mason review did, however, lead to the closure of the separate biological defence establishment at Porton and a cut in the chemical budget. In the following years, Watson had to prune Porton's expenditure, reducing the number of staff and facilities, to stay within budget, amid a feeling that the existence of the establishment always had to be justified to Whitehall. According to one account, he left Porton with some relief – 'the closure of the officers' mess was among the unpopular measures which earned him an unsought reputation as a hatchet man'.[91]

This intervention by the Americans, however crucial it was, underlines how closely the two countries collaborated over chemical warfare. Watson said, 'It was one of the few establishments in defence that you could go as director of Porton to the [United] States and be in a position where you were regarded as an equal. We were as good as they were in the sense of chemical defence.' Right up to the present day, this collaboration has persisted. The network of agreements, meetings and exchange of information has continued as strongly as ever.[92] (Graham Pearson, Porton's director between 1984 and 1995, said that during his time, the co-operation was revitalised and focused more tightly on the key issues of the day in chemical and biological defence).[93]

The chemical side of Porton had been retained because the government felt that Britain faced a specific threat from the Soviet Union. The political atmosphere changed in the 1980s, as the Cold War heightened. The Americans had stopped producing chemical weapons in 1969, but under the administration of US President Ronald Reagan, they resumed in 1987. Supporters of rearmament had argued that, while the West stood still, the Soviet Union had been galloping ahead and expanding its chemical arsenal, thereby gaining a significant lead in this field. It was an argument which was received favourably by Margaret Thatcher's Conservative government which had come to power in 1979. The following year, Francis Pym, the new Defence Minister, declared that he was 'haunted' by the Soviet Union's growing chemical stockpile, openly flirting with the idea of re-equipping Britain with poison gas in a blaze of publicity.[94] (It transpires that during the 1980s, Britain hugely over-inflated its assessment of the Soviet stockpile of nerve gas.)

The issue appeared to be dropped, but then burst into the public domain once again in 1985 following a leak to the left-wing magazine, the *New*

Statesman.[95] The magazine reported that Thatcher was 'on the point of forcing through a decision that Britain should restart production of nerve gases'. The leak immediately unleashed a political rumpus. Thatcher declared that she did not propose to change the policy, but 'as a responsible government, we have a duty to keep defence policy under review in the light of the massive Soviet capability in chemical weapons'. Any move to rearmament was presumably squashed.

By the late 1980s, signs of real progress in the negotiations to agree on a global treaty banning chemical weapons began to appear. These talks had started in earnest in 1968 and had been trundling on ever since in varying degrees of optimism. Britain had a good record on promoting and pushing forward these negotiations, for example, tabling a draft agreement in 1976 and coming up with a series of initiatives to break logjams. The final abandonment of plans to obtain a chemical capability in the late 1960s undoubtedly enabled Britain to play a leading role in these talks. The end of the Cold War opened the way for the superpowers to eliminate poison gas from their arsenals. It is also believed that the fear of Iraq's chemical weapons – highlighted in the 1991 Gulf War – reinforced the feeling that it was time to stop the growing number of countries who were alleged to be seeking to acquire such weapons. A treaty was finally signed in 1993, coming into force four years later. This treaty bans the production, stockpiling and use of chemicals weapons, and also places controls on chemicals from which these weapons can be made. Although the treaty may not rid the world of chemical weapons completely, it is a major and historic agreement which at least plugs some of the gaps left by the 1925 Geneva Protocol.

It should not be forgotten that many military commanders do not favour chemical weapons in their armouries for several reasons. They believe that although it is quite easy to protect a modern army against gas, the masks, suits and antidotes are cumbersome and do reduce a soldier's efficiency. Chemical weapons are also considered to be generally less effective than conventional munitions. Moreover, chemical weapons exert their effects more slowly than other weapons and so they are harder to integrate with the overall war-fighting capability. Similarly, their effects are unpredictable because their impact is affected by the direction of the wind and the prevailing temperature. Countries need to have a reasonable degree of expertise and skill to produce chemical weapons properly, and then be able to disseminate them in sufficiently harmful concentrations. Between evenly-matched armies, gas can be used advantageously in only a few circumstances. As noted before, chemical weapons have usually been used by well-equipped nations against forces with poor defences against gas. This is the reality of gas, not the myth of the 'superweapons' which causes so much alarm. Gas has in fact been used in only a small number of the hundreds of wars fought since the First World War.

CHAPTER EIGHT
Britain's Psychedelic Soldiers

The film of 'Operation Moneybags' must surely be one of the most bizarre ever made by the British military. The blue-tinged pictures show a unit of Royal Marine commandos staging a mock attack. Such exercises were routine for trained troops, but this attack had one crucial and unusual difference – the soldiers were tripping on the hallucinogenic drug, LSD. One khaki-clad commando is seen climbing up a tree trying to feed imaginary birds, two others have collapsed onto the ground in unconstrained fits of laughter – one of them had earlier hacked his way through half a tree with a spade. The scenes are described in a monotone by a plummy-voiced commentator, who at one point notes in his characteristically flat manner that 'men with no specific task have relapsed into laughter and inconsequential behaviour'.

That experiment was just one in a concerted series of tests carried out by Porton during the 1960s to see if a chemical could be used to befuddle the mind of the enemy in order to win a military advantage. The tests took place in a decade which has become a byword for drug-taking, the so-called Swinging Sixties. It is richly ironic that while 'peace-nik' hippies were being busted by police for getting high on acid and other drugs, military scientists in a top-secret laboratory were investigating whether the same sort of drugs could knock out future foes. It was all part of a new non-lethal concept for fighting conflicts: war without death, or how to disable the enemy without killing them. This was to be done with a category of chemical weapons which were to become known as incapacitating agents. Such chemicals would literally incapacitate the enemy physically or mentally for a period of time, but not terminate their life.

Nowadays, these experiments with LSD and other so-called pyscho-chemicals appear comical and are more likely to make many people giggle. However back then, there were those within British government circles who believed that mind-altering drugs could be exploited as a military weapon. LSD was just one of the chemicals which was tested on volunteers, often without their knowledge. The MoD subsequently admitted that these tests with mind-bending chemicals are 'particularly contentious'.[1]

The early impetus in developing pyscho-chemicals as a weapon of war came in fact from the American military.[2] The US Chemical Corps started studying pyscho-chemicals themselves in 1951.[3] Initially, the US scientists selected three drugs and their related compounds for investigation – LSD, mescaline, and marijuana.[4] The scientists wanted to investigate how effectively the chemicals caused a host of medical effects, such as hallucination, mania, delirium, psychosis, suicidal tendencies, and convulsions.[5]

The Americans were by 1958 moderately pleased with their efforts. Their assessment of progress was optimistic: it seemed possible that the mind-bending agents 'could be valuable in softening enemy troops, causing them to lose their morale and judgement, putting them in an euphoristic state where they have no interest in warfare, making them halt any offensive action and prevent them from resisting attack and capture.' The chemical warriors even raised the possibility that 'entire enemy forces' – dosed with mind-warping drugs – could be 'captured without resistance or casualties.'[6]

The focus of the American research had shifted onto LSD – mescaline was ruled to be an 'impractical' chemical weapon 'because the doses needed to bring about the mental effects were too large.' (An innocent civilian died in 1953 after he was given a mescaline-like drug in US Army tests.)[7] Scientists warned that marijuana 'may bring on pathological changes, and if this proves to be true, the testing of the compounds on volunteers will have to be done with great caution'.[8] The US Chemical Corps had been given permission in 1955-56 to test psycho-chemicals on humans.[9]

The Corps saw pyscho-chemicals and other drugs as a huge opportunity to transform the public's attitudes to chemical warfare. Most people were revolted by gas warfare because of the enduring image of the horror wreaked by mustard gas in the First World War. But these drugs were marketed as weapons which would 'incapacitate, but not kill', ushering a new era of 'humane warfare'. Such chemicals could turn brave men into cowards – 'a merciful alternative to the atomic bomb', as one magazine described it.[10]

In a propaganda offensive in the late 1950s, the US Chemical Corps sought to manipulate public opinion through a variety of ways: favourable articles appeared in the press with headlines such as 'Mickey Finn on the battlefield' and 'Off the rocker and on the floor'; previously-classified information was carefully and strategically leaked; generals spoke to a host of selected clubs and societies; travelling exhibitions were sent around the country; and officials addressed hearings of the US Congress.

Politicians and the press were particularly captivated by a film – shown to a Congressional committee – in which a cat dosed with a psycho-chemical is reduced to a trembling wreck in front of a mouse. One government scientist was quoted as saying, 'Ideally we'd like something we could spray out of a small atomiser that would cause the enemy to come to our lines with his hands behind his back, whistling "The Star-spangled Banner". I don't think we'll achieve that effect, but we may come close.'[11]

The American campaign to soft-sell the 'humane weapons' was creating waves across the Atlantic in the British military. In top-secret papers, Whitehall officials commented that the hallucinogenics had aroused widespread interest, adding that there was a 'growing awareness of the potential of this type of agent in warfare'. One paper noted dryly, 'There is a certain attraction in being able to achieve military objectives by affecting the mind of the enemy.'[12] Officials recommended that more money should be poured into researching the incapacitating agents. In 1960, the Master-General of the Ordnance in the War Office proclaimed that in the previous two years, the 'military potential of new incapacitating agents has been recognised. If the promise of present research is fulfilled, the introduction of these might revolutionise the attitude to the use of chemical agents'.[13] By 1961, the British government had begun to review its abandonment of a chemical arsenal. This far-reaching review – held in total secrecy – was started as many officials argued that two comparatively recent discoveries, the pyscho-chemicals and the more potent V-agent nerve gases, could be militarily useful.[14]

Through the usual channels of the regular Tripartite Conferences, Porton and its Canadian counterparts had been kept informed of the Americans' progress on uncovering the elusive perfect incapacitating chemical.[15] Throughout the 1950s, the Americans had been in the driving seat in the hunt for such a chemical, although Porton had carried out a small amount of research itself.[16] But by 1960, priorities were changing, as the British authorities became increasingly interested in an apparently bloodless weapon.[17] LSD appeared particularly appealing because it was so potent, and a minuscule amount could have a huge impact on a person's mind. In an initial set of experiments, LSD and other drugs had been tested on animals, in particular rats and rabbits. These experiments showed that, among other effects, LSD made rats defecate less.[18] Porton found that it was 'extremely difficult' to draw solid conclusions from the animal tests that could be applied to humans.

Inevitably LSD would have to be tested on humans if its potential as a weapon was to be evaluated. This raised ethical questions, since the dangers of the chemical were by then known within the medical and scientific community. LSD had been accidentally discovered in 1943 by Swiss chemist, Albert Hofmann, who on his first proper 'acid trip' had a frightening experience. He began to feel threatened, as if a demon had invaded him and taken control of his mind, body and soul, and his neighbour had became 'a malevolent, insidious witch with a coloured mask.' At one point, he feared that he had gone permanently insane. However, he had recovered by the next morning, and, walking into the garden after a spring rain, 'everything glistened and sparkled in a fresh light'.[19]

Within a decade, psychiatrists had begun to experiment with it as a possible cure for people suffering mental problems. LSD was administered to thousands of mental patients in hospitals and centres in several countries over the next two decades. But warnings about the hazards of LSD had started to appear in scientific journals. For example, three academics wrote to the *Lancet* in 1955 urging colleagues not to use the drug on patients until more was known about its effects. They cautioned that those under the influence of LSD were a danger to themselves and others and that the drug could aggravate psychotic illnesses.[20] This caution was noticed by Dr Van Sim, the American scientist who later played a prominent role in US chemical warfare experiments and who had recently spent a year at Porton (see chapter five). In a report circulated to the American military and the British government, Dr Sim called the *Lancet* letter a 'word of caution to those who would like to see immediate large-scale experiments' with psycho-chemicals.[21]

Porton staff grappled with the ethics of administering psycho-chemicals such as LSD to volunteers. In 1957, two Porton scientists noted that hallucinogenic drugs provoked 'a period of profound mental disturbance'. They wrote that 'unfortunately' human tests were then the only available method of assessing the mind-bending potency of such chemicals, but warned that, 'this could be a dangerous procedure'.[22] At a meeting of a Porton advisory committee in 1959, Porton scientist Roger Brimblecombe said the only certain method of selecting a drug which would be suitable for the heat of battle would be 'by tests on humans, but there were many objections to that'.[23] The committee's chairman, Professor Henry Rydon, wondered 'whether permission would be given for human experiments', and, to even apply for permission, they would have to know beyond reasonable doubt 'whether the effect of psychotomimetics [drugs which induce a psychotic state in people] was always temporary and entirely reversible, even in persons liable to develop psychoses without the administration of drugs.' In response, a colleague, Professor Jack Gaddum, explained that 'the effect of a few doses was usually reversible but if repeated doses were given, an irreversible effect might be produced'. During 1960, Porton and senior military officials debated the rights and wrongs of trying out mind-bending drugs on volunteers, and there were indeed 'slight misgivings in various quarters'.[24] However, their conclusion, as one former Porton scientist said, was that since 'quite a lot was known about LSD, it was thought to be potentially safe to expose people to it.'[25]

To ease ethical worries, Porton proposed a safety net – a series of checks which would exclude volunteers with 'inherent psychotic tendencies' as well as 'psychopaths and schizophrenics' so that 'only normal people would be used'.[26] Porton insist that these checks were 'stringent' in making sure that potent drugs such as LSD did not 'aggravate a pre-existing mental disorder.'[27] Such psychometric tests would evaluate the personality, intelligence and co-ordination of a potential volunteer, along with an interview with a psychiatrist. One former Porton scientist explained why it was undesirable to use the rejected men as experimental subjects: 'Those with criminal records might claim their exposure to the psychotomimetic as an excuse for subsequent crime, and malcontents might use it as a means of getting out of the Services, whereas those who were depressed or worried could have a very unpleasant experience.'[28]

The LSD experiments on humans kicked off in autumn 1961, when four of Porton's staff were injected with acid under psychiatric supervision: 'They were alone for most of the time in a darkened room and were asked to tape-record their experiences. Three of these had fairly pleasant experiences and one had an unpleasant one and still dislikes recalling it.'[29] They had been given a dose of 50 microgrammes. As one of the most powerful drugs known, a dose as small as 10 microgrammes can produce a change in people, such as mild euphoria and loosening of inhibitions. An average dose for a full-blown trip is between 100 and 150 microgrammes. The trip begins within an hour of taking the acid, peaks after two to six hours and fades out after about 12 hours.

Porton admits that a number of scientists themselves took LSD as part of these experiments. Dr Maxwell Hollyhock, one of the scientists who organised the human trials, even had some of the drawings which he made under the influence of LSD reproduced in the *New Scientist* magazine.[30] (He had written an article arguing that psycho-chemicals were safe and humanitarian weapons.) One drawing was of a scary weird monster, often seen by those tripping on acid, while another showed Einstein's famous equation of $E=mc^2$ apparently poking through curtains. The caption notes that 'drugs like LSD can sometimes create a feeling of transcendental truth'.

This must have been carried out within the rules on self-testing (see chapter six). Indeed, one Porton scientist considered that 'an experimenter who had taken the drug himself would have greater moral authority for its administration to volunteers'.[31] It was also felt that by taking LSD, the scientists could understand better the mental effects which were being experienced later by the volunteers. It would also help them to plan the tests and analyse their results more easily.

During 1962, twenty-three volunteers were given the same dose of 50 microgrammes, either injected or through the mouth, and instructed to attempt a set of tests.[32] Their performance in these tests was unsurprisingly worse than undrugged volunteers — Porton reported that eight of them 'had moderate subjective effects, mood changes and disturbances of perception.' (These experiments had been carried out in a special laboratory unit which had been set up in Porton's hospital.[33]) The programme of experiments was soon to move up a gear after the then Conservative government under Prime Minister Harold Macmillan secretly changed Britain's chemical warfare policy in May 1963. For more than two years, military chiefs and mandarins had been kicking around the possibility of rearming Britain with chemical weapons. This thorny issue had been reviewed, particularly through a working party chaired by Nobel Prize-winner, Sir Alexander Todd. In November 1962, the Chiefs of Staff had agreed that they 'required' chemical weapons back in their armoury since they believed that the Soviet Union could produce poison gas 'in large quantities'.[34]

The Chiefs believed that stocks of both lethal nerve gas and incapacitating weapons were necessary, foreseeing several scenarios where incapacitating agents would be useful. One was in all-out global war — to delay an enemy nation from escalating to nuclear weapons after an initial clash. This would either buy time for fruitful negotiations or else 'keep the battle under control'.[35] Incapacitating agents could be used 'on friendly territory which has been overrun without inflicting permanent harm on the civilian population'. Controversially, they also proposed that incapacitating chemicals could be fired off first in a limited, localised war 'in a sensitive area, such as South-East Asia'. It was argued that such a first strike would be 'politically acceptable' if the only other alternative was to unleash nuclear weapons, thereby avoiding an atomic conflagration. 'In such situations, an effective incapacitating agent, which would save casualties, would be a humane method of warfare,' the Chiefs reasoned.[36]

The decision was now in the hands of the politicians. The then Conservative Defence Minister Peter Thorneycroft commented that there was the 'possibility of developing extremely interesting incapacitating agents on which much work is being carried out in America'. The Cabinet's Defence Committee authorised an increase in the research and development of both lethal and incapacitating chemical weapons, 'and the means for their dissemination'. The committee approved the 'limited' production of nerve gas and added, 'if a successful incapacitating agent is developed, we should produce a certain amount of this also'.[37]

Porton started to administer higher doses to the volunteers, often more than once, in November 1963.[38] The doses rose to 200 microgrammes – more than the 100-150 microgrammes which would trigger a fully-blown trip. Once drugged, the men were given tasks to measure their reading ability, their vigilance and drawing. In one test, for example, they had to pick out three consecutive odd numbers from a tape recording of random numbers; in another, they had to mark all the letter 'e's in a sheet of jumbled-up letters. Their performances when they were tripping were compared to previous tests when they had not been drugged – as before, those on acid performed worse than those who were not. Porton concluded that the results of the tests were not directly related to the amount of LSD taken, although they found that it needed at least 100 microgrammes 'to incapacitate the majority to an obvious degree'. The drugged men were back to normal within twenty-four hours of taking the LSD, 'but one member of staff complained of a feeling of mild depression and inability to concentrate on his work for up to 48 hours after his dose, and there was a clinical impression among those who conducted these trials that most subjects felt depressed and generally "below par" for up to 48 hours after their dose.'[39]

Until December 1964, all the LSD experiments on humans had been carried out inside a laboratory. However, Porton now held the first of three trials outside in the open air to see how LSD would affect soldiers on the battlefield. This trial was called Operation Moneybags – the name may have been a coincidence, or it could have a play on the initials of LSD and old sterling money.

A detachment of seventeen Royal Marines commandos and three officers took part in the operation. The experiment was run as an internal security operation, just like those the commandos had performed in British colonies such as Borneo and Cyprus. The scenario was that 'following a political uprising, Porton had been attacked by rebels during the night. They had been repulsed and had sought refuge in the open country of Porton's ranges and were thought to be trying to escape westwards where they hoped to gain support.'[40] The commandos' mission was to capture as many of the raiders and their stores as possible.

The exercise was to be run over three days. The commandos knew that they were to be given some sort of a drug on one of the days, but they knew neither what it would be nor when. On the first day, the commandos were 'moderately successful' in executing the operation, capturing some prisoners and stores. On the second day, the scenario was altered slightly – enemy troops were now trying to infiltrate the area which had been cleared by the commandos the day before. As on the previous day, the commandos were given a drink of water before they moved off, but this time it had been spiked with 200 microgrammes of LSD.

Within twenty minutes, the commando unit had begun to fall apart and got worse and worse: radio operators were babbling gibberish and whistling down the handset; men were standing around giggling in the open in full view of the supposed enemy; one man was alternately laughing and retching; the soldiers were unable to aim the rocket-launcher properly and would have been as great a hazard to their own side as the opposing troops – one sergeant was 'apparently having considerable difficulty in maintaining realistic contact with the outside world.'

In the next half an hour, the men completely went to pieces. The film of Operation Moneybags shows the marines incapable of remembering what to do or even how to use their equipment. One marine became very agitated, saying 'I'm dying – it can't go on'; he had to be taken immediately into medical care.

The unit commander had begun to lose control of his troops after thirty-five minutes – he could not concentrate and was so distracted by the 'undisciplined antics' of his men that he could not even give orders to them. After an hour, two of the enemy walked into the headquarters unobserved and were not captured until they set off several thunderflashes. The commander later reported that he had seen them, but 'felt incapable of doing anything about it'. He had felt so detached that he punched a tree to see if it would hurt. He then lapsed into giggling, watching his men.

After seventy minutes, he gave up and relinquished his command, announcing, 'I'm wiped out as an attacking force.' He is filmed at Porton's hospital two hours later still tripping: 'Everything he looks at appears to be patterned. While looking at the white ceiling he describes geometrical patterns which are coloured and three-dimensional. They appear to move in and out of each other,' comments the voice-over on the film. According to Porton, the worst effects on the men were over within six hours; twenty-four hours later, all of them regarded themselves as back to normal. Sometime later, the commanding officer watched the film of the trial twice or three times and on each occasion, it 'produced a disturbing effect on him with profuse sweating'. Six of the other men were either unmoved by the film or amused by the capers of their comrades.[41]

Porton's report of Operation Moneybags – finally made public in 1996 – found that the LSD 'totally neutralised' the detachment as a fighting force. 'The whole force would have been annihilated by modest enemy action within an hour of starting the exercise.' It concluded, 'The results of this experiment show that men under a drug such as LSD would be incapable of effective military action, no matter how well-trained or well-motivated they might be.'

But the trial had highlighted the hurdles which needed to be overcome before LSD could be deployed in warfare. LSD was a solid material and therefore could only be dispersed on the battlefield if it was to be fired at the enemy as an aerosol. Moreover LSD would only pack a punch if the enemy then inhaled it in a large enough quantity. Porton scientists noted that experiments by their American counterparts had suggested that humans absorbed only small amounts of LSD by breathing it in, and therefore 'for comparable effects, the inhaled amount would have to be three or four times' the 200 microgrammes dose that the volunteers had swallowed in their drinks during Operation Moneybags. Finally, LSD was not easily available on the open market – the MoD would have to build a special plant if it wanted to manufacture enough LSD to load into weapons. But the authors of the report wrote that LSD could be 'an ideal incapacitating' weapon, especially since it was very safe – only an incredibly high amount would actually kill, rather than disable, a person.[42]

Porton claims that before its human experiments, volunteers have 'always as a matter of course' been informed of the name, nature and possible short-term effect of the chemicals to which they are about to be exposed. As we have seen from chapter six, this is a claim disputed by many volunteers who say that they had no idea what was being administered to them. Porton itself concedes that the 'only exception' to this practice was during the experiments with hallucinogenic drugs, such as LSD, in the 1960s.[43]

The reports of the LSD experiments do not spell out exactly what the volunteers were told beforehand. In the outdoor exercises – such as Operation Moneybags and Recount – it appears that the volunteers were informed that they would receive some sort of drug at some time during the experiment, but not what that drug was.[44] Porton says that the effect of acid was not explained to the volunteers prior to these outdoor exercises because of the risk that they would then react as they believed they should do, and not as they would if they did not know they had been drugged with LSD.[45] In this sense, the ethics of these experiments occupy a grey area. What the volunteers knew preceding the experiments goes to the heart of the first principle of the 1947 Nuremberg Code. Under this principle, it is 'absolutely essential' that the subjects of human experiments freely give their consent to take part in the test with 'sufficient knowledge and comprehension' of what is going to happen to them. It is questionable whether or not the volunteers understood enough before the experiments with mind-altering drugs to make that 'enlightened' decision. A member of Porton's staff at this time said there was also a further factor – after 'considerable discussion', it was decided to keep the identity of the drug from the volunteers, since LSD was too controversially associated with hippies during the 1960s.[46]

Volunteers routinely say that the Porton staff did not disclose details of the chemical before it was tested on them, unless the chemical was already a well-known weapon such as mustard gas. Porton's need for secrecy ensured that volunteers were told nothing about newly discovered chemicals which could turn out to be a decisive weapon. To this day, many volunteers who were tested with incapacitating chemicals and who endured curious and weird experiences have little idea of what caused them. Typical is John Stevens, a regular in the Army for nine years. In late 1962, he volunteered for what he believed were medical experiments. He had never heard of Porton and had no idea what it did. He says that during his two weeks at Porton, the staff told him virtually nothing.

One afternoon, he had what he calls a 'violent reaction' after having been given a tablet to swallow. 'It was a bland white colour. The next thing I knew I was laying on the bed. My bed was surrounded with people in white coats, asking questions and taking notes. I was just giggling. I was just out of it really. I should imagine I was hallucinating. I don't know if I collapsed or what.' He tried, but could not, answer the questions of the white coats, whom he took to be scientists. 'I felt stupid, giggly, I just could not control myself. I don't know how long it went on for.' His memory of that afternoon is just blank. A patriotic man, he feels that he was badly treated by Porton – 'I cannot honestly say that I can now trust my government,' and he would now be dubious about volunteering for such experiments. 'I would want to know a lot more about what I was letting myself in for. Back then, I was 20-ish, you were gung-ho. You would go anywhere and do anything you wanted. As you get older, you do start thinking twice about things.'[47]

The sensitivity of the trials with mind-bending chemicals was crystal clear. The LSD tests were scrutinised by the Applied Biology Committee, the official advisory group which had become responsible for overseeing the ethics of experiments at Porton. At its meeting in late 1965, one member, Dr O G Edholm, commented that the tests were 'ethically delicate', and Professor

Robert Thompson, the chairman of the committee, went on to warn that the experiments with incapacitating agents were a 'relatively uncharted field'. A third member, Professor Andrew Wilson, warned that the testing of new chemicals, whose 'effects could not be forecast', was risking another serious accident – like the death of Ronald Maddison in 1953.[48]

In fact, LSD experiments on humans had been temporarily halted at Porton in January 1965 – shortly after Operation Moneybags. This self-imposed ban was to run for at least eighteen months until September 1966, and Porton staff argued long and hard over how and whether the LSD tests should be reactivated. According to one account, some members of the Committee on the Safety of Human Experiments (COSHE) – Porton's internal body for monitoring the experiments – were, in late 1965, 'unsure of the justification for restarting the LSD trials until more was known of the persistence of mood effects.'[49] The reason for the stoppage is ambiguous – rather mysteriously it was attributed by one senior Porton official to 'disconcerting results in one particular case of multiple self-administration and concern over possible addiction.'[50] This implies that someone had been dropping so much acid that his or her mental health was being brought into question. It is, however, unclear why this should have an effect on the experiments in general.

Converting LSD into a viable weapon presented problems. The main obstacle, according to a Porton update in early 1966, was that there was 'currently no absolutely satisfactory method of disseminating LSD in the air'.[51] Put bluntly, since the enemy could not swallow the LSD in a battle situation, the acid would have to be projected at their lines so that it would explode as an aerosol and envelop them. But Porton was still unaware of how much acid would be inhaled by a person in that situation and, without knowing what dose would be effective, it was almost impossible to gauge how much would have to be loaded into a weapon to have any impact in the heat of the battle.

The first priority for future experiments was therefore to investigate how much LSD could be absorbed through the mouth and nose. It was suggested that volunteers should be placed in a wind tunnel in which LSD in an aerosolised form was blown over them.[52] Results of initial tests on this were encouraging.[53] Porton's second most pressing priority was to determine exactly how much LSD would bewilder the mind of an enemy, and critically, to what extent a tripping soldier is influenced by his surroundings. In particular, the scientists were keen to discover 'the differences between the effects of the drug on a solitary, isolated individual and those on a subject in the company of his fellows.' A second field trial was therefore to be held as a follow-up to Operation Moneybags, in which only some of the volunteers would be given the LSD. In keeping with the old money theme, it was called Recount.

However, there was a row over the safety of this second trial. At first, it had been assumed that the subjects would receive the same dose – 200 microgrammes – as those in Operation Moneybags. But Dr Ladell, then the senior scientist running the human experiments, objected to conducting the trial with 'such a large dose' because there was now nobody at Porton 'with any personal detailed clinical experience of looking after men under LSD'. Without such experience, it was 'unwise if not dangerous' to give them this dosage and so, against the views of Porton's internal human safety committee, he was not prepared to allow the proposed trial with such a high dose.[54] Eventually the trial was approved after it was agreed that only half the dose – 100 microgrammes – should be used.

It is evident that the hazards of the doses of LSD and other incapacitating chemicals used in the experiments were a significant issue within Porton. Like other human tests of the era, the experiments were controlled by the Applied Biology Committee, the external group of respected scientists monitoring the tests, and COHSE, the internal body responsible for safety. Both spent considerable time discussing how much could be administered to the human volunteers without incurring any possible risks. This was in line with the trend within Porton since the 1950s to tighten up on the ethics and safety of the human tests. For example, at one point, doses in all LSD experiments were restricted to 100 microgrammes after it had been discovered that twice that amount was still affecting the volunteers forty-eight hours after the experiment.[55] Later, a proposal to increase the doses beyond 200 microgrammes was withdrawn.[56]

In Exercise Recount, a unit of volunteers from the 37th Heavy Air Defence Regiment (Royal Artillery) were instructed to carry out the same military task – surveying a site to place radar and missile equipment – on three days on the Porton ranges.[57] As in Operation Moneybags, the troops were offered and drank orange squash at the start of each day, but did not know on which day they were to receive the undisclosed drug. On day two, sixteen of them were given between 63 and 97 microgrammes of LSD, without them knowing what it was; the drinks of another twelve did not contain the acid. As they tripped, all but two realised that something 'wrong' was happening to them and that this was caused by a drug of some sort. They started to complain of feeling 'unwell' or 'peculiar', and, of the two, one showed no sign of tripping at all, while the other believed that he was labouring under a severe hangover. One of the men who had not been slipped the LSD did, however, believe that he had been drugged. Porton observed that 'the general signs of intoxication were mainly boisterous and excessively cheerful activity, but one man felt depressed and voluntarily withdrew from the group.'

Gunner Barry Coates took part in the exercise, but was not drugged with LSD.[58] He remembers that 'there were a lot of funny things going'. Some men were 'making fools of themselves, running around like headless chickens, not performing to their best, put it that way'. Some leaders issued 'stupid commands' – one man was given the hopeless task of camouflaging a truck in an open plain. LSD was at that time a bit of mystery to Coates (as it was to many, and probably most of the other human 'guinea pigs' in Porton's LSD experiments). He did not know what effect it would have on people, nor which of his colleagues had been drugged in the exercise. 'You had never seen people take drugs. We never knew what [LSD] was. It had never come into our lives.' This exercise was held in September 1966 – the same year in which the British government outlawed LSD in an attempt to curb the widespread use of the chemical by hippies and young people rebelling against the established order.

As the exercise ended, several of the drugged men gathered together and became 'excessively hilarious', according to the trial report. Some of the junior officers were laughing and 'did not behave with the propriety expected of them when in the presence of their seniors.' After the exercise, the tripping men were taken to Porton's hospital. One man 'removed most of his clothes and sat on his bed wearing only his underclothes and a seraphic smile'. Two hours later, however, he had put his clothes back on and was feeling 'tensed up'. The psychiatrist reported that seven had an 'unpleasant' time; eleven hallucinated, some experiencing 'altered perception of time'; one person was 'mildly paranoid and unduly suspicious of the motives of his colleagues'; some had vague feelings of detachment, while others felt 'intense unreality', reporting 'no stomach', 'no mouth', or 'another body'.

It is apparent that the design of the experiment was flawed and few conclusions could be drawn from it. The unit managed to take most of the vital decisions and complete their measurements within ninety minutes before the full effects of the acid had gripped them, and there was only a minor drop in the efficiency of the unit. The trial was also 'not perfect' for studying how drugged men influenced the behaviour of undrugged men, and vice versa. Porton scientists commented that the men had not been given sufficient LSD to 'produce florid symptoms', and it was tentatively concluded that good discipline and mutual support could enable a unit to

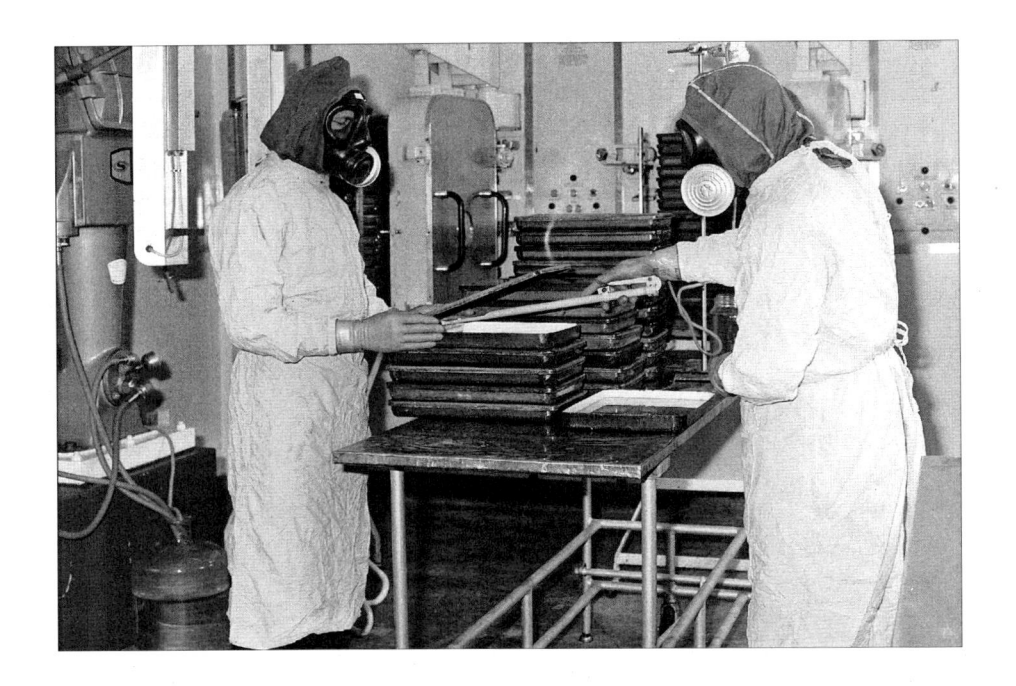

Experimental work at Porton in the sixties.

function, even when 'a substantial' proportion were 'mildly' tripping. Porton therefore accepted that the value of Exercise Recount was 'limited'.

Over the next twelve months, Porton lifted the restriction on the amount of LSD which could be administered to volunteers. In a series of laboratory tests, the scientists strove to establish how much LSD could be relied upon to knock out a person. Porton surveyed the behaviour of the men at different doses from 40 microgrammes to 160 microgrammes. At the highest dose, four out of ten men were 'incapacitated', and one report observed that 'five hours after dosing, three men continued to show fairly severe effects and definite signs or symptoms were present in five others'.[59] In another experiment, thirteen subjects were fed 160 microgrammes of LSD to see how small amounts of the chemical could be measured in human blood.[60] The third – and final – open-air trial with LSD was called Small Change and held in early 1968, with twenty-eight infantrymen from the 1st Stafford Regiment. One of the men who took part in the trial does not believe that they were 'true volunteers'. Sgt John Stubbs, then thirty-three, says one of the regiment's platoons were ordered to go.[61] 'From what I remember of it, we were never asked to volunteer. All of a sudden I was told that we were going.' He did not really know what Porton did. The purpose of the trial was only explained to the platoon once they arrived at the establishment.

This trial was different from Porton's usual experiments since, because the aim was to see how the LSD would affect the military efficiency of that unit, it was felt that the trial would work best if an already functioning unit of soldiers was used.[62] It seems that members of the platoon were therefore not given the option to opt out. (Porton's usual experiments only required individuals who could be drawn from a wide range of military units.) Although Stubbs has since grown dubious of Porton's experiments, he was at the time 'not too worried' about taking part in the tests. 'It was a job of work. I thought it was probably a useful thing. Somebody had got to do it.'

For the Small Change trial, Porton believed that it was logical to repeat the Recount exercise, but with a stronger dose – 160 microgrammes – to ensure that the volunteers would be 'high'.[63] Over five days, the troops carried out a simulated anti-terrorist operation, advancing over wide parts of the Porton ranges, 'with periodic opposition from a concealed enemy equipped with small arms and blank ammunition'. At the start of each day, before the three-hour exercise, all the men drank a draught of water, and as with Moneybags and Recount, the men did not know that the water would be laced with LSD on one of the days. Half the men consumed the LSD-filled water on day four. After thirty minutes, all but one of the men began to show signs of being 'high'.

Sgt Stubbs was in charge of the platoon on that day.[64] He remembers that he started to feel slightly drunken and bemused, and experienced a form of 'tunnel vision'. He describes it as like looking down the 'wrong end of a telescope' – he could not see on either side, while everything seemed a lot further away than it actually was. Since he knew that he was under the influence of some sort of drug, he concentrated more on doing his job. 'I could not really trust my judgement.' (He added that it would have been 'very disturbing' if it had been a real battle situation and he was unaware that it was LSD which was affecting him.) His colleagues told him afterwards that he became more aggressive – 'unusually loud and abrupt'– in issuing his orders. On one occasion, he was sitting down and trying to figure out how his platoon was going to capture an enemy position, and then, 'I suddenly decided what I was going to do, jumped to my feet, and said, "Right, on your feet" [to the others]'. One of the other soldiers 'leapt off the ground three feet. He definitely thought that I was going around the twist. He seemed scared as though I was going to grab hold of him and attack him.'[65]

During the exercise, he saw that a corporal in charge of one of the platoon's sections was 'acting stupid'. 'He reminded me of a little boy when we used to play cowboys and Indians – when you go into action with a toy pistol in your hand and slapping your hip or backside, pretending you were riding a horse. He was going backwards and forwards. Most of the section were looking at him in amazement.' They were 'very amused to see their section commander prancing around like that. There was a lot of laughter.' The section leader was taken away so that he could recover.

A private also had to be withdrawn from the trial after thirty-five minutes because he was tripping so badly. He was described as 'lying as though asleep'. The effects on the men were graded by Porton – four were classed as 'severe', six 'moderate' and the rest 'trivial'. They reacted in different ways to the LSD – men in the 'severe' category were, for instance, argumentative and 'completely detached'. Of the moderates, three complained of dizziness, nausea, and 'being unwell'; others were 'drunk and hilarious', 'drunken appearance talking nonsense – much rubbing of face', or 'shouting nonsense'. Two men who were not given LSD behaved as if they had been – one dragged his rifle 'with an unsoldierly appearance', the other laughed at his leader's orders and was reported lost.

Porton's 'substantial' experience of testing men in the laboratory with doses up to 160 microgrammes had shown that the 'subjects tend to become withdrawn, quiet and contemplative'. But in out-door experiments, men in a group behaved differently – together they often broke into 'uncontrolled hilarity'. Porton wanted to know whether undrugged men could rein in and control those who were tripping. Not enough LSD had been given to the men in the Recount exercise to prove anything conclusively, but this time around, the dose had been upped. Porton believed that the military performances of the four sections showed clearly that drugged men could be controlled by their sober comrades. For example, a glance from the commander in some sections 'would rapidly subdue the ebullient behaviour of the drugged subjects'. Mutual support and good discipline could 'mitigate' the effects of the drug. Overall, the men performed adequately, although their efficiency had dropped a little. These results meant that, in Porton's judgement, the value of LSD as a chemical weapon was 'doubtful' since the enemy could overcome the impact of the drug and continue fighting.

Porton maintains that the LSD experiments on humans were stopped in 1968 when the Small Change field trial 'confirmed that LSD was not a serious threat' to the security of the nation.[66] After all the experiments, Porton concluded that the concept of LSD as a weapon was dogged by three problems: it would be difficult to disseminate because it was a solid; it was extremely expensive to buy the sizeable amounts necessary for a significant arsenal; and its effects on the enemy were too erratic.[67]

Porton scientists observed that pyscho-chemicals such as LSD produced 'widely varying responses in different people so that one man might have an experience he considers pleasant, while others are terrified to an extent that they dread a repetition'.[68] Military commanders need weapons which they know with some certainty will have a predicted impact on the enemy. Neville Gadsby, Porton's director between 1968 and 1972, also commented that the appeal of reducing enemy forces to fits of giggles was not 'the sort of effect one wanted to achieve,' adding, 'you wanted something a little more dramatic than that.'[69] Indeed, as one former Porton scientist commented, 'Being wise after the event, it suddenly looked – after Moneybags – as though LSD might in fact have a future. Then people started asking awkward questions. But it became clear as time went on, and it was investigated, that things were not so clear as they ought to be.'[70]

By 1968, it had become clear that British plans to re-equip itself with chemical weapons were fading and would not be implemented. Five years earlier, the Macmillan government had authorised the drive to develop lethal weapons and if possible, an incapacitating agent, such as LSD. But, as already described, this effort fizzled out during the Labour government under Prime Minister Harold Wilson.

The lack of political will from the Cabinet dovetailed with a growing realisation that LSD was useless for inserting into Britain's military armoury. It is, however, unclear just how serious the British government actually was in its desire to develop incapacitating weapons. Declassified official papers indicate that at the high levels of Whitehall, some politicians were keen to produce such a weapon, but it is not certain that such enthusiasm ever filtered down to the lower echelons at Porton. One official who worked at Porton at this time said he was unaware of the 1963 decision taken by the Macmillan government to manufacture an incapacitating weapon if one could be perfected.[71] He says, 'Porton was not making the running. Nobody sat down at Porton one morning and said, "I have got a bright idea". It was always a response to some perceived threat. What we were looking at were stories which came from the intelligence agencies that certain people were apparently investigating incapacitating agents. The indications were that there were incapacitating agents – mental, physical, psychological – somewhere out there. One had to try to find out what sort of effects they might possibly have. Did they disorganise a unit, and if they did, was there any therapy possible for it?' It is evident that during this time, British officials perceived that the Soviet Union was developing incapacitating weapons, but it is very much less clear how far the Russians actually went down this road.[72] Soviet scientists were undoubtedly aware of the potential of such weapons, but this does not mean that the politburo would have ordered that they be manufactured. The documents detailing Western intelligence on Soviet intentions are scant, and so even now, it is difficult to determine the reality and seriousness of those intentions.

Porton has steadfastly claimed that all its work on LSD and the other incapacitating compounds was 'solely' defensive, aimed at designing protective measures in case these chemicals were used by Britain's enemies.[73] As an example of the flexible line between defensive and offensive work (see introduction), Porton's research on incapacitating chemicals would have been very useful had politicians decided to press ahead and manufacture such weapons on a large scale. Maybe they would have more willing to do so, if an effective chemical had been discovered by Porton.

The Ministry of Defence does not appear to be sure how many servicemen were dosed with LSD during the Porton experiments. When the LSD tests popped up as a public issue in late 1994, Dr Graham Pearson, then Porton's director-general, said a total of seventy-two volunteers had taken part in the field trials and laboratory experiments between 1962 and 1968.[74] Porton was, however, forced to revise this figure after a Channel Four programme in 1996 found that more than 100 servicemen had been involved in the experiments.[75] The programme makers had derived their figure from Porton's own documents which had been released to the public. Following the programme, the MoD announced that after a comprehensive search of its records, 'we now believe that the total number of all exposures to LSD was 136. A small number were second exposures of the same individual.'[76]

But this still may not amount to a full disclosure – it is highly likely that there was a separate set of LSD experiments on humans carried out at Porton in the 1950s. These trials were driven by Britain's spies who believed that LSD could be exploited as a so-called truth drug to loosen prisoners' tongues during interrogations. The clearest evidence comes from Peter Wright, the first scientific officer to be employed by the internal espionage agency, MI5. The Thatcher government lost a huge battle to suppress his memoirs, *Spycatcher*, in the late 1980s. In his best-selling book, Wright revealed that he had attended meetings with MI6, Britain's overseas spies, at Porton Down to discuss 'technical research for the intelligence services'. Wright discloses, 'The whole area of chemical research was an active field in the 1950s. I was co-operating with MI6 in a joint programme to investigate how far the hallucinatory drug LSD could be used in interrogations, and extensive trials took place at Porton. I even volunteered as guinea pig on one occasion.'[77] This strongly indicates that LSD was tested on humans in the 1950s – earlier than 1961 which Porton has claimed was the start of its LSD experiments on humans.

The details of these joint MI5/MI6 trials are still swathed in secrecy because the British government habitually refuses to disclose information or documents on the activities of its spies, even if they took place decades ago. When Wright's statement was put directly to the MoD in 1997, Porton replied that its staff could not find any documents on this set of trials.[78] And yet Porton hedged its bets by highlighting one of its old documents which, it said, 'indicates that some work on LSD may have occurred prior to 1961'.[79]

Buried deep in declassified official papers are snippets of information which back up the claim that Porton carried out human experiments in the 1950s for the espionage agencies. The most notable is an uncustomary mention of MI5's work, which has slipped past the censors. In 1964, the second most senior Army officer queried whether it was possible to improve British interrogation techniques in counter-insurgency and internal security operations.[80] (He added that 'some years ago, I took part in experiments with a truth drug', although he does not say when and where.) In a hand-written note of a telephone conversation with another mandarin, a Whitehall official scribbled that in the past, Porton had investigated 'incapacitating' chemicals as possible truth drugs in interrogations. He added, 'Position v. doubtful – not a worthwhile project. MI5 are in possession of facts'. MI6 were also informed of the Army's query. This information was so sensitive that the official did not want to 'reply in writing' in a formal note. In 1965, during a discussion of Operation Moneybags in a Porton advisory committee, Dr Ladell, then in charge of Porton's human experiments, commented that 'previous trials on LSD had been carried out at Porton many years before, but these had been tentative and inadequately controlled'.[81] In *Spycatcher*, Wright describes Ladell as the Porton scientist 'who handled all MI5 and MI6 work'.[82]

One volunteer from the RAF remembers going to Porton Down in 1958 and being injected with an unknown chemical which induced vivid hallucinations. Royston Clarke says he was strapped by his legs and arms onto a bed by five men in white smocks.[83] 'There was a screen in front of me which showed everything, and then they injected me (in my left arm) and I was looking at the thing on the screen...I said "What's happening now then?" And one says "Oh my God" and they gave me another shot in the right arm.' He recalls that he then started to think that something was wrong. 'My brain was going round and...I was beginning to think that I could fly and at one time I thought I was flying.' He says that he was on the bed for around an hour before they unstrapped him.

He had never felt like this before. He thought that he had floated back to his billet at Porton, without walking. 'I woke up on my bed. I was having a terrible, terrible nightmare on the bed, awful.' Royston had been a wireless operator on Lancaster bombers during the Second World War, going on twenty-nine raids over Germany. While on his bed, he recalled a plane crash in the Peak District which had happened when he was training. 'I lost all my crew but one. They all got killed and all that was coming back to me. I was having these images of the crash. I thought I was back on that crash site, looking for my crew, could hear my crew shouting and I was trying to find them.' He then thought that he could see the white-smocked scientists peering in at him and 'gibbering'. It appeared as if their eyes were coming out of their heads. 'It was frightening and then their eyes were changing colour.'

Nowadays, he suffers frequent nightmares triggered by the traumas of the air raids during the Second World War. In 1945, he was shot down on a raid over Berlin and captured, but soon escaped. He says that the Porton Down experience causes nightmares about once every fortnight. He was never told what the chemical injected into him was, but suspects that it was LSD. While at Porton Down, he underwent five or six other experiments within a week, but again he was not informed what was being tested on him. As we have seen in chapter six, like other human 'guinea pigs', he volunteered to go to

Porton because he believed that he was going to take part in experiments to find a cure for the common cold.

The intelligence agencies of Britain and the United States of America enjoyed close relations during the Cold War. Throughout much of that time, the Central Intelligence Agency (CIA) ran a huge – and now notorious – research programme in the hope of finding a way to control human behaviour (dubbed the 'search for the Manchurian Candidate'). The CIA had started its extraordinary hunt in 1950 because it believed that the Soviet Union had found a wonder drug that could turn someone into a robot who would do anything they were ordered to do. This belief had been triggered by the case of Hungarian dissident, Cardinal Josef Mindszenty. The cardinal had been a vocal critic of the Soviet-controlled regime in his country, but after he was arrested in 1949, he stood in the dock and, with glazed eyes, confessed to crimes he had not committed.

Until 1973, the CIA organised a series of programmes – with code names such as Bluebird, Artichoke, and MKULTRA – which explored a variety of potential brainwashing techniques. These included hypnosis, electric shocks, lie detectors and a range of chemicals. LSD was one of the drugs which especially interested the CIA. The agency had received reports that the Soviet Union 'was engaged in intensive efforts to produce LSD, and that the Soviet Union had attempted to purchase the world's supply of the chemical'. Years later – in 1975 – a CIA officer described the agency's reaction to these reports: '[it] is awfully hard in this day and age to reproduce how frightening all of this was to us at the time, particularly after the drug scene has become as widespread and as knowledgeable in this country as it did. But we were literally terrified because this was the one material that we had ever been able to locate that really had potential fantastic possibilities if used wrongly.'[84]

These attempts to discover an effective way of controlling a person's mind came to nothing, although there was a price for this failure. An in-depth Congressional inquiry discovered that the CIA had perpetrated widespread abuses on humans who had been tested with LSD and other chemicals. The inquiry found 'substantial violations of the rights of individuals'; the experiments 'exposed numerous individuals in the United States to the risk of death or serious injury without their informed consent, without medical supervision, and without necessary follow-up to determine any long-term effects.'[85] Their rights had been sacrificed by the CIA who believed that curbing the Russian threat was more important. The CIA funded the experiments in all sorts of laboratories including universities and prisons, and in one of the most astonishing tests, seven convicts were fed LSD for seventy-seven days non-stop.

The most infamous case concerned Army scientist, Dr Frank Olson. He jumped to his death in 1953 from the tenth floor of a hotel after the CIA had spiked his drink with 70 microgrammes of LSD – without his knowledge.[86] The Senate committee were very critical of the CIA for continuing to surreptitiously test unwitting subjects who had not volunteered for the experiments – even after the dangers had been made clear by Dr Olson's death. In the most colourful experiment, men were lured off the street into a brothel which had been set up and funded by the CIA. Once in there, these unsuspecting civilians had their drinks spiked with drugs, while having sex with prostitutes. CIA officers would watch through two-way mirrors as they sought to find out all kinds of information, such as whether some chemicals could be used to make people more talkative and give away secrets and how prostitutes could be used in spying. George White, who organised these experiments, later wrote, 'I toiled wholeheartedly in the vineyards because it was fun, fun, fun. Where else could a red-blooded American boy lie, kill, cheat, steal, rape and pillage with the sanction and blessing of the All-Highest?'[87]

But the CIA's pursuit of the Manchurian Candidate is believed to have had an unpredicted, and certainly unintended, consequence. It is suggested that the experiments helped to spread the allure of drugs among American students, thereby fostering the rebellions of the 1960s and the growth of the anti-authority hippy movement. Many students and academics were the human 'guinea pigs' in the drug experiments in universities and research institutions that were funded by the CIA and the American military. It was the first time that they had been introduced to the power of the hallucinogenic trip, and some were, in the famous phrase, 'turned on' by the trip, and persuaded others, in and outside of campuses, to try the drugs. 'It would become a supreme irony that the CIA's enormous search for weapons among drugs – fuelled by the hope that spies could, like Dr Frankenstein, control life with genius and machines – would wind up helping to create the wandering, uncontrollable minds of the counterculture,' commented one author.[88]

The CIA's intensely sensitive programme had been deliberately concealed from many of its own officers and any kind of democratic scrutiny. Sustained investigations by Congress and the media managed to uncover some of the details years afterwards. How far British spies investigated mind control techniques is simply not known because of this country's all-embracing secrecy laws. American government documents, however, do offer a tantalising glimpse. In June 1951, the CIA met with representatives of the British and Canadian governments to discuss possible mind control methods. According to the minutes, the unnamed Briton was sceptical at first, announcing at the outset that nothing new had been found in the whole business since the days of the Inquisition and that there was little hope of achieving any profound results through research. The CIA, however, records that by the end of the meeting, the Briton was 'evidently impressed' and had agreed to co-operate with the Americans and Canadians to investigate mind control methods because of their importance to Cold War operations.[89]

LSD was extensively tested on humans by Porton during its quest for a suitable incapacitating agent. There were, however, other disabling chemicals which were tried out on volunteers. In the late 1950s, Porton had set up a new committee – the so-called 'search party' – to seek out new compounds which could potentially be transformed into chemical weapons. In order to pinpoint leads, the committee set about scouring the scientific literature and visiting commercial companies and other research institutions. Porton hoped that pharmaceutical companies would 'open their files' to the establishment 'so that the type of compound which is too toxic for pharmaceutical use might not be lost altogether'.[90] Suggestions for the potential poisons came from far away – for example, the leaves of the Malayan reghas tree were reported as yielding a toxic substance, the fruit of a Jamaican tree was said to induce vomiting, extracts of an Australian fruit ('Finger Cherry') and a Brazilian plant were sent to Porton, and various types of snake venoms were also considered.

Some of these were obviously lethal, but as time went on, the focus concentrated on locating incapacitating chemicals. A substantial number were examined by Porton scientists; many of them being tested on animals and some tested on humans. One was pyrexal, a toxin derived from a strain of Salmonella bacterium. Porton scientists noticed scientific reports which showed that pyrexal could induce symptoms of fever, including headache, malaise, shivering, sweating and aching of back and limbs.[91] Since Porton believed that the toxin could be used to debilitate a person physically, it was administered to at least eighty-one men during 1959 and 1960.

In the first batch of tests, twenty-seven volunteers were injected with pyrexal. On average, the toxin caused their temperatures to rise to 101°F within four hours, stay above 100°F for nearly five hours, and then return back to normal within ten hours. The volunteers complained of a severe headache and were sick, wanting only to stay in bed, with a third of them suffering 'weakness, muzziness, and lack of energy'. Nearly half said they would not have been able to carry on working; the rest said they might have managed to, but only with a great struggle.[92]

Two more groups of twenty volunteers were tested with varying amounts of pyrexal in the following year. All of them were afflicted with headaches, many very severely.[93] National Serviceman Bob Bates was one of those who was administered pyrexal in July 1960, although he was not told at the time what it was. He had volunteered because the extra money he would receive was a considerable addition to his income at the time. In the first week, he and the other volunteers were put through a manual dexterity test – using tweezers, he had to pick up and move ball bearings on a rotating machine. As he was one of the most adept, he was asked to stay on for the second week. The pyrexal was injected into his biceps during week two. He recalls, 'This gave you a raging headache – it was like an axe had been driven through your head. They got you out of bed when the temperature was at its worst.'[94] He had to do the same manual dexterity test while he was in agony from the headache. In other experiments, men were made to do performance tests when the effects of pyrexal were at their height. From this, Porton concluded that on the whole, the subjects 'could still do complicated tasks when suffering from its [pyrexal's] influence'. In the following month, Gordon Bell, a young RAF National Serviceman, who believed he had volunteered for common cold experiments (see chapter six), was instructed to sniff pyrexal. But Porton found that administering pyrexal through the nose – as opposed to injecting it – had no effect on the volunteers.[95]

Pyrexal was dropped as a possible incapacitating weapon because its effects were too short-lived, lasting no more than five hours. There was, however, another reason why the pyrexal experiments were halted – Porton feared the risk of an accident if the men's temperatures were being pushed up to such very high levels.[96]

A new compound also attracted the attention of the Porton scientists, who found that it was 'at least 1,000 times more potent' than the powerful narcotic, morphine.[97] The chemical in question had been discovered by a Scottish company, Macfarlane and Co. of Edinburgh, and in February 1961, they secretly passed the details to Porton even before securing a patent to protect the commercial value of their discovery.[98] The compound – derived from thebaine and related to oripavine – was given the code name TL2636 by Porton, and by 1963, Porton had tested it on nearly 150 men.[99]

One Porton veteran remembers the human experiments with this compound as lots of 'dashing around with buckets of vomit'.[100] According to declassified documents, the human 'guinea pigs' experienced 'a transient euphoria and then severe malaise, vomiting…rather like a hangover'; 'it was not possible to sit quietly and concentrate for more than a few minutes'; 'any attempt to stand resulted in a sensation resembling motion sickness'.

The volunteers were 'uncomfortable and unhappy' after being administered with TL2636. Porton scientists admitted that the fall in blood pressure in some of the men 'did give some cause for concern'. One of the four men given the highest dose 'was not himself' thirty-six hours later – 'he had made up his mind not to vomit for 15 hours and this might have been his undoing'. For five hours, his blood pressure fell to a worrying level. Dr Ladell, then in charge of human experiments, also took TL2636 himself, at a dose one fifth of the highest given to the subjects and was 'incapacitated for four hours'. Dr Hollyhock, the Porton scientist whose LSD-influenced drawings appeared in the *New Scientist,* sampled TL2636 five times and reported that 'the unpleasant effects had not improved with successive doses.'[101]

Porton also tested volunteers with other compounds related to TL2636. However, experiments on these other compounds in 1963-64 were stopped after a 'few cases in which there was marked and quite unpredictable' depression of the subjects' heart rates and breathing. The experiments were suspended until Porton could do more animal tests to shed light on the basic way in which these compounds harmed the human body.[102] It is not known if these experiments were ever resurrected.[103]

In the mid-sixties, Porton was devoting more and more effort to uncovering an incapacitating chemical to knock out the enemy temporarily either physically or mentally. TL2636 was one of the main leads in this search, as Porton believed that it could be a useful physical incapacitant. Defence officials described it as being 'effective at very low dosages and would clearly give effects which would last and which would be of military significance'. 'Extensive' research therefore continued on TL2636 until 1968.[104] But this work was eventually curtailed as the British government lost its appetite to rearm the country with chemical weaponry and so shelved the offensive work in that year. In any case, Porton had spotted flaws in TL2636 – Dr Ladell suggested that even at large doses, 'a man might still pull himself together for short periods and do a job with intervals for vomiting'.[105]

The British never got as far as actually loading psycho-chemicals into weapons, unlike its ally, the United States of America. After the mid-1950s, the political will to maintain a chemical armoury was stronger in the US than in Britain, and with its huge military budget, the US could afford to build both categories of weapons of mass destruction – chemical as well as nuclear.

The US produced a formidable array of poison gases until 1969 when President Nixon called a formal halt. (This ban was lifted in the 1980s.)

From the thousands of compounds studied, the US selected a psycho-chemical known as BZ as its incapacitating weapon in 1961.[106] Within a year, they had erected a $2 million factory which would produce ten tons of BZ to load into cluster bombs and other weapons by the end of the decade. The Americans were attracted by BZ because it could 'induce a complex of incapacitating mental and physical effects, including hallucinations, unco-ordinated muscular movement and confusion'.[107] It has a greater effect than LSD on the victim. In the first four hours, victims feel very parched in their nose, mouth and throat, while their skin becomes dry and flushed. They may want to vomit while their head aches, their eyes are blurred, they become dizzy and bewildered, sliding into a stupor, and they may stumble about and mumble incoherently. In the following four hours, they become very disorientated, hallucinating and unable to move or react to what is going on around them. They slowly return to normal over the next one or two days, but, similarly, they may still behave in an unpredictable or even maniacal way during that time.[108] It was alleged, but not proved, that BZ was used by the US in Vietnam.[109]

More than 300 US servicemen were exposed to BZ in tests between 1960 and 1969 in laboratory experiments and outdoor exercises. Porton's programme of BZ tests on humans was much smaller, since the British did not want to duplicate the work being carried out by the Americans, exemplifying the closeness of the co-operation between the two nations in chemical warfare. Although the bulk of the BZ research was carried out by the Americans, the resulting data was automatically passed to Britain. Porton did, however, carry out some spot checks of the American results.[110]

It appears that the British believed BZ was unsafe and could kill people, instead of incapacitating them, as intended. A British liaison officer in Washington reported back to London in 1961, saying that the Americans had spent 'a great deal of money' on BZ, but 'the outcome remains very far from certain. Its effects on human beings are proving unpredictable and there is, without doubt, danger, in its use, of fatal casualties.'[111] By 1965, Porton's research had 'confirmed' that the safety of BZ was 'less than previously envisaged'.[112] Two years later, Porton was reporting that even some of the Americans believed that BZ was 'too dangerous...as a simple incapacitant because of its very slow onset and prolonged effect'.[113] Moreover, Porton noted that the results of its tests on BZ differed from the Americans, even though on one occasion the same sample was used.[114]

Porton administered BZ to around twenty-five men in the 1960s.[115] According to Porton, the experiments, 'caused confusion and other psychotic effects incompatible with serving as part of a military unit', confirming the power of BZ. For example, one human 'guinea pig' who swallowed a high dose of BZ was 'disorientated at nine hours after dosing, became completely confused and psychotic, and was not fully rational again until 50 hours after dosing'. During that time, he experienced visual and aural hallucinations and, at one point, became aggressive.[116] In a later trial, another individual was 'very restless', complaining likewise of hallucinations in his sight and hearing, and 'was completely dissociated from his surroundings' for thirty-six hours.[117] It appears that, as with LSD, volunteers were not informed of the name of the drug which they were about to receive. Instead they were told that they were taking part in tests to 'assess the effects of a potential agent which might affect their behaviour'.[118] Porton also exposed 113 human 'guinea pigs' to a glycollate – a compound closely related chemically to BZ, but more potent – in the late 1960s and early 1970s. Some of this work remains classified secret.[119]

The drive by the American and British governments to exploit drugs as weapons dissolved into nothing, as it was realised that these chemicals were simply too unpredictable. Military commanders obviously need to know the exact outcome that a particular weapon will produce if it is to be useful on the battlefield. Who knows what the enemy might do if they were high on a mind-bending drug – fire off all their weaponry or lay down their arms? Come out fighting like crazed banshees or roll over like kittens? But there may be an unfortunate legacy for the volunteers who took part in the experiments to try and perfect such weapons.

There have been a raft of lawsuits against the US military and the CIA over their human experiments, but one is most relevant. In a long-running legal battle, a US Army sergeant, James Stanley, won $400,000 compensation in 1996 after he complained that his life had been ruined by LSD experiments.[120] In 1958, he had volunteered to take part in chemical warfare clothing trials at the American equivalent of Porton, Edgewood Arsenal in Maryland. But he was tested at least four times with LSD and drugs to induce amnesia. In the first experiment, he was sent into an isolation room with barred windows, padded walls and furniture bolted to the floor. A doctor offered him a drink, promising him that it was 'only water, nothing more'. It was laced with LSD. After an hour, the young soldier thought he had gone mad, as his head filled with terrifying visions. Then he erupted into a rage, breaking down the door and running screaming down the hall. In a second experiment, he was given an even stronger dose of LSD which made him violently ill.[121] Within a year, he started to get flashbacks – the common LSD experience of reliving the original hallucinations – and waking up at nights giggling and staring at the ceiling. He once violently abused his wife and kids without reason. He also often 'lapsed into periods of incoherency', and was eventually drummed out of the army and his marriage broke down.

Stanley only discovered that he had been tested with LSD in 1975 when he received a letter from the US Army. The letter asked him to take part in a study of the long-term health effects of LSD on those who had been administered acid by the Army. After reading the letter, he broke into tears, as he finally began to realise that he may have found the cause of his long-running odd behaviour. The study had been launched following 'widespread concern' that there were prolonged illnesses among the LSD human 'guinea pigs'. Of the 741 US servicemen who were believed to have received LSD between 1955 and 1967, 320 were traced and were either examined at a military medical centre or filled out a questionnaire. Another 149 did not want to take part, while the others had either died or could not be located. The US Army reported that the 'majority did not appear to have sustained any significant damage', while for those who were suffering illnesses, the LSD could not be 'identified conclusively' as the culprit. The US Army pleaded that there were too many 'confounding variables' such as the length of time since the tests, exposure to other chemicals, the 'motivations' of those seeking examination, to reach a conclusive verdict.[122] The credibility of this study is, however, tainted since it was carried out by the very same organisation that had conducted the LSD experiments in the first place.

As we shall see in chapter ten, this was one of a series of studies to establish whether the health of American subjects of chemical warfare had been damaged in subsequent years. In Britain, Porton has never had a systematic programme for monitoring the health of volunteers after experiments, claiming that there is absolutely no evidence in the last forty years that any of them have been harmed in the long run.[123] The MoD maintains that there has been no need to check the mental and physical health of any of the LSD volunteers in the years following the experiments for two reasons. Firstly, they point out that all the subjects had undergone the screening tests so all those who were susceptible to developing mental disorders would have been weeded out beforehand. (It does appear that a significant number of men were excluded from the experiments.)[124] Secondly, further assessment was not considered appropriate because 'published clinical studies had not identified long-term effects with single, low doses of LSD.'[125]

The only information on the long-term health of the LSD volunteers comes from a limited study which was done nine months after the 1964 Operation Moneybags trial. Porton examined seven of the sixteen men who had been in the trial and, as a Porton scientist reported, 'All claimed to have been back to normal after 48 hours and willing to take part again in a similar experiment.' A consultant psychiatrist had found 'only trivial' personality changes in two of the men, 'one of whom was more relaxed than he was before the trial, and the other (who had married since the trial) was more ambitious.' The commanding officer of the Royal Marine unit, which had provided the subjects for the trial, was not approached for his assessment of the men since their return 'in view of the undesirability of suggesting the possibility of prolonged effects'. However, one of the members of the advisory committee which oversaw Porton's human experiments did comment that such follow-up studies were 'crucial and should be undertaken after one or two years'.[126] Yet – on its own admission – Porton has made no other effort to keep track of the mental state of the LSD volunteers. Despite this, the establishment still confidently asserts that 'there is no evidence to link controlled administration of single doses of pure LSD with any long-term effects'.[127]

A proper follow-up study by the MoD might establish the true picture and uncover cases similar to James Stanley. And yet for all Porton's certainty of the long-term harmlessness of LSD, the lasting effects of the drug have in reality been a matter of some controversy for many years, with no real consensus within the scientific community. At least some research was carried out by Porton on the long-term effects of LSD. But as for the other chemicals which were tested on volunteers during Porton's quest for an incapacitating weapon, even less is known about any ill effects that they may cause in later years.

The concept of non-lethal warfare may have died out by the 1970s, but it has enjoyed a revival in the 1990s, led by the police and military in America. Once again it has generated a slew of admiring articles – with headlines such as 'Non-lethal weapons change face of war' and 'Star Trek plan for a non-lethal weapon – Pentagon chiefs put "phasers on stun" to spare the enemy'. The familiar hyperbole hails the concept as 'the biggest breakthrough in combat since the slingshot,' with the new weapons including low frequency ultrasound to sicken the enemy, high-powered microwaves to neutralise electronic systems, superglue spread on roads to stick vehicles to the ground, and corrosive materials to melt aircraft wings.[128] In 1995, American forces deployed to keep the peace in Somalia were armed with non-lethal weapons, such as guns which fire tiny beanbags and sticky foam to immobilise rioters.[129] The British military has so far carried out research into the latest non-lethal warfare technologies, but has 'no present plans' to buy the latest weapons.[130]

CHAPTER NINE

Tears of Volunteers

CS sprays have attracted mounting criticism since British police forces started using them regularly in 1996. The Police Complaints Authority (PCA), the official watchdog, received more than 400 complaints about these CS sprays from the public in one year alone.[1] The watchdog was 'concerned' that CS spray was being used in ways 'neither justified nor appropriate'. It highlighted the case of a sixty-six-year-old man who parked on a double-yellow line so that his disabled wife could go into a hairdresser's. He had forgotten to display his orange disabled person's badge, so when police asked him to move, he refused to budge. During the subsequent scuffle, a police officer sprayed the pensioner with CS from a yard away, temporarily blinding him before arresting and handcuffing him. The pensioner was held for eight hours in a police cell until he was charged and released. He needed to be treated in hospital for damage to his eyes. The pensioner's complaints were vindicated by a PCA investigation – the policeman was later acquitted of assault, although the judge called it a 'disturbing and upsetting case'.[2]

A series of incidents has generated a persistent rumble of discontent about the chemical sprays. For example, twenty children who were bystanders had to be treated in hospital for the effects of CS gas after police used it to arrest a man at a show.[3] A four-year-old girl was squirted in the face as police tried to detain two suspects at a relative's house, causing her father to comment, 'It is appalling. She was in agony and screaming in pain. I want an apology – [the police] cannot get away with this.'[4] Police sprayed fourteen-year-olds who were disrupting children's homes. A mother was gassed after she violently resisted police who were attempting to take her child into care.[5] A forty-strong coach party claim that they were indiscriminately sprayed on a night out when a fracas erupted nearby; they say that police filled the coach with the gas and shut the doors.[6] Police forces have also been criticised for resorting to CS spray to subdue mental patients.[7] Newly-weds were sprayed and arrested on the day of their wedding after the groom was accused of stealing sunglasses,[8] and local councillors were furious when Merseyside police decided to issue the spray to all officers at Liverpool and Everton football matches.[9]

CS spray was authorised for everyday use in 1996 to help protect police officers from violent assaults. However even police officers have been critical of the spray, with at least three police instructors launching lawsuits for compensation, claiming that they had been injured by the spray in training.[10] One inspector suffered bad burns in his eyes and forehead after he volunteered to be sprayed in the face in a demonstration; this incident in fact delayed the introduction of CS spray.[11] Police officers in Yorkshire complained that in confined cells, they were suffering the effects of CS emanating from prisoners who had been sprayed. At least two police forces refused publicly to deploy CS spray when the government sanctioned it in 1996. Peter Sharpe, the head of Hertfordshire, one of the forces involved, declared that the long-term health risks of the spray were uncertain.[12] Three police forces in England and Wales still do not issue the sprays to their officers.[13] CS sprays were alleged to have been implicated in the deaths of three members of the public since 1996.

These modern-day disputes over CS spray are not isolated instances. Tear gases, such as CS, have often been mired in controversy for two reasons. Firstly, these gases are contentious because many people have criticised governments for resorting to chemical weapons to control their populations and squash riots and disorder. Tear gas has progressed from being used in faraway parts of the British Empire, to Northern Ireland, to mainland Britain on rare occasions, and now across the whole country on a very frequent basis. Secondly, there have been continual doubts over the safety of such gases, with many arguments over the question of whether they can cause lasting illnesses. Porton has been at the heart of researching and developing tear gases ever since the installation was established in 1916, and once again, human experiments, often painful, have been a crucial part of such work. Porton first tested tear gases on humans during the First World War and continued do so – as and when needed – in the decades that followed. Porton has now admitted that at least three of these tear gases can cause ill health, but the safety of these gases is important not only to Porton's human 'guinea pigs', but also the wider British public.

Tear gases were used in the First World War to harass the opposing side. Called lachrymators (because they produced lachrymation, or a copious flow of tears), their primary purpose was not to kill the enemy, but to compel them to don their gas masks, thus disrupting their military efficiency for short periods. All sides employed a range of tear gases in the battlefield during the Great War. Britain's main lachrymator was SK; as described in chapter one, it was named after South Kensington, the location of Imperial College, where its military potential was discovered by scientists in late 1914.[14] Human 'guinea pigs' had testified to its irritant power during the Imperial College experiments.

Porton's first trials with artillery shells took place with SK on 21 July 1916, just a few months after the installation had been founded. Shells filled with the tear gas were fired into a wood and Porton staff were dispatched into the wood to see how long the gas remained in the target area.[15] It was the beginning of regular tests by Porton on humans with SK and other tear gases during the war.

Chemical-filled hand grenades were found useful for driving the enemy out of dugouts.[16] These grenades were burst by a detonator, but because they were dangerous, only tear gases or non-lethal chemicals capable of penetrating German masks were loaded into them. Porton carried out 'numerous trials with a variety of fillings' to discover how much gas was needed to empty a dugout and to pierce German respirators.

Tear gas was useless on the battlefield if it dispersed too quickly, so in an experiment to see how long various tear gases remained in the air, 'unprotected' men went into dugouts, carrying sample bottles which they opened in the gas cloud. The 'captured' air was then analysed to see how much of it contained tear gas. In other trials with observers, these grenades were burst in the open, trenches and woods.

Tear gases were also compared to other chemical weapons. In one trial, for example, 'a continued slow bombardment of gun positions in the open was carried out for several hours' with shells loaded with two kinds of chemical weapons. One was SK, the other a lethal compound.[17] The two weapons were fired at different positions, with men 'actually exposed during the whole period to the gas clouds produced by the bursting shell'. The men 'had their eyes fully exposed' since the object of the trial was to establish whether they would be stopped from continuing with their military duties.

Tear gas did not disappear once the war had finished. It appears that in the 1920s, the American government and police forces in particular became increasingly attracted to the idea of using chemicals in peacetime 'following a marked increase in the crime rate and in urban gangster warfare'. It stimulated other countries around the world to adopt tear gases as an effective way of maintaining civil order and quelling riots.

The Americans were especially keen on one chemical – CN gas – which was to become widely deployed by many governments in years to come.[18] The effects of CN are striking – victims are afflicted by burning sensations in the throat, eyes and nose within seconds, followed by excessive watering of the eyes, a runny nose, stinging on the skin, difficulty with breathing, and gagging.

The Americans had begun to develop CN in early 1918, but the war ended too quickly for it to be exploited in combat. They therefore devoted much time and energy to researching CN after the war, and an official US report declared that by 1933, the American chemical warfare establishment at Edgewood Arsenal, Maryland 'had more experience with CN than any other known agency in the world'.[19] Edgewood had been manufacturing CN-filled munitions since the early 1920s. 'It has conducted field tests, closed-chamber tests, demonstrations and inspection drills using CN munitions and CN solutions in sprays,' added the report. During the experiments, Edgewood had exposed 'research personnel' to 'high concentrations of CN vapours' during 'research work of various types'.

Britain too had set up a manufacturing plant for CN in the early 1920s; by 1927, output had to be increased twenty-fold.[20] Police forces did not use CN on mainland Britain, but it did come in useful in the British Empire. In February 1936, Britain had authorised its colonial governments to fire tear gas at unruly mobs, and they did so for the next twenty or so years on a 'widespread' scale. Tear gas was viewed 'as one of the most effective and humane weapons available against rioting crowds'.[21] According to the British, the main objective of using tear gas in the colonies was to 'break up and disorganise violent mobs without having to resort to firearms'.[22] Colonial authorities in Mauritius, for example, expected riots in 1947 'as a result of subversive propaganda or scarcity of food' so it was thought 'advisable' for the police to be 'well-prepared and equipped' to face the rioters. The police were instructed not to fire their rifles at the rioters, but instead 'lavishly' use tear gas and go in with baton charges.[23]

Porton 'extensively studied' CN from at least 1924.[24] The establishment is no longer able to calculate the number of human subjects who were tested with CN, but it is estimated that around 4,000 human subjects were exposed to tear gases – including CN – between 1925 and 1936. CN was also being used widely for testing gas masks in the military and civil defence, and it was also being used as an aid in training the armed forces – new recruits would be exposed to the gas to enable them to recognise it in battle.[25]

Porton took a hard line in the 1930s against those who complained that they had been harmed by clouds of CN.[26] In one such case in 1939, a civil defence worker named Gertrude Bramall was exposed to CN and subsequently developed a rash upon her neck, arms and legs, which her doctor diagnosed as dermatitis. Porton, however, replied that over a 'considerable number of years', it had not seen any cases of 'actual dermatitis arising from exposure to CN'. In another case in 1939, a man alleged that he suffered permanent damage to his left eye after being exposed to CN. His eyes had run for the two days after his exposure and on the third day, he developed a pain in the eye which 'then became inflamed and swollen and the condition became progressively worse'. Asked for an opinion, Porton replied that the 'very many thousands of exposures' to CN had shown that the effects on the eyes faded away completely after an hour and no injuries developed after that.

An instruction circulated around the army in 1934 – presumably on the advice of Porton – stressed that CN posed no danger to health. In 1933, the Americans similarly were confident that, even with high concentrations of CN, 'no after effects have been observed more serious than a temporary skin rash lasting a few days'.[27]

However the assessment of the safety of CN has changed over time, and nowadays, it is no longer seen to be as harmless as it was once viewed. In its current evaluation, Porton says that in the majority of cases, symptoms disappear 'spontaneously' thirty minutes after a person is exposed to a single dose of CN. Porton, however, does accept that 'high concentrations can cause long-term clinical effects, namely damage to the eye and a dermatitis of the skin', resulting in reddening, swelling and in severe cases ulcers or open sores on the skin.[28] Indeed, former Porton scientists who have worked on tear gases echo the appraisal that CN can damage humans.[29]

It is unclear when Porton first became aware or conceded that this was the case. A Porton report in 1959 did at that time accept that CN was known to be capable of 'injuring the skin and of causing permanent damage to the eyes', attributing the evidence to a German scientific paper in 1931,[30] and in 1968, Porton scientists ruled that 'CN was a danger to eyes' and could not be tested on human volunteers.[31] Currently, the British government believes that CN is too hazardous to be used by police forces to control rioters in this country.[32]

Many people have been exposed to CN over the years, since it was employed for a panoply of different purposes. However, it will never be known how many have suffered lasting ill effects after they were exposed. Some people may have received a higher dose of CN than was in fact intended, and it is even conceivable that colonial police forces released stronger doses than planned during the heat and chaos of civil disturbances. British police carried on using CN in its colonies until at least 1965, even though Porton had concluded by 1959 at the latest that CN was capable of causing permanent damage to humans.[33]

During the Second World War, Britain maintained a small stockpile of CN, but relied chiefly on another highly irritating compound –BBC – as its main tear gas for military purposes. This compound was tested on a number of humans.[34] The British manufactured around 1,200 tonnes of BBC in the war, and considered a variety of ways in which it could be used – it could force enemy gunners to put on their respirators, thus reducing the accuracy of their shooting, or it could conceal the smell of the more deadly mustard gas.

Porton staff, with the help of scientists at Imperial College, London University, searched for a better tear gas during the war.[35] They believed that although BBC and CN were both potent, they had disadvantages in military situations. The scientists therefore tested more than 200 chemicals on men and animals as they sought possible replacements. Indeed such tests with tear gases were 'routine', according to one Porton document.[36] It however proved to be a fruitless search, as they could not settle on a satisfactory alternative before the war ended.

Like the other poison gases, BBC and CN were not employed in the Second World War. However, the British government did approve the use of BBC in military operations in its colony of Malaya (now Malaysia) in 1953. The British were locked in a war against Communist insurgents, and some officials floated the idea of laying down BBC as a miles-long barrier to prevent these insurgents, known as Communist Terrorists (CTs), moving stealthily around the Malay jungle.[37] Porton organised trials on the deserted, hilly island of Tenggol off Malaya in April 1953. In 'Operation Crusoe', British planes dropped the tear gas on parts of the jungle on the island, and 'British, Malay and Chinese' military personnel were sent in several times over some weeks to see how they fared in the gas barrier. (According to declassified documents, the team of thirteen human 'guinea pigs' were volunteers who had been told that they would experience 'no danger, but some discomfort'.)

Some individual volunteers had been chosen because they were as close to the insurgents 'in race and general characteristics as feasible, because of the possible differences in racial reaction to BBC'. The remainder of the volunteers had to be Europeans 'as a check on the results and to avoid giving grounds for adverse inter-racial propaganda'. As it turned out, no firm conclusions as to the 'relative toughness of British, Malay and Chinese' could be drawn. The human 'guinea pigs' suffered the effects of BBC – a flood of tears, burning sensation in the mouth and throat, and stinging on the face, neck and sometimes arms. They tried to cope with the gas in several ways – 'running through the intense vapour, opening one eye at a time, breathing only though the nose, following the noise of the man in front, and so on'.

Although the trials showed some promise, the British surmised that BBC would not stop a determined man once he knew what to expect from the chemical, and the extent of the gas clouds. The 'desperation of hunted men' would probably be enough to drive them on and withstand the pain of the tear gas. (It appears that BBC was never actually used in Malaya during this war.)[38] As well as its uncertain effectiveness, the British only had limited stocks of BBC by then and were not manufacturing any more. They also feared that they would be castigated if the use of the gas leaked out and became public. (The British did however spray herbicides in Malaya; one of the aims being to destroy the food crops of the insurgents in an effort to starve them into surrender. The Americans were later to use massive quantities of defoliants, such as the infamous Agent Orange, during the Vietnam war.)

The British began to realise after the war that CN gas would often not deter determined rioters in its Empire. The Governor of Trinidad wrote in 1948 that 'volatile crowds can quickly become criminally dangerous' on his island, but 'tear smoke is not invariably effective especially against crowds who have experienced it before and know how to smother it'.[39] Two years later, a senior official at the Colonial Office also reported that tear gas had little effect on rioters during disturbances in Jamaica. 'The strikers appear to have become "tear gas conscious". Some, by shielding their faces with outer garments, and others, by climbing on to the roofs of buildings, were able to avoid the full effects and their violence and aggression was undiminished'. He added that in a strike in Kenya, the crowds were dispersed at first, but then gathered again within fifteen minutes. He wondered whether there was a more powerful chemical which could act as a tear gas.[40] A War Office official replied that tear gas had not been 'used sufficiently liberally' on these occasions. He warned, however, of one danger of resorting to a stronger gas – the present tear gas grenades were meant not only for use against crowds in the colonies, but also 'possibly against Englishmen'. 'Use of unnecessarily potent anti-riot grenades in Great Britain would certainly not be tolerated by the public,' he added.

Porton scientists also recognised that CN was not up to the job, commenting that although one of the most painful tear gases around, CN was not 'adequate for incapacitating or even seriously discouraging fanatical or highly motivated rioters.' It had on several occasions been observed that crowds could tolerate the impact of CN after they had being exposed to it repeatedly or for prolonged periods.[41]

Porton had been working on an alternative to CN for a few years, but it had only been given a very low priority. (Some work had been done on improving riot gas grenades, which were tried out on police in the colonies.)[42] This changed in early 1956 when the War Office ordered a new, stronger gas for quelling rioters. Officials laid down some rigorous and exact requirements for the new gas: it should be capable of inflicting pain quickly, but also of knocking out rioters for longer periods than CN gas; it should incapacitate rioters within two minutes 'to such an extent that the rioter is no longer interested in hostile activity and is capable only of escape, but he must remain physically capable of escape'; it should also be able to 'transcend high degrees of motivation and morale' of rioters and dissuade them from rejoining the mob. 'Delayed recovery after exposure would be an additional asset in undermining morale and in discouraging reassembly', noted officials.[43]

But why did the War Office decide at this particular point to discard CN gas after all its years of service? According to one analysis, there were political motivations behind the urgent need for a more powerful riot gas. 'It is reasonable to suppose it was the times, not the gas, which had changed. 1956 was the year of Suez; it was also the year which saw the beginning of the Campaign for Nuclear Disarmament (CND). There was an upsurge of anti-imperialist struggles abroad and political struggles at home. Foreign bases would need protection, and the withdrawal from the colonies in favour of local ruling classes had to be accomplished delicately.'[44]

In the next two years, Porton scientists therefore examined ninety-one compounds as they searched for the ideal riot gas.[45] Of these, thirty-nine were eliminated early because they were too weak. The remaining fifty-two were thought to be sufficiently promising to be examined more fully by testing them on volunteers in the gas chamber. The chemicals were tried on teams of usually six volunteers, aged between eighteen and thirty, who were exposed either to several chemicals one after another, or different dosages of the same chemical. There were around 300 exposures, although Porton's report of the experiments does not specify how many human 'guinea pigs' in total took part.

One of them was Leonard Sellick, a nineteen-year-old National Service conscript at the time, who hated the army. He jokes that he had to be dragged into National Service 'screaming',[46] and readily admits that he volunteered for Porton because he believed it was a chance to skive. 'We were promised a week's leave. There didn't seem to be any reason to worry about it at all.' He says that there was nothing in the notices appealing for volunteers which scared them off. 'In fact it seemed like a good wheeze – to get out of the boring routine of being a National Serviceman. It was monotony.' He adds that like others, he had the attitude that he was young, nothing could hurt him, and he was going to live forever. 'It might sound foolish. I think if somebody offered me the chance now, I would turn it down very thankfully. I would be more scared, a little more worldly-wise.'

Sellick was in a batch of twelve men who were exposed one morning in August 1956, according to Porton's records. He had replaced another volunteer who, for an undisclosed reason, 'was unable to continue' in the experiment.[47] He went into the gas chambers three times. The first couple of times were not too painful, but the third time was excruciating. They were instructed to walk around and then remove their gas masks and try to remain in the chamber for as long as possible. 'It was as if somebody had jumped on your chest, all in seconds. The eyes just exploded with water. Thinking back on it, it was just unbelievable.' However, in a spirit of bravado, none of the young men in the circle wanted to be seen to be 'chicken' and flee the chamber first – 'So we stood there and suffered. I think somebody moved a foot towards the door and there was just one mass exodus.'[48] When he came out, he vomited 'for quite a lot of time'.

The whole group refused to go back into the chamber when an officer ordered them to do so, even offering them the equivalent of a week's wages as an incentive. Although they had committed a court martial offence by refusing the order, no action was taken against them. 'It was psychological. It was just to see how strongly you felt about handling that again.' He also underwent three other types of experiments over five days while he was at Porton.[49]

Sellick went to Porton with a friend from his unit, Roy Jemmett, who had also volunteered because he was 'a bit bored' with life as a National Serviceman.[50] Jemmett was told to try and stay in the gas chamber as long as he could without a gas mask. He says that the Porton staff told him that the gas would not hurt him. 'It was not too bad when you were in there. It was just a bit stingy. But it was murder when you came out. When you breathed in fresh air, you couldn't breathe, you felt as if you were going to throw up – just as ill as you could be. It went after about ten minutes, but God, it was terrible. You would not have gone back if someone had threatened to shoot you.'

At the time, both were not told what gases were to be tested on them. Sellick says, 'You just did what you were asked to do.' He only found out thirty years later when he wrote and asked Porton for details of his experiments.

Using the results of these human tests, Porton scientists were able to classify and grade the compounds according to how severely and painfully they affected people. In the subsequent experiments, the dosages of the more striking gases were increased in the gas chambers, and as the months passed, they began to whittle down the list of chemicals. In April 1957, Derek Payton, an RAF administrator, was tested with six of these more promising compounds.[51] He had been keen to go to Porton, since he had been attracted by the extra pay and leave, especially as his home was near to the establishment. 'It sounded like a good idea. To me, it was a holiday. I was a young bloke and would try anything once. Obviously you don't expect to be put in a position of danger by your employers.'

Payton had not really heard of Porton, nor was he was informed beforehand of what he was to be tested with. In one experiment, he went into the gas chamber in a group of six with gas masks and walked around in a circle. They were told to take their masks off by a scientist who was also in the chamber, but who kept his gas mask on. 'It was very uncomfortable, with burning in the chest and eyes, heck of a difficulty in breathing. It seemed like years, but it was probably more like 30 seconds or a minute at most. When they said put your masks back on, I don't think that I have moved so fast in my life.' When the scientist asked him whether he would prefer ten minutes in the chamber or six months in a military prison, he said would choose the latter. (Payton developed a serious eye disease, retinitis pigmentosa (RP), in the late 1960s and was registered blind in 1978.)

From this process (a sort of chemical warfare beauty contest), Porton chose CS gas as the best riot control gas to replace CN.[52] CS was named after the two American scientists, Corson and Stoughton, who had discovered it in 1928. Ironically Porton had briefly examined CS gas back in 1934 and tested it on humans, but then dropped its interest at that time.[53]

Porton now believed that CS was far superior to CN gas. The main difference was that at comparable concentrations, 'CN is at best a nuisance and cannot be relied upon to incapacitate rioters within a reasonable time or to discourage reassembly, while CS causes acute distress and incapacitation, in less than 30 seconds, of such severity that it is most unlikely that rioters would risk re-exposure'. The experiments with the human 'guinea pigs' had confirmed that 'within 20 seconds, all the subjects were quite incapable of any hostility whatsoever and were released from the chamber after 40 seconds' exposure'. By that time, all of them had been deemed to be 'incapacitated'. Porton also insisted that, as originally stipulated by the War Office, CS was safer than CN and would not inflict permanent damage on humans. (It was also advantageous in that it was easily dispersed, stable when stored, and its main ingredients were plentiful.)

The Americans were highly impressed by Porton's new gas. In September 1958, the British passed details of CS to their allies across the Atlantic, in line with the close co-operative agreements in chemical warfare between the two countries.[54] (CS was later cited by London as one of best examples of this collaboration, and, more particularly, of Britain's 'considerable scientific' contribution.)[55] Within months of learning of the new gas, the Americans had set up a crash programme – code-named 'Black Magic' – to manufacture CS in bulk to load into an array of munitions, such as grenades and spray tanks on planes and helicopters. The Americans quickly saw that the CS could be used on the battlefield 'in evicting enemy troops from foxholes, etc'.[56] As it turned out, the Americans did not wait long to use the new gas in just this way.

From 1964, the Americans fired off thousands of tons of CS in the Vietnam War. This provoked much controversy, bringing back memories of poison gas in the First World War. US officials argued that the tear gas was a humane weapon which would minimise casualties among the Vietnamese enemy and civilians. However, CS was in fact most commonly used to drive out the Vietnamese fighters from their concealed bunkers and tunnels into the open where they could be bombed or shot. One US Army official explained to a Congressional committee why the American troops liked CS very much: 'It flushes out Charlie [slang for the Viet Cong], gets him out of the bushes, and they are able to see who they are fighting.'[57] The Americans treated CS gas like any other weapon of war and placed no restrictions on the ways it was used in Vietnam. Massive quantities of CS were used as the US commanders began to realise the military value of the gas. Virtually every kind of weapon delivery system was capable of firing CS and so the Americans could spread the tear gas over any size of target, at any range, and in conjunction with other munitions. Many of the CS weapons were being tested for the first time in the south-east Asian country. Furthermore, it has been the most consistent use of tear gas in a war. (The Americans were also heavily criticised for relying on another form of chemical warfare – defoliants such as Agent Orange – during this war).

The trail of the new weapon from incubation in Porton's research laboratories to full-scale use on the battlefields of Vietnam underlines the ambiguity of the co-operation between Britain and America for a time. As described in chapter seven, Britain was committed only to defensive work in the field of chemical warfare during some of this era. But it was allied closely with a nation intent on producing chemical weapons and deploying them in combat. Since research data and information was passed freely between the chemical establishments of both nations, it was not surprising that the Americans picked up on Porton's breakthroughs and exploited them for their own advantage. Indeed, the British government now admits that 'collaboration with the US up to 1964 resulted in some of the results of UK research being used by the US in the development of its offensive programme'.[58]

The British were also making much use of CS, this time to maintain civil order and disperse rioters in their receding Empire. Colonial police forces, for instance, resorted to tear gas 124 times between 1960 and 1965.[59] Several tons of CS a year were being manufactured at the former nerve gas factory at Nancekuke, Cornwall. Britain also capitalised on its new weapon by selling CS gas around the globe. A top secret memo for the Prime Minister Harold Wilson reckoned that by 1965, it was 'probable that the majority of police forces in the world are equipped with CS from British sources'.[60] Britain sold CS to at least forty-six countries between 1962 and 1964, according to one confidential list, and military attaches in British embassies were encouraged to lubricate these sales.

The human tests during the selection of CS as the new riot gas were only the start of Porton's experiments on the volunteers. From 1959 to 1973, 460 human 'guinea pigs' were exposed to CS in a host of different experiments.[61] In one large test starting in 1960, 176 servicemen were tested to compare how CS particles of varying sizes affected humans through inhalation.[62] The results were needed to help develop riot control weapons. At the time, Porton was faced with the 'continuing and often urgent' demand for new types of munitions to shoot riot gases at insurgents. CS was being disseminated through hand grenades and cartridges fired from signal pistols, but the military chiefs wanted a weapon which could spread the gas on the ground from aircraft.[63]

The human 'guinea pigs' were placed in front of a wind tunnel. (According to Porton, the men had been informed beforehand that they were to be exposed to a new riot control gas.) The CS was then driven down the tunnel and over the head and shoulders of the volunteers. At a given signal, they were told to remove their gas masks and read random numbers aloud from a card mounted above the tunnel. They were to remain there reading the numbers for as long as possible, up to a maximum of four or five minutes. Throughout that time, a Porton medical officer 'stood close to the subject during his exposure and gave him such encouragement as he thought necessary'.[64] Some wore goggles and noseclips as a partial form of protection. The size of the CS particles and the strength of the dosages were varied throughout the experiment, and from this, Porton deduced that the smallest particles had the greatest effect on the volunteers.

The amount of time the volunteers could tolerate the CS fluctuated greatly. After the experiment, Porton asked some of the men whether the CS would have forced them to turn back if they had been advancing in a real riot. One man, who withstood the smaller particles of CS for five minutes, said: 'At first, it seemed as if I had swallowed something red hot, and it had gone straight into my lungs. There was a searing hot pain in my chest for two minutes, I was coughing badly, and felt sick. Later my throat also had this same sensation. My eyes watered a great deal despite the goggles, and I was salivating markedly. At first, I would probably have turned back, but not later.' Another man, who was exposed for nearly two minutes to larger CS particles, said, 'The gas caused a burning pain in my throat and chest, and I wanted to breathe through my nose. I kept trying to swallow as my mouth was full of saliva, and I had a bad cough. This gas would have made me turn back.' A third stayed for five minutes in a cloud of the largest particles. 'In the first minute, I was worried by coughing, and there was a burning sensation in the throat. Breathing was difficult because of tightness in the throat, and I was salivating excessively. There was no burning or tightness in the chest. After a minute, the cloud seemed to drift away, and I thought I was breathing normal air. Even at its worst, the cloud would not have stopped me.'

A key question facing Porton was whether or not determined rioters exposed repeatedly to CS could develop some degree of tolerance to the gas and carry on rioting. In one set of tests, groups of around six unprotected 'young male service volunteers' were exposed to a similar dosage of CS on either five consecutive days or alternate days during that period.[65] Each man had to carry out the simple repetitive task of sorting playing cards into suits for as long as possible (up to six minutes) in the CS gas cloud. Porton staff had explained to the forty men that they were testing a new riot gas and that 'although it would cause some physical discomfort, the effects were neither dangerous nor lasting'.

A Porton officer – 'wearing [a] well-fitting respirator' – went into the gas chamber with the men and 'exhorted the subjects to stay in as long as possible but if a man wanted to leave he was free to do so'. Each time they went into the gas cloud, the men were 'exhorted to try and stay in the chamber longer than on previous occasions' and offered the incentive of extra pay, more than the usual amount which they received for the experiments. The men suffered the standard symptoms of CS gas; they bolted early from the chamber 'usually because of nausea and in some cases vomiting or difficulty in breathing'. 'Several' of the volunteers exposed to the highest dosages 'were unable or unwilling' to return to the gas chambers after the first or second time 'because of difficulty in breathing'.

By correlating the length of time the men stayed in the chamber, the dosages they received, and how well they managed to sort the cards, Porton concluded that the men developed a tolerance to the gas the more they were exposed to it. In other words, on each successive occasion they could stay in the chamber longer and sort the cards better. This was obviously a disadvantage of an anti-riot gas, especially since some politically motivated rioters may gird themselves to withstand the gas longer than the volunteers who were driven merely by the lure of extra money.[66] Perhaps Porton should have realised this phenomenon of tolerance earlier, but it was understandably difficult to ensure that the volunteers' motivation to remain in the CS-filled atmosphere in the somewhat artificial experiments would be the same as fired-up rioters in a real disturbance. A Porton scientist who organised some of the human trials with CS commented, 'What surprised us was that there was a considerable degree of tolerance developed during actual exposure, which of course has been demonstrated in riots subsequently. People can go on rioting quite merrily in the presence of tear gas, once they get over that initial exposure. They get adapted to it.'[67]

Porton also exposed volunteers to CS to try and solve a problem encountered by the American military in 1959.[68] During early US trials to check how effectively CS could be used in attacking troops in dug-in positions, some American soldiers complained that their respirators had not shielded them from the gas. Porton scientists wondered why this was happening since the masks were in no way defective, and it was suggested that perhaps the American troops had in fact been hurt by CS trapped in the mask when it was being donned. However, in order to investigate this further, Porton sent seventeen men into a CS-filled gas chamber in a series of tests. In one, four unmasked men had to go into the chamber and, on a table, find the respirator with their name on. They then had to put it on and stay in there as long as possible. The men were severely hurt by the CS at first and – after putting on the masks – could only remain there for between seventeen and forty-two seconds.

In another test, four men entered the chamber with respirators, but had to remove them and then march on the spot for twenty seconds before putting a second mask back on. Three fled after ten seconds of donning the second mask. In the last test, four were sent in without any protection for thirty seconds. Then, 'when all were showing marked symptoms' of gassing, they were told to leave the chamber, don their respirators and return the chamber. Two were in too much pain to pull on their respirators, while the others managed to get back into the chamber, but once there, had to wrench off their respirators. From this, Porton scientists concluded that CS trapped in a respirator would have little effect on humans. They also observed that once the CS had taken a grip on people, they could not tolerate wearing a respirator because they were coughing and salivating too much.

In an unusual diversion from its core work, Porton investigated whether CS could be used to repel sharks.[69] Trials on dogfish caught off Plymouth had indicated that CS had the potential for warding off sharks. Porton also used volunteers to see if humans would be affected by CS-filled water. Men, 'clad only in thin trunks', sat in a tank up to their necks with increasing amounts of CS. Within ten minutes, they all 'complained of stinging of the neck, crotch and armpits, but in no case was the stinging so severe that the men were unable to remain in the tank'. These results proved the same for fresh and sea water. Porton drew the conclusion that unprotected men in water would find CS 'unpleasant', but the pain was only 'transitory' and would not incapacitate people in the dosages used.

Porton's other CS tests had different aims: volunteers were given CS-contaminated food to see if they could eat it (this experiment had to be ended early because the food proved so repulsive)[70]; CS was smeared on the skin of volunteers after it was reported that American workers has suffered ill health[71]; volunteers were exposed to CS to work out the 'safety distances' so that unprotected bystanders would not be affected by the gas during training exercises.[72]

On the question of the ethics of the human tests with tear gases, it is possible to see the trials in a different light from the experiments with the more pernicious chemical weapons such as the nerve gases. Indeed, as Porton staff have pointed out, tear gases are painful at the time of exposure, but wear off quite quickly. They knew the effects well. Dennis Swanston, a toxicologist involved in some of the CS experiments in the 1970s, said 'the chaps would feel pretty awful for fifteen minutes', but 'we knew that everything was reversible' and they would get over it. He added that he and his colleagues explained to the volunteers 'exactly' what was going to happen and they could withdraw if they wanted to.[73] Another scientist who organised these experiments said that watching a volunteer coughing and spluttering in the testing chamber was 'absolutely ghastly', but they recovered within minutes in the fresh air. 'One does not laugh. CS is an emotional subject.'[74] He added that the tests were invariably on fit, young men – old people with lung problems or very small children would have been another matter.

A political row erupted in August 1969 when police fired CS gas at rioters in Northern Ireland. It was a crucial landmark, since it was the first time that tear gas of any kind had been used to crush civil disturbance in Britain, as opposed to the colonies of the British Empire. One Porton scientist admitted, 'The colonies were different. Now, that's a very cynical thing, but you know what I mean. What went faraway in the Far East might not go for Britain on home ground.' The Labour government – which had previously insisted that CS would never be used to control crowds in Britain – hesitated before finally giving its authorisation.[75] In the same week, the government took the fateful decision to deploy British troops on the streets of Ulster to restore order in the province after sectarian violence between Catholics and Protestants descended into open warfare. As the Irish troubles intensified, government forces unleashed CS gas forty-three times to quell riots in the region between August 1969 and October 1970.[76]

In a groundswell of opposition, the government came under serious criticism for authorising the use of CS gas for a number of reasons. One dispute raged over whether or not it was even legal to fire CS gas at the rioters. In 1930, Britain had signed up to the 1925 Geneva Protocol in which countries were banned from employing chemical weapons first in a war. The government had clearly declared then that it believed that tear gas was outlawed in war under this treaty. Four decades later, the government reversed this long-standing position, since it was in an embarrassing pickle. How could the government use CS gas on its own citizens when it was maintaining that the same gas was illegal under the treaty? Moreover, it would also be awkward to condemn a gas which was at that time being widely used by the Americans in Vietnam.

The solution was to redefine CS so that it now fell outside the scope of the 1925 treaty. The then Foreign Secretary Michael Stewart announced that the gas was in fact a '*smoke* which, unlike the tear gases available in 1930, is considered to be not significantly harmful to man in other than wholly exceptional circumstances'. (This was a curious claim, since CS had replaced CN precisely because it was more potent than the older gas.) In this way, the accusation of hypocrisy was deflected, allowing the police forces to carry on using the gas to squash civil disorder in Ulster. However, these linguistic contortions did come with a price – Britain's international standing had been damaged. A key Labour minister in the row has candidly admitted that this wriggling 'was received with a mixture of anger and distress' in the international conference rooms, 'where Britain had built up a solid reputation for its vigorous pursuit of effective measures of arms control and disarmament'.[77]

The government also came under pressure over the possible damaging medical effects of CS gas. Reports from Northern Ireland indicated some distressing cases; for instance a baby had developed acute bronchial disorder, another baby suffered from a tight chest, young kids had to be treated for eye-burning, and people had lost consciousness.[78] James Callaghan, the then Home Secretary, had quickly set up an official committee under the chairmanship of distinguished scientist Sir Harold Himsworth to investigate whether the gas could cause lasting damage to humans.[79] Callaghan has since disclosed that after CS had been used on the streets of Ulster, he discovered that 'the scientists did not know as much about the effects of the gas as I thought' and that is why he set up the committee.[80]

Porton had originally pronounced that CS caused 'no permanent harm', but later conceded that this was only on the basis of 'limited' experiments which were 'by no means comprehensive'.[81] The Himsworth committee 'initiated years of studies at Porton', on both animals and humans, to investigate more thoroughly the toxicity of CS.[82] In a sense, Porton went back and conducted in the 1970s many studies which should have been done in the 1950s before the gas was issued. Dennis Swanston, who was involved in these later studies, said the original work on the toxicity of CS was 'a bit thin and highly insufficient' in the circumstances which later arose, catching Porton out to some extent. But he argued that back in the 1950s, the standards and requirements of health and safety were lower – even 'cavalier' – throughout scientific and industrial laboratories in general, not just at Porton. He added that in those days, there was often the attitude that 'if something seemed okay, it was okay... It is amazing. The stuff you get away with under that culture, there's no way you would get away with it these days, but you must judge it by the culture.'

Swanston believes that the whole episode around CS and Himsworth produced a 'sea change' in Porton's outlook. 'Certainly, it brought Porton up with a jerk. It brought the realisation that the old way at this time was not ever going to be good enough, and would not do. Socks would have to be pulled up.' The procedures for testing products which emerged from Porton would have to be improved so that they became even more rigorous.

The Himsworth committee produced an important recommendation – the possible damaging effects of riot control gases should be scrutinised as if they were a new drug rather than a military weapon. In its view, new riot gases should be investigated for their potential harm not only on healthy people (assumed to be the bulk of rioters), but also on 'the young, the elderly and those with impaired health, who may inadvertently be exposed' in the areas surrounding a riot. By this yardstick, Porton's investigation into the toxicity of CS in the 1950s was inadequate. For example, the effect of CS on people with chronic bronchitis was a source of controversy in Northern Ireland after the gas had been deployed in 1969. Porton's claim that CS would not unduly affect chronic bronchitics was based on experiments with just two rabbits. The Himsworth committee later concluded that there was 'a real possibility' that CS could trigger short-term attacks of bronchitis 'superimposed on the chronic condition'. The committee had seen cases of this in middle-aged and elderly people who had been exposed to CS in Northern Ireland three weeks earlier.[83]

The Himsworth committee announced in 1971 that it was 'highly improbable' that in a civil disturbance, any citizens would be exposed to the high dosages of CS which 'might cause serious injury or death'. It added that, although CS presented some minor hazards, the government could carry on using the gas. Porton believed that this judgement 'in effect vindicated' its earlier selection of CS as 'a more effective and safer replacement' for CN.[84]

'Fire gas weapon on Ulster stand-by' ran the headline in the *Daily Express* in June 1973.[85] The paper revealed that the government was producing a new anti-riot gas 'so incapacitating that it makes people feel as though they are on fire'. The new weapon – called CR gas – was being lined up for possible use in Ulster, although this would 'provoke a violent reaction in Parliament' since many believed that it should be banned.[86] However, by October of the same year, the government had authorised CR gas for use in Northern Ireland.[87]

Like CS, CR gas too had been tested and developed by Porton, and again, as with CS, details of CR were passed to the American military which added the new gas to its armoury. Even though Porton had taken much credit for discovering CS gas back in 1958, the establishment had launched a new search for an even stronger riot gas within a year. CS gas was judged to be only an 'interim solution to the main problem' of uncovering the ideal gas to suppress rioters. CS gas was flawed because it failed one of the rigorous requirements laid down by the War Office in 1956 – its effects wore off too quickly and rioters could recover in fresh air within a few minutes. Porton was thus charged with finding an even 'more potent and persistent' riot gas.[88]

By chance, scientists at the Royal Technical College, Salford came across CR and in 1961, privately passed details of 'an intensely irritant compound' to Porton. A batch of twelve volunteers were soon sent into the gas chamber to test the potency of the new find. They had to take off their gas masks in a CR cloud and 'were instructed to remain in the chamber until the effects became intolerable'. At the highest dose, none could stay in for longer than twenty seconds. Porton was therefore encouraged that CR could be much more intolerable than CS.

However, two of the subjects in the test developed blotches on their skin which disappeared after a day. Porton decided to suspend human tests with CR in order to carry out further investigation into the sensitivity of skin to the chemical. Scientists sought advice from an outside expert, who believed that there was 'no foreseeable risk' in exposing volunteers and that the chemical did not obviously cause cancer. Porton commissioned a research institute to conduct long-term studies to see if CR could cause cancer. The initial indications showed that CR 'probably' did not, but the work was still continuing. In the meantime, Porton, 'with this reassurance', smeared a paste of CR on the arms of forty-one volunteers for seven hours. 'Apart from intermittent stinging, no other skin effects were noted,' Porton concluded.[89]

Over a thirteen-year stretch from 1963, Porton scientists tested CR gas on hundreds of volunteers. Porton has told Parliament that a total of 190 humans were exposed to the gas during that time, but this seems to be an underestimate.[90] Many tests were designed to compare CR and CS gases, and in one early experiment, the harassing power of both gases was tested on seventy-five volunteers.[91] According to Porton, volunteers had been told the object of the experiment. They were exposed once to each gas on different days and asked which one was 'the most unpleasant'. They had to go into the gas chamber with their masks on and sit down at a table. Then, they had to take off their masks and rearrange fifty-five dominoes. The longer they stayed in the chamber (up to four minutes), the more money (or reward) they would be given. Every thirty seconds a buzzer sounded and an illuminated sign lit up, showing the amount of money they had already earned (displayed in green as 'go for £XX') and the total cash they would earn if they stayed longer (displayed in red as 'stay for £XX').

The young men suffered the familiar symptoms of the gases in varying degrees. In particular, 'there was intense salivation in more than a third of the men' exposed to either gas, and 'rather more nausea and vomiting' with CR than CS gas. 'The nausea and vomiting was brought on in part by swallowing the contaminated saliva, those subjects who spat rather than swallowed were less nauseated, and in part by the intense coughing,' Porton scientists observed. From this, they found that CR gas was around six times more potent than CS gas,[92] and recommended that 'serious consideration' could be given to replacing CS with CR as Britain's main riot control gas.

One set of trials was held to contrast how the two gases affected a soldier's ability to fire a rifle accurately.[93] Fred Pitchers, a Royal Artillery bombardier, remembers going to Porton in July 1966, at about the same time that the England football team won the World Cup.[94] 'You got extra money for doing it and that's why we went,' he says. The amount of money depended on the type of experiments undertaken by the volunteers. He knew little of what he was going to be doing until he got there. 'We knew that it was something to do with firing small arms.' He says he was not informed that he was being exposed to riot gases, but he recognised CS gas. 'They don't tell you anything,' he said.

The men were instructed to enter an enclosed shed – which had been filled with riot gas – and shoot at targets out of the window. At first, they shot with their gas masks on, but then they took them off and carried on shooting for as long as they could before having to leave the shed. He repeated this every day for around ten days. He recalls that the tear gas was not particularly painful, but he was forced to focus on the effects of the gas, rather than his marksmanship. 'You lose your concentration. All you are interested in is getting out of it quick. You are trying to hit the target, but it is impossible'. He was not firing as well as he could, and these trials did indeed reveal that there was 'marked impairment' in the shooting performances of men when exposed to either gas. But once again, CR gas was found to be around six times more powerful than CS gas in harassing the men.

Porton scientists also tested solutions of both gases on the eyes of human 'guinea pigs'.[95] In October 1969, Tony Lyons – then a captain (rising eventually to be a Lieutenant Colonel after three decades of service) – was on a nuclear, biological and chemical course at nearby Winterbourne Gunner.[96] Although they received no payment, he and others agreed to take part in some short experiments at Porton. He was seated in a sort of dentist's chair, with two people either side apparently to restrain him if necessary. He put his head back and drops of a chemical were placed in one of his eyes. He was never told what the substance was, but suspected it was some kind of riot control gas – 'something upmarket from CS'. Porton, which does not have records of his participation in this experiment, believes that it was CR gas.

The chemical was excruciating. He 'let rip' and swore hard as he was gripped by the pain. He was well used to CS, since he had been subjected to it 'countless times' during army training. 'It was certainly more intense than CS. It was significantly stronger than CS. Although CS is very uncomfortable, it is possible to carry on and do things if you have the determination. But with this, there was no chance of doing anything. Your mind was totally, totally occupied with getting rid of the pain in the eye. It was like any other acute pain – nothing else matters at that moment.' The pain persisted for about five minutes, and he suffered a headache for the following two days. He says he would have adamantly refused to undergo the experiment again. It appears that at one time, Porton scientists were actually barred from dropping solutions containing tear gas into human eyes 'as it was felt that this test could be misrepresented outside' Porton.[97]

As well as being more powerful than CS gas, CR has an added advantage – it dissolves more easily in water and can therefore be dispersed more accurately by water cannons. Tear gases disseminated in a smoke can float away from the areas of civil unrest and strike down bystanders, but Porton scientists observed that this disadvantage 'could be limited by the use of aimed jets of irritant solution'. Porton therefore tried out solutions of both CS and CR gas on 146 human 'guinea pigs' who were drenched in a set of experiments.[98] The 'lightly clothed' volunteers stepped into cubicles where they were saturated from head to toe. Others were thoroughly soaked out in the open in groups of up to twelve at a time. Many suffered 'extremely unpleasant experiences' after being soaked with 'dilute' solutions. The two gases caused about the same amount of 'immediate discomfort' to the eyes of the volunteers – stinging and 'profuse' watering for a few minutes, along with runny nose and 'excessive salivation'. But CR gas inflicted much more intense pain, and for longer, on the skin of the human 'guinea pigs' than CS. The volunteers felt burning, for up to twenty minutes, most severely on the face, back and genitalia. This was aggravated by the chafing of wet clothes – many 'exhibited a characteristic "penguin" gait, in which arms were held away from the body and the legs slightly apart'.

When the government authorised CR gas for use in Ulster in 1973, the MoD insisted that an 'intensive' testing programme over several years had given 'no cause for concern'. People could not suffer any permanent damage from the so-called 'fire gas', asserted the MoD.[99] (At the time, the MoD was criticised for ignoring a key recommendation of the Himsworth committee by failing to publish the scientific reports underpinning its confident assertion that CR was safe.)[100] But like CN gas, Porton's evaluation of the safety of CR has also shifted over time, and this gas too is no longer proclaimed to be as harmless as it once was. Porton now concedes that CR is not backed by 'extensive health and safety assessments', and that information about the long-term effects of CR is 'sadly lacking', particularly its potential to cause cancer and genetic defects.[101]

Apart from one disputed incident in Ulster, CR gas has never been used in public anywhere by the British government since the 1970s. (During a riot at the Maze prison in October 1974, 'prisoners, used to the effects of CS gas, claimed that a new agent was used on them'. They say they suspected it was a new agent being used against them and not CS gas because they found it 'more irritating to the eyes and [it] had a paralysing effect'. The use of CR gas was denied by the government. It appears, however, that on a few occasions, the armed forces have been prepared and equipped to use it to counter disturbances in Ulster, but it did not prove necessary. Since 1992, the MoD secretly authorised the use of CR on two occasions 'where the armed forces have responded to a request for assistance for law enforcement purposes' from police, but the ministry was unwilling to give any details of when or where this happened for reasons of 'national security'. Some service personnel were exposed to a 'small amount' of CR 'for training purposes in the past', but details of this are sparse.)[102]

Nowadays, the government considers that CR, like CN gas, is too hazardous to be used by British police forces on the general population. Currently, the MoD is the only government department to stockpile CR gas. The gas is solely approved for use against terrorists, but – crucially – not for controlling disturbances by ordinary members of the public.[103] It appears that so far, the government has recognised that CR gas is too politically controversial to be used in public.

Dr Rex Watson, Porton's director between 1974 and 1983, stressed that the overriding concern of all Porton's work on tear gases during the 1970s was to develop chemicals which would deter rioters without causing them any personal harm. 'One deplored the fact that people should riot. It does not seem to be a very sensible way of conducting politics. Given that you had to contain it, then we sought to make the containment as safe as possible for the people who were doing it.' He said that safety was the key issue. 'What we were being asked to do was pretty impossible – to find some way of discouraging people from rioting which was significantly less damaging to them than a rifle bullet.'[104] He added, 'In my life, I have seen a tendency for people in this country to riot to grow and grow and grow because people are less well-behaved.'

A significant amount of Porton's work in the 1970s was aimed at 'internal security' – devising technologies for subduing political and civil unrest within Britain. Neville Gadsby, Porton's director between 1968 and 1972, says that this research had 'quite considerable priority' after the Troubles in

Northern Ireland broke out,[105] and that as well as perfecting tear gases, Porton also carried out research on rubber bullets and water cannon.

The forerunner to rubber bullets was the wooden bullet which had been developed by the British in 1958 in Hong Kong. The wooden or 'baton round' was seen as a way of striking demonstrators without the colonial police having to put themselves in danger by charging into crowds with their wooden sticks. According to Gadsby, Porton had 'responsibilities for crowd control, and of course we were well aware of the various types of non-explosive bullets that had been used in other parts of the world'. However the wooden bullet was felt to be too dangerous for Northern Ireland (but not, it seems, for the colonies) because it splintered. Since the wooden bullet was 'highly unacceptable', Porton started to look at other materials, mainly rubber or plastic. As Gadsby said, 'We agreed that we would develop a few prototypes for them to be demonstrated in Northern Ireland.' Ulster officials requested rubber bullets to be produced quickly. Gadsby says the original bullets were developed from the same rubber as that used in chemical warfare respirators. Porton delivered the first batch 'on time' in 1970, and over the next four years, the Ulster security forces fired around 55,000 rubber bullets during disturbances.[106]

Rubber bullets may sound like squashy pellets, but they are dangerous. According to one description, they are 'made of black rubber, rather harder than that in car tyres', are 'blunt nosed cylinders' around five inches high and more than one inch in diameter, weighing over five ounces, fired rapidly from guns and are 'unstable in flight, and highly inaccurate'.[107] They are supposed to be fired in accordance with certain guidelines (for example, laying down the minimum distance between the gun and the target), but in the heat of the street battles in Northern Ireland, these were sometimes cast aside. At least fifteen people have died after being struck by rubber (and plastic) bullets fired by the Ulster security forces since 1970. Officials argue that despite this death toll, rubber or plastic bullets are considerably safer than using rifle bullets to deter rioters. Dr Watson, ex-Porton director, said it was unrealistic to believe that no one would be killed with rubber or plastic bullets: 'People talk about safety as if it is an absolute. There is no such thing as total safety – there's a lack of hazard. It's not safe to cross the road.'

In the mid-1980s, the then Northern Ireland minister, Nicholas Scott, declared that the rubber bullets were the only effective method of protecting the security forces against rioting since both 'water cannon and CS have both proved to be ineffective'.[108] Water cannon knocks people to the ground, but it has proved to be limited as a riot control weapon. It is basically a motorised water-tank with a high-pressure hose. They were wheeled out in Cyprus in the 1950s and then again in Northern Ireland between 1968 and 1970.[109] Its disadvantages are that the tanks of water run out quickly (within around five minutes), the vehicles are hard to manoeuvre, and the rioters can duck behind small walls to avoid the jets of water. Furthermore, although they knock people over at less than thirty yards, they do inflict relatively little pain or discomfort, compared to other riot control weapons, and once a person has been soaked, they may as well stay in the area.

In the 1970s, Porton carried out trials with human 'guinea pigs' to test the medical effects of water cannon, the results of which remain secret.[110] Porton is also believed to have developed a special dye which was sprayed in the jets of the water cannon in Ulster. The purpose of this dye – which, according to one account, 'was difficult to wash off the skin and impossible to get out of clothes' – was to identify rioters for later arrest or possibly stigmatise them in the eyes of parents or employers. The colour of the dye was specifically chosen – not red, since it looks like blood on television; not green or orange, because these were deeply symbolic in Ireland, so it became blue.[111]

Porton's work on internal security appears to have tailed off since the 1970s. It is known that in the 1980s, the eyes of nineteen volunteers were exposed to a new potential tear gas, which was eventually dropped since it was judged to be no better than CS.[112]

CS gas has steadily encroached from being used in the colonies, then Northern Ireland, onto the rest of Britain in limited circumstances, and now on a widespread scale throughout the country. Back in 1971, police declared that CS gas 'will not be used to quell riots or rowdy demonstrations'.[113] Another milestone was passed when CS was fired for the first time in a civil disturbance on mainland Britain, during the Toxteth riots in Liverpool in the summer of 1981. Willie Whitelaw, the then Home Secretary, pronounced that the use of CS in these riots was 'necessary and justified'. However he asserted that police forces could only use the tear gas 'as a last resort' where conventional policing had failed and there was 'a risk of loss of life or serious injury, or widespread destruction of property'.[114] Over the next decade or so, police forces resorted to CS sparingly, mainly in sieges.[115]

Yet police chiefs and officers were lobbying to be allowed to wield CS on a much more regular and routine basis. They argued that they needed a 'non-lethal weapon' to combat the rising number of armed attacks on police officers. Their pressure paid off in April 1995 when Michael Howard, Conservative Home Secretary at the time, approved a series of trials in selected police forces in which bobbies on the beat carried CS spray every day to protect themselves. The trials had to be postponed when a police instructor suffered bad burns in his eyes and forehead after he was sprayed in the face in a demonstration (as noted earlier in this chapter), but they eventually got underway in March 1996. Before they were due to end, Howard announced in August 1996 that all police forces were permitted to use CS if they wished. Official statistics indicate that nowadays, individual police forces are using CS sprays hundreds of times a year.[116]

Before CS spray was adopted in 1996, senior police chiefs had for a few years been advocating another disabling chemical – pepper spray.[117] This spray is derived from capsaicin, the main ingredient in paprika and cayenne pepper. According to one description, pepper spray is more severe than CS, since it can blind for up to thirty minutes, cause a burning pain on the skin for around an hour, and trigger spasms and uncontainable coughing making it difficult to breathe or speak for between three and fifteen minutes.[118] Porton tested pepper gas on an unknown number of human 'guinea pigs' between the First World War and the mid-1950s. These tests showed that it was capable of inflicting great distress on humans; indeed in one experiment in 1956, volunteers found it 'quite intolerable in less than 10 seconds'.[119]

Porton now accepts that over the long term, a single exposure to pepper sprays can damage the nervous system, making a person insensitive to pain, and may also harm the body's ability to regulate its temperature.[120] Scientists have privately warned that there 'remains a considerable risk to the use of pepper sprays on a large and varied population'.[121]

After scrutinising demands from police chiefs for pepper sprays, the government decided in late 1995 that 'not enough' was known about their effects on human health to be reassured that they were safe enough to be used by British police forces.[122] In a leaked letter, a Home Office scientist had commented in 1994 that there was 'considerable interest in using oleoresin capsicum (OC) pepper sprays in this country, however there are still a number of questions regarding the safety of OC that have not yet been satisfactorily answered.'[123] Department of Health officials had judged that 'the available experimental data' indicated that pepper sprays caused cancers.[124] Although British police forces are at the moment not armed with pepper sprays, many countries around the world do use them.

How effective are tear gases? On the military battlefield, they appear to be very efficient in forcing the enemy out of concealed bunkers where they can be shot and bombed, as the Americans demonstrated in Vietnam. Tear gas was proclaimed by the Americans to be a humane weapon which would avoid deaths among the Vietnamese, but this was not how it was used.

The worth of tear gases in civil situations is questionable. Governments often resort to disabling chemicals to contain political dissent among its citizens when the usual, more benign methods of control have not worked. In Britain, until the last few years, the most widespread use of CS has been in Northern Ireland. If the aim of the authorities was to dampen down the disturbances in Ulster, it appears to have badly backfired and actually inflamed the situation. According to one authoritative study of the IRA, the tear gas 'proved particularly effective in manufacturing resentment. Many of those who went on to take up guns cite their first experience of tear gas as the moment their alienation from the State became complete'.[125] One Porton scientist observed of the use of tear gas in the 'highly emotive, powder-keg' situation of Ulster that 'violence begets violence'. It seems that tear gas – like any riot control technology – is a poor method of solving political and social problems. In recent times, the number of riots and the use of tear gas in Northern Ireland have diminished since the so-called 'peace process' – a political solution to the unrest – has materialised.

Today, the government's justification for the routine use of CS sprays nowadays is that the tear gas was necessary to combat the rising tide of armed attacks on police officers. As it happens, the number of serious assaults on police actually fell in the five years before the CS trials began in 1996. Officially, CS sprays are meant to be used only to protect police officers when they are under attack. However police have been criticised for resorting to the sprays for other reasons – to make it easier to arrest people and to subdue people, whether or not they are being violent. The official watchdog, the Police Complaints Authority (PCA), has warned that while the sprays have provided 'much-needed protection for police officers', some police officers are tempted to use CS 'as an easy way of resolving difficult situations when other means might be more appropriate'. The PCA also suggested that some police forces 'have used the spray to a much greater extent than others'.[126] Citizens can become angry and resentful towards the police if they believe that CS sprays have been wrongly used on them or people they know personally. The persistent doubts over the safety of CS can also foster grievances among the public. Reports in scientific journals have shown a number of ill effects on humans, including severe blistering on the face.

CS is currently being used by the British police as a spray; the CS is dissolved in a solvent and then dispersed as a liquid solution from a canister. Previously, in Ulster, CS was disseminated in a different way – a small explosive charge in a cartridge or grenade propelled and dispersed the powdered irritant in a cloud over the target. Critics have argued that the

Himsworth committee approved CS in this previous form of powdered cloud, but the government was scientifically ill-advised in 1996 to extrapolate this approval to CS as a *liquid spray*. The sprays, for instance, leave a deposit on the skin, which is difficult to remove and can therefore continue to cause injury over a longer time. For the police, the advantage of sprays is that they can be more easily directed towards the target, while CS clouds often drift away.

Critics also point out that the proportion of CS in the spray, as opposed to solvent, is very high and excessive compared to police forces in other countries. The concentration of CS in Britain is five percent, while in other countries it is only one percent. (Spot checks have found that some sprays used by British police had concentrations of CS even higher than five percent.) The Home Office contends that concentrations of less than five percent are simply ineffective.[127] In an experiment in the 1970s, Porton drenched 146 volunteers with CS and CR gases (described earlier in the chapter). It is noticeable that a solution of just 0.005 percent CS was enough to produce quickly the usual discomforting symptoms of this tear gas. The CS solvent which is currently employed by British police has also been questioned, with even Porton recommending a switch to a 'safer and more acceptable' alternative.[128]

The latest inquiry by two official committees into CS sprays – launched following persistent criticisms of the weapon – implored police to obey the operational guidelines for using the spray.[129] The committees expressed concern that 'certain groups of the population, comprising individuals with bronchial asthma, chronic obstructive pulmonary disease, and those suffering from hypertension or other cardiovascular disease, might be particularly susceptible to the effects of CS spray'. They ruled that the data on the mixture of CS and its solvent was sparse at the moment, but on that basis, the sprays did not pose a danger. Interestingly, the committee members considered that more information about the effects of the spray was needed, but noted that 'systematic studies in volunteers to investigate the toxicity of CS spray may present insurmountable difficulties'. Thirty years ago, Porton scientists were called upon to carry out human experiments to investigate the safety of CS gas. Now with the changing atmosphere of the times, it would appear that the government no longer believes that such tests are politically possible. The committees ruled that CS itself – on its own – was by and large regarded as being safe.

It is clear that three tear gases – CR, CN, and pepper gas – which were tested on human subjects at Porton were once believed to be harmless. But nowadays this has changed; the British government, including Porton, has accepted that these three gases are dangerous and can damage human health. In this light, Porton's repeated assurances that none of the human 'guinea pigs' could have suffered long-term illnesses may prove to be questionable.

CHAPTER TEN
A Solitary Battle

Thousands of people have been subjected to British chemical warfare experiments from the First World War onwards. It is now impossible to calculate the true total of volunteer 'guinea pigs' who have taken part in Porton's experiments in the past eight decades. Officials put the total at 'more than 20,000', although this is almost certainly an underestimate.[1] A more accurate figure would be around 30,000 (see appendix one). Porton's own figures show that since 1945, over 14,000 have taken part in the tests. Yet remarkably, it was not until the 1990s that significant numbers came forward to tell their stories in public. Before then, there had been only sporadic press and political interest in the issue.

Chemical and biological warfare is an inherently secretive subject, as is Porton. The establishment has always been guarded about disclosing information to the public. One of its most tightly-held secrets is undoubtedly its long programme of human experiments – a topic which is especially emotive and therefore sensitive for the establishment.[2] One of the main reasons why volunteers have been reticent about airing their experiences in public is the Official Secrets Act. It is likely that many still fear that they could be prosecuted under the Act if they were ever to speak out. Take, for instance, one volunteer who took part in tests at Porton Down in the 1970s. He said, 'We are not allowed to talk about them as we signed the Official Secrets Act which they could use against us if we talked.'[3]

Others are likely to have kept quiet out of a sense of duty to their country. For example, Richard Meakin, who served in the Wiltshire Regiment, underwent a 'pretty awful' nerve gas experiment in 1954 from which he experienced bad headaches and vision for up to three days.[4] But he feels that, although the likelihood of being prosecuted is remote, he would not blab about his experiment because of 'my love of my country', especially since he comes from a family of soldiers. He said his experiment was 'part of our national defence. Had Saddam [Hussein] attacked our troops in the Gulf War with nerve gas and the antidotes which they found from our experiments proved effective to save chaps' lives, I would have been very proud and pleased.' He feels that the experiment was his small contribution towards enhancing the country's defences. 'I respect the army's code of secrecy. I signed the [official secrets] papers. You play by the rules, like when you play football or rugby. The referee is right.'

Some of the volunteers, particularly those who went to Porton during the Cold War days of the 1950s, say that they were required to sign a 'gagging' document when they first arrived at the establishment. Leonard Sellick, who was tested with riot gases in 1956 (see chapter nine), recalls that on the first morning, he was given a 'pretty detailed' document – 'about three pages long' – setting how they could not pass any information about the tests to anybody outside of Porton. He had to sign it, or else return to his unit.[5]

Others say that they were required to sign the usual short declaration of the Official Secrets Act. This declaration warns of the 'serious consequences' of divulging government information. John Nelson, who passed out in a nerve gas experiment in the 1950s (see chapter five), says that he and other volunteers were told to sign it because they were at a restricted establishment. He adds that on a number of occasions, Porton staff stressed that they faced a long stretch in prison if they disclosed anything to anybody.[6]

All government employees sign the Official Secrets Act declaration, when they start their job. Making the volunteers sign the declaration again is almost worthless in legal terms.[7] It seems that the point of insisting that the volunteers all sign it, was to reinforce the secrecy of the experiments to the human 'guinea pigs' so that they would not even mention the existence of their visit to outsiders. The need for secrecy in all matters is, of course, constantly drilled into military personnel. Bob Marsden, who volunteered for Porton when he was stationed at an RAF signals station in the late 1960s, believes that he was not required to sign any pieces of paper, but recalls that while he was there, 'You were told that what everyone was doing was confidential – not for other ears, but you were used to that sort of thing in the forces.'[8] The irony is that often the volunteers never in fact knew any real secrets simply because they were told very little about the chemicals which were being tested on them.

It is virtually certain that the government would not prosecute a volunteer for talking about experiments which he or she experienced (nor incidentally, the former Porton staff who organised the tests). In early 1998, the Ministry of Defence launched a new initiative in which volunteers could contact Porton for details of their tests (see appendix four). It would therefore be extremely odd for the government to hand out such details and then arrest a volunteer who discussed them in public or the media. Since the high-profile trials of Clive Ponting and Peter Wright during the 1980s, the government has in any case appeared to be reluctant to launch legal action under the Official Secrets Act against people who leak information, except those who are directly involved in espionage.[9] Moreover, it would be a public relations disaster to prosecute former servicemen who had volunteered for experiments and who are now claiming that their health had been damaged by these tests. If nothing else, it would draw attention to a subject the government wants to keep quiet and under control.

Until the mid-1990s, the government had done reasonably well in keeping the human trials out of the media. Indeed, one War Office mandarin noted that 'our technique' in 'getting volunteers' and 'keeping the experiments fairly quiet' had been successful.[10] The first serious dose of bad publicity about the experiments came in 1953 after the death of Ronald Maddison. The press reported how the government was covering up the death, whilst the fatality was aired in Parliament. Six months later, the *Daily Express* revealed, apparently for the first time, the existence of the nerve gas experiments on humans. Headlined 'Nerve gas secret out', the *Express* disclosed how 'scores' of servicemen were being exposed to the deadliest known poison gases so that scientists could experiment with antidotes.[11] It added that the men 'suffered "extra harassment" while braving the gases with no form of protection'.

Over the next decade, there seems to have been little or no coverage. One of the first human 'guinea pigs' to go to the press about the nerve gas experiments was an RAF man from Hull in March 1960. Under the headline, 'I tried killer nerve gas', Daine Bryce Kelman, then twenty-six, described how in 1955 he and others 'had to go through two air-locks before entering the gas chamber. Once inside, we were ordered to take off our gas masks and expose ourselves to the nerve gas for exactly 60 seconds. The horrifying thing about the gas was that no one could see it, smell it or feel it. But once out in the fresh air, our chests tightened up, we got severe headaches and our eyes became dilated.'[12]

Public concern about chemical and biological warfare rose in the 1960s, largely because of the American use of CS gas and defoliants in Vietnam and the British deployment of tear gas in Northern Ireland. Due to increased scrutiny of Porton's activities, the establishment held some open days in the late 1960s in an attempt to allay public disquiet. These 'open days' triggered press articles on Porton's LSD tests on humans. In the 1970s, media coverage was muted even though the secrets of the American tests were tumbling out mainly through US congressional inquiries. The next bout of publicity does not appear to have come until 1984, when Tony Banks, Labour MP, received

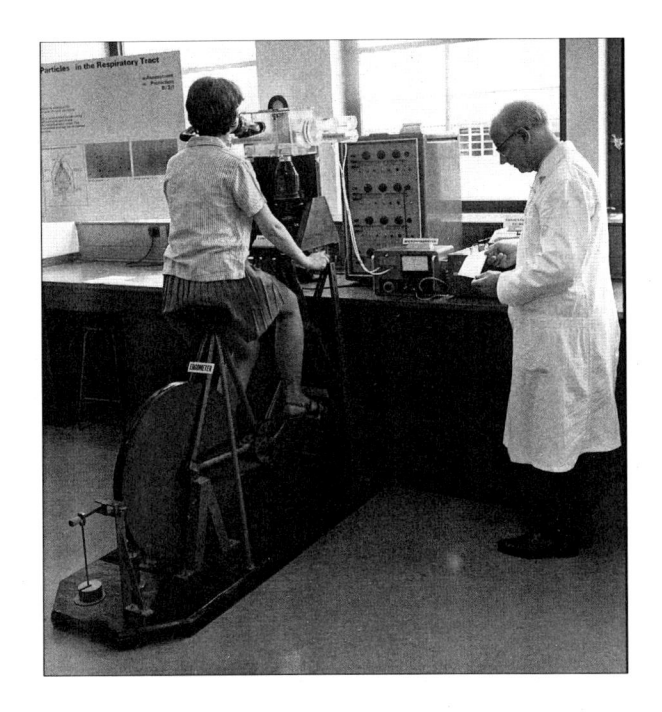

A young visitor tests out Porton's equipment at one of Porton's open days in the late sixties.

Porton's laboratories in the sixties.

an unsigned letter from a man who claimed to have volunteered to take part in tests seeking a cure for the common cold, but was instead exposed to nerve gas. Tony Banks tabled questions in the House of Commons, causing widespread coverage when the MoD confirmed the experiments, adding that they had been going on for some years.[13] Banks commented that the answers had 'given the lie' to people who could not believe that 'experiments were taking place on humans' at Porton Down.[14] In 1987, the *Mail On Sunday* newspaper ran a front-page 'world exclusive' revealing that servicemen were being shut in Porton's gas chambers and exposed to nerve gas.[15] This precipitated another round of publicity. *Chemistry in Britain*, a magazine which has often covered chemical and biological warfare issues, caustically noted that the paper's 'world exclusive' has 'shocked many people, but the story first leaked out over 30 years ago'.[16]

Since at least the 1930s, Porton has been receiving complaints from servicemen exposed to chemicals, but few, if any, went to the press. For many decades, aggrieved volunteers were pressing their case privately to the authorities, but on the whole they were isolated, coming against dead ends as they struggled against the bureaucracy. The first step of their campaign was of course to discover what they had been subjected to during their experiments at Porton. This information was essential to establishing whether their illnesses were connected to their tests at Porton. For a long time, this was a difficult task.

Some say that they wrote to Porton asking for details of their experiments, but were rebuffed or ignored. One was Eddie Roberts (see chapter six). His doctors wrote to Porton in the early 1970s, but after some months, were told that his medical details were 'lost'.[17] Lewis Birt contacted Porton in 1973, asking for information about the nerve gas experiment in which he had been blinded for two days in 1951 (see chapter four). He received no reply. Although he is not claiming compensation, he does confess to getting 'a little niggled' when the government tries to 'weasel out' of its responsibility to look after those whose health has been damaged while serving their country.[18]

Another volunteer given the brush-off by Porton was Bill Clavey, who was a teenage National Serviceman, and was tested with sarin nerve gas in 1950.[19] In the experiment in question, he and others were led into the gas chamber without any protection. The officer in the chamber with them wore a gas mask, while various high-ranking officials watched from behind a glass screen. He endured chest pains and then, for the next three or so days, restricted vision, since the pupils of his eyes had been reduced to pinpoints. '[Your] eyes prevented you reading and doing anything. You wore these glasses to keep any light off because you could not see. Your eyes were too tender for light.' Beginning a decade later, Clavey suffered a succession of nervous disorders and two heart attacks. It was around 1970 that he first thought that his illnesses may been connected to the Porton experiments. His doctor wrote to Porton asking 'in view of the suggested long-term effects of some of the nerve gases' whether his patient had been exposed to nerve gas or another chemical. He received a holding reply stating that the inquiry has been passed 'to our Medical Division, i.e. those responsible for experimental work, who when records have been checked will communicate direct with you', but nothing appeared after that.[20] Clavey sees this as an outrage – 'That's very wrong. I feel that it was an assault on my body' – and he regrets going to Porton, especially since he only volunteered to get a pass for a weekend break from the RAF.

Another volunteer now suffering from a string of illnesses is Gerry Ashton, who was tested with nerve gas in 1951 (see chapter four). He managed to persuade his new doctor in the 1970s to write to Porton to establish the type of chemical that had been administered to him. He says that the MoD at first denied that he had ever been to Porton: 'Of course my doctor thought I had been telling him lies.' However, when his doctor wrote again soon afterwards, the MoD this time did admit that he had been to Porton, but added that the experiments were 'very innocuous' and could therefore not be the cause of his medical problems.[21] For many years, he believed that there was little point pressuring the MoD about his experiments or illnesses because he had come up against this stonewalling. He feels strongly, however, that this lack of information from the MoD has hindered his doctors from treating his illnesses. It was not until 1994 that he wrote again to Porton and finally received a reply confirming that he had been exposed to tabun nerve gas and giving other important details.[22]

Porton insists that it has 'always' been its policy to release information about experiments to the doctors of former volunteers when requested.[23] Despite this claim, it is apparent that in the past, Porton has been reluctant to hand over details of experiments to either volunteers or their doctors. This has now changed, as Porton is making more effort to answer volunteers' inquiries and relax its tight hold on information (see appendix four), and nowadays, former volunteers are routinely given a description and the particulars of their experiments. Undoubtedly Porton finds it increasingly difficult to disregard such requests, especially since the establishment has come under more and more pressure from disgruntled volunteers in the 1990s. The ending of the paranoid atmosphere of the Cold War may also have made it easier to be freer with such data. It also has been suggested that for some time, there was confusion between Porton and Whitehall over who exactly should be responsible for answering volunteers' requests for information.

It was not until recently that the isolated individuals were able to form themselves into some sort of a collective force. The catalyst behind this change was Mick Roche, one of the more persistent campaigners, who founded the Porton Down Volunteers Association in early 1994. As described in chapter seven, Roche was tested with nerve gas in 1963 in experiments which broke the official safety rules laid down by government ministers. A Royal Engineer for fourteen years, Roche says he 'foolishly' chose to go to Porton twice as a human 'guinea pig'. After seeing a notice asking for volunteers, he 'mulled it over before I finally decided going. Looking back what really decided it in my case is that I remember as a small child watching my father's father slowly dying from the effects of gas that he had in the First World War. And I suppose it was perhaps that and, dare I mention the word – patriotism, and [that] I wanted to do my little bit, that I decided to volunteer.'

In the 1980s, when Roche was in his forties and running a small building company, he 'started getting breathing problems. I put it down to approaching old age. I didn't take a great deal of notice of it. But it was gradually getting worse and worse'.[24] He went to see his doctor who took a series of tests and quickly sent him to hospital. 'I had blood pressure that was absolutely astronomical...nurses and doctors said [that] at that pressure your head should explode. And this...[was]...what was causing the breathing problems.' After ten days in hospital, Roche's blood pressure had come down and he went back to his doctor who wanted to prescribe a long-term treatment. 'He just casually remarked, had I ever been exposed to a dangerous chemical in a working environment. And I said "I can do better than that, doc – I attended Porton Down as a human guinea pig for gas testing."' His doctor told him that he needed to know what chemicals he had been exposed to before he could treat him. He advised him to ask the MoD for his military medical records as well as the scientific information on his experiments which were held by Porton Down.

It was, however, to be some time before he would get a proper answer from the MoD. He says that the initial medical records released by the MoD omitted any reference to his Porton tests. He resorted to going on hunger strike and camping outside Porton Down. This he began on Remembrance Sunday in 1989. In an angry letter to the then Defence Minister, Tom King, he wrote, 'For nearly four years now I have knocked politely on the doors of power requesting information. I have now finished knocking. I am now kicking the door down and placing the matter before the nation's conscience.' He added, 'On Remembrance Sunday, we honour all our war dead, but hold a special place in our hearts for the few remaining 'Old Contemptibles' of the First World War. I think I am now a 'New Contemptible'. For your department has treated all my requests with cold, callous contempt.'

The bold move produced a response. Within four days, Porton had sent a letter to his doctor, outlining the experiment, the name of the nerve gas in the test, and the immediate effect of the gas on him.[25] By this time, Roche had been registered as an invalid, suffering from hypertension and chronic bronchitis. His breathing problems had been steadily getting worse. 'I used to be full of zip and drive. I could run around a building site with two bags of cement. Now I couldn't run round with two bags of sugar.' His claim for a war pension had been refused.

Roche had the idea of starting an association after he saw an American television programme in 1993 on the US mustard gas tests. 'I was amazed to find out that the American government had now, after all these years, finally accepted that the testing they've done on their men may have injured their health and they've been compensated. Looking back on my lone voyage, crying in the wilderness over all these years and getting nowhere I thought that the best thing I could do was to form an association.'

He sent a round-robin letter to local papers all over the country, appealing for former Porton Down volunteers to come forward and join the association. These letters, along with an hour-long ITV television programme in October 1994, triggered a sizeable amount of media coverage, and helped swell the association's membership to more than 200.[26] In the following years, the media showed occasional interest in the issue of Porton's human experiments, with a concentrated burst of publicity in 1999 when Wiltshire police launched its investigation.

The human 'guinea pigs' have faced a tough legal battle to win compensation and recognition. The Porton Down Volunteers' Association achieved a breakthrough in late 1994 when Roche won legal aid to sue the Ministry of Defence for compensation for damage to his health caused by the Porton Down tests. It is known that there had been legal claims over Porton Down's experiments in the 1930s; but it appears that Roche's lawsuit was the first for many decades.[27] He was represented by Leigh, Day and Co., a law firm with a reputation for championing causes challenging the establishment and the status quo. This was to be a test case for members of the association, around sixty of whom joined in the group action.

But their legal action was effectively blocked by the Ministry of Defence under a law dating from the 1940s. For years the Crown Proceedings Act 1947 prevented all servicemen and women, and their relatives, from suing the Ministry of Defence for compensation for injuries caused during their military service.

Ironically the act was originally passed by the Labour government as a liberalising measure to allow, for the first time, the state to be sued by citizens. However a fateful clause was added to the bill as it passed through Parliament. Section 10 specifically banned any member of the armed forces from suing for any damages which originated while they were serving in the military. The clause was drawn up because the government maintained that, in contrast to civilians, the armed forces were regularly engaged in dangerous activities, even in peacetime, such as training with live bullets or flying in close formation. As Lord Shawcross, then the Attorney-General, claimed in 1947, such activities were necessary 'to secure the efficiency of the Forces', but would be 'extremely blameworthy if done by private citizens'.[28] The justification for the clause can also be seen in a declassified letter written in 1959 by Sir Jocelyn Simon, then the Financial Secretary to the Treasury. He wrote, 'The need for Section 10 is obvious. A member of the forces, whether on active service or not, runs risks which a civilian does not normally encounter... The courts could not easily determine whether the degree of risk which a serviceman was called upon to undergo on any particular occasion was justifiable or not. Again, the requirements of discipline and service morale forbid a situation in which servicemen could institute proceedings against other servicemen in respect of acts performed on duty.'[29]

Many Porton Down volunteers were deeply dismayed when their legal action was stopped by Section 10, feeling that it was injustice in the extreme. Alan Care, a lawyer who has represented the association, called the effect of Section 10 'draconian and indefensible', adding, 'Section 10 was not intended to serve as a convenient immunity from prosecution of civil claims for the MoD. It was a policy provision to prevent civil legal actions arising from ordinary military activity.'[30] He told members, 'Quite frankly, I believe that Porton Down Volunteer Association members have received shabby treatment by the MoD, given their undoubted selfless contribution to British defence and security in the area of chemical and biological warfare.'

There had been long-standing doubts about the fairness and justice of Section 10 ever since it had come into force. Many MPs voiced concern about it even as it was passed through Parliament. Indeed, an Air Ministry official noted in 1947 that his department had 'expressed grave doubts' about the section when it was first drafted.[31] He wondered if, 'in the face of adverse public opinion', it would be possible to maintain the government's exemption from legal action. The official believed that the position of the military would be difficult to maintain in the long run. A few years later, a Whitehall working party noted that the clause had 'attracted a good deal of criticism' in cases which 'might be considered as being rather removed from the primary intention of the Act'. In particular, these were the type of cases 'where it is clear beyond doubt that the injury is the direct result of gross negligence' by the MoD.[32]

Section 10 was finally repealed in 1987 after a series of cases highlighted the injustice of the clause. But the repeal of Section 10 was scant comfort for human 'guinea pigs' who were tested years or decades earlier because it was not retrospective. In other words, those Porton volunteers who had been in experiments before 1987 are still barred from launching a legal action for compensation; only those who have been in tests after 1987 can bring a lawsuit. (Since the late 1980s, written consent forms have been given to volunteers before they agree to take part in an experiment. Two sample forms released by Porton show that the volunteers are specifically told that they can claim compensation if anything goes wrong. One section of the form spells out how, 'in the unlikely event of your suffering injury or disability as a consequence of your attendance' at Porton, the volunteers can submit a claim for a war pension. They are also told that 'if you feel whatever injury you suffered was caused by the negligence of the MoD', they can submit a claim for common law compensation.)[33]

The civil action by Roche had been brought to a halt in 1995 when the MoD issued what is known as a Section 10 certificate. This is a curious mechanism with all the hallmarks of bureaucratic stonewalling. The certificate can only be served by the government if it admits that the injury or illness suffered by the claimant is 'attributable' to military service, in this case the Porton Down experiments. But this was a hollow victory for the Porton human 'guinea pigs'. The certificate meant that Mick Roche could no longer continue his legal action to sue the MoD for a lump-sum compensation payment. Instead he and other volunteers had to apply for a weekly war pension – and that has been a tough obstacle.

By serving the certificate, the MoD in effect conceded that volunteers were entitled to *apply* for a war pension. But that is very different from conceding that the volunteers were entitled to actually *receive* one. The wording of the certificate offers false hope to claimants – it says that the government 'certifies' that the suffering is 'treated as attributable to service for the purposes of entitlement to an award'. It amounted to an illusion that volunteers would get compensation quickly. However, the volunteers had fallen foul of Section 10 just as many service men and women had done in previous years. Indeed, the true impact of Section 10 was not lost on one minister who had been in charge of war pensions. During a discussion about the clause in the late 1950s, John Boyd-Carpenter, the then Tory Minister of Pensions and National Insurance, had written in a secret memo about Section 10 certificates, 'Although of course the terms of the certificate contain no promise that a pension will be paid, it seems to me that to people unused to the niceties of legal and official draftsmanship, it might well seem that it was being suggested that a pension would be paid.'[34]

The War Pension Agency, an independent body answering to the Department of Social Security, is responsible for awarding payments on a sliding scale to members of the armed forces who have been injured during their military service.[35] The weekly pensions are a form of recognition of service to the nation, and the amount awarded is dependent on how badly the applicant has been injured. In its policy towards Porton Down volunteers, the War Pension Agency does not lay out a defined list of diseases and illnesses which it recognises as being caused by specific chemical weapons, but instead considers claims 'individually and according to their specific circumstance'.[36]

Many volunteers are discouraged from even applying for a war pension because they see it as basically a waste of time. (Others do not apply because they feel that they deserve a lump-sum compensation, rather than a weekly pension). Those who do apply often do so with a very pessimistic attitude. They believe that in order to be awarded a pension, they have to demonstrate to the War Pension Agency that their illness was caused by a particular chemical. Proving the medical connection between an illness and a specific chemical is often complicated and lies at the heart of the volunteers' plight (see chapter eleven). Faced with this daunting task, they sense a heavy burden on themselves. This is not the case, however, in theory since the War Pension Agency insists that the 'benefit of any reasonable doubt is always given to the claimant'.[37]

This rule on the benefit of doubt may appear to offer Porton volunteers hope of winning some sort of compensation, but the reality is in fact different. The government claims that it cannot confirm how many Porton Down volunteers have successfully won a war pension, as it would cost too much money to locate the relevant information.[38] However the Porton Down Volunteers Association knows of only one human 'guinea pig' who has won a war pension for a claim based solely on the chemical warfare experiments. This is Harry Hogg who was tested at Porton during the Second World War and has endured various illnesses for many years (see chapter three). His application for a war pension in 1991 was initially turned down, but his appeal was successful three years later.[39]

Three other cases have come to light in which volunteers have won some sort of pension. The first case is Eric Watts who was a conscientious objector in the Second World War, serving in a non-combatant unit on duties such as bomb disposal.[40] In the middle of the war, he volunteered for what he was told would be 'only a mild test', and since it did not sound much, he was happy to go. The Porton scientists put mustard gas and, he believes, lewisite on either arm, producing 'slight' blisters, which were then dressed. The tests did not hurt too much and after a few days, he returned to his unit. But a week or so later, he 'broke out in bubbles all the way up my arms and my face', and for months, he was in and out of several hospitals. 'The bubbles were itchy and slightly painful, but mostly itchy. You wanted to scratch them, but you could not. You were bandaged right up the arms.' At one time, he had a 'huge sack of yellow pus' hanging down from his arms. He believed that the Porton experiments had possibly made his skin allergic to the dye in his khaki uniform. He was discharged in early 1945. For two or three years, he could not return to his previous job as a compositor in the printing trade and struggled to get work elsewhere. In 1947 he was awarded a pension for two years, followed by a final pay-off of a lump sum of £40. The official form shows that the money was awarded for dermatitis (a disease or inflammation of the skin).[41] He has occasionally had outbreaks of skin rashes since then, and regrets doing the tests because of the ill effects he experienced afterwards. 'I realise that they were not sure themselves what they were up to. But I thought that I was helping the peace of the world. I was a bit idealistic in those days.'

The second case also concerns a volunteer who went to Porton in the Second World War. Hubert Brocklesby was a nineteen-year-old private in the Sherwood Foresters Regiment when he responded to a notice asking for volunteers for a chemical establishment in early 1942.[42] 'I thought I was doing something for my King and Country. It looked interesting.' He had never heard of Porton and believed that the experiments would be harmless. He was one of seven who went into the gas chamber without any protective equipment – 'There were two sides of plate glass windows. Five scientists with jotter boards and stopwatches were looking at us. A fully-clad technician switched on the gas at a given signal from one of the scientists.'

Immediately one of the men 'hit the deck as if pole-axed, face downwards. As Brocklesby and the sergeant bent down to help him, the gas hit them in turn. He said that like the others, he was struck by 'terrible' pains all over his body. 'It was like a convulsive fit, like electric shocks. They would switch from one part of your body to another. You could not concentrate on anything. You had got no control whatsoever.' He and the sergeant pleaded with the scientists to turn off the gas, but they remained 'pokerfaced and were taking down notes until the allocated time on their stopwatches had ended'. At the end, two stretcher-bearers carried out the pole-axed human 'guinea pig'. Brocklesby described the experiment as 'the worst thing that has ever happened to me in my life. It boils down to nothing but torture.'[43] Porton has no records of the substance to which he and the other volunteers were exposed.

During the following week, he and others were taken to some nearby hills where mustard gas vapour was blown over them. The gas felt 'mild and warm' and was 'not unpleasant', although there was a 'burning effect' on their skins. They were protected with gas masks. Afterwards, they discarded their battledress which had been impregnated with an experimental mixture. He had some blisters on his head and neck. He believed that his health has been affected by the Porton tests, and said that he had suffered painful periods of being irritable and highly-strung 'like a nervous disposition'. He sweated, and felt panicky and helpless. The skin on his throat had also been sore when he shaved. In 1992, he was awarded the smallest war pension – twenty percent – for four conditions which had been caused by his military service. These were a gunshot wound in the face, hearing loss and post-traumatic stress disorder, and the fourth, exposure to mustard gas. Curiously, his case notes show that the War Pension Agency doctors appear more willing to attribute this exposure to the usual gas training, rather than the Porton tests. He, however, claimed that he had not been exposed to mustard gas outside of Porton. He died in 1999.

The third case is an RAF man who went to Porton in the late 1970s and does not want to be named.[44] He says that he was tested with 'several' chemicals during his stay, particularly anti-nerve gas tablets. One experiment he took part in took place in a chamber which had been heated to resemble a hot climate. He was testing equipment which could have been used in a chemical-contaminated environment. In the chamber, he dozed off inside what looked like a sleeping bag and woke up sweating. Towards the end of his visit, he began to experience breathing difficulties, and one morning, he woke up but could neither breathe nor speak, and was stricken in his bed. He was immediately injected with adrenaline to revive him, and taken to a military hospital, where he started vomiting. He remained on oxygen and a saline drip for nearly a week, and was off military duty for months. A year later he was forcibly discharged from the Armed Forces for being medically unfit. He was mystified about why he was being discharged since he had not wanted to leave and felt healthy. He was given a £400 pay-off and awarded a small weekly pension from the War Pension Agency, although he is uncertain why he was awarded these and wonders whether it was because of what had happened at Porton. He still feels very bitter about the episode, since he had set his heart on a career in the military.

These cases are, at best, ambiguous precedents of the continuous weekly pension awarded by the War Pension Agency for ailing Porton Down volunteers. The last two cases in particular are mystifying since it is not even certain whether the awards are connected to Porton. To some extent, confusion is caused by the War Pension Agency's policy of treating each claim as an individual case, rather than laying down a blanket policy setting out a prescribed list of diseases which are acknowledged to be caused by particular gases. Without official figures from the War Pension Agency, it is difficult to determine how many volunteers have been successful in winning pensions. Such data would help other Porton volunteers who could use the cases of other volunteers as precedents for their claims.

Until the early 1990s, war pension claims from Porton Down volunteers appear to have been spasmodic. It was not until 1993 that the War Pension Agency felt it necessary to draw up any kind of specific instructions for its staff on how to process Porton Down claimants.[45] An indication of the volume of claims is apparent from official figures showing that around 122 volunteers have requested information from Porton in support of their war pension applications since 1990. (This a good gauge of the number of actual claims, since volunteers need particular information, for example confirmation of dates of their attendance and details of their experiments, to pursue their claims.)[46]

The question of financial compensation for volunteers who suffer ill health many years after the experiments has from time to time been discussed by the MoD, according to declassified records. However, it is likely that the files containing the most frank discussion of this touchy issue have not, and will never, be released to the public, if only because they could be used against the MoD in a court case.

It appears that as far back as 1922, the Commandant of Porton suggested that the sub-committee in charge of the tests should make recommendations on 'the provision of adequate compensation in the event of lasting damage to health'.[47] Despite opposition from some quarters, the Army Council, recognising that the experiments were 'special, dangerous and unpleasant', recommended that compensation claims should be treated relatively generously.[48] It is not known what precise arrangements were adopted at that time. It was, in theory, possible to win compensation from the government, but in practice, it proved more difficult. At the start of the Second World War, when the question arose again, Porton reported that 'past attempts to procure financial compensation for severe mustard [gas] burns had failed'. (It was also noted that this issue 'was obscured by the fact that the relevant file at the War Office had been mislaid'.)[49] As shown in the previous chapter, Porton had also refused to award compensation to those suffering from tear gas exposure before the Second World War. Indeed, the MoD has confirmed that it has not paid any financial compensation to volunteers in the past forty years.[50]

The authorities have always understandably been anxious to avoid publicity over any sort of compensation claims. For instance, in 1960, the ministry then in charge of war pensions was 'concerned at the possibility of receiving claims at a much later date, alleging a connection with the tests, where the medical evidence of such connection might be inconclusive or completely lacking. They feel that they would have to accept such claims to avoid an appeal to the Pensions Appeal Tribunal and disclosure of these secret matters.'[51] A year later, the War Office mulled over ways of 'keeping cases out of the courts' during the long debate on whether to test the V nerve gases on volunteers (see chapter six). Mandarins suggested that claimants, in return for dropping public legal actions, could be paid an appropriate amount of money. They were keen to prevent the government 'from being "blackmailed" into paying more than we consider reasonable in order to prevent a case going to court'.[52] (Of course, one of the consequences of bad publicity is that potential volunteers are deterred from taking part in the experiments. It is difficult to quantify how many service personnel have been put off from going to Porton as a result of these bouts of media coverage. However it is known that in 1995, two service personnel pulled out after they had volunteered because 'of bad publicity (following a television report on ITV)'.)[53]

At the time of writing, the volunteers have renewed their attempts to win legal redress. In 1995, they had been thwarted by the Ministry of Defence which, in effect, blocked their lawsuit through the Section 10 certificate. They stood little chance of winning any appeal against the certificate in a British court. Their lawyers, searching for ways of overcoming this brick wall, saw some possibility in Europe and with the help of the civil rights group Liberty, Roche (on behalf of the Porton Down Volunteers Association) took a case in 1996 to the European Commission of Human Rights. He contended that his rights had been violated on two grounds – Porton was refusing to release his medical records to him and the Ministry of Defence prevented him from suing for compensation. However, this challenge fizzled out. The volunteers' pursuit of justice was given fresh impetus in 1999 when Wiltshire police began their investigation into the death of Ronald Maddison and the alleged hoodwinking of human 'guinea pigs'. In October 1999, Alan Care, now with solicitors Russell Jones and Walker, won legal aid to represent the Maddison family and another Porton Down volunteer, Michael Paynter. Paynter is one of those who claims he was duped into taking part in Porton's poison gas tests in the 1950s when he believed he had volunteered for common cold research. The volunteers hold out that the Wiltshire police investigation will give them a new opening to pursue their campaign in the courts.

Roche and many other volunteers are bitter at the way they have been fobbed off by the MoD, despite all their efforts in serving the nation. Roche said, 'I've been in contact with people who've volunteered to help this country and some are in a hell of a mess and they've not had one penny.' He is angry that the MoD has not even investigated their complaints properly, but instead just tried to sweep their grievances under the carpet. 'I've always maintained that it may be that what I underwent at Porton Down has nothing whatsoever to do with my present medical condition. But on the other hand it may have a lot to do with it and at the back of my mind and other people that I've been in contact with, similar volunteers, is always the question – if I hadn't attended those trials, would my health be a lot better than what it is now?'

Typical are the views of another volunteer, Gerald Fitzgerald, who was tested with mustard gas at Porton in the middle of the Second World War.[54] During the war, he was happy and prepared to take part in the tests. 'It was wartime. You hoped that you were doing a bit of good. There was a sense of your patriotic duty to the King. It sounds foolish. I did not regret it at the time. But the way they have treated us since then, I regret it. We have been treated abominably.' He adds, 'We are not getting anywhere at all. I am getting fed up with it.' He kept quiet about the tests for five decades, after being told at Porton that it was all secret.

The Porton Down volunteers' battle for compensation and recognition follows a familiar pattern. Two other groups of service men and women have also waged a long battle with the MoD over their ill health – the A-Bomb test veterans from the 1950s and 1960s and those suffering from the mysterious Gulf War Syndrome after the conflict in Kuwait in 1991.

More than 22,000 British servicemen and civilians, and 15,000 Australians, participated in twenty-one nuclear tests in Australia and islands in the south Pacific between 1952 and 1958. There was also a series of more than 550 minor trials, involving five different kinds of experiments, carried out in Australia between 1953 and 1963. The explosions and trials were conducted as Britain strove to develop nuclear weapons and retain its status as a great power in the world.

Since radiation-linked diseases take years to materialise, it was not until the 1970s that the servicemen in Britain and Australia began to wonder why an unusually high number of them were suffering from illnesses such as cancer, cataracts and skin diseases. They started to ask questions about their illnesses and the tests themselves, taking their cases to the media. The resulting publicity brought forward more servicemen who had been involved in the tests, and they organised themselves to promote their cause and enlist the help of sympathetic politicians. Throughout the 1980s, the issue refused to die away as the test veterans lobbied and took legal action. Supportive MPs, from all parties, took up their cause in Parliament, asking questions, starting debates and so on. But all the time, the MoD stuck to its same line – the safety arrangements for the tests were effective and stringently enforced and no one at all received a sufficient dose of radiation to have caused cancers and illnesses. None of this would surprise many members of the Porton Down Volunteers Association.

But the pressure from the nuclear test veterans appears to have paid off to some extent. Early on in the campaign, the MoD were forced to commission a medical inquiry, conducted by the National Radiological Protection Board (NRPB), to ascertain whether there was an excessive amount of cancer among the test veterans and whether this could have been caused by the tests. After five years, the NRPB scientists concluded in 1988 that on the whole, the tests did not have a 'detectable' effect on the heath of the veterans, 'apart from possibly causing small risks of developing' two illnesses – leukaemia and multiple myeloma (tumour of the bone marrow).[35] So far, the War Pensions Agency has awarded pensions to at least twenty-four test veterans (or their widows) who have been suffering from those two illnesses. The War Pension Agency says that the NRPB study, while not being categorical proof, did raise 'a reasonable doubt' that the two illnesses were caused by the tests, thus satisfying the War Pension Agency's rules on the burden of proof when deciding awards.[36] The atomic bomb veterans' campaign therefore does show that it is possible to win something from the government, although the gains may be small.

It has been claimed that the veterans of the atomic tests were deliberately exposed to radiation to see its effects on humans. This has been denied by the MoD.[37] However the MoD has admitted that Porton Down volunteers were intentionally exposed to radioactive substances during experiments, but strenuously insists that the exposures were so small that the danger was 'virtually non-existent'.[58] The ministry claims that since so few records of these experiments actually still exist, it is not possible to give information on how many volunteers took part in these tests.[59] According to the MoD, the volunteers were used in two kinds of experiments in the 1950s and 1960s.

The first type of experiment was part of a long-running investigation into the decontamination of radioactive materials. In co-operation with other military scientists, Porton staff studied different methods of removing radioactive fallout of a nuclear weapon explosion from people and their clothing, a variety of surfaces such as roofs and paved areas, and vehicles and other equipment.[60] In one set of eight trials in 1960, volunteers crawled across up to twenty-four feet of ground which had been strewn with irradiated beads.[61] The trials were designed to see how much radioactive fallout would stick to the clothing of soldiers and whether radioactive material could be cleaned by brushing it off or vacuuming it. The volunteers wore various kinds of battledress, such as khaki serge, along with linen skull caps, gloves, overshoes, and masks. Afterwards, they went into a dark room and were examined with a UV lamp to see which parts of their clothing had been contaminated. The beads had been irradiated with a simulant, sodium-24, to imitate the radioactive fallout.[62] The scientists concluded that the trials showed that 'very high levels of contamination can result on various parts of the clothing. As would be expected, the heaviest deposits occurred on knees and forearms though considerable contamination was also found on some occasions over the thighs and abdomen'. However it appears that the skin of the volunteers underneath the clothing was not contaminated, and it does seem from the trial report that the radiation from the simulant was so small that the volunteers were probably in no danger.[63]

In another trial, seven volunteers from a nearby Civil Defence unit rescued dummy casualties from mock rubble onto which irradiated beads had been scattered.[64] Wearing either serge battledress or denims, along with boots, gloves and masks, the volunteers received 'moderate to heavy' contamination on their clothes in the wet conditions. According to the report of the trial, none of the radiation reached the skin of the volunteers. In a later experiment, Porton's fire brigade hosed down a road onto which irradiated sand had been distributed.[65] The firefighters, 'directing hoses at a low angle', were required to remove the 'realistic amounts of radioactive particles' that were simulating the fallout from a nuclear bomb. By doing this, they were testing whether the fallout could be 'hosed effectively down roadside drains'.

One doctor believes that one of his former patients may have died as a result of Porton's radiation experiments. Bill Dyer was serving in the Somerset Light Infantry in 1957 when he volunteered for Porton. According to his doctor, Richard Lawson, Dyer and others 'were given denim overalls and ordered to crawl across ground that was covered in a dust. At the end of this crawl, dosimeter readings were recorded. The overalls were then taken away'.[66] It appears that, if this experiment with radioactive material did take place in that particular year, it was unauthorised, since Porton was still pursuing permission from the War Office in 1960 to test service personnel in radiation trials.[67]

Twenty years later, Dyer developed a cancer – Hodgkin's disease – and after prolonged treatment, died in 1987, aged forty-nine. Dr Lawson said, 'The link between exposure to radiation and development of cancer is well-documented. He told me he had taken part in these experiments and my gut feeling is that they are what caused his cancer.'[68] The MoD has argued that since the half-lives of the radioactive materials were 'relatively short', the experiments were not considered by Porton to be dangerous and so the volunteers' health was not monitored in the years afterwards.[69] Dyer's widow, Jeanette Chilcott, feels 'very angry' that there was no subsequent monitoring of the volunteers' well-being. 'He was offered extra money and never told what the risks were. It's simply a disgrace that they can do that sort of thing with people's lives.'[70] Dr Lawson added, 'There may be many other people with similar experiences who have not made the connection between events which seem unrelated in time. The morality of this kind of experimentation apart, is it not irresponsible to expose soldiers to radiation and not to arrange for long-term follow-up?'[71]

The second type of experiment was to 'establish the mechanism of penetration of compounds through the skin' and to 'trace the fate of compounds in the body'. Chemicals were tagged with radioactive substances so that their progress around the body would be monitored with a Geiger counter. How many volunteers and which chemicals or radioactive substances were used in these experiments is now difficult to establish, given the MoD's claim that few of the records have survived. As described in chapters five and six, it is evident that nerve gas tagged with phosphorus-32 was dropped onto the skin of humans in the 1950s and early 1960s. At the time, many scientists believed that it was safe to expose humans to minor amounts of radioactive substances below a 'threshold' level, but nowadays, it is accepted that there is no dose so small that it cannot produce cancer or genetic defects in the future – the higher the dose, the higher the chance of producing them. Phosphorus-32 emits beta radiation which, if it gets inside the body, can harm live soft tissue.

One of the few existing reports of these human experiments concerns an experiment in 1953 in which the highly toxic insecticide TEPP – tagged with Phosphorus-32 – was tested on the skin of volunteers, all aged between nineteen and twenty-two. TEPP is an organophosphate – the same family of chemicals as nerve gases. It had been discovered as an insecticide in 1938 by German scientist Gerhard Schrader, who also unearthed tabun and sarin. It appears that the Nazis dismissed TEPP as a nerve gas since it was not quite as potent as the other G-gases which have become more well-known. However TEPP is recognised as being too dangerous to use as a pesticide in public areas.[72] The test was conducted by Porton to see how a toxic substance would penetrate through skin – a key question in chemical warfare. Two milligrams of the radioactive TEPP were placed on the forearm of six men and left for thirty minutes. The same procedure was repeated on the palm of three men's hands. A 'small amount' was also injected into the top layers of the skin of five volunteers.[73] A white weal was caused by the injection. The experiment showed that the toxic chemical disappeared from the skin into the body at a clearly predictable rate, depending on the speed of blood-flow. It vanished quickly from areas of the body where the blood-flow was plentiful, and vice versa. It was also found that the top layer of the skin – the epidermis – would provide a barrier to slow down the penetration of the poison into the body.

David Sleeman was a young aircraftsman at RAF Wyton near Huntingdon when he was tested in Porton experiments in 1959.[74] The scientists 'put a clear liquid down my arm, said it had some radioactive content, swabbed it off and then just ran a dosimeter down me'. He was not told what the liquid was. The liquid was dropped though a retort onto his arm which had been placed on a bench. He felt no pain from the test. Another experiment left him bemused. On one day, he was trying out gas masks and suits, and went into a gas chamber with an artificial membrane in his mouth and a clamp over his nose. 'The idea was that whatever went through the respirator was trapped by the membrane. That was meant to be a harmless agent.' When he came out of the chamber, he was led into another room. The membrane was removed with a rubber glove. 'Then we were hosed down outside. You actually went through a decontamination. Don't ask me why, how or what, but it did strike me that, with a harmless agent, it was all a bit over-the-top.' On the last day of his stay, he received a thorough medical examination during which Porton staff 'stuck a Geiger counter up your rear-end'.

Another young RAF volunteer who was tested with an unknown radioactive liquid was Keith Hopwood who went to Porton in the early 1960s.[75] He was told to hold out his arm perfectly still. Porton scientists placed a bottomless rubber cup onto his arm, 'then they put this liquid into the cup which they said there was a radioactive element in it.' He did not know what else was in the solution. 'They said that the dosage was so small that it would not do any damage to you. It was just to monitor how far it went for an amount of time, how your body absorbed it.' He was told to 'do nothing and wait for it to soak through'. The liquid was 'allowed to seep through the pores' of his bare skin. Hopwood found this 'extremely boring'. Four hours later, the scientists came and took a blood sample from near his ankle. The experiment was 'not painful', and 'to be perfectly honest,' says Hopwood, 'I don't think that it has done me any damage.'

The British government considered conducting around 100 trials at Porton to test-fire critical components of British nuclear weapons in 1956. According to one official account, this would not have involved the fissile material within the bomb, but 'some radioactivity would, however, inevitably be carried beyond the boundaries' of Porton.[76] Conducting these trials at Porton would have been much cheaper than at Britain's regular site in Maralinga, Australia. Officials also argued that it would be embarrassing to expose the Australian population to such radioactivity but not Britons. Government officials concluded that these tests could be done safely at Porton, but ministers refused to allow any tests in Britain on political grounds. Despite this, another set of purely non-nuclear explosions were conducted at Porton as an 'essential' part of the development of British atomic bombs.[77]

A huge furore erupted in 1994 when details of widespread, distasteful and unethical radiation experiments that had been carried out in America between the 1940s and the 1970s emerged in the press.[78] It was disclosed that, among other experiments, sick patients were deliberately injected with plutonium and uranium, pregnant women and mentally ill children were fed milk and cereals laced with radioactive iron, and radioactivity from bomb blasts was intentionally released into the atmosphere. More than 200,000 humans were subjected to at least 200 radiation tests.[79] In Britain, scientists at the atomic establishments at Aldermaston and Harwell also carried out a much smaller number of human radiation tests from the 1950s to the 1980s, some in collaboration with the Americans.[80] Curiously, the gist of the American experiments was revealed by a US congressman in the mid-1980s, but no public outcry was provoked.[81] It appears that the Congressman's report was ignored in the Cold War climate, particularly since the experiments had largely taken place because of the nuclear arms race with the Russians. It seems that, by 1994, the American government and press were more willing to face up to consequences of such experiments.

The radiation tests in Britain and America are a further illustration of how attitudes change. Many scientists believed that the Cold War was a sufficient justification for such experiments, many of which broke the Nuremberg Code of ethics. Nowadays, however, it would be hard to justify many of those tests.

The Allied coalition which beat Saddam Hussein's Iraq in the 1991 Gulf War suffered few casualties during their victory. However, after the war, British and American veterans alike began to experience mysterious illnesses which have become known collectively as 'Gulf War Syndrome'. According to their lawyers, the veterans have complained of a variety of unexplained illnesses – fatigue, diarrhoea, irritability, headache, poor appetite, sleep disturbances, weight loss, rashes and so on. Some have such severe symptoms that they can no longer work or lead a normal life.[82]

The Ministry of Defence has come under heavy criticism for seemingly dragging its feet over this issue when the first reports of Gulf-related illnesses began to emerge in 1993. Typical of the official attitude was the comment of the then junior defence minister, Nicholas Soames, who said that the veterans' claims were a 'mixture of unsubstantiated rumour [and] incorrect information' and that there was 'no evidence of any medical condition peculiar to service in the Gulf'.[83] One of the sternest critics was the all-party House of Commons Defence Committee which concluded in 1995 that the Ministry of Defence had been 'quick to deny but slow to investigate' the allegations of a Gulf War Syndrome. The committee added that while the United States government had shown 'compassion, commitment, and determination' to help their ailing veterans, the response of the British government had been 'characterised throughout by scepticism, defensiveness, and general torpor'.[84]

The MoD's dismissive stance has fuelled the public perception that perhaps the government was covering up something, which, in turn, caused a host of conspiracy theories to flourish. In reality, however, it is more likely that the MoD was reacting in its usual manner when accused of being responsible for some mishap – the ministry automatically denies that it is the cause and is reluctant to release information. It is unlikely that the MoD knows what the reasons for the Gulf War Syndrome are and has been hiding the information. But its disdainful posture has left many of the veterans bitter and resentful. The MoD has created the impression among veterans that it does not care about their health. Their feelings are similar to those of other groups of military personnel, such as the Porton volunteers and the A-bomb veterans, who have blamed the MoD for causing their ill health.

The specific symptoms reported by the veterans are so diverse that there is unlikely to be one single cause behind Gulf War Syndrome. Five theories have been touted the most as possible explanations: the large number and mixture of vaccinations administered in a short time; organophosphate pesticide poisoning; exposure to chemical and biological weapons during the conflict; depleted uranium contained in shell tips and tank armour; and the Nerve Agent Pre-treatment Set (NAPS) tablets. It has also been mooted that the illnesses could have been caused by a combination of these explanations.

Much controversy has surrounded the safety of NAPS tablets, the last of the above explanations, which were developed by Porton Down with the help of human experiments. The NAPS tablets are taken before a nerve gas attack, if it can be anticipated, to help protect the victims.[85] Between 1970 and the early 1980s, 300 Porton volunteers were tested with pyridostigmine bromide, the main ingredient of the NAPS tablets, to see if the compound was safe or whether it caused side-effects which would hinder the fighting efficiency of troops.[86] The results of these trials are still secret.[87]

Porton discovered that NAPS tablets caused nausea and abdominal pain, increased urination and 'frequency of bowel action but rarely overt diarrhoea', and the worsening of any existing infection in the mouth or throat, runny nose and cough. However, these effects were found to last only a short time and they did not 'interfere with military duties'. Since the compound gave 'considerable protection' against all nerve gases, it was officially approved for use by the Armed Forces in 1981.[88] The MoD has conceded that some of the illnesses recounted by the Gulf veterans are the same as those caused in the short term by pyridostigmine bromide. But the ministry argues that these symptoms cease when the tablets are stopped being taken and insists that 'there is no medical evidence of continuing long-term effects'.[89]

NAPS were first used on a large scale in a real combat zone in the 1991 Gulf War. As Foulkes had observed right back in the First World War, the theoretical work was not always the same as the practical experience on a battlefield. The Porton experiments on volunteers had concentrated on the short-term side-effects of NAPS and had lasted not more than four weeks, since Porton had intended the tablets should be taken for not longer than *two* weeks, only when the threat of nerve gas attack was feared to be imminent. But some of the troops swallowed the tablets for *six* weeks while they were in the Gulf. Some took more than the stated dose of one every eight hours, claiming that there was no supervision from doctors or superiors and that instructions were vague. Overdosing on pyridostigmine has well-established dangers. In extreme cases, it causes profound weaknesses, with the usual symptoms being muscle cramps, diarrhoea, sweating and hypersalivation. These have been some of the symptoms experienced by the sick veterans, as the House of Commons Defence Committee commented in a 1995 report.[90]

The MoD has maintained that the existing evidence, including Porton's trials, was enough to satisfy them that NAPS were safe to use and, apart from one new test in 1993, it has not deemed it necessary to carry out more work into the possible side-effects.[91] The House of Commons Defence Committee however was not 'convinced' that NAPS had been 'adequately tested in the UK for use over a long period in the type of conditions prevalent in the Gulf'. The committee also found it 'incredible' that the MoD only sought and obtained an official safety licence for NAPS from the proper authorities in 1993. Porton claimed that this was 'simply a question of putting through the paperwork', since all its tests had shown that it was safe. The Defence Committee, however, commented that if NAPS had been licensed before the Gulf War, many of the doubts which later surfaced would not have arisen.[92]

Porton has recently developed a replacement for the NAPS tablets.[93]

Many veterans have questioned whether their illnesses have been caused by a 'cocktail' of anti-biological warfare vaccines and NAPS tablets being administered in a short space of time. It has been suggested that the tablets and multiple injections together could have damaged their immune system, making them vulnerable to a variety of apparently unrelated illnesses. The tablets and vaccines had been studied individually, but, as the House of Commons Defence Committee pointed out, 'the lack of comprehensive and convincing research on the long-term effects of such combinations of drugs administered rapidly and in unusual conditions means that it is impossible to rule out this explanation with complete certainty'.[94]

The current Labour government has been spending more than £2 million on a research programme which investigates such combinations.[95] This research was just one of a series of measures announced by the new Labour government in 1997 in what it billed as a 'new beginning' in dealing with the veterans. This fresh start was to be based on three principles – the veterans would be given medical help quickly; research into the possible causes of the illnesses would be carried out; and any information 'of potential relevance' to the veterans' illnesses would be made public.[96] It could be argued that Porton's NAPS trials in the 1970s and 1980s, which are still classified, and a follow-up study into the health of the volunteers who took part in those trials might shed new light on the possible causes of the Gulf veterans' ill health. However, as we shall see in the next chapter, the MoD is unwilling to track down any Porton volunteers to check on their health.[97]

More than 1,840 Gulf veterans are lining up to sue the British government for compensation for their illnesses. Unlike most Porton volunteers, this legal route is open to them since their illnesses are alleged to have been caused after the infamous Section 10 of the Crown Proceedings Act was abolished in 1987.

Many Porton volunteers, like the Gulf and Atomic bomb veterans, feel that they have been badly treated by monolithic officialdom which has stubbornly ignored and rejected their claims. The Ministry of Defence's refusal to give any ground is motivated by two reasons. One is that, in these seemingly cash-strapped times, the ministry does not want to be landed with a huge bill for compensation. If the MoD was to admit that it was responsible for the illnesses, it would come under heavy pressure to set up a special compensation scheme for the volunteers. The second reason is the government's traditional reluctance to concede that it is at fault. Many government ministers fear that their authority is undermined if they admit blunders. Whitehall mandarins too are very slow to own up to mistakes, whenever they may have happened. However such attitudes often backfire if the public are led to believe that the government is guilty of stonewalling and covering up the truth, and public cynicism and disdain towards the government grows as a result.

The Army's own research shows that the Gulf War Syndrome controversy has made many people believe that soldiers are simply expendable in the eyes of their superiors.[98] The MoD's stance on disputes such as the Gulf, Porton volunteers and Atomic bomb veterans creates a particular danger for the ministry. Military personnel will no longer believe that their commanders will protect them if anything goes wrong while they are serving the nation. This lack of faith in authority depresses morale and efficiency among the armed forces and may also deter others from joining up in the first place.

CHAPTER ELEVEN
In Whose Interest?

Porton has frequently declared that it is 'very grateful' to all the human 'guinea pigs' who have taken part in its experiments through the decades, and acknowledges that the volunteers have made an 'immense' and 'valuable contribution' to Britain's defences. The volunteers, Porton says, have helped to provide the country with safe and effective protection against chemical and biological weapons and that such human experiments 'are vital to the defence of the realm'.[1]

Despite this high praise, volunteers who complain that these invaluable experiments have in fact damaged their health receive a far less gratifying response from Porton Down. The MoD has rigidly stuck to its claim that there is 'no evidence' that any of the human 'guinea pigs' have suffered any harm to their health.[2] The same line is trotted out to volunteers and MPs alike whenever they protest or make inquiries. Some volunteers may be forgiven for feeling that on the one hand, the MoD is patting them on the back for their selfless contribution, but on the other hand, kicking them in the teeth if they ask for compensation for their damaged health.

Porton's human 'guinea pigs' have often complained about their ill health, going back to the 1930s. Nowadays, as more and more volunteers are prepared to go public with their stories, the complaints of damaged health have mounted up. From time to time, MPs and volunteers have pressed the MoD to launch an independent inquiry into the allegations, but these have been rejected by both the previous Conservative government and the current Labour administration. As is so often the case in politics, the Labour Party in opposition had demanded, 'at the very least', an impartial investigation into the long-term illnesses of the volunteers, but once they were elected and had the power to set one up, they refused to do so.[3]

The current Labour government cited three reasons for rejecting a call for an inquiry from Labour MP (and later a government minister), Chris Mullin.[4] Firstly, the experiments 'would not have taken place if either scientists or their advisers had believed that there was a long-term risk to health'. Secondly, 'after careful thought and consideration, it has to be concluded that it is just not feasible or practical, given the length and timescale of the Porton Down programme and the diverse range of trials that have been conducted, to devise a valid study'. (Mullin commented that this was 'code for saying that the possible conclusions of any such inquiry might be embarrassing...for the mighty vested interests at the heart of the defence establishment'.)[5] Thirdly, the MoD wished to avoid the 'undue anxiety and stress that such a recall of former volunteers may cause in many thousands of elderly, but otherwise healthy, ex-servicemen'.

Similarly Nicholas Soames, the previous Conservative Armed Forces Minister, had rejected calls for an independent inquiry, saying that he could 'assure' MPs that none of the volunteers' health had been damaged.[6] This 'assurance' is, however, surely undermined by the fact that the MoD has failed to monitor the health of volunteers on a regular basis in the years after they were subjected to experiments. Porton has never run a systematic programme for tracking and checking the condition of the subjects of their tests afterwards. Only four small-scale and limited surveys on 100 volunteers tested with either nerve gas or LSD have been conducted. Many believe that, without such a systematic programme, the MoD's reassurances look threadbare. One does not have to be a cynic to conclude that if you never look, then obviously you will not find any evidence of damaged health.

Porton believes that there is no need to monitor the volunteers over a long period. In a television programme in 1994, Graham Pearson, the then director of Porton, said, 'You could argue that you should call back people who've been exposed to, say, passive smoking and see if that's got effects on them. I mean it's a question of what is the best and appropriate use of resources and one endeavours to use resources to the best effect to ensure that our armed forces have effective protective measures. There are a lot of things that you could carry out research on, but it would be wasting the government's money if you put effort into things that have little prospect of benefit to those concerned.'[7]

Instead of a comprehensive monitoring programme, Porton has claimed that 'from time to time, volunteers have been recalled so that checks on their medical health can be made'. But Porton has admitted that 'there is no particular frequency or pattern to such recalls', nor has it been able to put a figure on the number of volunteers who have been recalled for this purpose.[8] Some volunteers are called back to Porton after a year or two, but for another reason – to undergo further tests to check that the measurements and methods used in their earlier experiments are giving consistent results.[9] Porton claims that none of the volunteers who have been recalled have shown any signs of ill health caused by the tests.[10]

The government's refusal to launch an independent inquiry creates a vacuum in one sense. It means that there is not a credible and respected verdict on the claims of ill health which are advanced by the volunteers. One effect of this is evident. Military veterans may be suffering from some illnesses for some time and have no idea what has caused their sickness. It is perfectly natural to wonder what has caused their ill health. One day, they may hear an item about the Porton experiments in the media, and remember that they too were once a human 'guinea pig' at Porton. Steadily, an idea begins to dawn on them. They then connect their illness with Porton and suggest that the chemical warfare tests could be the reason for their disease. Most do this out of a genuine belief that Porton may be responsible, some out of a selfish desire to jump on a bandwagon and gain some extra money through a compensation claim. An independent inquiry should end all this uncertainty and help to settle these allegations of ill health.

Porton routinely dismisses any volunteers who claim that the experiments have caused their ill health. It appears that, in Porton's eyes, this evidence is simply not worth investigating or taking seriously. This in turn breeds anger, resentment and cynicism among the volunteers and often inflames, rather than soothes, their worries.

Ultimately, to win their battle for a war pension or lump-sum compensation, the human 'guinea pigs' have to demonstrate clearly that their illnesses have been caused by the experiments. This is a far from easy task. For a start, there has been relatively little research in general to establish the long-term effects of chemical warfare agents after the victim has been exposed once or perhaps twice. Military establishments around the world have carried out most of the existing research to find out how chemical weapons attack the human body – and their concern is with the short-term (acute) effects, and not long-term (chronic) illnesses.[11] These establishments have been concentrating mainly on the questions of how to inflict and treat battlefield injuries. Clearly, a raft of potentially useful experimental data was lost when these establishments failed to organise sustained medical monitoring programmes of those who underwent experiments. If an independent inquiry into Porton's experiments was set up, it would be a rare thing and could yield some important information for many around the world. The volunteers are also hampered because in most cases, the illness which they believe resulted from the experiments has appeared years or even decades after their spell at Porton. As with many illnesses, it is difficult to single out the cause for a specific malady from all sorts of possible factors which may have had an influence over many years.

The question of whether people can develop delayed illnesses from limited exposures to chemical weapons is far more complex than the MoD's automatic assurances would suggest. In what is a poorly understood field of science, Porton's unflinching certainty that the tests have not damaged any volunteers rings hollow. Rather than treating all chemical weapons in a blanket fashion, it is necessary to isolate each gas in turn to see if it can result in chronic illnesses.

The most compelling of the chemicals involved is mustard gas. Porton's position on the dangers of mustard gas has been contradictory. In public, Porton says that its mustard gas experiments have not been responsible for the ill health subsequently suffered by volunteers. But secretly, Porton banned the testing of mustard gas on humans in 1978, after decades of human experiments with this chemical weapon. This permanent ban was not made public for twenty years, and was not volunteered by Porton until the establishment was specifically asked by an MP. Indeed, on one occasion, the MoD had misled Parliament over the ban.[12] Porton decided to stop testing mustard gas on humans because of scientific evidence which indicated that 'repeated' exposures to the gas caused certain kinds of cancers in later years.[13] It is now widely recognised among scientists that sulphur mustard gas, the most common type of mustard gas, is a carcinogen (a compound which causes cancer). Porton insists that there was no evidence that a *single* exposure to mustard gas, which was what was most commonly experienced by the human 'guinea pigs', could cause cancer. However the permanent ban does seem to indicate that Porton was sufficiently alarmed about the health risks of mustard gas to stop its tests on volunteers. One Porton scientist from this time recalled that it was a prudent decision: 'There were all sorts of slightly alarming stories about the long-term effects of mustard gas, none of which were ever in fact really confirmed. It was regarded as possibly not a good idea to continue with these tests.'[14] Under questioning in Parliament, Porton has conceded that a single exposure of mustard gas can cause particular long-term illnesses, but only after high dosages of the gas.[15]

Further evidence of the hazards of mustard gas comes from the chemical, biological and nuclear training centre at Winterbourne Gunner (situated next door to Porton, but run separately). Set up in 1926, the centre has over the years been responsible for training military personnel in these types of warfare, both defensively and offensively.[16] For many years, the military personnel on these courses had a 'small amount' of mustard gas – 'equating to the size of a pinhead' – dabbed onto the inside of their wrists.[17]

Mike Underhill, a lance corporal in the Staffordshire Regiment at the time, remembers attending Winterbourne Gunner around 1970.[18] 'They used to put a drop on your arm with an eye-dropper,' before quickly removing it with a decontaminating agent. He felt no pain or after-effects from the gas, and says that the point of the procedure was 'to give you trust' in the decontamination process.[19]

In 1980, Winterbourne Gunner permanently stopped these exposures, two years after Porton had halted its own tests on humans with mustard gas. Winterbourne Gunner acted following advice from Porton that the exposures were 'not compatible with health and safety guidelines'. Porton has been unable to explain more fully why it was no longer safe to place mustard gas on the arms.[20]

Other governments have acknowledged that their mustard gas tests are responsible for the long-term illnesses of their human 'guinea pigs', and have started to pay them compensation as a result. The most notable is the United States of America. In the US, claims from service men and women who believe that their disability or injury has resulted from their military service are dealt with by the Department of Veterans' Affairs (the VA). (Some of the equivalent functions are carried out in Britain by the War Pensions Agency.)

In the 1980s and 1990s, the US VA began to receive more and more claims from those who had been subjected to the American mustard gas tests, mainly in the Second World War. Individual claimants in the US had to prove that their medical problems had resulted from participating in the experiments, as happened with volunteers in Britain. The VA admits that this task was 'nearly impossible' for the veterans,[21] and recognised that it was hard for the human 'guinea pigs' to prove their case because they found it difficult to get information about the secret experiments. The department therefore launched an 'aggressive' review of the way it was handling the mustard gas claims, and as they began to adopt a more generous attitude in the early 1990s, they started implementing a series of initiatives to help claimants.

In a breakthrough in July 1992, the VA Department instituted a new policy which significantly tilted the balance of proof in favour of the claimants. The department ruled that from then on, the veterans would win compensation in specific circumstances – i.e. if they had been completely exposed to mustard gas in chamber or outdoor experiments during the Second World War and then had subsequently developed any of seven chronic illnesses. (These were bronchitis, laryngitis, emphysema, asthma, conjunctivitis, keratitis of the eye and corneal opacities – damage to the lens of the eye.) It meant that in order to win compensation, the veterans who were suffering from any one of those seven specified illnesses would only have to prove that they took part in tests in which the whole of their bodies had been exposed to mustard gas.

The VA Department also commissioned a huge study from an independent group of scientists since it recognised that it needed more information to clarify the issues. A respected body, the Institute of Medicine (IoM) of the National Academy of Sciences, therefore carried out an intensive study on the long-term health effects of mustard gas.[22] In January 1993, the IoM committee delivered a strongly worded 400-page report.[23] They ruled that the American programme of mustard gas experiments demonstrated a 'well-ingrained pattern of abuse and neglect' of the human subjects. It believed that although the subjects were called 'volunteers', they had actually been recruited through 'lies and half-truths'.

The committee was most appalled by the fact that there was no formal long-term medical care or monitoring, even though, by 1933, military doctors had published papers showing that chronic bronchitis, chronic asthma, emphysema, corneal opacities and chronic conjunctivitis resulted from mustard gas (see chapter two). It was dismayed to learn that the human 'guinea pigs' had not even been cared for in the weeks after the experiments. 'Subjects in the chamber tests were sworn to secrecy and simply released on leave at the conclusion of the experiments. Some of these men still had blisters or evidence of skin burns upon release, but were not given any instructions about how to obtain knowledgeable medical care if they had needed it,' the committee lamented.

The report went on to comment that, although the experiments had been conducted 'in a wartime climate of urgency and secrecy,' it was clearly a mistake to continue to hush up the tests after the war. 'These men risked their health and safety to help develop better means of protection against chemical warfare. Yet, in most cases, their participation in these experiments was not even acknowledged in their service records and was, in fact, officially denied for decades. Further, these men were ordered to keep their participation secret. They did so for nearly fifty years, in some cases despite serious, disabling diseases that they believed were caused by their exposures. There can be no question that some veterans, who served our country with honour and at great personal cost, were mistreated twice – first, in the secret testing and second, by the official denials that lasted for decades.'

The IoM committee agreed with the VA Department's original list of seven chronic illnesses which resulted from mustard gas exposure. But it recommended that several more sicknesses (including various cancers and psychological disorders) should be added to the list.[24] Consequently, the VA

Department expanded the catalogue of diseases for which the subjects of mustard gas experiments automatically receive compensation. Publishing the new list in August 1994, VA secretary Jesse Brown said, 'Many brave members of our armed forces have waited far too long for this day, but I am proud and pleased at last to announce some relief from their pain and suffering.'[25]

The IoM report and the sympathetic attitude of the US VA Department represents substantial evidence for the British volunteers who are trying to gain recognition and compensation from their own government. This evidence challenges the intransigence of the British government. Disappointingly, the War Pension Agency has admitted that it did not even obtain a copy of this comprehensive report until four years later, and only then after being prompted by an MP.[26] The agency's subsequent evaluation of the report is ambiguous. It stated that 'most of the conclusions of the report on scientific and medical matters are known and agreed by us,'[27] but added that 'it is not possible to give a categorical answer' to the question of whether it would award a war pension to a British volunteer who had taken part in mustard gas experiments and was subsequently suffering from one of the illnesses identified by the IoM report.[28] Porton has so far avoided giving a specific, direct comment on the section of the IoM report which concludes that a string of chronic illnesses can be caused by the mustard gas experiments.[29]

The human 'guinea pigs' who took part in the Australian mustard gas experiments in the Second World War have made some progress in gaining compensation, and at least thirty-five claimants have been successful in winning pensions.[30] In awarding these payments, the Australian government has recognised that eight illnesses have been caused by the mustard gas tests. (These were squamous cell carcinoma of lower lip; bronchial asthma; atrophic (wasting away) area under chin; chronic bronchitis and emphysema; ischaemic heart disease; hardening of the arteries leading to the brain; carcinoma of lung; and burns to scrotum. However, unlike the Americans, the Australians have not specified the diseases which would automatically win compensation.) Tom Mitchell, one of the Australian volunteers (see chapter three), reached an out-of-court settlement with the Australian government in 1990, receiving a small payment and a pension after a nine-year legal battle. He has endured a succession of illnesses, including a bad heart for fifteen years, hypertension, skin cancer and leukaemia. The government did not accept that mustard gas had been causing his illnesses. Richard Gillis, one of the Australian scientists in the tests, said the volunteers have had 'a lousy deal' in getting compensation. In

Canada, servicemen who were exposed to mustard gas in the 1940s have also been awarded disability pensions.[31]

The British War Pension Agency accepted that mustard gas can cause long-term illnesses in one specific case – the victims of the Bari harbour disaster during the Second World War.[32] In December 1943, German planes attacked and quickly sunk seventeen Allied ships in the Italian harbour. Unknown to the survivors, one of the ships was carrying mustard gas, which seeped out into the sea and air. More than 600 military personnel were poisoned, and about eighty of them died. There were also as many as a thousand casualties among the civilians in the town. In the aftermath, the Allied High Command clamped tight secrecy over the tragedy, straining to hush up the fact that poison gas had been on the ship and killed so many.

In the 1980s, some of the military personnel who were at Bari emerged to tell their stories and claim war pensions for their disabilities.[33] One man, Bertram Stevens, won an important victory over his claim. At Bari, he had been blinded and covered in blisters. Over the years, he suffered from chronic conjunctivitis, chronic bronchitis, cancer of the lip and a gland in his neck, and blistered feet. It was not until 1983 that he first became aware that he had been exposed to mustard gas at Bari and that it could have been the cause of these illnesses. Within a year, he had been awarded a war pension as a gas victim. Backed by his MP, Stevens went on to complain that his war pension should have been backdated to the time when his symptoms first became evident, many years earlier. He argued that he would have claimed earlier had he known then that he had been exposed to mustard gas. In an 'exceptional decision', the government caved in.[34] He then won a further victory in 1990 when Parliament's Ombudsman ruled that the government should pay interest (amounting to around £8,000) on the outstanding amount.[35]

His campaign also forced the government to review the cases of other casualties who had been contaminated with the mustard gas at Bari.[36] An investigation was set up in 1986 to see if other claimants should have their pensions backdated and to look again at claims which had previously been refused. In all, 105 claims (out of a total of 184) were approved.[37] Although the Bari victims suffered extreme mustard gas poisoning, their pension awards are significant to the Porton Down volunteers, since they amount to official admissions that long-term illnesses can result from a single exposure to mustard gas.

Long after the end of the Second World War, gas victims from the First World War were still claiming war pensions for their illnesses. Like many others, the veterans from the Great War faced the problem of proving satisfactorily that one, or maybe two incidents of gassing had caused their sicknesses many decades afterwards. Their difficulties provoked unrest among the local war pension committees. (For example, members of the Coventry, Nuneaton and District War Pension Committee passed a resolution in 1963 recording their 'considerable disquiet and displeasure' about the 'extreme difficulty' experienced by Arthur Hems and other gas victims in winning pensions for their 'chest troubles'.[38]) The Ministry of Pensions, then in charge of war pensions, believed in the 1960s that mustard gas could produce 'permanent damage to eyes or lungs, although disablement might not be evident for some years'. The illnesses which could result from the gas were bronchitis and keratitis, consistent with the ministry's opinion in the 1920s and 1930s (see chapter two).[39]

Experienced chemical warfare scientists have also stated publicly that mustard gas causes long-term illnesses. Two long-serving Porton scientists, Timothy Marrs and Robert Maynard, and an American colleague, Frederick Sidell, published an authoritative book on the medical effects of chemical warfare agents in 1996.[40] They list at least six illnesses which they believe can result from mustard gas poisoning. (These are permanent blindness; visual impairment; scarring of the skin; chronic bronchitis; bronchial stenosis (a narrowing or constriction of this passage); and sensitivity to mustard gas. They add that mustard gas may also produce psychological effects which may persist for some time.) The trio also say that sulphur mustard gas – the type of mustard gas used most frequently in Porton's experiments – is 'known' to cause cancer in humans. They cite the 'strongest evidence' as being a series of studies on factory workers who produced mustard gas during the Second World War. Indeed, they add that one study on British factory workers in particular revealed a 'clear increase' in respiratory cancers.

Workers in these factories are likely to have been exposed to mustard gas several times over a long period of time, although this is not always clear. This means that their specific circumstances may often be different from those of the Porton human 'guinea pigs' who typically received one or two doses of the gas over a few weeks. Nevertheless, the factory studies are useful indications of the cancer-inducing power of sulphur mustard gas.

The three scientists add that 'a more difficult question concerns the likelihood of developing cancer' by being exposed to sulphur mustard gas on the battlefield (this by implication would involve a limited number of exposures). They believe that in these conditions, 'the evidence is suggestive, but not absolutely clear-cut', highlighting one study of First World War veterans which does not demonstrate a rise in respiratory cancers after suffering one dose of sulphur mustard gas. But on the other hand, they point to another study of mustard gas victims from the same war which did suggest an increase in lung cancer.

One of the trio, Sidell, has stated that a single exposure to mustard gas can lead to long-term illnesses, such as chronic bronchitis along a gas victim's airway.[41] He added that several eye diseases, for instance chronic conjunctivitis, appear after a short, but usually severe, attack of the gas. He singled out delayed keratitis of the eye which could emerge as long as twenty-five years after the original injury. He has accepted that 'skin scarring, pigment changes, and even cancer' can later develop at the site of mustard gas burns.

The opinions of Marrs, Maynard, and Sidell are significant since they have spent many years working for Porton or the equivalent organisation in the United States of America. Their views, along with the other evidence described above, throw doubt on Porton's cast-iron certainty that mustard gas exposure has never damaged the health of the Porton human 'guinea pigs' in later years. The cumulative evidence indicates that the chances of developing illnesses from short exposures, far from being zero, are, in fact, all too real.

Porton exudes much conviction and confidence that short-term exposures to mustard gas do not produce chronic or delayed illnesses. But, remarkably, it appears that Porton scientists have carried out relatively little research into possible long-term illnesses.[42] This is surprising since Porton scientists have exposed such a large number of human 'guinea pigs' to the gas, but the only time that Porton has investigated this issue appears to be in the late 1920s (described in chapter two).

At that time, even Porton accepted without doubt that mustard gas could cause, at the very least, chronic lung diseases, particularly bronchitis. But now in a U-turn, Porton has renounced this position; instead it states that a link between sulphur mustard gas exposure and chronic respiratory illnesses such as bronchitis or laryngitis has not been scientifically proved. 'We are aware that First World War veterans were awarded disability compensation for respiratory disorders which were believed to have resulted from sulphur mustard [gas] poisoning. However other factors such as cigarette smoking, influenza and other environmental effects were not taken into consideration.'[43]

The long-term health effects of nerve gases are unclear, since there is no scientific consensus. Some scientists have suggested that nerve gas can damage the nervous system and brain, and lead to behavioural and psychological problems, and in a few cases, liver and kidney failure. They have suggested that damage to the body's central nervous system can result in a lack of oxygen supply to the brain. This harmful effect on the brain would cause depression, anxiety, drowsiness, dizziness, fatigue, slurred speech and mental confusion over the years.[44]

Once again, it appears that, for all its certainty, Porton has not conducted very much research into whether nerve gas can cause long-term illnesses, even though more than 3,000 people have been exposed to the deadly gas by the establishment. Questioned by an MP, Porton could point to only a few studies which it has conducted in recent times.[45]

Declassified records show that Porton researched the possible delayed effects of the nerve gases in 1952-53. This research into 'an awkward problem' was prompted by various reports showing that people were being poisoned by various organophosphorus (OP) compounds and suffering paralysis. (As outlined in chapter four, nerve gases are part of the family of chemicals known as organophosphorus compounds). Porton believed that it was a 'matter of great importance to determine' whether the G-nerve gases were also capable of inflicting such paralysis.[46] In a series of animal experiments, Porton scientists concluded that the G-nerve gases did not produce paralysis. However they did discover that 'well within the lethal range', one OP compound did cause paralysis 'repeatedly' and 'consistently'. This was PF-3 (also known as DFP) which, as seen in chapter four, was tested on humans by both Porton and the Americans during the Second World War before being discarded as a chemical weapon.[47]

Towards the end of the 1950s, Porton scientists once again looked at the issue of the neurotoxicity of OPs.[48] It was evident from scientific reports that victims of OP poisoning could suffer a 'particularly unpleasant and long-lasting' illness. Typically, the victim would be free of symptoms from the poisoning for between five and thirty days. Then they would feel a tingling or cramping pain in the calves for a few days, followed by the rapid onset of complete or partial paralysis and weakness in the muscles of the foot. A week later this spread to the muscles of the hand and forearm. 'The curse of the malady is chronic and little improvement can be observed for months after onset and even when it occurs, progress is slow', commented one Porton report. Many victims never recover completely. This condition is known as organophosphate-induced delayed neuropathy (OPIDN).[49] Porton scientists judged that the G-nerve gases (but not the V-nerve gases) were capable of causing this illness in humans, but *crucially* only at amounts higher than the lethal doses. In other words, the victims would die before they had time to develop OPIDN.[50]

More recently, Porton scientists have studied whether tabun (GA), sarin (GB), soman (GD) and VX could induce OPIDN, this time in experiments with hens. They concluded that OPIDN was only brought on by one of the gases, sarin (GB), but, once again, only in amounts 'well in excess of the lethal dose'.[51] Interestingly, Porton did warn that in the future, OPIDN could develop in nerve gas victims because improvements in antidotes and treatments would keep them alive.[52]

The question of long-term effects of nerve gases is inconclusive because generally it is an under-researched subject, and no clear-cut conclusions have been reached. Marrs, Maynard and Sidell comment that 'there is very little doubt, on theoretical, experimental and epidemiological grounds that severe OP poisoning can cause long-term irreversible changes in brain function. In less severe poisoning, the data are conflicting.'[53] They add that 'further work upon the subject is required'.

The controversy over Gulf War Syndrome has provided the spur for more research into this issue, with suggestions that former Gulf troops are now suffering because they were exposed to Iraqi chemical weapons in the war. This has been mooted as just one of the possible causes of the syndrome. Veterans have testified that on various occasions, their equipment for detecting chemical attacks was triggered, but the American and British governments have maintained that there is 'no confirmed evidence' that chemical weapons were used in the conflict. The most likely incident occurred after the war, in March 1991 when the Americans destroyed an Iraqi munitions dump containing at least 8.5 tonnes of nerve gas in Khamisiyah. Although initially sceptical, the American government eventually accepted that thousands of its troops may have been exposed to the gas released into the air by the demolition. The British government now says that up to 9,000 of its military personnel could have been exposed to the nerve gas, but the dose would have been so minute that it could not possibly have caused any health problems in the long run.[54] This, and other incidents, have provoked much debate, particularly in the US, over the long-term effects of nerve gases. It seems that the exposed troops did not experience symptoms of nerve gas poisoning at the time, and so scientists have questioned whether it is possible to develop chronic illnesses subsequently if victims had not suffered visible signs of poisoning at the time they were supposed to have been exposed. This point has influenced much of the debate. In the case of the Porton volunteers, many of those exposed to nerve gas in the chambers certainly did experience symptoms at the time, although some did not.

An inquiry by the US official watchdog body, the General Accounting Office, maintained that there was 'substantial' evidence to show that delayed, long-term illnesses can be caused by OPs, including sarin (GB).[55] This finding is challenged by the conclusions of another inquiry team – the US Presidential Advisory Committee on Gulf War Veterans' Illnesses. This committee argued that although long-term illnesses resulted from *severe* nerve gas poisoning, the available scientific information did not indicate that similar illnesses were in fact caused by *low* doses of the gas. However the committee acknowledged that the data from both human and animal studies was 'minimal' and recommended more research.[56]

It is ironic that valuable information could be gained from an independent study of the 3,000 or so human 'guinea pigs' who were exposed in Porton's nerve gas experiments since 1945. They would, after all, fulfil the criteria for a useful scientific study. Porton would be able to supply the details of the experiments in which they were exposed, and they could be traced through their service records. This would be a long, but not impossible, task. In a comparable study, more than 22,000 service personnel who took part in Britain's nuclear weapon tests in the 1950s and 1960s were tracked down by scientists. As detailed in the previous chapter, these scientists had been commissioned by the MoD to assess whether the tests had caused deaths and cancers among these military personnel.[57] Since few other countries have run such an extensive programme of nerve gas experiments on humans, such a study would be an important contribution to scientific knowledge. It would also help to clear up the concerns of the volunteers themselves.

So far Porton has carried out limited monitoring of the human 'guinea pigs' who were exposed to nerve gas. Porton scientists have deemed it necessary to initiate three secret surveys since the early 1970s, examining in total the military medical records of ninety-three volunteers tested with nerve gas. To avoid 'speculation and possible undesirable publicity', the volunteers themselves were not contacted and questioned about their health during the survey, nor were they told that their medical histories were being examined by Porton. Moreover, Porton did not attempt to obtain and inspect the civilian medical records of the volunteers after they had left the armed forces, which inevitably restricted the scope of the surveys. Porton complained that the quality of the military medical records was 'very poor in far too many cases' and in their judgement, the results of the three surveys 'showed nothing out of the ordinary in the subsequent health records' of these volunteers.[58]

The American government commissioned a follow-up study into 1,136 human 'guinea pigs' who had been exposed to nerve gases in its military experiments during the 1950s and 1960s.[59] Following its investigation, a US National Academy of Sciences panel ruled that there were no lasting health effects caused by these nerve gas tests.

Information about the effect of nerve gases on real battlefield casualties is sparse, especially since the gases have rarely been used in warfare. Allegations of chemical attacks have often been bandied around by opposing sides in conflicts, but verifying the claims is difficult amid the propaganda and chaos of war. Monitoring victims of gas attacks over long periods of time is seldom undertaken. The most large-scale use of chemical weapons since the First World War occurred during the Iran-Iraq war in the 1980s. The Iraqi forces, under the control of Saddam Hussein, resorted to chemical weapons on many occasions, allegedly employing nerve gas (particularly tabun), and mustard gas. Iranian health officials have said that 60,000 Iranian troops were wounded by gas during the war. Although the details were sketchy, the officials said that a decade later, up to sixty percent of these were suffering pulmonary diseases, some thirty percent ocular problems and the rest skin diseases.[60]

In the late 1980s, the Iraqis also unleashed chemical weapons on Kurdish fighters and villages in a series of assaults. It appears that at least nerve gas and mustard gas were used on those occasions.[61] The most notorious attack was in March 1988 on the town of Halabjah in Iraqi Kurdistan, when thousands of civilians, many women and children included, were killed in massive assaults from fighter planes. It is believed that at least nerve gas and mustard gas were dropped on the defenceless Kurdish villagers. It was a watershed in chemical warfare since it was the first time that a regime had unleashed lethal gases on such a huge scale on their own citizens. A decade later, a British television film-crew investigated the health of Halabjah residents, since they believed that the long-term effects of the chemical attack had been ignored by official organisations and aid agencies. The documentary makers, accompanied by scientist Christine Gosden, found strikingly high rates of leukaemia, respiratory disease, birth abnormalities, neurological disorders and other illnesses. Intensely moved by the suffering of the residents, Gosden reported experiencing a 'deep and lasting chill' which grew stronger as she 'met the people, heard their stories and saw the extent of the long-term illnesses caused by the attack'. 'The terrible images of the people of Halabjah and their situation persist and recur in my nightmares and disturb my waking thoughts,' she added.[62] The British government has recently acknowledged that the Halabjah residents are still suffering illnesses from the gas attack and, as a result, has started to give them aid.[63]

Nerve gas has been deliberately inflicted twice on civilians outside of a war, and both times in Japan. In the first incident, sarin (GB) killed twelve people and injured many others in an attack by the religious cult Aum Shinrikyo, meaning Supreme Truth Sect, on the Tokyo subway in March 1995. In an earlier incident, at Matsumoto in June 1994, sarin was also released by the cult, killing seven and injuring more than 200. Doctors have reported data on the symptoms of those poisoned in March 1995.[64] Although horrific, the attacks also present a rare opportunity to monitor the chronic effects of nerve gas poisoning over a period of years. The British government has undertaken to monitor and assess the data produced from the long-term follow-up programme of the casualties.[65]

Three cases of chronic illnesses among staff at both Porton and Britain's former nerve gas plant at Nancekuke have often been cited as evidence of the long-term effects of nerve gases. In all three, however, the MoD has consistently refused to accept that nerve gas was responsible for their lingering ill effects.

Flight Lieutenant William Cockayne collapsed during a nerve gas trial at Porton in 1953.[66] He said that nerve gas shells were being fired at animals and that his role was to inspect the target area after it appeared to be clear. But his gas mask and protective gear failed to work since he fell to the ground and was unable to move. When he came round he found himself in a hospital where he was discharged from the RAF. He was later diagnosed as a psychiatric case. For years, he experienced bouts of depression (attempting suicide several times), loss of memory, nervous tension for long periods, and became almost comatose in cold weather. The MoD said he had received a 'mild dose' of nerve gas.

Tom Griffiths, a fitter at Nancekuke, was exposed to leaking sarin (GB) in 1958 without any protective clothing while cleaning a cubicle that he had been assured was clean of the deadly liquid. He could hardly breathe or see anything and had a tight chest and bad headache. He got better within weeks, but then gradually his health began to deteriorate, with loss of memory, fainting attacks, muscle spasms all over his body, lack of energy and concentration, and pains in the head, neck, chest and back. He was declared unfit to work at the age of forty-three and received a small disability pension. He spent years seeking proper compensation through medical tribunals, hearings and appeals. (The MoD paid £110 to compensate for the five initial weeks of his illness, but argues that it is not responsible for any ill effects after then). 'We were told that in the unlikely event of an accident, we and our families would be well looked after – well, in the event, they did not want to know,' he said bitterly.[67]

Another Nancekuke fitter, Trevor Martin, believes that he was exposed to nerve gas in 1961. On the day in question, he felt dizzy, flushed and breathless, with incoherent speech. He recovered, but later that week developed uncontrollable twitches and paralysis in his face. After a year, he was unemployable at the age of thirty-seven and had to endure years of headaches, muscle cramps, fatigue, twitches in his arm, blurred vision, depression, and severe breathlessness.[68]

The disbanded nerve gas factory at Nancekuke has a similar public image to Porton. The media invariably contrasts its beautiful location on the holiday coast of north Cornwall with its 'sinister' work as a nerve gas factory during the Cold War.[69] Even though it was closed down in the mid-1970s, Nancekuke still seems to inspire awe among many locals as a mysterious 'cloak-and-dagger' place, with many dark secrets that are better left undisturbed. It is not worth poking around or asking awkward questions, they mutter. All sorts of rumours and claims still envelop Nancekuke.

This enduring suspicion and controversy was revived in 2000 when local MP Candy Atherton took up the campaign of the ill workers. There has been much dispute over an inconclusive official study into sickness levels and death rates among Nancekuke workers. The government maintained that this study gave the plant a clean bill of health, while campaigners believed that the results had been manipulated.[70]

It is not known if there are other cases of former Nancekuke and Porton staff who have suffered long-term illnesses because of their work at the secret establishments, especially since any further victims would have felt under great pressure not to go public. Tom Griffiths, a patriot who believed in Nancekuke's work, did not even tell his wife for twelve years what the cause of his accident was. The MoD claims that there is no evidence that anybody at Nancekuke suffered long-term illness from their work 'as great care was taken to ensure that they were not exposed to toxic chemicals.'[71] It further says that Nancekuke had a 'commendable' accident record, since 'there were no major accidents' with toxic chemicals.

Similarly, says the MoD, staff at Porton were not 'generally' exposed to chemical warfare substances because all work was, and is, conducted according to the 'appropriate health and safety guidelines.'[72] The MoD therefore believes that there is no need to launch follow-up studies to check the health of staff after they left both establishments.

A very different picture has, however, been given by former Porton scientists, Timothy Marrs and Robert Maynard, and an American counterpart, Frederick Sidell. They comment that at the height of the nerve gas research and production programmes in Britain and the US, staff experienced 'many accidental exposures', mainly to sarin (GB) vapour.[73] Most of the effects were mild – 'the sudden onset of "dim vision", a runny nose and tightness of chest was not considered the serious matter that it might be today', and staff generally preferred to continue working, rather than go to the doctor. Some of the reports which document the hundreds of accidental exposures at US chemical warfare installations have been analysed, but only three of the most severe cases appear to have been monitored for any length of time after the initial exposure. One member of staff lost consciousness within seconds of inhaling a large dose of sarin (GB), while another alarmingly sucked some soman (GD) into and around his mouth while using a pipette. The three 'resumed their normal work after 6-8 weeks with no known decrements,' commented the authors.

In the absence of clear evidence about the nerve gases themselves, scientists have turned to looking at the medical effects of other chemicals in the organophosphorus (OP) family for clues. OP pesticides are used on a large scale in agriculture as well as the homes and gardens of ordinary Britons. OPs are also found in household products such as fly killers, flea collars for pets, garden pesticides and headlice treatments for children. Public concern in Britain about these chemicals began to rise in the 1980s as hundreds of farmers reported that their health had been damaged by OP sheep dips. Until 1992, it was compulsory for farmers to dip their sheep to rid them of parasites. Many farmers, including former Conservative Defence Minister Tom King, have reported persisting symptoms such as dizziness, nausea, exhaustion and depression, resulting from either one or many exposures to the pesticides, and campaigners for the farmers believe that OP poisoning has even caused some to commit suicide. Hundreds have reported that they had suffered some sort of adverse reaction to OP sheep dips. (OP pesticides have also been suggested as a possible cause of Gulf War Syndrome.) However, Whitehall officials have maintained for a long time that the chronic effects of OP poisoning, either from single or repeated exposures, have not yet been established.[74] The MoD has dismissed the 'alleged' health problems of farm workers from OP sheep dips as being irrelevant to the long-term effects of nerve gases on the grounds that the two types of compounds act in different ways.[75]

So far, this chapter has only looked at the chronic effects of two major chemical weapons, mustard gas and nerve gas. It is apparent from the available information that mustard gas can lead to long-term illnesses. While there are no settled conclusions about nerve gas, Porton's own research shows that PF-3 – one of the early organophosphorus compounds tested on humans – can 'consistently' cause lingering paralysis.

What about the other chemicals which have been tested on the Porton human 'guinea pigs'? Again, the lasting effects of many of the other major chemical weapons are not clear-cut because of a lack of research. The existing evidence is patchy. The 1993 IoM study on mustard gas (described above) also scrutinised lewisite, concluding that this particular blister gas could cause some chronic respiratory diseases. The data on a further weapon, phosgene, is meagre, although it is reported to be capable of bringing on chronic lung diseases such as bronchitis and emphysema.[76] Porton itself records that several staff, who tested gas masks after the First World War by breathing in the arsenical smoke adamsite (DM), suffered ill health long afterwards, although this does appear to have resulted from repeated exposures (see chapter two).[77] Doubts about the safety of tear gases, such as CN gas and pepper gas, have been highlighted in chapter nine. Very little however is known about many of the experimental chemicals which were tested on humans and were then rejected as gas weapons.

Research into the long-term effects of chemical weapons has evidently not been one of Porton's top priorities. As we have seen, Porton scientists have carried out only a limited amount of investigation into the potential chronic illnesses resulting from mustard gas and nerve gases. Similarly, it also appears that comparatively little research has been done into the delayed consequences of the other major chemical weapons, such as chlorine and adamsite (DM).[78] Equally, the possible lasting effects of the large number of potential poison gases, which were rejected as weapons, do not seem – by Porton's own admissions – to have been explored.[79] Nevertheless, Porton claims that it has 'always taken the most careful account' of possible long-term damage before exposing volunteers to chemicals.[80]

It is apparent that Porton has neither monitored the health of the volunteers in the years after the experiments, nor devoted much effort to researching the long-term effects of the chemicals used in such tests. Given this, it seems that rather than displaying absolute certainty, Porton should be rather more tentative in its attitude towards the possibility that some of its test subjects could still be suffering long after the actual experiments had taken place.

There is a further element of uncertainty. Many volunteers were exposed to two or more chemicals during their visits to Porton, and indeed some speak of being tested with a string of different compounds within days. Porton has confirmed that in the 1950s and 1960s, 'many volunteers took part in several different experiments during a single visit and that some were exposed to more than one chemical agent. For example, there are records of volunteers being exposed to mustard gas on one day and CS gas some days later. By the 1970s, this was much less common and by the 1980s most volunteers were taking part in highly specific studies which involved exposure to no more than one chemical.'[81] The impact on the human body of a combination of poison gases and chemicals is also a much under-researched field. It is difficult to establish whether Porton scientists were even aware of the dangers of such combinations and what steps were taken to protect against them. In 1998, Ken Livingstone MP asked the MoD what assessments of the dangers of administering two or more chemicals to volunteers during one stay had been made by Porton. The reply from Porton was very limited and specific, 'As far as drugs are concerned, Porton has a clear policy which is that no volunteer can take part in a drug study within six months of participating in the same study. With respect to studies involving more than one drug, many of the studies conducted at Porton have been designed to evaluate the interaction of current medical countermeasures.' Porton added that, for these experiments, there 'has never been, and never will be' any policy, since approval of such tests would be 'a scientific and ethical decision which is made on a study by study basis'. Porton made no reference to any of the wide range of poison gases and experimental chemicals which have been tested on volunteers over the decades. It added: 'There is no documentary evidence that Porton Down has ever had a specific policy on the administration of two or more chemicals to a volunteer during one stay.'[82] However, as noted before, the interactions of various chemicals have been suggested as possible causes of the unforeseen illnesses experienced by veterans of the 1991 Gulf War.

A key factor in all this controversy is the amount of chemicals to which the volunteers were exposed. The dosage used in an experiment must surely be above a certain level if the chemical is to be capable of inflicting long-term harm on an individual. Porton indeed accepts that chemical weapons can cause chronic health effects, but only at high dosages. The Porton hierarchy argues that the dosages administered to the volunteers in its experiments have always been within a safe limit. Clearly, however, Porton has much more confidence in this assertion than many of the human 'guinea pigs'. As we have seen in chapter three, the lungs and eyes of some volunteers were exposed to mustard gas during the Second World War – and this happened *after* Porton had accepted that the gas could cause chronic lung diseases, and while war pensions were being awarded to First World War victims for eye ailments. In these circumstances, Porton now has to argue that the dosages in the wartime tests were low enough in *each* experiment not to cause similar illnesses.

Many Porton scientists who conducted the human experiments are now in retirement, living out the last of their years. From time to time, they hear the persistent complaints of the volunteers aired in the media, but remain dubious as to whether such grievances are valid. Take one former scientist who organised many Porton human experiments during the Cold War (and who did not want to be named). At the time, he believed that the experiments would not cause any harm to the volunteers in the long run. He considers that this is still 'probably true', but acknowledges that nobody can be 100 percent certain of that.[83] However he says that if he is wrong about this, he would be 'very sorry and horrified'.

This scientist is sceptical about some of the volunteers' claims, which he describes as more like 'Star Trek than Porton'. He believes that some are 'confused or sensationalised'. In the past, he has personally checked some of the volunteers' accounts against the archives, and found them to be inaccurate. These were experiments which he himself had organised. For instance, some volunteers claimed in the press that they had been exposed to nerve gas, when, according to the archives, they had been given placebos (inactive compounds in those particular tests). He says it is very hard to prove a firm connection between a disease and its cause in a Porton test.

Some Porton staff suggest that a number of volunteers may be following the current trend in British society where someone else always has to be blamed for their misfortune – the so-called 'blame culture'. Rex Watson, Porton's director between 1974 and 1983, said, 'We did all we possibly could at Porton to take advice and make sure that what we were doing would not jeopardise people's long-term health. You have to face up to the fact that if somebody is suffering from something or other, and if they can blame somebody else for it and get some compensation, they will do so.'[84] He does accept that compensation must be paid if the volunteers' claims are well-founded. 'If it is true, obviously they must be looked after and be compensated, but is it true? I find it difficult to believe that it can be true, given the weight of care that went into the work we did.'

Scientists from outside the installation have questioned the safety of some chemicals, but it appears that Porton staff have, in the main, sincerely believed that the compounds would probably not damage the health of the volunteers in the long term. But as so often in science, certainty about anything can be elusive, particularly in the complex area of the effects of chemicals on the human body. Porton staff may have believed that the chemicals were safe at the time of the experiments, but later, more scientific evidence has emerged which challenges and discredits the safety of the compounds. For instance, many human 'guinea pigs' were exposed to CN tear gas up to the 1940s, but Porton began to accept from the 1950s that this gas could damage humans. It is evident that the boundaries of scientific knowledge (and the sophistication of techniques) are not static and can fluctuate. It may be that sometime in the future, scientists may uncover conclusive proof showing that nerve gas can cause chronic illnesses.

The government's refusal to launch an independent inquiry into the health claims of the volunteers helps neither the human 'guinea pigs', nor officialdom. Such an inquiry may benefit Porton, as it could dispel the long-running allegations of ill health caused by its scientists. By ignoring the volunteers, the government appears to be treating them unfairly. An inquiry would certainly give the impression that the volunteers' campaign had won some justice from this government. Tony Blair's New Labour government, of all governments, knows that perception is all – the appearance of doing something is as important as actually doing it.

CHAPTER TWELVE

Into the Twenty-first Century

Today, Porton is much changed from the days of yesteryear. Instead of being a self-contained establishment managing itself, Porton is now run by the Defence Evaluation and Research Agency (DERA), a semi-autonomous Ministry of Defence organisation. Billing itself as 'one of Europe's largest research organisations', DERA is responsible for a string of military establishments with an annual turnover of £1 billion and more than 11,500 staff. These establishments carry out research, development and testing for a wide range of military projects, from electro-magnetic guns to high resolution imagery.

DERA projects a slick, modern image of an organisation at the cutting edge of science. Its glossy brochures portray DERA as a 'dynamic' organisation which 'harnesses science and technology to ensure that Britain's defence and security services maintain their superiority – always'. Its work across many scientific disciplines produces 'a compelling synergy'. In keeping with the zeitgeist of the modern world, DERA too has a mission statement: its vision is 'to be recognised as the world's foremost defence science and technology organisation and thus be a source of pride to our owners, our customers and our staff'.

For what is essentially a state-owned organisation, DERA advertises itself more like a commercial company. But it has to. It receives a set sum of money from the government to fund its main military work, but then has to raise a significant proportion of its income from other sources. In an era of diminishing government budgets, DERA is under a burden to make money by selling its own innovations and technical expertise. It must seek to win contracts from industrial companies, other government departments and overseas organisations to carry out research and development. (It is certainly a sign of the new times that DERA has a business office in Moscow.)[1] At one level, this means exploiting profitably the spin-offs from military science which have applications in the civilian world. For instance, liquid crystal displays were originally developed by military scientists at a DERA establishment and are now everywhere in ordinary, everyday life being used in calculators, watches, electronic notebooks and other hand-held gizmos. The talk is all of buzzwords: pathfinder initiatives, dual use technology centres, beacon scheme, offset agreements, and hotelling. In the past, government research establishments were given a budget from Whitehall and then got on with their work with barely a thought of making money from outside sources.

Porton has endured many spells of upheaval and turbulence in recent years. The current Labour government spent much time contemplating whether to sell off DERA in some sort of form to commercial firms. The idea ran into opposition from many quarters. The US government, for example, was worried that privatisation would jeopardise its secret collaboration with DERA, not least in the field of chemical and biological defence. After many months of these and other protests, the Ministry of Defence decided in 2000 that Porton and other sensitive establishments would be kept in the public sector, but the rest of DERA – three-quarters of the organisation – would be converted into a private company in the near future. Porton and the remaining rump of DERA will probably continue under the same commercial pressures as before.

The Porton management, imbued with the forward-looking DERA spirit, seeks to present a positive face to the world. It sends out regular press releases to highlight achievements, in an effort to persuade outsiders to view Porton in a particular light. The very fact of these press releases is a marked departure from the old days. These releases also give an indication of what the Porton officials want us to think about the establishment. For instance, they highlighted how a camera crew from the BBC science programme, *Tomorrow's World*, filmed an item at Porton about a new flame-resistant jacket which protects people in fires; how Porton and collaborating companies had won an award for 'turning part of its science park into a nurturing centre for fledgling biotechnology businesses'; and how Porton scientists were co-operating with the Ministry of Agriculture, Food and Fisheries to 'develop a rapid microbiological test for specific bacteria, which promises to have great exploitation potential'.

The past, however, still plagues Porton. Some of the things which went on at the establishment are distant memories, but they are, in a sense, like uncontrollable skeletons in the cupboard. They can pop out at any time to cause trouble for the current management. This is especially true of the experiments with human 'guinea pigs'. The death of Ronald Maddison in 1953 suddenly came back to haunt Porton in August 1999 when Wiltshire police decided to launch a criminal investigation into the case. Over the past decade, the controversy over the human experiments has been steadily growing – more and more human 'guinea pigs' are emerging with their own horror stories of gas chambers and lingering illnesses. The allegations over the common cold research have recently surfaced with vigour, and the media took a renewed interest in the LSD experiments. Other aspects of the experimental work have also come under scrutiny lately – the unresolved question of ill health among Nancekuke workers, the chemical contamination of land close to Porton, the dumping of old poison gas munitions in the sea, and germ warfare trials conducted over public areas of Britain.

Today's management at Porton have to deal with all these issues, the enduring legacy of other people's work and attitudes. They are in a sense cleaning up someone else's mess. But, according to one source, the current scientists are most irritated because this diverts them from their work. As scientists, they are, of course, primarily interested in doing their own science, and do not want to waste their time on sorting out something which happened a long time ago. If nothing else, it destroys Porton's concerted efforts to shake off the bad image of the installation – this is a far from trivial concern, since bad PR could hinder their attempts to win much-needed contracts for DERA.

Porton has gone through a series of name changes over the last decade, during which time it was taken over by DERA. Since 1991, it has officially been known as the Chemical and Biological Defence Establishment, DERA's Protection and Life Science Division (PLSD), and now the Chemical and Biological Sector of DERA. But in the public's mind, it is still the same old, mysterious Porton Down, the establishment which, it seems, is perpetually tarred with a murky reputation. (Unkind souls have drawn a parallel with the infamous nuclear complex in Cumbria, whose name was allegedly altered from Windscale to Sellafield after a barrage of bad publicity about the 'World's Nuclear Dustbin'.) When Wiltshire police announced in 1999 that they were going to investigate Maddison's death from forty-six years earlier, even respectable figures criticised Porton. Bruce George, the chairman of the House of Commons defence select committee – something of a key position within Britain's military community – said senior ministers were being kept in the dark about many aspects of Porton. 'It would be misleading for me to say that we know everything that is going on in Porton Down. It is too big for us to know and, secondly, there are many things happening there which I am not certain ministers are fully aware of, let alone parliamentarians'.[2] Within days, the media was again making hay when it emerged that Porton scientists were developing a vaccine against plague, produced by using a genetic engineering technique which was to be tested on human volunteers.[3]

This combined two great scare stories of the modern age – genetic modification and biological warfare – at an establishment already renowned for its seemingly alarming and furtive activities. Naturally, Porton saw it differently. According to their interpretation, this was 'pioneering research' in an area in which Porton was already leading the world. The episode showed how its past hangs like a great, long foreboding shadow over the installation.

It is apparent that as a general rule, the harsher of the human experiments were carried out some years ago. Privately, staff who have worked more recently at Porton have been appalled by the tests which had been done before they joined. One scientist who joined in the 1960s said of the nerve gas tests in the 1950s, 'I certainly would have had considerable reservations about them. I certainly would not have wanted to be involved in them either as a volunteer or a researcher. But [comparing] the standards of the 1950s and the standards in the 1970s, things have moved on. People are far more concerned with the well-being of the subject.'[4] This scientist pointed out that the ethical practices of many scientific establishments as a whole in the 1950s could be criticised nowadays, and that some of the experiments in those institutions would not have been approved in the modern era.

Criticism may also be detected in the public statements of government ministers. Nicholas Soames, the then Conservative Armed Forces Minister, commented in 1996 that the nature of the experiments 'have developed in response to changing principles and practices' over the last eighty years. 'There has also been a considerable advance in the understanding of the hazards to health of many of the chemicals to which individuals are exposed. It is therefore possible that some of the activities carried out in the past will raise concern when viewed through the eyes of scientists at the end of the 20th century,' he added.[5] Similarly, John Reid, who held the same post under the present Labour government, observed that the tests had 'evolved in response to changes in thinking, and it is quite possible that some activities carried out in the past at Porton Down might be carried out differently today'.[6] Both ministers ritually protested that Porton scientists have always followed the highest standards of the time and done their best to protect the health and safety of the volunteers. However such statements are tantamount to a tacit admission of malpractices in the past.

Porton's current trials reflect a changing climate in which the public are less willing to tolerate the use of human volunteers in chemical warfare tests. Compared to the past, the public are more suspicious about clandestine government activities, and less inclined to trust the authorities. These shifting attitudes must have exerted a restraining influence on Porton, and fostered a new political atmosphere in which extensive testing is harder to justify. Human 'guinea pigs' have not been exposed to any poison gas of any kind, including nerve gas, since 1989. According to Porton, there have been two types of human tests in recent years as the scientists concentrate on their main task of developing defences against chemical and germ weapons.[7] The first has been to assess the effects of various drugs on the performance of military personnel. Such drugs are used to protect and treat battlefield victims under attack from chemical or biological weapons. 'The effects that are investigated in such studies would be trivial or go unnoticed in a civilian population but may be important in a military context because they could possibly degrade overall performance. An example of this type of study is the evaluation of the effects of antibiotics on the performance of those involved in such tasks as map reading,' says Porton.

Over the years, Porton scientists have devoted enormous efforts towards seeking to develop antidotes, known as medical countermeasures, against specified chemical weapons. This has always been a complex area, particularly when complete defence against an attack is sought. It took a long time to develop satisfactory countermeasures against nerve gases, and volunteers were used in numerous experiments.[8] As described in chapter ten, Porton scientists developed the Nerve Agent Pre-Treatment Set (NAPS) tablets which are taken before an anticipated attack. They were also behind another success, the idea of taking atropine, pralidoxime mesylate (P2S), diazepam in combination in order to reverse the effects of nerve gas poisoning in victims after an attack. (The antidotes for other known poison gases are not as advanced as those for nerve gases. For instance, as noted in chapter two, there is no specific therapy for mustard gas burns, and so victims are essentially treated in the same way as they were many decades ago, despite all the research which has been conducted.)[9]

The other type of recent human testing has been to evaluate the 'physical and psychological burden imposed on (military) personnel by wearing various items of personal protective equipment', such as gas masks and NBC suits, in hot and cold temperatures. Typically, volunteers have worn the equipment while on a treadmill, so that scientists can measure the effects on their breathing rates, body temperature and circulation. This kind of work has been the mainstay of Porton's research for many years. Porton has been unwilling to list exactly which items of defensive equipment have been tested using volunteers since 1980, pleading that 'items of new equipment under development...are subject to both defence security and commercial sensitivities'.[10] However it is known that the S10 respirator and the Mark 4 NBC suit had been tested on volunteers. The S10, according to Porton, a 'considerable improvement on its predecessor', became the standard gas mask for the British military in 1986-7.[11] Around 250 volunteers had taken part in trials with these respirators a few years earlier to check that they would fully protect military personnel.[12] Since the early 1980s, around 500 volunteers have also been involved in trying out the Mark 4 NBC suit, which covers the body from head-to-toe. The Porton trials investigated how well troops can function in various temperatures wearing the suit.[13] Porton believes that this suit is capable of blocking all chemical and biological weapons from reaching the body of the wearer. Unfortunately such 'noddy suits', as they are called, are notoriously sweaty and uncomfortable in hot weather, enormously hindering troops from actually fighting properly in a real combat zone. This inevitably slows down troops on the battlefield, and they succumb to one of the advantages of the use, or even threatened use, of chemical weapons. Porton scientists have therefore spent considerable time and effort trying to fulfil a key principle – to design clothing which gives the greatest amount of protection, but imposes the least amount of burden and discomfort on the wearer.

The number of human 'guinea pigs' used in Porton's experiments has declined since the early 1980s. The annual totals have slowly been sliding from between 100 and 300 people to fewer than 100 nowadays. These totals are noticeably smaller than previous decades. Aside from the changing political atmosphere, there are probably other reasons why the number of experiments has been running at a lower ebb than before. The lack of an offensive chemical weapons policy has removed one motivation behind the trials. Fewer experiments are needed if only defensive equipment needs to be tested. (For example, the human experiments ballooned to 700-800 a year in the 1950s during the energetic drive to produce nerve gas weapons.) Furthermore, many experiments have already been done in the previous decades, producing a substantial body of scientific data. This is particularly so in the cases of nerve and mustard gases, the two chemical weapons most likely to be used in a war. Indeed, Tom Inch, who worked at Porton as a chemist between 1965 and 1986, said, 'One found out most of the information you wanted to know. There's no point in going on and on finding out this information. You have so much of it.'[14] He said that once you had discovered a certain amount about individual poison gases, 'what you realise then is that you really are not going to find out any more without unnecessary risks.' He added that also, the human trials were costly. As with experiments in any laboratory, 'it gets more and more expensive as you move from animals to men,' he said.

It is also clear that Porton's own ethical standards and controls appear to have markedly tightened in recent times, in line with the evolving rules throughout the scientific world. For instance, one set of safety regulations covering the use of the gas chambers appeared to be comprehensive and intricate (if observed properly), stretching to sixteen dense pages.[15] It seems that some Porton scientists believed that the safety regulations may have even gone too far. One, who worked at the establishment around 1990, said the process of getting proper permission for human trials, and the paperwork involved, inhibited enthusiasm and initiative; this bureaucracy acted as a barrier and slowed down the scientific work. He admitted being cynical, as he commented, 'You could not give someone a glass of water without getting approval.'[16] He believed that an approach of being 'super-safe' had been adopted as the Porton management feared being sued by volunteers, at a time when health and safety had become an important issue within government. 'It did not contribute to the well-being of the (volunteers), as we were always looking after the well-being of individuals. It did not necessarily achieve anything at all, except paperwork.'

As we have seen, the possibility of testing human 'guinea pigs' with poison gases has not been officially ruled out. At a cost of £3.5 million, a new gas chamber which can be used for exposing human 'guinea pigs' has been built.[17] This replaced gas chambers which 'had reached the end of their useful life and become too expensive to refurbish'. Porton estimates that the new chamber, opened in 1994, can be used for 'at least' 20 years.

Official documents reveal that the old gas chambers had 'deficiencies' and 'shortcomings', and had been criticised in 1984 by the watchdog body, the Health and Safety Executive (HSE), in its first inspection of Porton.[18] The HSE found that the chambers were difficult to clean and decontaminate; there were for example 'unsealed surfaces and cracks around tiles'. The chambers were not designed to be 'fail safe' – meaning that they would not automatically revert to a safe condition if there was some sort of accident. The report therefore advised that, as safety relies upon the exercise of effective control, it was essential that detailed, written protocols for operation of the chambers should be prepared. In all, the HSE made fifty-eight comments and criticisms of the establishment. Graham Pearson, then Porton's director, admitted that the 'deficiencies' of the existing chambers were recognised and that 'action has commenced to replace them'. He added, 'We believe that cosmetic treatment would not improve safety and may detract from experimental work.'

However, the HSE remained unimpressed with Porton in its next inspection in 1988. The watchdog came close to issuing an official order forcing the establishment to improve its health and safety standards to meet legal requirements.[19] Across the establishment as a whole, the HSE 'had to record our concern that your present organisation and arrangements were not effective at ensuring the health and safety of your employees and others'. The HSE made further criticisms of the gas chambers, in particular the lack of any system of mechanical and electrical interlocking doors which would restrict exposure in the case of any unexpected spillages. Once again, the then Porton Director, Graham Pearson, conceded that the 'shortcomings of the existing chambers are known', but it was not worth spending large sums of money on them since work to build new chambers had already started.[20]

The existence of Porton, once under severe threat in the 1970s, is quite safe for the foreseeable future. It would indeed be a surprise if the establishment were not around to celebrate its 100th birthday in 2016. As Porton's official historian Gradon Carter has commented, Porton can be reasonably confident of reaching its centenary, although the establishment would invariably 'suffer uncertainties and vicissitudes as it has in the past'.[21] Porton's future is secure, as long as the British authorities, along with other governments, remain fearful of the threat of chemical and biological weapons. Carter has commented, 'Because of the considerable military utility of chemical and biological warfare, the vulnerability of the military and civilian population of the United Kingdom to clandestine attacks and the particularly unpleasant hazards that would arise, it is certain that Porton will continue to be seen as an essential part of the national defence programme, whatever levels of arms control appear in the future.' The overall number of countries seeking to develop these weapons appears to have grown over the past thirty years; and anything up to twenty nations have been suspected of possessing, or having sought to produce, poison gas or germ weapons. The most notable country in recent times has been Iraq, which manufactured a huge arsenal of chemical and biological weapons. Under the brutal regime of dictator Saddam Hussein, the Iraqi military unleashed a series of chemical attacks on Iran during its war in the 1980s, as well as the notorious assault on thousands of Kurdish civilians in the village of Halabjah in 1988. The spectre of poison gas and germs hung over the Allied troops during the 1991 Gulf War, but as it turned out, they were never employed. The potential of terrifying clandestine attacks on ordinary citizens was highlighted in 1995 when an obscure sect released nerve gas in a Tokyo subway, killing twelve people and injuring many others.

The threat from all these different sources has helped to secure government funding for a flourishing Porton.[22] Officials believe that Porton had 'a good war' in the operation to remove Iraqi troops from Kuwait in 1991. Graham Pearson, director at the time, noted that 'the value of the

United Kingdom's investment over a number of years in research, development and procurement of chemical and biological defence equipment...was confirmed'.[23] The full scope of Porton's contribution was apparent, consuming the energies of many members of staff during the conflict. They gave advice to military commanders and politicians on a number of issues – analysing the nature of Iraq's chemical and biological arsenal, assessing the likely impact of a chemical or biological attack by Allied forces, calculating the hazard if a Scud-type missile containing deadly poison gas or germs was shot down, and so on. In three months, a system for identifying and collecting samples of biological weapons was developed and deployed so that any attacks could be confirmed. Porton staff also advised how the effects of chemical weapons may be more persistent in the heat of the Gulf, compared to European temperatures, and scientists devised a surgical technique to quicken the rate at which mustard gas wounds would heal. British troops deployed equipment which had been invented at Porton, such as detectors and protective equipment. Even after the war, Porton scientists were part of the United Nations team which toiled hard for some years to oversee the destruction of Iraq's chemical and biological munitions. Pearson said, 'Despite the very different climatic conditions from Western Europe, our physical preparedness to fight in a chemical and biological warfare environment compared very favourably with that of allies with whom close collaboration was maintained. The United States Marine Corps purchased substantial quantities of the British Mark 4 NBC suit and S10 respirator. Saudi Arabia also procured British chemical defence equipment.' Carter wrote of the magnitude of Porton's work: 'Acknowledgement of the establishment's role in the Gulf War was both widespread and at the highest level, the ability to act as well as advise within a short time scale was particularly appreciated.'[24] He added, 'The ability of Porton to respond so successfully to wide-ranging problems was dependent on the existence of multi-disciplinary teams of civilian and military personnel, backed by efficient trials, engineering and administration staff.' This was a 'reflection of the tradition laid down at Porton after the Great War of 1914-18'.

Porton's job is to ensure that British troops are protected against poison gas or germ weapons, whatever the conflict or whoever the enemy. Porton believes that the British armed forces are 'probably' equipped with the best defences against chemical and biological attack in the world. 'The newest S10 respirator, the No 1 NBC suit Mark 4 and the array of sophisticated detection and monitoring equipment available (in military service) are unsurpassed,' Carter has said.[25] This equipment has been researched, developed and provided by Porton scientists. The technical ingenuity and designs behind this protection have evolved from much perspiration and inspiration from Porton staff over the decades since 1916. The current gas mask is, for example, the culmination of waves of research into respirators which goes back as far as the First World War. Within thirty-six hours of the first use of gas by the Germans in 1915, some kind of improvised mouth-pad had been distributed to all British troops. These were soon discarded as the idea of a helmet covering the head with a small window for the eyes was conceived. That in turn was jettisoned when an improved mask was invented. This process has continued ever since, as scientists experimented with different materials, designs and filters in the hunt for even better respirators. The same process is evident in the evolution of protective clothing.

For some years, British troops have been in the fortunate position that they could depend on some of the most up-to-date protection against the horrors of gas and bugs. To a large extent, this protection could not have been developed without the huge volume of human tests. This 'vital' role of the human 'guinea pigs' was expressly acknowledged by John Reid, the then Armed Forces Minister, when he aired the government's official view in 1998: 'I am in no doubt that our knowledge and our technology in the very complex field of chemical and biological defence could not have been advanced without the contribution of volunteers participating in the trials as part of the programme.' He specifically emphasised the government's gratitude to the human 'guinea pigs'.[26] Equally, the experiments conducted on volunteers between 1916 and the 1960s proved extremely useful for the time when Britain was interested in manufacturing chemical weapons.

After all, the volunteers have participated in the longest-running and most continuous programme of chemical warfare tests on humans in the world. There was a temporary pause in these human trials in 1919 and then the nerve gas tests (but not other experiments) were halted for some months in the aftermath of the tragic death in 1953. Aside from these interruptions, human experiments of some sort at Porton have stretched more or less non-stop from 1916 to the present day. These experiments were so interwoven into the ordinary day-to-day life of the installation that Porton is likely to have used the highest number of human subjects of any chemical warfare testing programme in the world.

Unfortunately, the price of having some of the best defensive equipment against chemical and biological weapons appears to have been paid by these volunteers down the years. Many human 'guinea pigs' suffered much pain and agony in these tests. One twenty-year-old was killed, a life cut short at an early age. Volunteers now complain that they were mistreated by Porton.

Many, young and naïve, had little idea what they were letting themselves in for. Some say that they were forced to take part in the trials. Others claim that they were tricked into participating in gas experiments when they believed that they were helping research to uncover a cure for the common cold. A significant number have come forward to say that they believe their health has been damaged by the trials. Many are aggrieved that the government has neither admitted their illnesses, nor paid them compensation for their troubles. They feel shunned and ignored by the Ministry of Defence, a sense of being used and abused. It is not known how many have died with their complaints left dangling and disregarded.

On 5 May 2000, a memorial to the human 'guinea pigs' who had been subjected to gas tests was unveiled by the defence minister at a chemical warfare establishment. But this was not at Porton. Instead it took place many, many miles away – in Canada. After some years of pressure, the Canadian government agreed to honour the 2,000 human 'guinea pigs' who had been involved at its huge chemical warfare base at Suffield. The vast majority of them went there during the Second World War to take part in experiments run jointly by Canadian and Porton scientists, and some of them are now receiving compensation from their government. In a simple ceremony attended by a small crowd of human 'guinea pigs' and their families, Art Eggleton, the Canadian Defence Minister, unveiled a bronze plaque which eloquently pays tribute to them. It reads: 'In recognition of those who suffered so that their comrades in arms might be spared the horrors of chemical warfare – they also served'. Eggleton added, 'They put their lives on the line in those early days of research', and the memorial was a 'chance to show our gratitude and to acknowledge the debt we owe' to the human volunteers. As for Porton volunteers, the British government has no plans at present to erect a similar kind of memorial outside the Wiltshire establishment.[27] Perhaps this is a telling example of the difference in attitudes between the two governments.

The so-called 'man on the Clapham bus' would agree that if the Porton volunteers are now suffering, they should be given help. Like the legal system, justice must be seen to be done, otherwise people lose confidence in the system of government. The scientific evidence on whether chemical weapons can cause long-term illnesses is mixed – it may be that the illnesses suffered by some of the volunteers are not caused by the Porton trials; it may be that some are. However, at the moment, it appears that for many, it is no more than an unresolved, quietly festering question repeatedly being swept under the proverbial carpet by Tony Blair's government. Such an approach could foster more anger and disillusionment among the volunteers in the future. If this New Labour government were to treat the claims of the volunteers in an open and fair manner, then this outstanding sore could be healed. An inquiry would most likely settle the dispute once and for all. The volunteers served a purpose at the time of their experiments, but Porton and the rest of government now has a responsibility to make sure that they are treated properly. Ultimately, it comes down to a question of integrity. Tony Blair was elected in 1997, promising to clean up government and be open and honest with the people of Britain. To many volunteers, this government seems no different from the previous Conservative administration.

Many of these experiments may have been completed in the past, but they are still very much a part of the present. Human 'guinea pigs' who thought that they were serving this country now believe they are left with a sad legacy of illnesses from the experiments they undertook during that service. They deserve a fairer hearing from those in power in this country.

AFTERWORD

Clouds of Deceit over Britain

The British government insists that unlike chemical weapons, Porton has never tested 'live' biological weapons on human subjects. In a letter to Matthew Taylor MP on 25 January 2000, the Ministry of Defence stated that no volunteers from the armed forces or Porton staff have 'ever been deliberately exposed to live biological agents'. This denial is supported by former Porton staff who have been interviewed for this book. However, from the mid-1950s to the late 1970s, Porton scientists carried out more than 150 top-secret trials with germ warfare simulants which were dispersed over large, populated tracts of Britain.[1] It was as if whole chunks of the country had been turned into an experimental laboratory during the Cold War. The full details of this considerable number of trials have only recently been revealed to the British public and have provoked much controversy about the secrecy and safety of these tests. It has led the current Labour government to set up two inquiries into the trials.

The recent furore has nettled Porton staff. Rex Watson, Porton's director between 1974 and 1983, deplored the attitudes of some Britons. 'So much is being raked up that was necessary at the time, but is now presumed not to have been necessary and is now presumed to be something that should not have [been] done. But if, in fact, biological or chemical warfare had been used against the population of this country, and we had not done those experiments, then there would have been uproar that we had not bothered to work it out. It is a no-win situation. You either get pilloried because you do not do it and people are upset because they are not protected, or you get pilloried because you did do it, and donkey's years later, people say "we think that you must have affected us in some way".'[2]

Britain began to take the threat of biological warfare attack seriously in the 1930s. During the Second World War, Porton developed biological weapons to retaliate against the Nazis if they resorted to germ warfare. In particular, Porton produced five million cattle cakes filled with deadly anthrax spores. The idea was to drop the cattle cakes over Germany so that their livestock would eat them and be killed, further weakening the enemy's agricultural sector. German people would almost certainly have died in the ensuing massive outbreak of anthrax. The Allies drew up serious plans to drop anthrax-filled bombs on six German cities. If these plans had been executed, many Germans would have been killed, and the cities rendered uninhabitable for years. Experiments on the Scottish island of Gruinard revealed the destructive power of anthrax. During the war, Porton scientists had conducted anthrax experiments on Gruinard, leaving the land so contaminated that it was declared out of bounds for man and beast until the late 1980s.

Biological weapons had not been used in the war, but the potential of producing such weapons in the future seemed feasible and genuine. In great secrecy, top levels of the British government decided that Porton's research into biological weapons should be continued in peacetime. Indeed, the development of a biological arsenal was accorded a high priority for some time by the government. Five major large-scale experiments with real biological warfare organisms were carried out at sea between 1948 and 1955. Three of these – Operations Harness, Ozone, and Negation – were located in Caribbean waters, whilst the other two – Operations Cauldron and Hesperus – were conducted off the Scottish coast. Like the wartime tests, only animals and not humans were used as subjects in these trials. (It has been reported that a British civilian trawler accidentally sailed through a cloud of plague germs in one trial, but miraculously none of the crew fell ill.)[3]

In the early 1950s, Britain's policy on germ warfare appears to have started to slide slowly from an offensive stance of developing biological weapons towards a position of concentrating on producing defensive measures against such weapons from the 1960s. According to one academic, this gradual shift over some years was 'characterised by ambiguity, uncertainty and a general drift between policy stances'.[4] In British chemical warfare policy after 1945, the key Cabinet decisions of 1956 and 1963 are easily identifiable, but the comparable decisions in British biological warfare policy are not so visible.

One of the few direct references to biological warfare experiments on human subjects dates from 1953, in the wake of the death of Ronald Maddison. Following his death, the committee leading the inquiry made various recommendations, including that the Biology Committee (reporting to the Chemical Defence Advisory Board) should be the 'authoritative' arbiter on all questions relating to chemical warfare tests on humans. It was decided that an equivalent arrangement should also be put in place for *biological* warfare experiments on human subjects. The key committee was the Biological Research Advisory Board (known colloquially as BRAB), which, like the Biology Committee, was made up of distinguished scientists from outside Porton who advised the establishment. BRAB would have to consulted if Porton scientists wanted to conduct any experiments 'involving the administration to human beings of substances or organisms which are likely to be harmful'. BRAB would then decide whether the proposed tests were 'desirable and safe'. Although not spelt out, it appears that BRAB would have the final approval over whether an experiment of this sort could proceed.[5] These documents imply that Porton had not carried out experiments with 'live' germ weapons on humans up until that point.

Some questions have been raised about one particular experiment which was a collaboration between two Porton scientists and two staff from St Thomas's Hospital in London in the 1960s. Over a four-year period, thirty-three patients suffering from terminal cancers were experimentally infected with Langat Virus and Kyasanur Forest Disease Virus to see whether the viruses would alleviate the effects of the cancers. As it turned out, only four patients experienced 'transient therapeutic benefit', and all of them eventually died. The two Porton scientists involved were Dr Gordon Smith, the director of the biological warfare section of Porton between 1964 and 1971, and senior scientist Dolores McMahon. All the cancer patients were said to have given their consent to the experiment. But this begs the question as to why the Porton duo were involved in such an experiment in the first place. It is apparent that during the 1960s and 1970s, many of Porton's biological warfare scientists were increasingly engaged in research which was essentially civilian in its aims (and, according to many, was well-respected in scientific circles). A high proportion of this work, including this particular experiment, was published in open journals. It is likely that this experiment was one of those civilian projects. Indeed, it is noticeable that the two viruses in the experiment are not among those most commonly associated with biological warfare.[6]

Human experiments with real biological weapons are thankfully rare in the world. Details of such experiments are, however, often kept secret for years, so it is difficult to establish the existence and extent of such tests around the world. The most widespread and gruesome tests appear to have been organised by the Japanese germ warfare establishment, Unit 731, before and during the Second World War (see chapter six). The Americans exposed humans to disease-causing organisms (pathogens) during the Cold War. Between 1959 and 1974, around 2,200 people were tested with pathogens such as Venezuelan Equine Encephalitis and Tularaemia, as part of research to find vaccines.[7] For much of that time, the Americans were immersed in a long programme to develop a biological warfare arsenal.

Remarkably, many of the subjects in the germ warfare tests were soldiers from a religious group, the Seventh Day Adventist Church. As conscientious objectors, they served in the army as non-combatants. However, they were apparently happy to take part in these experiments. (As one of their leaders explained, 'We like to look at ourselves as conscientious co-operators, not conscientious objectors.') In one set of tests, they were infected with airborne Tularaemia and became ill within a week, although they were all said to have later recovered.[8] More recently, evidence has emerged that under the brutal and cruel regime of the Iraqi dictator Saddam Hussein, prisoners were exposed to biological weapons. However, this has yet to be fully substantiated.[9]

The controversial open-air trials over large swaths of Britain began in the 1950s. Porton scientists wanted to investigate how easily a huge cloud of deadly germs could be dispersed over Britain from a ship or plane off the coast. There was a very real concern that Britain as a small, vulnerable island could be devastated by this kind of biological warfare attack.[10] They decided that a marker chemical – zinc cadmium sulphide – should be released to simulate the path of the cloud. The scientists could then track the progress of the cloud by tracing and counting the fluorescent particles of the zinc cadmium sulphide at sampling points. In all, Porton scientists are believed to have conducted at least seventy-six trials with zinc cadmium sulphide over most of England and Wales.

In the initial batch of trials, the chemical was sprayed over picturesque towns and villages across the shire counties of Middle England – Wiltshire, Hampshire, Berkshire, Dorset, Somerset and Surrey.[11] In the first trial in November 1953, it was emitted in an arc from a disused RAF station near Beaulieu in Hampshire northwards for up to fifty miles over Winchester towards Newbury, Berkshire and Devizes, Wiltshire. In March 1954, it was again disseminated from Beaulieu, but this time over Shaftesbury and Blandford, Dorset, to Yeovil, Somerset, fifty miles away. Two months later, Porton scientists released the chemical from an RAF base near Yatesbury, Wiltshire, southwards over Warminster, Shaftesbury and Blandford. The sampling points were erected in lines twenty-five miles away between Salisbury and Mere, Wiltshire, and fifty miles away between Hurn and Cerne Abbas, Dorset. In July 1954, the chemical was dispersed from RAF Hullavington near Chippenham, Wiltshire, eastwards, with the rows of samplers placed firstly twenty-five miles away near Hungerford, Berkshire, and then fifty miles away between Pangbourne and Basingstoke in Hampshire. A week later, the chemical was sprayed over eighty miles. A generator was towed along a road near Frome, Somerset, while it spewed out the chemical for an hour. Thirty miles away, sampling machines between Salisbury and Marlborough, Wiltshire, were used to monitor the cloud. Another line of samplers had been positioned between Ottershaw, near Woking in Surrey, and Selsey Bill on the Sussex coast.

The experiments changed tack in 1955. On six occasions, Porton scientists disseminated large quantities of the zinc cadmium sulphide for twenty-five miles around the establishment so that RAF planes could fly through the clouds and measure their progress. Sampling equipment fitted onto vehicles also tracked the particles on the Wiltshire roads.

The scale of these trials was greatly expanded in 1956. Over the next three years, the fluorescent particles were sprayed out of planes flying long distances, usually 250 miles, along the British coast. The zinc cadmium sulphide clouds then drifted over most of the country. Declassified documents in the Public Record Office describe at least twelve trials of this scale between April 1957 and November 1959.[12] For example, in one trial in September 1958, the fluorescent particles were discharged from a military plane while it flew from a point off Cornwall through the English Channel to a point off Beachy Head in Sussex. Samples from the cloud were collected at a network of monitoring stations throughout south-west England, central England, parts of Wales and as far north as Yorkshire. This trial was part of a series to see if it was possible to hit a specified target, centred on Coventry, with the particles.

Virtually every region within England and Wales was blanketed with the zinc cadmium sulphide clouds at one time or another during the trials. The planes dispersing the clouds overland flew along different routes – for instance, from East Anglia right up to the Scottish borders, or from Newcastle overland to the Irish Sea and then down to a point off south-east Eire. As an indication of the enormous scale of the tests, Porton estimated that in just one of the trials, the cloud would have settled over twenty-eight million Britons, if the sampling equipment 'gave a true picture'.[13]

Taken as a whole, a large proportion of the British population is likely to have breathed in the particles during these trials.[14] The compound could also have contaminated the environment and ended up in the food eaten by British people. All this happened completely without their knowledge or consent since the trials were carried out in total secrecy at the time. Indeed, the entire scope of the trials only came to the public's attention in the late 1990s.[15] Similar large-scale tests were carried out across enormous sections of America in the 1950s and 1960s by the US military. Zinc cadmium sulphide was released from aeroplanes, rooftops and moving vehicles over

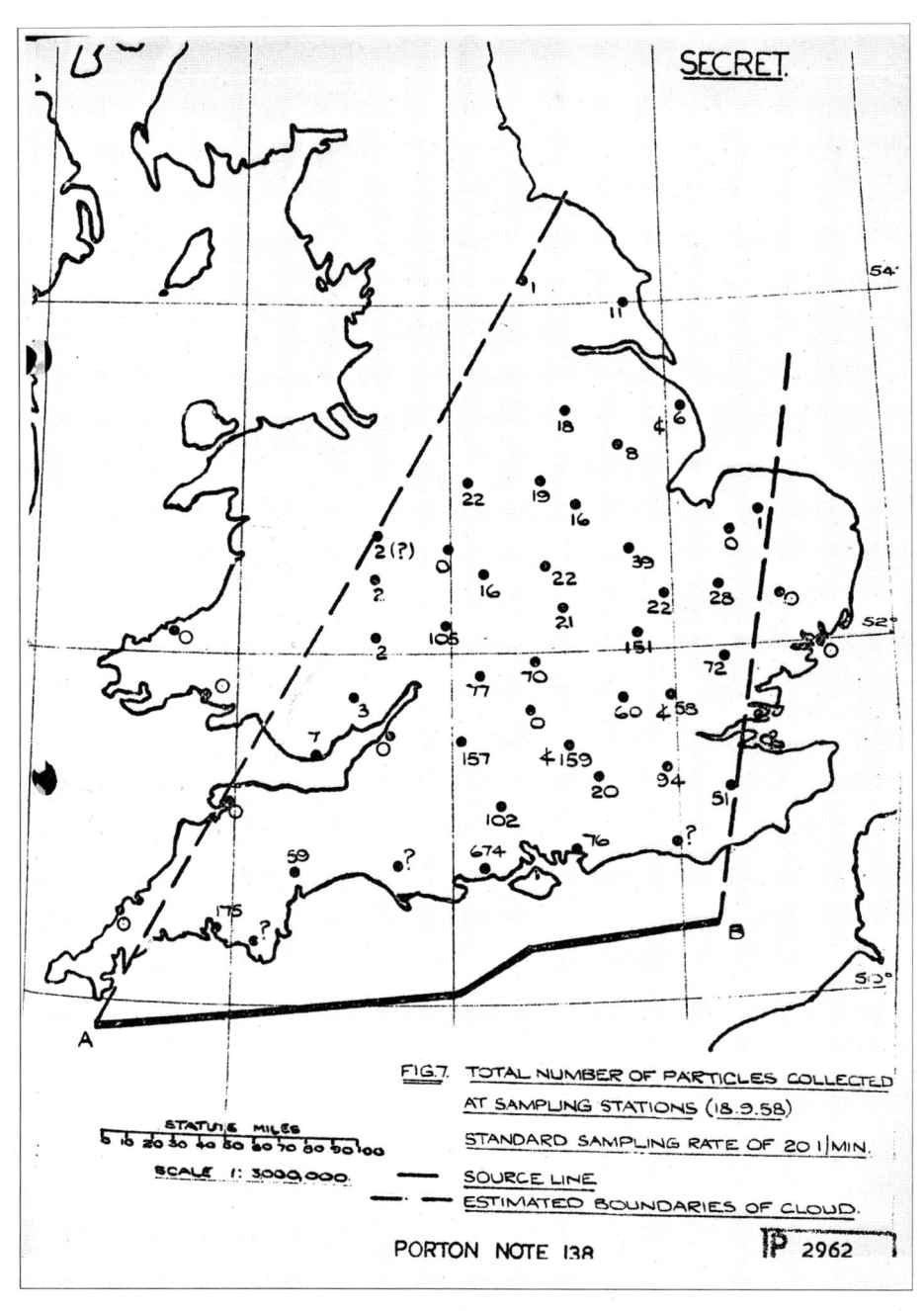

Official Porton map showing how far zinc cadmium sulphide was sprayed over Britain during one of the trials.

thirty-three urban and rural areas in the US and Canada, including Minneapolis, St Louis and Winnipeg. Porton and its US counterparts shared the results of their respective trials. Once again, US citizens only learnt about the trials in their country many years later. The resulting furore forced the American Congress to commission an independent inquiry into the toxic hazard to American people in the trial areas.

An expert committee of the US National Academy of Sciences observed that the amount of published information on the hazards of zinc cadmium sulphide is 'sparse', with no reports in the scientific literature on the potential toxicity of the compound if inhaled by humans. The committee concluded that this was a compound with a 'largely unknown toxic potential'. However the committee in its report in 1997 ruled that the list of disorders reported by citizens in the trial areas could not have been caused by zinc cadmium sulphide.[16] 'People were outraged at being exposed to chemicals by the government without their knowledge or consent,' noted the committee.

It appears that at the time of the Cold War trials, Porton scientists regarded zinc cadmium sulphide as so safe that there barely seems to have been any discussion about its possible toxic hazards to the public. According to Porton, 'it was not considered necessary to undertake any preliminary tests on the safety aspects of the compound'. It was 'a recognised air movement tracer in meteorology and was widely used, at the time of these trials, in many different countries'. However Porton conceded that, since the end of the trials, 'doubts' about the safety of the compound had arisen. Citing the US National Academy study, Porton argued that the compound was 'probably harmless' and 'probably caused no human illness', since British people only inhaled 'trivial' amounts of the compound.[17] In the modern era, it would have been politically damaging for Porton to have to admit any degree of uncertainty about the safety of a compound sprayed over so many unwitting British citizens. Following criticisms and publicity in the media, the Ministry of Defence, with relatively little prompting, set up an independent inquiry in 1999 into the zinc cadmium sulphide trials, as the Americans had done.

This inquiry, headed by Peter Lachmann, a retired professor of immunology at Cambridge University, focused in particular on cadmium, the component within the spray which could have caused ill health. By the late 1940s, it was known that cadmium was harmful to humans. A scientific report in 1932 had warned, for instance, that cadmium is a 'dangerous substance' and that people should avoid inhaling or swallowing 'even small amounts' of it.[18] Indeed, a range of cadmium compounds had been examined by the Allies as potential chemical weapons during the Second World War.[19] Cadmium oxide was proposed for use in special incendiary bombs. It could be added to normal incendiary bombs with the advantage that enemy firefighters would breathe it in and suffer severe lung oedema (abnormal accumulation of fluid in the lungs, similarly resulting from phosgene exposure). A Porton paper from 1967 stated that short-term exposure to cadmium affects the respiratory system of humans, causing irritation, cough and laboured breathing.[20] High doses of cadmium over long periods of time are believed to cause bone and kidney problems and lung cancer.

The inquiry by Professor Lachmann, made public in March 2000, concluded that the trials had not harmed the health of the British public.[21] He found that over the course of the trials, they had been responsible for just over one percent of the total amount of cadmium which had been released by British industry into the atmosphere. He concluded that 'the cadmium exposure arising from these trials did not significantly increase the level to which the population is normally exposed', adding, 'Although we fully understand the public unease that ensued when it was discovered, many years after the event, that large areas of Britain had been subjected to this form of experimentation, the existing evidence shows that no public health danger arose.'

Many of the British trials were designed by Mr R A Titt, a Porton scientist for forty years who was, by the early 1960s, head of the establishment's munitions research division. Mr Titt was reluctant to talk about the trials on the grounds of national security.[22] He acknowledged that 'cadmium itself is poisonous. Everybody knows that.' Asked if the cadmium in the trials posed a hazard to the British population, he replied: 'Not to my knowledge. I took advice on that. A lot of work had been done on this before I ever touched it. I am not a medical man.' He said that 'other people' had previously chosen zinc cadmium sulphide for trials which had already taken place in this and other countries. He added that the trials were done for 'the defence of the country' and 'discussed and considered at a very high level'. 'I was not privy to that,' he said.

Zinc cadmium sulphide was chosen for use in the trials because it was thought that its fluorescent particles could be easily detected under ultraviolet light.[23] Unfortunately, Porton discovered an 'intrinsic error' in the trials – up to half the zinc cadmium sulphide particles lost their fluorescence, particularly during daylight and over longer distances.[24] This flaw meant that the number of particles counted at the sampling stations could not be relied upon to be an accurate measurement of the dissemination of the chemical during the trials. It has also become clear that quite a few of the trials –

possibly as many as a third – were not in fact recorded by Porton scientists in reports. As a result, no one can be sure how much zinc cadmium sulphide was actually dispersed around the country.

Zinc cadmium sulphide was 'gradually discarded' by Porton scientists in the early 1960s.[25] (It appears that the last trial with the chemical took place over Norwich in 1963.)[26] Porton switched to using micro-organisms in large-scale tests in public areas. Instead of dangerous pathogens, Porton relied on simulants – organisms which they believed to be harmless, but which would mimic genuine biological weapons. In this way, the scientists aimed to study the behaviour of virulent germ weapons, but obviously avoid the harmful effects of such weapons among the British people.

Some officials voiced their opinions that such trials could cause a stir if their existence leaked out. One BRAB member believed that 'it was not possible to carry out large-scale trials in this country with pathogens, and probably not with simulants either'[27], and a senior scientific adviser warned, 'I am convinced of the vital need for these trials which impose no hazard to the public, although clearly knowledge of them by unauthorised persons could be politically embarrassing.'[28] In May 1963, the Cabinet authorised a set amount of money to be spent on the trials, as part of a 'small increase' in biological warfare research.[29]

One strand of the trials took place in the London Underground in July 1963 and May 1964. These were done 'in great secrecy under the covering title of "ventilation trials".'[30] Two simulants – one of which was *Bacillus globigii* – were released along the Northern Line at lunchtime on two days.[31] Millions of spores were dropped between Colliers Wood and Tooting Broadway stations, and sampling equipment measured how many of the organisms had been dispersed at different points along the line, as far north as Camden Town, about ten miles away.

A second type of trial involved the exposure of the simulants to the open air in boxes between 1963 and 1967.[32] The bacteria were held on tiny spider's threads in the boxes to see how the organisms would survive in different environments (such as built-up or rural areas) and at different times of the days. These test locations included Waterloo Bridge and Thames Embankment in central London, Southampton, Swindon, Portland Bill, Osmington Mills and Maiden Castle in Dorset. Not all these experiments were static. The boxes full of organisms were driven on top of vehicles, termed 'mobile sampling stations', from the Dorset coast as far as Taunton and Frome, Somerset. The Porton scientists wanted to transport the bacteria 'in the same parcel of air' to measure how they would decay. Few of the bacteria are believed to have escaped from the boxes in this particular kind of experiment.

Another set of trials entailed the spraying of huge quantities of simulants from a ship inland over populated areas of Britain. A military experimental ship, the *Icewhale*, steamed around Lyme Bay and Weymouth Bay spraying micro-organisms in a five- to ten-mile radius over Dorset, showering Weymouth, Dorchester and the surrounding countryside.[33] The simulants used were *Bacillus globigii* and a strain of *E. Coli*, known as MRE 162. (This strain of *E. Coli* is not the one which has been responsible for recent food poisoning and deaths; instead it is a strain isolated by Porton from a toilet seat in 1949.) These trials were carried out fourteen times in 1963 and 1964, and fourteen times again between February 1966 and January 1968.[34]

A more extensive version of these trials was also conducted. The *Icewhale* ship sprayed large amounts of the same organisms over two more counties – Hampshire and Devon – in two arcs twenty to thirty miles inland from Lyme Bay. One arc stretched from Totnes in Devon, over Torquay and along the coast to Lyme Regis in Dorset, the other was from Weymouth as far as Ringwood in Hampshire. These two arcs were spread over an estimated one million unsuspecting people living in the countryside and in conurbations such as the Torbay area and parts of Poole and Bournemouth. Porton scientists had set up around sixty sampling stations across the three counties of Devon, Hampshire and Dorset to measure how many of the two organisms had travelled to each one. These more widespread trials were carried out thirteen times between October 1964 and May 1965.[35]

American germ warfare scientists also carried out 200 or so trials in more than fifty public places of their own country – ranging from entire cities to rural areas – during the Cold War with simulants which they maintain are innocuous. In 1971, American biological warfare scientists collaborated with their Porton colleagues in a series of trials over Dorset. *Bacillus globigii* and another bacteria, *Serratia marcescens*, were sprayed sixteen times from the *Icewhale* over the Portland peninsula. These were aimed at testing British and American equipment for detecting the presence of biological weapons in the environment.[36]

In another strand of these trials, large amounts of organisms were sprayed from aircraft in 1967. In five trials, the planes sprayed more than 200 gallons of *Bacillus globigii* and *E.Coli* MRE 162 over an RAF airfield at Tarrant Rushton near Blandford in Dorset. Porton accepts that some of the load was deposited outside the boundaries of the RAF base.[37]

Military personnel were also exposed to the simulants in some of the experiments. In the mid-1970s, human subjects were sent into clouds of

Bacillus globigii at Porton and a training centre in Portsmouth. In the latter trial, they were exposed to a large number of micro-organisms, whilst wearing different types of clothing to find out how many of the spores would stick to them. Indeed, in one experiment, the spores 'contaminated' their hair.[38]

A small number of Porton staff were involved in tests with a more controversial simulant in 1977. The aim of the experiment was to explore how samples of organisms could be collected from the human body and other surfaces as a method of verifying whether or not a biological attack had taken place. The simulant *Serratia marcescens* was sprayed into a wooden hut at Porton. Staff then entered and remained in the hut for an hour. It appears that the Porton staff wore an experimental mask and boiler suits or duffel coats, and inhaled some of the organisms.[39] It is, however, unclear to what degree the Porton staff were actually exposed to the *Serratia marcescens* and if indeed any fell ill.

Serratia marcescens was extensively sprayed by the American military in their tests over populated areas between 1950 and 1969. (The Americans used a strain of the organism called '8UK' which had been developed by Porton during the Second World War. The advantage of the organism was that its red colour made it easy to monitor and track in the trials.) In six mock attacks in September 1950, American naval ships sprayed large quantities of the organisms over San Francisco. Military scientists estimated that almost the entire 800,000 inhabitants of the city would have breathed in the organisms. At least eleven people fell ill with infections caused by *Serratia marcescens*; one of them died. Military scientists concluded that the death and the illnesses were 'coincidental', although these infections were the first such recorded cases at their hospital. In general, the scientific community believed in the 1950s and 1960s that the organism was harmless to humans. But this assessment began to change in the 1960s as the organism became recognised 'as a cause of serious infection in man'. In 1969, the US military, while continuing to insist that its trials had not harmed any members of the public, decided that *Serratia marcescens* was dangerous in a 'limited' way and 'should not be used for study of experimental infections in man'.[40] The *Serratia marcescens* used in the joint US-UK trials over Portland peninsula in 1971 (described above) was, according to Porton, 'inactivated' or killed.

Another series of tests took place on Royal Navy ships. The crews inhaled varying amounts of bacterial spores in these trials. In Operation Kolanut, HMS *Andromeda* sailed through a big cloud of *Bacillus globigii* and *E. Coli* MRE 162 off Portland in 1970 to discover how many of the organisms would penetrate the ship. It showed that unprotected service personnel in all parts of the ship could be at 'considerable risk' if attacked with real germ weapons.[41] Three years later, a similar trial, Operation Varan, confirmed that ships and their crews could easily be attacked with germs. Some of the sailors on HMS *Achilles* had protective clothing in this test.[42] The last trial of this kind took place off Plymouth in 1976. In Operation Hazelwood, sailors were exposed to *Bacillus globigii* clouds on the flight deck of HMS *Galatea*, inhaling a 'high' dose of the bacteria.[43] These off-shore tests highlighted the danger of a biological attack on naval vessels. But what did the panoply of tests over land actually prove? According to Porton, the trials with zinc cadmium sulphide established that Britain was indeed vulnerable to biological attacks off its coastline from ships and planes which could effortlessly spread lethal germs over much of the country.[44] The London Underground trials confirmed that bacterial spores could be carried for several miles in the tube system and could persist in heavy concentrations at certain points for considerable periods of time. Trains travelling through such clouds would become contaminated inside the carriages.

As for the trials over open land in southern England, Porton insists that these were 'extremely useful', and provided much important information about the progress and survival of micro-organisms released close to Britain, as if in a real biological attack. Porton says for example that 'scientists were able to calculate the concentration of living organisms at different times and different distances from their source of release, and how that related to their size and meteorological conditions'. The MoD also argues that the results 'proved invaluable for assessing what measures would be needed to protect Britain and its people from a biological attack'. This information, adds the MoD, contributed to the development of computer models that were used as late as the 1991 Gulf War to help plan the protection of British armed forces if the Iraqi regime had used germ weapons.[45]

Military planners may be loath to admit it publicly, but the tests served to show that a germ warfare attack from off the coast of Britain would sweep over the country, leaving the government powerless to protect the British people and resulting in massive casualties.

Disclosure of the full details of these trials in 1997 and 1998 triggered protests and complaints, particularly from residents, MPs and local councillors in Dorset.[46] Concerns were especially acute in the picturesque coastal village of East Lulworth, where, according to residents, there was a mysterious and heart-breaking cluster of miscarriages and birth abnormalities, such as severe handicap, lung problems, and learning difficulties.[47] They suggested that the experiments could have been responsible. Like others in the region, the villagers pressed for a public inquiry into the tests. Their campaign was backed by the family of one of the Porton scientists who had helped organise the germ warfare trials. The scientist, Robin Southey, had died suddenly in 1970,[48] and his family have been demanding to know if his death was connected to the trials.

British residents had undoubtedly inhaled thousands of micro-organisms released into the air during the trials, but had this caused any ill health? Although Porton had been consistently arguing that these trials had been 'entirely benign', the Ministry of Defence commissioned a microbiology expert to conduct an inquiry into the safety of the trials with micro-organisms over southern England.[49] Porton did not completely pass with flying colours from this inquiry by Professor Brian Spratt of Oxford University. Pleasingly for Porton, he stated in his report in 1999 that the trials were 'unlikely' to have affected the 'overwhelming majority' of healthy citizens.[50] However, he concluded that the trials had put 'a small number of individuals at risk of infection'. He could not estimate this number, but added that 'inhalation of *E. Coli* MRE 162 could have caused a lung infection in a few individuals with underlying lung disease [e.g. cystic fibrosis patients], or a blood infection in individuals who were particularly susceptible to infection'. This finding that some vulnerable people could have suffered ill health because of the trials was potentially embarrassing for the government, but reaction from the media and politicians to the report was largely muted.

Surviving Porton scientists who organised these trials are reticent about talking publicly. Some say that they signed the Official Secrets Act and are therefore prevented from speaking about them to outsiders. On the whole, like their colleagues on the chemical side of Porton, they are defensive, weary and exasperated. They believe that years later, their work has been distorted and taken out of context in a welter of bad publicity by the media and protesters who seek to stir up unnecessary controversy. For instance, George Harper, who worked at Porton for many years in the Cold War, would not speak because he considered that anything he said would be manipulated. Now in his eighties, he added, 'I did my job as a civil servant for what I thought were good, ethical grounds. I have got no worries, no concern. I am not going to now try at this great age, so many years after the event...to defend what we did then.'[51] Keith Norris, a senior Porton official during the 1960s and 1970s, argued that discussing these experiments in public helped to spread information which could be used by enemy nations keen to develop deadly biological weapons: 'Consider what the possibilities are now for the misuse of this technology.'[52]

Afterword

Both the Soviet Union and the Americans devoted huge budgets to developing biological weapons in the Cold War, in a classic 'arms race' response to each other's efforts. In a surprising move, the US unilaterally renounced its germ weapons in 1969, helping to produce a world-wide treaty banning biological warfare. It now transpires that, although the Russians signed up to this treaty in 1972, they comprehensively broke it and continued to develop biological weapons for years afterwards. This they finally admitted in 1992, after many denials.

In the furtive and chilly atmosphere of the Cold War, Porton staff believed that they were justified in conducting secret germ warfare trials over populated areas without telling the British people.[53] The scientists wanted to avoid giving any help or information to the Russians, who, they thought, could launch a biological attack on Britain. Mike Hood, a scientific officer in Porton's biological warfare section between 1953 and 1978, said, 'If the Ministry of Defence had informed the public, all the trials would not have been worth doing. The public is so ill-informed, and of course, you would let a potential enemy know what you were doing.'[54] He added that Porton staff were 'extremely concerned' about the threat from the Soviet Union, and he personally feels that these trials were 'for the public good'. There was much discussion among Porton staff to ensure that the experiments were not in any way hazardous to the public. 'Otherwise, we would not have done them,' he said.

Another scientist, who worked at Porton for much of the Cold War (and did not want to be named), echoes these views.[55] He said there was no question of details of the trials being made public in the middle of the Cold War: 'We would have been giving our work, our efforts to the enemy to use against us. We did not want them to know what we had found out.' He was surprised that the existence of the large-scale, costly trials – a 'hush-hush affair' – did not leak out to the press at the time. He added that internal discussions over the safety of the trials were 'a big, big part of the whole thing'. The trials, particularly the type of micro-organisms released over the public, were 'strictly controlled' by 'top-notch' scientists on the Biological Research Advisory Board (BRAB), which had to scrutinise and approve the tests beforehand. 'It was not a question of just popping out and doing something,' he said.

Rex Watson, Porton's director between 1974 and 1983, argued that the scientists had to be judged in the context of the Cold War and the pressing questions that needed to be answered. He also questioned what the public would have done had they been told in advance about the tests: 'Gone inside and shut their windows?'

A recent review of the zinc cadmium sulphide trials by Porton bluntly defends the 'valid' decision to conceal the 'highly-classified' trials: '...the Cold War was extant and the needs of defence security were paramount – there was no option beyond secrecy...'.[56] This report argues that revealing the trials 'would obviously have led to public unease and anxiety about the susceptibility of the UK's population and armed forces to biological warfare attack'. It also points out that once it is known how to produce biological weapons, that specific scientific knowledge does not vanish; it could be used by the Russians – or any other hostile nation – at any point in the future to attack Britain. This meant that the trials had to be kept secret for decades to prevent the nation's defences from being compromised.

As Porton itself concedes, the debate on the ethical dilemmas is 'unending'. Although ordinary citizens were not the primary targets of the experiments, they unavoidably became subjects of the tests up to a point since they were to some degree exposed to the sprays used in the trials. It could be argued that ethically, Porton should have tried to obtain the informed consent of the British public to be participants in the tests. However, in the strange circumstances of the Cold War, Porton of course could not have done this without letting the Russians know what they were doing. Equally, it could be argued that the British public – members of a democracy – should have been given the chance of weighing up the pros and cons of the trials and deciding whether the experiments were worth risking people's health, or even if there was a potential threat to people's well-being. In a parallel with the Porton human 'guinea pigs', there was a direct clash between the need for secrecy and the principle of informed consent. As with the Porton volunteers, the scientists decided that the former prevailed over the latter. It could also be argued that the trials had to be kept secret to help defend Britain and thereby benefit the public. In this sense, the public were being sprayed 'for their own good' so that they could be protected from a germ warfare attack.[57]

In hindsight, it appears that the price of acquiring the results of these experiments, which Porton argues have been very useful, was the possible ill health of an unknown number of people, and the delayed disclosure of tests involving the public for many years. It seems ironic that the government may have harmed its own citizens in trials which were aimed at devising protection for them.

Officially, MoD ministers refuse to rule out the possibility of conducting this kind of huge open-air trial once again at some point in the future.[58] However, Porton staff themselves are sceptical that such trials would now be politically acceptable. One commented privately that they would not dream

Afterword

of organising this type of trial nowadays, fearing the inevitable public outcry. In previous years, many Britons trusted, and were deferential towards authority and officialdom. But these attitudes have undoubtedly been disappearing, leaving many people more suspicious and cynical about the antics of the authorities. It is apparently the weight of this changing public opinion which has forced the government finally to disclose the extent of these trials, even though it could be argued that these details could be turned against Britain by a hostile nation and used to inflict a massive germ warfare attack on the country.

APPENDIX 1

Annual totals of military personnel who have taken part in experiments at Porton Down

It is impossible to calculate a reliable total of exactly how many military personnel have been subjected to Porton's experiments since they began in 1916. Porton Down has conducted so many human experiments in the last eight decades that a precise total can no longer be compiled from its archives.

The only dependable figures exist for experiments conducted after 1945. Porton Down's own history of the human experiments – written in 1959 – was unable to find out the number of humans used in the years before 1945.[1] However the figures below, taken from official sources, show that since the end of the Second World War, 14,727 human subjects have passed through Porton's doors to take part in experiments.[2]

The Ministry of Defence estimates that around 20,000 military personnel have taken part in Porton's experiments since 1916.[3] This figure, however, appears to be too low. It would have to mean that there were only 6,000 volunteers before 1945, but this is almost certainly an underestimate. It is apparent, for example, that a substantial number took part in Porton's experiments during the First World War, and between the wars, around 4,000 humans are estimated to have been exposed to tear gas alone between 1925 and 1936, while 1,500 were tested in just one experiment with mustard gas over a five-year period in the 1930s. As chapter two shows, hundreds more were tested with all sorts of chemicals during that era. It is known that in 1929 alone, 524 volunteers were exposed in experiments. The numbers of volunteers used in the Second World War is not known, but it is worth noting that Porton wanted around 1,000 human subjects a year for experiments.

The picture is further complicated because a proportion of the human subjects took part in experiments more than once. Moreover, not all British chemical warfare tests on humans took place at Porton – some tests in the First World War were conducted at other government laboratories, while Porton staff have also organised experiments in Australia, Canada and India.

APPENDIX 1

As a rough estimate, therefore, it seems that the total number of military personnel who have been subjects of Porton's experiments from 1916 to the present day is more likely to be around 30,000.

For many years, Porton was unwilling to give a year-by-year breakdown of human subjects in its experiments 'for security reasons – since such data could enable an informed observer to gain a useful insight into the scope and direction of our chemical defence programme'.[4] Indeed, there are sometimes discrepancies in the annual totals given by Porton on different occasions.

Below are the annual totals of military personnel who have taken part in experiments at Porton Down. (The figures in brackets below are the number of volunteers who were exposed to nerve gases.)[5]

1945-46	297	(34)
1946-47	168	(0)
1947-48	118	(0)
1948-49	129	(129)
1949-50	326	(159)
1950-51	637	(234)
1951-52	789	(384)
1952-53	836	(531)
1953-54	704	(64)
1954-55	724	(8)
1955-56	606	(303)
1956-57	536	(184)
1957-58	624	(203)
1958-59	372	(201)
1959	440[6]	
1960	426	
1961	381	
1962	313	
1963	328	
1964	298	
1965	146	
1966	149	(24)
1967	244	(106)
1968	263	(42)

1969	181	(22)
1970	327	(22)
1971	225	(40)
1972	358	(35)
1973	264	(48)
1974	304	(10)
1975	137	(4)
1976	254	(8)
1977	117	(0)
1978	104	(4)
1979	153	(17)
1980	340	(30)
1981	303	(41)
1982	161	(16)
1983	177	(26)
1984	131	(9)
1985	181	(0)
1986	96	(0)
1987	93	(5)
1988	136	(12)
1989	110	(24)
1990	83	(0)
1991	50	(0)
1992	112	(0)
1993	64	(0)
1994	96	(0)
1995	58	(0)
1996	42	(0)
1997	60	(0)
1998	72	(0)
1999	84	(0)

APPENDIX 2

Chemical weapons and their effects

Listed below are some of the main chemical weapons, with a broad description of their effects on humans and their lethal dosages. These figures give an idea of how potent the classical poison gases are in relation to each other.

Common/code-name	Chemical name	lethal dosage (mg min m^{-3})
Nerve gases		
These cause sweating, vomiting, cramps, chest tightness, coma, convulsion, death from asphyxiation.		
Tabun GA	ethyl NN-dimethyl-phosphoramide-cyanidate	150-400
Sarin GB	iso-propyl methyl-phosphono-fluoridate	70-100
Soman GD	1,2,2-trimethylpropyl methylphosphono-fluoridate	40-60
VX	ethyl S-2-diisopropyl aminoethyl methylphosphono-thiolate	10

APPENDIX 2

Common/ code-name	Chemical name	lethal dosage (mg min m^{-3})

Blister gases
These cause skin and eye blisters, lung damage, broncho-pneumonia and respiratory failure.

Mustard	bis (2-chloroethyl) sulphide	1500
Lewisite	2-chlorovinyl-dichloroarsine	1300

Choking gases
These cause giddiness, disorientation, broncho-pneumonia.

Phosgene CG	carbonyl chloride	3200
Chlorine		1900

Blood gases
These cause hyperventilation, loss of consciousness, convulsions, cardiac/respiratory arrest.

Hydrogen cyanide AC		2-5000

Tear gases
These cause a burning feeling, tears, respiratory difficulty, nausea.

CN	2-chloroacetophenone	7-11000
CS	2-chlorobenzylidine malononitrile	25000
CR	dibenzoxazepine	25000

It is difficult to calculate accurately the dosages of poison gases which will kill or injure humans. Scientists can only define dosages which have a specified probability of producing a particular effect in humans. Listed above

APPENDIX 2

are the lethal dosages of airborne poison gases which are likely to kill fifty percent of people exposed if they are unprotected. These approximate figures are expressed as units of milligrams-minutes/metre cubed (mg min m^{-3}). This list relates only to dosages which are inhaled, the most likely route by which a victim will absorb poison gas. This table is based on pages 111-112 of *No fire, no thunder - the threat of chemical and biological weapons*, Sean Murphy, Alastair Hay and Steven Rose (Pluto Press, 1984). Although the two terms may seem interchangeable, there is a distinction between the *dosage* to which a person is exposed (also termed the exposure) and the *dose* which is taken into the body.

APPENDIX 3

The 1947 Nuremberg Code

1. The voluntary consent of the human subject is absolutely essential. This means that the person involved should have legal capacity to give consent; should be so situated as to be able to exercise free power of choice, without the intervention of any element of force, fraud, deceit, duress, overreaching, or other ulterior form of constraint or coercion; and should have sufficient knowledge and comprehension of the elements of the subject matter involved as to enable him to make an understanding and enlightened decision. This latter element requires that before the acceptance of an affirmative decision by the experimental subject there should be made known to him the nature, duration, and purpose of the experiment; the method and means by which it is to be conducted; all inconveniences and hazards reasonably to be expected; and the effects upon his health or person which may possibly come from his participation in the experiment.

The duty and responsibility for ascertaining the quality of the consent rests upon each individual who initiates, directs or engages in the experiment. It is a personal duty and responsibility which may not be delegated to another with impunity.

2. The experiment should be such as to yield fruitful results for the good of society, unprocurable by other methods or means of study, and not random and unnecessary in nature.

3. The experiment should be so designed and based on the results of animal experimentation and a knowledge of natural history of the disease or other problem under study that the anticipated results will justify the performance of the experiment.

4. The experiment should be so conducted as to avoid all unnecessary physical and mental suffering and injury.

APPENDIX 3

5. No experiment should be conducted where there is an *a priori* reason to believe that death or disabling injury will occur, except, perhaps, in those experiments where the experimental physicians also serve as subjects.

6. The degree of risk to be taken should never exceed that determined by the humanitarian importance of the problem to be solved by the experiment.

7. Proper preparations should be made and adequate facilities provided to protect the experimental subject against even the remote possibilities of injury, disability or death.

8. The experiment should be conducted only by scientifically qualified persons. The highest degree of skill and care should be required through all stages of the experiment of those who conduct or engage in the experiment.

9. During the course of the experiment the human subject should be at liberty to bring the experiment to an end if he has reached the physical or mental state where continuation of the experiment seems to him to be impossible.

10. During the course of the experiment the scientist in charge must be prepared to terminate the experiment at any stage, if he has probably cause to believe, in the exercise of good faith, superior skill, and careful judgement required of him, that a continuation of the experiment is likely to result in injury, disability, or death to the experimental subject.

APPENDIX 4

How the human 'guinea pigs' can find out more information about their experiments

Until relatively recently, the human 'guinea pigs' have found it difficult to prise any information out of Porton about the experiments which they underwent. Several volunteers who contacted Porton in the 1970s for details of their tests received little or no response (see chapter 10). Their experiences appear to be typical. Mick Roche, who set up the Porton Down Volunteers Association, had a long struggle in the 1980s to get any data about his tests until he resorted to a one-man hunger-strike outside Porton. After all those years of pressure, Roche eventually succeeded in persuading Porton to release some information in 1989. But the letter containing this information was sent to his GP, and not shown to Roche until another five years later.

For many years, Porton said that its 'long-standing policy' was to disclose information to the volunteers' doctors when requested.[1] But this was done on a 'medical-in-confidence' basis so that it was up to the doctors to decide how much or little to pass on to the volunteers. An outline, containing less information, was also sent to the volunteers themselves – it seems that this was done because officials believed that the volunteers would not understand complicated medical data and it would be best if their doctors interpreted it for them.

Porton's attitudes seem to have changed in the 1990s and the establishment began to release more details of its human experiments directly to volunteers. This change, however, seems to have been forced on Porton, as a result of more and more human 'guinea pigs' coming out of the woodwork and demanding to know what happened to them when they visited the establishment many years previously. Another catalyst may have been the 1990 Access to Health Records Act, which gave individuals a better chance of getting copies of their medical records.

In February 1998, the Ministry of Defence announced a number of initiatives to help volunteers discover details of their experiments. After meeting some of the human 'guinea pigs', the then Armed Forces Minister,

APPENDIX 4

John Reid, admitted that the volunteers had faced a 'fundamental problem' in obtaining this information. He added, 'In some cases, they have not known where to go for information, or they believe that it is being withheld.' He hoped to provide 'many individuals with the answers and assurance they seek'.[2] Reid said later, 'I was convinced that the secrecy and mystery surrounding Porton Down served only to encourage views that a conspiracy had been afoot. That was frustrating and disturbing for those with questions, and did not reflect well on the MoD, which was perceived as over-secretive and paranoid, and consequently as having something to hide.'[3]

The MoD set up a special helpline which is answered by Porton staff. (It is 0845 603 9140; calls charged at local rate). A leaflet was also produced to explain what information is available. Volunteers can either ring this helpline or write to Porton if they want to find out more about their experiments. The address is:

Porton Down Volunteers
Room 37, Building 106,
DERA Porton Down
Salisbury
Wiltshire
SB4 0JQ

Porton advises volunteers to include their full name, service number, and the date or approximate time that they were involved in experiments. The leaflet is available from this address, and also from Porton's website at www.dera.gov.uk.

Porton has been quite frank in admitting that its records from the past are not comprehensive. Documents from before approximately 1940 or 1942 have either been destroyed or are patchy. Porton has warned, 'Regrettably, individuals may have to accept that old records are in some cases very sparse. It is also the case that record-keeping in years gone by did not reach the same high standards that we expect today.' This inevitably lays Porton open to criticism that its record-keeping should have been better when its scientists were testing human subjects with some of the most deadliest substances in the world. (Porton has also admitted that records which detail its medical examinations of volunteers before and after experiments in the early 1950s have also gone missing, and were probably destroyed. It is unclear how many other of these medical examinations from other years are no longer recorded by Porton.[4]) According to Porton, the general trend is that the more recently the experiment occurred, the more comprehensive and detailed the information available.[5]

From 1940-2 to 1990, Porton maintained a kind of ledger, or summary book, of each volunteer. These included a volunteer's name, service number, dates of attendance, and a brief title of the experiments in which they participated.[6] The entry in the summary book is effectively a gateway into the archives. From this entry, Porton staff will then attempt to trace other information which is held about the individual at the establishment. This will come either from laboratory notebooks which were kept by staff, or from technical reports of the experiments. Porton says there tends to be more information on volunteers who were exposed to chemical weapons, rather than those who took part in experiments without gas (for example, testing protective equipment in hot conditions or on a treadmill). For some volunteers, the only surviving information may be the short entry from the summary book. Over the last decade, Porton has kept a paper folder on each volunteer which includes written copies of all medical examinations carried out before and after the tests and notes of any health issues arising during their visit.

Having searched their records, Porton will then send the individual a letter describing the key aspects of the experiments. Normally, this letter will include the names and dosages of the chemicals used in the tests, some sort of description of these chemicals, the duration of the experiments, a brief explanation of the purpose of the test, and symptoms experienced by the individual. Porton will also express their thanks to the human 'guinea pig' for taking part in the experiments and contributing to Britain's defences. To a certain extent, Porton is seeking to put a favourable gloss on this response and paint as positive a picture of themselves as possible, often, for example, underplaying the pain inflicted on volunteers in the tests.

It seems to be the case that the more the volunteers push for information, the more they will get back. Volunteers need to ask specifically for the names of the chemicals in their tests, the amounts used, and how long they were exposed to these substances. Moreover, volunteers have even received photocopies from the summary books and laboratory notebooks after putting in a request for them.

The Ministry of Defence also announced an important concession when the helpline was set up in February 1998 – from then on, volunteers, on request, would be given copies of technical reports of the experiments in which they participated. These technical reports are accounts and analyses of experiments written by Porton scientists which put individual tests into context. They will give volunteers the general background to why particular

Appendix 4

tests were being done, what the results of the tests were, and how the scientists interpreted the data from the trials.[7] At the time this was announced, the then Defence Minister John Reid commented, 'In the past, while volunteers were told about the experiments in which they took part, many of the actual records and reports of the experiments were, quite justifiably, kept secret in the interests of national security. Understandably, this has fuelled the concerns and uncertainties'.

Volunteers who wish to pursue their inquiries can also ask to visit Porton, accompanied by a friend, relative, lawyer, doctor, member of parliament, or other supporter. They can then inspect the relevant records at Porton, or discuss the experiments with a member of staff in person.

It appears that more volunteers now want to find out about their experiments. In the 'few years' before the helpline was established in February 1998, 'about 150' volunteers had enquired about the tests, and, according to Porton, 'sometimes out of curiosity, but sometimes because they have concerns about their health and wonder whether there is a link'.[8] However, in the two years since it was opened, around 250 former volunteers have contacted the helpline requesting information, and around ten have gone further and visited Porton to discuss their tests.[9]

The Ministry of Defence has also admitted that its keeping of another set of crucial documents which are important to the human 'guinea pigs' has not been as rigorous as it should have been. Each member of the armed forces has a Service Medical Record, which should be a complete account of all the medical examinations and illnesses which he or she has experienced during their time in the military. These documents are maintained by the army, navy, airforce – depending which service the individual was in – and are stored outside of Porton. These papers could have recorded details of the experiments and medical examinations which the volunteers underwent at Porton, but unfortunately, they do not. The MoD says that before the late 1980s, these Service Medical Records were only marked to show that an individual had attended Porton, and nothing else. 'And in some cases, even that did not happen,' the ministry adds.[10] Porton has admitted that 'concern has been expressed, from time to time' that these medical records fail to show that individuals have been volunteers at the installation.[11]

NOTES

The letters PRO in front of a reference mean that the document is in the Public Record Office. The letters PQ stand for Parliamentary Question. Unless specifically stated that the PQs were answered in the House of Lords or were oral replies, this refers to written answers in the House of Commons.

INTRODUCTION

1. Interview with the author, 11 February 2000.
2. Author's interview with former scientist who requested to remain anonymous.
3. Interview with the author, 1 June 2000.
4. The debate was initiated by the Countess of Mar on 12 December 1994.
5. Ministry of Defence manual 'Instructions for Record Reviewers', (annex B, appendix 7, chemical and biological warfare records). This manual is often updated. It was originally released to the Campaign for Freedom of Information (and later to the author in 1996) under the Code of Practice on Access to Government Information.
6. Public Record Office (hereafter PRO), PREM 13/1952, note to Prime Minister Harold Wilson, 27 February 1968.
7. PRO, AB 16/3680, letter from Ministry of Aviation to United Kingdom Atomic Energy Authority, 9 March 1961. As described in chapter 10, a series of non-nuclear explosions were done at Porton around this time to help the development of Britain's nuclear weapons. A local trader complained in 1961 that the explosions were damaging his windows, walls and ceilings. Under pressure from the trader's MP to solve this problem, a Whitehall official commented that 'the War Office's chief concern in all this must be to avoid any public outcry since our Porton establishment, dealing in chemical and biological warfare, is already sufficiently unpopular'. Any ideas from other civil servants would 'be most welcome since our efforts so far have clearly failed to silence all critics'.
8. *Veterans at Risk: the health effects of mustard gas and lewisite*, Institute of Medicine (National Academy Press, 1993), page 28. This states that the subjects of these tests were mainly scientists and other personnel at Edgewood Arsenal, the American equivalent of Porton.
9. *Human Experimentation – an overview on Cold War era programs*, US General Accounting Office, 28 September 1994 (GAO/T-NSIAD-94-266).
10. Speech by Art Eggleton, Defence Minister, 5 May 2000.
11. See, for instance, *Sunday Telegraph*, 25 July 1999.
12. *The Times* (1 April 1995) suggests that 'several thousand Kurdish prisoners' were used as human 'guinea pigs' and killed in chemical warfare tests in about 1990.

NOTES

13. *Jerusalem Post*, 15 January 1997.
14. Following the end of apartheid, the official Truth and Reconciliation Commission was set up to investigate the human rights abuses of the white-controlled regime. It held public hearings to interview people and scrutinised government documents. The TRC questioned scientists and staff involved in the programme (code-named Project Coast) and inspected internal papers. In its final report published in October 1998, the TRC makes no explicit reference to the existence of human tests. From the tone of the report, it would be surprising if the TRC had uncovered evidence of human experimentation, and then not mentioned them. (The results of the TRC's investigation into the CBW programme are in volume two, chapter six of its final report).
15. *Unit 731 – The Japanese Army's secret of secrets*, Peter Williams and David Wallace (Hodder & Stoughton, 1989), pp 45-7.
16. *The Times*, 29 March 2000. The protesters had discovered that sheep were being shot with high-velocity bullets to test the effects on skin and tissue at Porton.
17. Robert Maynard, quoted in *General and Applied Toxicology*, volume two, edited by Bryan Ballantyne, Timothy Marrs, and Paul Turner (Stockton Press, 1993), p. 1281.
18. 'Chemical Warfare Agents', précis no 10, 12 Training Regiment RCT, 'restricted', undated, but believed to be sometime in 1980s.
19. PRO, WO 188/802, 'History of Porton' by Lt Col Tony Kent, late 1950s, p. 100.
20. PRO, WO 32/20843, 'Experiments with physiological observers at Porton Down', note by the Director of Chemical Defence Research and Development, 2 February 1962.
21. Obviously, this refers to anti-personnel weapons, not the anti-plant agents such as defoliants.
22. PRO, WO 189/234, 'Physiological methods employed in testing war gases', Porton Memorandum 16, March 1942.
23. PRO, WO 188/802, 'History of Porton' by Lt Col Tony Kent, late 1950s, page 106. The comment was made in particular on the 'important contribution' of the human 'guinea pigs' in the Second World War, but it could equally apply to all the human subjects since 1916.

CHAPTER ONE *Pioneers of Pain*

1. Chemicals had been used in warfare many times prior to 1914, but it was not until the First World War that chemical science and military technology could be combined to influence a conflict significantly.
2. *Gas - the Story of the Special Brigade*, Major-General C H Foulkes (William Blackwood & Sons Ltd, 1934), p. 19 (hereafter referred to as Foulkes).
3. In his comprehensive study of gas in the Great War, Ludwig Haber points out that both sides manipulated the casualty figures for their own propaganda. For a detailed discussion of gas casualty figures throughout the war, see Haber's *The Poisonous Cloud: Chemical warfare in the First World War* (Clarendon Press, Oxford, 1986), chapter 10.
4. *An authentic account of the military history of Canada from the earliest days to the close of the war of the nations*, (Toronto, 1919), Volume three, chapter three on the Second battle of Ypres by A T Hunter, p. 71.
5. Foulkes, p. 28. It appears that the Germans only used the gas as an experiment 'to try it out thoroughly'. Another reason that the Germans were unable to capitalise on their success was that their own troops – some of whom did not have protective masks –

feared advancing into the gas cloud only 15 minutes after it had been unleashed. This was an early lesson in the limitations of chemical warfare.
6. ibid, pp. 19-20; PRO, WO 142/241.
7. ibid, p. 20.
8. His life is sketched in *Chemical Soldiers, British Gas Warfare in World War One*, Donald Richter (Leo Cooper, 1994), pp. 18-21. This book is an evocative account of the British Special Brigade, the 6,000-strong unit, led by Foulkes, which carried out more than 700 gas attacks, involving some 5,700 tons of chemicals, during the war.
9. Foulkes, pp. 17-18.
10. ibid, p. 22.
11. PRO, WO 142/284, notes by Leslie B Turner, 'Some of the more important developments in offensive chemical warfare in diary form', 1919.
12. *A Brief History of the Chemical Defence Experimental Establishment, Porton*, (March 1961), p. 1 (hereafter referred to as Trotman). This booklet was a shortened version of a longer history which had been written in the 1950s by Lt Col A E Kent (hereafter referred to as Kent). Porton superiors were unhappy with Kent's version and asked Cyril (C G) Trotman to produce a shortened version. An account of this incident is given in a foreword to Kent's history which is currently held in the PRO at WO 188/802; Trotman's booklet is at WO 188/785. He is not shown as the author in the booklet.
13. Foulkes, pp. 37-8.
14. ibid, pp. 42-4.
15. The trials showed, he believed, that the most effective way of discharging the chlorine was from a line of cylinders, placed 25 yards apart. If grouped like that, two cylinders opened at the same time would generate a 'very intense cloud' which 'clings to the ground in a remarkable manner and sinks into trenches.'
16. A British general later reported that 'the use of gas is not popular amongst our own men'. He believed that the military value of the cylinders was 'questionable' since the disadvantages outweighed the 'uncertain and varying' advantages. (PRO, WO 158/270, letter from General Barrow, commanding First Army, to adviser GHQ, 18 August 1916).
17. *A Higher Form of Killing – The Secret Story of Gas and Germ Warfare*, Robert Harris and Jeremy Paxman, (Triad Paladin, 1983), p. 15. This book is a good introduction to the whole subject of chemical and biological warfare since 1915, even though it was published some years ago.
18. Trotman, p. 2.
19. *Porton Down – 75 years of chemical and biological defence,* Gradon Carter, (HMSO, 1992), p. 7 (hereafter referred to as Carter).
20. Trotman, p. 2; PRO, WO 142/284, Notes by Leslie B Turner.
21. Trotman, p. 5.
22. Foulkes, pp. 87 and 237. According to the obituary of Livens in *The Times* on 5 February 1964, his 'expert knowledge of both chemistry and engineering was very useful in the development of new kinds of warfare.'
23. ibid, p. 105.
24. ibid, p. 273.
25. Trotman, p. 2. It was believed to be the 'best site on all counts (availability, suitability of the terrain, convenience to London, etc)'.
26. Carter, p. 8.

27. *ibid*, pp. 9-10; Trotman, p. 4; PRO, WO 32/11375.
28. Trotman, p. 4. Hydrogen sulphide however turned out to have little use in chemical warfare – it was prone to catching fire, corroded the cylinders, was too light to cling to the ground and could be easily smelt, quickly alerting the enemy.
29. Carter, pp. 9-10; Trotman, p. 11. He had been professor of organic chemistry at King's College in London.
30. PRO, WO 142/264, 'Report of Porton's activities in First World War by the establishment's Commandant Arthur Crossley' (hereafter referred to as Crossley Report), p. 9. Crossley wrote that the first experiment with artillery shells took place on 21 July 1916 when shells filled with an tear gas known as SK were fired into a wood and staff were sent in to discover how long the gas persisted.
31. Trotman, p. 9.
32. PQs, 13 January 1998; 5 November 1992
33. One Porton history states that 'some' early work on the toxicity of gases to man was done at Cambridge, but no details are given. (Trotman, p. 6).
34. Carter, p. 17.
35. PRO, WO 142/264, Crossley Report, p. 63. (A copy of the Crossley Report can also be found in the PRO at MUN 5/386/1650/14).
36. The 800 reports are kept in PRO, WO 142/209-211. The reports are known as the CCP series – Colonel Commandant Porton. Confusingly, the numbers in this series run up to 7798. The reports in the Public Record Office are not consecutive and it appears that other kinds of written material, such as letters and memos, were also given a number in the series.
37. The exact number is not certain. One Porton historian, Carter, says that 'some 147' toxic substances were studied, while Trotman suggests that it was 'nearly 200'.
38. PRO, WO 142/238, 'Report upon certain gases and vapours and their physiological effects, 1918', Chemical warfare department of the Ministry of Munitions of War. This report outlines the effects on humans and animals of 160 chemicals in total. One category – termed 'action on man' – implies that the chemical has been tested on humans; 96 compounds are listed in this category. Some of the data in the report appears to have been supplied by Britain's allies.
39. PRO, WO 142/332, List of compounds investigated as possible offensive agents by the Chemical Warfare Committee, but not recommended for adoption, between October 1917 and June 1919.
40. Trotman, p. 4.
41. Carter, p. 23.
42. PRO, WO 142/264, Crossley Report, p. 52.
43. Carter, p. 20.
44. PRO, WO 142/264, Crossley Report, p. 42.
45. *ibid*, pp. 32-3.
46. *ibid*. (See also PRO, WO 33/850 and 851).
47. PRO, WO 142/264, Crossley Report, p. 63. Although not stated, it is most likely that these people would have been exposed to gas in some way.
48. PRO, WO 142/264, Crossley Report, p. 82. A War Office official also praised the Porton staff who 'were constantly obliged by the nature of their work to expose themselves to gas in order to ascertain what its effects were likely to be on the enemy, and to

undertake experiments in cold blood, which involved risks at least as great as any they might have to face in the Field'. (PRO, WO 142/284, Notes by Leslie B Turner, 15 May 1919).

49. Trotman, p. 9.
50. The activities of the informal group known as the Old Portonians is recorded in the Royal Engineers Journal, (volume 109, 1995, pp. 162-7).
51. PRO, WO 142/264, Crossley Report, p. 82. He was later to describe Porton's 'organised effort' as a 'body of men working in perfect harmony as one man, each one with a single purpose in his daily work'. (Old Portonians, Royal Engineers Journal, (volume 109, 1995), p. 165).
52. Kent, p. 7.
53. ibid, p. 7.
54. 'Some recollections of Porton in World War One', Sir Austin Anderson, Journal of Royal Army Medical Corps, volume 118 (3), ps 173-7 (1972); Kent, p. 7. (Kent's comment about the mess bills was edited out by Porton, although it is still visible in the text).
55. Trotman, p. 8; *Joseph Barcroft, 1872-1947*, Kenneth J Franklin (Blackwell, Oxford, 1953), p. 103. He was to remain associated with Porton until his death in 1947. Porton paid tribute to him when he died, saying 'this great gentleman and great man of science...did much to assist the cause of chemical warfare'. (PRO, WO 195/9354).
56. This description is by Sir Rudolph Peters (*Joseph Barcroft, 1872-1947*, Kenneth J Franklin (Blackwell, Oxford, 1953), p. 104).
57. This account is drawn from several sources, including Kent, p 15; The Armed Forces Chemical Journal, September-October, 1959, p. 31; J B S Haldane, *Callinicus: A Defence of Chemical Warfare* (London, 1925), pp. 75-77; *Joseph Barcroft, 1872-1947*, Kenneth J Franklin (Blackwell, Oxford, 1953), pp. 107-9, Journal of Hygiene, 1931, volume 31, pp. 1-34, and PRO, WO 188/361. Barcroft's own report of this experiment – dated 10 December 1917 – can be found among Porton's official reports in PRO, WO 142/210 (CCP 2989). Interestingly, he does not name himself as being the human in the experiment.
58. The chamber was said to have filled with at least one part in two thousand of hydrogen cyanide. More recently, Porton scientists have commented that the experiment 'appeared conclusive', but was 'marred' by the survival of the dog the next morning. 'Some doubt has been cast on the concentration of hydrogen cyanide to which Barcroft was exposed, in the light of his almost complete absence of symptoms'. (*Chemical Warfare Agents: Toxicology and Treatment*, Timothy C Marrs, Robert Maynard and Frederick Sidell, (John Wiley & Sons, 1996), p. 206).
59. Barcroft's papers, letter to his wife, 3 June 1918. Barcroft added that after the King's remark, 'I felt like the clown in the circus with all the generals standing around whom I felt would be the legitimate objects for such language.'
60. Barcroft's papers, letter from Lloyd George, 10 January 1919.
61. Kent, p. 15.
62. J B S Haldane, *Callinicus: A Defence of Chemical Warfare* (London, 1925), p. 74.
63. PRO, WO 142/264, Crossley Report, pp. 29-30.
64. *Chemical Warfare Agents: Toxicology and Treatment*, Timothy C Marrs, Robert Maynard and Frederick Sidell, (John Wiley & Sons, 1996), p. 185.
65. Foulkes, p. 52.

Notes

66. The estimate of six comes from p. 43 of *The Problem of Chemical and Biological Warfare*, volume 1 (the rise of CB weapons), Stockholm International Peace Research Institute (SIPRI), Almqvist & Wiksell, Stockholm, 1971, (hereafter referred to as SIPRI, volume 1). Foulkes, p. 112, gives the figure of 10. He adds that the Germans believed that it was 20 times as toxic as chlorine.
67. *ibid*, pp. 112-3.
68. PRO, WO 142/266, Special Brigade Operations on the enemy, Transcript of notes dictated by Colonel Cummins, June 1917.
69. PRO, WO 142/99.
70. PRO, WO 95/121, War Diary, Third Battalion, Special Brigade, 30 June / 1 July 1916.
71. Foulkes, pp. 112-3.
72. PRO, WO 142/210, with 'Concentrations of phosgene produced in the open by the explosion of Livens' Drums filled with phosgene', CCP 2781, November 1917.
73. PRO, WO 142/210, 'Report on the experiments on the penetration of German respirators by dilute gas', CCP 3439, February 1918.
74. PRO, WO 142/211, 'Chamber experiments on the penetration of German respirator by phosgene', CCP 5675, September 1918.
75. Foulkes, p. 114.
76. A M Prentiss, *Chemicals in War* (New York, 1937), quoted on p. 41 of SIPRI volume 1.
77. The chemical names are diphenylchloroarsine (DA), diphenylcyanoarsine (DC) and 10-Chloro-5,10-dilhydrophenarsazine (DM).
78. PRO, WO 142/211, 'Chamber experiments on the penetration of the German respirator by DA and DM', CCP 4676, June 1918. In one respect, the results were mixed – the respirators were more effectively penetrated by DM (adamsite) than DA at the weaker concentrations, but the other way round when the dose was stronger.
79. PRO, WO 142/211, 'The persistence of the "effective state" of concentrations of DA and DM in chamber experiments', CCP 5266, July 1918.
80. Foulkes discusses the M devices and DA/DM on pp. 249-254.
81. The M device worked on the thermo-generator principle – the chemical was distilled into the atmosphere as a vapour which immediately condensed into an aerosol cloud. The 'germ' of the 'new and very valuable' idea of the M devices had originated from one of Foulkes' officers who, in a 'spirit of investigation', put a pinch of DA on the hot plate of a stove in his room. 'The result was so remarkable that everyone was driven out of the house immediately,' recalled Foulkes, p. 250.
82. PRO, WO 142/210, 'Trials of chemical thermo-generators', (CCP 3616), February 1918.
83. PRO, WO 142/211, 'Trials of chemical thermo-generators', (CCP 4543/6110).
84. *ibid*.
85. *ibid*.
86. *ibid*.
87. SIPRI, volume 1, p. 46.
88. *The Problem of Chemical and Biological Warfare*, volume 2 (CB Weapons Today), Stockholm International Peace Research Institute (SIPRI), (Almqvist & Wiksell, Stockholm, 1973), p. 46 (hereafter referred to as SIPRI, volume 2).
89. Foulkes, p. 263.
90. PRO, WO 142/99; WO 32/5176.

91. This version of the story is reproduced from *Callinicus: A Defence of Chemical Warfare*, J B S Haldane, (London, 1925), pp. 48-9.
92. PRO, WO 142/264, Crossley Report, p. 73.
93. PRO, WO 142/211, 'The sensitiveness of the skin to lewisite and HS in normal persons and in persons previously exposed to HS', CCP 5817, September 1918.
94. Foulkes, pp. 272-3.
95. *ibid*, p. 266.
96. PRO, WO 142/211, 'Experiments on the influence of certain other odours on the detection of mustard gas by the sense of smell', CCP 6062.
97. PRO, WO 142/211, 'Experiments in the chamber on the "fatigue" of the sense of smell in atmospheres of mustard gas', CCP 5206. There were 54 exposures of observers in these experiments, although this may not be the total number of observers used in these tests.
98. PRO, WO 142/211, 'Experiments to determine the concentrations of mustard gas in relation to the times of exposure necessary to produce eye effects on man', CCP 5376.
99. PRO, WO 142/211, 'Errors in the data regarding concentrations given in former reports on chamber experiments with mustard gas', CCP 6002.
100. SIPRI, volume 1, p. 57.
101. 'Medical Manual of Defence against chemical agents', Ministry of Defence, HMSO, 1987, quoted in *Chemical Warfare Agents: Toxicology and Treatment*, Timothy C Marrs, Robert Maynard and Frederick Sidell, (John Wiley & Sons, 1996), p. 185.
102. PRO, WO 142/254, 'History of the Anti-Gas Department', Lieutenant-Colonel H S Raper, Superintendent, January 1919; WO 142/284, Notes by Leslie B Turner, May 1919. Dr B R W Pinsent served as a captain in the Anti-gas Department during the war. He later published a privately printed 31-page history of the department, in which he describes a variety of tests. It is kept in the Imperial War Museum (P374T). His papers appear to be the only ones available in the museum relating to the scientific side of chemical warfare in the First World War.
103. It cannot be stated definitely when Britain first conducted chemical warfare experiments on humans. Before the First World War, some experiments had been conducted in Britain after the question of using chemicals for military purposes was raised. However official accounts do not show whether or not the chemicals used in the experiments were tested on humans, (PRO, WO 188/357; WO 142/240).
104. PRO, WO 142/266. J B S Haldane, a well-known scientist (and in time a noted defender of chemical warfare), has also described some of the early tests in which chlorine was released in a makeshift laboratory – a small glass-fronted room, like a greenhouse – in a converted hospital. He had been sent over to France by the British high command to investigate possible protection against gas immediately after the first German chemical assault in April 1915. *Callinicus: A Defence of Chemical Warfare*, J B S Haldane, (London, 1925), pp. 67-9.
105. Ernest Rudge, Chemistry in Britain, 20: 2, February 1984, pp. 138-140.
106. *ibid.*
107. PRO, WO 142/284, notes by Leslie B Turner, May 1919.
108. PRO, WO 33/1072, 'Report on German chemical warfare organisation and policy, 1914-18', Brigadier General Harold Hartley, (probably written 1921-2 and secret until 1976), p 45; WO 142/284, Notes by Leslie B Turner, May 1919. Hartley, who was a

legendary figure in British chemical warfare for some years, went to Berlin in 1921 to debrief German scientists.
109. Brig-Gen Sir J E Edmonds and Lieutenant-General R Maxwell-Hyslop, 'Military Operations, France and Belgium, 1918', volume 5, *History of the Great War*, (HMSO, 1947).
110. For more discussion of the success or failure of gas on the war, see chapter 11 of Ludwig Haber's *The Poisonous Cloud – Chemical Warfare in the First World War* (Clarendon Press, Oxford, 1986) and SIPRI, volume 1, pp. 140-1.
111. According to the most reliable calculations, there were at least 1.2 million gas casualties in the war, of which only seven percent – 90,000 – died. It is estimated that gas killed around two percent of all those who died in the Great War.
112. Carter, p. 25.
113. PRO, WO 142/275, an account of the development of weapons used in trench warfare, 1914-18, Lt Col Brothers, August 1918, introduction of chapter four, The Livens gas projector – its use and development.
114. Trotman, p. 9. He records: 'The frustration arose through lack of clear definition of responsibilities vis-à-vis other departments concerned with gas warfare and the absence of channels for direct liaison with the users of gas in France.'
115. PRO, WO 142/264, Crossley Report, p. 78.
116. Foulkes, pp. 272-5.
117. Carter, pp. 24 and 26.
118. Barcroft's papers, letter to his wife, 12 November 1918.

CHAPTER TWO *The Pursuit of Bodies*

1. *Porton Down – 75 years of chemical and biological defence*, Gradon Carter, (HMSO, 1992), p. 27 (hereafter referred to as Carter).
2. PRO, WO 32/5185, 'Policy regarding use of poison gas in warfare and of its possible use in India'. Minute (no. 73) to Secretary of State from CIGS, March 1920.
3. It was chaired by Lieutenant-General Sir Arthur Holland. The report of the committee on the chemical warfare organisation is a declassified document, but it is unclear if it is in the PRO.
4. PRO, T 161/171.
5. PRO, WO 33/1014, 'Second report of the Secretary of the chemical warfare committee, for the year ending March 31, 1922', p. 55.
6. PRO, WO 33/1028, 'Third report of the Secretary of the chemical warfare committee, for the year ending March 31, 1923', p. 11.
7. PRO, WO 142/211, 'Report on chamber experiments to determine duration of "effective penetrative state" of DA and DM clouds at low temperatures', CCP 6523, January 1919. This report was a record of previous experiments, since 'it has been ruled that observers are not to be utilised for the present'.
8. PRO, WO 33/987E, 'Report of the Secretary of the chemical warfare committee, for the period ending March 31, 1921', pp. 59-60. (This was the first in a series of annual reports – covering Britain's chemical warfare organisation – for the years between the First and Second World Wars. Collectively, they offer the most complete account of the work of Porton and other chemical warfare activity between 1921 and 1938).

9. PRO, WO 195/14846, 'History of the Service Volunteer Observer Scheme at Porton Down' (Porton Note 119), November 1959.
10. PRO, WO 33/1028, 'Third report of the Secretary of the chemical warfare committee, for the period ending March 31, 1923', p. 61.
11. Author's interview with former Porton scientist who requested to remain anonymous.
12. As an 'urgent' priority, Porton was trying to develop alternatives to exposing humans to chemicals in their testing of gas masks. (PRO, WO 33/1028, 'Third report of the Secretary of the chemical warfare committee, for the period ending March 31, 1923', pp. 61-2).
13. PRO, WO 163/29, 'Memorandum by the conditions of employment of personnel engaged in chemical warfare research and experiment by the Master-General of the Ordnance (with assistance from the Porton Commandment)', December 1923, précis 1158, p. 369.
14. PRO, WO 163/29, 'Decisions of the 326th meeting of the Army Council, December 1923', p. 25.
15. PRO, WO 163/30, 'Memorandum on the exposure to gas of personnel of the chemical warfare experimental station' by Porton's Commandant, Colonel S W H Rawlins, January 1924, précis 1163, pp. 40-5; 'Decisions of the 328th meeting of the Army Council, January 1924', p. 4; WO 33/1049, 'Fourth annual report of the chemical warfare committee, for period ending 31 March, 1924', p. 70.
16. PRO, WO 33/1049, 'Fourth annual report of the chemical warfare committee, for period ending 31 March, 1924', p. 70.
17. PRO, WO 33/1078, 'Fifth annual report of the chemical warfare committee, for period ending 31 March, 1925', p. 77.
18. PRO, WO 33/1128, 'Sixth annual report of the chemical warfare research department, for period ending 31 March, 1926', p. 117.
19. PQ, 11 January, 1996. DCIs were introduced in 1964 when the ministries in charge of the individual military services were merged to form the new Ministry of Defence.
20. Defence Council Instructions 8/98 and 76/98, 'Volunteers for studies at CBD Sector, Porton Down, unclassified, programme for the periods 1 January to 5 June, and 29 June to 27 November 1998'. These were released to the author under the Code of Practice on Access to Government Information.
21. Defence Council Instructions numbers 41 and 76 from 1994. The latter is reprinted in a parliamentary question on 8 February, 1996. Other special requirements in recent years have been 'must bring own well-worn boots', 'no glasses or contact lenses' and must be '5ft 8ins-6ft tall'. All the DCIs have more or less the same wording. Until 1996, these DCIs appear to have been classified documents of some description; DCI 41/94 is for example marked 'restricted'.
22. Author's interview with former Porton scientist who requested to remain anonymous.
23. PRO, WO 195/14846, 'History of the Service Volunteer Observer Scheme at Porton Down' (Porton Note 119), November 1959. This document is 'mainly concerned with the difficulty of obtaining human volunteers and the efforts that have been made to surmount them'. An addendum covering the years from 1959 to 1965 is in PRO, WO 195/16136.
24. PRO, WO 33/1174, 'Eighth annual report of the chemical warfare research department, for period ending March 31, 1928', p. 107. This report added that once the supply of volunteers was rectified, it 'enabled progress to be made with the investigations'.

Notes

25. PRO, WO 195/15643, 'annual review of the work of the Chemical Defence Advisory Board to 30 June 1963'. The volunteers were needed for tests with incapacitating chemicals, such as LSD (see chapter eight).
26. These are the percentages of the numbers of volunteers who actually took part in the experiments, compared to the number which had been initially requested by Porton: 1994 – 73%; 1995 – 77%; 1996 – 47%; 1997 – 71%; 1998 – 67% (see *Guardian*, 10 March 2000). These figures do not strictly reflect the actual number of volunteers as some military personnel volunteer for the experiments, but are then unable to take part for a variety of reasons.
27. Interview with the author, 2 February 2000.
28. Interview with the author, 6 June 2000.
29. Sections of this film were broadcast by Observer Films in *The Secrets of Porton Down*, 11 October 1994. This film – originally classified as 'restricted' – has now been declassified by Porton, and a copy was obtained by the author, who worked on the Observer programme.
30. Interview with the author, 25 February 2000 and letter to the author, 17 September 1999.
31. PRO, WO 195/16686, statement on volunteer observer scheme at Porton, 1968.
32. Author's interview with former scientist who requested to remain anonymous.
33. *The Times*, 25 February 1984, and *Observer* 26 February 1984.
34. *New Scientist*, 22 March 1984.
35. The testimonies of volunteers interviewed for this book underline that many of them were under 25 when they went to Porton. This is backed up by evidence from Porton documents with two of their studies into the motives of volunteers (outlined later in this chapter) giving the average age of volunteers as 22.
36. It is known, for example, that in February 1937, the question of the age of the volunteers was raised by commanding officers 'since it was considered undesirable to use [Naval] ratings under 18 years of age'. In the following year, however, Porton's Commandant had to stipulate that the volunteers must be over 18. (PRO, WO 195/14846, 'History of the Service Volunteer Observer Scheme at Porton Down', Porton Note 119, November 1959.)
37. It seems that the appeals for the years before 1945 have not been retained in the Public Record Office. However, it would be unlikely that the wording of such appeals would be more explicit before 1945 than afterwards. It is noticeable that any detail given was of Porton's defensive research, with no hint of its offensive work to develop chemical weapons.
38. Letter from J C Baker (for Air Commodore, Director of Manning) to commanding officers of units dated 12 February 1953 (copy of letter released to David Atkinson, MP for Bournemouth East, by Porton Down, 6 December 1996).
39. PRO, WO 195/16136, the service volunteer observer scheme at CDEE from 1959 to 1965, addendum to Porton Note 119. The 'administrative instructions for the attachment of army personnel to Porton as volunteers for tests, December 1963' are reproduced as an annex.
40. Defence Council Instruction (Army) no. 37 of 1964, covering the period May to August 1964, reproduced as an annex in PRO, WO 195/16136. The version which was posted on the units' notice board was also reproduced as an annex.

NOTES

41. Noticeboard information for chemical warfare – volunteers for tests at Porton, date stamped September 1967. Copy – along with Defence Council Instruction 439 – released to David Atkinson MP by Porton Down, 6 December 1996. Porton stated that this DCI had been issued in 1967.
42. PRO, WO 32/20843, 'Conditions for experiments with physiological experiments at CDEE', attachment to letter from Porton director, Eric Haddon, to War Office, 17 August 1961. It is uncertain who wrote the attachment.
43. As before, it is difficult to judge what warnings were given in appeals before 1945 since they do not seem to have been retained in the Public Record Office. But once again, it would seem improbable that the warnings would be clearer before 1945 than afterwards.
44. A Porton document from the 1950s shows that each of the three military services used different wording in the appeals which were circulated around their units. The Army and RAF mention that the tests are 'carried out under expert medical supervision and any physical discomfort which may result from them is usually very slight', whereas the Navy simply says that the tests 'are carefully planned and are carried out under medical supervision', without mentioning any 'physical discomfort' of any kind. (Letter from J C Baker, for Air Commodore, Director of Manning, to commanding officers of units, 12 February 1953; untitled and undated document from the 1950s 'outlining the procedures followed for recruitment and day-to-day administration of the volunteer programme' – both released to David Atkinson MP by Porton Down, 6 December 1996).
45. PRO, WO 195/16136, 'The service volunteer observer scheme at CDEE from 1959 to 1965,' addendum to Porton Note 119.
46. Noticeboard information for chemical warfare – volunteers for tests at Porton, date stamped September 1967, released to David Atkinson MP.
47. Figures taken from Defence Council Instructions 41/1994 and 8/1998 and PQ, 7 March 1995. The PQ stated that at that time, the rate of payment per test before tax was £1.70 and that 'the number of tests in any study vary between about a minimum of 100 to a maximum of 400 as studies vary between three days to four weeks in duration'.
48. PQ, 22 March 1984.
49. Author's interview with former Porton scientist who requested to remain anonymous.
50. PRO, WO 195/14846, 'History of the Service Volunteer Observer Scheme at Porton Down,' Porton Note 119, November 1959. This document, along with an update for the years between 1959 and 1965 (PRO, WO 195/16136), charts the amounts of pay and leave received by Porton volunteers over the years.
51. PRO, WO 195/16136, 'The service volunteer observer scheme at Porton Down from 1959 to 1965', addendum to Porton Note 119.
52. Interview with the author, 3 March 1996. In a letter on 16 April 1996, Porton confirmed that during 14-18 July 1952, Ross did indeed take part in a 'study to assess the effects of inhalation of sarin (GB) on respiration and the level of activity of the enzyme, acetyel cholinesterase, present in blood' during which he breathed in a concentration of sarin for two and a half minutes.
53. Interview with the author, 5 February 1997. He does not believe that he has suffered any ill problems because of these experiments.
54. PRO, WO 195/15070, 'The "Volunteer" personality', Porton Note 173, November 1960. The volunteers' answers were compared with a control sample of 63 other military personnel.

NOTES

55. The psychological character of the volunteers had became an important question in the early 1960s when Porton started to test mind-altering drugs, such as LSD, on the men (see chapter eight).
56. PRO, WO 195/15638, 'A study of the personality and intelligence of service volunteers at Porton', Porton Technical Paper 857, June 1963. The study was conducted between August 1960 and November 1961.
57. PRO, WO 189/167, 'Further studies of the service volunteer at Porton', Porton Technical Paper 950, March 1966. According to Porton, this was the last formal piece of research into the motives of volunteers.
58. PRO, WO 195/12218, 'Psychological effects of a G-agent on men', Porton Technical Paper 322, March 1953.
59. PRO, WO 195/12493, 'Psychological effects of a G-agent on men', Second Report. Porton Technical Paper 378, September 1953.
60. Author's interview with former Porton scientist who requested to remain anonymous.
61. PRO, WO 195/15638, 'A study of the personality and intelligence of service volunteers at Porton', Porton Technical Paper 857, June 1963. As part of this study, 471 individuals were questioned about their motives for volunteering between August 1960 and November 1961. A 1965 report stated that 'some 15 percent' of volunteers 'return for a second period of attachment' (PRO, WO 195/16136).
62. PQ, 24 June 1994. This stated that 'there is no restriction on the number of times a volunteer may return to Porton to participate in studies, but a volunteer cannot re-attend to participate in the same study for scientific and statistical reasons'.
63. Interview with the author, 9 March 1996.
64. PQs, 24 June 1994; 20 December 1994. The MoD stated: 'Female service personnel have been invited to participate in the human volunteer programme since May 1972'. The first did so in November of that year. The only reason identified for the lifting of the bar was 'a change in perception of the importance of female Service personnel'.
65. It is also known that at the Suffield chemical warfare establishment run jointly by Porton and the Canadians, women volunteers were barred from being human 'guinea pigs' in gas tests during the Second World War. They were 'not acceptable for scientific reasons', although again no explanation is apparent. (PRO, WO 195/14846, 'History of the Service Volunteer Observer Scheme at Porton Down', Porton Note 119, November 1959; *Deadly Allies: Canada's Secret War 1937-47*, John Bryden (1989, McCelland & Stewart Inc), p. 167).
66. PRO, WO 195/15697, 33rd meeting of the Biology Committee, September 1963.
67. PRO, WO 195/16161, first meeting of the Applied Biology Committee, November 1965.
68. Interview with the author, 31 May 2000.
69. *A Brief History of the Chemical Defence Experimental Establishment, Porton*, (March 1961), p. 11 (hereafter referred to as Trotman).
70. ibid, pp. 17-18.
71. Gradon Carter and Graham Pearson, *Journal of the Royal United Services Institute*, February 1996, p. 60.
72. Trotman, p. 18.
73. ibid, pp. 16-7; Carter, p. 32.
74. Trotman, p. 17.

NOTES

75. PRO, WO 195/14846, 'History of the Service Volunteer Observer Scheme at Porton Down', Porton Note 119, November 1959.
76. The physiological sub-committee, along with the medical sub-committee, of the main chemical warfare committee were responsible for human experiments. The minutes and papers of these two committees do not appear to be in the PRO; they have either been destroyed or not passed over to the PRO. (PRO, WO 33/1443, 'Sixteenth annual report of the chemical defence research department, March 31, 1936', p. 36).
77. PRO, WO 195/14846, 'History of the Service Volunteer Observer Scheme at Porton Down', Porton Note 119, November 1959.
78. PRO, WO 188/470, Letter from Porton's commandant, 22 May 1936. The commandant stated: 'During the past five and half years, 2,106 exposures to [tear gases] have been carried out in this station – 1,114 in the field, and 992 in the gas chamber.' He estimated that a similar number had been exposed between 1925 and 1930. Some of these totals included respirator fitting tests.
79. In 1931/2, military officials reported: 'Tests have been made of the sensitivity to mustard gas of 302 members of the Porton staff... Further experiments are in hand.' In the following year, they reported that 'the sensitivity of normal persons to mustard gas has been investigated by tests on 681 volunteers from the three Services'. In 1934/5, they reported that 'large scale trials to determine the sensitivity to mustard gas of British and Indian troops in India have now been carried out...a total of 590 observers being employed'. It may be possible that some of the subjects in these tests have been counted twice. (WO 33/1298, 'Twelfth report of the chemical defence research department, for the period ending March 31, 1932', p. 49; WO 33/1330, 'Thirteenth report of the chemical defence research department, for the period ending March 31', 1933, p. 46; WO 33/1389, 'Fifteenth report of the chemical defence research department, for the period ending March 31, 1935', p. 44).
80. 'Not a Proper Doctor', David Sinclair, (The Memoir Club, *British Medical Journal*, 1989), pp. 84-5.
81. Interview with the author, 11 June 1996.
82. Lewisite, an arsenical, had been discovered as a war gas by the Americans towards the end of the First World War. Like mustard gas, lewisite is a blister gas which burns the skin and eyes of humans. After much exploration, involving many human subjects being exposed to lewisite, it was recognised by Porton and others that mustard gas was the superior chemical weapon. (Descriptions of human experiments involving lewisite between the early 1920s and 1940 can be found in PRO, WO 188/52, WO 188/53, WO 188/472, and AVIA 15/891).
83. Interview with the author, 6 September 1999.
84. Interview with the author, 6 July 1996.
85. These cards were called jump cards. A picture of military personnel carrying them in a 1938 trial can be found in Carter, p. 34.
86. PRO, WO 208/2174, 'Classified list of compounds examined physiologically since 1919'. Porton Memorandum 15 (October 1941), part five.
87. Fraser receives a war pension, but it is not attributed to the Porton tests.
88. PRO, WO 33/1028, 'Third report of the Secretary of the chemical warfare committee, for the period ending March 31, 1923', pp. 61-2; WO 163/29, 'Memorandum by the Master-General of the Ordnance, December 17, 1923', précis 1158, pp. 369-371; WO 163/30, 'Memorandum by Porton's Commandant, Colonel S W H Rawlins, January 1924', précis 1163, pp. 40-5.

Notes

89. Rawlins argued other nations' ownership of 'new compounds, or known ones improved and reintroduced, must form a potential source of danger' to Britain's defences.
90. PRO, WO 33/1049, 'Fourth annual report of the chemical warfare committee, for period ending March 31, 1924', pp. 67-8; WO 33/1128, 'Sixth annual report of the chemical warfare research department, for period ending March 31, 1926', p. 107.
91. PRO, WO 188/54. Naturally-occurring poisons were just one of the sources for identifying putative poison gases. Another was monitoring the new compounds which were emerging from academic and industrial laboratories.
92. See for instance PRO, WO 188/54, 'Physiological examination of new compounds'.
93. PRO, WO 106/1148, letter from GHQ North Russia, Archangel, 7 September 1919; WO 32/5749, Churchill's handwritten note on 19 April 1919; WO 33/987, 'Report of the secretary of the chemical warfare committee, for period ending 31 March 1921', pages 42-6. Churchill was forced to defend the use of gas in Parliament in May 1919 when it came out into the open. For more details on how the M devices were used, see WO 106/1170.
94. PRO, WO 188/471, 'Abstract of report on harassing effects of particulate clouds of DC', Porton Report 1055, December 1932; also note on harassing effects of DC by N K Johnson, chief superintendent, to War Office, March 1933.
95. PRO, WO 188/53, 'Preliminary report on the detectability and tolerability of DM', Porton Report 329, March 1926; WO 188/49, symptomatology of action of DA in low concentrations on man, undated. Also WO 188/51, note on experiment on detectability by Surgeon Commander, RN, G R McCowen, superintendent of physiological department, June 1924.
96. PRO, WO 188/51, Report on T346 (a & b), Porton Report 143, April 1924. See also further experiments recorded in Porton Report 143A, June 1924. Many human experiments with these arsenicals can be found in WO 188/49, WO 188/50, 188/51 and WO 188/52.
97. See for example, PRO, PIN 15/4039, memorandum on gassing and its alleged relationship to the development of tuberculosis and other disabilities, J H Hebb, Director-General of Medical Services, Ministry of Pensions, January 1938.
98. PRO, WO 188/165; PIN 15/126.
99. PRO, PIN 15/127, extracts from ministerial meetings with representatives of war pensions committees, 3 July and 14 April 1930.
100. PRO, WO 188/265, 'After-effects of war gases (R/290/7)', Surgeon Commander Archibald Fairley, Superintendent, physiological department, July 1929. Fairley, of the Royal Navy, was head of the physiological department – and the human experiments – until 1951.
101. PRO, PIN 15/127, letter from Fairley to Dr G B Price, Ministry of Pensions, June 1929.
102. Discussion between Porton and the Ministry of Pensions over the arrangements can be found in PRO, PIN 15/126.
103. PRO, WO 188/265, 'Disability due to gas poisoning', (Porton Report 490), Surgeon Commander Fairley, acting superintendent, physiology department, June 1927; PRO, WO 33/1174, 'Eighth report of the chemical warfare research department, for the period ending March 31, 1928', page 109.
104. A month later, the War Office reiterated this view in a secret letter to the Ministry of Pensions: the pensioners examined at the medical boards had been 'few but it is generally agreed that the majority of gas pensioners are chest cases and that most of

these are due to mustard gas'. (PRO, PIN 15/126, Letter from the War Office, 25 July 1927 to Secretary of the Ministry of Pensions).

105. PRO, WO 188/265, 'After-effects of war gases' (R/290/7), Surgeon Commander Fairley, Superintendent, physiological department, July 1929.

106. PRO, WO 188/293, 'The after history of some cases of mustard gas poisoning', report by Colonel J C Kennedy, April 1928; WO 33/1204, 'Ninth annual report of the chemical warfare research department, for the year ending March 31, 1929', pp. 87-8.

107. PRO, WO 33/1204, 'Ninth annual report of the chemical warfare research department, for the year ending March 31, 1929', p. 88; WO 188/265, 'Residual effects of war gases', Porton's account of the American work, September 1928. Both accounts state that the board's conclusions were preliminary.

108. *Medical Aspects of Chemical Warfare* (Baltimore, Williams and Wilkins, 1925), quoted in *Veterans at Risk: the health effects of mustard gas and lewisite*, Institute of Medicine (National Academy Press, 1993).

109. His research was contained in two publications, *A Comparative Study of World War Casualties from Gas and other Weapons*, (US Government Printing Office, Washington DC, 1928) and *The Residual Effects of Warfare Gases* (with Philip Matz), (US Government Printing Office, Washington DC, 1933). Both are quoted in *Veterans at Risk: the health effects of mustard gas and lewisite*, Institute of Medicine (National Academy Press, 1993).

110. PRO, PIN 15/2959, Letter from Chief Superintendent of the Chemical Defence Research Department (London) to Ministry of Pensions, 16 March 1934 (in response to submissions by Dr W N Abbott, of Auckland Hospital, New Zealand – see also PIN 15/2960 and PIN 15/129).

111. PRO, PIN 15/2962, Letter from Ida Mann, FRCS, of Harley Street to British Legion, 15 January 1946. This file deals with the treatment of mustard gas keratitis between 1936 and 1949. Further cases, and discussion of the illness, can be found in PRO, PIN 15/4039.

112. Exact figures are difficult to divine. It appears, for example, from Ministry of Pensions files that 165 pensions were awarded between 1937 and 1944. A 1948 Porton report noted the work of a scientist, Ida Mann, who had analysed the records of one of the large London eye hospitals and found that between 1937 and 1943, 89 cases of delayed keratitis had been diagnosed in veterans of the 1914-18 war. Of these, 63 had been awarded pensions, with the majority of the rest under investigation. (PRO, PIN 15/2962, Note by Ministry of Pensions official, 24 March 1945; letter from Ministry of Pensions official H Parker to Douglas Veale, University Registry, Oxford, 26 March 1945; WO 188/723, eye lesions due to mustard gas, monograph 9.134, pp. 5 & 6).

113. It was highlighted by Reginald Bickerton, an ophthalmic surgeon, in an article 'New cases of war blindness due to mustard gas' in the British Medical Journal (27 October 1935, volume 3851, pp. 769-770). British chemical warfare officials drew attention to the article in their annual report for that year (PRO, WO 33/1389, 'Fifteenth report of the chemical defence research department, for the period ending March 31, 1935', p. 45).

114. PQ, 4 December 1996. Porton cites two papers for this observation – one in 1940 by T J Phillips in the *Proceedings of the Royal Society of Medicine*, volume 33, pages 229-232 and the other in 1942 by W F Hughes in the *Archives of Ophthalmology*, volume 27, pages 582-601. It is highly unlikely that Porton would have been unaware of these developments in the scientific literature.

115. The main thrust of human experiments with mustard gas occurred before 1945. Even after the mid-sixties, mustard gas experiments 'were undertaken to determine the

effectiveness of decontamination procedures and protective measures'. Although exact figures are not available, Porton estimates that 'about 70 percent of volunteers in the late 1960s and 1970s were involved' in mustard gas experiments. This estimate however appears to be too high. (PQ, 5 July 1995).

116. PRO, WO 33/987E, 'Report of the Secretary of the chemical warfare committee, for the period ending March 31, 1921', p. 63; WO 33/1153, 'Seventh report of the chemical warfare research department, for the period ending March 31, 1927', p. 106.

117. See, for example, discussion on page 107 of 'Eighth annual report of the chemical warfare research department, for period ending March 31, 1928' (PRO, WO 33/1174).

118. See for example, PRO, WO 188/293, 'Effects of the vapour of H on the human skin', Porton Report 483, May 1927; 'Interim report on the absorption of H vapour by clothing', Porton Report 527, October 1927.

119. PRO, WO 188/294, 'Experiments to ascertain the length of time heavy winter clothing will protect the skin from large drops of liquid mustard gas', Porton Report 710, March 1929, and further report, Porton Report 727, June 1929.

120. PRO, WO 188/293, 'Observations on the exposure of personnel in service dress to mustard gas vapour in a closed chamber', Porton Report 785, February 1930; WO 33/1272, 'Eleventh annual report of the chemical defence research department, March 31, 1931', part 2, paragraph 416.

121. PRO, WO 188/293, Letter from Porton's commandant to the controller of chemical warfare research, 13 April 1927. His comments were based on the observations of the head of the physiological department, which was responsible for the human tests.

122. PRO, WO 188/294, 'Report on experimental mustard gas burns sustained by Privates G Allmark and G Evans, both of the 2nd Bn, Cheshire Regiment, March 1928'.

123. There were frequent reports on this work, for example in PRO, WO 188/294; WO 188/51; WO 188/52 and the annual reports in WO 33.

124. PRO, WO 188/294, 'An investigation of the use of certain remedies in the mitigation or prevention of a mustard burn', Porton Report 726, June 1929.

125. For example, at least 81 men were tested in two experiments (PRO, WO 188/294, 'Further report on the use of bleach to prevent or mitigate mustard burns on the skin', Porton Report 756, October 1929; 'Bleach Ointment as a decontaminating agent – present position', Porton Report 792, March 1930).

126. PRO, WO 188/294, 'Experiments to investigate the use of bleach (dry or in paste form) in the prevention or mitigation of liquid mustard burns', Porton Report 676, January 1929.

127. For examples, see PRO, WO 188/68, 'Contamination of boots with mustard gas', Porton Report 334, 1926; WO 188/66, 'Fifth Report on Protection against mustard gas', Porton Report 312, November 1925; PRO, WO 188/293, 'Report on the physiological examination of HS manufactured from cracked oil gas', February 1928.

128. *Air Power and colonial control, the Royal Air Force 1919-39*, David E Omissi, (Manchester University Press, 1990), pp. 206-7. Long accounts of the Italian use of chemical weapons in this war appear in SIPRI, volume 1, pp. 142-6, and volume 4 (CBW disarmament negotiations 1920-70), pp. 175-186), Stockholm International Peace Research Institute (SIPRI), (Almqvist & Wiksell, Stockholm), 1971.

129. A detailed account is given by Paul Harris in 'British Preparations for offensive chemical warfare 1935-9', Journal of the Royal United Services Institute, 125: 2, June 1980, pp. 56-62, especially various Treasury files in PRO, T161. See also Gradon Carter and Graham Pearson, Journal of the Royal United Services Institute, February 1996, pp. 60-

1 and p. 2 of 'The United Kingdom's declaration of past activities relating to its former offensive chemical weapons programme to the Chemical Weapons Convention', May 1997.
130. PRO, WO 195/10217, A review of compounds studied in chemical warfare research, Porton Memorandum 33, (by A E Childs, Porton's chief superintendent), February 1949.
131. Carter, p. 34.

CHAPTER THREE Burning Issues

1. From a memo to Lord Cherwell, his scientific adviser, in August 1941, quoted in *British Army Review*, Major Ian Toler, August 1990.
2. PRO, WO 106/1626, Telegrams (numbers 11 and 12) from Vauban Madelon (British Mission in France) to War Office, 17 September 1939.
3. Later in the war, the Germans became very concerned when they mistook American stocks of Gas – in reality, petrol – for chemical weapons. (*Porton Down – 75 years of chemical and biological defence*, Gradon Carter, (HMSO, 1992), p. 41 (hereafter Carter); *A Brief History of the Chemical Defence Experimental Establishment, Porton*, (March 1961), p. 22 (hereafter referred to as Trotman); *Most Secret War – British scientific intelligence 1939-45*, R V Jones, (Hamish Hamilton, 1978), pp. 125-6).
4. Responsibility for protecting the civilian population against gas attack had become Porton's concern as early as 1926 (PRO, WO 188/144).
5. By spring 1940, military chiefs again warned that it would be impossible to retaliate with chemical weapons until the following year, unless production was immediately speeded up (Trotman, p. 23; PRO, WO 163/49, memorandum by CIGS on offensive chemical warfare, OS 41, no date, but sometime between January and May 1940).
6. Paul Harris, Journal of the Royal United Services Institute, 125: 2, June 1980, p. 61.
7. PRO, PREM 3/88/3.
8. PRO, AVIA 22/1218.
9. Trotman, pp. 21, 23; Carter, pp. 39-40.
10. PRO, AVIA 15/361, 'Report outlining Porton's organisation and structure', January 1940, Sir Keith Price to Brigadier Goldney (pp. 32-4 cover the physiology department). Porton was reorganised at about this time.
11. PRO, WO 188/624, 'Porton priority programme of research: brief review: 12 July 1940'. It adds that twenty volunteers a week were required at that time.
12. PRO, WO 188/802, Kent history, p. 100. Very few documents describing Second World War experiments are in Porton's classmarks at the Public Record Office (WO 188 and 189), and almost all of these cover the years 1939 and 1940.
13. PRO, WO 195/14846, 'History of the Service Volunteer Observer Scheme at Porton Down' (Porton Note 119), November 1959.
14. *ibid.*
15. PRO, WO 166/7952, 'War Diary of the Second Chemical Warfare Group, Royal Engineers, March 1942'. This, and the war diaries of other chemical warfare companies, describe various trials and activities with Porton, some of which took place around the country.

16. Interviews with the author, 8 July 1996, 24 July 1996, and 2 October 1996. Hall was tested at Porton between January and April 1940, and has since claimed a war pension as he has been suffering badly from bronchitis.
17. Interview with the author 21 October 1998.
18. Interview with the author, 10 October 1998.
19. Interview with the author, 25 November 1995; Interview and correspondence with Observer Films, 1994.
20. Interview with the author, 21 October 1998. Case believed that he was at Porton for over a week. He could not recall the chemical to which he exposed in the gas chamber, nor did he remember if he was told before the test what the gas was. He was winded by the gas and had to run around to regain his breathing properly. He said the other tests, with mustard gas and lewisite, were to find a treatment for the blisters. He did not think that the experiments harmed him in the long term.
21. PRO, WO 195/14846, 'History of the Service Volunteer Observer Scheme at Porton Down' (Porton Note 119), November 1959.
22. *'Collar the lot!' – How Britain interned and expelled its wartime refugees*, Peter and Leni Gilman, (Quartet Books, 1980), p. 257.
23. Interview with the author, 25 January 1997.
24. Interview with the author, 29 January 1997; letter to the author, 24 January 1997. Henson still has a copy of an official certificate which was given to him after the experiment. Signed by two Porton staff, it 'certifies' that he 'was exposed to a chemical warfare agent at the Chemical Defence Experiment Station, Porton, on 26 April 1941'. It adds that the 'nature of the CW agent was blister gas'. Another word before blister gas has been blanked out.
25. Interview with the author, 25 January 1997.
26. Arsine was dismissed as a possible replacement to phosgene in the war because it was less lethal and more difficult to turn into a liquid. One Porton report warned that 'although arsine is less lethal than phosgene, the danger of permanent ill effects is greater...even small doses of arsine are sufficient to cause anaemia'. (Carter, pp. 41-2; Trotman, pp. 21-2; SIPRI, volume 1, p. 80; PRO, WO 193/727 and WO 189/234, p. 27).
27. PRO, WO 195/14846, 'History of the Service Volunteer Observer Scheme at Porton Down' (Porton Note 119), November 1959.
28. Letter to Ken Livingstone MP, 3 December 1996. Porton stated that the general guidelines governing the employment of volunteers have developed since the 1920s. 'Changes have been made to them in response to the evolving requirements for ethical control of such studies which have also developed since the 1920s. We do not hold a detailed record of how guidelines have altered over this whole period.'
29. This account of these Australian experiments and the quotes of the participants are derived from four main sources. The first is a 1985 official report, 'Australian Field Trials With Mustard Gas', 1942-45, known as the Gillis Report, after its author Dr Richard Gillis. (He had been one of the chemists who worked on these trials, and was commissioned by the Australian government to produce a report on the experiments.) The second is a book by Bridget Goodwin, *Keen as Mustard: Britain's horrific chemical warfare experiments in Australia*, (University of Queensland Press, 1998). She also produced a documentary of the same name which was shown on Australian television in 1989 and in an adapted form as a BBC Horizon programme on 14 January 1991. The third is the autobiography of David Sinclair, *Not a Proper Doctor* (The Memoir Club, British Medical Journal, 1989). His memories of Porton and the Australian tests

comprise four chapters of his book. The fourth is from the series of official reports written during the war. These are entitled 'Chemical Defence (Australia) Reports or Notes'. It seems that at least 27 reports relate to the human experiments. These documents were sent back to Porton; none appear to have been placed in the British Public Record Office. Some of these reports have been obtained by the author from other sources, including CD Australia Reports 15, 20, 21 and 61.

30. This portrait comes from David Sinclair, his British deputy, in *Not a Proper Doctor*, (pp. 108-9). Australian member of the unit, Jack Legge, called him 'quite a remarkable man'. Gorrill has since died.

31. The human 'guinea pigs' at Townsville were the scientists themselves, some of whom 'sometimes suffered very severe internal and external injuries from toxic gases'. Before the move to Townsville, some human experiments had been carried out on students from Melbourne University. *Australia in the war of 1939-45: The role of science and industry* (series 4 (civil), volume 5), Professor D P Mellor (Canberra, Australian War Memorial, 1958), p. 378).

32. PRO, AVIA 15/893, Summary and conclusions of a report on 'Chemical warfare physiology under tropical conditions', March 1943.

33. Both the American and British anti-gas ointments failed to give substantial protection. Even the best ointments which were later developed in the war were not that successful in the tropics.

34. This description was by Sinclair, in *Not a Proper Doctor*, (p. 107), who added that Legge was 'subtle in argument and persuasive in direction'.

35. 'A clinical analysis of a series of mustard burns occurring under tropical conditions', C.D (Australia) Report 65, October 1944. Sinclair wrote that 'a considerable number' of volunteers had been exposed to mustard gas under tropical conditions at Innisfail between November 1943 and May 1944. Out of 258 men, at least 98 wore no protective clothing; all but seven were affected in their scrotum.

36. Details of the new system are contained in C.D Australia Report 42 (May, 1944), 'The assessment of casualties from vesicant agents'.

37. By exposing so many men to mustard gas in a controlled way, the scientists were able to shed more light on the incidence and type of symptoms caused by mustard gas. They showed that mustard gas could be absorbed through human skin and cause systemic poisoning in the body, most commonly nausea and in the more severe cases, vomiting. This systemic poisoning was more obvious because the gas had a greater effect on humans in the tropics. Sinclair commented that it was 'difficult to demonstrate the occurrence of systemic manifestations in cases of slight or moderate mustard burns in temperate climates'. By publishing this work in the British Medical Journal after the war, he believes that he was able to disseminate factual information about mustard gas, and the treatment of burns, to medical officers and doctors who may need it. (British Medical Journal 7 August 1948, pp. 290-4 and 19 March 1949, pp. 476-8).

38. Impregnated battledress was seen as an alternative to the heavy impervious oilskin clothing which tired out soldiers quickly in hot weather or arduous exercise. For more details of impregnites, see an official monograph written in 1948 (PRO, WO 188/738) and Carter, pp. 46-8.

39. The impregnite was named Anti-Verm (a ruse to fool the enemy into believing that the substance was connected to anti-louse or insecticides). It turned into aniline. Sinclair describes how he later apologised to the men as he had had no idea that this would happen. A subsequent experiment involving eighteen men wearing the same clothing showed results of tiredness, weakness, unsteadiness and headaches amongst the men.

NOTES

One 24-year-old man collapsed and was taken to hospital, suffering 'mental confusion and unsteady gait', but he recovered rapidly once the clothing had been removed. A description of the incident and later experiment are in C.D Australia Report 18 (January, 1944), 'The toxicity of AV impregnated clothing, part one'.

40. A former British RAF Group Captain, John Hampshire, alleged in 1975 that 15 American convicts were killed in the experimental gas bombing of a small Australian island just before the Brook Island trial, but this claim has not been supported by other evidence. The US Department of Defence stated at the time that it had launched an investigation into his claims. However the department said in 1999 – in response to a request under the US Freedom of Information Act by the author – that no records or documents relating to this investigation could be found. (*Daily Mail*, 15 April 1975).

41. *Australia in the war of 1939-45: The role of science and industry* (series 4 (civil), volume 5), Professor D P Mellor (Canberra, Australian War Memorial, 1958), p. 377.

42. Their cases appear to be described in C.D Australia Report 37, May 1944, 'The systemic effects of mustard gas under tropical conditions, as seen in four cases of liquid contamination.'

43. *The Sun-Herald* (Australia), 19 June 1994. He had burns on his arm and neck from his time on the island.

44. Less is known about these trials. One is described in C.D Australia 60, February 1945, 'The comparative assessment of persistent traversing hazard in jungles contaminated with HT, HBD, and Levinstein H from dropped 65-lb bombs.'

45. Bridget Goodwin in her book, *Keen as Mustard* (p. 229), says that around 2,000 Australian service men had been tested. The Australian government does not have exact figures, but estimates the total to be around 750.

46. PRO, WO 106/4594A, Chemical warfare interim report 23, 29 November 1943, by Major General J S Lethbridge, GS Commander. This report commented that the conception of chemical warfare as an offensive weapon had changed dramatically since the First World War when its main attribute was 'nuisance value'. This enhanced offensive value was due, among other factors, to the greater effect of mustard gas on the human skin and the huge difficulties of protection in the tropics.

47. Early work in 1920/1 is described in PRO, WO 188/58. It seems to have been based in a small laboratory at the well-known resort of Dehra Dun in the foothills of the Himalayas in northern India. Humans were exposed to gas in a few tests.

48. At the start, staff doubted that 'suitable laboratory assistants will be forthcoming at the present rate of remuneration and on the temporary basis of employment; especially in the case of assistants for physiological work'. (PRO, WO 188/370, 'Progress report on CDRE (India) for the quarter ending March, 31 1930').

49. The Chemical Defence Research Establishment (India) 'pursued a programme, co-ordinated with that of Porton Down, on the problems of chemical warfare and chemical defence in hot climates and in the context of military action in India as well as the particular problems of individual protection for Indian troops'. In 1944, the Rawalpindi establishment was moved to Wellesley Barracks, Cannanore on the Kerala coast, south-west India (to be, it seems, in a more humid area). Ten more Porton scientists were sent out to the new station. This facility was closed before Indian independence in 1947, as Wellesley Barracks were given over to the new Indian Army. ('Britain's declaration of past chemical warfare activities to the Chemical Weapons Convention, May 1997', p. 136; Trotman, p. 26; other details of chemical warfare work in India during the war are in PRO, AVIA/888).

NOTES

50. Details of gas warfare in the British Empire just after the First World War are somewhat sketchy. In the Middle East, RAF chiefs wanted to drop gas bombs on 'recalcitrant Arabs' as an experiment in 1919. This was authorised by Churchill who believed that it was 'not necessary to use only the most deadly gases', advocating gases 'which cause great inconvenience and would spread a lively terror and yet would leave no serious permanent effects on most of those affected'. But there was a problem – the Air Ministry noted that 'although considerable time and trouble was expended on research during the war, we have not yet evolved suitable and practicable gas bombs for use from aircraft'. It appears that although the RAF did not drop chemical weapons, the Army did fire gas shells in 1920 against rebels in what is now Iraq. (PRO, WO 32/5184; WO 32/5191; *Air Power and Colonial Control, the Royal Air Force 1919-39*, David E Omissi, (Manchester University Press, 1990), especially pp. 160 and 206; SIPRI volume 1, p. 142).

51. Some officials were worried that the use of gas against the Afghans 'would have political and moral consequences of a very serious kind'. Churchill fumed that such objections were 'unreasonable', since 'gas is a more merciful weapon than high explosive shell, and compels an enemy to accept a decision with less loss of life than any other agency of war'. He argued, 'If it is fair war for an Afghan to shoot down a British soldier behind a rock and cut him in pieces as he lies wounded on the ground, why it is it not fair for a British artilleryman to fire a shell which makes the said native sneeze? It is really too silly.' By April 1920, the British authorities in India were still not prepared to use gas 'until the general question of the legitimacy or otherwise of the use of gas in warfare has been decided by the Cabinet'. However they did agree that the 'Army in India should be in a position to study gas warfare and to use it, if necessary, in retaliation'. (PRO file WO 32/5185; WO 188/58; *A Higher Form of Killing – the secret story of gas and germ warfare*, Robert Harris and Jeremy Paxman, (Triad Paladin, 1983), pp. 43-4).

52. PRO, WO 188/58, 'Report on Chemical warfare in India', Major W A Salt, Chemical Adviser, General Staff, Delhi, November 1920.

53. PRO, WO 33/987E, 'Report of the Secretary of the chemical warfare committee, for the period ending March 31, 1921', p. 63; WO 33/1298, 'Twelfth annual report of the chemical defence research establishment, for the period ending March 31, 1932', p. 48.

54. PRO, WO 33/1174, 'Eighth annual report of the chemical warfare committee, March 31, 1928', p. 107.

55. The complete reports of these experiments have evidently not yet been declassified. It is not known how the human subjects were exposed, or the full range of dosages they received. A preliminary 'small-scale' test was carried out in 1934 with 60 Indian and British soldiers. The British were also interested to find out if the susceptibility of the Europeans to the gas was related to the length of service in the dominion. It is unclear how this series of experiments continued after 1937. (PRO, WO 188/640 and 641, Quarterly progress reports of the Chemical Defence Research Establishment (India) between 1930 and 1940; WO 33/1330, 'Thirteenth report of the chemical defence research department, for the period ending March 31, 1933', p. 18; WO 33/1359, 'Fourteenth report of the chemical defence research department, for the period ending March 31, 1934', p. 14; WO 33/1389, 'Fifteenth report of the chemical defence research department, for the period ending March 31, 1935', p. 48; WO 33/1443, 'Sixteenth report of the chemical defence research department, for the period ending March 31, 1936', p. 37; WO 33/1484, 'Seventeenth report of the chemical defence research department, for the period ending March 31, 1937', p. 44)

56. PRO, WO 188/640 and 641. The Rawalpindi establishment produced at least 271 reports in a series known as CDRE (India) Reports, but few of them have been declassified.

NOTES

57. PRO, WO 33/1176, 'The effect of mustard gas vapour on eyes under Indian hot weather conditions', CDRE (India) Report 241, November 1942.
58. PRO, WO 33/1773, Research programme of CDRE (India) for first six months of 1943.
59. PRO, AVIA 15/893 and WO 33/1799, 'The appearances and treatment of mustard gas burns of the skin under Indian conditions', CDRE (India) Report 255, July 1943.
60. *Deadly Allies: Canada's Secret War 1937-47*, John Bryden (Toronto, Ontario, 1989), p. 173. This experiment is described in a British report dated 18 November 1943 which is in the US National Archives and Research Administration (NARA). Gas warfare reports were routinely distributed to other Allied nations. It seems that this report has not yet been placed in the British PRO.
61. Some of this account is drawn from *Deadly Allies: Canada's secret war 1937-47* by John Bryden, McCelland & Stewart Inc. (Toronto, Ontario), 1989. This is a well-researched book of Canada's chemical and biological activities around the Second World War. See chapter seven for descriptions of the human experiments at Suffield.
62. Papers detailing the initial discussions and arrangements of setting up Suffield, including the aims of the new establishment, can be found in PRO, AVIA 15/1071. The large-scale testing site was needed to replace a French site in Algeria.
63. See PQ on 19 June 1992. Around 10 British scientists went to Canada to help set up the new establishment.
64. Examples of such requests are, for instance, evident in the regular progress reports which were sent back to Porton from Suffield (PRO, AVIA 15/1072).
65. *Deadly Allies*, p. 171. The British stopped funding Suffield in 1946.
66. Military officials noted that 'the risk of casualties (chiefly blindness) to personnel outside Porton' was too great to allow any trials with high-flying modern aircraft (PRO, AVIA 15/1071; T 164/180/22).
67. For further discussion of the development of aerial gas warfare in this period, see SIPRI, volume 1, pp. 98-100.
68. Human subjects were used to sample the potency of the poison gas after the bombs had landed. In 1921, for example, 2,200 tear gas bombs were dropped near gun-pits which sheltered eight men. Immediately, they dashed out into the cloud; five of them reported an 'immediate and painful' effect. The Air Ministry officials believed that such bombs would be 'of considerable value against semi-civilised personnel'. Officials added that such bombs would have a 'very great psychological effect on natives', but that Porton's 'trained observers' were made of hardier stuff mentally to withstand these munitions. (PRO, WO 188/318; WO 33/1014, 'Second report of the Secretary of the chemical warfare committee, for the year ending March 31, 1922', pp. 54-5).
69. It seems that the British saw the opportunity of spraying humans in tests right from the moment Suffield was set up. (PRO, AVIA 15/1071).
70. *Deadly Allies*, p. 170.
71. PRO, AVIA 15/1072, cable from Davies to Porton on 8 August 1942.
72. PRO, AVIA 15/896, 'Abstract and appreciation of Suffield Reports 39 and 47 on mustard spray, March 10, 1943'. The two Suffield reports are not contained in this file. Instead Porton has analysed and commented on the Suffield reports in this paper.
73. *Deadly Allies* (p. 170). According to this source, the test was Field Experiment 68.
74. PRO, AVIA 15/896, 'Summary of the casualty-producing power of thickened lewisite sprayed from aircraft on troops', Suffield Report 115, June 1944. Out of 35 men, 30 were hit with lewisite. Seven developed 'numerous and prominent' burns. Each day for

nine days, these seven took part in a six-mile route march and an hour's gun drill. 'None of the men failed to complete his task successfully,' notes the report.

75. John Bryden in *Deadly Allies* (p. 169) comments that the trial reports 'do exist, but are among those documents still unavailable' in the Canadian government archives. 'It is doubtful this is because they contain experimental information that is still a military secret...It is more likely it is because they contain descriptions of experiments the average person would find horrific.' Experiments were written up in a variety of Suffield reports; none of these are in Porton's classmarks at the British Public Record Office (WO 188/189), although a few have been located in other Whitehall files of the time. Some of the communications between Suffield and Porton during the war are contained in the PRO files, AVIA/1071-3.

76. *Deadly Allies*, (pp. 167-9). In 1940 – in tests outside the yet-to-be established Suffield – the Canadian military had 'approved' experiments on the arms of soldiers, with formal rules on the amount of mustard gas and the amount of medical supervision. The new regulations were drawn up in the summer of 1942, although Bryden says that Suffield 'did not wait for formal authorisation (from the higher-ups) to expand the mustard gas tests'.

77. In 1942, Suffield wanted 100 volunteers a month for the human experiments.

78. It is not known how many human subjects took part in the American tests during the war. It appears that the total would be in the region of 5,000 and above with at least 2,500 being tested in gas chambers and a further 1,000 or so involved in open-air trials. Others took part in patch tests in which poison gases were dropped or placed on the arm so that some kind of putative treatment could be tried out. The Institute of Medicine – which scrutinised these tests in the 1990s (see chapter 11) – estimated that 'at least 4,000 of these subjects had participated in tests conducted with high concentrations of mustard agents or lewisite in gas chambers or in field exercises over contaminated ground areas'. (*Veterans at Risk: the health effects of mustard gas and lewisite*, Institute of Medicine (National Academy Press, 1993); *Washington Post*, 7 March 1993; *Independent on Sunday*, 14 March 1993; *Bulletin of Atomic Scientists*, March 1993).

79. No servicemen did die in these experiments, as far is known. However it is interesting to note the perceptions of the human 'guinea pigs' who believed that such deaths were possible.

80. 'North Atlantic collaboration (Part 1: The War Years)', Gradon Carter and Graham Pearson, 'The ASA newsletter' (Applied Science and Analysis Inc), 5 December 1996 (issue 57, 96-6). This article provides an account of the co-operation in chemical and biological warfare from the First World War to the end of the Second World War. The authors wrote that in the arena of gas warfare, 'there was indeed a 'special relationship', a product not of political inspiration, but arising from the mutual enthusiasm of practical scientists, engineers and servicemen'. Trotman (p. 27) commented, 'It was said that during the war liaison in chemical warfare was better than in any other field.'

81. Interview with the author, 16 June 2000.

82. *Nature*, 16 September 1993, p. 218.

83. This information had been gathered mainly through experiments at Porton and its offshoot in India. In 1937, for instance, human subjects in India had been exposed to mustard gas vapour to study any difference in hot and cold weathers. The scientists wrote that 'all the experiments to date point to the fact that arms exposed to the same concentration of mustard vapour over the same lengths of time, react much more severely in the hot rather than in the cold weather'. (PRO, WO 188/641; WO 208/2174).

NOTES

84. 'Chemical warfare agents and related chemical problems' (summary technical report of Division 9, National Defense Research Committee, part 1, editor Birdsey Renshaw, Washington 1946), chapter 5, p. 57.
85. *Deadly Allies*, pp. 177-8.
86. The bare outlines of some of these wartime tests were made public in the late 1940s and 1950s, (in particular, Sinclair's articles in the British Medical Journal in 1948/9 and Mellor's chapter on chemical warfare in the 1958 official history in the case of the Australian tests). These accounts were quite anodyne reports which did not describe the experiences of the human 'guinea pigs' in any vivid detail. The experiments did not attract much mainstream media attention until the 1970s and 1980s when the volunteers began to come forward in Australia and the US and supply the discomfiting details. Porton volunteers started to go public in numbers in the 1990s. It appears that the Indian human 'guinea pigs' have not openly spoken about the tests.
87. As already shown, many of the reports on Porton's human experiments during the Second World War are still classified secret. It is not known precisely how many human subjects were exposed to mustard gas through their eyes and lungs, nor the dosage of gas on each occasion. Brief accounts of some mustard gas experiments on the eyes (and some accidental exposures) during the war are given in a summary report produced by Porton in 1948. (PRO, WO 188/723; AVIA 15/893; WO 189/234; 'Chemical warfare agents and related chemical problems' (summary technical report of Division 9, National Defense Research Committee, part 1, editor Birdsey Renshaw, Washington 1946), chapter 5, p. 56).
88. A useful guide to British consideration of gas at various points of the war is contained in *Effects of Chemical Warfare – a selective review and bibliography of British state papers*, Andy Thomas, (SIPRI, 1985). This includes a list of references in the Public Record Office for many official documents which describe the policy and contingency plans for gas warfare during the conflict.
89. PRO, PREM 3/89, note by Churchill to Chiefs of Staff on 6 July 1944; report by Chiefs of Staff, 28 July.
90. Carter, p. 43.
91. Trotman, pp. 23-4. Some of these weapons were accepted by the military services, but none were produced in great quantities 'because the possible military situation for which it had been intended was no longer likely to arise, or the diminishing likelihood towards the end of the war of gas being used did not justify bulk manufacture'.
92. David Sinclair, *Not a Proper Doctor*, pp. 86 and 98. He recalls, 'One Canadian general reckoned it wasn't nearly so bad as we pretended – his "boys" would have no trouble in carrying on. He was very put out when they had to open up like the rest.'
93. PRO, WO 189/258, Porton Memorandum 37.
94. Trotman, p. 23. For an account of the poison gas factories and their wartime output, see Britain's declaration of past chemical warfare activities to the Chemical Weapons Convention, May 1997.
95. The official commented that 'it would be worthwhile having a short list of 20 compounds from which something might arise whereby we could pull a quick one on the Hun'. (PRO, AVIA 15/374, letter from G M Rambaut, RD Arm 6, to Porton, 26 March 1943; Trotman, p. 24).
96. Important chemical warfare research outside of Porton was conducted at the Cambridge Extra-Mural Testing unit at the university's department of physiology. The unit built a gas chamber – described as 'a complete testing unit' – at the university for

human and animal experiments. Relatively little is known about the work of this unit. Some papers from the early part of the war have been declassified to the PRO. These show that in mid-1940, 'about 20 volunteers have been enrolled as observers for the Chamber experiments'. In an article in *Nature* on 30 March 2000, former scientists told how they tested compounds on themselves as part of the war effort. Fred Pattison said, 'I remember being ushered into the gas chamber for 10-minute exposures, armed with paper and pencil to note down any symptoms'. Distinguished chemist Bernard (B C) Saunders carried out pioneering work on organophosphorus, and other, compounds and nearly uncovered the lethal nerve gases. The unit regularly sent reports of its work to Porton (see PRO, WO 188/ 454, WO 188/455 and WO 188/457). It appears that scientists at Cambridge University did some kind of poison gas work for Porton before the Second World War, but a file on this – covering the period 1934-7 – is still being kept shut at the PRO (WO 188/692). Some discussion of the programme of research projects outside Porton in 1940 can be found in WO WO 188/ 475, 188/627 and AVIA 15/374. An official overview of these university projects appears in *Medical Research*, edited by F H K Green and Major-General Sir Gordon Covell, (HMSO, 1953), chapter ten.

97. It is not known how many chemicals were tested on humans during the Second World War. However one report shows that around 500 chemicals were tested on humans and animals between September 1941 and February 1945 at Porton (excluding the trials abroad). A snapshot of the wartime effort shows, for example, that in spring 1940, around 50-60 compounds were being studied to see if they were suitable new chemical weapons. (PRO, WO 188/631; WO 189/232).

98. SIPRI, volume 1, p. 272.

CHAPTER FOUR *Cleaning up after the Nazis*

1. BIOS report 138, interrogation of German chemical warfare medical personnel (August and September 1945), appendix four on interview with Schrader, 30 August 1945; BIOS Report 44, examination of various German scientists, p. 10; *A Higher Form of Killing – the secret story of gas and germ warfare*, Robert Harris and Jeremy Paxman, (Triad Paladin, 1983), p. 53. After the war, the Allies scrutinised every aspect of the German war machine. The Anglo-American teams of intelligence experts worked under the auspices of the Combined Intelligence Objectives Sub-committee (CIOS). Reports of CIOS and the British Intelligence Objectives Sub-committee (BIOS) are held in the Imperial War Museum, London and the Public Record Office.

2. SIPRI, volume 1 pp. 84-5.

3. There appears to be no consensus on the actual amounts of tabun and sarin produced there.

4. In 1941, scientists at Cambridge University – in collaboration with Porton – had begun to examine the organophosphorus compounds. The Americans lagged behind, only becoming interested towards the end of the war. Both the British and Americans exposed men to one of the chemicals in particular, known as PF-3 (diispropyl fluorophosphate), which had attracted the most attention. Three other organophosphorus compounds were also tested on around 20 subjects by the British. For descriptions of these experiements, see *Clinical and Experimental Toxicology of Organophosphates and Carbamates* (edited by Bryan Ballantyne and Timothy C Marrs, Butterworth-Heinemann, 1992), p. 374; 'Chemical warfare agents and related chemical problems' (summary technical report of Division 9, National Defense Research Committee, part 1, editor Birdsey Renshaw, Washington 1946), chapter 9, pp. 147-150; 'An investigation into the potentialities of diisopropyl fluorophosphate vapour in

respect of the production of eye casualties', Porton Report 2592, February 1942; Obituary of B C Saunders, *Chemistry in Britain*, 20 (10), 917, October 1984).

5. Porton concluded that PF-3 'had little to recommend it as a lethal agent', adding, 'it appears, therefore, to have value in CW only as a semi-persistent harassing agent'. (PRO, AVIA 15/374; 'Chemical warfare agents and related chemical problems' (summary technical report of Division 9, National Defense Research Committee, part 1, editor Birdsey Renshaw, Washington 1946), chapter 9, p. 132).

6. *A Brief History of the Chemical Defence Experimental Establishment, Porton*, (March 1961), p. 32 (hereafter referred to as Trotman).

7. 'Chemical warfare agents and related chemical problems' (summary technical report of Division 9, National Defense Research Committee, part 1, editor Birdsey Renshaw, Washington 1946), chapter 9, p. 140.

8. Trotman, p. 29.

9. PRO, WO 193/723. His debriefing is printed in 'Chemical warfare' (CSDIC (UK)/SIR 14), July 1943.

10. For forceful criticism of the Allies on this issue, see *Deadly Allies: Canada's secret war 1937-47*, John Bryden (Toronto, Ontario, 1989), chapter eight.

11. Unnamed official quoted in *A Higher Form of Killing – the secret story of gas and germ warfare*, Robert Harris and Jeremy Paxman, (Triad Paladin, 1983), p. 67.

12. PRO, WO 32/21200, 'Capture and disposal of German chemical warfare material, second progress report on German shell filling', 12 April 1945.

13. PRO, WO 32/21200, Note dated 16 April 1945 on German gas shell.

14. PRO, CAB 81/128, Reports by the Joint Intelligence Sub-Committee of the War Cabinet on the use of chemical warfare by the Germans, 28 March and 23 April 1945. Britain's spy chiefs were continually monitoring for any sign that the Germans might use chemical weapons. These assessments in 1945 can be found in CAB 81/127-131. Further material on such assessments is in WO 193/724 and PREM 3/89.

15. PRO, WO 195/14846, 'History of the Service Volunteer Observer Scheme at the Chemical Defence Experimental Establishment', Porton Note 119, November 1959, appendix eight. According to this account, 34 volunteers were exposed to nerve gas in 1945/6. (However this is contradicted by the figure of 49 subjects in the first study with tabun which is described in this chapter).

16. *Chemical Warfare Agents: Toxicology and Treatment*, Timothy C Marrs, Robert Maynard and Frederick Sidell, (John Wiley & Sons, 1996), pp. 115-6. According to this account, the scientists had been accidentally exposed to tabun.

17. The report is believed to be 'Toxicity, symptoms, pathology and treatment of T2104 (tabun)', Porton Report 2693, 16 August 1945 (addendum 1, 27 September 1945).

18. According to one account, Porton scientists suffered miosis as they elucidated the pharmacology and toxicity of tabun and documented the antidotal activity of atropine over the weekend. (*Chemical Warfare Agents* edited by Satu Somani, Academic Press, 1992, p. 157; *Chemical Warfare Agents: Toxicology and Treatment*, Marrs, Maynard and Sidell, p. 116. Both accounts attribute their information to personal communications from K Wilson).

19. In late 1996, Ken Livingstone MP asked for copies of three reports which were believed to contain accounts of the nerve gas experiments on humans and animals in 1945/6. In a letter on 4 February 1997, Porton replied that while the reports were not classified, 'they contain information which might be of value to terrorist groups and we would prefer not to place them in the public domain'.

NOTES

20. Details of the experiments come from PRO, WO 32/21200, undated interim report on substance T2104 (tabun); 'Chemical warfare agents and related chemical problems' (summary technical report of Division 9, National Defense Research Committee, part 1, editor Birdsey Renshaw, Washington 1946), chapter 9, pp. 146-7; and *Chemical Warfare Agents: Toxicology and Treatment*, Marrs, Maynard and Sidell, p. 117. The official account of this experiment is in the still-classified 'eye effects of T2104 (tabun)', Porton Report 2698, 28 September 1945.

21. The figure of 150 mg min m^{-3} is derived from appendix two of *Chemical Warfare Agents: Toxicology and Treatment*, Marrs, Maynard and Sidell. The estimate of 400 mg.min.m^{-3} comes from pp. 86-7 of SIPRI, volume 1. At the end of 1946, Porton was estimating the lethal dosage as being between 400-500 mg min m^{-3} (PRO, WO 195/9236).

22. *Porton Down – 75 years of chemical and biological defence*, Gradon Carter, (HMSO, 1992), pp. 48 and 55-6 (hereafter referred to as Carter).

23. *ibid*, pp. 48 and 55.

24. The results of these trials are contained in PRO, WO 208/2174.

25. PRO, CAB 131/3, 'Gas offensive policy and disposal of German war stocks', report by the Chiefs of Staff to the Defence Committee of the Cabinet, June 1946.

26. The bombs had to be adapted to be carried on British planes, but this was problematic. (Declaration of past chemical weapons activities by the United Kingdom for the Chemical Weapons Convention, May 1997, p. 4; PRO, WO 189/263).

27. For details of British dumping, see PRO, WO 32/21200; *Chemistry in Britain*, October 1995 (pp. 782-6); 'Sea Dumping of chemical weapons by the United Kingdom in the Skagerrak waters post-World War Two', CHEMU 2/2/5, a report submitted to the Ad Hoc Working Group on Dumped Chemical Weapons, Helsinki Commission (HELCOM CHEMU), 28-30 October 1993 (released to the author on 10 October 1996 by the MoD); *New Scientist*, 1 October 1987; *Sunday Times*, 5 April 1992.

28. Tommy Griffiths, a fitter, was part of a small team who helped build Nancekuke in the early 1950s. He says that his superiors told them that plant for Nancekuke had come from Germany. (PRO, WO 32/21200, letter from War Office, 7 March 1946; WO 208/2182, German CW experimental installation at Raubkammer, report of visit on 13-14 May 1945).

29. PRO, AIR 20/8730 and WO 189/263, 'German KC 250 III bomb – charged tabun', Porton Memorandum 42, April 1951. This includes a summary of the toxicological assessment of 165 Luftwaffe trials between 1935 and September 1944.

30. CIOS report (item number 8, file number 16-86) on the chemical warfare installations in the Munsterlager area, 23 April to 3 June 1945.

31. PRO, WO 195/9678; *The Nazi Doctors and the Nuremberg Code, Human Rights in Human Experimentation*, edited by George J Annas and Michael A Grodin (Oxford University Press, 1992), pp. 97-100.

32. PRO, WO 208/2182, Report by Lt Colonel Albert E Link of the US Chemical Warfare Service on Raubkammer, 13-14 May 1945. He added, 'The method used was to expose the portion of a uniform to be tested, then have a man put it on and observe his reactions. Such testing was checked by exposing small animals with shaved bellies in the same general area as the clothing, and assaying the animal reaction.'

33. CIOS report (item number 8, file number 16-86) on the chemical warfare installations in the Munsterlager area, 23 April to 3 June 1945. Of the 17 investigators, 14 were British/Porton, two Americans and one Canadian.

34. In the German experiments, the human subjects, with their face and neck exposed, would stand or lie in a shallow trench for up to an hour downwind of poisoned ground. Their hands would be covered with some kind of treatment. They would wear the clothes for four hours before removing them, taking a hot bath and having their hands treated. Outside of the concentration camps, the subjects of the German gas tests seem to have been drawn from the personnel of the various chemical warfare laboratories, motivated by the lure of extra cash and apparently volunteers. Details of the types of German tests can be found in the CIOS and BIOS reports; for instance, BIOS report 138, 'Interrogation of German chemical warfare medical personnel' (August and September 1945) pp. 14-19.

35. PRO, CAB 158/2, Memorandum 74 by Joint Intelligence Sub-Committee of the Chiefs of Staff, November 1947.

36. PRO, WO 195/9678, 'German CW experiments on human beings by Major D C Evans', received by the Chemical Defence Advisory Board on 12 January 1948.

37. The prosecutors at Nuremberg war crimes trials submitted that at one camp alone, Auschwitz, 4.5 million prisoners were exterminated with Zyklon B (a powder form of HCN). In 1948, Major Evans reported that during his trip: 'Considerable time was spent in trying to discover reliable data on which to calculate what concentrations of HCN were used for the extermination of the victims.'

38. PRO, WO 195/9714 and WO 195/9727, minutes and report of the sixth meeting of the Chemical Defence Advisory Board, February 1948.

39. PRO, WO 195/9714, minutes of the sixth meeting of the Chemical Defence Advisory Board, February 1948.

40. See, for example, appendix two of a 1946 Porton report (PRO, WO 195/9236), which lists German data on the toxicities of the nerve gases to humans and various animals through three different routes into the body. One experiment with nerve gases which had come to light was to determine the minimum amount of tabun which would cause eye effects. Ten German medical officers were exposed and suffered contraction of their pupils. However no accurate results could be concluded from the experiment. (BIOS report 138, 'Interrogation of German chemical warfare medical personnel', August and September 1945).

41. Robert Maynard and Frank Beswick, *Clinical and Experimental Toxicology of Organophosphates and Carbamates* (edited by Bryan Ballantyne and Timothy C Marrs), Butterworth-Heinemann, 1992, p. 380. It is apparent that the Americans did capture some records showing that the Germans had tested nerve gases on concentration camp inmates to investigate their effects and toxicity and to test possible antidotes. Some, if not all, of this captured information was passed onto Porton by the Americans (see PRO, WO 195/16811). It seems that the Americans analysed this concentration camp data in a report in 1954, but the US Department of Defense refused to release a copy following the author's request under the Freedom of Information Act in 1998.

42. *The Paperclip Conspiracy – the battle for the spoils and secrets of Nazi Germany*, Tom Bower (Michael Joseph, London, 1989), pp. 93-4.

43. For more details, see *Unit 731 – the Japanese Army's secret of secrets*, Peter Williams and David Wallace (Hodder & Stoughton, 1989).

44. *Secret Agenda: The United States Government, Nazi Scientists and Project Paperclip, 1945 to 1990*, Linda Hunt, (St Martin's Press, New York, 1991), chapter 10.

45. See, for instance, the papers of the defence research policy committee in PRO, DEFE 10/18-22.

46. 'Nazi science – the Dachau hypothermia experiments', Robert Berger, New England Journal of Medicine, 17 May 1990 (322: 20, pp. 1435-40).
47. PRO, FO 1031/81, 'Report on German chemical warfare personnel', 15 September 1945.
48. PRO, WO 208/2182, 'Information on a new group of toxic war gases', 28 April 1945; 'CIOS Report on a new group of war gases', (item number 8, file number 23-7, 23 April 1945).
49. The Russians had also managed to find valuable laboratory notebooks and documents which had been hidden down a mineshaft. (PRO, DEFE 5/37, 'Review of Chemical warfare development up to end of 1951', by Chiefs of Staff committee, March 1952; Gradon Carter and Graham Pearson, 'RUSI Journal', February 1996; *The Paperclip Conspiracy – the battle for the spoils and secrets of Nazi Germany*, Tom Bower (Michael Joseph, London, 1989), p. 91).
50. PRO, CAB 81/131, memorandum 305 by the Joint Intelligence Sub-Committee of the Chiefs of Staff, 24 October 1945; WO 32/21200, 'Appreciation of the information on sarin-type compound available to the USSR', 10 October 1945; WO 208/2183, 'Complementary information on tabun and sarin, anabasine', 20 July 1945. Although concrete information was hard to obtain, Britain's intelligence chiefs were consistently warning in the late 1940s and early 1950s that the Russians were capable of producing at least one of the nerve gases in great quantities. The assessments by the Joint Intelligence Committee are available in CAB 158 and CAB 159 at the PRO.
51. PRO, WO 32/21200, Note dated 13 October 1945 from the No. 1 chemical warfare investigation detachment, Porton to the War Office.
52. Carter, p. 56. For contemporary assessments of nerve gas, see PRO, DEFE 2/1857 and 1858.
53. Author's interview with former Porton scientist who requested to remain anonymous.
54. PRO, WO 195/9103, Résumé of work on nerve gases, received by the Chemical Defence Advisory Board in July 1945.
55. PRO, WO 195/14846, 'History of the Service Volunteer Observer Scheme at the Chemical Defence Experimental Establishment', Porton Note 119, November 1959, appendix eight. This shows a gap in the numbers of people exposed to G nerve gases in the two years 1946/7 and 1947/8.
56. One scientist commented that although 'very little effort was being put into investigations concerning the vesicants', they 'still possessed some importance' particularly in tropical climates. This had 'encouraged him to utilise the supply of "volunteer subjects"' to continue some 'interesting' research into mustard gas. (PRO, WO 195/9240, 'Statements on nerve gases, received by the Biology Committee', January, 1947; WO 195/9287, first meeting of the Biology Committee, February 1947).
57. Interview with the author, 13 April 1996. Porton confirmed in a letter to Mr Mills on 16 December 1994 that he had been a volunteer between 16 September and 5 October and had taken part in 'studies involving exposure to mustard gas... Our records relating to Mr Mills indicate that there was reddening of his arms, but no blistering'.
58. Letter to his MP, 9 November 1994.
59. PRO, CAB 131/1, Minutes of the defence committee of the Cabinet, 20 June, 1946; CAB 131/3, memorandum on gas – 'offensive policy and disposal of German war stocks', DO (46) 75. The committee wanted to achieve this position within five to ten years.
60. 'Declaration of past chemical weapons activities by the United Kingdom for the Chemical Weapons Convention', May 1997, p. 37.

Notes

61. PRO, WO 195/9236, Preliminary report on the potential value of nerve gases as chemical warfare agents – based on information available up to 31 December 1946. (Porton Report 2747, appendix three). The Nazis had been able to produce tabun satisfactorily, but had run into difficulties with sarin.
62. For discussion of the search for the new site, see the papers of the Defence Research Policy Committee for 1949 in PRO, DEFE 10/24 and DEFE 10/37, and for its early development, WO 185/315.
63. A full description of the Nancekuke site is on pp. 41-59 of the 'Declaration of past chemical weapons activities by the United Kingdom for the Chemical Weapons Convention, May 1997'. It seems that Nancekuke's existence first attracted major public attention in 1968 when CND published photographs and a map of the site in its magazine (*Sanity*, June 1968). For an interesting account of the aura surrounding the installation see *New Society*, 11 December 1969.
64. PRO, WO 195/9910, 'The industrial hazards of nerve gas intermediates, Porton Technical Paper 73, July 1948, Part One: the toxicity of the intermediates to animals; Part Two: the effect of repeated applications of small amounts to the human skin'. The report states that the intermediates were not a 'serious hazard to operatives provided that attention is given to general cleanliness of the hands and forearms, and normal precautions are taken to prevent the compounds coming into contact with the eyes'.
65. PRO, CAB 131/7, paper by the Defence Research Policy Committee to the Defence Committee of the Cabinet, 15 December 1948.
66. PRO, WO 188/706, 'Programme of research, 1948 for Porton and Sutton Oak', pp. 3 & 13, January, 1948 (see also WO 189/257 and WO 189/258).
67. Restarting human experiments with nerve gases may have been delayed in part until 1948 by the 'serious shortage of suitable personnel' for key posts at Porton, including physiologists. This lack of staff was raised frequently at meetings of the Chemical Defence Advisory Board at this time. See, for instance, PRO, WO 195/10037, 'Review of the board's work for 1948'.
68. PRO, WO 195/14846, 'History of the Service Volunteer Observer Scheme at the Chemical Defence Experimental Establishment', Porton Note 119, November 1959, appendix eight.
69. Interview with the author, 3 March 1996. Smith was also tested with mustard gas, but he does not believe that his health has been damaged by the tests.
70. Interview with the author, 25 November 1995; transcript of interview with Observer Films, 1994. In a letter dated 7 December 1994, Porton confirmed that Ashton went to Porton between 29 January and 2 February 1951 and that he was exposed to tabun vapour 'at a dosage of 9.5 mg.min/m^3 for five minutes'. The exact purpose of his experiment is not clear, but is thought to have been a comparison of the value of the various G-agents. (PRO, WO 195/10906, sixth meeting of the Biology Committee, March 1950; WO 195/11344, seventh meeting of the Biology Committee, February 1951).
71. During his stay, Aston was issued with a pair of RAF underpants – 'what you call passion-killers' – which he had to wear all week. They had been impregnated with an unknown yellow powder. He claims that Porton wanted to find out how much powder had been lost during the week, but Porton denies any record of this experiment. This was likely to have been connected with Porton's experiments on impregnating clothing to prevent poison gas seeping on skin (see previous chapter). It is known that during the Second World War, Porton considered the 'development of an impregnated "pantee" to protect the vulnerable groin area; the special problems of kilted troops were also studied'. Experiments, apparently with human subjects, showed that 'impregnated

knickers and stockings' – worn under Highland dress – 'afforded good protection against mustard gas vapour'. (PRO, WO 188/630, Progress Report, November 1939, p. 6; Carter, p. 47).

72. Robert Maynard and Frank Beswick, *Clinical and Experimental Toxicology of Organophosphates and Carbamates* (edited by Bryan Ballantyne and Timothy C Marrs (Butterworth-Heinemann, 1992, p. 377.

73. PRO, WO 195/10813, 'Exposures of unprotected men and rabbits to low concentrations of nerve gas vapour', Porton Technical Paper 143, December 1949.

74. Porton concluded that a dosage of just 3.3 mg min m^{-3} (the 'threshold' amount) was enough to produce an effect in humans. This conclusion may however be incorrect, as discussed in chapter seven.

75. PRO, WO 195/10581, 'Cholinesterase as an aid to the early diagnosis of nerve gas poisoning', Porton Technical Paper 136, September 1949. The five volunteers were exposed to 3.3 mg min m^{-3} of sarin, with an interval of two days between the first and second exposure, and four days between the second and third. The clinical effects were less well marked in the second and third exposures,' wrote the scientists.

76. See appendix two of *Chemical Warfare Agents: Toxicology and Treatment*, Timothy C Marrs, Robert Maynard and Frederick Sidell, (John Wiley & Sons, 1996), p. 233 and SIPRI, volume 1, pp. 86-7.

77. Interviews with the author, 25 November 1995 and 7 October 1996.

78. PRO, WO 195/11264, 'Exposure of men to sarin vapour, Part one: general symptomatology; Part two: effects on the eyes', Porton Technical Paper 218, January 1951.

79. PRO, WO 189/260, 'Physiological assessment of the nerve gases', Porton Memorandum 39, August 1950.

80. To 'simulate more closely actual [battlefield] conditions', these men were exposed to the sarin for a short time – between 30 seconds and two and a half minutes.

81. Porton commented that although fighting soldiers would be troubled by the 'considerable harassment' of their eyes, 'real casualties will not be produced from eye effects alone'.

82. Interview with the author, 22 November 1995.

83. Interview with the author, 8 March 1997. Mallard does not believe that the Porton tests have damaged his health in later years.

84. PRO, WO 195/14846, 'History of the Service Volunteer Observer Scheme at the Chemical Defence Experimental Establishment', Porton Note 119, November 1959.

85. A succinct summary of the progress of Porton's human experiments is contained in PRO, WO 189/260, 'Physiological assessment of the nerve gases', Porton Memorandum 39, August 1950.

86. Virtually no reports of Porton's human experiments with GA, GE, and GF from this time are in the public domain. Two Porton scientists have commented that in general, British and American experiments with these three nerve gases throughout its human programme are 'very poorly reported'. (Robert Maynard and Frank Beswick, *Clinical and Experimental Toxicology of Organophosphates and Carbamates* (edited by Bryan Ballantyne and Timothy C Marrs (Butterworth-Heinemann, 1992), p. 380.)

87. Author's interview with former Porton scientist who requested to remain anonymous.

88. A number of documents dating from the late 1940s and early 1950s on British plans to produce nerve gas in great quantity, and progress towards this goal, have been released

NOTES

into the PRO. The discussions of nitty-gritty aspects are contained in the papers of the Defence Research Policy Committee in DEFE 10/18-34 and DEFE 10/36-39. A few papers appeared before the Chiefs of Staff Committee in DEFE 5, particularly a comprehensive review in 1952 in DEFE 5/37. Interestingly, the only part of this document which has been censored appears to be a section on Porton's nerve gas experiments on humans (p. 43). Nerve gas production was discussed three times by the defence committee of the Cabinet, the highest political authority, between 1947 and 1954, but the papers for all of them are still closed (CAB 131/8, CAB 131/13 and CAB 131/14).

89. A snapshot of the position in late 1952 showed that a full-scale nerve gas factory – capable of producing 50 tons a week – had been authorised and was projected to start operating by 1955. (PRO, DEFE 41/157, meeting of Chemical Warfare sub-committee of the Chiefs of Staff committee, November 1952 and memo 23 October 1952).

90. Gradon Carter and Graham Pearson, RUSI Journal, February 1996.

91. Interview with Observer Films, 1994.

92. From 1947 to 1964, the collaboration was channelled mainly through 16 Tripartite conferences held virtually every year, the venue rotating around the countries. The picture becomes more complicated from the mid-1960s onwards, since co-operation flowed through several agreements. Much of the discussion and decisions of the collaboration is still clothed in secrecy. However some documents dealing with the Tripartite conferences in the 1950s and 1960s have been declassified and are in PRO, WO 195 and WO 188/709. Some information is also recorded in the annual 'summaries of major events and problems' produced by the US Army Chemical Corps from the early 1950s until 1962. In 1992, the author submitted a series of Freedom of Information requests for memos and minutes of meetings relating to collaboration in the 1970s and 1980s, but these were blocked on 'national security' grounds by the US government. Britain and Canada had also objected to the release of the information. One authoritative but sketchy account of the co-operation is an article by former Porton staff – Dr Graham Pearson and Gradon Carter – in Journal of Strategic Studies, March 1996, (pp. 74-103). As Porton's director, Dr Pearson lifted some of the secrecy by disclosing basic details of the co-operation, such as the dates and locations of meetings, in answers to Parliamentary Questions in the 1990s.

93. The discovery of the nerve gases was a major impetus behind the need for continuing collaboration. One memo records that in early 1947, British officials found that the work on the new gases and other recent developments 'appeared so wide...that in the light of the many competing claims on the limited scientific manpower of the country, it was clear that it would require larger staffs than could possibly be allotted'. (PRO, DEFE 10/20, memo by chemical warfare sub-committee, 3 October 1947).

94. In March 1947, representatives from the three countries agreed that the British would concentrate on GE, and the Americans on sarin. It was suggested that, although GE was less toxic than sarin, it was easier to produce. By 1950, Britain and American had chosen sarin in a joint decision. (PRO, WO 195/9476; PQs, 3 February 1995 and 16 March 1995).

95. PRO, WO 195/11540, 'The retention of inhaled GB vapour', Porton Technical Paper 244, July 1951.

96. PRO, WO 195/12218, 'Psychological effects of a G-agent on men', Preliminary report on an exploratory study of the effects of GB vapour on unprotected men, Porton Technical Paper 322, March 1953.

97. 'Recovery was rapid after treatment at the end of the experiment', says the report of the test.

98. Interviews with the author, 24 January and 2 October 1996.

99. In a letter dated 16 February 1996, Porton confirmed that Harper had been a volunteer between 14 and 18 July 1952 and had taken part in a study to 'assess the psychological effects of exposure to nerve agent vapour', in this case sarin. Their records indicated that he experienced physical symptoms consistent with the level of nerve agent exposure, but he recovered fully within 48 hours.
100. PRO, WO 195/12493, 'Psychological effects of a G-agent on men', Second Report. Porton Technical Paper 378, September 1953.
101. This experiment showed that the men's intellectual ability was not impaired, as shown by the tests for reasoning and reading comprehension (although the effect of the gas on the eyes – blurred vision, miosis and so on – 'caused some mechanical difficulty in seeing print clearly').
102. PRO, WO 195/15189, 'An old demonstration with GD', Porton Note 212. The exposures took place in December 1951, but were not written up in any sort of report until a decade later. This is virtually the only Porton report of a human experiment with soman which has been made public. (See also PRO, WO 195/15217, 27th meeting of the Biology Committee, July 1961).
103. The men were exposed to 5.5 mg min m^{-3} 'for a demonstration at the Director-General's Exercise at Mytchett'. The approximate lethal dose of soman is currently estimated to be between 40 and 60 mg min m^{-3}. (See *Chemical Warfare Agents: Toxicology and Treatment*, Marrs, Maynard and Sidell, p. 233, and SIPRI, volume 1, pp. 86-7. The latter gives the dose which produces casualties among unmasked people as 35 mg min m^{-3}.
104. PRO, WO 195/12084, 'An evaluation of the functional changes produced by the inhalation of sarin vapour – part one', Porton Technical Paper 321, December 1952.
105. PRO, WO 195/11264, 'Exposure of men to sarin vapour, Part one – general symptomatology; Part two – effects on the eyes', Porton Technical Paper 218, January 1951.

CHAPTER FIVE *Death of an Airman*

1. Interview with the author, 13 May 2000.
2. Letter from J C Baker (for Air Commodore, Director of Manning) to commanding officers of units dated 12 February 1953 (released to David Atkinson MP, 6 December 1996).
3. Interview with Observer Films, 1994.
4. Letter from J C Baker (for Air Commodore, Director of Manning) to commanding officers of units dated 12 February 1953.
5. Letter, 18 November 1994 to Priscilla and Eric Foster, Maddison's cousins.
6. Interview with Observer Films, 1994.
7. PRO, WO 195/12612, 'Percutaneous toxicity of the G compounds', Porton Technical Paper 399, January 1954.
8. It is not known when the first of the 396 volunteers were exposed in the experiment. Even with the large numbers of volunteers available to Porton at that time, it would have taken some months to test this number of people. A progress report for the six months to March 1952 records that 'some experiments using human experiments have been carried out on the percutaneous absorption of undiluted sarin'. (PRO, WO 188/710, Progress report number 19, p. 16).
9. Some of the teams wore one layer of khaki, known as serge, while another tranche of men had a combination of one layer of serge and another layer of flannel.

NOTES

10. PRO, WO 189/260, 'Physiological assessment of nerve gases', Porton Memorandum 39, August 1950, paragraph 40, pp. 13-15. The same conclusion was also made in a previous report, 'Appreciation of the potential chemical warfare value of nerve gases based on information available up to 30 June 1949', Porton Memorandum 34, paragraph 10, p. 3. (PRO at WO 189/254).
11. The report is known as Porton Technical Paper 373. It was written by Major R H Adrian, G L D Henderson, D R Davies, J P Rutland, and H Cullumbine. The authors are given in a list of technical reports. This list (at PRO, WO 195/12505) has been subjected to crude censorship – the last part of the report's title has been blanked out so that it reads 'A fatal case of poisoning with…'
12. Interview with the author, 8 August 1999.
13. This account comes from appendix one of 'Percutaneous toxicity of the G compounds', Porton Technical Paper 399, January 1954 (PRO WO 195/12612), record of the Court of Inquiry into his death (released by Porton to Ken Livingstone MP, 13 October 1997), and Porton's summary of events (sent to the Maddison family's lawyers, 21 September 1999).
14. PRO, WO 195/12549, 24th meeting of the Chemical Defence Advisory Board (CDAB), November 1953. This meeting was discussing the minutes of its subsidiary committee, the Biology Committee. It was the Biology Committee that dealt primarily with Porton's human experiments. However the minutes of the first meeting after Maddison's death – WO 195/12402 – are being kept secret by the Ministry of Defence, most probably because they contain discussion of his death. There is also discussion of the fatality in the minutes of CDAB's parent body, the Advisory Council on Scientific Research and Technical Development, at its 115th meeting in November 1953 (PRO, WO 195/12596).
15. This, and the other cholinesterase measurements quoted from this experiment, are for red blood cell cholinesterase. This is one of two ways of measuring cholinesterase levels.
16. PRO, WO 195/12989, 'Vomiting and sarin poisoning – a review', November 1954.
17. The report is known as Porton Technical Paper 361. The man in question is no longer alive.
18. It is unclear why the men were given subject numbers which were higher than the total number in the experiment.
19. Letter from Porton, 10 October 1996. Porton merely says that the sarin was dropped on the 'outside of your clothing'.
20. Interview with the author, 7 September 1996.
21. Porton's records indicate that his cholinesterase fell by 40 percent. The establishment added: 'This level of depression is not unexpected and would return to normal levels within a short time.'
22. On the first occasion, he was part of a similar experiment in which 100 milligrams of a nerve gas called GF was applied to his bare skin. Porton said his only symptom was a headache 10 hours after he had been exposed. 'This reaction is often noticed for this type of exposure.'
23. Virtually no other volunteers have mentioned that they were asked to write an account of their time at Porton. It appears that Mike Cox and others were asked to do so because of the impending inquiry into Maddison's death.
24. PRO, WO 195/14846, 'History of the Service Volunteer Observer Scheme at Porton Down' (Porton Note 119), November 1959.

NOTES

25. The evidence from these witnesses to the Court of Inquiry is still being kept secret by the authorities.
26. This is a figure which is most commonly quoted by scientists; however it is difficult to know if this figure is reliable. Porton refuses for reasons of national security to publish its current estimate of the lethal dose of sarin through skin (see PQ on 8 March 2000). It is apparent that its estimate has fluctuated over the years from the 1950s onwards.
27. Former Porton scientists Robert Maynard and Frank Beswick, *Clinical and Experimental Toxicology of Organophosphates and Carbamates* (edited by Bryan Ballantyne and Timothy C Marrs, Butterworth-Heinemann, 1992), p. 381. See also *Chemical Warfare Agents: Toxicology and Treatment*, Timothy Marrs, Robert Maynard and Frederick Sidell, (John Wiley & Sons, 1996), p. 118. They write that there had been 'many observations that there is no relationship between the effects caused by direct contact of the nerve gas vapour [on the eye, nose and airways] and inhibition of the [red blood cell] cholinesterase activity'. (For more discussion of this point, see for instance a Porton paper in 1965 at PRO, WO 195/16138).
28. See, for example, one of Porton's earlier experiments, in which two groups of five volunteers were exposed, either once or a succession of three times, to sarin in 1949. It was concluded that 'quite clearly' the variations in cholinesterase levels were 'too indefinite' to be used for diagnosing nerve gas poisoning. (PRO, WO 195/10581, WO 195/10580 and WO 195/11411).
29. Early work by Porton from the late 1940s was to see if monitoring and measuring cholinesterase levels would be a useful way of checking the health of workers who would manufacture the nerve gas. (See also WO 195/11596 and WO 195/11619).
30. PRO, WO 195/16808, paper by Bill Ladell, head of Porton's human experiments in the 1950s and 1960s, on 'impracticability of deducing blood cholinesterase depression from clinical condition in organophosphorus poisoning' in 1961.
31. This question was later investigated without the use of volunteers and reported in 'Penetration of clothing by sarin', Porton Technical Paper 492, July 1955. (PRO, WO 195/13343).
32. PRO, WO 189/254, 'Appreciation of the potential chemical warfare value of nerve gases based on information available up to 30 June 1949', Porton Memorandum 34 (paragraph 10, p. 3). A key summary in 1947 stated that 'restriction of evaporation of the liquid, by covering with impervious material (e.g. gloves, facepiece, dressings) dangerously increases the effect of contamination, particularly in the case of the relatively volatile sarin, with which covering the site of contamination increases the toxic absorption ten-fold'. (PRO, WO 195/9236).
33. PRO, WO 195/12614, 'Observations on the percutaneous absorption of liquid GB', Porton Technical Paper 396, January 1954. Further experiments – on cats and dogs – are recorded in PRO, WO 195/12704.
34. A progress report in 1952 noted that 'samples of radio-active sarin of high purity are being used to study percutaneous penetration in man'. It is unclear if this is the same or a separate experiment. (PRO, WO 188/710, 'Progress report number 20 for Porton and Sutton Oak for half-year ended 30 September 1952', p. 17).
35. Maddison's body was identified by his father on 8 May. At 5.30p.m. on the same day, the Wiltshire coroner started the inquest in Porton's main conference room, and then reconvened it eight days later. The inquest was held in camera on the instructions of the Home Office. At the time of writing, the Wiltshire coroner's file on the case is still being kept secret.
36. *The People*, 24 May 1953.

Notes

37. *Sunday Express*, 24 May 1953.
38. The death certificate is held in the General Register Office of Salisbury.
39. PQ, 9 June 1953.
40. His death is briefly recorded in the station logbook of RAF Ballykelly. It reads: 'May 6, 1953 – 3509906 LAC Maddison R. died whilst on voluntary duty detachment from Ballykelly at the Chemical Defence Experimental Establishment at Porton Down.' (PRO, AIR 28/1181).
41. Interview with the author, 3 March 1997.
42. Interview with the author, 16 April 1996.
43. PQ, 26 October 1994.
44. Author's interview with former Porton scientist who requested to remain anonymous.
45. *Porton Down – 75 years of chemical and biological defence*, Gradon Carter, (HMSO, 1992), p. 70. There was more bad publicity, for example, in 1962 when Porton microbiologist Geoffrey Bacon was infected with plague and died – the inquiry went as high as the Prime Minister at the time.
46. PRO, WO 195/14846, 'History of the Service Volunteer Observer Scheme at Porton Down' (Porton Note 119), November 1959. It appears that the Ministry of Supply, to whom Porton was accountable, launched an investigation which was separate from the Court of Inquiry. The results of this inquiry are unknown. A search of the Ministry of Supply files (called SUPP) at the PRO by the author yielded no obvious reference to this inquiry nor a report of its findings.
47. The Court also proposed that the decision to resume tests 'will be influenced by the outcome of further fundamental studies on the permeability of human skin to chemical substances'.
48. PQs, 26 October 1994; 7 March 1995.
49. During the Second World War, Dr Adrian was one of the leaders of the chemical warfare testing laboratories at Cambridge University (see chapter three) which carried out work for Porton. Sir Roy Cameron worked at Porton during the Second World War. Sir Rudolph Peters' association with Porton went back as far as the First World War and he was one of the first recruits to the Porton department which conducted human experiments.
50. In the decade up to 1956, all three were chairmen of one of these committees, and in 1953, Peters was the chairman of the Biology Committee of the Chemical Defence Advisory Board.
51. According to the surviving records, a Royal Army Medical Corps medical officer, Major R H Adrian, was observing the Maddison experiment and 'immediately took charge of the situation' when Maddison started to fall ill. Adrian played a key part in the emergency effort to revive Maddison. He later gave evidence to the Court of Inquiry and was one of the authors of the still-secret report on Maddison's death.
52. Like Porton's own report on Maddison's death, two of the documents relating to the work of this committee have also been subjected to crude censorship. In the documents – released to the Public Record Office – the word 'nerve' in what is obviously 'nerve gases' has been blacked out with a pen. This is curious since the censorship has been imposed on descriptions of the committee's remit, yet from other published documents – including the committee's final report – it is obvious that the three scientists are looking at the question of nerve gas experiments. The censored documents are in PRO, WO 195/12436 and WO 195/12437.

NOTES

53. PRO, WO 195/12435, report of Dr Edgar Adrian's special committee, 12 August 1953.
54. PRO, WO 286/77, notes by chief scientist and other officials, September 1953. These papers refer to two 'incidents' – presumably meaning Maddison and the volunteer who nearly died.
55. It is apparent that, for example, parliamentary questions about Porton and its experiments were habitually answered with bland uninformative replies until the early 1990s when the establishment's then director Graham Pearson attempted to be more open and provide fuller replies.
56. PRO, DEFE 7/1451, 'tests of chemical warfare agents (G&V)', W A Drummond, DGAMS, 6 November 1959.
57. PRO, WO 32/20843, 'Memorandum on percutaneous and intravenous tests on men with G and V agents', approved by Professor Jack Gaddum, Chairman of the Biology Committee, 19 February 1960.
58. Interview with the author, 14 February, 1997. Stacey died in June 1999.
59. Interview with the author, 4 December 1995; interview with Observer Films, 1994.
60. PRO, WO 195/14846, 'History of the Service Volunteer Observer Scheme at Porton Down' (Porton Note 119), November 1959.
61. There is no mention of the restarting of the nerve gas experiments in House of Commons Hansard between 3 November 1953 and 25 November 1954.
62. PRO, WO 195/14846, 'History of the Service Volunteer Observer Scheme at Porton Down' (Porton Note 119), November 1959, appendix eight.
63. Interview with the author, 13 March 1997.
64. PRO, WO 195/12917, 'Effects of a minor exposure to GB on military efficiency', Porton Technical Paper 438, August 1954.
65. PRO, WO 195/13341, 'The effects of atropine and wearing respirators on the military efficiency of troops exposed to GB', Porton Technical Paper 485, July 1955; WO 195/13220, Recommendations and conclusions of the Ninth Tripartite Conference.
66. Interview with the author, 30 May 2000. Given that he was in the 1st Battalion of the Wiltshire Regiment around this time, it is very likely that he took part in one of these two exercises, or indeed something very similar.
67. He took charge of the human tests at Edgewood in 1956 and was still in command in 1975. It is not known when he retired.
68. PRO, WO 195/13584, 'Effect on pupil size of exposure to GB vapour', Porton Technical Paper 531, January 1956.
69. PRO, WO 195/13434, 'Cognitive and emotional changes after exposure to GB', Porton Technical Paper 488, September 1955.

CHAPTER SIX *Breaking the Code*

1. A fuller description of these awful tests is given in *The Nazi Doctors and the Nuremberg Code, Human Rights in Human Experimentation*, edited by George J Annas and Michael A Grodin (Oxford University Press, 1992), particularly pp. 97-100.
2. For more information on this ghastly story, see *Unit 731 – the Japanese Army's Secret of Secrets*, Peter Williams and David Wallace (Hodder & Stoughton, 1989) and *Factories of Death: Japanese Biological Warfare 1932-45 and the American Cover-up*, Sheldon Harris (Routledge, 1994).

3. PQ, 11 January 1996. See also, for example, the then junior MoD minister Nicholas Soames in an adjournment debate on 16 October 1996; letter from then junior MoD minister Earl Howe to David Atkinson MP, 9 October 1996. In a more recent PQ (19 January 1998), the MoD stated firmly that 'studies at Porton Down have always been conducted to the highest standard of ethical practice prevailing at the time and volunteers would have been required to give their informed consent to take part in a study'.
4. Obviously, the volunteers would have been no better off if they had been told the technical or chemical name of a chemical warfare agent, such as *bis*-(2-chloroethyl) sulphide, but they would have had a better idea if they had been told the common name of that agent, in this case mustard gas.
5. PRO, DEFE 7/1451, notes of a meeting held on 21 December 1959 to discuss chemical tests on service volunteers at Porton.
6. In the publicity film produced to recruit volunteers in the 1960s (see chapter two), Porton deliberately warns volunteers about leaking secrets. A staff member is shown talking to a group of volunteers before they leave Porton. He tells them that they should not talk to their 'pals or civilians [about] anything which they have seen or heard during their stay,' adding that 'this is of great concern to us.'
7. In the immediate post-war period, they sat on two committees – the Biology Committee and its parent body, the Chemical Defence Advisory Board.
8. Interview with the author, 15 January 1996.
9. Author's interview with former Porton scientist who requested to remain anonymous.
10. Interview with the author, 8 October 1997. According to Porton, Shave took part in one experiment in which he was exposed to a 'low concentration' of nerve gas for nearly two hours and suffered various effects for several days, including a headache and painful eyes.
11. Interview with the author, 1 September 1999.
12. Interview with the author, 10 March 1996.
13. Interview with the author, 7 October 1997.
14. Interview with the author, 15 May 2000.
15. Interviews with the author, 26 November 1995 and 12 May 2000, and other correspondence over the years.
16. Letters from Porton, 7 December 1995 and 28 February 1995.
17. In the 1950s, Porton scientists took part in a government research programme to 'investigate the causes and effects of the problem and possible solutions' the London smog which had claimed an estimated 4,000 deaths from chronic breathing problems. At the time, there was much doubt over what the toxic chemical in the smogs actually was, and so Porton exposed hundreds of the volunteers to some of the likely substances, such as sulphur dioxide, for up to an hour in a gas chamber. There were more than 1,500 exposures over a year. It appears that the volunteers were used for such research since there was a handy pool of them, and since most of them were young, fit individuals, they would be able to withstand these exposures with being harmed. According to the government, these Porton trials helped to bring about the 'clean air legislation of the 1960s, which considerably improved the atmosphere in our large cities and saw the disappearance of the London fogs of old'. (Adjournment debate in House of Commons, 16 October 1998; Porton's smog work is recorded in four reports, Porton Technical Papers 525, 535, 547 and 645).

18. Interview with the author, 15 October 1997, and his various correspondence with Porton over the years.
19. Interview with Royston Clarke for *Dispatches* programme, broadcast on 3 April 1996. In another case, an unnamed person wrote to Labour MP Tony Banks in 1984, saying that he had volunteered for tests seeking a cure for the common cold, which turned out to involve nerve gas. The letter was 'unsigned and could not be authenticated'. No date was given for the tests. (*Daily Telegraph*, 25 February 1984).
20. Interview with the author, 6 May 1998.
21. Interview with the author, 13 June 1998. Despite the offer of extra money, Underhill did not volunteer because he 'could not be bothered'.
22. Interview with the author, 7 May 1998. The man did not want to be named.
23. Letter from the individual to David Atkinson MP, 18 October 1996; House of Commons adjournment debate, 17 March 1998. The man served at RAF Wattisham, Suffolk.
24. PQ, 8 February 1996; letter from Armed Forces Minister Dr John Reid to Chris Mullin (Gordon Bell's MP), 30 November 1997.
25. Author's interview with former Porton scientist who requested to remain anonymous.
26. PQ, 9 May 1996. Up to the early 1960s, this unit recruited volunteers 'largely as a result of favourable press coverage and talks and lectures in colleges and voluntary groups, as well as through word of mouth'. In the late 1960s, the publicity drive became more 'systematic' with leaflets in libraries and workplaces and adverts in the media.
27. PQ, 8 February 1996.
28. PRO, WO 32/20843, 'Conditions for experiments with physiological experiments at CDEE', attachment to letter from Porton director, Eric Haddon, to War Office, 17 August 1961. It is not clear who wrote the attachment.
29. The MoD has stated that 'although Porton cannot comment on the wording used to recruit volunteers by RAF stations, the information and advice from Porton Down would not have mentioned common cold research'. (Letter from Armed Forces Minister Dr John Reid to Chris Mullin MP, 30 November 1997).
30. In 1960/1, Porton carried out research to find out why servicemen volunteered for its chemical warfare tests (see chapter two). From those questioned, two volunteers stated that they came by 'mistake' since they believed that they were going to the Common Cold Unit in Salisbury. Porton commented that this was 'odd, but apparently true'. (PRO, WO 195/15638).
31. Porton has also never issued any written directives to its staff to implement another important code of ethics, the 1964 Declaration of Helsinki. The establishment has claimed that it 'has always conducted its experimental work involving human volunteers in accordance with the current standards both scientifically and ethically'. (Letters to Ken Livingstone MP, 10 June and 4 November 1998).
32. See the report of a Committee of Inquiry into radiation in Medical Research Committee-supported research in the 1950s and 1960s, published in May 1998; New England Journal of Medicine, 274, 1966, pp. 1354-60; Yale Journal of Biology and Medicine, 26, June 1964, pp. 455-476.
33. 'Use of volunteers in chemical agent research', Colonel James Taylor and Major William Johnson, Office of the Inspector-General, US Army, 10 March 1976 (DAIG-IN 21-75), chapter six.
34. Their conclusions are backed up by another official watchdog body, the United States General Accounting Office (GAO) which is roughly equivalent to Britain's National

NOTES

Audit Office in scrutinising government expenditure and actions. The GAO found that with regard to the Nuremberg Code, 'According to defense officials, some of the rules, including those related to the quality of informed consent and the capability of the subjects to withdraw without prejudice, were not followed in the 1950s and 1960s'. (*Human Experimentation: an overview on Cold War era programs*, 28 September 1994, GAO/T-NSIAD-94-266).

35. PQ, 11 January 1996.
36. Details on how many volunteers have pulled out of experiments are cursory. According to Porton, 10 volunteers withdrew between 1979 and 1984; half were on 'compassionate grounds, i.e. where domestic circumstances have necessitated an early departure'. More recently, Porton stated in 1994 that in the previous three years, only one volunteer had exercised his right to withdraw from an experiment after it had been explained to him. He was to have taken part 'in a climatic study whilst wearing Individual Protective Equipment', but was uneasy about blood samples being taken from him. (PQs, 5 March 1984; 24 June and 20 December 1994.
37. PRO, AIR 20/10719, Note of a meeting held on 23 September 1959 to discuss nerve gas tests on human observers.
38. According to Porton, the spur to setting up this committee is believed to have been 'the concern expressed internationally regarding the ethics of human experimentation, reflected in the 1964 Declaration of Helsinki'. Declassified records show that it came about following an apparently off-the-cuff remark at a meeting of a Porton advisory committee by one of the outside scientists.(PQ, 6 July 1963; PRO, WO 195/15697, 33rd meeting of the Biology Committee, September 1963; WO 195/15900, 34th meeting of the Biology Committee, July 1964; WO 195/16131, report by the chairman of COSHE, November 1965).
39. Porton has acknowledged that 'formal supervision of the use of human subjects in studies is an important element in protecting individuals'. It has claimed that this supervision was carried out by one of Porton's advisory bodies, the Biology Committee (of the Chemical Defence Advisory Board), from 1946 until the 1960s. A mixture of outside scientists, Porton staff and assorted officials sat on these committees. However the minutes of the Biology Committee show very little discussion of the ethics and safety of the human tests. One university scientist who was a member of the Biology Committee for some years said, 'I don't think that the committee actually dealt with that very much...I don't think that ethics really came into it.' Instead the discussions tended to focus on the objectives of experiments and how to solve particular problems which went along with its original remit. (PRO, WO 195/9124, minutes of the second meeting of the Chemical Defence Advisory Board, August 1946; letter from Porton to Ken Livingstone MP, 3 December 1996; the minutes of the Biology Committee, which met 35 times between 1947 and 1964, are at the PRO in the classmark WO 195. At the time of writing, one meeting has been kept secret by the Ministry of Defence – 11th).
40. PRO, WO 195/16131, report by the chairman of COSHE, November 1965; PQ, 6 July 1995.
41. PQ, 18 July 1995.
42. Author's interview with former Porton scientist who requested to remain anonymous.
43. PRO, WO 195/16131, report by the chairman of COSHE, November 1965. Since COSHE was an internal body, its work was reviewed by one of Porton's external advisory bodies, the Applied Biology Committee. At the first meeting of the Applied Biology Committee in 1965, Porton's director, Eric Haddon, said he hoped that 'in addition to giving support to the experiments with human volunteers, the committee

NOTES

would act as a watchdog to ensure that the experiments did not go too far'. From the limited number of minutes so far published, the discussions in this committee focused more on ethics and safety than its predecessor body, the Biology Committee, had done. The Applied Biology Committee was later replaced by a similar body, a sub-group of the medical committee of the Defence Scientific Advisory Council, until 1991, this sub-committee monitored Porton's human experiments. (PRO, WO 195/16161, 'First meeting of the Applied Biology Committee', November 1965; PQ, 3 July 1996).

44. At the time of writing, a few papers covering the early work of COSHE are in the WO 195 classmark in the PRO because they had outlived the 30-year ban on releasing official papers.

45. PQs, 6 July 1995 and House of Lords, 7 February 1994. The other two members are Porton staff – its technical director and senior military officer – who act as a sort of liaison between the establishment and the committee. These two withdraw from the committee so that the outside members can carry out their deliberations in private (like other ethics committees).

46. Interview with the author, 2 February 2000. Professor Dudley, who had been a member of the previous ethical committee since the mid-1980s, served as chairman until 1996.

47. Interview with the author, 6 June 2000.

48. PQ, 1 March 1995.

49. Letter to Ken Livingstone MP, 14 October 1997. Porton staff who fail to take heed of suggested modifications to their proposed experiment would almost certainly later have it rejected by the Independent Ethics Committee.

50. The committee members have to sign the Official Secrets Act as they have 'unrestricted access to any classified information' which may relate to their decisions. The minutes of the committee are secret because they contain 'matters which are of commercial and defence sensitivity'. The committee meets three or four times a year. The MoD is reticent about making public the members of the committee, although the chairman is openly identified.

51. Interview with the author, 2 February 2000. Professor Lader, of the Institute of Psychiatry in London, had been an ordinary member of the committee.

52. PQ, 1 March 1995; 'Guidelines on the practice of ethics committees in medical research involving human subjects' (second edition), published by the Royal College of Physicians of London, January 1990.

53. PQ, House of Lords, 7 February 1994.

54. Letter from Porton to Ken Livingstone MP, 14 October 1997. Porton cannot put a date on the actual introduction, but believes that they were brought in 'gradually' in the late 1980s and certainly since 1991.

55. Two sample forms were disclosed to Ken Livingstone on 14 October 1997. One – CBDE VP 58/96 – concerns a study to develop possible antibiotics against biological weapons (the effects of doxycycline and ciprofloxacin on human performance). The second was the effect of wearing protective suits and equipment while driving a car. Both forms are undated. According to Porton, the forms are 'not all the same, particular forms being specific to individual studies'. (PQ, 19 January 1998).

56. *Sunday Telegraph*, the author and Andrew Gilligan, 2 November 1997.

57. The V-agents had been discovered by scientists at the industrial giant ICI Ltd in 1953. ICI sent samples of the new compounds to Porton, which in turn passed the secret information onto the Americans early in 1953. ('Summary of Major Events and Problems, United States Army Chemical Corps, Fiscal Year 1958', pp. 97-100, obtained

58. 'Summary of Major Events and Problems, United States Army Chemical Corps, Fiscal Year 1958', p. 98.
59. By September 1953, Porton's scientific advisors were noting that the new compounds 'opened up a potentially interesting and valuable new field' of chemical warfare and appeared to be 'in quite a different category'. (PRO, WO 195/12495; WO 195/12596).
60. Dr Ted Perren, Porton's director, wrote that in recent years, the offensive value of the chemical weapons had been 'largely overshadowed' by nuclear weapons, but he speculated that the new V-agents could change that military perception. (DEFE 10/281, 'The offensive potential of V-gases', February 1956; 'Summary of Major Events and Problems, United States Army Chemical Corps, Fiscal Year 1955', p. 46, obtained through a request under the United States Freedom of Information Act on 10 July 1992).
61. Another official also commented that V-gases 'have not been tested directly on man and probably never will be in an experimental manner'. (PRO, DEFE 10/282, 'Use of chemical agents in war', 21 February 1957).
62. Porton argued that injecting into the vein was the only way of ensuring that they knew how much nerve gas had actually gone into the body. (PRO, WO 195/14086, 'Proposal to administer anti-cholinesterase agents by intravenous injection to man', June 1957; WO 195/14422, 'Human experiments with anti-cholinesterase agents', September 1958).
63. PRO, WO 195/14048, 18th meeting of the Biology Committee, April 1957.
64. PRO, WO 195/14095, informal meeting of the Chemical Defence Advisory Board and its parent body, July 1957.
65. PRO, WO 195/14086, 'Proposal to administer anti-cholinesterase agents by intravenous injection to man', June 1957; WO 195/14422, 'Human experiments with anti-cholinesterase agents', September 1958.
66. PRO, WO 195/14422, 'human experiments with anti-cholinesterase agents', September 1958.
67. PRO, WO 195/14321, 20th meeting of the Biology Committee, March 1958. It consisted once again of Lord Adrian, Sir Rudolph Peters and Sir Roy Cameron, and two other outside scientists.
68. It is highly likely that the WL in the experiment was Ladell. (PRO, WO 195/14441, 'Rate of absorption of V agents through human skin', Porton Note 44, September 1958; WO 195/14514, 21st meeting of the Biology Committee, November 1958).
69. The first experiment, with VX, in the US was in 1959. The only other countries which may have discovered the V-agents by then were the then Soviet Union and France, but little is known about their respective human experiments. It is notable that the first public disclosure of significant information about the toxicity of the V-agents through the skin was by a Soviet Union academic in 1959 (at a Pugwash conference). This may well mean that the Soviet Union had tested the chemicals on humans to reach these figures. (*Chemical Warfare Agents: Toxicology and Treatment*, Tim Marrs, Robert Maynard and Frederick Sidell, (John Wiley & Sons, 1996) p. 127; SIPRI, volume 2, p. 177).
70. It was concluded that between 6 micrograms and 20 micrograms of the VX had penetrated through the skin. (PRO, WO195/14654, 'Percutaneous experiments with V', Note by Dr W S S Ladell, Superintendent of Porton's Medical Division, May 1959).

NOTES

71. Information from a confidential Porton source. Ladell appears to have succeeded Harry Cullumbine as superintendent of the medical division, with responsibility for the human tests. Ladell's health was breaking down during his time at Porton. He has since died.
72. PRO, WO 195/14654, 'Percutaneous experiments with V', Dr Bill Ladell, Superintendent of Porton's Medical Division, May 1959.
73. In the memo, he wrote that 'although...the lower limit for toxic effects has not been found, there is sure knowledge of a limit below which toxic effects will not take place.'
74. PRO, WO 195/14514, 21st meeting of the Biology Committee, November 1958; WO 195/14824, 23rd meeting of the Biology Committee, November 1959. This had been agreed at the 13th Tripartite Conference between the two countries and Canada in September 1958. It was reiterated at the following year's conference in September 1959.
75. PRO, WO 195/14704, 22nd meeting of the Biology Committee, June 1959.
76. PRO, DEFE 7/1451, notes of a meeting held on 21 December 1959 to discuss chemical tests on service volunteers at Porton.
77. PRO, AIR 20/10719, note of a meeting held on 23 September 1959 to discuss nerve gas tests on human observers; letter from H T Smith to A C W Drew, War Office, 24 November 1960.
78. PRO, AIR 20/10719, notes by P B Lee-Potter, DGMS, 16 March 1961 and AUS (P), 20 March 1961.
79. PRO, DEFE 7/1451, note of a meeting held on 21 December 1959 to discuss chemical tests on service volunteers at Porton.
80. For example, see paragraph nine of the notes of a meeting held on 21 December 1959 to discuss chemical tests on service volunteers at Porton (PRO, DEFE 7/1451).
81. PRO, AIR 20/10719, note by J F Mayne, 15 September 1959.
82. PRO, WO 32/20843, 'Personal and secret' letter from Eric Haddon, director of Chemical Defence Research and Development (London), to Dr Walter Cawood, Chief Scientist, War Office, 16 May 1961. Later in the year, Haddon was to become director of the Chemical Defence Establishment at Porton. Since 1929, he had been working in a variety of posts within Britain's chemical warfare effort.
83. PRO, WO 195/16811, 'Human exposures to GB', 1968.
84. PRO, AIR 20/12171, note by T C G James, head of F2, 27 January 1961.
85. PRO, WO 32/20843, Letter from Ladell to Eric Haddon, director of Chemical Defence Research and Development (London), 12 May 1961.
86. PRO, AIR 20/10719, note of a meeting held on 23 September 1959 to discuss nerve gas tests on human observers.
87. PRO, DEFE 7/1451, 'Tests of chemical warfare agents (G&V)', W A Drummond, DGAMS, 6 November 1959. Echoing that point, this official wrote that of the intravenous tests with sarin, 'the danger...does not lie in an overdose but in the possibility of undue susceptibility of the volunteer'. The actual degree of risk of this possibility in Porton's experiments is open to debate. On the one hand, it could be argued that since there is no test for spotting a similar idiosyncrasy in another volunteer, then Porton scientists were jeopardising the lives of the human subjects who were exposed to nerve gas after 1953. Porton has also stated (in a Parliamentary answer on 8 March 2000) that the establishment 'has not undertaken any work to develop a test to identify the relative sensitivity of different individuals to the effects' of nerve gases. On the other hand, it could be argued that the dosages of nerve gases used in the post-1953 experiments were so much reduced that the risk was negligible. Even with

419

a great variation in the cholinesterase depression among a group of human 'guinea pigs', the cholinesterase would not be reduced by such a percentage that would approach the levels which were dangerous and life-threatening.

88. PRO, WO 195/14422, 'Human experiments with anti-cholinesterase agents', September 1958.
89. PRO, WO 32/20843, 'Human experiments with nerve gases', note by Jack Gaddum, Chairman of the Biology Committee, February 1960.
90. PRO, AIR 20/10719, letter from I Montgomery, Ministry of Defence, to Sir Charles Key, War Office, 14 January 1960. The letter reproduces a section of the Joint Intelligence Committee's assessment of the Soviet threat written in 1959.
91. PRO, AIR 20/10719, note by J F Mayne, 15 September 1959.
92. PRO, AIR 20/10719, note of a meeting held on 23 September 1959 to discuss nerve gas tests on human observers.
93. PRO, DEFE 7/1451, letter from PD Nairne, Private office, 27 November 1959.
94. PRO, DEFE 7/1451, paragraph seven of a draft paper prepared by Sir Charles Key of the War Office, attached to a letter of 16 December 1959 to H T Smith of the Air Ministry.
95. PRO, DEFE 7/1451, letter by J A Drew, CB of the Ministry of Defence to the War Office, 29 November 1960.
96. PRO, WO 195/15335, minutes of 49th meeting of the Chemical Defence Advisory Board, February 1962. Profumo had made his views known in a meeting in July 1961 with two senior Porton officials, director Eric Haddon and Ladell. The second condition was that 'all three Services must be in complete agreement on the conduct of the experiments'. At that time, the War Office and the Admiralty were in favour, but the Air Ministry 'had expressed some doubts'.
97. RO, WO 32/20843, Letter from A C W Drew, War Office, to the Home Office, 28 July 1961; note by A C W Drew, 11 August 1961; reply by Home Office, 23 November 1961.
98. PRO, AIR 20/10719, loose minute by J F Mayne, 16 November 1959.
99. PRO, WO 32/20843, 'Memorandum on percutaneous and intravenous tests on men with G and V agents', Professor Jack Gaddum, chairman of the Biology Committee, 19 February 1960.
100. PRO, WO 32/20843, Letter from Dr Bill Ladell to Eric Haddon, director of Chemical Defence Research and Development, 12 May 1961.
101. Author's interview with former Porton scientist who requested to remain anonymous.
102. The reports on the Committee on the Safety of Human Experiments show glimpses of how staff wanted to test on themselves and were turned down. For instance, one scientist wished to take LSD in 1966, but the reasons given were inadequate. (PRO, WO 195/16311 and 16798).
103. Porton is now unsure when exactly this ban was introduced. Porton stated that any staff who broke the ban could be disciplined in the same way as if they had infringed any other workplace regulation. The establishment added it was not aware of any staff testing chemicals on themselves since some LSD experiments in the early 1960s (see chapter eight). Bill Ladell said in November 1965 that 'self-experimentation with any agent was banned at Porton'. (PQs, 23 November 1995; 9 May 1996; PRO, WO 195/16161, first meeting of Applied Biology Committee, November 1965).
104. PQ, 6 June 1996.

105. PRO, DEFE 7/1451, note of a meeting held in the War Office to discuss chemical tests on service volunteers, 21 December 1959.
106. Interview with the author, 6 June 2000.
107. PRO, AIR 20/10719, note of a meeting held on 23 September 1959 to discuss nerve gas tests on human observers.
108. PRO, WO 32/20843, letter from Dr Ladell to Porton's director, Dr Ted Perren, 11 May 1961.
109. PRO, WO 32/20843, minutes of meeting on 9 May 1960 to discuss the subject of human tests with G- and V-agents, point one 'Experiments in the USA'.
110. PRO, WO 32/20843, letter from Dr Bill Ladell to Eric Haddon, director of Chemical Defence Research and Development, 12 May 1961.
111. Officials argued that the experiments could not be left to their American or Canadian allies 'because on a matter so important as this, on which all appraisals, defence planning, etc must be based, the UK must have its own data even if only as a cross-check on American results'. (PRO, AIR 20/10719, letter from A C W Drew of War Office to H T Smith of the Air Ministry, 15 March 1961: draft note by the War Office on tests with V-agents and G-agents on human volunteers, undated).
112. *Chemical Warfare Agents: Toxicology and Treatment*, Marrs, Maynard and Sidell. The experiments are summarised on pp. 127-131, with their references on p. 136. The Americans gave the VX the code-name EA1701, the 'experimental VX-like compound' was known as EA3148. For the total number of subjects tested, see 'Possible long-term health effects of short-term exposure to chemical agents', National Research Council, volume 1 (National Academy Press, Washington DC, 1982), p. 37.
113. PRO, WO 195/14824, 23rd meeting of the Biology Committee, November 1959. The account was given by Dr Ladell. Dr Sim's blood cholinesterase level was reported to have dropped by 88 percent, but 'within a few hours, he had made a spontaneous recovery without treatment'.
114. Joint hearings of the subcommittee on health of the committee on labor and public welfare and the subcommittee on administrative practice and procedure of the committee of the judiciary, United States Senate, 10 & 12 September and 7 November 1975, p. 212.
115. PRO, WO 32/20843, 'Experiments with physiological observers at CDEE', note by Mr James, Director of the Chemical Defence Research Department (DCDRD), 2 February 1962.
116. PRO, WO 195/15335, minutes of 49th meeting of the Chemical Defence Advisory Board, February 1962; WO 32/20843, 'Experiments with physiological observers at CDEE', note by Mr James, Director of the Chemical Defence Research Department (DCDRD), 2 February 1962.
117. Letter to Matthew Taylor MP, 25 January 2000. It states that 'no experiments have ever been carried out at Porton Down in which nerve agents have been injected into human subjects'.
118. PRO, WO 32/20843, 'Experiments with physiological observers at CDEE', note by Mr James, Director of the Chemical Defence Research Department (DCDRD), 2 February 1962.
119. PRO, WO 195/15105, 'Penetration of VX through clothing', Porton Technical Paper 753, January 1961; WO 195/15154, 26th meeting of the Biology Committee, February 1961; *Chemical Warfare Agents: Toxicology and Treatment*, Marrs, Maynard and Sidell, pp. 130 and 136. One of them was almost certainly Dr Ladell (identified by the initials

Notes

WSSL in the trial report) who had tested himself with VX in the previous experiment in January 1958.

120. *Chemical Warfare Agents: Toxicology and Treatment*, Marrs, Maynard and Sidell, p. 130; 'The long-term health effects of nerve agents and mustard' by Frederick Sidell and Col Charles Hurst, submission to the DSB Task Force on Gulf War CW, December 1993, p. 3.
121. All except one of the staff had previously been exposed to nerve gas, emphasising once again how often staff were taking part in experiments.
122. PRO, WO 195/15492, 11th meeting of the Offensive Evaluation Committee, November 1962.
123. PRO, WO 195/15450, 'Vapour toxicity of VX to man', November 1962 (early draft); WO 195/15527, 'Human exposure to VX vapour', Porton Technical Paper 830, January 1963.
124. The early trials were organised to determine how little VX would cause noticeable effects in man. It was found that an exposure of just 1 mg min m^{-3} started miosis, the contraction of the pupil in the eye, compared to 3.3 mg min m^{-3} for sarin.
125. The figure of 10 mg min m^{-3} is given on pp. 86-7 of SIPRI, volume 1. The figure of 50 mg min m^{-3} comes from appendix two of *Chemical Warfare Agents: Toxicology and Treatment*, Marrs, Maynard and Sidell. These authors worked for considerable periods of time for either Porton or its American equivalent.
126. PRO, WO 195/15576, 32nd meeting of the Biology Committee, March 1963.
127. PRO, WO 195/15492, 11th meeting of the Offensive Evaluation Committee, November 1962. In the reports of the trials, the staff are identified only by three letters – presumably the first three letters of their names. Since this individual is denoted by the letters LAD, it is likely that it was Dr Ladell.
128. PRO, WO 195/15576, 32nd meeting of the Biology Committee, March 1963.
129. PRO, WO 195/15526, 'Passage of VX through human skin', Porton Technical Paper 839, January 1963; WO 195/15576, 32nd meeting of the Biology Committee, March 1963. The VX was tagged with P-32. Porton noted that the results more or less tallied with those done by Dr Van Sim at Edgewood Arsenal.
130. PRO, WO 195/15335, minutes of 49th meeting of the Chemical Defence Advisory Board, February 1962.
131. PRO, WO 195/15576, 32nd meeting of the Biology Committee, March 1963.
132. PRO, WO 195/15609, 53rd meeting of the Chemical Defence Advisory Board, June 1963.
133. PRO, WO 195/15576, 32nd meeting of the Biology Committee, March 1963.
134. PRO, WO 195/15826, 'Cutaneous absorption and desorption of VX vapour', Porton Technical Paper 899, March 1964. These experiments were mainly on models and pigs. (For later V-agents experiments using excised human skin, see PRO, WO 189/496, Porton Technical Paper 998, February 1969. The excised skin came from post-mortems or from operations in local hospitals, usually from the mid-abdomen region).
135. Letters from Porton to Ken Livingstone MP, 10 August 1992 and 4 February 1997. In the former, Porton stated that 'no studies involving British service personnel have been carried out using VX nerve agent'.
136. Unwanted attention would also have been drawn towards Britain's secretive chemical warfare policy, which – as described in chapter seven – was in a state of flux in the late 1950s and early 1960s.

CHAPTER SEVEN Conscience Explored

1. *Porton Down – 75 years of chemical and biological defence*, Gradon Carter, (HMSO, 1992), p. 31 (hereafter referred to as Carter).
2. Interview with the author, 1 June 2000.
3. Interview with the author, 6 June 2000.
4. Author's interview with former Porton scientist who requested to remain anonymous.
5. Author's interview with former Porton scientist who requested to remain anonymous.
6. Interview with the author, 7 April 2000. Cookson sat on the Chemistry Committee.
7. Interview with the author, 6 June 2000.
8. Interview with the author, 7 April 2000.
9. Carter, p. 70.
10. Author's interview with former Porton scientist who requested to remain anonymous.
11. Confidential source.
12. The precise title of this, and other divisions, often changed over the years.
13. Conversation with the author, 25 February 2000.
14. Conversation with the author, 14 April 2000. Beswick took over from Ladell around 1966 as the official in charge of the human trials.
15. Quoted in the *Mail on Sunday*, 12 July 1987. Gall died in 1993.
16. Quoted in *New Scientist*, 16 July 1987.
17. Author's interview with former Porton scientist who requested to remain anonymous.
18. Interview with the author, 11 February 2000.
19. Obituary in *The Times*, 29 March 2000.
20. This total has been compiled from official figures and declassified papers, although it is likely to be a slight under-estimate. The exact total is not known. Porton has stated that the figure is 'some 3,000'. (*Guardian*, 3 September 1999; PQ, 18 July 1995. The figure is misprinted as '300'; the correct figure is given in the original answer sent as a letter to Ken Livingstone, the MP who raised the question.)
21. 'Possible long-term health effects of short-term exposure to chemical agents', US National Academy of Sciences, volume 1, (National Academy Press, Washington DC, 1982 and 1985), p. 37. It breaks down as follows: VX 740, sarin (GB) 246, soman (GD) 83, an experimental VX-like compound known as EA 3148 30, tabun (GA) 26, GF 21, DFP/PF-3 11.
22. Letter from Perrin Beatty, Minister of National Defence, to Pauline Jewett MP, 15 September 1988.
23. *Chemical Warfare Agents: Toxicology and Treatment*, Timothy C Marrs, Robert Maynard and Frederick Sidell, (John Wiley & Sons, 1996), p. 116.
24. PRO, WO 195/14846, 'History of the service volunteer programme at Porton', November 1959, Porton Note 119, appendix 8.
25. Letter to Ken Livingstone MP, 10 June 1998. Porton added that its records of human experiments were not complete.
26. According to the MoD, these GF tests were 'designed to examine the effects of the compound on the airway of the subject'. The volunteers breathed in the nerve gas deeply and held their breath for two seconds. This experiment 'revealed short-term changes occurred in airway resistance which were resolved in 24 hours'. It is not clear

NOTES

why Porton was testing GF at this particular time. (Letters from Earl Howe, the then junior defence minister, to Ken Livingstone MP, 13 November 1995 and 29 February 1996; PQ, 18 July 1995).

27. His account is based on interviews with the author and with Observer Film Company, 1994, and his article in Chemistry and Industry magazine, 7 March 1994. During his experiment, his cholinesterase level dipped by 40 percent at its peak.
28. PRO, WO 195/16227, 'Report on human safety committee', 1966.
29. PRO, WO 195/15108, 'Fate of liquid G and V on the skin', Porton Technical Paper 756, 1961; WO 195/15154, 26th meeting of the Biology Committee, February 1961.
30. For example, in 1967, Porton was again discussing injecting sarin into human volunteers. The Committee on the Safety of Human Experiments considered 'unanimously' that this was safer and more accurate than tests in which the volunteers breathed in the nerve gas. But a senior Porton official pointed that intravenous injection 'had been discussed at great length some years ago' and referred 'to very high authority and permission had been refused'. (PRO, WO 195/16431).
31. PRO, WO 195/14268, 'The desirability of human experiments on the effects of exercise during or after exposure to anticholinesterase agents', Porton Note 2, February 1958.
32. PRO, WO 195/14321, 20th meeting of the Biology Committee, March 1958. Ladell proposed that these tests would be done first with sarin 'but would be extended to other [nerve gases] when permission was obtained to do so'.
33. PRO, WO 195/16809, 'Limit on exposure of man to GB only', 1968; WO 195/16431, Committee on Safety of Human Experiments, report of meetings 28-32, 1967.
34. PRO, WO 195/15625, 'Physical performance following inhalation of GB', Porton Technical Paper 855, 1963.
35. Details of this test are contained in CDE Technical Note 237, 'Effects of a single exposure to sarin on human physical performance'. This report is still being kept secret by Porton, but the key information has been given on pp. 121-2 of *Chemical Warfare Agents: Toxicology and Treatment*, Marrs, Maynard and Sidell.
36. PRO, WO 195/14268, 'The desirability of human experiments on the effects of exercise during or after exposure to anticholinesterase agents', Porton Note 2, February 1958. Once again, Porton and the Americans had suggested doing these tests at one of the regular Tripartite conferences.
37. PRO, WO 195/15244, 'GB exposure during simultaneous experimental acclimatisation to heat and cold in man', Porton Technical Paper 780, August 1961.
38. PRO, WO 32/20843, letter from Ladell to Professor J L M Morrison, 31 August 1959.
39. PRO, WO 195/16530, report of meetings 33-37 of the Committee on Safety of Human Experiments, 1967; WO 195/16809, 'Limit on exposure of man to GB only', 1968; WO 195/16811, human exposures to GB, 1968; WO 195/16690, report of meetings 38-43 of the Committee on Safety of Human Experiments, 1968; WO 195/16855, seventh meeting of the Applied Biology Committee, December 1968.
40. Author's interview with former Porton scientist who requested to remain anonymous.
41. PRO, WO 195/14442, 'Special senses and GB vapour in man hearing', Porton Note 45, 1958.
42. PRO, WO 195/15101, 'The action of anticholinesterases and pressor amines on the capacity veins of the leg', Porton Technical Paper 745, 1960.
43. PRO, WO 195/14997, 'Changes in cardiac output following the administration of sarin and other pharmacological agents (part 3)', Porton Technical Paper 736, 1960.

44. PRO, WO 195/14748, 'The intercostal muscles and GB inhalation in man', Porton Technical Paper 693, 1959.
45. PRO, WO195/14763, 'Symptomatology and cholinesterase depression in man resulting from exposure to GB vapour', Porton Technical Paper 695, 1959.
46. PRO, WO 195/14823, 'The single-breath administration of sarin', Porton Technical Paper 702, 1959 (see also WO 195/15069, Porton Note 172, 1960).
47. Author's interview with former scientist who requested to remain anonymous.
48. For a review of Porton's human experiments on the effects of nerve gas on the eyes, see a paper written in 1967 at PRO, WO 195/16531.
49. PRO, WO 195/16527, 'The effect of nerve agents on the eyes – the "problem" ', 1967.
50. PRO, WO 195/16532, 'Experimental investigation of the military significance of miosis', 1967. Back in 1949, Porton had estimated that 3.3 mg.min.m^{-3} was the lowest dosage which would cause nerve gas symptoms (see chapter four). This report comments that this figure 'appears to be incorrect and it is felt that insufficiently sensitive methods of pupil measurement may have been used'.
51. 'The effects of a chemical agent on the eyes of aircrew', CDE Technical Paper 137, 1973. This report is still classified secret, but some information can be found in *Chemical Warfare Agents: Toxicology and Treatment*, Marrs, Maynard and Sidell, p. 125.
52. 'Estimation of the concentrations of nerve gas vapour required to produce measured degrees of miosis in rabbit and human eyes', CDE Technical Paper 64, 1971. Once again, Porton has refused to publish this report, but the salient details are available in *Chemical Warfare Agents: Toxicology and Treatment*, Marrs, Maynard and Sidell, pp. 125-6. The number of volunteers in this experiment is unknown.
53. Interview with the author, 25 November 1995. In a letter to his MP on 16 January 1996, Porton confirmed that Knowles underwent a series of experiments and 'skin sensitivity tests for materials for use in protective clothing and decontamination studies'.
54. Porton has been unable to 'locate very much data' on his experiments, but adds that 'the records we have do not indicate that he experienced any unexpected reactions'.
55. British Journal of Pharmacology (1973), 48, pp. 309-313.
56. 'Experimental Eye Research' (1975), 20, pp. 15-21. There appears to be a still-classified report of this experiment, entitled 'a comparative study of central visual field changes induced by sarin vapours and physostigmine salicylate eyedrops'.
57. The two reports are CDE TP 64 and CDE TN 237 which have already been described in this chapter using information in the 1996 book by ex-Porton scientists, Timothy Marrs and Robert Maynard.
58. Private information.
59. Porton argued that when the two reports were originally produced in the 1970s, Britain was facing the threat of chemical attack from hostile countries (in the old Communist Bloc) which already knew much about the effects of nerve gases on humans. The reports were then not classified. But, 'over the past 20 years', as Porton explained, 'the situation has changed quite significantly and our assessment of the perceived threat to the UK from chemical and biological weapons is now different'. Although not spelt out, the government was implying that the threat now comes from a host of Third World countries which are seeking to develop chemical weapons, and, compared with the Soviet Union of old, these countries are starting from scratch with only a small body of technical knowledge. This is surely a classic case of shutting the stable door after the horse has bolted. A large amount of research illuminating how nerve gases attack the

NOTES

human body has already been published in a variety of places, and scientists from Porton and other chemical warfare installations around the world have made public all sorts of information on this subject in books and scientific journals. A series of internal Porton papers have also been released to the Public Record Office. All these sources are open and have been quoted in this book and elsewhere. It therefore seems that the results of the two reclassified reports of nerve gas experiments in the 1970s represent a tiny proportion of research compared to the total amount which has been previously published – a proverbial drop in the ocean. (Letters from Porton to Ken Livingstone MP, 3 July and 21 October 1996).

60. PQ, 24 June 1994.
61. Letter to Ken Livingstone MP, 14 October 1997.
62. The impetus behind the proposal came from the RAF, which wanted to know how pilots would be affected if they were exposed to 3 mg min m^{-3} of nerve gas for a long period after an attack on an airbase. 'Such an effect would clearly be of more significance in a fast jet pilot than, for example, in a soldier in the field.' The proposal was approved by Porton's Independent Ethics Committee, but, as it turned out, the MoD decided on an alternative – to use a 'technique whereby the effects of the nerve agent were simulated using eyedrops and corrective blurring lenses'. (Letter to Matthew Taylor, 10 December 1999; *Guardian*, 20 October 1999).
63. PQ, 7 February 1996.
64. Interview with the author, 2 February 2000. The Independent Ethics Committee approved the 1995 proposal to test volunteers with nerve gas 'on the grounds that the detailed information gained would be vitally important to our knowledge about the operational effectiveness of aircrew' after a chemical attack. According to Porton, the committee decided that 'the risk of any adverse effects at such a low vapour concentration was negligible'.
65. PQ, 7 February 1996.
66. The decision in 1956 had originally applied to nerve gas. The government followed through the implications of that decision and decided in 1957 to get rid of the remaining mustard gas stocks and munitions.
67. PRO, CAB 131/17, minutes of the defence committee, 10 July 1956 and accompanying memorandum DC (56) 13.
68. See, for example, PRO, WO 286/77.
69. PRO, WO 286/77; DEFE 13/440; DEFE 10/355.
70. PRO, DEFE 10/34, review of defence R&D, 23 January 1956.
71. This committee had been unsure about nerve gas in a review two years earlier. On that occasion, in November 1954, it had recommended that 'if, but only if, the Services can reasonably expect to use chemical weapons from the beginning of a war, there is strong justification for producing toxic agents in quantity and stock-piling weapons as war reserves.' (PRO, DEFE 10/33).
72. House of Commons, oral answers, 6 March 1990. For many years, the British government rarely elaborated on the reasons behind the 1956 decision. A handout given to the press during the open day at Nancekuke on 29 October 1970 said that 'international tension relaxed to the point where it was not judged necessary' to produce nerve gas on a large scale. Something approaching the truth was finally given by the Ministry of Defence in a parliamentary answer on 18 July 1995 when the MoD stated that the 1956 decision had been taken 'after reassessment of the most effective deterrents to aggression in keeping with national financial capabilities'.

NOTES

73. Ministry of Defence manual 'Instructions for Record Reviewers', (annex B, appendix 7, chemical and biological warfare records).
74. In those two years, a small machine for filling shells with the sarin had been installed, but only ran with a simulant, not actual nerve gas.
75. The Ministry of Defence has given substantial details of this dumping – code-named Operation Sandcastle – in letters to the campaigning group, the Celtic League, on 30 January 1995 and Plaid Cymru MP Dafydd Wigley on 24 January 1995. The MoD said the letters were written after an investigation of files in the PRO (AIR 29/2017, AIR 25/1537 and ADM 1/26657). See also the *Scotsman*, 9 October 1994; *New Statesman*, 24 March 1995; *Guardian*, 28/29 March 1995.
76. PRO, DEFE 41/157, note by Air Ministry on chemical warfare reserve policy for the chemical warfare sub-committee of the Chiefs of Staff Committee, 30 July 1952; DEFE 10/26, Defence Research Committee Policy paper on chemical warfare research and development policy, 24 February 1950; Gradon Carter and Graham Pearson, RUSI Journal, February 1996.
77. See, for example, PRO, CO 537/2702.
78. According to Porton, details of the trials are recorded in Porton Technical Papers 420, 421, 477-480 and Porton Reports 2761, 2763 and 2765. Some of these have been declassified and are in the PRO. For instance, the report of the third expedition is located at WO 189/149.
79. PQ, 24 June 1997. The MoD claims that 'all efforts were made to retrieve any unexploded munitions', adding that although it does not have full records, the site was only used 'on a relatively small scale and would not have been expected to leave any traces'. There was one experiment in which five Nigerian soldiers were injected with atropine, the antidote to nerve gas, to assess its effect in a warm, moist climate, but they were not exposed to the gas itself (PRO, WO 195/12999).
80. For official papers on this debate, see PRO, DEFE 4/156, DEFE 13/440, DEFE 5/131 DEFE 24/31 and defence research policy committee documents in DEFE 10/282, 283, 355, 358, 382, 450, 490, 491.
81. PRO, CAB 131/28, Minutes of Cabinet Defence committee, 3 May 1963 and memorandum on chemical and biological warfare policy by Minister of Defence, 16 April 1963, D (63) 14.
82. For more details, see papers in PRO, WO 32/20163, DEFE 13/440, DEFE 24/6 and 31, DEFE 10/570, DEFE 5/162 and 176, DEFE 6/97 and 104.
83. RUSI Journal, February 1996, Gradon Carter and Graham Pearson; declaration of past chemical weapons activities by the United Kingdom for the Chemical Weapons Convention, May 1997, p. 5.
84. PRO, DEFE 4/224, confidential annex of Chiefs of Staff committee, 30 January 1968.
85. PRO, FCO 10/181, memo on 2 July 1968.
86. RUSI Journal, February 1996, Gradon Carter and Graham Pearson. They state that the question was reviewed 'in the light of evolving international circumstances, including the perceived threat, but proposals were never again put before the Cabinet'.
87. After the 1956 decision, Nancekuke staff switched tack. They investigated whether it was possible to manufacture new potential lethal and incapacitating agents as part of Britain's overall work to assess the threat from other countries. Among other tasks, they also supplied nerve gas and other compounds to Porton for its research, produced chemicals and other material for chemical defence, and manufactured CS tear gas.
88. See, for example, discussions in PRO, WO 32/21686.

NOTES

89. The final closure of Nancekuke was witnessed in March 1979 by representatives of 19 nations as a way of boosting conference in the talks to achieve a treaty banning chemical weapons. Nancekuke was returned to the RAF and is now a control and reporting post within RAF Portreath.
90. Carter, p. 79.
91. Obituary in *The Times*, 29 March 2000.
92. For an official description, see the MoD's publication, 'Defending against the threat from chemical and biological weapons', July 1999, pp. 21-2.
93. Interview with the author, 6 June 2000.
94. *The Times*, 4 October 1980.
95. *New Statesman*, 11 January 1985.

CHAPTER EIGHT *Britain's Psychedelic Soldiers*

1. Ministry of Defence manual 'Instructions for Record Reviewers', (annex B, appendix 7, chemical and biological warfare records), version written probably in 1992. It cautioned that human experiments are a sensitive topic with regard to releasing records, adding, 'Work with incapacitants such as LSD, BZ and other gylcollates which produce behavioural changes is particularly contentious'.
2. A key report was made in 1949 by L Wilson Greene, an Edgewood Arsenal scientist. Greene speculated that the enemy – if exposed to such drugs – would lose their will to resist and instead succumb to mass hysteria and panic. He listed a series of compounds which ought to be investigated. ('Psychochemical warfare – a new concept of war', Army Chemical Centre report, August 1949).
3. 'Summary of Major Events and Problems', United States Army Chemical Corps, Fiscal Year 1958, p. 100 (obtained by the author under the United States Freedom of Information Act on 1 May 1991).
4. 'Summary of Major Events and Problems', United States Army Chemical Corps, Fiscal Year 1955, pp. 48-49, (obtained by the author under the United States Freedom of Information Act on 10 July 1992).
5. The full list also included 'symptoms of delusion, depression, paralysis, unco-ordination, listlessness, weakness, headache, nausea, dizziness, defects in hearing, sight or judgement and (skin-affecting) disorders'. ('Summary of Major Events and Problems', United States Army Chemical Corps, Fiscal Year 1955, pp. 48-49).
6. 'Summary of Major Events and Problems', United States Army Chemical Corps, Fiscal Year 1958, p. 101.
7. Tennis professional Harold Blauer was undergoing psychiatric treatment at a New York hospital. Unfortunately this hospital was also receiving money from the US Army Corps to investigate the effects of mescaline and its derivative compounds. One of these was given to Blauer on the morning of 8 January 1953. Within 30 minutes, he was rigid all over and had fallen into a deep coma. By lunchtime, he was dead. The doctors had injected him with a drug about which they knew virtually nothing. One later said, 'We didn't know if it was dog piss or what it was we were giving him'. His family only found out the truth in the late 1970s (like the Olson case which is described later in this chapter).
8. 'Summary of Major Events and Problems', United States Army Chemical Corps, Fiscal Year 1957, pp. 97-99 (obtained by the author under the United States Freedom of

NOTES

Information Act on 14 June 1991). The Americans had been examining tetrahydrocannabinol – the main ingredient of marijuana.

9. 'Summary of Major Events and Problems', United States Army Chemical Corps, Fiscal Year 1958, p. 100-1.
10. 'Germs and gas – the weapons nobody dares talk about', Brig Gen J H Rothschild, *Harper's magazine*, June 1959, pp. 29-34.
11. Wall Street Journal, 16 August 1963, quoted in *A Higher Form of Killing: The secret story of gas and germ warfare*, Robert Harris and Jeremy Paxman, (Triad Paladin, 1983), p. 186.
12. PRO, DEFE 10/382, 'Incapacitating Agents' note by Eric Haddon (then in Whitehall, but later Porton's director), December 1959.
13. PRO, DEFE 13/440, Note for the Defence Research Policy Committee, 31 August 1960.
14. Graham Pearson and Gradon Carter made the same point in their survey of Britain's chemical weapons policy in the RUSI Journal, February 1996, pp. 64-5.
15. As early as July 1951, the Americans had sent over to Porton documents on pyscho-chemicals, particularly LSD. (PRO, WO 195/11532).
16. According to a progress report in December 1956, Porton had in the last six months started to investigate LSD and related compounds 'with a view to assessing the potentialities of drugs of this type as CW agents', and an academic who served on Porton's advisory committees had done some initial work on LSD in 1954. (PRO, WO 188/710, progress report no 28 for the half-year ended December 1956, paragraph 49; WO 195/12778, 'Studies with LSD' by Professor Robert Thompson, Guy's Hospital Medical School; *Science*, 120, pp. 990-1, 1954).
17. PRO, WO 188/710, a progress report on research and development at Porton in December 1959 states that 'the programme of research on incapacitating agents has been expanded'; PRO, WO 188/706. A similar review in July 1960 notes in the foreword that 'more and more attention is being paid to the potential use in war of non-lethal incapacitating agents'.
18. RO, WO 195/15170, 'The biological testing of incapacitating agents, part two – the results of tests using drugs with known effects on man', Porton Technical Paper 766, January 1961.
19. *Independent*, 16 April 1993.
20. *Lancet*, 2 April 1955, p. 719, volume 268.
21. 'Psycho-chemicals' by Dr Van Sim, 14 September, 1956, Chemical Warfare Laboratories Report number 2071, US Army Chemical Centre, Maryland.
22. PRO, WO 195/14232, 'Inhibition of monoamine oxidase or pseudo-cholinesterase as a possible mode of action of hallucinogens', Porton Technical Paper 624, November 1957.
23. PRO, WO 195/14637, 32nd meeting of the Chemistry Committee, March 1959.
24. PRO, WO 195/15026, 'Screening tests prior to administration of psychotomimetic drugs in human subjects', Porton Note 166, September 1960.
25. Author's interview with former Porton scientist who requested to remain anonymous.
26. PRO, WO 195/15289, 28th meeting of Biology Committee, November 1961. WO 195/15026 (Porton Note 166) describes the tests in detail. The scientific validity and value of such tests may be questioned. On a lighter note, one volunteer who went to Porton around 1968 recalls that he was bemused when he was questioned by a psychologist at Porton. One of the questions was, 'Do you masturbate?'. He says, 'God

knows why they asked that. It's the sort of question which does stick in your mind. The rest of the questions were nothing unusual.'
27. PQs, 3 November 1994; 7 December 1994. In a two-week stay, a volunteer would spend the first seven days undergoing these checks, and if he passed, he would then be given the drug in the second week.
28. PRO, WO 195/16161, first meeting of the Applied Biology Committee, November 1965.
29. PRO, WO 195/16213, Summary of work on LSD at Porton in the last five years.
30. Dr WM Hollyhock, *New Scientist*, 22 April 1965.
31. PRO, WO 195/16371, third meeting of the Biology Committee, 1966.
32. To get an indication of the nature of these tests, see PRO, WO 195/16290 and WO 195/16212.
33. At one stage in 1962, staff reported that the programme had been interrupted for nearly two months because the hospital was being redecorated. 'It seemed inadvisable to have men under [mind-altering] drugs possibly under observation by the decorators,' it was noted dryly. (PRO, WO 195/15381.)
34. PRO, DEFE 5/131, Memorandum on chemical and biological warfare (COS 62/432), 6 November 1962.
35. The other scenario was straightforward retaliation in a limited war. The Chiefs also recommended that the War Office should study the potential for using both incapacitating and lethal chemical weapons in an all-out war in Europe. For further discussion of how the British military believed incapacitating chemicals could be used in warfare, see PRO, WO 32/20163, particularly, a policy paper by Porton official M A P Hogg in August 1963 discusses the pros and cons of incapacitating chemicals in combat. The compounds that were tested on human 'guinea pigs' in the 1960s feature in this paper.
36. The RAF top brass were not fully convinced at the time about the advantages of chemical weapons in these scenarios. One briefing paper commented, 'Regrettably the arguments are not as sound as one would wish.' (PRO, AIR 8/1936, 19 March 1963).
37. PRO, CAB 131/28, Minutes of Cabinet Defence committee, 3 May 1963 and memorandum on chemical and biological warfare policy by Minister of Defence, 16 April 1963, D (63) 14.
38. PRO, WO 195/16213, Summary of work on LSD at Porton in the last five years.
39. *ibid*
40. PRO, WO 195/16137. 'A field experiment using LSD25 on trained troops', Porton Technical Paper 936, August 1965.
41. PRO, WO 195/16161, first meeting of the Applied Biology Committee, November 1965.
42. PRO, WO 195/16137, 'A field experiment using LSD25 on trained troops', Porton Technical Paper 936, August 1965.
43. PQ, 11 January 1996.
44. PRO, WO 195/16137, 'A field experiment using LSD25 on trained troops', Porton Technical Paper 936, August 1965; WO 195/16660, 'Recount – a second field experiment to assess the effects of T3456 (LSD) on trained troops', Porton Technical Paper 979, September 1967. The report of Operation Moneybags states that 'the men knew they would be "drugged" on one day'. The Recount report states that the purpose of the trial was explained to the men – 'the nature of the compound to be tested was

not mentioned neither was any clue given as to what symptoms might be expected from its administration'. T3456 is Porton's code-name for LSD.
45. PQ, 18 July 1995. The declassified documents in the Public Record Office do not throw much light on what the volunteers in the laboratory tests were told, although it's likely to be similar to the volunteers in the outdoor exercises.
46. Author's interview with former member of Porton's staff who requested to remain anonymous.
47. Interview with the author, 30 March 1996.
48. PRO, WO 195/16161, first meeting of the Applied Biology Committee, November 1965.
49. *ibid.*
50. PRO, WO 195/16273, second meeting of the Applied Biology Committee, April 1966.
51. PRO, WO 195/16214, Proposals for future work on LSD in medical research division – animal and human work, 1966.
52. *ibid.*
53. WO 195/16427, progress report on work with T3456, 1967; WO 195/16528, T3456 by inhalation progress report, 1967. In January 1996, under pressure from MPs, Porton – in a gesture of openness – released a batch of 11 files on the LSD tests. Porton stated in a PQ on 25 January 1996 that eight papers 'which include references to laboratory work involving LSD and other substances being tested on animals' remain classified. The work was 'primarily concerned with analytical methods'.
54. PRO, WO 195/16311, Report on meetings 23-27 of the CDEE Human Safety Committee by the chairman, 1966.
55. PRO, WO 195/16131, report by the Chairman of the Committee on the Safety of Human Experiments (COSHE), November 1965.
56. PRO, WO 195/16690, report of the meetings 38-43 of the Committee on the Safety of Human Experiments, 1968; WO 195/16699, progress report on laboratory experiments with T3456, 1968.
57. PRO, WO 195/16660, 'Recount – a second field experiment to assess the effects of T3456 (LSD) on trained troops', Porton Technical Paper 979; WO 195/16312, 'Exercise Recount – preliminary report of a field experiment', 20 September 1966; PQ, 16 January 1995.
58. Interview with the author, 24 April 1998. Coates also tested gas masks in clouds of tear gas.
59. PRO, WO 195/16529, 'Progress report on laboratory experiments with T3456', October 1967.
60. 'The determination of T3456 in human plasma following oral administration.' Technical Note 5, May 1969 (released to Ken Livingstone MP on 13 October 1997). The results of the paper had been published in a scientific journal in 1972 (*Clinica Chimica Acta*), volume 36, pp. 67-73).
61. Interview with the author, 12 April 1998.
62. It is unclear whether the human 'guinea pigs' in the previous two open-air trials were true volunteers. The report of Operation Moneybags states that 'all the men were spontaneous volunteers, and although they came from the same unit, the men had not previously worked together as a group and the officer was relatively inexperienced. These facts influenced the design of the trial'. The report of the second trial – Recount – also states that 'all the men...were volunteers who submitted themselves only after a

senior member of Porton staff had visited [their] regiment and talked to the men, explaining, in general outline, the purpose of the trial'. Gunner Barry Coates, who took part in Recount, but was not drugged with LSD, says of the volunteers, 'Nobody was forced to go', adding that there were enough from the regiment as a whole to make up the required numbers. He went because he wanted to escape the tedium of his military routine for a little while.

63. PRO, WO 189/122, 'Small Change – a brief preliminary report', Porton Technical Note 53, February 1968; PQ, 8 March 1995.

64. Stubbs also took part in other Porton experiments – one was to measure the size of tablets which could be swallowed by a person. He does not believe that the Porton tests caused any long-term illnesses, but is, however, worried that his participation in the tests is not recorded on any of his military service records.

65. The only sergeant who received LSD in the trial was number 33 (each person was allocated a number). He is judged by the official observers as being 'severely' affected by the drug after an hour – 'quiet, very indecisive and uncertain of himself'. During the exercise, he was 'perfectly aware of the axis of advance and yet appeared to be completely uncertain of the tactics being employed. This uncertainty caused him to withdraw from his responsibilities and for the hour in question, he refrained from giving any orders.'

66. PQ, 18 April 1996.

67. PQ, 3 November 1994; PRO, WO 195/16855, seventh meeting of the Applied Biology Committee, December 1968.

68. PRO, WO 195/16429, 'A review of some concepts of incapacitation', 1967. In this paper, three Porton scientists speculate on possible future avenues of uncovering chemicals which will incapacitate humans on the battlefield.

69. Untransmitted interview with Observer Films, 1994. The author has relied on this taped interview since Neville Gadsby was unable to be reinterviewed for medical reasons.

70. Author's interview with former Porton scientist who requested to remain anonymous.

71. Author's interview with former Porton official who requested to remain anonymous.

72. For a typical view, see the comment by Porton's then director, Eric Haddon, that the manufacture of LSD 'in quantity might now be possible' and that 'Iron Curtain countries were known to be very interested in it'. (PRO, WO 195/16273, second meeting of the Applied Biology Committee, April 1966).

73. See for example, PQ, 3 November 1994.

74. PQ, 21 November 1994. A year earlier, Dr Pearson had told a member of the public that 'LSD was administered to about 70 volunteers between 1961 and 1972' (Letter, 21 January 1993).

75. The *Dispatches* programme 'Purple Haze' was broadcast on 3 April 1996. It was made by Granada Television. As well as the Porton Down trials, it looked at how psychiatrists administered LSD to many patients in mental hospitals from the 1950s to the 1970s. The author worked as a researcher on the programme.

76. PQ, 18 April 1996.

77. *Spycatcher*, Peter Wright with Paul Greengrass, (William Heinemann Australia, 1987), p. 160. It appears that many within Porton did not know about these spy tests.

78. There were, for example, no entries for the MI5/MI6 tests in its register which records the names of volunteers and their experiments. On another occasion, Porton said it had

'no record of any work being carried out to assess whether and how LSD could be used in interrogations'. (Letter to Ken Livingstone MP, 14 October 1997; PQ, 14 May 1996).

79. This document, produced in 1966, summarised Porton's LSD human experiments for the previous five years. It states that 'the present interest in LSD dates from the autumn of 1961'. The words 'present interest' may be unintended, or they may actually reveal the true picture. (PRO, WO 195/16213).

80. PRO, WO 32/20163, R&D for counter-insurgency and internal security operations, memo by Geoffrey Baker, Vice Chief of the General Staff, 19 June 1964; correspondence dated 1 & 8 July 1964. Baker, who served in the military for more than three decades, rose to become Chief of the General Staff and a Field Marshal. He knew about counter-insurgency since he had led British operations against Cypriot rebels in the 1950s and arrested their leader, Archbishop Makarios (Obituary, *Daily Telegraph*, 10 May 1980).

81. PRO, WO 195/16161, first meeting of the Applied Biology Committee, November 1965. In another snippet, Britain's spymasters – the Joint Intelligence Committee – suggested in 1956 that there should be research into pyscho-chemicals; this was authorised and was to be carried out at Porton. The Ministry of Defence has blocked the release of a memorandum on this initiative into the Public Record Office, although some details have slipped out.

82. *Spycatcher*, p. 161. Wright writes of his disgust at a demonstration of a new James Bond-style gadget at Porton. Ladell and his assistant showed how quickly a sheep could be killed by the cigarette packet which had been modified to shoot a poison-tipped dart. As the sheep died agonisingly, 'white-coated professionals discussed the advantages of the modern new toxin around the corpse.' Wright adds that the horrifying incident proved that his love for animals was stronger than his passion for spying.

83. Interview with Royston Clarke for *Dispatches* programme 'Purple Haze' broadcast on 3 April 1996.

84. Final report of the Select Committee to study government operations with respect to intelligence activities, United States Senate (April 1976), pp. 392-3.

85. ibid, pp. 393 & 399.

86. ibid, pp. 393-403. The case is also described in the most comprehensive book on the CIA's mind control experiments, *The Search for the 'Manchurian Candidate'*, by John Marks (Allen Lane, 1979). The book was based on documents prised out of the CIA through the US Freedom of Information Act. The CIA had destroyed many of the key documents in 1973.

87. *The Search for the 'Manchurian Candidate'*, p. 101.

88. ibid, p. 121.

89. ibid, p. 30. *Freedom* magazine (published by the Church of Scientology) reproduced part of the minutes in its 63rd edition, May 1979.

90. Reports of the committee are located in the Public Record Office at classmarks WO 195/14272; WO 195/14656; WO 195/15180; WO195/15322; WO195/15388; WO195/15786.

91. 'Effects of pyrexal in man', Porton Technical Paper 841, February 1963. This paper describes Porton's human experiments with pyrexal which drew to a close by 1963. A copy of this report – under the title of 'Oripavine derivative as a potential incapacitating agent' – is in the PRO at WO 195/15503.

92. PRO, WO 188/710, 'Directorate of Chemical Defence Research and Development, progress report for the half-year ended June 30, 1959', paragraph 42.

NOTES

93. PRO, WO 188/710, 'Directorate of Chemical Defence Research and Development, progress report for the half-year ended June 30, 1960', paragraph 11.
94. Interview with the author, 16 January 1996; letters to him from Porton, 12 February 1996 and 25 March 1996. According to Porton, he was given either 0.3 microgrammes or 0.5 microgrammes of pyrexal.
95. Letter from Porton to Gordon Bell, 28 November 1996. According to Porton, 34 people sniffed a spray containing pyrexal in this experiment, producing no reaction in any of them. He cannot remember anything of this test. Porton concluded that sniffing pyrexal in this way 'was an ineffective method of administration'.
96. PRO, WO 195/15217, 27th meeting of the Biology Committee, July 1961; WO 195/15576, 32nd meeting of the Biology Committee, March 1963; WO 195/15077, 25th meeting of the Biology Committee, November 1960.
97. PRO, WO 195/15786, UK progress report on the search for new agents for 17th Quadripartite CBR Conference, (March 1964), p. 45. This same report states that of all the new compounds being examined by Porton at that time, none approached the potency of TL2636.
98. Through the Industrial Liaison Programme, Porton was quietly in touch with commercial firms in case they turned up a chemical which would be useful in warfare.
99. PRO, WO 195/16131, Report by the chairman of the Committee on the Safety of Human Experiments (COSHE), November 1965; for a description of the early trials, see PRO 189/357, 'An oripavine derivative (TL2636) as a potential incapacitating agent', Porton Technical Paper 835, 1963.
100. Author's interview with former Porton scientist who requested to remain anonymous.
101. PRO, WO 195/15477, 31st meeting of the Biology Committee, November 1962; PRO, WO 195/15498, 43rd meeting of the Chemistry Committee, November 1962. According to Dr Ladell, TL2636 did not produce a state of catalepsy in any of the human subjects, nor had it acted like a painkiller.
102. PRO, WO 195/16131, Report by the chairman of the Committee on the Safety of Human Experiments (COSHE), November 1965.
103. Details of the earlier tests are sketchy. One compound, code-named T2833, apparently had a 'rapid knock-down' effect when injected. (PRO, WO 195/15381; WO 195/15697).
104. It is not known how many men were tested with this compound in total, but it appears to be at least 175. (PRO, DEFE 10/571, Defence Research committee memorandum DR/P (64) 35, December 1964; WO 195/16065, Summary of Porton's annual report 1964-65; for a description of the later experiments on 27 men around 1968, see PRO, WO 195/16691).
105. PRO, WO 195/15477, 31st meeting of the Biology Committee, November 1962.
106. 'Summary of Major Events and Problems', United States Army Chemical Corps, Fiscal Years 1961-2, pp. 124-5 (obtained by the author under the United States Freedom of Information Act on 16 May 1990).
107. *ibid*, pp. 125-6.
108. SIPRI, volume 2, p. 47.
109. A 1990 film, *Jacob's Ladder* portrays a frightening rollercoaster of bad trips and hallucinations suffered by an American soldier years after he was allegedly exposed to a chemical in Vietnam; it appears that this chemical was based on BZ.

110. PRO, WO 195/16131, report by the chairman of the Committee on the Safety of Human Experiments (COSHE), November 1965.
111. PRO, WO32/21379, letter on 22 March 1961 from British Joint Services Missions (Army staff) to the Under-Secretary of State, War Office. BZ is referred to by its American code-name, EA2277. Like Porton, the Americans assigned numbers to the chemicals which were examined for their toxicity. EA stood for Edgewood Arsenal. (Porton's equivalent number for BZ was T2532). The real name for BZ is 3-quinuclidinyl benzilate.
112. PRO, DEFE 6/97, Memorandum on chemical and biological warfare by the defence planning staff of the Chiefs of Staff, July 1965.
113. PRO, WO 195/16432, Porton report on the US experience with BZ and other benzilates and glycollates, April 1967.
114. PRO, WO 195/15900, 34th meeting of the Chemistry Committee, July 1964; WO 195/16462, fourth meeting of the Applied Biology Committee, April 1967.
115. PQs, 16 March 1995; 5 July 1995. The figure is given in a letter from Porton's former Director-General, Dr Graham Pearson, 21 January 1993, to a member of the public. The aim of the tests was to 'identify the symptoms arising from exposure to BZ'.
116. In the early phase of the trials with BZ, 17 human subjects were given BZ between 1962 and 1964. It was noted, for example, that 'in contrast with the US experiments, some men could remember afterwards some of their activities during the drugged condition'. (PRO, WO 195/16428, early exploratory work with BZ in the UK, 1967; WO 195/16462, fourth meeting of the applied Biology Committee, 1967).
117. PRO, WO 195/16533, 'Preliminary report on human laboratory tests of BZ', September 1967. This test involving four subjects was apparently Porton's last human experiment with BZ.
118. PQs, 12 May 1993; 19 July 1993. Porton maintains that, as with the LSD tests, the subjects were 'screened for normality' before and after the tests to exclude anyone who may be mentally vulnerable.
119. Brief descriptions of Porton's human experiments with this glycollate, known as MPIPG, and BZ are given in a report – an overview of research carried out on glycollates and related compounds at Porton Down, published in September 1999. The last exposures with the glycollate occurred in 1971/2 – curiously late for this kind of work at Porton which had tailed off by the late 1960s. The early human experiments, around 1968, with the glycollate (code-named T3436) are discussed in PRO, WO 195/16695, WO 195/16799 and WO 195/16804. In 1998, the Ministry of Defence announced that Iraq had produced 'large quantities' of a 'mental incapacitant' agent known as Agent 15. The MoD believed that Agent 15 was a glycollate. In the 1960s, Porton tested Agent 15 on animals, but not humans.
120. Stanley started his legal action in 1979, won it in 1984, but then lost it on appeal in 1987 when the US Supreme Court ruled that the military were protected from such lawsuits. He won compensation following a special bill in the US Congress. A panel of arbitrators awarded him the sum of money to settle his legal battle with the government. For details of his case, see the *New York Times*, 9 December 1986, the *Washington Post*, 9 August 1987, the *High Times*, March 1992, and Associated Press report, 5 March 1996.
121. *Secret Agenda, The United States Government, Nazi scientists and Project Paperclip, 1945 to 1990*, Linda Hunt (St Martin's Press, New York, 1991), p. 158, based on interviews with James Stanley.

NOTES

122. LSD follow-up study report, October 1980, US Army Medical Department, US Army Health Services Command, Project Director Lieutenant Colonel David McFarling.
123. A Dorset businessman has claimed that servicemen had to be treated in a hospital for mental patients because of chemical experiments. Robert Owen said that in the late 1950s and early 1960s, he occasionally visited his uncle, Brigadier John McGhie, who was in charge of a military hospital at Netley near Southampton, and that he used to accompany his uncle on his rounds. 'During his rounds, I would see and hear patients, as if it were a lunatic asylum of the worst kind. John explained that these poor young soldiers were victims of chemical experiments, such as LSD, from both grenade canisters and artillery shells, "to see what effect they have on the human mind in a battle situation". As a soldier, a medical doctor, and leading psychiatrist, it angered him to have to clear up the after-effects of such experiments'. Mr Owen could add no further detail, nor evidence for his claim. It is however confirmed that Brigadier John McGhie was in charge of the now-demolished hospital, the Royal Victoria, between 1956 and 1961, and his name crops up on declassified Porton documents. These documents show that staff from the Netley hospital assisted the Porton experiments with incapacitating chemicals, mainly by giving medical advice – for example, in 1961/2, they helped screen volunteers to make sure that they were suitable for the experiments. (PRO, WO 195/16579 and WO 195/15381).
124. For example, four volunteers out of 20 were screened out 'as unsuitable' from Operation Moneybags in 1964; 34 out of 80 were eliminated 'for clinical or psychiatric reasons' from the 1966 Recount exercise. Less information is available about the laboratory tests which stretched over six or seven years. It is however known that in one four-month stretch in the early 1960s, 21 out of 46 volunteers were turned away as ill-suited. One report from 1965 noted that 'with the commencement of experimental programmes concerned with exposure to incapacitating drugs, it has become apparent from the initial screening tests that the men reporting are not representative of a Service population, over two-thirds being found unsuitable for employment in this field'. Bill Ladell commented in 1967 that fewer than 20 percent had passed the screening tests in the past, but this had then risen to 'nearer 50 percent'. He added that the standard had not been relaxed, but 'with increasing experience borderline could now be accepted' when they used to be rejected. (PRO, WO 195/15381; reports of the three exercises; WO 195/16136; WO 195/16462).
125. PQ, 18 July 1995.
126. PRO, WO 195/16161, first meeting of the Applied Biology Committee, November 1965.
127. PQ, 21 November 1994.
128. *The Sunday Times*, 19 December 1993; *Mail on Sunday*, 25 September 1994.
129. *Guardian*, 16 February 1995; *The Times*, 1 March 1995.
130. PQs, 13 November 1997; 12 January 1998.

CHAPTER NINE *Tears of Volunteers*

1. The 1997/98 annual report of the Police Complaints Authority, pp. 51-3; PQ, 4 March 1999. Set up in 1985, the PCA supervises police investigations into complaints made by the public against the police.
2. The PCA's description of the case does not give the names of those involved. However the case is almost identical to an incident in Bedfordshire which went to court in June 1998. The PCA-supervised inquiry substantiated the 66-year-old man's complaints

'about the use of force and the length of time he had been detained'. (*Guardian*, 10 June 1998).
3. *Daily Telegraph*, 29 July 1997.
4. *Daily Telegraph*, 31 August 1998.
5. *Guardian*, 8 January 1998; *Guardian*, 28 August 1996.
6. *Daily Telegraph*, *Guardian*, 28 March 1996; *Sunday Times*, 26 January 1997.
7. Mental Health Care journal, August 1998, (volume 1, number 12), pp. 402-4. For one such incident, see *Daily Telegraph*, 7 February 1997.
8. *Daily Telegraph*, 19 August 1997.
9. *Guardian*, 28 July 1998.
10. *Independent*, 1 March 1996.
11. *Independent*, 16 June 1995; Review of police trials of the CS aerosol incapacitant, Police Research Series Paper 21, November 1996, Home Office Police Research Group; *Police Review*, 12 January 1996.
12. *The Times*, 22 August 1996. The two police forces were Hertfordshire and Surrey. (Other dissenting police forces did not appear to declare their position in public). In April 1998, both forces deployed the spray, although Hertfordshire said it was only an interim measure while their staff researched into alternatives.
13. PQ, 7 July 2000. The forces are Northamptonshire, Nottinghamshire and Sussex.
14. The British mixed SK with alcohol to increase its volatility on the battlefield. This mixture was known as KSK. For some earlier discussion of the effects of tear gases, see PRO, WO 142/299.
15. PRO, WO 142/264, Crossley Report, p. 9. Reports of Porton's experiments with SK and tear gases during the First World War are in WO 142/209-211 in the PRO.
16. PRO, WO 142/264, Crossley Report, pp. 69-70.
17. The other chemical weapon was known to the British as NC. This was a mixture of chloropicrin and stannic chloride. Chloropicrin appealed to chemical warfare commanders for a number of reasons – as with chlorine and phosgene, it killed by damaging the lungs (although its toxicity was somewhere between the two); it was a strong tear gas, although not so intense as, say, SK; and it was capable of penetrating German gas masks from early 1917. First exploited by the Russians in 1916, it was adopted by all sides during the war, usually in a variety of mixtures with other chemicals, and used in great quantities. Porton carried out many human experiments with chloropicrin and its mixtures in the war. Again, reports of these tests are in WO 142/209-211 in the PRO.
18. Its chemical name is choracetophenone; it is also known by the initials CAP.
19. 'The Toxicology of CN', Edgewood Arsenal Technical Report EATR 4207, December 1968, p. 19 (released to the author under the US Freedom of Information Act on 1 May 1997).
20. In 1923, a commercial company – which was to be taken over by ICI Ltd within three years – had erected a plant for manufacturing CN. By 1927, it was capable of producing 2,000 kg of CN each month.
21. PRO, CO 537/2712, circular 14452/48 to colonial governments from Arthur Greech-Jones, Secretary of State for the Colonies, June 1948. Information on the total number of times CN was used in the colonies appears to be sparse. One Porton report from 1958 noted that there had been 'widespread use' for a long period. More recently,

NOTES

official Porton historian Gradon Carter commented that for police forces in the Colonies, tear gases had been 'available and occasionally used for many years'. (PRO, WO 195/14415, 'Agents for riot control – the selection of CS as a candidate agent to replace CN', Porton Technical Paper 651, October 1958; *Porton Down – 75 years of chemical and biological defence*, Gradon Carter, (HMSO, 1992), p. 73).

22. See for example, PRO, CO 537/5346, letter from B D Edmonds, Colonial Office, to Lt Col N A C Croft, Essex Regiment, War Office, 19 October 1950.

23. PRO, CO 537/2717, minutes of police officers' conference, Mauritius, 21 February 1947.

24. It is evident that British chemical warfare scientists had tested CN on humans before then. In a report dated January 1919, the Anti-Gas Department in central London (see chapter one) reported on the 'offensive properties' of CN. Three people were exposed to the gas in ever-increasing dosages for three minutes. As the dosages grew stronger, they began to cry more and more from the gas. At the strongest dosage, 'no observer was able to keep his eyes open after two minutes'. (The Toxicology of CN, Edgewood Arsenal Technical Report EATR 4207, December 1968, pp. 30-1).

25. PQ, 20 December 1994; PRO, WO 188/470, Letter from Porton's commandant, 22 May 1936. In this letter, the commandant stated, 'During the past five and half years, 2,106 exposures to lachrymators (including CAP) have been carried out in this station – 1,114 in the field, and 992 in the gas chamber. Respirator fitting tests employing CAP are included in the above. The figures for five years prior to 1930 cannot be quoted with the same exactitude but the numbers are approximately the same'. In 1994, Porton said that, although records no longer remained, it was 'probable' that volunteers were exposed to CN in the inter-war years.

26. Papers relating to such complaints are contained in PRO, WO 188/470, physiological effects of lachrymators, 1931-40.

27. The Toxicology of CN, Edgewood Arsenal Technical Report EATR 4207, December 1968, pp. 13-19. This report remarks that 'in view of the known high toxicity of CN the absence of serious effects from exposure to CN vapours is remarkable. The reason for this is twofold. First, due to the low vapour pressure of CN it is very difficult to secure concentrations of CN in air which are dangerous to life or health. Second, dangerous concentrations of CN are many times higher than intolerable concentrations for the same exposure and no person will voluntarily remain in intolerable concentrations. This fact affords a very high factor of safety in dealing with CN.'

28. PQs, 30 October 1996; 27 October 1997. The Defence Evaluation and Research Agency, which took charge of Porton in April 1995, says that it has not 'assessed the concentrations of CN that cause long-term clinical effects'. It adds, 'Most of the information concerning long-term effects in man is based on case reports from the United States, following widespread use during the 1960s civil rights riots. These reports contain no reliable information regarding the concentrations of CN that produced such effect'.

29. Bryan Ballantyne, who worked at Porton in the 1970s, says, 'Aerosols of CN cause mild conjunctivitis and blepharitis except at high concentrations when corneal epithelial damage and chemosis may occur.' (Corneal epithelial damage is the loss of the protective membrane covering the outside of the eye, leading potentially to permanent scarring). He adds that CN may also cause dermatitis – 'erythema, oedema, vesication, purpura and necrosis have all been described'. In another scientific paper, he and another Porton scientist, David Gall, state that, 'If irritants are to have their place in the control of civil disorder, their safety is of paramount importance. In this respect, the use of CS an alternative to CN was to be preferred. CN, for example, can damage the eye

438

and skin.' Two other Porton scientists in the 1980s, Timothy Marrs and Robert Maynard, have said, 'CN can produce corneal epithelial damage as well as chemosis'. 'Riot control agents – biomedical and health aspects of the use of chemicals in civil disturbances', Bryan Ballantyne, Medical Annual 1977, ed by Scott RB and Frazer J (Wright, Bristol); 'Effects on man of drenching with dilute solutions of CS and CR', Medicine, Science and the Law, 1976, volume 16, number 3, pp. 159-170; Chemical Warfare Agents: Toxicology and Treatment, Timothy C Marrs, Robert L Maynard and Frederick R Sidell, (John Wiley & Sons, 1996), p. 227).

30. PRO, WO 195/14561, Agents for riot control, a study of the toxicity of T792 (CS gas), Porton Technical Paper 672, January 1959. Citing the same 1931 paper, this report also comments, 'Contamination of human skin and of animal eyes with CS demonstrated that the material did no specific damage to these tissues. This compares favourably with the topical trauma which is known to result from similar use of CN.' The official committee under Sir Harold Himsworth – which investigated the medical effects of CS gas (described later in this chapter) – noted that CN 'has been shown to be capable of causing serious damage to the eyes when used in concentrations that could occur in operational situations'. This committee based its conclusion on this Porton Technical Paper.

31. PRO, WO 195/16798, report on meetings 44-49 of the Committee on the Safety of Human Experiments, 1968; WO 195/16855, seventh meeting of the Applied Biology Committee, December 1968.

32. This view was based on a report commissioned by the Home Office which was completed by Porton in December 1994. In the report, Porton scientists noted that at high concentrations, 'CN causes corneal epithelial damage, contact dermatitis consisting of oedema (swelling), blistering and loss of the skin surface and allergic contact dermatitis'. They added that there was a lack of information about the long-term effects of CN and that doubts surrounded its 'potential for chronic lung toxicity'. (PQ, 12 May 1998; the Porton report – 'Review of the toxicology of the riot control agent CS gas' – was obtained by the author after a seven-month delay from the Home Office under the open government code in January 1999).

33. Oral questions, House of Commons, 1 April 1965. Questioned about the use of CN gas in the colonies in the last five years, Anthony Greenwood, then the minister in charge of the colonies, claimed that CN did not produce 'permanent harmful effects', since victims recover within three minutes. He further claimed that 'there is not known to be any case within the period in question where permanent harmful effects have been caused'.

34. BBC – bromobenzyl cyanide – was initially uncovered and adopted for military use by the French in the last five months of the First World War. It is a persistent gas which can powerfully affect the eyes and produce many tears. It is not known how many humans were exposed to BBC or exactly when, although, according to the MoD, volunteers would have been exposed to BBC between the First and Second World Wars when Porton believed that it was an irritating compound which 'would be a useful tear gas'. Experiments with BBC were also carried out in World War Two. (PQ, 19 July 1995; PRO, AVIA 15/596; AVIA 15/891; AVIA 15/896; AVIA 15/374, Porton's Red Book entry for BBC, 1943).

35. This wartime work is documented at some length in a 1948 monograph (PRO, WO 188/730). It is not known how many human 'guinea pigs' were exposed during this work, although the monograph states that 'some 250 compounds have been prepared, most of which have been tested physiologically'. Reports of human experiments with tear gases in 1939 and 1940 (as well as earlier in the 1930s) are in PRO, WO 188/452.

NOTES

36. PRO, AVIA 15/361, Report outlining Porton's organisation and structure, January 1940, Sir Keith Price to Brigadier Goldney, p. 34.
37. PRO, AIR 23/8593, 'Use of non-lethal gas in Malaya'; DEFE 4/59, confidential annex to Chiefs of Staff meeting on 2 February 1953.
38. The MoD has stated recently that 'although the results of the trials showed some potential, available records indicate that the limited stocks of agent available were not in fact used in operations'. (UK declaration of past Chemical warfare activities to the Chemical Weapons Convention, May 1997, p. 138).
39. PRO, CO 537/2712, letter from the Governor of Trinidad, 31 July 1948.
40. PRO, CO 537/5346, letter from B D Edmonds, Colonial Office, to Lt Col N A C Croft, Essex Regiment, War Office, 19 October 1950; reply by Lt Col Croft, 26 October 1950.
41. PRO, WO 195/14415, 'Agents for riot control – the selection of CS as a candidate agent to replace CN', Porton Technical Paper 651, October 1958. CN was also deficient because it was unstable and tended to melt in tropical climates.
42. PRO, CO 537/2711, 'Tear smoke', 1948; CO 537/5346, 'Tear smoke', 1950.
43. The War Office also wanted a new gas which would 'not produce permanent harmful physical effects' and 'not be more likely to produce fatal casualties than CN'. At the same time, the War Office also ordered a 'complete range of riot control equipment and munitions'. (PRO, WO 195/14415, 'Agents for riot control – the selection of CS as a candidate agent to replace CN', Porton Technical Paper 651, October 1958; PRO, WO 32/16608, 'Anti-riot general stores – development 1956-65').
44. *The Technology of Political Control*, Carol Ackroyd, Karen Margolis, Jonathan Rosenhead and Tim Shallice, (Penguin Books, 1977), pp. 213-4.
45. PRO, WO 195/14415, 'Agents for riot control – the selection of CS as a candidate agent to replace CN', Porton Technical Paper 651, October 1958.
46. Interview with the author, 26 March 1996. Sellick does not believe that he has suffered any ill effects from his tests and is more or less in good health for his age.
47. Letter from Porton, 30 April 1996. Sellick was 'exposed to CN and adamsite (DM) both at concentrations of one part per million in air', and although it is not clear, it appears that they were exposed to both chemicals at the same time. None of the twelve could stay in the chamber longer than two minutes and 50 seconds.
48. According to Porton, the importance and purpose of the tests was explained to the men before they were exposed – 'it is considered that their standard of discipline and self-respect, especially in the presence of their fellows, provided a degree of psychological resistance and determination which was comparable to that of well-motivated rioters'. (PRO, WO 195/14415)
49. In one test, he went on a treadmill in a very hot room. Mustard gas was dropped on his inner thigh, producing a blister the size of a 50 pence piece. The blister hurt and then disappeared after a few days. According to Porton, this was a 'trial of A.G. cakes to the thighs'. Porton staff believe it 'probably concerned an alternative approach for administering anti-gas ointment to protect against the effect of mustard gas'. They believe that this idea was not 'explored any further'.
50. Interview with the author, 6 January 1996. For the past fifteen years or so, Jemmett has experienced mystifying spasms.
51. Interview with the author, 28 November 1995; Letters from Porton Down to Mr Payton's MP Ian Bruce, 21 December 1995, 29 January 1996, and 28 February 1996. According to Porton, he was exposed 'for a few minutes' to six chemicals 'at low concentrations (0.1 or 1 part per million in air)'.

NOTES

52. The chemical name of CS is ortho-chlorobenzylidene malononitrile. Porton's code-name for CS is T 792. Several of Porton's reports on CS from this time are available in the PRO in classmark WO 195 (including, WO 195/14428, 15110, 15165, 15212, 15221, and 15234).

53. In late 1934, Porton tested CS on human subjects who found it pretty intolerable. Porton scientists certainly established how powerful CS was, but for some reason, they did not take it further. In May 1935, Porton commented that the 'lachrymatory and irritant properties' of CS were 'interesting'. (For reports of these experiments, see PRO, WO 188/452 and 188/476).

54. The British informed the Americans and Canadians about CS during the regular Tripartite conference in September, 1958. In late 1958, a British liaison officer in Washington noted the 'real enthusiasm' of the Americans for CS. ('Summary of Major Events and Problems', United States Army Chemical Corps, Fiscal Year 1959, pp. 96-8, obtained by the author under the United States Freedom of Information Act on 1 May 1991; PRO, WO 188/709, munitions/TW letter number 33).

55. PRO, DEFE 10/356, note by Defence Research Policy staff on biological and chemical warfare, 28 January 1959.

56. PRO, DEFE 10/382, note on incapacitating agents for defence research policy staff by War Office, December 1959.

57. For a full discussion of the use of CS in the Vietnam war, see SIPRI, volume 1, pp. 185-202. See also PRO, WO 195/16840.

58. UK declaration of past chemical warfare activities to the Chemical Weapons Convention, May 1997, p. 138, p. 5.

59. Oral questions, House of Commons, 1 April 1965.

60. According to official statements, CS was not sold directly to foreign countries. From 1962, CS gas manufactured by Nancekuke was sold to a commercial company which made riot control equipment. This company then exported CS weapons – in the form of grenades and cartridges – abroad under licences issued by the government. This company was Schermuly, a Surrey-based firm. (PRO, PREM 13/221; PQs, 30 May 1968; 19 June 1968; 21 June 1968).

61. PQ, 24 June 1994.

62. PRO, WO 195/15193, 'The influence of particle size in the subjective effects of CS', Porton Technical Paper 776, May 1961; WO 195/15034, 'Relation between particle size and speed of action of CS', August 1960; WO 188/706, 'Review of research and development at Porton and Nancekuke in the last six months', July 1960, p. 11; WO 188/710, 'Progress report for the half-year ended December 31, 1959', p. 36.

63. PRO, DEFE 10/382, note on incapacitating agents for defence research policy staff by War Office, December 1959 and note on chemical warfare, July 1960; WO 188/706, 'Review of research and development at Porton and Nancekuke in the last six months', July 1960, foreword; WO 195/15193, 'The influence of particle size in the subjective effects of CS', Porton Technical Paper 776, May 1961; PRO 195/14774, 'The search for new riot control agents', Porton Note 120, 28 October 1959.

64. Porton scientists hoped such encouragement 'would give confidence to the subject and counteract the lack of group competition'.

65. PRO, WO 195/15835, 'Some experiments on the growth of tolerance to CS', Porton Technical Paper 903, June 1964; WO 195/15077, 25th meeting of the Biology Committee, November 1960. (It appears that these experiments started in 1960.)

NOTES

66. A further experiment on 35 volunteers, reported by Porton in the open literature in 1972, confirmed that people can tolerate relatively low concentrations of CS if the exposure is gradual. (British Journal of Industrial Medicine, 1972, 29, pp. 298-306).
67. Author's interview with former Porton scientist who requested to remain anonymous.
68. PRO, WO 195/15096, 'The ability of troops to mask and remain masked in a cloud of CS', Porton Note 169, December 1960; WO 195/15154, 26th meeting of the Biology Committee, February 1961.
69. PRO, WO 195/14939, 'Investigations into the use of CS as a potential shark repellent', Porton Technical Paper 725, March 1960; WO 195/14514, 21st meeting of the Biology Committee, November 1958.
70. Porton noted that one consequence of using CS in urban areas was that food in homes and shops could become seriously contaminated with CS and would then harm people if inadvertently swallowed. Porton therefore used 22 volunteers to find out if such contaminated food would be sufficiently foul that people would not eat it, and therefore save themselves from being hurt by the CS. The food in the experiment included bread, butter, cheese, biscuits and apples. From the outset, Porton had 'considerable difficulty' in recruiting enough volunteers for the experiment. Many withdrew from the tasting panels because the contaminated food was so vile, causing the experiment to be cut short. The tasting panels were required to indicate if they could detect CS-contaminated food and then grade it as being 'tainted', 'unpleasant' or 'offensive'. One person ate slices of bread which had been exposed to massive concentrations of CS. The bread slices gave off a 'strong aura of CS' and 'only by a considerable exercise of willpower could they be placed in the mouth, where they produced an intolerable burning sensation and were immediately rejected'. The subject's mouth was sore for two days. From these tests, Porton believed that people would notice that food was contaminated with CS at levels far below those which could harm them. (Medicine, Science and the Law, 12: 2, April 1972, pp. 113-120; Himsworth report, part two, p. 28).
71. PRO, WO 195/14561, 'Agents for riot control, a study of the toxicity of T792 (CS gas)', Porton Technical Paper 672, January 1959; WO 195/15109, 'Skin reaction and sensitivity to CS', Porton Technical Paper 757, February 1961; 'Interim Report of CS exposures in plant workers', CWL Technical Memorandum 24-50, June 1960, (obtained by the author through the US Freedom of Information Act on 16 October 1996); PRO, WO 189/124, 'Cutaneous reaction produced by fumaronitrile, CS and the isomers of CS in human subjects', CDE Technical Note 38, June 1970; British Journal of Dermatology, (1972), 86, pp. 150-4.
72. PRO, WO 195/15468, 'Safety distance for grenade, hand, anti-riot, irritant, L1A1', Porton Field Trial Report 603, October 1962.
73. Interview with the author, 1 June 2000.
74. Author's interview with former Porton scientist who requested to remain anonymous.
75. The Royal Ulster Constabulary has requested CS gas on or around 12 July 1969, but authorisation was refused by the government until 13/14 August when the fighting between the Catholic nationalists and the police had grown increasingly bitter and violent. James Callaghan, the then Home Secretary and later Prime Minister, 'had said that we would never use such gas on a crowd in Britain'. (*The Diaries of a Cabinet Minister – Secretary of State for Social Services 1968-70 (volume 3)*, Richard Crossman, (Hamish Hamilton and Jonathan Cape, 1977), p. 570; *The Technology of Political Control*, Carol Ackroyd, Karen Margolis, Jonathan Rosenhead and Tim Shallice, (Penguin Books, 1977), p. 216; *The Provisional IRA*, Patrick Bishop and Eamonn Mallie, (Corgi Books, 1989), pp. 97 and 100).

76. PQ, 11 November 1970.
77. Alan Chalfont (who was minister for disarmament), *New Statesman*, 31 July 1970; (*The Diaries of a Cabinet Minister – Secretary of State for Social Services 1968-70 (volume 3)*, Richard Crossman, (Hamish Hamilton and Jonathan Cape, 1977), pp. 655-6, 802 and 834.
78. *The Technology of Political Control*, Carol Ackroyd, Karen Margolis, Jonathan Rosenhead and Tim Shallice, (Penguin Books, 1977), pp. 218-220 (this contains a critique of the Himsworth committee's work and conclusions); *Lancet*, 20 September 1969, p. 635.
79. Callaghan established the committee on 30 August 1969, within three weeks of CS gas first being used in Northern Ireland. Originally the committee consisted of three members and was charged with investigating if anyone exposed to CS in Derry on 13/14 August could suffer long-term medical effects. On 5 September, Callaghan widened the scope of the committee to examine more fully the evidence concerning the toxicity of CS, and a further five members joined the committee. The first part of the committee's report was published on 22 September 1969 (Command paper 4173) and its second (Command paper 4775) on 9 July 1971 (hereafter referred to as the Himsworth reports).
80. *A House Divided*, James Callaghan, (Collins, 1973), p. 29, quoted in 'Westminster Scene' by Tam Dalyell MP, *New Scientist*, 6 September 1973.
81. PRO, WO 195/14561, 'Agents for riot control, a study of the toxicity of CS', Porton Technical Paper 672, January 1959.
82. Some experiments were carried out at the direct request of the Himsworth committee. Other work seemed to have evolved through consensus between the committee and Porton. It is apparent that the Himsworth inquiry led Porton to publish the results of some of its human experiments with CS gas in scientific journals, which would otherwise not have happened. (*Porton Down – 75 years of chemical and biological defence*, Gradon Carter, (HMSO, 1992), p. 73; Himsworth report, part two, pp. 28 and 70; *Medicine, Science and the Law*, 12: 2, April 1972, pp. 121-8).
83. Himsworth report, part two, pp. 32-3.
84. *Porton Down – 75 years of chemical and biological defence*, Gradon Carter, (HMSO, 1992), p. 73.
85. 7 June 1973. See also *The Times* and *Financial Times*, 7 June 1973.
86. The chemical name of CR is dibenzoxazepine. Porton's code-name for CR is T 2806.
87. The MoD authorised the use of CR in 'certain special circumstances only, particularly when it may enable the use of firearms to be avoided when the armed forces have been called in to help deal with terrorists' (PQs, 18 March 1974; 17 December 1998; *Sunday Times*, 11 November 1973).
88. In late 1959, Porton commented that 'a compound with more persistent deterrent effects would appear particularly desirable for the effective use of aircraft in security operations'. By mid-1960, Porton's work on riot control was growing, and as well as pursuing a new and improved gas, Porton was also faced with the 'often urgent' demand for new types of munitions to shoot such gases at insurgents. (PRO, 195/14774, 'The search for new riot control agents', Porton Note 120, 28 October 1959; WO 188/710, 'Progress report for half-year to 30 June 1960', p. 36; WO 188/706, 'Review of programme of research and development', July 1960, introduction.
89. 'The identification of dibenzoxazepine – a new sensory irritant', Porton Technical Paper 812, June 1962; 'Analogues of dibenzoxazepine', Porton Technical Paper 813, June 1962; PRO, WO 195/16085, 'A direct comparison between CS and CR as harassing

agents', Porton Technical Paper 930, March 1965; WO 195/15609, 53rd meeting of the Chemical Defence Advisory Board, June 1963. Porton's experiments with CR on the skin of volunteers are also reported in the British Journal of Dermatology: 90, pp. 657-9, 1974. It concluded that CR 'even under adverse and unrealistic conditions' could not produce blisters.

90. PQ, 24 June 1994. Figures culled from published and declassified Porton papers indicate that the total is over 300. However, it is difficult to be certain about the absolute total, since some volunteers may have been exposed more than once, while the reports of some experiments are opaque.

91. PRO, WO 195/16085, 'A direct comparison between CS and CR as harassing agents', Porton Technical Paper 930, March 1965.

92. More recently, Porton has said that the tests with human 'guinea pigs' indicated that CR was ten times more potent than CS gas. (PQ, 19 July 1995).

93. PRO, WO 195/16313, 'The effect of harassing agents on marksmanship – report of field trials by Porton'. These trials took place between 18-26 July 1966 with sixteen men of the 37th Heavy Air Defence Regiment, Royal Artillery. According to this report, the volunteers recovered completely from both gases within five minutes.

94. Interview with the author, 18 June 1998. He was in the 37th Heavy Air Defence Regiment, Royal Artillery at the time.

95. PQ, 24 June 1995.

96. Interview with the author, 15 April 1996; letter to the author, 16 March 1996. Tests with 'dilute solutions' of CR on human eyes took place between 29 September and 17 October 1969. Lyons was on a three-week course at Winterbourne Gunner learning how to instruct others to defend themselves against nuclear, biological and chemical attack.

97. PRO, WO 195/16131, report by the chairman of the Committee on the Safety of Human Experiments, November 1965. This states that 'after preliminary tests, the Committee decided to disallow the instillation of irritant solutions into the human conjunctival sac'.

98. 'Effects on man of drenching with dilute solutions of CS and CR', Medicine, Science and the Law: 16, 3, 1976, pp. 159-170. It is unclear exactly when this series of experiments were conducted. Some tests must have occurred after November 1972 since 23 women took part in them (see chapter two). These experiments were also aimed at evaluating the safety of the solutions. Porton noticed that the volunteers' blood pressure rose during 'the period of intense skin irritation'. They surmised that it was 'probably due to the intensely uncomfortable nature of the experience'.

99. PQ, 13 June 1973; oral questions, 3 July 1973; PQ, 18 March 1974; Daily Express, The Times and Financial Times, 7 June 1973.

100. The Himsworth committee recommended that if the government decided in the future to introduce a new chemical to control civil disorders, it should promptly publish all the relevant research. The government accepted this and the other recommendations. But by November 1973 – when the government authorised CR gas in Ulster – only one scientific paper from Porton had been published in the scientific press. The respected journal, the Lancet, described this paper as being 'so incomplete that, in fairness to its three medically qualified authors, one must assume that it was written in a security straitjacket'. The journal added that this paper was shorn of crucial details and that 'of longer-term studies, teratogenicity [malformations in foetuses], carcinogenicity [cancer-causing] and so on, nothing is said'. One member of the original Himsworth committee commented that 'it seems premature to authorise the use of CR'. (Himsworth report,

part two, p. 48; *Lancet*, 16 June and 24 November 1973, pp. 1371 and 1184; <u>British Medical Journal</u>, 7 July 1973, p. 5; the Porton paper was reproduced in <u>Medicine, Science and the Law</u>, 13: 4, October 1973, pp. 265-8; *Sunday Times*, 11 November, 1973; *Guardian*, 14 March 1974; *New Scientist*, 31 May 1973).

101. In 1994, Porton was commissioned by the Home Office to assess the health effects of riot control gases which could be used on the general British population. In its report, Porton scientists observed that, 'To date, little is known about the chronic health effects of CR as well as its genotoxic and carcinogenic potential'. ('A review of the toxicology of riot control agent CS gas', Porton, December 1994, released to the author under the Code of Practice on Access to Government Information; PQs, 26 February 1998; 18 November 1998).

102. *Sunday Times*, 27 October 1974; PQs, 17 December 1998; 19 November 1998; 28 January 1999; author's request under the Code of Practice on Access to Government Information, 10 March 1999.

103. Nancekuke began work on producing CR gas in the early 1960s and continued until 1977. 'Approximately two tonnes of CR' were manufactured at Nancekuke, 'most of the production occurring in the mid-1970s'. In March 1998, the Ministry of Defence held 'stocks of approximately 260 kg for use if necessary by those units responsible for maintaining an effective counter terrorist capability'. CR gas was selected 'some decades ago' for use against terrorists. The government has stated that CR gas is not to be used for 'domestic riot control purposes'. (PQs, 24 February 1995; 19 July 1995; 12 March 1998; 11 January 1999; letter from John Reid, then the armed forces minister, to Ken Livingstone MP, 25 March 1998).

104. Interview with the author, 11 February 2000.

105. Interview with Observer Films, 1994.

106. *Britain's military strategy in Ireland – the Kitson experiment*, Roger Faligot (Zed Press/Brandon, 1983), p. 139.

107. 'The New Technology of Repression, Lessons from Ireland', pamphlet by the British Society for Social Responsibility in Science, 1974.

108. Oral questions, 1 May 1986.

109. According to the Northern Ireland Office, water cannons were 'withdrawn from operational use in or around 1970' by the Royal Ulster Constabulary. They have, however, been used at least once since then – in the summer of 2000. (PQs, 10 July 1997; 11 June 1997; 26 February 1998, Lords, 19 November 1985; *The Technology of Political Control*, Carol Ackroyd, Karen Margolis, Jonathan Rosenhead and Tim Shallice, (Penguin Books, 1977), pp. 205-7).

110. According to the MoD, Porton 'carried out research involving the use of water projection devices during the 1970s. Some field trials of devices were conducted involving human volunteers... This work did not indicate that any medical effects were experienced as a result of the use of the water delivery system.' Other tests were conducted with animals 'to assess the effects of high pressure water on the eyes'. Porton scientists concluded that 'there appeared to be a low risk of damage to eyes from the use of such equipment'. (PQs, 19 November 1976; 5 February 1997; 18 June 1997; *Observer*, 24 August 1997).

111. *The Technology of Political Control*, Carol Ackroyd, Karen Margolis, Jonathan Rosenhead and Tim Shallice, (Penguin Books, 1977), p. 206.

112. The potential tear gas – 1-methoxycycloheptatriene (1-MCHT) – was reported by the Canadians to be a potent irritant. Porton 'therefore considered it as an alternative to the

use of pyrotechnically-generated CS tear gas in hostage situations', and investigated the compound 'intermittently' between 1974 and 1985. According to Porton, 'The studies concluded that 1-MCHT had no significant operational advantage over more conventional sensory irritants such as CS and considerable investment in terms of studies to obtain a complete set of data for safety clearance would be necessary before it could be considered for operational use'. (PQs, 27 October 1997; 21 July 1998; Letter from Porton to Ken Livingstone MP, 10 June 1998; *Human and Experimental Toxicology*, 1991, volume 10, pp. 93-101).

113. *The Times*, 31 July 1971.
114. *Daily Telegraph*, *Guardian*, 20 October 1981; PQ, 19 October 1981.
115. *Independent*, 15 March 1989; *Guardian*, 18 October 1996; PQ, 31 March 1994.
116. Whitehall does not collect statistics from all 43 police forces in England and Wales, showing how many times a year each of the forces have used CS. Some parliamentary questions give an indication of how often the spray is released – 300 times by Merseyside police between March 1996 and March 1997; 120 and 190 times by London's Metropolitan police in 1996 and 1997 respectively; 138 times by Gloucestershire police officers between April 1997 and July 1998. The Police Complaints Authority has observed that from the breakdown of complaints which it has received from the public about the spray, it 'appears to suggest that some forces have used the spray to a much greater extent than others'. (PQs, 29 July 1998; 21 July 1998; 12 March 1998; 29 January 1998; 4 and 11 March, 1997; the 1997/98 annual report of the Police Complaints Authority, p. 52).
117. In 1991, the Association of Chief Police Officers had requested pepper sprays 'to incapacitate ferocious dogs used by drug dealers.' Later, they began to urge the government to issue pepper gas for the same reason as CS sprays – to protect police officers from criminals armed with guns and knives. (PQs, 5 July 1993; 11 February 1997; *The Times* and *Guardian*, 15 April 1994; *Guardian*, 4 January 1996; *Sunday Telegraph*, 18 June 1995).
118. Pepper gas dispersed as a spray is known as oleoresin capsicum (OC). In Porton's assessment, 'it is reported in the technical literature than short-term exposure to OC causes pain and irritation of the membranes lining the eyes, nose and mouth. Ingestion of capsicum may cause acute stinging of the lips, tongue and mouth, and may lead to vomiting and diarrhoea with large doses. Inhalation of the vapours may also cause significant irritation of the airways and [a] prolonged cough.' (*Statewatch* magazine, March-April 1996; PQ, 27 October 1997).
119. Soon after the Germans initiated chemical warfare in April 1915, the British searched for ways of retaliating with poison gas. Before long, 'a small quantity' of capsaicin was added to grenades and sent to France, although they appear to be little used, if at all. Humans were exposed to capsaicin at Porton during the First World War, and the chemical once again came under scrutiny in the early 1920s (and again, occasionally in the 1930s). From these tests, capsaicin was found to be the most potent and 'unquestionably superior' to the related compounds. In a report in March 1923, Porton suggested that capsaicin was 'highly irritant in very low concentrations', but its effects subsided relatively quickly. There also appeared to be 'considerable difficulty' in disseminating the substance. When Porton was searching for a replacement for CN gas in 1956, capsaicin was once again resurrected and tested on volunteers. The 'extremely potent' chemical was however dismissed by Porton because it was difficult to prepare and unstable when heated. It does not appear to have been tested on humans since then. (Descriptions of these tests can be seen in the PRO in files WO 142/209, WO 142/323, WO 142/332, WO 188/49, WO 188/50, WO 188/51, WO 188/452, and WO

195/14415; *Gas – the Story of the Special Brigade*, Major-General C H Foulkes (William Blackwood & Sons Ltd, 1934), p. 36).
120. PQ, 27 October 1997.
121. In its 1994 report for the Home Office (already referred to), Porton noted that there was 'currently political pressure' from several British police forces who wanted pepper sprays. But their evidence was 'based on no more than anecdotal testimony' from various American law enforcement agencies who were equipped with the sprays. 'Objective examination' of the evidence showed that these sprays were capable of 'producing mutagenic and carcinogenic effects, sensitisation, neurotoxicity and cardiovascular or pulmonary toxicity'. Porton also noted, 'Serious concern must still be expressed about OC in the light of approximately 30 deaths that have occurred in police custody in the US following the use of this compound'.
122. Scientists at the Home Office's Police Scientific Development Branch reviewed the safety of pepper sprays. By June 1994, they had reported that, 'While pepper sprays are used extensively in the United States of America, there were a number of unanswered issues relating to the safety of these sprays,' and further research was commissioned from the Department of Health. The press later reported that pepper sprays were shelved by the Home Office because of 'concern' that they could 'adversely affect pregnant women and asthmatics, or people with other respiratory or neurological conditions'. It is interesting to note that the US Army (but not the other military services) stopped squirting pepper sprays in the face of new recruits as part of their training after their own officials warned in October 1996 that the sprays were dangerous. (PQs, 15 June 1994; 28 November 1995; 25 January 1996; 20 February 1996; 12 May 1998; *Guardian*, 19 June 1994 and 16 March 1995; *The Times* 8 April 1995).
123. Letter from Dr Jill Tan, Police Scientific Development Branch (St Albans) to R W Hamdorf, Chief Superintendent, National Police Research Unit, South Australia, 3 August 1994. I am grateful to Outsider Television for passing on this document. The attached report comments that, aside from its potential to cause cancer, two other properties of capsaicin have also been questioned – its effects on the control of body temperature and its ability to cause an insensitivity to pain.
124. *Genetic toxicity and carcinogenic potential of oleoresin capsicum*, Toxicology Branch of Department of Health, 1993. This report was obtained by the author through a request under the Code of Practice on Access to Government Information on 19 February 1997.
125. *The Provisional IRA*, Patrick Bishop and Eamonn Mallie, (Corgi Books, 1989), pp. 150-1.
126. The 1997/98 annual report of the Police Complaints Authority, pp. 52-3.
127. The Home Office argues that 'operational use of this [five percent] concentration by French police for many years has been found to be effective in delivering the required amount of incapacitation in a short time'.
128. The solvent is methyl isobutyl ketone (MIBK), which is commonly used in paints, varnishes, lacquers and industrial processes. During the police trials with CS in 1996, Porton was commissioned by the Home Office to compare the toxicology of MIBK and methylene chloride (MC), another potential solvent for CS spray. Porton recommended that, although there were also doubts about the safety of MC, the police forces should switch from using MIBK to MC. According to Porton, MC would be 'less hazardous' and 'pose a significantly reduced risk' than MIBK. A second Porton report in November 1997 reiterated that MIKB was too toxic. But the government decided to keep using MIBK in CS sprays. According to the Home Office, MIBK has been used in CS sprays

NOTES

by French police 'for many years without serious difficulty'. However, Home Office scientists have for some time carried out research to find an alternative, more suitable solvent. Porton has not carried out any human experiments with MIBK. (The two Porton reports were released to the author under the Code of Practice on Access to Government Information; *Sunday Telegraph*, 19 April 1998, the author and Andrew Gilligan; PQ, 31 July 1997; letter to Ken Livingstone, 4 November 1998.)

129. In September 1998, the government asked two official committees to review the safety of CS sprays – the Committee on Toxicity of Chemicals in Food, Consumer Products and the Environment (COT) and the Committee on Mutagenicity of Chemicals in Food, Consumer Products and the Environment (COM). The results of their inquiry were announced a year later.

CHAPTER TEN *A Solitary Battle*

1. PQ, 13 February 1998.
2. Equally emotive are its experiments on animals which have attracted frequent protests. Porton sources have often indicated that nowadays, animal experimentation is one of its most sensitive subjects, arguing that its staff could be attacked by animal rights extremists in acts of terror.
3. Letter to the author, 27 March 1996. For obvious reasons, the name of the individual is being withheld.
4. Interview with the author, 24 February 1997.
5. He went to Porton with a friend, Roy Jemmett, who also says he 'had to sign the Secrets Act' at the start of his stay (see chapter nine). He believes that he was security-vetted before he went. (Interviews with the author, 6 January and 26 March 1996).
6. Interview with the author, 4 December 1995; interview with Observer Films, 1994.
7. *Official Secrets – the uses and abuses of the Act*, David Hooper, (Coronet Books, Hodder and Stoughton, 1988), pp. 4/5. He comments that signing the Official Secrets Act in the first place is of no particular legal significance, since government employees could still be prosecuted if they had not signed it. He believes that there are two purposes of making people sign it. Firstly, it would be useful evidence in any trial to show that the employee knew that he was bound by the Official Secrets Act, and secondly, it helps to initiate the employee into the culture of official secrecy.
8. Interview with the author, 20 February 1997.
9. Clive Ponting was a high-ranking civil servant who leaked secrets about the Falklands War to an MP. He was acquitted by an Old Bailey jury in 1985. As noted in chapter eight, Wright was the MI5 officer who wrote the best-selling book *Spycatcher*.
10. PRO, WO 32/20843, note by A C W Drew, War Office, 11 August 1961.
11. 2 November 1953.
12. *Evening News*, 17 March 1960. This was the first time that the government appears to have officially confirmed that nerve gas was being tested on humans (*Daily Mail*, 14 March 1960).
13. PQs, 23 and 28 February; 5 and 22 March. Press articles include *The Times*, 25 February; *Observer*, 25 February; *Daily Telegraph*, 6 March; and *Daily Telegraph* and *The Times*, 23 March.
14. *Daily Telegraph*, 25 February 1984.
15. *Mail On Sunday*, 12 and 19 July, 1987; *New Scientist*, 16 and 23 July, 1987.

NOTES

16. August 1987, p. 732.
17. Interview with the author, 15 January 1996.
18. Interview with the author, 22 November 1995. Birt had been advised to write to Porton – more as a precautionary measure – by the doctor who examined him when he left the armed services. He had served for 25 years, mainly with the Royal Electrical and Mechanical Engineers (REME).
19. Interview with the author, 18 January 1996.
20. Letter from his doctor, 23 January 1970; reply from Porton in January 1970, stating that the enquiry had been passed 'to our medical division, i.e. those responsible for experimental work, who when records have been checked will communicate directly with you.' Porton eventually confirmed details of his tests in 1999.
21. Medical history compiled by Gerry Ashton and made available to the author; interview with the author, 25 November 1995.
22. Letter from Dr Graham Pearson, then Director-General of Porton, 7 December 1994.
23. PQ, 11 January 1996.
24. This account is based on interviews with the author and with Observer Film Company, 1994, and his article in Chemistry and Industry magazine, 7 March, 1994. Roche's first visit had been in 1962.
25. Letter from Frank Beswick, Porton's deputy director (Biomedical), 14 November 1989.
26. *The Secrets of Porton Down*, 11 October 1994, (Network First film by Observer Films in association with Ray Fitzwalter Associates).
27. It is unclear whether there have been other lawsuits since 1945. The MoD claimed in 1988 that there had been none in the previous ten years, but in 1996, the MoD said that it was 'not possible to establish the number of service personnel who have claimed in the period 1966 to 1989...since records of claims are not held in a way that would readily provide the data requested'. It added that since 1989, there had been only two claims – one by Roche, the other by a volunteer who had attended Porton in 1957. According to the MoD, this volunteer was 'suffering from sweating and breathing difficulties and furthermore was suffering from an unexplained virus'. The lawyers of this volunteer had submitted his claim to the MoD in May 1995. The MoD responded three months later 'pointing out that the individual was prevented by Section 10 of the (1947) Crown Proceedings Act from making a claim because of the timing of his military service'. According to the MoD, the individual did not pursue the case. The identity of this individual has not been made public. (PQs, 22 January 1988 and 1 July 1996; letters from the then MoD minister James Arbuthnot to Ken Livingstone MP, 20 August 1996 and 1 April 1997).
28. Quoted by Winston Churchill MP during the Second Reading of the Crown Proceedings (Armed Forces) Bill, 13 February 1987.
29. PRO, WO 32/17180, Interpretation of Section 10 of the Crown Proceedings Act 1947, 1957-60, letter to John Boyd-Carpenter, the Minister of Pensions and National Insurance.
30. Letter to members of the association, 8 June 1995 and 19 July 1995; letter to volunteers, 28 May 1998.
31. PRO, T 213/88, letter from H A Good of the Air Ministry to Treasury, 20 November 1947.
32. PRO, PIN 59/55, Crown Proceedings Act 1948-1962. The minutes of the working party are undated, but appear to have been written in early 1950s.

449

NOTES

33. The two sample forms were released to Ken Livingstone MP on 14 October 1997.
34. PRO, WO 32/17180, 'Interpretation of Section 10 of the Crown Proceedings Act 1947, 1957-60', draft memo to the Home Affairs Committee on compensation for injuries or deaths of members of the services.
35. The agency was set up on 1 April 1994 and took over from the War Pensions Directorate of the Department of Social Security. As of April 2000, war pensions ranged from £116 a week for a full 100 percent pension to £23 a week for the lowest, 20 percent pension. A war pension can be paid at any age and is unaffected by the state pension.
36. This is its policy across the board for any claim. (Letter from Kevin Cardwell, chief executive of the War Pension Agency, to Ken Livingstone MP, 1 July 1996; PQ, 20 March 1997).
37. PQ, 20 February 1997. The War Pension Agency applies different rules to claimants depending on when they submit their claim. If it is submitted within seven years of leaving military service, the onus is on the War Pension Agency to 'show beyond reasonable doubt that service has played no part in the cause or course of the claimed disablement.' However, if the claim comes after seven years, the onus is on the claimant, but he or she is 'required only to raise at least a reasonable doubt, based on reliable evidence, that a condition may be due to service.' Most members of the Porton Down Volunteers Association are submitting claims more than seven years after their military service, since the illnesses are mainly appearing years, or decades, later.
38. In October 1997, the War Pension Agency said it 'does not hold any statistics on this issue. Claims relating to Porton Down are not identified separately and there are presently no plans to do so. To obtain this information would involve manual examination of the many hundreds of thousands of war pension files which would not be practical'. This view has been echoed by the Ministry of Defence. (PQs, 2 February 1995 and 2 March 1999; letter from Kevin Caldwell, chief executive of the War Pension Agency, to Ken Livingstone MP, 8 October 1997).
39. Hogg was awarded a fifty percent war pension.
40. Interview with the author, 29 June 1996.
41. Notice of decision signed by the Ministry of Pensions official, 4 June 1947, copy of original kept by Watts.
42. Interview with the author, 8 June 1996. Brocklesby had also made available to the author his extensive notes and official papers on this case.
43. Porton confirms that Brocklesby was one of a group of 25 servicemen who, in the week beginning 30 March 1942 were exposed in an experiment. 'Unfortunately the substance that he was exposed to was not recorded.' Porton adds that, according to the notebooks of the experiment, the volunteers wore gas masks which were removed 'for a measured time to perform the required exposure'. (Letter from Porton, 12 November 1991, kept within his War Pension Agency case notes).
44. Interview with the author, 1 March 1997.
45. There are two stages when an individual makes a claim. In the first stage, officials have to check that the individual did in fact take part in the experiments, as alleged. Officials ask Porton for details of those tests. A manual setting down the relevant procedures covers this first stage. According to a PQ on January 13, 1997, this manual did not contain a section relating solely to Porton Down cases in the version which existed in 1986. A section was only later included when the manual was rewritten in 1993. In the second stage of a claim, War Pension Agency officials, having checked that the claimant

took part in the experiments as alleged, pass the case on to doctors in the War Pension Agency who decide whether an award is justified. These doctors also have a manual to guide their decisions. The latest version of this manual has no specific reference to Porton Down cases, although it has a section on gas poisoning in wartime, particularly for the First World War. (Sections of both manuals were made available to Ken Livingstone MP in 1997).

46. PQs, 12 March 1998; 8 March 2000 and 25 July 2000; House of Commons adjournment debate, 16 October 1996.

47. PRO, WO 195/14846, 'History of the Service Volunteer Observer Scheme at Porton Down' (Porton Note 119), November 1959.

48. Military officials noted in 1923 that the question of 'compensation to be given to an individual who may suffer as the result of exposure to gas has not until recently been faced'. They added that this question had now been 'taken up and is receiving sympathetic consideration. Discussion is at present proceeding on matters of detail of a financial matter, but it is hoped that the whole question will be satisfactorily settled at an early date'. (PRO, WO163/29, 326th meeting of the Army Council, 19 December 1923, pp. 25, 369-372; T 164/71/28; T 164/72/10; T 162/507; WO 33/1028, 'Third Report of secretary of the chemical warfare committee, for the year ending March 31, 1923', pp. 61-2).

49. PRO, WO 195/14846, 'History of the Service Volunteer Observer Scheme at Porton Down', Porton Note 119, November 1959. This document described 'an important decision' made by the War Office in late 1942. Some military chiefs wanted a Court of Inquiry to investigate why one of their men had suffered mustard gas burns, but Porton complained that 'if this was approved, it [would] set a precedent which would involve the formation of a permanent Court of Inquiry which would have to investigate nearly all the experiments at Porton'. The issue was adjudicated by the War Office which decided that no Court was necessary, provided that full records of the tests were kept in the military medical records of each human 'guinea pig'.

50. PQ, 25 April 1995.

51. PRO, AIR 20/12171, handwritten note on 7 December 1960. At the time, the Ministry of Pensions and National Insurance had yet to reach a firm conclusion on the matter. The papers on its further deliberations seem not to have survived.

52. PRO, WO 32/20843, note on 18 September 1961 by official on behalf of Assistant Secretary, F3 (absent on leave).

53. It appears that this television report was *The Secrets of Porton Down*, an hour-long documentary made by Observer Films and broadcast on 11 October 1994. (Annual report of Porton ethics committee, 1995, annex B).

54. Interview with the author, 17 February 1997. At 21, he was a gunner in the Royal Navy. The appeal for volunteers mentioned Salisbury Plain – 'I thought "that looks a nice quiet country place".' He thought that he was going to be doing some kind of tests, but he knew nothing about Porton, nor that the tests were concerned with chemical warfare. He was part of a group of around 25 to 30 volunteers and was there for three weeks. He believes that liquid mustard gas was dropped on both shoulders through a military uniform, which he then had to wear, even sleeping in it, for several days. Every two hours – during the night and day – Porton staff photographed the progress of his 'painful and very uncomfortable' blisters, which were filled with yellow pus. In another test, patches of khaki clothing, contaminated with a chemical, were placed in his arms, also producing blisters. Afterwards, he was given two weeks' leave. He says that he was told little about the tests. Later, the uncertainty fuelled his fears that the tests may have

451

affected his four children. His claim for a war pension has been rejected. He appealed, but without much optimism.
55. British Medical Journal, 296, 30 January 1988.
56. PQs, 6 March 1997; 13 March 1998; 20 April 1988. The awards (except one) were made following the NRPB report.
57. *Clouds of Deceit, the deadly legacy of Britain's bomb tests*, Joan Smith (Faber and Faber, 1985), p. 110; *A Very Special Relationship, British atomic weapon trials in Australia*, Lorna Arnold, (HMSO, 1987), p. 155.
58. Letters from the then Defence Secretary Michael Portillo to Ken Livingstone MP, 8 February, 25 March, and 15 May 1996; the author and Andrew Gilligan, *Sunday Telegraph*, 16 June 1996.
59. Letters from the then Defence Secretary Michael Portillo to Ken Livingstone MP, 8 February, 25 March, and 15 May 1996. Much of Porton's radiation work between 1956 and 1964 is recorded in 50 reports in the Porton Technical Papers (Radiological) series. According to a parliamentary question on 3 July 1996, five of these reports remained classified at that time. The unclassified reports can be found at the Public Record Office in either WO 189/114-118, WO 189/193-211 or scattered throughout WO 195. Only a few of these reports detail experiments involving humans. Some of these reports were placed in the PRO following inquiries by the author in 1996.
60. PRO, WO 195/14611, 'Radiological defence work at Porton, Note on collaboration between organisations', Porton Note 84, April 1959.
61. PRO, WO 189/118, 'Radiological decontamination: clothing trials', Porton Technical Paper (R) 33, March 1961; WO 195/15058, 'Radiological decontamination – clothing trials', Porton Note 168, undated, but 1960. In an earlier version of these trials, two 'civilian officers' tried out this experiment to check that the experiment was viable and safe. Porton commented that safety was 'particularly important since permission has to be obtained from the War Office for the exposure of Service volunteers in future trials'. There would be 'no appreciable hazard' from any radioactivity, concluded the scientists.
62. The MoD pointed out that sodium-24 is a short-lived gamma emitter with a half-life of 15 hours. For Porton's discussion of which simulants to use in these trials, see PRO, WO 189/204, 'Dry Fallout simulants', Porton Technical Paper (R) 29, April 1960.
63. Letter dated 12 March 1998 to the author from Dr Alice Stewart, of Birmingham University, the renowned epidemiologist who first revealed that X-raying pregnant women caused childhood leukaemia. She points out that the doses were so small that special techniques and very sensitive instruments had to be used to measure the contamination on the clothes.
64. PRO, WO 195/15302, 'Radiological decontamination – fallout contamination during a rescue operation', Porton Technical Paper (R) 38, November 1961.
65. PRO, WO195/15792, 'Radiological decontamination of roads by hosing', Porton Technical Paper (R) 49, March 1964.
66. Letter in the *Lancet*, 12 December 1987. Dr Lawson said his patient gave him permission to disclose details of his case.
67. PRO, WO 195/15058, 'Radiological decontamination – clothing trials', Porton Note 168, undated, but 1960.
68. *Sunday Telegraph*, the author and Andrew Gilligan, 16 June 1996.
69. Letter from former Defence Secretary, Michael Portillo, to Ken Livingstone MP, 15 May 1996.

Notes

70. *Sunday Telegraph*, the author and Andrew Gilligan, 16 June 1996.
71. Letter in the *Lancet*, 12 December 1987.
72. Robert Maynard and Frank Beswick (former Porton scientists), *Clinical and Experimental Toxicology of Organophosphates and Carbamates* (edited by Bryan Ballantyne and Timothy C Marrs, Butterworth-Heinemann, 1992), pp. 372-385.
73. PRO, WO 189/123, 'The clearance of tetra ethyl pyrophosphate (TEPP) from skin and tissue, as measured by radioactive tracer techniques', Porton Technical Paper 345, April 1953. (This paper was released into the PRO in early 1997 following inquiries by Ken Livingstone MP).
74. Interview with the author, 27 January 1996.
75. Interview with the author, 10 April 1996.
76. *A Very Special Relationship, British atomic weapon trials in Australia*, Lorna Arnold, (HMSO, 1987), pp. 203-4.
77. A description of this work is given in a note, dictated by the Atomic Weapon Establishment, Aldermaston, on 16 March 1961 (PRO, AB16/3680). In a letter to Ken Livingstone MP on 15 May 1996, Michael Portillo, the then Defence Secretary, wrote, 'I can confirm that the firing trials conducted at Porton Down in the late 1950s and 1960s involved the use of conventional explosives to test their behaviour and to record seismic and other signals from the detonations. Porton Down was used as it provided a convenient and capable instrumented range for the work and no radioactive materials were employed in these trials.'
78. For British coverage, see for example *Guardian*, 1 January 1994; *Observer*, 2 January 1994; *Independent on Sunday*, 16 January 1994. For a resumé see *The Bulletin of Atomic Scientists*, January/February 1996, pp. 32-40.
79. *Human experimentation: An overview on Cold War Era programs*, United States General Accounting Office, 28 September 1994 (GAO/T-NSIAD-94-266); *Status of Federal efforts to disclose Cold War radiation experiments involving humans*, US GAO, 1 December 1994, (GAO/T-RCED-95-40). Following the 1994 furore, the American government ordered that all the records of these experiments be collated and published. These can be found on a US Department of Energy website.
80. *The Nuclear Guinea Pigs – secret human radiation experiments in Britain*, a report by the Campaign for Nuclear Disarmament, November 1996.
81. *American nuclear guinea pigs: three decades of radiation experiments on US Citizens*, a report published by Congressman Edward J Markey, chairman of the subcommittee on energy conservation and power, on 24 October 1986.
82. Press release issued on behalf of Donn and Co solicitors, 7 November 1995.
83. Adjournment debate on Gulf War Syndrome, 20 December 1994; PQs on 22 May 1995 and 20 June 1995; and oral defence questions, 28 February 1995.
84. Gulf War Syndrome, House of Commons Defence Committee, 11th report, session 1994-5, (HC 197), published on 7 November 1995, paragraph 60.
85. The way nerve gases kill is detailed in chapter four. Pyridostigmine bromide mimics the action of nerve gases by binding to acetylcholinesterase at exactly the same site as the nerve gases. This blocks the nerve gas, but only temporarily. The pyridostigmine bromide can protect 30 percent of the body's acetylcholinesterase, enough to prevent death.
86. PQs, 3 February and 15 February 1995. Some of these trials were conducted in collaboration with other MoD establishments. For instance, in 1980, 28 military

NOTES

personnel on a training course at the Royal Military College of Science, Shrivenham took part in one NAPS study. In 1981, 25 military personnel participated in a study at Bordon, of which 15 received NAPS tablets. Porton collaborated with the Institute of Aviation Medicine 'in the analytical methods used in carrying out' NAPS studies. Trials also took place at Dover and the Cambridge Military Hospital. (PQs, 16 February 1995 and 16 March 1995).

87. When asked, Porton stated that the results of its trials on NAPS had been published in four articles in scientific journals. Three of these articles however describe experiments on animals, not humans. The fourth article could not be located by the author in the Science Library in London. Furthermore, in a letter to Ken Livingstone MP on 3 July 1996, Porton provided a list of its technical papers which described human studies between 1969 and 1991 and were currently unclassified. None of the papers mentioned featured the NAPS studies. During its investigation into Gulf War Syndrome in 1995, members of the House of Commons Defence Committee were given 'the detailed results' of the NAPS trials which were classified secret. The committee was satisfied that, on this basis, the studies confirmed Porton's stated evidence to the committee on the safety of the NAPS tablets. (Gulf War Syndrome, House of Commons Defence Committee, 11th report, session 1994-5, (HC 197), published on 7 November 1995, p. 48; PQ, 6 July 1995).

88. PQ, 16 March 1995.

89. Point 10 C (1) of Memorandum by MoD, 9 December 1994 submitted to the House of Commons Defence Committee investigation into Gulf War Syndrome; printed on pp. 46-50 of 11th report, session 1994-5, (HC 197). On this occasion, the MoD cited the side-effects as being vomiting, diarrhoea, increased salivation and sweating.

90. 'Gulf War Syndrome', House of Commons Defence Committee, 11th report, session 1994-5, (HC 197), published on 7 November 1995, paragraphs 41-2.

91. Giving evidence to the House of Commons Defence Committee on 1 February 1995, Porton's then Director-General, Graham Pearson, said, 'Since the Gulf we have not actually mounted any major new programme. I think we did one trial involving taking NAPS for eight weeks just to see if there was any sign of anything unusual. Nothing unusual showed up in that trial. We have done nothing further because NAPS is licensed.' In a later PQ, he said, 'The administration of NAPS during the Gulf conflict of 1990/1 confirmed the results of the NAPS studies previously carried out at Porton and in various external trials in that the side-effects from the taking of NAPS were minimal and did not interfere with military efficiency.' He added, however, that the MoD wanted to study any side-effects from taking NAPS over a longer period. The experiment was carried out over eight weeks at the Cambridge Military Hospital. According to the MoD, the experiment confirmed the conclusions of the earlier trials. ('Gulf War Syndrome', House of Commons Defence Committee, 11th report, session 1994-5, (HC 197), published on 7 November 1995, p. 17, PQ, 16 March 1995).

92. Gulf War Syndrome, House of Commons Defence Committee, 11th report, session 1994-5, (HC 197), published on 7 November 1995, paragraph 41.

93. The replacement uses a combination of the drugs physostigmine and hyoscine which is a 'more effective treatment' against nerve gas. According to Porton, 'tests have shown that this treatment can be delivered using an adhesive skin plaster which is preferable to tablets'. The idea of using this combination was first reported by Porton in 1984; since then, the establishment has conducted a series of studies 'into its effect against a range of different nerve agents and its electrophysical, biochemical and behavioural effects'. In early 1997, Porton stated that 'studies to assess the military acceptability of the commercially licensed drugs which are combined in the proposed pre-treatment

have recently commenced'. This work was going to 'continue for some years' before any decision could be made on whether to approve it for use by the Armed Forces. (The MoD was not at that stage planning to withdraw NAPS from military service). In late 1997, Porton stated that it was 'currently carrying out a programme of work to examine any possible side-effects of these substances when delivered as a transdermal patch. To date, no unacceptable side-effects have been identified, but the programme of work is not yet complete'. (Annual report and accounts of the Defence Evaluation and Research Agency, 1995/6; PQs, 13 January 1997 and 16 March 1998; letter to Ken Livingstone MP, 14 October 1997).

94. 'Gulf War Syndrome', House of Commons Defence Committee, 11th report, session 1994-5, (HC 197), published on 7 November 1995, paragraphs 51-3.

95. By March 1998, preliminary research into the combinations had been started at Porton Down. It was planned that other elements of the research programme would be carried out by the National Institute for Biological Standards and Control and 'a number of other scientific and academic bodies'. The research was expected to take three and a half years to complete. (PQ, 27 March 1998).

96. Labour's 20-point plan to help sick veterans was announced on 14 July 1997. The details were set out in a 13-page policy statement entitled 'Gulf veterans' illnesses: A new beginning'.

97. Porton stated in 1996 that it was neither monitoring the health of the volunteers who took part in its NAPS experiments, nor conducting any studies to assess the long-term health effects of the tablets. The establishment said, 'The active ingredient of NAPS tablets is pyridostigmine bromide, which is licensed for use in the clinical treatment of myasthenia gravis. Adults with this complaint take dosages far in excess of that found in NAPS tablets over extended periods, in some cases for life. There are no indications that these high doses over a long period of time give rise to long-term health effects.' (PQ, 6 June 1996).

98. 'Images of the Army (1997)', opinion poll research commissioned by the Directorate of Public Relations (Army), released to the author under the Code of Practice on Access to government Information, 16 March 1998.

CHAPTER ELEVEN In Whose Interest?

1. See, for example, letters to the volunteers who request information about their experiments; PQ, 7 March 1995; Porton's annual reports and accounts for 1994-5, p. 24 and 1993-4, p. 22. (Between 1991 and 1995, Porton published four annual reports of its work and accounts. This initiative by Graham Pearson, the then Director-General, was aimed at removing some of the secrecy surrounding the establishment).

2. See, for instance, PQs, 26 January 1994; 7 March 1995; 4 April 1995; 25 April 1995; 2 May 1995.

3. Press release by the late Derek Fatchett (shadow defence spokesman at the time and later a Foreign Office minister), 25 April 1995; Independent on Sunday, 12 March 1995. He said that the then Conservative government's attitude was a disgrace. 'We need a full independent medical inquiry to find out what happened. It should be in two stages, to establish the causal link between the illnesses and the experiments, and then once that has been achieved, immediately set compensation'.

4. Letter from John Reid, the then Armed Forces Minister, to Chris Mullin MP, 30 November 1997. The MP was taking up the case of his constituent, Gordon Bell.

5. Adjournment debate on Gordon Bell, 17 March 1998.

Notes

6. Letter to Ken Livingstone MP, 4 November 1994.
7. *The Secrets of Porton Down*, ITV Network First documentary by Observer Films, October, 1994. Dr Pearson has also stated, 'It is important to recognise that the human body is remarkably effective in dealing with toxic pollutants to which we are exposed in our daily lives and the participation in a study at Porton Down involving a short exposure to chemical warfare agent has to be considered in the context of whole life exposures to other toxic pollutants.' (PQ, 7 March 1995).
8. PQs, 26 January 1994; 17 March 1994; 24 June 1994. Asked how many volunteers on average each year were recalled to have their health checked, Porton replied that 'there is no set pattern of recalls or selection of volunteers for recall. The number of volunteers recalled and the time after the study are varied, according to the objective of recalling the volunteers'.
9. PQs, 7 March 1995; 26 January 1994. Porton states that 'from time to time after specific studies, those volunteers that participated in them are called back to Porton for a further set of tests or measurements in order to check on the consistency of the method used in the tests or measurement and to demonstrate invariance with time'. Porton did not specify how many volunteers are recalled for this reason. Comparatively recently, Porton has started the practice of reading the following statement to volunteers: 'It is [our] policy to call back some volunteer subjects for re-testing from time to time to ensure that the techniques used give consistent and reproducible results and that no changes in the way we apply the tests have occurred with time'.
10. In other strands of its defence, Porton has pointed that some human 'guinea pigs' have volunteered 'repeatedly' to undergo experiments. This occurs at 'irregular intervals', but it provides Porton staff with 'spontaneous and sporadic' opportunities to examine the volunteers medically. Porton argues that the health of none of these enthusiastic returnees has suffered. However it appears extremely unlikely that any volunteers would go back for more experiments if they believed that they had been harmed first time around. Porton has also claimed that when the volunteers have returned to their units after the experiments, there is no history of military doctors seeking advice from the establishment about illnesses which may have resulted from the tests. Nor, according to the establishment, have there been any reports of Porton-induced illnesses during the regular health checks which are carried out on military personnel.
11. 'Chronic' illnesses are defined as being those which last a long time or recur frequently. The symptoms can be caused by a single, repeated, or long-term exposure to a chemical. In contrast, 'acute' illnesses begin soon after exposure and stop shortly afterwards.
12. In a PQ on 5 July 1995, the MoD said human experiments with mustard gas 'ceased in the 1970s when reliable laboratory tests which did not require the use of this type of testing were developed'. The ban was not mentioned at all. Aside from mustard gas, Porton does not have a current list of chemicals which are banned from being tested on human subjects, since the Independent Ethics Committee scrutinises and approves each proposed experiment on a case-by-case basis.
13. In 1978, Porton scientists decided to stop exposing humans to sulphur mustard gas in clothing tests. According to Porton, 'Whilst there was no evidence to suggest, either from animal studies or epidemiological surveys, that a single exposure could cause cancer, the epidemiological evidence did suggest an association between repeated exposures to mustard and the subsequent development of certain cancers.' The decision by the Porton scientists was endorsed by the establishment's Committee on the Safety of Human Experiments (COSHE), resulting in the permanent ban (Letter to Ken Livingstone MP, 4 November 1998).

14. Author's interview with former Porton scientist who requested to remain anonymous.
15. PQs, 30 October 1996, 4 December 1996, 18 November 1997.
16. A history of the centre is given on p. 133 of the United Kingdom's declaration of past activities relating to its former offensive chemical weapons programme to the Chemical Weapons Convention, May 1997. See also PQ, 18 July 1995.
17. PQ, 15 May 1996.
18. Interview with the author, 13 June 1998.
19. The MoD also says that the procedure was aimed at giving the personnel on the courses 'confidence' in the process for removing gas from their bodies, since they would have to instruct their colleagues back in their own units. (PQ, 15 May 1996).
20. Porton has stated that in the late 1970s, it informed Winterbourne Gunner that 'in the light of new advice from the Health and Safety Executive (HSE), it was advisable to discontinue the routine use of mustard for training purposes. It is assumed by Porton staff that this would have been the reason why Winterbourne Gunner stopped using the substance routinely'. However, Porton had been unable to find any documents from that time to explain the nature of this new advice. The HSE was also unable to shed any light on this matter. It has stated that, 'As far as we can find out, HSE was unaware that mustard gas was being used on students and therefore no specific advice was issued on that issue.' The HSE adds that the 'emerging health and safety guidelines' cited by the MoD 'may have been general advice on controlled use of toxic substances that HSE put out in the late 1970s'. (Letter from Porton to Ken Livingstone MP, 14 October 1997; PQ, 29 April 1998; letter from the Health and Safety Executive to Ken Livingstone, 26 November 1997).
21. Testimony by John Vogel, Deputy Under-Secretary for benefits, US Department of Veterans' Affairs, before the sub-committee on compensation, pension and insurance of the Committee on Veterans' Affairs, House of Representatives, 10 March 1993.
22. It formed a committee of scientists drawn from many fields including toxicology, epidemiology, occupational and environmental medicine, ophthalmology, dermatology, oncology, chemistry and psychology. This committee scrutinised nearly 2,000 technical reports, by military and non-military scientists, and heard the stories of more than 250 affected veterans.
23. *Veterans at Risk – the health effects of mustard gas and lewisite*, Institute of Medicine, edited by Constance Pechura and David Rall, National Academy Press, January 1993.
24. The committee believed that the available evidence indicated that the following illnesses are caused by exposure to mustard gas (sulphur mustard unless stated): respiratory cancers (nasopharyngeal, laryngeal, and lung); skin cancer; pigmentation abnormalities of the skin; chronic skin ulceration and scar formation; leukaemia (typically acute non-lymphocytic type from nitrogen mustard); chronic respiratory diseases (asthma, chronic bronchitis, emphysema, chronic obstructive pulmonary disease, chronic laryngitis); recurrent corneal ulcerative disease (including corneal opacities); delayed recurrent keratitis of the eye; chronic conjunctivitis; bone marrow depression and (resulting) immunosuppression (an acute effect that may result in greater susceptibility to serious infections with secondary permanent damage to vital organ systems); psychological disorders, such as mood and anxiety disorders, and other traumatic stress disorder responses (resulting from traumatic or stressful experiences of the experiment, not the toxic effects of the gases themselves); dysfunctions in sexual performance as a result of severe burns and scarring of sexual organs.
25. Added to the list were squamous cell carcinomas of the skin, scar formation of the skin, nasopharyngeal, laryngeal and lung cancers (except mesothelioma), acute

NOTES

non-lymphocytic leukaemia, and chronic obstructive pulmonary disease. (Press release from the Department of Veterans Affairs, 25 August 1994).

26. The agency requested a copy of the report on 6 February 1997. According to the PQ, 'no steps had been taken to evaluate' the report up until that point. Until January 1998, the agency's policy advisers were also 'not aware of the details' contained in the US VA Department press release of 25 August 1994 which announced that, in response to the IoM report, the list of illnesses caused by mustard gas was being expanded. (PQ, 20 February 1997; letters to Ken Livingstone MP from the War Pensions Agency, 20 March 1997 and 21 January 1998).

27. Letter to Ken Livingstone MP from the War Pensions Agency, 8 October 1997. This letter describes the agency's evaluation of the report: 'First, there is a review of the existing medical and scientific literature. Particular attention is drawn to the fact that most studies consider only short-term acute effects of exposure and that the few longer-term follow-up studies are British or Japanese. Most of the conclusions of the report on scientific and medical matters are known and agreed by us. The second part of the report discusses in detail the US mustard gas/lewisite testing programme from the earliest days after World War Two. It notes that the programme participants were not volunteers, that the studies were secret and that there was a lack of documentation and long-term follow-up of the health of those taking part. These circumstances do not precisely reflect the British experience.'

28. Letter to Ken Livingstone MP from the War Pensions Agency, 21 January 1998.

29. When asked specifically by Ken Livingstone MP in 1997, Porton responded by directing his attention to a review of the IoM report by the then Porton Director-General, Dr Graham Pearson, in a scientific magazine in 1993. 'This still reflects the position of Porton Down,' it added. Although Dr Pearson makes a series of criticisms of the IoM's 'bias' and lack of judgement in this review, he does not appear to address directly whether the list of illnesses which the IoM attributed to mustard gas exposure is right or wrong. At one point, Dr Pearson criticises the IoM committee for failing to present any evidence of long-term health risks arising out of the 'patch tests'. Under this procedure, drops of mustard gas were applied to the arms and removed soon afterwards with a decontaminant. The IoM committee later replied that the US Department of Veterans' Affairs accepts skin cancer in the scars of patch test participants as being caused by mustard gas. (Letter from Liz Peace, DERA company secretary, to Ken Livingstone, 14 October 1997; review of IoM report by Dr Pearson, 16 September 1993, *Nature*, p. 218, volume 365; ripostes to the review appeared in *Nature* on 2 December 1993, pp. 398-9, volume 366).

30. Under the Australian system, claimants have to establish a 'reasonable hypothesis' that their illness is connected to the experiments. This is considered to be a 'generous standard of proof' by the Australian Department of Veterans' Affairs. 'In effect, this means that there is no onus on the veteran to prove a connection between the claimed condition and their service. They simply have to establish that there is a reasonable hypothesis linking the condition to the particular circumstances of the veteran's service.' Between 750 and 2,000 Australian servicemen were subjected to the wartime experiments, and according to the Australian Department of Veterans' Affairs, 173 of them had submitted claims for illnesses suffered as a result of the tests by June 1985. Of those, 35 had been accepted, 125 rejected and 13 undecided at that time. After that date, the veterans' affairs department did not collect information on the claims specifically related to the mustard gas experiments, but estimates that another 80 claims were lodged in the years to 1992. The outcome of these later claims is not known.

NOTES

31. Details of these disability payments are sparse, since the Canadian Department of Veterans' Affairs is unable to produce the relevant statistics from its files. The department believes that some of the human 'guinea pigs' have been awarded disability payments for respiratory and skin problems. It is known that around 1989, 19 veterans applied for disability pensions when the Canadian government set up a hotline for the human 'guinea pigs' following a bout of publicity about the wartime tests. The Department is unable to provide any other details of claims before or after that period in 1989. Under the Canadian system, the cases of veterans who claim disability payments are treated individually, since the Canadians do not lay down the illnesses which they believe were caused by the mustard gas experiments. (Information from the Canadian Department of Veterans' Affairs, 9 November 1998).

32. This account of the catastrophe is drawn from several sources: *A Higher Form of Killing*, Paxman and Harris, pp. 119-123; *New Scientist*, 30 January 1986; *After the Battle* magazine, number 79, 1993; report by Lt Colonel Stewart F Alexander (Consultant, chemical warfare medicine) on the toxic gas burns sustained in the Bari Harbour catastrophe, 27 December 1943 (PRO, WO 193/712; this classmark also contains other material on the disaster). The full story is told in the book, *Disaster at Bari*, by Glenn B Infield, (Macmillan Company, New York, 1971).

33. See, for example, *New Scientist*, 30 January and 13 March 1986; *Guardian*, 6 March 1986; *Independent*, 1 September 1990.

34. PQs, 5 March 1986; 30 October 1996. In 1984, he was awarded a 40 percent war pension – this was increased to 100 percent two years later.

35. Case number C170/88 – refusal to compensate war pensioners for loss in value of back-dated war pension, Parliamentary Commissioner for Administration (Ombudsman). See also *Daily Telegraph*, 27 April 1990.

36. PQ, 5 March 1986.

37. PQ, 30 October 1996. A breakdown of the illnesses suffered by the successful claimants is given in a PQ on 11 December 1996. Following a request by the author under the Code of Practice on Access to Government Information, the War Pension Agency – in its response on 10 January 1997 – gave more details about the 1986 investigation, but added that it was unable to say how many of the awards were made for 'the effects of exposure to mustard gas only and how many included disablement/death due to other causes'.

38. PRO, PIN 59/19, resolution in April 1963 by Coventry, Nuneaton and District War Pension Committee, sent to the Ministry of Pensions and National Insurance. This file was opened in 1997 by the Department of Social Security following a request from the author.

39. PRO, PIN 59/19, letter from T S Ferguson of the Ministry of Pensions and National Insurance to the General Secretary of the Federation Mondiale des Anciens Combattants (Paris), 1 September 1964.

40. *Chemical Warfare Agents: Toxicology and Treatment*, Timothy C Marrs, Robert L Maynard and Frederick R Sidell, (John Wiley & Sons, 1996), pp. 169-170. Sidell has worked in the American chemical warfare organisations for many years.

41. 'The long-term health effects of nerve agents and mustard' by Frederick Sidell and Col Charles Hurst, submission to the DSB Task Force on Gulf War CW, December 1993, pp. 31-2. In this paper, they wrote that repeated exposures to mustard gas over a period of years seem 'well-established' as causing an increase in airway cancer. However, 'the association between a single exposure to mustard and airway cancer is not as well-established'. They add that the 'association between one-time mustard exposure and

NOTES

other chronic airway problems, such as chronic bronchitis, seems more clearly established, based on World War One data. In some cases this long-term damage was probably a continuation of the original insult resulting from insufficient therapy in the pre-antibiotic era'. They also note that 'skin scarring, pigment changes, and even cancer have either followed the initial wound as a continuation of the process (scarring) or later appeared at the site of the lesion'.

42. PQs, 8 November 1995; 3 & 22 July 1996; 18 November 1997; 21 July 1998.
43. PQ, 4 December 1996.
44. See in particular memorandum on medical effects of chemical warfare agents on pp. 70-6 of House of Commons Defence Select Committee report on Gulf War Syndrome (11th report, session 1994-5, (HC 197), 7 November 1995).
45. PQs, 8 May 1996; 6 June 1996; 4 December 1996; 3 & 22 July 1996; Letter to Ken Livingstone MP, 14 October 1997; Report of the official group on OPs to ministers, 25 June 1998, pp. 116 and 141-2.
46. PRO, WO 195/12335, 'An investigation of possible delayed effects of the G agents and DFP', Porton Technical Paper 350, May 1953; WO 188/710, 'Progress report number 19 for Porton and Sutton Oak for half-year ending 31 March 1952', p. 16 and 'Progress report number 20 for Porton and Sutton Oak for half-year ending 30 September 1952', p. 18. For further discussion of this research, see the eighth, ninth and tenth meetings of the Biology Committee (PRO, WO 195/11699, WO 195/11903, and WO 195/12139).
47. Porton does not appear to have repeated any human experiments with this compound after the Second World War. In a 1983 paper, Porton described DFP as a 'potent' compound for causing OPIDN (*Archives of Toxicology*, 1983, volume 52, p. 73).
48. PRO, WO 195/14875, 'Neurotoxicity of OP compounds', Porton Technical Paper 706, December 1959; WO 195/15029, 'Neurotoxicity as an incapacitating effect of G agents', Porton discussion paper for 15th Tripartite conference on toxicological warfare with US and Canada, July 1960; WO 195/15328, 'Neurotoxicity of OP compounds', Porton Note 240, January 1962.
49. The initial effects of OP poisoning, suffered by many Porton Down volunteers exposed to nerve gas since 1945, wear off within a few days. However two specific syndromes resulting from OP exposure have been identified. One, the Intermediate Syndrome, appears a few days to a week after the exposure and results in weakness or paralysis of the limbs, neck and respiratory muscles. It disappears after three weeks. The other is OPIDN.
50. Marrs, Maynard and Sidell state that 'it is extremely unlikely that nerve agents possess the capability to cause OPIDN'. (*Chemical Warfare Agents: Toxicology and Treatment*, Marrs, Maynard and Sidell, p. 93).
51. PQ, 4 December 1996.
52. This suggestion was echoed by researchers at a Belgian chemical warfare laboratory. ('Delayed neuropathy by OP nerve agents', J L Willems, D M Palate, M A Vranken, and H C De Bisschop, (laboratory of medical toxicology, Department of NBC protection, Belgium), *Proceedings of International Symposium on Protection Against Chemical Warfare Agents*, Stockholm, June 6-9, 1983, pp. 95-100).
53. *Chemical Warfare Agents: Toxicology and Treatment*, Marrs, Maynard and Sidell, pp. 94-5. They write that previous research had provided 'some evidence of persistent EEG effects', 'few of the relevant studies are above criticism'. They add that the 'most impressive studies relate to sarin (GB), but even here there is room for doubt'.

NOTES

54. The British MoD states that the Khamisiyah incident is the only time when Coalition troops could 'potentially' have been exposed to chemical weapons. For an official view of this episode, see the British Ministry of Defence paper published on 7 December 1999, 'Review of events concerning 32 Field Hospital and the release of nerve agent arising from US demolition of Iraqi munitions at the Khamisiyah depot in March 1991.'

55. *Gulf war illnesses – improved monitoring of clinical progress and re-examination of research emphasis are needed*, GAO/NSIAD-97-163, June 1997 (see pp. 43-45 and 118-120) and GAO/T-NSIAD-97-190 and GAO/T-NSIAD-97-191.

56. The Presidential Committee's final report was published in 1997. One British Parliamentary report commented that the 'widely different interpretations' between the PAC and the GAO 'stem from the fact that PAC placed greatest weight on the few studies involving short-term exposures to low-levels of OPs (on the grounds that these were most relevant as far as possible exposure during the Gulf War was concerned)'. The PAC was particularly interested in the American nerve gas experiments on humans in the 1950s and 1960s. The report added, 'In contrast, GAO placed more weight on studies involving animals, or long-term exposure to low levels in humans, to project possible effects from Gulf War exposures. The scientific basis of some of these studies has been questioned by PAC and others'. ('Gulf War Illnesses – dealing with the uncertainties,' Parliamentary Office of Science and Technology, report 107, December 1997).

57. The military personnel were identified using the MoD's archives, NHS and social security records. (British Medical Journal, 296, 30 January 1988).

58. These surveys were released to Ken Livingstone MP in September 1998. (CDE Technical Note 120, February 1972; CDE Technical Note 175, July 1973; CDE Technical Note 1010, August 1989; Letters from Porton to Ken Livingstone MP, 14 October 1997 and 10 June 1998).

59. *Possible long-term health effects of short-term exposure to chemical agents*, volumes 1 and 2, National Academy Press, Washington DC, 192 and 1985.

60. Broadcast by IRNA news agency in Tehran, 14 March 1998. The statement was made by Farzad Panahi, deputy head of the oppressed and the war-disabled foundation for health and medical treatment affairs at a conference on the long-term effects of chemical weapons. He added that these chemical casualties were being treated in the foundation's medical centres. Given relations between Iran and the West, it has been difficult to obtain information about the long-term effects of the chemical weapons on their casualties. One researcher has suggested that mustard gas attacks in the war have damaged the genes of the victims, producing a high number of foetal deaths and upsetting the natural balance between boys and girls in their offspring ('Secondary sex ratios in progenies of Iranian chemical victims', *Veterinary Human Toxicology*, 36 (5), October 1994, pp. 475-6).

61. CBDE Technical Paper 702, April 1993; CBDE Technical Paper 716, September 1993; CBDE Technical Paper 780, March 1995; *Times*, 28 November 1988; PQ, 2 March 1995.

62. It is difficult to discern which health conditions are attributable to which type of chemical weapon. (*Washington Post*, 11 March 1998; *Sydney Morning Herald*, 14 March 1998; *Dispatches*, Channel Four, 23 February 1998).

63. Clare Short, the minister in charge of the Department for International Development, said, 'We share the widespread concern for the people of Halabjah, who are suffering from the continuing effects of the chemical weapons attack.' (PQ, 29 July 1998; letter to the author by DFID in response to request under the Code of Practice on Access to Government Information, 13 August 1998).

64. *Lancet*, Volume 345, 15 April 1995 (pp. 980-1) and 3 June 1995 (pp. 1146-7). The figure of 12 dead in the Tokyo subway attack is given in a paper in Toxicology and Applied Pharmacology, 144, pp. 198-203, 1997.

65. PQs, 13 February 1997; 30 July 1998; 17 December 1998; 3 February 1999; and House of Lords, 5 April 1995. In July 1998, the Department of Health said its officials had 'studied published material' on the two nerve gas attacks, and 'some of these papers relate to the delayed effects of nerve agents'. Japan has instigated a long-term follow-up programme to monitor the health of the individuals involved in the attacks.

66. A fuller account of his case is given in *Rage Against the Dying*, Liz Sigmund (Pluto Press, 1980), pp. 20-27. An MoD file on this case is located at the PRO at classmark WO 32/21597, but has yet to be opened. Two Porton reports on its trials with nerve gas shells in 1953 have been released (WO 189/147 and WO 189/148), but do not contain any reference to the incident with Cockayne.

67. Interview with the author, 27 January 2000. A longer account of this case is also given in *Rage Against the Dying*, Liz Sigmund (Pluto Press, 1980), pp. 28-38.

68. In a PQ in 1994, the MoD said that there are two unnamed Nancekuke staff who 'claimed that they were suffering from work-related illnesses.' One obviously refers to the case of Tom Griffiths; the other may be Trevor Martin or could indeed be another case altogether. The MoD described it thus: 'One claim was rejected, although the employee was later retired on medical grounds, his symptoms being considered to have been caused by "psychoneurosis" or anxiety'. (*Birmingham Post*, 2 & 5 December 1969; *Daily Telegraph*, 5 December 1969; *Sunday Times*, 7 December 1969; *A Higher Form of Killing*, Jeremy Paxman and Robert Harris, (Triad Paladin, 1983), p. 181; PQ, House of Lords, 11 April 1994.)

69. See, for example, *Independent on Sunday*, 16 January 2000.

70. The argument centred around a study by government statisticians in the General Register Office in 1970 (see PRO, RG 26/449). It emerged in May 2000 that the Ministry of Defence was going to re-examine the data on sickness among Nancekuke workers. (Adjournment debate, House of Commons, 18 January 2000; PQ, 11 November 1999; *Daily Telegraph*, 3 November 1970).

71. PQ, House of Lords, 11 April 1994. The MoD added that between 1955 and 1979, there were 98 'lost time incidents' in which Nancekuke workers had to leave their posts; the majority were accidents 'concerned with physical injury due to mechanical causes 'very few accidents occurred involving chemicals.'

72. PQ, 4 December 1996.

73. *Chemical Warfare Agents: Toxicology and Treatment*, Marrs, Maynard and Sidell, pp. 132-3; 'The long-term health effects of nerve agents and mustard' by Frederick Sidell and Col Charles Hurst, submission to the DSB Task Force on Gulf War CW, December 1993, pp. 15-18 and 30-31.

74. ee, for example, PQ, 18 March 1997. This view was based on 'evaluation of the medical and scientific literature and discussion with expert toxicologists in academic departments, Porton Down and the Veterinary Medicines Directorate'.

75. PQ, 4 April 1995; PQ, Lords, 11 April 1994. Nicholas Soames, then a junior MoD minister, said, 'The structure and purpose of OP nerve agents differ significantly from those of OP sheep dips.' The nerve gases are intended to injure and kill quickly, attacking the body mainly through the skin, he said. 'For full effect, the nerve agent will need to vaporize over time and result in a downwind hazard.' On the other hand, OP sheep dips are much less toxic to humans and have an 'extremely low volatility, thus rendering any inhalation exposure insignificant'.

NOTES

76. Samuel Cucinell (1974), 'A review of the toxicity of long-term phosgene exposure', Archives of Environmental Health, 28, 272-5; *Chemical Warfare Agents: Toxicology and Treatment*, Marrs, Maynard Sidell, p. 201. It should be noted that the article by Cucinell, an Edgewood Arsenal scientist, discusses the toxicity of long-term exposure to phosgene. He states that 'it is reported that phosgene is responsible for the development of long-term lung disease in man' and cites a study from 1947 into the residual effects of phosgene poisoning in humans subjects after chronic exposure. He adds, 'There are no quantitative data available on what dosage might cause permanent lung damage in man'.

77. Porton has recently stated that people who are exposed to adamsite suffer symptoms for several hours, which 'then disappear leaving no obvious long-term effects'. (PQ, 22 July 1996).

78. See, for instance, various statements by the MoD. On chlorine, the MoD stated that Porton 'has not carried out any research into possible long-term effects' of short-term exposure to this chemical. On adamsite (DM), the MoD said that 'no assessment of possible long-term health effects resulting from short-term exposure to adamsite has been made'. (PQs, 21 July 1998; 21 October 1998).

79. Throughout the decades, Porton has tested hundreds, if not thousands, of these chemicals on humans. But any research into, or discussion of, the long-term effects of these substances does not show up in the documents released by Porton into the public domain. When asked about individual chemicals tested on humans in the years after 1945, Porton has replied that its staff have not done any research into such effects. For example, Porton staff did not carry out any research into the possible long-term effects of the morphine-like compound TL2636, pyrexal, BZ, and a glycollate before these compounds were tested on many volunteers in the 1960s. As described in chapter eight, Porton considered these compounds to be potential incapacitating weapons. Porton did not conduct any assessment of the possible long-term effects of the putative tear gas, 1-MCHT, which was tried out on volunteers in the 1980s. (Letters to Ken Livingstone MP, 10 June and 4 November 1998; PQs, 21 July 1998; 8 March 2000).

80. PQs, 3 and 22 July 1996.

81. Letter to Ken Livingstone MP, 10 June 1998.

82. *ibid.*

83. Author's interview with former Porton scientist who requested to remain anonymous.

84. Interview with the author, 11 February 2000.

CHAPTER TWELVE *Into the Twenty-first Century*

1. PQ, 4 April 2000. DERA and Russia have been involved in joint research projects.

2. *Guardian*, 21 August 1999.

3. According to Porton, the plague vaccine was not itself genetically-modified, but is 'produced by a genetic engineering technique widely used in civilian microbiology laboratories'. Clinical trials will be carried out by a commercial organisation and will not involve human volunteers from the armed forces.

4. Author's interview with former scientist who requested to remain anonymous.

5. Adjournment debate, 16 October 1996.

6. Letter to Mick Roche, chairman of the Porton Down Volunteers Association, 2 December 1997.

7. PQ, 6 April 2000. (See also PQ on 7 March 1995).

NOTES

8. These have been recorded, for instance, in internal Porton reports, such as CDE Technical Note 46 (September 1970), CDE Technical Note 58 (January 1971), CDE Technical Note 68 (March 1971), CDE Technical Note 84 (July 1971), CDE Technical Note 127 (March 1972) CDE Technical Note 342 (November 1977).
9. 'The development of immunohistochemical techniques to determine the mechanism of action of sulphur mustard in human skin', CBDE Technical Paper 759, July 1994.
10. PQ, 5 July 1995.
11. PQ, 16 March 1995.
12. PQ, 3 February 1995. Another set of trials in military units around the country – involving 1,500 volunteers – had shown up some 'minor' design faults. Further trials involving up to 40 volunteers confirmed that the modified design was up to the required standards. A harmless aerosol was used in these tests.
13. PQs, 16 March and 5 July 1995. In experiments, non-toxic aerosols were used to see if the suit could be penetrated. Porton has said that none of the volunteers in the Mark 4 suit trials were exposed to toxic chemicals. The Mark 4 suit passed into service as the standard 'noddy suit' in 1987.
14. nterview with the author, 6 June 2000.
15. These regulations related to the two old chambers which were demolished in the early 1990s. The regulations were released to the author under the open government code in 1998.
16. Author's interview with former Porton scientist who requested to remain anonymous.
17. Porton said that 'equipment and volunteers can be exposed to a steady low level of test materials which may be simulants or actual agents' in the new chamber. The new facility replaced four buildings which formed a complex for testing humans. This complex consisted of 'a respirator fitting and testing building, two chambers and a bathhouse/store'. Two of the buildings dated from 1918. (*Independent on Sunday*, the author, 27 August 1995; letters to Ken Livingstone MP, 30 November 1994 and 30 March 1995).
18. Porton released to Ken Livingstone MP copies of HSE inspections and its responses to these reports.
19. The HSE said it would 'normally have issued an Improvement Notice requiring the setting up of an effective organisation and arrangements to meet the legal requirements'. However the inspectors resisted this, only on the 'personal assurance' of Dr Pearson that things would be put right. Under health and safety law, HSE inspectors have the power to issue an Improvement Notice – in effect, a legal warning to employers to rectify health and safety breaches in a given time. If they flout the order, employers can be prosecuted.
20. He wrote, 'Work has already started on the new chamber complex so that investment on interlocks for the present chamber is hard to justify. The shortcomings of the existing chambers are known and are taken into consideration when planning and writing the protocols for chamber trials'. The interlocking system was never installed in the old chambers before they were replaced.
21. orton Down – 75 years of chemical and biological defence, Gradon Carter, (HMSO, 1992), p. 97 (hereafter referred to as Carter).
22. See, for instance, budget figures in PQ, 10 March 1994.
23. Porton's annual report and accounts, 1991/2, p. 3.
24. Carter, pp. 91-4. This describes in full Porton's activities in the war.

25. *ibid* p. 89.
26. Adjournment debate, 17 March 1998.
27. *Guardian*, 6 May 2000. The plaque was the result of many years' pressure by John Bryden, who wrote a book on Canadian chemical and biological research work and later became an MP.

AFTERWORD

1. This approximate figure is derived from analysis of declassified reports of these trials. The Ministry of Defence has not officially estimated the total, but has stated in a PQ on 1 May 1995 that between 1964 and 1977, simulants of radioactive substances or chemical or biological warfare agents 'were used in some 100 experiments'. A large number of germ warfare trials were held before 1964.
2. Interview with the author, 11 February 2000.
3. *Observer*, 21 July 1985.
4. 'The drift of biological weapons policy in the UK 1945-1965', Brian Balmer, The Journal of Strategic Studies, 20: 4, December 1997, pp. 115-145.
5. PRO, WO 195/12530, Experiments on volunteers, 3 November 1953; WO 188/668, 30th meeting of BRAB, November 1953.
6. British Medical Journal, 29 January 1966, pp. 258-266; *Rage Against the Dying*, Elizabeth Sigmund, (Pluto Press, 1980), pp. 61-2; *CBW Chemical and Biological Warfare – London Conference on CBW* (edited by Steven Rose), (George G Harrap, 1968), pp. 107 and 116; *Porton Down – 75 years of chemical and biological defence*, Gradon Carter, (HMSO, 1992), pp. 75-6; obituaries of Smith, *The Times*, 10 August and *Guardian*, 21 August 1991.
7. *An Overview on Cold War Era Programs*, US General Accounting Office (GAO/T-NSIAD-94-266), 28 September 1994, p. 6.
8. *Chemical and Biological Warfare, America's Hidden Arsenal*, Seymour Hersh (MacGibbon & Kee, London, 1968), p. 124.
9. *Saddam's Secrets, the hunt for Iraq's hidden weapons*, Tim Trevan (HarperCollins, 1999), p. 365; *Plague Wars*, Tom Mangold and Jeff Goldberg (Macmillan, 1999), pp. 299-300.
10. In military jargon, this was known as the large area concept. Previously, biological weapons were perceived for use on a relatively limited scale; the lethal germs were to be released over a matter of miles from small bursting munitions. By the 1950s, it was realised that the germs could be disseminated over a massive area, tens of thousands of square miles, from missiles, planes or ships. This meant that the threat of such weapons was much greater.
11. Reports of these trials were released to Matthew Taylor MP by Porton on 26 April 1999; *Guardian*, 2 November 1999.
12. For reports of these trials, see WO 195/14593, WO 195/14594, WO 195/14970, WO 195/14973, WO 195/15132, WO 195/15133, WO 195/15134, WO 195/15135, WO 195/15142, and WO 195/15158. These reports are discussed at various meetings of the Offensive Evaluation Committee, whose minutes are also in the WO 195 classmark.
13. PRO, WO 195/14405, 41st meeting of BRAB, July 1958.
14. Officials estimated in 1960 that the trials 'had covered areas of the UK with not less than 1 million, and up to 38 million inhabitants' (PRO, WO 195/14995, 48th meeting of BRAB, July 1960).

NOTES

15. A brief description of these trials appeared in *A Higher Form of Killing – the secret story of gas and germ warfare*, Robert Harris and Jeremy Paxman, (Triad Paladin, 1983), p. 158. The official reports of the trials began to emerge into the PRO in the 1990s, with some media publicity in late 1998.
16. *Toxicological assessment of the Army's zinc cadmium sulphide dispersion tests*, Subcommittee of the National Research Council (Washington DC: National Academy Press), May 1997.
17. Letter from Porton to Matthew Taylor MP, 28 August 1998; *Sunday Telegraph*, the author and Andrew Gilligan, 1 November 1998; 'Review of zinc cadmium sulphide (FP) field trials conducted by the UK – 1953-64', Gradon Carter, April 2000, p. 5.
18. For a more detailed discussion of the toxicity of cadmium and zinc cadmium sulphide, see *The Eleventh Plague – the politics of biological and chemical warfare*, Leonard Cole, (W H Freeman, 1996), pp. 19-28.
19. Porton is known to have exposed small animals to various concentrations of cadmium oxide fumes in 1940. Porton reported: 'The results suggest that cadmium oxide fumes are similar in degree of toxicity to phosgene'. Most of the Allied work on cadmium during the war was done by the Americans and Canadians. Like the rest of the chemical warfare effort, the results of this work would have been shared with Porton (PRO, WO 188/631, Progress Report, October 1940, p. 17; WO 195/10217, 'A review of compounds studied in chemical warfare research', Porton Memorandum 33, February 1949).
20. PRO, WO 195/16429, 'A review of some concepts of incapacitation', April 1967, p. 9.
21. The report was published on 24 March 2000.
22. Interview with the author, 30 October 1998. Mr Titt refused to give his first name.
23. There were other reasons – it was cheap, relatively stable in the atmosphere, and its particle size was similar to biological warfare organisms. Titt commented, 'Zinc cadmium sulphide had certain advantages and certain disadvantages. It was available in very fine particle sizes. Its fluorescence was distinctive. It was extremely difficult to dissolve'.
24. Letter from Porton to Matthew Taylor MP, 28 August 1998; PRO, WO 195/15390 and WO 189/378.
25. Letter from Porton to Matthew Taylor MP, 28 August 1998. Porton says that this loss of fluorescence did not detract from the value of trials, but that the next step was to use bacteria to validate the earlier results.
26. PRO, WO 195/15813, 'Penetration of built-up areas by aerosols at night', Porton Field Trial Report 610, May 1964. The aim of the trial was to see how the heat generated by industrial firms and homes would disrupt the flow of a large cloud over a city and whether the chemical would fall in greater quantities in the urban area than the countryside. The chemical was released some 20 miles from Norwich, with sampling equipment dotted around the city.
27. RO, WO 195/14405, 41st meeting of BRAB, July 1958.
28. RO, WO 32/20457, note by Sir Walter Cawood, War Office's chief scientist, 30 May 1963.
29. PRO, CAB 131/28, minutes of meeting of the Cabinet's defence committee, 3 May 1963, D (63) 6th meeting, with accompanying memorandum D (63) 14, 16 April 1963.
30. PRO, WO 195/15751; WO 195/15982; WO 32/20457; *Independent*, 28 March 1995. According to these documents, in the early 1950s, 'as a preliminary to testing the vulnerability of the London Underground system to covert biological warfare attack, trials were carried out with biological warfare simulants in ventilation and service

NOTES

tunnels under governmental buildings in Whitehall. These proved that there would be a wide dissemination of biological warfare agents throughout such a system.'

31. *Bacillus globigii* is now more commonly known as *Bacillus subtilis*.
32. PRO, WO 195/16081, WO 195/16147;WO 195/16176; WO 195/16292; DEFE 55/82, 'The visible decay of *E.Coli* on microthreads – exposures carried out in the open air on the coast and inland in Great Britain', MRE Field Trial Report 7, May 1969. Following pressure, the government decided in 1998 to release early the reports which document Porton's experiments in public places up to 1977. This was a departure from the official rule that state papers should be kept closed for 30 years and was done in the spirit of open government. These reports are in a series of 27 technical papers known as MRE Field Trial Reports and are in the PRO at DEFE 55. (MRE stands for the Microbiological Research Establishment, the germ warfare section of Porton which was closed in 1979). At the time of writing, only two of the MRE Field Trial Reports remain classified, since they deal with tests with new equipment.
33. PRO, WO 195/16195. Other information and papers on all these trials in public places can be found in the minutes and memos of BRAB in the PRO classmark, WO 195.
34. PRO, DEFE 55/80, 'Comparison of the viability of *E.Coli* in airborne particles and on microthreads exposed in the field', MRE Field Trial Report 5, April 1969; DEFE 55/81, 'Influence of a protective agent upon the viability of *E.Coli* in aerosols and on microthreads – tests in the field', MRE Field Trial Report 6, May 1969.
35. PRO, DEFE 55/79, 'The viability, concentration and immunological properties of airborne bacteria released from a massive line source', MRE Field Trial Report 4, September 1968; *Sunday Telegraph*, the author and Andrew Gilligan, 17 May 1998.
36. PRO, DEFE 55/87, 'Collaborative US/UK biological detection trials', MRE Field Trial Report 12, August 1972. For details of the American tests in their own country, see *Clouds of Secrecy – the Army's germ warfare tests over populated areas*, Leonard Cole (Rowman & Littlefield, New Jersey, 1988).
37. 'Preliminary proving trials of the Icing Tanker aircraft, Parts 1 and 2', MRE Development Notes 67 and 71, February 1968 and January 1969, (Part 1 is in the PRO at WO 195/16647); *Sunday Telegraph*, the author and Andrew Gilligan, 16 November 1997; Letter from Porton to Ken Livingstone, 29 October 1997. An earlier set of airborne trials with dead bacteria took place at an RAF site in Odiham, Hampshire in 1959 and 1960 (see PRO, WO 195/15111).
38. PRO, DEFE 55/90, 'Decontamination and cleansing in biological operations – studies on the deposition of an airborne biological agent simulant on clothing and hair, and of its subsequent re-aerolization', MRE Field Trial report 15, August 1974; DEFE 55/96, 'Decontamination and cleansing in biological operations – studies in the protection training unit', Phoenix NBCD School, Navy Trial Gondolier, MRE Field Trial Report 21, July 1976; Spratt report (see below), pp. 31-2. Although not specifically stated, it is likely that the human subjects in these tests were drawn from the armed forces.
39. PRO, DEFE/101, 'Assessment of indirect methods for detecting the release of airborne micro-organisms', MRE Field Trial Report 26, December 1977. This report states that the test subjects in the trials were Porton staff.
40. *Clouds of Secrecy – the Army's germ warfare tests over populated areas*, Leonard Cole (Rowman & Littlefield, New Jersey, 1988), pp. 52-4, 167-8 and chapters 7 and 8.
41. PRO, DEFE 55/86, 'The penetration of an airborne BW simulant into HMS *Andromeda*', MRE Field Trial Report 11, October 1971.

NOTES

42. PRO, DEFE 55/89, 'Ship defence against biological operations', MRE Field Trial Report 14, January 1974.
43. PRO, DEFE 55/99, 'Decontamination and cleansing in biological operations – tests in a ship at sea', MRE Field Trial Report 24, June 1977; Spratt report (see below), pp. 32-3.
44. Letter from Porton to Matthew Taylor MP, 28 August 1998. By 1968, Porton was able to state with much certainty that 'as we are surrounded by sea, a sufficiently long line aerosol source to blanket any or all of Britain could be laid down by a very small number of aircraft or ships'. The British public did not know at that time that Porton scientists had secretly carried out the large-scale tests to establish this. (*Nature*, 219, 3 August 1968, pp. 537-9).
45. Former Armed Forces Minister John Reid, in the adjournment debate on the germ warfare tests (West Country) in House of Commons, 12 November 1997.
46. *Sunday Telegraph*, the author and Andrew Gilligan, 2 February 1997; Adjournment debate in House of Commons, 12 November 1997. The issue has led to much coverage in the local media, such as the *Dorset Evening Echo* and regional television programmes.
47. See, for example, *Daily Express*, 26 May 1998. The Spratt report (see below) decided that the trials did not cause the village's health problems, while the Dorset Health Authority ruled that there was not a cluster (see its report on 23 March 1999).
48. *Daily Express*, 6 July 1998.
49. DERA press release announcing exhibitions in Dorset, 18 September 1997.
50. Professor Spratt of the Wellcome Trust Centre for the Epidemiology of Infectious Disease was appointed in August 1998. His report was made public on 28 January 1999. At one point in his report, Spratt implies criticism of Porton's safety practices. He notes that in MRE Field Trial Report 3 – which describes 14 trials over Dorset in 1963/4 – an unknown organism contaminated the bacteria which was sprayed from the Icewhale ship over populated areas. He says that this was 'surprising', 'as there was a possible risk that the contaminating bacteria had a significant ability to cause disease in humans'.
51. Conversation with the author, 7 January 2000.
52. Conversation with the author, 7 January 2000.
53. The Ministry of Defence refused to give substantive details of the trials when the issue was raised in 1979, after documents on similar American tests were disclosed. With end of the Cold War and the inevitable (if slow) release of Porton's trial reports to the Public Record Office after the required 30-year lapse, the Ministry of Defence was prepared to reveal some of these secret details when requested by Ken Livingstone in 1996. (Letter from then Defence Secretary Michael Portillo to Ken Livingstone MP, 6 August 1996; *Guardian*, 28 & 29 September 1979).
54. Conversation with the author, 7 January 2000.
55. Interview with the author.
56. 'Review of zinc cadmium sulphide (FP) field trials conducted by the UK – 1953-64', Gradon Carter, April 2000, pp. 44/5.
57. See paper presented by Brian Balmer, Department of Science and Technology Studies, University College, London, to conference on Using Bodies: humans in the service of Twentieth century Medicine, Wellcome Institute, London, 3-4 September 1998.
58. Letter from the then Ministry of Defence Minister Lord Gilbert to Matthew Taylor MP, 2 February 1999. Lord Gilbert said there was no need for such trials at the moment because 'much of the data from the previous trials is still valid and useful'. But he

NOTES

added, 'I do not think that we should rule out the need to conduct further trials to ensure the protection of the UK from attacks by people or states using biological or chemical weapons. Indeed, events of the last few years, such as the chemical attack on the Tokyo Underground, have shown the need to be prepared for similar acts of terrorism.' According to the Spratt report, non-pathogenic bacteria have been released on MoD sites in small-scale tests in the 1980s and 1990s, but 'no significant exposure to bacteria would have occurred outside MoD land'.

APPENDIX 1

1. PRO, WO 195/14846, 'History of the Service Volunteer Observer Scheme at the Chemical Defence Experimental Establishment', Porton Note 119, November 1959. More recently, the Ministry of Defence stated in a PQ on 16 July 1987 that 'a precise figure for the total number of volunteers over the years is not available'.
2. The figures for the number of volunteers tested between 1945/6 and 1958/59 are contained in the 1959 history of the Service Volunteer Observer Scheme at the Chemical Defence Experimental Establishment. The totals between 1959 and 1964 come from an update to the 1959 history – the Service Volunteer Observer Scheme at the Chemical Defence Experimental Establishment from 1959 to 1965, addendum to Porton Note 119, October 1965 (PRO, WO 195/16136). The figures for the years between 1964 and 1996 are from PQs on 11 January and 24 June 1994; 30 October 1996; 27 October 1997. The figures for 1997 and 1998 are given in the annual reports of the Porton's Independent Ethics Committee. The total for 1999 is given in a PQ on 8 March 2000. (Of this total, 13 took part in an experiment at HMS *Phoenix*, the Naval Nuclear and Biological centre and fire training school in an experiment described in a PQ on 3 May 2000).
3. See, for example, statements by defence ministers in House of Commons debates on 16 October 1996 and 17 March 1998.
4. 6 July 1987.
5. The earlier figures, up to 1958/9, are given in the 1959 history of the Service Volunteer Observer Scheme at the Chemical Defence Experimental Establishment. According to this history, between 1948 and 1950, Porton staff were exposed to nerve gases 127 times. For the year 1948/9, the staff exposures have been subtracted to leave the total of volunteers who were exposed to nerve gas. For 1949/50, it is not possible to make this differentiation and so the figure for this year may not been accurate. The figures after 1966 were disclosed in a letter from Porton to Ken Livingstone MP on 10 June 1998.
6. During 1959, 97 volunteers had been exposed to nerve gases up until 27 October of that year – the cut-off date for the compilation of statistics for the 1959 history of the Service Volunteer Observer Scheme at the Chemical Defence Experimental Establishment.

APPENDIX 4

1. PQ, 6 July 1995.
2. Letters to various MPs, 30 January 1998.
3. ouse of Commons adjournment debate, 17 March 1998.
4. Letter to David Atkinson, MP for Michael Paynter, 7 December 1995.

Notes

5. PQ, 27 June 2000.
6. A photocopy from these summary books from 1960, for instance, shows handwritten entries in a series of columns headed (in order) date joined, service number, rank, name, age, weight, height, blood number, unit to which they belonged, experiments in which they participated, and pay received. Since 1940, Porton has also maintained an alphabetical list of individuals who attended the establishment to take part in experiments.
7. These technical reports were produced by Porton in series; for example Porton Technical Papers, Porton Notes, Porton Memorandum, CDE Technical Papers. On the whole, they do not contain the names of individual volunteers in the trial, and so it can be difficult to match up a volunteer with their experiment. At the time of writing, relatively few volunteers have been given technical reports. Porton says that reports which are still classified cannot be released to volunteers, although details are often extracted and disclosed to them.
8. In October 1996, 'fewer than 100' had written to Porton requesting details of their tests. By March 1998, this figure had steadily risen to 'some 170' volunteers (PQ, 13 February 1998; House of Commons adjournment debates, 17 March 1998 and 16 October 1996).
9. PQ, 8 March 2000.
10. According to Porton, no volunteer has been allowed to start an experiment in recent times unless their Service Medical Records have been reviewed by Porton staff. A reference to the tests is automatically included in these records nowadays. Under the Access to Health Records Act 1990, individuals can obtain copies of their Service Medical Records, but only those documents which have been compiled after 1 November 1991.
11. For one survey covering volunteers between 1975 and 1980, any note in the records was 'exceptional' and even then, threadbare ('Possible long-term sequelae of exposure to nerve agents – a retrospective survey', CDE Technical Note 1010, August 1989).

INDEX

Page numbers in italics refer to photographs

A

A-Bomb tests 304-5
Abyssinia: use of gas in 76
Access to Health Records Act 373
Achilles, HMS 360
adamsite *see* arsenical smokes
Adie, Captain W J 35
Adrian, Dr (later Lord) Edgar 153
Adrian committee 153-6, 157, 183-4, 185, 210, 213
Afghans: use of gas against 98
Agent Orange 271
aircraft: spraying gas from 102-3
Aldermaston 309
Allmark, Private 74
Anderson, Sir Austin 31-2, 39, 46
Andromeda, HMS 359-60
animals: experiments on 18, 32-4, 35-6, 67, 118, 177, 183, 188, 233, 255, 325, 329, 342, 350
anthrax 349-50
Anti-Gas Department 27-8, 43, 44
antibiotics 341
antidotes 17
    semi-automatic injector 160
    to biological warfare 341
    to nerve gases 11, 127, 132, 142, 143, 160, 161, 191, 341
Antler, Operation 1
Apollo missions 122
Applied Biology Committee 240-1, 242
Army Council 49, 89, 302
arsenical smokes:
    deployment 38, 68-9
    effects of 37, 68, 69
        long-term 332
    experiments 31-2, 37-9, 63-4, 68, 69, 89-90
arsine: experiments 88
'Arthur' 88
Artichoke programme 251

INDEX

Ashton, Gerry 127, 294
assault courses 93-4
Atherton, Candy 330
atropine 127, 142, 143, 160, 161
Attlee, Clement 125
Aum Shinrikyo 329
Australia:
   chemical warfare tests 7, 9, 90-7, 105, 106, 209, 321-2, 365
      ending 220
   collaboration with 104-5, 220
   compensation payments 321-2
   nuclear tests 304-5, 309

B

bacteria: used as germ warfare simulants 357-61
Baird, Jack 92, 94
Banks, Tony 55, 291-3
Barcroft, Professor Sir Joseph 32-3, 46, 120, 190
Bari harbour disaster 107, 322
Barnes, Terence 83
Bates, Bob 254
BBC *see* tear gases
BBC (television) 338
Beaulieu, Hampshire 352
Beck, Michael 161-2
Beech, Gerry 128-30
Bell, Gordon 1-2, 173, *174*, 254
Berrecloth, Sue 62
Beswick, Frank 204
Biological Research Advisory Board (BRAB) 350-1, 357, 362
biological warfare 289, 344, 345, 349-64
   antidotes 341
   definition 14
   experiments 350
      military volunteers 358-60
   human experiments 350-2, 358-60
   trials over civilians 352-8
   trials with simulants 13, 349, 352-61
   used on prisoners of war 11, 166
Birt, Lewis 132, 293
Black Magic 271
Blair, Tony 347, 348
blister gases 14, 65-7, 332, 369
blood circulation: effect of nerve gas on 214
blood gases 14, 369
Bluebird programme 251
Boyd-Carpenter, John 299

INDEX

BRAB *see* Biological Research Advisory Board
brainwashing 251-3
Bramall, Gertrude 264-5
Brazill, Fay 93
breathing tests: definition 89
Brimblecombe, Roger 234
British Expeditionary Force: Central Laboratory 43-4
Brocklesby, Hubert 300-1
Brook Island, Queensland 96-7
Brown, Jesse 321
bullets: rubber and plastic 283
Buxton, Jim 175

C

Caldicutt, Private RH 102-3
Callaghan, James 277
Cambridge University 109
Cameron, Professor Sir Roy 153-4
Campaign for Nuclear Disarmament (CND) 226, 268
Canada:
   chemical warfare testing 7, 9, 90, 100-4, 107, 185, 210, 365
   collaboration with 104-5, 133, 220, 252-3
   plaque to volunteers 347
Cannock Chase, Staffordshire 24
Care, Alan 152, 297, 304
Caribbean: biological warfare experiments 350
Carter, Gradon 27, 45, 77, 117, 153, 203, 344, 345
Case, Thomas 85
Castner Kellner, Runcorn 23
Cauldron, Operation 350
Cazalet, Rupert 182
Central Laboratory, British Expeditionary Force 43-4
Channel Four 248
Chemical Defence Advisory Board 350
chemical warfare:
   see also nerve gases; tear gases, etc
   antidotes 341
   committee on 47
   countries developing 344
   definition 14
   deployment among military units 224-5
   dumping weapons 118, 223-4, 339
   effects: summary 368-9
   filling weapons 75
   'ideal' weapons 17-18
   lack of stock 225
   lethal dosages 368-70

INDEX

    military objections to 228
    offensive weapon testing 108-9
    range of weapons 14-15
    reasons for not using 108, 113-14
    tests: definition 14
Chemical Warfare Committee 49
chemical warfare companies 82-3
Chemistry in Britain 293
Chilcott, Jeanette 307
China:
    use of chemical weapons against 90, 107
    weapons held 12
chlorine gas:
    deployment of 21-3, 24
    effects of 21-2, 369
    experiments 23-4, 43
    release methods 23-4
chloroform 31-2
choking gases 14
    effects of 369
cholinesterase levels 141, 143, 144, 146-7, 190, 193, 194, 212
Churchill, Winston 69, 79, 80, 98, 100, 108, 123
CIA (Central Intelligence Agency) 9, 251-3, 257
Clarke, Royston 175, 250-1
Clavey, Bill 293-4
Clutterbuck, David 171
CN gas *see* tear gases
CND *see* Campaign for Nuclear Disarmament
Coates, Gunner Barry 243
Cockayne, William 329
Cold War 1, 10, 56, 122-4, 163, 167, 170, 171, 182, 197-229, 251, 253, 290, 309-10, 349, 358, 362-3
Committee on the Safety of Human Experiments (COSHE) 178-80, 241, 242
common cold research 1, 5, 165, 170, 173, 175-6, 293, 304, 347
Communist Terrorists (CTs) 266
compensation:
    claims for 5, 10, 67, 296-304, 334, 347-8
    pensions 70-1, 72, 85, 107, 296-304, 305
concentration camps 12, 107, 120, 121, 122, 165-6, 206
consent forms 181-2, 189
Cookson, Richard 201-2
corporate manslaughter 1
Court of Inquiry 145, 153
Coventry, Nuneaton and District War Pension Committee 323
Cox, Mike 141-2, 145
CR gas *see* tear gases

Cross, E M 72
Crossley, Arthur 25, 26, 29, 30, 45, 68
Crown Proceedings Act: Section 10 297-9, 303
Crowther, Joseph 65
Crusoe, Operation 266
CS gas *see* tear gases
Cyprus 284

D

Dachau concentration camp 122
Daily Express 278, 291
Dale, Harold 150
Dalyell, Tam 55
Davies, Emlyn Llewelyn (E.Ll) 100, 102, 103
Daykin, Richard 87-8
decontamination methods 64, 306-7
Defence Council Instructions (DCI) 50
Defence Evaluation and Research Agency (DERA) 337-9
defence policy 220-2
Defence Research Policy Committee 222
defoliants 14-15, 271
demonstrations: at Porton 8
Department of Veterans' Affairs (VA) 319-21
detection devices 64
Devitte, Private L V 102-3
disability pensions *see* war pensions
disarmament 222-3
Dobbs, Seargeant Major 25
'Doctors' Trial' 165
dog: experiments on 32-3, 120, 190
Dorchester 358
Dorset 358, 360
Dudley, Hugh 180
Dyer, Bill 307
Dyhernfurth, Poland 113

E

E. Coli 358, 359, 361
East Lulworth 360-1
Eden, Sir Anthony 220
Edgewood Arsenal, USA 122, 202, 257-8, 264
Edholm, Dr OG 240
Eggleton, Art 347
Eisenhower, Dwight 222
ethics 165-96, 204-5
    clashing with secrecy 167-8, 240

INDEX

    during First World War 29-30
    during Second World War 90, 105-7
    Geneva Protocol 62, 76, 81, 220, 228, 276
    improvements 342-3
    Nuremberg Code 2, 29, 107, 165, 166, 167, 169, 173, 176-8, 182
        clauses 371-2
    of open-air tests 362-4
    of psycho-chemical testing 233-5, 239-41
    of radiation tests 309-10
    standards compared 340
    of tear gas tests 275
    using data from unethical tests 122
    using unwitting subjects 251-2
Ethiopia:
    use of chemical weapons in 10
    use of gas on 76
European Commission of Human Rights 303-4
Evans, Major DC 120
Evans, Private 74
eyes:
    effects of mustard gas on 40, 41, 42-3, 99-100, 103, 324, 333
    effects of nerve gases on 111, 116, 126, 127, 128, 130, 131-2, 135-6, 157, 162, 215-17, 218, 293-4
    effects of tear gases on 261, 262, 265, 270, 280-1
    keratitis 72, 73

F

Fairley, Surgeon Commander Archibald 70-1
film: promotional 52-4, 56
firing trials 27
First World War 4, 6, 10, 12, 21-46, 50, 62, 68-9, 73, 77, 79, 90
    disabilities from gassing 70-2, 322-4
Fitzgerald, Gerald 304
'Flying Cow' 109
'Flying Lavatory' 109
Forster, Ella 140, 149-50
Fortescue, Arthur 65
Fortescue, John 65-6
Foulkes, Major Charles Howard 22-5, 34, 35, 37, 38, 45, 311
France:
    chemical warfare programme 10, 210
    disputes with 31, 32
    recruiting Germans 121
Fraser, Daniel 66-7
Freedom of Information Act 9
French, Sir John 21, 22
Fudge, Henry 58

G

Gaddum, Professor Jack 188, 234-5
Gadsby, Neville 247, 282-3
Galatea, HMS 360
Gall, Dr David 206
gas chambers 4, 92, 343, 344
gas masks *see* respirators
gas shells 63
Gemmell, Captain Alexander 44
General Accounting Office 327
Geneva Protocol 62, 76, 81, 220, 228, 276
George V, King 33
George, Bruce 339
germ warfare *see* biological warfare
Germans:
    interned 85-6
    in Porton experiments 85
Germany:
    concentration camps 12, 107, 120, 121, 122, 165-6, 206
    confiscation of weapons from 118-19, 224
    development of nerve gas 111, 113-15
    human experiments 9-10, 44
        data from 119-21
    invasion of Britain: defence against 80
    suggested use of biological warfare on 349-50
    use of chemical warfare 21-2, 24, 34-5, 39-40, 45, 68
Gilchrist, Colonel Harry L 72
Gillis, Richard 321-2
Gorrill, Freddie 90, 91, 97
Gosden, Christine 328
Grandison, Robert 152, 158
Gray, Mike 144-5
Griffiths, Tom 329, 330
Gruinard, Scotland 350
Guest, William 158
Gulf War 12, 52, 196, 228, 310, 312, 313, 326, 344, 345, 360
Gulf War Syndrome 304, 310-13, 326, 331, 333

H

Haddon, Eric 61-2, 186, 191, 192
Haile Selassie, Emperor 76
Halabjah, Kurdistan 328, 344
Hall, Wilfred 82-3
hallucinogenic drugs 166-7, 231-59
    effects of 231, 234
    experiments 231, 234
        code for 235

INDEX

Hangover (mock exercise) 158-60
Hangover Two 160-1
Harness, Operation 350
Harper, George 361
Harper, Peter 135-6
Harrison, Colonel Edward 44
Harrower, Sergeant 35
Harwell 309
Hawkes, Nigel 2
Hay, Alastair 152, 370
Hazelwood, Operation 360
Health and Safety Executive (HSE) 343-4
hearing: effect of nerve gas on 214
heart rates: effect of nerve gas on 214
Heavy Air Defence Regiment (Royal Artillery) 242-5
Hems, Arthur 323
Henman, Godfrey 83-4
Henson, Kenneth 86-7
Hesperus, Operation 350
Himsworth, Sir Harold 276
Himsworth committee 276-7, 287
Hitler, Adolf 80, 113, 115
Hofmann, Albert 234
Hogg, Harry 84-5, 299-300
Holland committee 47-8
Hollyhock, Dr Maxwell 235, 255
Hong Kong 283
Hood, Mike 362
Hopwood, Keith 309
Hormats, Saul 133
House of Commons Defence Committee 310, 312
Howard, Michael 284, 285
Hullavington, Wiltshire 352
humane weapons 233, 236
Hutchins, Ray 170-1
hydrogen cyanide (HCN) 369
    testing 32-3, 120
        use in concentration camps 120
        weapon containing 109
hydrogen sulphide: trials 24, 25

I

Icewhale 358
Imperial College 263, 266
incapacitating weapons 236, 248, 259
Inch, Tom 199, 342
Independent Ethics Committee 52, 179-81, 219

INDEX

India: chemical warfare testing 90, 98-100, 365
Indians 98-9
    after tests *101*
injector: semi-automatic 160
Innisfail, Queensland 91, 92-5, 97
Institute of Medicine, National Academy of Sciences 320
interrogation 249-50
IRA 286
Iran: weapons 12
Iran-Iraq war 328
Iraq:
    chemical warfare testing 11, 210
    chemical weapons 196, 344
        destruction of 345
    use of nerve gases 326
Israel:
    drug testing 11
    weapons 12
Italians: interned 85-6
Italy:
    chemical warfare testing 10
    use of chemical weapons 76

J

Jamaica 267
Japan:
    gas experiments 12
    germ warfare experiments 12, 166, 351
    nerve gas used in 329
    use of chemical weapons 90, 107
Japanese:
    bravery 93
    tests for use of gas on 96-8
Jemmett, Roy 269

K

Kelman, Daine Bryce 291
Kennedy, Edward 192
Kennedy, Colonel J C 71
Kenya 267
Keynes, Professor Richard 202
Khamisiyah, Iraq 326
Kimber, Detective Inspector Sid 3
King, Tom 295, 331
Kitchener, Lord 22
Knowles, Alan 216-17
Kolanut, Operation 359-60

INDEX

Kurds 328, 344
Kuwait 344-5

L

Lachmann, Peter 355-6
lachrymators *see* tear gases
Ladell, Dr Bill 61, 183, 184, 185, 187, 190, 193, 194, 195, 212, 213, 215-16, 242, 250, 255
Lader, Professor Malcolm 52, 180, 219
Lancet 234
Lawson, Dr Richard 307
Legge, Jack 91, 92, 93, 94
Leigh, Day and Co 296
Lethbridge, Major General 97-8
lewisite 65
    effects of 332, 369
    experiments 85, 86
Libya: weapons 12
liquid crystal displays 337-8
Livens, Captain William Howard 24
Livens Projector 24, 27, 28, 63, 67
Livingstone, Ken 217-18, 333
Lloyd George, David 33
London Underground: biological weapon trials 357, 360
LSD 14, 231-59
    effects of 231, 234, 236, 237, 238-9, 240, 242-5, 246-7, 257-8
        long-term 258-9
    experiments 231, 234, 235-6, 237-53, 291
        code for 235
Luckett, Detective Superintendent Gerry 1, 3
lung irritants 14
Lyme Bay 358
Lyons, Tony 280-1

M

M device 38-9, 68, 102
McAndrew, Lawrence 171
McBray, Alan 53
Macfarlane and Co. 254
McKay, Henry 61
McMahon, Dolores 351
Macmillan, Harold 220, 224, 236, 247, 248
Maddison, John 139, 149-50
Maddison, Lillias 139, 149, 152
Maddison, Ronald 138, 139-54, 163, 170, 187
    aftermath of death 153-8, 168, 183, 184, 186, 210, 291
    death certificate 151

480

inquest 149, 150
investigation into death 1, 2, 152, 165, 304, 338, 339
Mail on Sunday 293
Malaya (Malaysia) 26, 267
Mallard, Tony 132
Manchurian Candidate 251, 252
Maralinga, Australia 309
Marrs, Timothy 323, 324, 326, 330-1
Marsden, Bob 290
Martin, Trevor 330
Mason, Roy 226, 227
Matsumoto, Japan: nerve gas attack 329
Maunder, Maurice 91, 93, 94
Mauritius 264
Maynard, Robert 323, 324, 326, 330-1
Maze prison 282
Meakin, Richard 289-90
medical countermeasures *see* antidotes
medical inquiries 315-35
Medical Research Council 176
mental faculties:
    effects of nerve gas on 134-5
        exercises to assess 158-63
    effects of psycho-chemicals on 234, 237, 241
mescaline 232
MI5 249-50
MI6 249-50
Milliken, John 140, 152
Mills, Steve 124-5
mind control 251-3
Mindszenty, Cardinal Josef 251
Ministry of Agriculture, Food and Fisheries 338
Ministry of Defence 218, 219, 223, 258, 259, 360
    compensation claims 296-309, 313, 329
    estimates of volunteers 365-7
    on Gulf-related illnesses 310-11
    helpline 374-6
    plans for DERA 338
    providing information 290, 295-6
    records 248, 249
    refusing inquiry 315-35
    reports 156
    secrecy 225, 282
    Service Medical Records 376
Ministry of Pensions 70-1, 72, 323
Ministry of Supply 145, 153, 157
Mirror 2

INDEX

Mitchell, Tom 97, 321
MKULTRA programme 251
Monckton, Sir Walter 220-1, 222
Moneybags, Operation 231, 237-9, 242, 247, 250, 259
monkeys 46
mortar bombs 63
Mullin, Chris 315-16
Murphy, Sean 370
mustard gas 14
   bombs containing 79-80
   on clothes 73-4
   concealing smell 266
   effects of 40, 41, 42-3, 74, 75, 82, 87, 93-4, 300
      assessing degree 94-5
      on different skin types 98-9
      on eyes 40, 41, 42-3, 99-100, 103, 324, 333
      long-term 70-3, 318-24, 331
      summary 369
   experiments 5, 41-2, 64-7, 69-70, 73-6, 82, 85, 86-8, 98-100, 124, 167
      on different skin types 98-9
      ending 318, 319
      'man-break' tests 104
      spraying from aircraft 102-3
      in tropical conditions 90-1, 92-7
   manufacture 80, 109
      dangers to workers 323
   treating burns 50, 74-6, 91, 99, 345
   use in war 39-40, 44, 45, 76, 328
   weapons containing 109

N

Nancekuke, Portreath, Cornwall 125, 133, 221, 223, 224, 225, 226, 272, 329-30, 339
NAPS (Nerve Agent Pre-treatment Set) tablets 311-13, 341
National Academy of Sciences (USA) 328, 355
   Institute of Medicine 320
National Radiological Protection Board (NRPB) 305
Natzweiler concentration camp 121
Nazis 10, 12, 29, 107, 111, 113-14, 117-22, 224
Negation, Operation 350
Nelson, John 156, 157, 290
nerve gases 14
   adding radioactive material to 148-9, 184, 185, 195
   antidotes 127, 142, 143, 191, 341
      testing 11, 132, 160, 161
   cholinesterase levels 22, 141, 143, 144, 146-7, 190, 193, 194
   in cold War 123-4

482

INDEX

death from 1, 113, 114-15
deployment among military units 224-5
dumping 223-4
effects of 111-13, 114-15, 116, 126, 127, 128, 130, 131-2, 134-7, 157, 159, 160-1, 162-3, 170, 215, 293-4
    exercise combined with 126, 212
    long-term 127, 130, 145, 157, 169, 294, 295, 296, 324-32
    on mental faculties 134-5, 158-63
    repeated exposures 128
    summary 348
experiments 10, 53, 111, 112, 114, 115-18, 124, 125-37, 155-63, 169, 190, 193-5, 209-20
    alternatives 219
    intravenous tests 183, 192
        seeking permission for 183-9, 192
    resulting in death 139-54, 163, 168, 170, 183, 186, 187, 210, 291
    in tropical conditions 212-13
lack of stock 225
manufacture 113, 125, 133, 221-2, 223, 224-6, 228
moved from Germany to England 118
NAPS (Nerve Agent Pre-treatment Set) tablets 311-13, 341
origin 111
single-breath administration 215
use on civilians 329, 344
use in war 326, 328
V-agents 182-96, 211
New Scientist 235, 255
New Statesman 227-8
No fire, no thunder – the threat of chemical and biological weapons 370
non-lethal warfare 231-60
Norris, Keith 361
Northern Ireland 208, 276, 277, 278, 281-4, 286, 291
Norwich 357
Nosworthy, Ron 96-7
nuclear tests 304-5, 309
nuclear weapons 117, 221
Nuremberg Code 2, 29, 107, 165, 166, 167, 169, 173, 176-8, 182, 240
    clauses 371-2

O

Obanakoro 224
Offences Against the Person Act 1
Official Secrets Act 198, 201-2, 203, 204, 289-91, 361
Olson, Dr Frank 252
organophosphorus compounds *see* nerve gases
Owen, Wilfred 44
Ozone, Operation 350

P

Pacific islands: nuclear tests 305
Paperclip, Operation 121-2
Paynter, Michael 172-3, 304
Payton, Derek 270
Pearson, Graham 52, 105-6, 181, 202, 218, 227, 248, 316, 343, 344-5
Peck, SC 49
Pensions Appeal Tribunal 303
Pepper, Sydney 86
pepper spray 285
Perren, Dr Ted 183
pesticides 331
Peters, Sir Rudolph (Captain 'Bunny') 31, 153-4
Petrenko, Vladimir 10
phosgene:
    effects of 34-5, 42-3, 113, 369
        long-term 71, 332
    manufacture 109
    testing 34, 35-8
    use in war 34-5
Pioneer Corps 85-6
Pitchers, Fred 280
plant toxins 253
Plymouth 360
police: riot control 253, 261-2, 265, 267-8, 276, 282, 283-5, 286-7
Police Complaints Authority (PCA) 286
    arrests 286
Ponting, Clive 291
Porton Down:
    animal testing 32-4, 35-6, 67, 177, 183, 188, 255, 325, 329
    Applied Biology Committee 240-1, 242
    bad publicity 303
    biological warfare trials 349-64
    Biology Committee 155, 183-4, 212, 213
    in Cold War 197-229
    Committee on the Safety of Human Experiments (COSHE) 178-80, 241, 242
    Court of Inquiry 145, 153
    criminal investigations 1-3, 145, 146, 152, 165, 296, 304, 338
    critical assessment 202
    demonstrations 8
    directors 207-9
    ethical standards 165, 166-96, 204-5, 208, 234, 235, 239-41, 340, 342-3, 362-4
    expansion 25-6
    experimental work 244
    in First World War 20
    future 344

gas chamber 4, 343, 344
geographical position 3
German scientists wanted 122
helpline 374-6
human experiments:
    arguments for 67-8
    intravenous tests 183
        permission for 183-9, 192
    placebo use 334
    resulting in death 139-54, 158, 163, 165, 168, 170, 183, 186, 187, 210
    on staff members 29, 32, 49-50, 103, 183, 190-1, 193-5, 208, 235-6, 329, 359
Independent Ethics Committee 52, 179-81, 219
laboratories 26, *292*
name changes 339
open days *292*
Physiology Laboratory 26, 30-1, 32, 48, 81
present-day activities 337-48
press releases 338
promotional film 52-4, 56
records 373-6
safety regulations 343-4
scientists' motivation 197-207
setting up 25-6
staff recruitment 48, 80
Technical Chemical Department (Offensive Munitions Department) 63
threat of closure 47, 226-7
volunteers 29, 32-9, 45, 81
    armed forces 50-62, 81-5, 86-8, 89, 139-40, 158, 169-76, 189, 204, 207, 210-11, 268-9, 327
        annual numbers 346-7
    civilians 189-90
    consent forms 181-2, 189
    gratitude to 346
    health monitoring 259, 315-18, 324, 325-6, 327, 330-4
    inducements 49, 57, 82, 140, 268, 269, 273, 279, 280
    motivation 57-9, 59, 60, 216, 268, 270
    numbers 289, 342, 365-7
    obtaining information 293-6, 373-6
    personality of 58-60
    recruiting 49-62
    refusal to return 82, 269
    releasing information to 293-6
    tricked into taking part 1-2, 165, 170-7, 188, 250-1, 293, 304, 347
    withdrawing 92, 178
    women 61-2
Porton Down Volunteers Association 61, 295, 296, 299, 373
prisoners: use as guinea pigs 190, 251, 352

INDEX

Profumo, John 189, 225
projectiles 24, 27, *28*, 34
Proserpine, Queensland 97
protective clothing 17, 66, 73, 74, 95-6, *200*, 228, 341-2, 345-6
   see also respirators
   use in tropics 95-6
psycho-chemicals 14, 232-59
   effects of 231, 234, 236, 237, 238-9, 240, 242-5, 246-7, 254-5, 256, 257-8
      long-term 258-9
   experiments 231, 234, 235-6, 237-59
psychotomimetics 234-5
Pym, Francis 227
pyrexal 253-4

Q

Quakers 32

R

radioactive material:
   adding to nerve gases 148-9, 184, 185, 195, 307-9
   decontamination tests 306-7
   diseases linked to 305-10
   penetration through skin 307-9
   testing 306-10
Randle, near Runcorn, Cheshire 76
Raubkammer, Germany 117-18, 124
Rawalpindi, India (now Pakistan) 98
Rawlins, Colonel SWH 67
Reagan, Ronald 227
Recount exercise 239, 242-5, 247
Reid, John 340, 346, 374, 376
respirators (gas masks) 29, 31, 36-9, 43, 53-4, 63-4, 79, 96, *200*, 274-5, 341-2, 345, 346
respiratory illnesses 10, 70-3, 361
riot control:
   gases 60, 262, 264, 267-8, 270, 272-3, 276-8, 282, 286
   rubber bullets 283
Roberts, Eddie 169, 293
Roche, Mick 61, 211, 295-6, 303-4, 373
Rodgers, Bill 152
Roosevelt, Franklin D 98, 108
Rose, Steven 370
Ross, Ron 58
Royal Army Medical College, Millbank 27-9
Royal College of Physicians 181
Royal Engineers:
   chemical warfare companies 82-3, 86
   Experimental Company 29

INDEX

Royal Marines 237-9
Royal Norfolk Regiment 85
Royal Technical College, Salford 278
Rudge, Ernest 43
Runcorn, Cheshire:
    Castner Kellner works 23
    mustard gas factory 76
Russell Jones and Walker 304
Russia:
    civil war 68-9
    deployment of chemical weapons in 102
    reducing weapons 12
Rydon, Professor Henry 234

S

Saddam Hussein 4, 11, 196, 289, 310, 328, 344, 352
St Thomas' Hospital, London 351
Salt, Major 98
San Francisco: biological warfare simulation trials 359
San Jose Island, Panama 104
Sandys, Duncan 190
Schrader, Dr Gerhard 111, 113, 308
scientists:
    motivation 197-8
    public's view of 13, 197
    publishing papers 198
Scotland: biological warfare experiments 350
Scott, Nicholas 283-4
Second World War 9, 10, 51, 61, 64, 77, 79-117, 165, 209, 266, 349-50, 356
secrecy 6-7, 15, 167-8, 220, 240, 362-3
    Official Secrets Act 198, 201-2, 203, 204, 289-91
Sellick, Leonard 268-9, 290
Serratia marcescens 359
Service Medical Records 376
Seventh Day Adventist Church 352
sharks: repelling 275
Sharpe, Peter 262
Shave, Douglas 170
Shawcross, Lord 297
sheep dips 331
Sidell, Frederick 323, 324, 326
Sim, Dr Van 162, 192, 234
Simon, Sir Jocelyn 297
Sinclair, Dr David 91-2, 93, 94, 95, 96, 105, 209
skin:
    effects on 10, 40-1, 42, 264-5, 279, 300
        for varying skin types 98-9

INDEX

    treating burns to 50
Sleeman, David 308
Small Change trial 245-6
Smith, David 126
Smith, Dr Gordon 351
smoke generators 63
sneezing, gases inducing *see* sternutators
Soames, Nicholas 310, 316, 340
Sobo Plain 224
Somalia 260
Somme, Battle of the 35
South Africa:
    apartheid 11
    chemical and biological warfare 11
Southey, Robin 361
Soviet Union 221
    see also Cold War
    biological weapons 362
    chemical warfare programme 10, 210
    compensation claims 10
    developing nerve gases 123-4
    incapacitating weapons 248
    LSD manufacture 251
    nerve gas stockpile 227
    obtaining information from Germans 123
    recruiting Germans 121
spies 249
Spratt, Professor Brian 361
Spycatcher (Wright) 249, 250
'Squirt' 109
Stacey, Frank 156-7
Stafford Regiment 245-6
Stanley, James 257-8, 259
sternutators 14, 37, 89-90
Stevens, Bertram 322
Stevens, John 240
Stewart, Michael 276
stomach disease 10
Stranks, Harold 105
Strasbourg University 121
Stubbs, Sgt John 245, 246
Suez Crisis 222
Suffield, Alberta 100-4, 202, 347
suicide gas 88
Sunday Dispatch 150
Sutton Oak 125
Swanston, Dennis 6, 198-9, 201, 275, 277
Syria: weapons 12

T

Tarrant Rushton, Dorset 358
Taylor, Matthew 349
tear gases (lachrymators) 14, 261-88
    concentrations 287
    disguising mustard gas 266
    dispersing 281
    dissemination 286-7
    effects of 261, 262, 263-4, 266, 269, 270, 273, 274-5, 279, 280
        on food 275
        long-term 265, 277-8, 279, 287-8, 332
        summary 369
        tolerance 273-4
        in water 275, 281
        wearing respirators 274-5
    experiments 60, 64, 81, 89, 190, 208, 252, 263, 264-5, 266-7, 268-70, 272-5, 278-81
        ethics 275
    manufacture 109, 264, 272
    people susceptible to 287
    use by police 253, 261-2, 265, 267-8, 272, 276, 282-3, 284-5, 286-7
    use in war 262-3, 263, 266, 271, 285, 291
Tenggol, off Malaya 266-7
Thatcher, Margaret 17, 227, 228
Thompson, Professor Robert 241
Thorneycroft, Peter 236-7
thyroid: effects on 10
Times 2, 76
Titt, RA 356
Todd, Sir Alexander 236
Tokyo: nerve gas attack 329, 344
Tomorrow's World 338
treaty: banning chemical weapons 228
Trinidad 267
Truman, Harry S 121
truth drug 249
Truth and Reconciliation Commission (TRC) 11

U

Underhill, Mike 175, 319
United States of America:
    biological weapons:
        development 362
        simulation trials 353-5, 358
    buying British protective clothing 345
    collaboration 104-5, 133-4, 191, 220, 221, 226-7, 251, 252-3, 256, 271-2, 309

INDEX

    compensation claims and payments 296, 319-21
    Department of Veterans' Affairs (VA) 319-21
    ethical standards 177, 251-2
    experiments 7-9
        germ warfare 351-2
        mustard gas 104-6
        nerve gases 162, 168, 185, 191-2, 210, 325
            ending 168, 220
        psycho-chemicals 232-3, 237, 239, 251-3, 256
        radiation 309-10
        on unwitting subjects 251-2, 309, 320
    'guinea pigs' from 51
    in Gulf War 326
    inquiries into long-term health problems 319-21, 327-8
    lawsuits 257-8
    manufacture of nerve gases 185, 221
    objections to Porton closure 226-7
    recognition of Gulf War Syndrome 310
    recruiting Germans 121-2
    recruiting Japanese 122
    reducing weapons 12
    Special Relationship 221
    spies 114
    use of chemical weapons 225, 255, 256
    use of tear gas 263-4, 271, 276, 285, 291
    volunteers: from prison population 190, 251
    working with DERA 338
University College, London 29, 43
US Chemical Corps 232
US Presidential Advisory Committee on Gulf War Veterans Illnesses 327

V

V-agents *see* nerve gases
vaccines 351
Varan, Operation 360
Vedder, Colonel EB 71
vesicants *see* blister gases
Vietnam War 225, 271, 276, 285, 291
volunteers 29
    armed forces 50-62, 81-5, 86-8, 89, 103-4, 139-40, 158, 169-76, 189, 204, 207, 210-11, 268-9, 327
        annual numbers 346-7
    civilians 189-90
    consent forms 181-2, 189
    gratitude to 346
    inducements 49, 57, 82, 104, 140, 268, 269, 273, 279, 280
    motivation 57-9, 59, 60, 91-2, 216

INDEX

obtaining information 293-6, 373-6
personality of 58-60
plaque to 347
recruiting 49-62
refusal to return 82
tricked into taking part 1-2, 5, 165, 170-7, 188, 250-1, 293, 304, 320, 347
withdrawing 92, 178
women 61-2

W

Walton, Alan 171-2
Wansborough-Jones, Sir Owen 187
War Pension Agency 299, 302, 305, 321, 322
war pensions 70-1, 72, 85, 107, 296-304, 305
'Warfin' 109
water cannon 283-4
Watkinson, Colonel 81
Watson, Dr Rex 5, 16, 207-9, 226, 282, 334, 349, 362
Watson, Lieutenant Colonel William 44
Watts, Eric 300
Weymouth, Dorset 358
Whitcher, Harold 204
White, George 252
Wilson, Professor Andrew 241
Wilson, Harold 225, 247, 272
Wilson, Jack 140, 149
Wiltshire Police 1-3, 145, 165, 175, 296, 304, 338, 339
Wiltshire Regiment 158-61
Wimmer, Dr Karl 121
Winterbourne Gunner 318-19
women:
    on gas chamber duty 93-4
    taking part in tests 61-2
Wright, Peter 249, 250, 291

X

X-Files 13

Y

Yatesbury, Wiltshire 352
Ypres 21

Z

zinc cadmium sulphide 352-7, 360, 363
    area of UK covered 354

HOUSE OF STRATUS

Internet: **www.houseofstratus.com** including author interviews, reviews, features.

Email: **sales@houseofstratus.com** please quote author, title and credit card details.

Hotline: UK ONLY: **0800 169 1780**, please quote author, title and credit card details.
INTERNATIONAL: **+44 (0) 20 7494 6400**, please quote author, title and credit card details.

Send to: **House of Stratus Sales Department
24c Old Burlington Street
London
W1X 1RL
UK**